# The History of The Decline and Fall of the Roman Empire by Edward Gibbon

## Volume VI (of VI)

For decades, perhaps centuries, the standard work of reference on Roman History has been courtesy of Edward Gibbon. In its original printing it was a best-seller and a publishing sensation. History was brought to the masses in vivid detail.

Within its massive six volumes Gibbon put into context the entire sweep of this huge and complex Empire. We visit its far-flung regions, its most charismatic characters as we travel through centuries of its existence and its eternal influence on Western and, most probably, World culture.

Considering the times and the resources at his disposal it quite incredible what Gibbon has been able to put together, to distil, to formulate and precisely plot in this most seducing of histories.

## Index of Contents
CHAPTER LIX - The Crusades
CHAPTER LX - The Fourth Crusade
CHAPTER LXI - Partition of The Empire by The French and Venetians
CHAPTER LXII - Greek Emperors of Nice and Constantinople
CHAPTER LXIII - Civil Wars and The Ruin of the Greek Empire
CHAPTER LXIV - Moguls, Ottoman Turks
CHAPTER LXV - Elevation of Timour or Tamerlane, And His Death
CHAPTER LXVI - Union of The Greek And Latin Churches
CHAPTER LXVII - Schism of The Greeks And Latins
CHAPTER LXVIII - Reign of Mahomet The Second, Extinction of Eastern Empire
CHAPTER LXIX - State of Rome From the Twelfth Century
CHAPTER LXX - Final Settlement of The Ecclesiastical State
CHAPTER LXXI - Prospect of the Ruins of Rome in the Fifteenth Century
Edward Gibbon – A Short Biography
Edward Gibbon – A Concise Bibliography


CHAPTER LIX

THE CRUSADES

PART I

PRESERVATION OF THE GREEK EMPIRE—NUMBERS, PASSAGE, AND EVENT, OF THE SECOND AND THIRD CRUSADES—ST BERNARD—REIGN OF SALADIN IN EGYPT AND SYRIA—HIS CONQUEST OF JERUSALEM—NAVAL CRUSADES—RICHARD THE FIRST OF ENGLAND—POPE INNOCENT THE THIRD; AND THE FOURTH AND FIFTH CRUSADES—THE EMPEROR FREDERIC THE SECOND—LOUIS THE NIGTH OF FRANCE; AND THE TWO LAST CRUSADES—EXPULSION OF THE LATINS OR FRANKS BY THE MAMELUKES

In a style less grave than that of history, I should perhaps compare the emperor Alexius [1] to the jackal, who is said to follow the steps, and to devour the leavings, of the lion. Whatever had been his fears and toils in the passage of the first crusade, they were amply recompensed by the subsequent benefits which he derived from the exploits of the Franks. His dexterity and vigilance secured their first conquest of Nice; and from this threatening station the Turks were compelled to evacuate the neighborhood of Constantinople. While the crusaders, with blind valor, advanced into the midland countries of Asia, the crafty Greek improved the favorable occasion when the emirs of the sea-coast were recalled to the standard of the sultan. The Turks were driven from the Isles of Rhodes and Chios: the cities of Ephesus and Smyrna, of Sardes, Philadelphia, and Laodicea, were restored to the empire, which Alexius enlarged from the Hellespont to the banks of the Mæander, and the rocky shores of Pamphylia. The churches resumed their splendor: the towns were rebuilt and fortified; and the desert country was peopled with colonies of Christians, who were gently removed from the more distant and dangerous frontier. In these paternal cares, we may forgive Alexius, if he forgot the deliverance of the holy sepulchre; but, by the Latins, he was stigmatized with the foul reproach of treason and desertion. They had sworn fidelity and obedience to his throne; but he had promised to assist their enterprise in person, or, at least, with his troops and treasures: his base retreat dissolved their obligations; and the sword, which had been the instrument of their victory, was the pledge and title of their just independence. It does not appear that the emperor attempted to revive his obsolete claims over the kingdom of Jerusalem; [2] but the borders of Cilicia and Syria were more recent in his possession, and more accessible to his arms. The great army of the crusaders was annihilated or dispersed; the principality of Antioch was left without a head, by the surprise and captivity of Bohemond; his ransom had oppressed him with a heavy debt; and his Norman followers were insufficient to repel the hostilities of the Greeks and Turks. In this distress, Bohemond embraced a magnanimous resolution, of leaving the defence of Antioch to his kinsman, the faithful Tancred; of arming the West against the Byzantine empire; and of executing the design which he inherited from the lessons and example of his father Guiscard. His embarkation was clandestine: and, if we may credit a tale of the princess Anne, he passed the hostile sea closely secreted in a coffin. [3] But his reception in France was dignified by the public applause, and his marriage with the king's daughter: his return was glorious, since the bravest spirits of the age enlisted under his veteran command; and he repassed the Adriatic at the head of five thousand horse and forty thousand foot, assembled from the most remote climates of Europe. [4] The strength of Durazzo, and prudence of Alexius, the progress of famine and approach of winter, eluded his ambitious hopes; and the venal confederates were seduced from his standard. A treaty of peace [5] suspended the fears of the Greeks; and they were finally delivered by the death of an adversary, whom neither oaths could bind, nor dangers could appal, nor prosperity could satiate. His children succeeded to the principality of Antioch; but the boundaries were strictly defined, the homage was clearly stipulated, and the cities of Tarsus and Malmistra were restored to the Byzantine emperors. Of the coast of Anatolia, they possessed the entire circuit from Trebizond to the Syrian gates. The Seljukian dynasty of Roum [6] was separated on all sides from the sea and their Mussulman brethren; the power of the sultan was shaken by the victories and even the defeats of the Franks; and after the loss of Nice, they removed their throne to Cogni or Iconium, an obscure and in land town above three hundred miles from Constantinople. [7] Instead of trembling for their capital, the Comnenian princes waged an offensive war against the Turks, and the first crusade prevented the fall of the declining empire.

*[Footnote 1: Anna Comnena relates her father's conquests in Asia Minor Alexiad, l. xi. p. 321—325, l. xiv. p. 419; his Cilician war against Tancred and Bohemond, p. 328—324; the war of Epirus, with tedious prolixity, l. xii. xiii. p. 345—406; the death of Bohemond, l. xiv. p. 419.]*

[Footnote 2: The kings of Jerusalem submitted, however, to a nominal dependence, and in the dates of their inscriptions, (one is still legible in the church of Bethlem,) they respectfully placed before their own the name of the reigning emperor, (Ducange, Dissertations sur Joinville xxvii. p. 319.)]

[Footnote 3: Anna Comnena adds, that, to complete the imitation, he was shut up with a dead cock; and condescends to wonder how the Barbarian could endure the confinement and putrefaction. This absurd tale is unknown to the Latins. Note: The Greek writers, in general, Zonaras, p. 2, 303, and Glycas, p. 334 agree in this story with the princess Anne, except in the absurd addition of the dead cock. Ducange has already quoted some instances where a similar stratagem had been adopted by Norman princes. On this authority Wilken inclines to believe the fact. Appendix to vol. ii. p. 14—M.]

[Footnote 4: 'Apo QulhV in the Byzantine geography, must mean England; yet we are more credibly informed, that our Henry I. would not suffer him to levy any troops in his kingdom, (Ducange, Not. ad Alexiad. p. 41.)]

[Footnote 5: The copy of the treaty (Alexiad. l. xiii. p. 406—416) is an original and curious piece, which would require, and might afford, a good map of the principality of Antioch.]

[Footnote 6: See, in the learned work of M. De Guignes, (tom. ii. part ii.,) the history of the Seljukians of Iconium, Aleppo, and Damascus, as far as it may be collected from the Greeks, Latins, and Arabians. The last are ignorant or regardless of the affairs of Roum.]

[Footnote 7: Iconium is mentioned as a station by Xenophon, and by Strabo, with an ambiguous title of KwmopoliV, (Cellarius, tom. ii. p. 121.) Yet St. Paul found in that place a multitude (plhqoV) of Jews and Gentiles. under the corrupt name of Kunijah, it is described as a great city, with a river and garden, three leagues from the mountains, and decorated (I know not why) with Plato's tomb, (Abulfeda, tabul. xvii. p. 303 vers. Reiske; and the Index Geographicus of Schultens from Ibn Said.)]

In the twelfth century, three great emigrations marched by land from the West for the relief of Palestine. The soldiers and pilgrims of Lombardy, France, and Germany were excited by the example and success of the first crusade. [8] Forty-eight years after the deliverance of the holy sepulchre, the emperor, and the French king, Conrad the Third and Louis the Seventh, undertook the second crusade to support the falling fortunes of the Latins. [9] A grand division of the third crusade was led by the emperor Frederic Barbarossa, [10] who sympathized with his brothers of France and England in the common loss of Jerusalem. These three expeditions may be compared in their resemblance of the greatness of numbers, their passage through the Greek empire, and the nature and event of their Turkish warfare, and a brief parallel may save the repetition of a tedious narrative. However splendid it may seem, a regular story of the crusades would exhibit the perpetual return of the same causes and effects; and the frequent attempts for the defence or recovery of the Holy Land would appear so many faint and unsuccessful copies of the original.

[Footnote 8: For this supplement to the first crusade, see Anna Comnena, (Alexias, l. xi. p. 331, &c., and the viiith book of Albert Aquensis.)]

[Footnote 9: For the second crusade, of Conrad III. and Louis VII., see William of Tyre, (l. xvi. c. 18—19,) Otho of Frisingen, (l. i. c. 34—45 59, 60,) Matthew Paris, (Hist. Major. p. 68,) Struvius, (Corpus Hist Germanicæ, p. 372, 373,) Scriptores Rerum Francicarum à Duchesne tom. iv.: Nicetas, in Vit. Manuel, l. i. c. 4, 5, 6, p. 41—48, Cinnamus l. ii. p. 41—49.]

[Footnote 10: For the third crusade, of Frederic Barbarossa, see Nicetas in Isaac Angel. l. ii. c. 3—8, p. 257—266. Struv. (Corpus. Hist. Germ. p. 414,) and two historians, who probably were spectators, Tagino, (in Scriptor. Freher. tom. i. p. 406—416, edit Struv.,) and the Anonymus de Expeditione Asiaticâ Fred. I. (in Canisii Antiq. Lection. tom. iii. p. ii. p. 498—526, edit. Basnage.)]

I. Of the swarms that so closely trod in the footsteps of the first pilgrims, the chiefs were equal in rank, though unequal in fame and merit, to Godfrey of Bouillon and his fellow-adventurers. At their head were displayed the banners of the dukes of Burgundy, Bavaria, and Aquitain; the first a descendant of Hugh Capet, the second, a father of the Brunswick line: the archbishop of Milan, a temporal prince, transported, for the benefit of the Turks, the treasures and ornaments of his church and palace; and the veteran crusaders, Hugh the Great and Stephen of Chartres, returned to consummate their unfinished vow. The huge and disorderly bodies of their followers moved forward in two columns; and if the first consisted of two hundred and sixty thousand persons, the second might possibly amount to sixty thousand horse and one hundred thousand foot. [11] [11/1] The armies of the second crusade might have claimed the conquest of Asia; the nobles of France and Germany were animated by the presence of their sovereigns; and both the rank and personal character of Conrad and Louis gave a dignity to their cause, and a discipline to their force, which might be vainly expected from the feudatory chiefs. The cavalry of the emperor, and that of the king, was each composed of seventy thousand knights, and their immediate attendants in the field; [12] and if the light-armed troops, the peasant infantry, the women and children, the priests and monks, be rigorously excluded, the full account will scarcely be satisfied with four hundred thousand souls. The West, from Rome to Britain, was called into action; the kings of Poland and Bohemia obeyed the summons of Conrad; and it is affirmed by the Greeks and Latins, that, in the passage of a strait or river, the Byzantine agents, after a tale of nine hundred thousand, desisted from the endless and formidable computation. [13] In the third crusade, as the French and English preferred the navigation of the Mediterranean, the host of Frederic Barbarossa was less numerous. Fifteen thousand knights, and as many squires, were the flower of the German chivalry: sixty thousand horse, and one hundred thousand foot, were mustered by the emperor in the plains of Hungary; and after such repetitions, we shall no longer be startled at the six hundred thousand pilgrims, which credulity has ascribed to this last emigration. [14] Such extravagant reckonings prove only the astonishment of contemporaries; but their astonishment most strongly bears testimony to the existence of an enormous, though indefinite, multitude. The Greeks might applaud their superior knowledge of the arts and stratagems of war, but they confessed the strength and courage of the French cavalry, and the infantry of the Germans; [15] and the strangers are described as an iron race, of gigantic stature, who darted fire from their eyes, and spilt blood like water on the ground. Under the banners of Conrad, a troop of females rode in the attitude and armor of men; and the chief of these Amazons, from her gilt spurs and buskins, obtained the epithet of the Golden-footed Dame.

[Footnote 11: Anne, who states these later swarms at 40,000 horse and 100,000 foot, calls them Normans, and places at their head two brothers of Flanders. The Greeks were strangely ignorant of the names, families, and possessions of the Latin princes.]

[Footnote 11/1: It was this army of pilgrims, the first body of which was headed by the archbishop of Milan and Count Albert of Blandras, which set forth on the wild, yet, with a more disciplined army, not impolitic, enterprise of striking at the heart of the Mahometan power, by attacking the sultan in Bagdad. For their adventures and fate, see Wilken, vol. ii. p. 120, &c., Michaud, book iv—M.]

[Footnote 12: William of Tyre, and Matthew Paris, reckon 70,000 loricati in each of the armies.]

[Footnote 13: The imperfect enumeration is mentioned by Cinnamus, (ennenhkonta muriadeV,) and confirmed by Odo de Diogilo apud Ducange ad Cinnamum, with the more precise sum of 900,556. Why must therefore the version and comment suppose the modest and insufficient reckoning of 90,000? Does not Godfrey of Viterbo (Pantheon, p. xix. in Muratori, tom. vii. p. 462) exclaim? —Numerum si poscere quæras, Millia millena militis agmen erat.]

[Footnote 14: This extravagant account is given by Albert of Stade, (apud Struvium, p. 414;) my calculation is borrowed from Godfrey of Viterbo, Arnold of Lubeck, apud eundem, and Bernard Thesaur. (c. 169, p. 804.) The original writers are silent. The Mahometans gave him 200,000, or 260,000, men, (Bohadin, in Vit. Saladin, p. 110.)]

[Footnote 15: I must observe, that, in the second and third crusades, the subjects of Conrad and Frederic are styled by the Greeks and Orientals Alamanni. The Lechi and Tzechi of Cinnamus are the Poles and Bohemians; and it is for the French that he reserves the ancient appellation of Germans. He likewise names the Brittioi, or Britannoi. Note: He names both—Brittioi te kai Britanoi—M.]

II. The number and character of the strangers was an object of terror to the effeminate Greeks, and the sentiment of fear is nearly allied to that of hatred. This aversion was suspended or softened by the apprehension of the Turkish power; and the invectives of the Latins will not bias our more candid belief, that the emperor Alexius dissembled their insolence, eluded their hostilities, counselled their rashness, and opened to their ardor the road of pilgrimage and conquest. But when the Turks had been driven from Nice and the sea-coast, when the Byzantine princes no longer dreaded the distant sultans of Cogni, they felt with purer indignation the free and frequent passage of the western Barbarians, who violated the majesty, and endangered the safety, of the empire. The second and third crusades were undertaken under the reign of Manuel Comnenus and Isaac Angelus. Of the former, the passions were always impetuous, and often malevolent; and the natural union of a cowardly and a mischievous temper was exemplified in the latter, who, without merit or mercy, could punish a tyrant, and occupy his throne. It was secretly, and perhaps tacitly, resolved by the prince and people to destroy, or at least to discourage, the pilgrims, by every species of injury and oppression; and their want of prudence and discipline continually afforded the pretence or the opportunity. The Western monarchs had stipulated a safe passage and fair market in the country of their Christian brethren; the treaty had been ratified by oaths and hostages; and the poorest soldier of Frederic's army was furnished with three marks of silver to defray his expenses on the road. But every engagement was violated by treachery and injustice; and the complaints of the Latins are attested by the honest confession of a Greek historian, who has dared to prefer truth to his country. [16] Instead of a hospitable reception, the gates of the cities, both in Europe and Asia, were closely barred against the crusaders; and the scanty pittance of food was let down in baskets from the walls. Experience or foresight might excuse this timid jealousy; but the common duties of humanity prohibited the mixture of chalk, or other poisonous ingredients, in the bread; and should Manuel be acquitted of any foul connivance, he is guilty of coining base money for the purpose of trading with the pilgrims. In every step of their march they were stopped or misled: the governors had private orders to fortify the passes and break down the bridges against them: the stragglers were pillaged and murdered: the soldiers and horses were pierced in the woods by arrows from an invisible hand; the sick were burnt in their beds; and the dead bodies were hung on gibbets along the highways. These injuries exasperated the champions of the cross, who were not endowed with evangelical patience; and the Byzantine princes, who had provoked the unequal conflict, promoted the embarkation and march of these formidable guests. On the verge of the Turkish frontier Barbarossa spared the guilty Philadelphia, [17] rewarded the hospitable Laodicea, and deplored the hard necessity that had stained his sword with any drops of Christian blood. In their intercourse with the monarchs of Germany and France, the pride of the Greeks was exposed to an anxious trial. They might boast that on the first interview the seat of Louis was a low stool, beside the throne of Manuel; [18] but no sooner had the French king transported his army beyond the Bosphorus, than he refused the offer of a second conference, unless his brother would meet him on equal terms, either on the sea or land. With Conrad and Frederic, the ceremonial was still nicer and more difficult: like the successors of Constantine, they styled themselves emperors of the Romans; [19] and firmly maintained the purity of their title and dignity. The first of these representatives of Charlemagne would only converse with Manuel on horseback in the open field; the second, by passing the Hellespont rather than the Bosphorus, declined the view of Constantinople and its sovereign. An emperor, who had been crowned at Rome, was reduced in the Greek epistles to the humble appellation of Rex, or prince, of the Alemanni; and the vain and feeble Angelus affected to be ignorant of the name of one of the greatest men and monarchs of the age. While they viewed with hatred and suspicion the Latin pilgrims the Greek emperors maintained a strict, though secret, alliance with the Turks and Saracens. Isaac Angelus complained, that by his friendship for the great Saladin he had incurred the enmity of the Franks; and a mosque was founded at Constantinople for the public exercise of the religion of Mahomet. [20]

[Footnote 16: Nicetas was a child at the second crusade, but in the third he commanded against the Franks the important post of Philippopolis. Cinnamus is infected with national prejudice and pride.]

[Footnote 17: The conduct of the Philadelphians is blamed by Nicetas, while the anonymous German accuses the rudeness of his countrymen, (culpâ nostrâ.) History would be pleasant, if we were embarrassed only by such contradictions. It is likewise from Nicetas, that we learn the pious and humane sorrow of Frederic.]

[Footnote 18: Cqamalh edra, which Cinnamus translates into Latin by the word Sellion. Ducange works very hard to save his king and country from such ignominy, (sur Joinville, dissertat. xxvii. p. 317—320.) Louis afterwards insisted on a meeting in mari ex æquo, not ex equo, according to the laughable readings of some MSS.]

[Footnote 19: Ego Romanorum imperator sum, ille Romaniorum, (Anonym Canis. p. 512.) The public and historical style of the Greeks was Rhx... princeps. Yet Cinnamus owns, that 'Imperatwr is synonymous to BasileuV.]

[Footnote 20: In the Epistles of Innocent III., (xiii. p. 184,) and the History of Bohadin, (p. 129, 130,) see the views of a pope and a cadhi on this singulartoleration.]

III. The swarms that followed the first crusade were destroyed in Anatolia by famine, pestilence, and the Turkish arrows; and the princes only escaped with some squadrons of horse to accomplish their lamentable pilgrimage. A just opinion may be formed of their knowledge and humanity; of their knowledge, from the design of subduing Persia and Chorasan in their way to Jerusalem; [20/1] of their humanity, from the massacre of the Christian people, a friendly city, who came out to meet them with palms and crosses in their hands. The arms of Conrad and Louis were less cruel and imprudent; but the event of the second crusade was still more ruinous to Christendom; and the Greek Manuel is accused by his own subjects of giving seasonable intelligence to the sultan, and treacherous guides to the Latin princes. Instead of crushing the common foe, by a double attack at the same time but on different sides, the Germans were urged by emulation, and the French were retarded by jealousy. Louis had scarcely passed the Bosphorus when he was met by the returning emperor, who had lost the greater part of his army in glorious, but unsuccessful, actions on the banks of the Mæander. The contrast of the pomp of his rival hastened the retreat of Conrad: [20/2] the desertion of his independent vassals reduced him to his hereditary troops; and he borrowed some Greek vessels to execute by sea the pilgrimage of Palestine. Without studying the lessons of experience, or the nature of the war, the king of France advanced through the same country to a similar fate. The vanguard, which bore the royal banner and the oriflamme of St. Denys, [21] had doubled their march with rash and inconsiderate speed; and the rear, which the king commanded in person, no longer found their companions in the evening camp. In darkness and disorder, they were encompassed, assaulted, and overwhelmed, by the innumerable host of Turks, who, in the art of war, were superior to the Christians of the twelfth century. [21/1] Louis, who climbed a tree in the general discomfiture, was saved by his own valor and the ignorance of his adversaries; and with the dawn of day he escaped alive, but almost alone, to the camp of the vanguard. But instead of pursuing his expedition by land, he was rejoiced to shelter the relics of his army in the friendly seaport of Satalia. From thence he embarked for Antioch; but so penurious was the supply of Greek vessels, that they could only afford room for his knights and nobles; and the plebeian crowd of infantry was left to perish at the foot of the Pamphylian hills. The emperor and the king embraced and wept at Jerusalem; their martial trains, the remnant of mighty armies, were joined to the Christian powers of Syria, and a fruitless siege of Damascus was the final effort of the second crusade. Conrad and Louis embarked for Europe with the personal fame of piety and courage; but the Orientals had braved these potent monarchs of the Franks, with whose names and military forces they had been so often threatened. [22] Perhaps they had still more to fear from the veteran genius of Frederic the First, who in his youth had served in Asia under his uncle Conrad. Forty campaigns in Germany and Italy had taught Barbarossa to command; and his soldiers, even the princes of the empire, were accustomed under his reign to obey. As soon as he lost sight of Philadelphia and Laodicea, the last cities of the Greek frontier, he plunged into the salt and barren desert, a land (says the historian) of horror and tribulation. [23] During twenty days, every step of his fainting and sickly march was besieged by the innumerable hordes of Turkmans, [24] whose numbers and fury seemed after each defeat to multiply and inflame. The emperor continued to struggle and to suffer; and such was the measure of his calamities, that when he reached the gates of Iconium, no more than one thousand knights were able to serve on horseback. By a sudden and resolute assault he defeated the guards, and stormed the capital of the sultan, [25] who humbly sued for pardon and peace. The road was now open, and Frederic advanced in a career of triumph, till he was unfortunately drowned in a petty torrent of Cilicia. [26] The remainder of his Germans was consumed by sickness and desertion: and the emperor's son expired with the greatest part of his Swabian vassals at the siege of Acre. Among the Latin heroes, Godfrey of Bouillon and Frederic Barbarossa could alone achieve the passage of the Lesser Asia; yet even their success was a warning; and in the last and most experienced age of the crusades, every nation preferred the sea to the toils and perils of an inland expedition. [27]

[Footnote 20/1: This was the design of the pilgrims under the archbishop of Milan. See note, p. 102—M.]

[Footnote 20/2: Conrad had advanced with part of his army along a central road, between that on the coast and that which led to Iconium. He had been betrayed by the Greeks, his army destroyed without a battle. Wilken, vol. iii. p. 165. Michaud, vol. ii. p. 156. Conrad advanced again with Louis as far as Ephesus, and from thence, at the invitation of Manuel, returned to Constantinople. It was Louis who, at the passage of the Mæander, was engaged in a "glorious action." Wilken, vol. iii. p. 179. Michaud vol. ii. p. 160. Gibbon followed Nicetas—M.]

[Footnote 21: As counts of Vexin, the kings of France were the vassals and advocates of the monastery of St. Denys. The saint's peculiar banner, which they received from the abbot, was of a square form, and a red or flaming color. The oriflamme appeared at the head of the French armies from the xiith to the xvth century, (Ducange sur Joinville, Dissert. xviii. p. 244—253.)]

[Footnote 21/1: They descended the heights to a beautiful valley which by beneath them. The Turks seized the heights which separated the two divisions of the army. The modern historians represent differently the act to which Louis owed his safety, which Gibbon has described by the undignified phrase, "he climbed a tree." According to Michaud, vol. ii. p. 164, the king got upon a rock, with his back against a tree; according to Wilken, vol. iii., he dragged himself up to the top of the rock by the roots of a tree, and continued to defend himself till nightfall—M.]

[Footnote 22: The original French histories of the second crusade are the Gesta Ludovici VII. published in the ivth volume of Duchesne's collection. The same volume contains many original letters of the king, of Suger his minister, &c., the best documents of authentic history.]

[Footnote 23: Terram horroris et salsuginis, terram siccam sterilem, inamnam. Anonym. Canis. p. 517. The emphatic language of a sufferer.]

[Footnote 24: Gens innumera, sylvestris, indomita, prædones sine ductore. The sultan of Cogni might sincerely rejoice in their defeat. Anonym. Canis. p. 517, 518.]

[Footnote 25: See, in the anonymous writer in the Collection of Canisius, Tagino and Bohadin, (Vit. Saladin. p. 119, 120,) the ambiguous conduct of Kilidge Arslan, sultan of Cogni, who hated and feared both Saladin and Frederic.]

[Footnote 26: The desire of comparing two great men has tempted many writers to drown Frederic in the River Cydnus, in which Alexander so imprudently bathed, (Q. Curt. l. iii c. 4, 5.) But, from the march of the emperor, I rather judge, that his Saleph is the Calycadnus, a stream of less fame, but of a longer course. Note: It is now called the Girama: its course is described in M'Donald Kinneir's Travels—M.]

[Footnote 27: Marinus Sanutus, A.D. 1321, lays it down as a precept, Quod stolus ecclesiæ per terram nullatenus est ducenda. He resolves, by the divine aid, the objection, or rather exception, of the first crusade, (Secreta Fidelium Crucis, l. ii. pars ii. c. i. p. 37.)]

The enthusiasm of the first crusade is a natural and simple event, while hope was fresh, danger untried, and enterprise congenial to the spirit of the times. But the obstinate perseverance of Europe may indeed excite our pity and admiration; that no instruction should have been drawn from constant and adverse experience; that the same confidence should have repeatedly grown from the same failures; that six succeeding generations should have rushed headlong down the precipice that was open before them; and that men of every condition should have staked their public and private fortunes on the desperate adventure of possessing or recovering a tombstone two thousand miles from their country. In a period of two centuries after the council of Clermont, each spring and summer produced a new emigration of pilgrim warriors for the defence of the Holy Land; but the seven great armaments or crusades were excited by some impending or recent calamity: the nations were moved by the authority of their pontiffs, and the example of their kings: their zeal was kindled, and their reason was silenced, by the voice of their holy orators; and among these, Bernard, [28] the monk, or the saint, may claim the most honorable place. [28/1] About eight years before the first conquest of Jerusalem, he was born of a noble family in Burgundy; at the age of three-and-twenty he buried himself in the monastery of Citeaux, then in the primitive fervor of the institution; at the end of two years he led forth her third colony, or daughter, to the valley of Clairvaux [29] in Champagne; and was content, till the hour of his death, with the humble station of abbot of his own community. A philosophic age has abolished, with too liberal and indiscriminate disdain, the honors of these spiritual heroes. The meanest among them are distinguished by some energies of the mind; they were at least superior to their votaries and disciples; and, in the race of superstition, they attained the prize for which such numbers contended. In speech, in writing, in action, Bernard stood high above his rivals and contemporaries; his compositions are not devoid of wit and eloquence; and he seems to have preserved as much reason and humanity as may be reconciled with the character of a saint. In a secular life, he would have shared the seventh part of a private inheritance; by a vow of poverty and penance, by closing his eyes against the visible world, [30] by the refusal of all ecclesiastical dignities, the abbot of Clairvaux became the oracle of Europe, and the founder of one hundred and sixty convents. Princes and pontiffs trembled at the freedom of his apostolical censures: France, England, and Milan, consulted and obeyed his judgment in a schism of the church: the debt was repaid by the gratitude of Innocent the Second; and his successor, Eugenius the Third, was the friend and disciple of the holy Bernard. It was in the proclamation of the second crusade that he shone as the missionary and prophet of God, who called the nations to the defence of his holy sepulchre. [31] At the parliament of Vezelay he spoke before the king; and Louis the Seventh, with his nobles, received their crosses from his hand. The abbot of Clairvaux then marched to the less easy conquest of the emperor Conrad: [31/1] a phlegmatic people, ignorant of his language, was transported by the pathetic vehemence of his tone and gestures; and his progress, from Constance to Cologne, was the triumph of eloquence and zeal. Bernard applauds his own success in the depopulation of Europe; affirms that cities and castles were emptied of their inhabitants; and computes, that only one man was left behind for the consolation of seven widows. [32] The blind fanatics were desirous of electing him for their general; but the example of the hermit Peter was before his eyes; and while he assured the crusaders of the divine favor, he prudently declined a military command, in which failure and victory would have been almost equally disgraceful to his character. [33] Yet, after the calamitous event, the abbot of Clairvaux was loudly accused as a false prophet, the author of the public and private mourning; his enemies exulted, his friends blushed, and his apology was slow and unsatisfactory. He justifies his obedience to the commands of the pope; expatiates on the mysterious ways of Providence; imputes the misfortunes of the pilgrims to their own sins; and modestly insinuates, that his mission had been approved by signs and wonders. [34] Had the fact been certain, the argument would be decisive; and his faithful disciples, who enumerate twenty or thirty miracles in a day, appeal to the public assemblies of France and Germany, in which they were performed. [35] At the present hour, such prodigies will not obtain credit beyond the precincts of Clairvaux; but in the preternatural cures of the blind, the lame, and the sick, who were presented to the man of God, it is impossible for us to ascertain the separate shares of accident, of fancy, of imposture, and of fiction.

[Footnote 28: *The most authentic information of St. Bernard must be drawn from his own writings, published in a correct edition by Père Mabillon, and reprinted at Venice, 1750, in six volumes in folio. Whatever friendship could recollect, or superstition could add, is contained in the two lives, by his disciples, in the vith volume: whatever learning and criticism could ascertain, may be found in the prefaces of the Benedictine editor.*]

[Footnote 28/1: *Gibbon, whose account of the crusades is perhaps the least accurate and satisfactory chapter in his History, has here failed in that lucid arrangement, which in general gives perspicuity to his most condensed and crowded narratives. He has unaccountably, and to the great perplexity of the reader, placed the preaching of St Bernard after the second crusade to which i led—M.*]

[Footnote 29: Clairvaux, surnamed the valley of Absynth, is situate among the woods near Bar sur Aube in Champagne. St. Bernard would blush at the pomp of the church and monastery; he would ask for the library, and I know not whether he would be much edified by a tun of 800 muids, (914 1-7 hogsheads,) which almost rivals that of Heidelberg, (Mélanges tirés d'une Grande Bibliothèque, tom. xlvi. p. 15—20.)]

[Footnote 30: The disciples of the saint (Vit. ima, l. iii. c. 2, p. 1232. Vit. iida, c. 16, No. 45, p. 1383) record a marvellous example of his pious apathy. Juxta lacum etiam Lausannensem totius diei itinere pergens, penitus non attendit aut se videre non vidit. Cum enim vespere facto de eodem lacû socii colloquerentur, interrogabat eos ubi lacus ille esset, et mirati sunt universi. To admire or despise St. Bernard as he ought, the reader, like myself, should have before the windows of his library the beauties of that incomparable landscape.]

[Footnote 31: Otho Frising. l. i. c. 4. Bernard. Epist. 363, ad Francos Orientales Opp. tom. i. p. 328. Vit. ima, l. iii. c. 4, tom. vi. p. 1235.]

[Footnote 31/1: Bernard had a nobler object in his expedition into Germany—to arrest the fierce and merciless persecution of the Jews, which was preparing, under the monk Radulph, to renew the frightful scenes which had preceded the first crusade, in the flourishing cities on the banks of the Rhine. The Jews acknowledge the Christian intervention of St. Bernard. See the curious extract from the History of Joseph ben Meir. Wilken, vol. iii. p. 1. and p. 63—M.]

[Footnote 32: Mandastis et obedivi.... multiplicati sunt super numerum; vacuantur urbes et castella; et pene jam non inveniunt quem apprehendant septem mulieres unum virum; adeo ubique viduæ vivis remanent viris. Bernard. Epist. p. 247. We must be careful not to construe pene as a substantive.]

[Footnote 33: Quis ego sum ut disponam acies, ut egrediar ante facies armatorum, aut quid tam remotum a professione meâ, si vires, si peritia, &c. Epist. 256, tom. i. p. 259. He speaks with contempt of the hermit Peter, vir quidam, Epist. 363.]

[Footnote 34: Sic dicunt forsitan isti, unde scimus quòd a Domino sermo egressus sit? Quæ signa tu facis ut credamus tibi? Non est quod ad ista ipse respondeam; parcendum verecundiæ meæ, responde tu pro me, et pro te ipso, secundum quæ vidisti et audisti, et secundum quod te inspiraverit Deus. Consolat. l. ii. c. 1. Opp. tom. ii. p. 421—423.]

[Footnote 35: See the testimonies in Vita ima, l. iv. c. 5, 6. Opp. tom. vi. p. 1258—1261, l. vi. c. 1—17, p. 1286—1314.]

Omnipotence itself cannot escape the murmurs of its discordant votaries; since the same dispensation which was applauded as a deliverance in Europe, was deplored, and perhaps arraigned, as a calamity in Asia. After the loss of Jerusalem, the Syrian fugitives diffused their consternation and sorrow; Bagdad mourned in the dust; the cadhi Zeineddin of Damascus tore his beard in the caliph's presence; and the whole divan shed tears at his melancholy tale. [36] But the commanders of the faithful could only weep; they were themselves captives in the hands of the Turks: some temporal power was restored to the last age of the Abbassides; but their humble ambition was confined to Bagdad and the adjacent province. Their tyrants, the Seljukian sultans, had followed the common law of the Asiatic dynasties, the unceasing round of valor, greatness, discord, degeneracy, and decay; their spirit and power were unequal to the defence of religion; and, in his distant realm of Persia, the Christians were strangers to the name and the arms of Sangiar, the last hero of his race. [37] While the sultans were involved in the silken web of the harem, the pious task was undertaken by their slaves, the Atabeks, [38] a Turkish name, which, like the Byzantine patricians, may be translated by Father of the Prince. Ascansar, a valiant Turk, had been the favorite of Malek Shaw, from whom he received the privilege of standing on the right hand of the throne; but, in the civil wars that ensued on the monarch's death, he lost his head and the government of Aleppo. His domestic emirs persevered in their attachment to his son Zenghi, who proved his first arms against the Franks in the defeat of Antioch: thirty campaigns in the service of the caliph and sultan established his military fame; and he was invested with the command of Mosul, as the only champion that could avenge the cause of the prophet. The public hope was not disappointed: after a siege of twenty-five days, he stormed the city of Edessa, and recovered from the Franks their conquests beyond the Euphrates: [39] the martial tribes of Curdistan were subdued by the independent sovereign of Mosul and Aleppo: his soldiers were taught to behold the camp as their only country; they trusted to his liberality for their rewards; and their absent families were protected by the vigilance of Zenghi. At the head of these veterans, his son Noureddin gradually united the Mahometan powers; [391] added the kingdom of Damascus to that of Aleppo, and waged a long and successful war against the Christians of Syria; he spread his ample reign from the Tigris to the Nile, and the Abbassides rewarded their faithful servant with all the titles and prerogatives of royalty. The Latins themselves were compelled to own the wisdom and courage, and even the justice and piety, of this implacable adversary. [40] In his life and government the holy warrior revived the zeal and simplicity of the first caliphs. Gold and silk were banished from his palace; the use of wine from his dominions; the public revenue was scrupulously applied to the public service; and the frugal household of Noureddin was maintained from his legitimate share of the spoil which he vested in the purchase of a private estate. His favorite sultana sighed for some female object of expense. "Alas," replied the king, "I fear God, and am no more than the treasurer of the Moslems. Their property I cannot alienate; but I still possess three shops in the city of Hems: these you may take; and these alone can I bestow." His chamber of justice was the terror of the great and the refuge of the poor. Some years after the sultan's death, an oppressed subject called aloud in the streets of Damascus, "O Noureddin, Noureddin, where art thou now? Arise, arise, to pity and protect us!" A tumult was apprehended, and a living tyrant blushed or trembled at the name of a departed monarch.

*[Footnote 36: Abulmahasen apud de Guignes, Hist. des Huns, tom. ii. p. ii. p. 99.]*

*[Footnote 37: See his article in the Bibliothèque Orientale of D'Herbelot, and De Guignes, tom. ii. p. i. p. 230—261. Such was his valor, that he was styled the second Alexander; and such the extravagant love of his subjects, that they prayed for the sultan a year after his decease. Yet Sangiar might have been made prisoner by the Franks, as well as by the Uzes. He reigned near fifty years, (A.D. 1103—1152,) and was a munificent patron of Persian poetry.]*

*[Footnote 38: See the Chronology of the Atabeks of Irak and Syria, in De Guignes, tom. i. p. 254; and the reigns of Zenghi and Noureddin in the same writer, (tom. ii. p. ii. p. 147—221,) who uses the Arabic text of Benelathir, Ben Schouna and Abulfeda; the Bibliothèque Orientale, under the articles Atabeks and Noureddin, and the Dynasties of Abulpharagius, p. 250—267, vers. Pocock.]*

*[Footnote 39: William of Tyre (l. xvi. c. 4, 5, 7) describes the loss of Edessa, and the death of Zenghi. The corruption of his name into Sanguin, afforded the Latins a comfortable allusion to his sanguinary character and end, fit sanguine sanguinolentus.]*

*[Footnote 391: On Noureddin's conquest of Damascus, see extracts from Arabian writers prefixed to the second part of the third volume of Wilken—M.]*

[Footnote 40: Noradinus (says William of Tyre, l. xx. 33) maximus nominis et fidei Christianæ persecutor; princeps tamen justus, vafer, providus' et secundum gentis suæ traditiones religiosus. To this Catholic witness we may add the primate of the Jacobites, (Abulpharag. p. 267,) quo non alter erat inter reges vitæ ratione magis laudabili, aut quæ pluribus justitiæ experimentis abundaret. The true praise of kings is after their death, and from the mouth of their enemies.]


PART II

By the arms of the Turks and Franks, the Fatimites had been deprived of Syria. In Egypt the decay of their character and influence was still more essential. Yet they were still revered as the descendants and successors of the prophet; they maintained their invisible state in the palace of Cairo; and their person was seldom violated by the profane eyes of subjects or strangers. The Latin ambassadors [41] have described their own introduction, through a series of gloomy passages, and glittering porticos: the scene was enlivened by the warbling of birds and the murmur of fountains: it was enriched by a display of rich furniture and rare animals; of the Imperial treasures, something was shown, and much was supposed; and the long order of unfolding doors was guarded by black soldiers and domestic eunuchs. The sanctuary of the presence chamber was veiled with a curtain; and the vizier, who conducted the ambassadors, laid aside the cimeter, and prostrated himself three times on the ground; the veil was then removed; and they beheld the commander of the faithful, who signified his pleasure to the first slave of the throne. But this slave was his master: the viziers or sultans had usurped the supreme administration of Egypt; the claims of the rival candidates were decided by arms; and the name of the most worthy, of the strongest, was inserted in the royal patent of command. The factions of Dargham and Shawer alternately expelled each other from the capital and country; and the weaker side implored the dangerous protection of the sultan of Damascus, or the king of Jerusalem, the perpetual enemies of the sect and monarchy of the Fatimites. By his arms and religion the Turk was most formidable; but the Frank, in an easy, direct march, could advance from Gaza to the Nile; while the intermediate situation of his realm compelled the troops of Noureddin to wheel round the skirts of Arabia, a long and painful circuit, which exposed them to thirst, fatigue, and the burning winds of the desert. The secret zeal and ambition of the Turkish prince aspired to reign in Egypt under the name of the Abbassides; but the restoration of the suppliant Shawer was the ostensible motive of the first expedition; and the success was intrusted to the emir Shiracouh, a valiant and veteran commander. Dargham was oppressed and slain; but the ingratitude, the jealousy, the just apprehensions, of his more fortunate rival, soon provoked him to invite the king of Jerusalem to deliver Egypt from his insolent benefactors. To this union the forces of Shiracouh were unequal: he relinquished the premature conquest; and the evacuation of Belbeis or Pelusium was the condition of his safe retreat. As the Turks defiled before the enemy, and their general closed the rear, with a vigilant eye, and a battle axe in his hand, a Frank presumed to ask him if he were not afraid of an attack. "It is doubtless in your power to begin the attack," replied the intrepid emir; "but rest assured, that not one of my soldiers will go to paradise till he has sent an infidel to hell." His report of the riches of the land, the effeminacy of the natives, and the disorders of the government, revived the hopes of Noureddin; the caliph of Bagdad applauded the pious design; and Shiracouh descended into Egypt a second time with twelve thousand Turks and eleven thousand Arabs. Yet his forces were still inferior to the confederate armies of the Franks and Saracens; and I can discern an unusual degree of military art, in his passage of the Nile, his retreat into Thebais, his masterly evolutions in the battle of Babain, the surprise of Alexandria, and his marches and countermarches in the flats and valley of Egypt, from the tropic to the sea. His conduct was seconded by the courage of his troops, and on the eve of action a Mamaluke [42] exclaimed, "If we cannot wrest Egypt from the Christian dogs, why do we not renounce the honors and rewards of the sultan, and retire to labor with the peasants, or to spin with the females of the harem?" Yet, after all his efforts in the field, [43] after the obstinate defence of Alexandria [44] by his nephew Saladin, an honorable capitulation and retreat [44/1] concluded the second enterprise of Shiracouh; and Noureddin reserved his abilities for a third and more propitious occasion. It was soon offered by the ambition and avarice of Amalric or Amaury, king of Jerusalem, who had imbibed the pernicious maxim, that no faith should be kept with the enemies of God. [44/2] A religious warrior, the great master of the hospital, encouraged him to proceed; the emperor of Constantinople either gave, or promised, a fleet to act with the armies of Syria; and the perfidious Christian, unsatisfied with spoil and subsidy, aspired to the conquest of Egypt. In this emergency, the Moslems turned their eyes towards the sultan of Damascus; the vizier, whom danger encompassed on all sides, yielded to their unanimous wishes, and Noureddin seemed to be tempted by the fair offer of one third of the revenue of the kingdom. The Franks were already at the gates of Cairo; but the suburbs, the old city, were burnt on their approach; they were deceived by an insidious negotiation, and their vessels were unable to surmount the barriers of the Nile. They prudently declined a contest with the Turks in the midst of a hostile country; and Amaury retired into Palestine with the shame and reproach that always adhere to unsuccessful injustice. After this deliverance, Shiracouh was invested with a robe of honor, which he soon stained with the blood of the unfortunate Shawer. For a while, the Turkish emirs condescended to hold the office of vizier; but this foreign conquest precipitated the fall of the Fatimites themselves; and the bloodless change was accomplished by a message and a word. The caliphs had been degraded by their own weakness and the tyranny of the viziers: their subjects blushed, when the descendant and successor of the prophet presented his naked hand to the rude gripe of a Latin ambassador; they wept when he sent the hair of his women, a sad emblem of their grief and terror, to excite the pity of the sultan of Damascus. By the command of Noureddin, and the sentence of the doctors, the holy names of Abubeker, Omar, and Othman, were solemnly restored: the caliph Mosthadi, of Bagdad, was acknowledged in the public prayers as the true commander of the faithful; and the green livery of the sons of Ali was exchanged for the black color of the Abbassides. The last of his race, the caliph Adhed, who survived only ten days, expired in happy ignorance of his fate; his treasures secured the loyalty of the soldiers, and silenced the murmurs of the sectaries; and in all subsequent revolutions, Egypt has never departed from the orthodox tradition of the Moslems. [45]

[Footnote 41: From the ambassador, William of Tyre (l. xix. c. 17, 18,) describes the palace of Cairo. In the caliph's treasure were found a pearl as large as a pigeon's egg, a ruby weighing seventeen Egyptian drams, an emerald a palm and a half in length, and many vases of crystal and porcelain of China, (Renaudot, p. 536.)]

[Footnote 42: Mamluc, plur. Mamalic, is defined by Pocock, (Prolegom. ad Abulpharag. p. 7,) and D'Herbelot, (p. 545,) servum emptitium, seu qui pretio numerato in domini possessionem cedit. They frequently occur in the wars of Saladin, (Bohadin, p. 236, &c.;) and it was only the Bahartie Mamalukes that were first introduced into Egypt by his descendants.]

[Footnote 43: Jacobus à Vitriaco (p. 1116) gives the king of Jerusalem no more than 374 knights. Both the Franks and the Moslems report the superior numbers of the enemy; a difference which may be solved by counting or omitting the unwarlike Egyptians.]

[Footnote 44: It was the Alexandria of the Arabs, a middle term in extent and riches between the period of the Greeks and Romans, and that of the Turks, (Savary, Lettres sur l'Egypte, tom. i. p. 25, 26.)]

*[Footnote 44/1: The treaty stipulated that both the Christians and the Arabs should withdraw from Egypt. Wilken, vol. iii. part ii. p. 113—M.]*

*[Footnote 44/2: The Knights Templars, abhorring the perfidious breach of treaty partly, perhaps, out of jealousy of the Hospitallers, refused to join in this enterprise. Will. Tyre c. xx. p. 5. Wilken, vol. iii. part ii. p. 117—M.]*

[Footnote 45: For this great revolution of Egypt, see William of Tyre, (l. xix. 5, 6, 7, 12—31, xx. 5—12,) Bohadin, (in Vit. Saladin, p. 30—39,) Abulfeda, (in Excerpt. Schultens, p. 1—12,) D'Herbelot, (Bibliot. Orient. Adhed, Fathemah, but very incorrect,) Renaudot, (Hist. Patriarch. Alex. p. 522—525, 532—537,) Vertot, (Hist. des Chevaliers de Malthe, tom. i. p. 141—163, in 4to.,) and M. de Guignes, (tom. ii. p. 185—215.)]

The hilly country beyond the Tigris is occupied by the pastoral tribes of the Curds; [46] a people hardy, strong, savage impatient of the yoke, addicted to rapine, and tenacious of the government of their national chiefs. The resemblance of name, situation, and manners, seems to identify them with the Carduchians of the Greeks; [47] and they still defend against the Ottoman Porte the antique freedom which they asserted against the successors of Cyrus. Poverty and ambition prompted them to embrace the profession of mercenary soldiers: the service of his father and uncle prepared the reign of the great Saladin; [48] and the son of Job or Ayub, a simple Curd, magnanimously smiled at his pedigree, which flattery deduced from the Arabian caliphs. [49] So unconscious was Noureddin of the impending ruin of his house, that he constrained the reluctant youth to follow his uncle Shiracouh into Egypt: his military character was established by the defence of Alexandria; and, if we may believe the Latins, he solicited and obtained from the Christian general the profanehonors of knighthood. [50] On the death of Shiracouh, the office of grand vizier was bestowed on Saladin, as the youngest and least powerful of the emirs; but with the advice of his father, whom he invited to Cairo, his genius obtained the ascendant over his equals, and attached the army to his person and interest. While Noureddin lived, these ambitious Curds were the most humble of his slaves; and the indiscreet murmurs of the divan were silenced by the prudent Ayub, who loudly protested that at the command of the sultan he himself would lead his sons in chains to the foot of the throne. "Such language," he added in private, "was prudent and proper in an assembly of your rivals; but we are now above fear and obedience; and the threats of Noureddin shall not extort the tribute of a sugar-cane." His seasonable death relieved them from the odious and doubtful conflict: his son, a minor of eleven years of age, was left for a while to the emirs of Damascus; and the new lord of Egypt was decorated by the caliph with every title [51] that could sanctify his usurpation in the eyes of the people. Nor was Saladin long content with the possession of Egypt; he despoiled the Christians of Jerusalem, and the Atabeks of Damascus, Aleppo, and Diarbekir: Mecca and Medina acknowledged him for their temporal protector: his brother subdued the distant regions of Yemen, or the happy Arabia; and at the hour of his death, his empire was spread from the African Tripoli to the Tigris, and from the Indian Ocean to the mountains of Armenia. In the judgment of his character, the reproaches of treason and ingratitude strike forcibly on our minds, impressed, as they are, with the principle and experience of law and loyalty. But his ambition may in some measure be excused by the revolutions of Asia, [52] which had erased every notion of legitimate succession; by the recent example of the Atabeks themselves; by his reverence to the son of his benefactor; his humane and generous behavior to the collateral branches; by their incapacity and his merit; by the approbation of the caliph, the sole source of all legitimate power; and, above all, by the wishes and interest of the people, whose happiness is the first object of government. In his virtues, and in those of his patron, they admired the singular union of the hero and the saint; for both Noureddin and Saladin are ranked among the Mahometan saints; and the constant meditation of the holy war appears to have shed a serious and sober color over their lives and actions. The youth of the latter [53] was addicted to wine and women: but his aspiring spirit soon renounced the temptations of pleasure for the graver follies of fame and dominion: the garment of Saladin was of coarse woollen; water was his only drink; and, while he emulated the temperance, he surpassed the chastity, of his Arabian prophet. Both in faith and practice he was a rigid Mussulman: he ever deplored that the defence of religion had not allowed him to accomplish the pilgrimage of Mecca; but at the stated hours, five times each day, the sultan devoutly prayed with his brethren: the involuntary omission of fasting was scrupulously repaid; and his perusal of the Koran, on horseback between the approaching armies, may be quoted as a proof, however ostentatious, of piety and courage. [54] The superstitious doctrine of the sect of Shafei was the only study that he deigned to encourage: the poets were safe in his contempt; but all profane science was the object of his aversion; and a philosopher, who had invented some speculative novelties, was seized and strangled by the command of the royal saint. The justice of his divan was accessible to the meanest suppliant against himself and his ministers; and it was only for a kingdom that Saladin would deviate from the rule of equity. While the descendants of Seljuk and Zenghi held his stirrup and smoothed his garments, he was affable and patient with the meanest of his servants. So boundless was his liberality, that he distributed twelve thousand horses at the siege of Acre; and, at the time of his death, no more than forty-seven drams of silver and one piece of gold coin were found in the treasury; yet, in a martial reign, the tributes were diminished, and the wealthy citizens enjoyed, without fear or danger, the fruits of their industry. Egypt, Syria, and Arabia, were adorned by the royal foundations of hospitals, colleges, and mosques; and Cairo was fortified with a wall and citadel; but his works were consecrated to public use: [55] nor did the sultan indulge himself in a garden or palace of private luxury. In a fanatic age, himself a fanatic, the genuine virtues of Saladin commanded the esteem of the Christians; the emperor of Germany gloried in his friendship; [56] the Greek emperor solicited his alliance; [57] and the conquest of Jerusalem diffused, and perhaps magnified, his fame both in the East and West.

[Footnote 46: For the Curds, see De Guignes, tom. ii. p. 416, 417, the Index Geographicus of Schultens and Tavernier, Voyages, p. i. p. 308, 309. The Ayoubites descended from the tribe of the Rawadiæi, one of the noblest; but as they were infected with the heresy of the Metempsychosis, the orthodox sultans insinuated that their descent was only on the mother's side, and that their ancestor was a stranger who settled among the Curds.]

[Footnote 47: See the ivth book of the Anabasis of Xenophon. The ten thousand suffered more from the arrows of the free Carduchians, than from the splendid weakness of the great king.]

[Footnote 48: We are indebted to the professor Schultens (Lugd. Bat, 1755, in folio) for the richest and most authentic materials, a life of Saladin by his friend and minister the Cadhi Bohadin, and copious extracts from the history of his kinsman the prince Abulfeda of Hamah. To these we may add, the article of Salaheddin in the Bibliothèque Orientale, and all that may be gleaned from the Dynasties of Abulpharagius.]

[Footnote 49: Since Abulfeda was himself an Ayoubite, he may share the praise, for imitating, at least tacitly, the modesty of the founder.]

[Footnote 50: Hist. Hierosol. in the Gesta Dei per Francos, p. 1152. A similar example may be found in Joinville, (p. 42, edition du Louvre;) but the pious St. Louis refused to dignify infidels with the order of Christian knighthood, (Ducange, Observations, p 70.)]

[Footnote 51: In these Arabic titles, religionis must always be understood; Noureddin, lumen r.; Ezzodin, decus; Amadoddin, columen: our hero's proper name was Joseph, and he was styled Salahoddin, salus; Al Malichus, Al Nasirus, rex defensor; Abu Modaffer, pater victoriæ, Schultens, Præfat.]

[Footnote 52: Abulfeda, who descended from a brother of Saladin, observes, from many examples, that the founders of dynasties took the guilt for themselves, and left the reward to their innocent collaterals, (Excerpt p. 10.)]

[Footnote 53: See his life and character in Renaudot, p. 537—548.]

[Footnote 54: His civil and religious virtues are celebrated in the first chapter of Bohadin, (p. 4—30,) himself an eye-witness, and an honest bigot.]

[Footnote 55: In many works, particularly Joseph's well in the castle of Cairo, the Sultan and the Patriarch have been confounded by the ignorance of natives and travellers.]

[Footnote 56: Anonym. Canisii, tom. iii. p. ii. p. 504.]

[Footnote 57: Bohadin, p. 129, 130.]

During his short existence, the kingdom of Jerusalem [58] was supported by the discord of the Turks and Saracens; and both the Fatimite caliphs and the sultans of Damascus were tempted to sacrifice the cause of their religion to the meaner considerations of private and present advantage. But the powers of Egypt, Syria, and Arabia, were now united by a hero, whom nature and fortune had armed against the Christians. All without now bore the most threatening aspect; and all was feeble and hollow in the internal state of Jerusalem. After the two first Baldwins, the brother and cousin of Godfrey of Bouillon, the sceptre devolved by female succession to Melisenda, daughter of the second Baldwin, and her husband Fulk, count of Anjou, the father, by a former marriage, of our English Plantagenets. Their two sons, Baldwin the Third, and Amaury, waged a strenuous, and not unsuccessful, war against the infidels; but the son of Amaury, Baldwin the Fourth, was deprived, by the leprosy, a gift of the crusades, of the faculties both of mind and body. His sister Sybilla, the mother of Baldwin the Fifth, was his natural heiress: after the suspicious death of her child, she crowned her second husband, Guy of Lusignan, a prince of a handsome person, but of such base renown, that his own brother Jeffrey was heard to exclaim, "Since they have made him a king, surely they would have made me a god!" The choice was generally blamed; and the most powerful vassal, Raymond count of Tripoli, who had been excluded from the succession and regency, entertained an implacable hatred against the king, and exposed his honor and conscience to the temptations of the sultan. Such were the guardians of the holy city; a leper, a child, a woman, a coward, and a traitor: yet its fate was delayed twelve years by some supplies from Europe, by the valor of the military orders, and by the distant or domestic avocations of their great enemy. At length, on every side, the sinking state was encircled and pressed by a hostile line: and the truce was violated by the Franks, whose existence it protected. A soldier of fortune, Reginald of Chatillon, had seized a fortress on the edge of the desert, from whence he pillaged the caravans, insulted Mahomet, and threatened the cities of Mecca and Medina. Saladin condescended to complain; rejoiced in the denial of justice, and at the head of fourscore thousand horse and foot invaded the Holy Land. The choice of Tiberias for his first siege was suggested by the count of Tripoli, to whom it belonged; and the king of Jerusalem was persuaded to drain his garrison, and to arm his people, for the relief of that important place. [59] By the advice of the perfidious Raymond, the Christians were betrayed into a camp destitute of water: he fled on the first onset, with the curses of both nations: [60]

Lusignan was overthrown, with the loss of thirty thousand men; and the wood of the true cross (a dire misfortune!) was left in the power of the infidels. [60/1] The royal captive was conducted to the tent of Saladin; and as he fainted with thirst and terror, the generous victor presented him with a cup of sherbet, cooled in snow, without suffering his companion, Reginald of Chatillon, to partake of this pledge of hospitality and pardon. "The person and dignity of a king," said the sultan, "are sacred, but this impious robber must instantly acknowledge the prophet, whom he has blasphemed, or meet the death which he has so often deserved." On the proud or conscientious refusal of the Christian warrior, Saladin struck him on the head with his cimeter, and Reginald was despatched by the guards. [61] The trembling Lusignan was sent to Damascus, to an honorable prison and speedy ransom; but the victory was stained by the execution of two hundred and thirty knights of the hospital, the intrepid champions and martyrs of their faith. The kingdom was left without a head; and of the two grand masters of the military orders, the one was slain and the other was a prisoner. From all the cities, both of the sea-coast and the inland country, the garrisons had been drawn away for this fatal field: Tyre and Tripoli alone could escape the rapid inroad of Saladin; and three months after the battle of Tiberias, he appeared in arms before the gates of Jerusalem. [62]

[Footnote 58: For the Latin kingdom of Jerusalem, see William of Tyre, from the ixth to the xxiid book. Jacob a Vitriaco, Hist. Hierosolem l i., and Sanutus Secreta Fidelium Crucis, l. iii. p. vi. vii. viii. ix.]

[Footnote 59: Templarii ut apes bombabant et Hospitalarii ut venti stridebant, et barones se exitio offerebant, et Turcopuli (the Christian light troops) semet ipsi in ignem injiciebant, (Ispahani de Expugnatione Kudsiticâ, p. 18, apud Schultens;) a specimen of Arabian eloquence, somewhat different from the style of Xenophon!]

[Footnote 60: The Latins affirm, the Arabians insinuate, the treason of Raymond; but had he really embraced their religion, he would have been a saint and a hero in the eyes of the latter.]

[Footnote 60/1: Raymond's advice would have prevented the abandonment of a secure camp abounding with water near Sepphoris. The rash and insolent valor of the master of the order of Knights Templars, which had before exposed the Christians to a fatal defeat at the brook Kishon, forced the feeble king to annul the determination of a council of war, and advance to a camp in an enclosed valley among the mountains, near Hittin, without water. Raymond did not fly till the battle was irretrievably lost, and then the Saracens seem to have opened their ranks to allow him free passage. The charge of suggesting the siege of Tiberias appears ungrounded Raymond, no doubt, played a double part: he was a man of strong sagacity, who foresaw the desperate nature of the contest with Saladin, endeavored by every means to maintain the treaty, and, though he joined both his arms and his still more valuable counsels to the Christian army, yet kept up a kind of amicable correspondence with the Mahometans. See Wilken, vol. iii. part ii. p. 276, et seq. Michaud, vol. ii. p. 278, et seq. M. Michaud is still more friendly than Wilken to the memory of Count Raymond, who died suddenly, shortly after the battle of Hittin. He quotes a letter written in the name of Saladin by the caliph Alfdel, to show that Raymond was considered by the Mahometans their most dangerous and detested enemy. "No person of distinction among the Christians escaped, except the count, (of Tripoli) whom God curse. God made him die shortly afterwards, and sent him from the kingdom of death to hell."—M.]

[Footnote 61: Benaud, Reginald, or Arnold de Chatillon, is celebrated by the Latins in his life and death; but the circumstances of the latter are more distinctly related by Bohadin and Abulfeda; and Joinville (Hist. de St. Louis, p. 70) alludes to the practice of Saladin, of never putting to death a prisoner who had tasted his bread and salt. Some of the companions of Arnold had been slaughtered, and almost sacrificed, in a valley of Mecca, ubi sacrificia mactantur, (Abulfeda, p. 32.)]

[Footnote 62: Vertot, who well describes the loss of the kingdom and city (Hist. des Chevaliers de Malthe, tom. i. l. ii. p. 226—278,) inserts two original epistles of a Knight Templar.]

He might expect that the siege of a city so venerable on earth and in heaven, so interesting to Europe and Asia, would rekindle the last sparks of enthusiasm; and that, of sixty thousand Christians, every man would be a soldier, and every soldier a candidate for martyrdom. But Queen Sybilla trembled for herself and her captive husband; and the barons and knights, who had escaped from the sword and chains of the Turks, displayed the same factious and selfish spirit in the public ruin. The most numerous portion of the inhabitants was composed of the Greek and Oriental Christians, whom experience had taught to prefer the Mahometan before the Latin yoke; [63] and the holy sepulchre attracted a base and needy crowd, without arms or courage, who subsisted only on the charity of the pilgrims. Some feeble and hasty efforts were made for the defence of Jerusalem: but in the space of fourteen days, a victorious army drove back the sallies of the besieged, planted their engines, opened the wall to the breadth of fifteen cubits, applied their scaling-ladders, and erected on the breach twelve banners of the prophet and the sultan. It was in vain that a barefoot procession of the queen, the women, and the monks, implored the Son of God to save his tomb and his inheritance from impious violation. Their sole hope was in the mercy of the conqueror, and to their first suppliant deputation that mercy was sternly denied. "He had sworn to avenge the patience and long-suffering of the Moslems; the hour of forgiveness was elapsed, and the moment was now arrived to expiate, in blood, the innocent blood which had been spilt by Godfrey and the first crusaders." But a desperate and successful struggle of the Franks admonished the sultan that his triumph was not yet secure; he listened with reverence to a solemn adjuration in the name of the common Father of mankind; and a sentiment of human sympathy mollified the rigor of fanaticism and conquest. He consented to accept the city, and to spare the inhabitants. The Greek and Oriental Christians were permitted to live under his dominion, but it was stipulated, that in forty days all the Franks and Latins should evacuate Jerusalem, and be safely conducted to the seaports of Syria and Egypt; that ten pieces of gold should be paid for each man, five for each woman, and one for every child; and that those who were unable to purchase their freedom should be detained in perpetual slavery. Of some writers it is a favorite and invidious theme to compare the humanity of Saladin with the massacre of the first crusade. The difference would be merely personal; but we should not forget that the Christians had offered to capitulate, and that the Mahometans of Jerusalem sustained the last extremities of an assault and storm. Justice is indeed due to the fidelity with which the Turkish conqueror fulfilled the conditions of the treaty; and he may be deservedly praised for the glance of pity which he cast on the misery of the vanquished. Instead of a rigorous exaction of his debt, he accepted a sum of thirty thousand byzants, for the ransom of seven thousand poor; two or three thousand more were dismissed by his gratuitous clemency; and the number of slaves was reduced to eleven or fourteen thousand persons. In this interview with the queen, his words, and even his tears suggested the kindest consolations; his liberal alms were distributed among those who had been made orphans or widows by the fortune of war; and while the knights of the hospital were in arms against him, he allowed their more pious brethren to continue, during the term of a year, the care and service of the sick. In these acts of mercy the virtue of Saladin deserves our admiration and love: he was above the necessity of dissimulation, and his stern fanaticism would have prompted him to dissemble, rather than to affect, this profane compassion for the enemies of the Koran. After Jerusalem had been delivered from the presence of the strangers, the sultan made his triumphal entry, his banners waving in the wind, and to the harmony of martial music. The great mosque of Omar, which had been converted into a church, was again consecrated to one God and his prophet Mahomet: the walls and pavement were purified with rose-water; and a pulpit, the labor of Noureddin, was erected in the sanctuary. But when the golden cross that glittered on the dome was cast down, and dragged through the streets, the Christians of every sect uttered a lamentable groan, which was answered by the joyful shouts of the Moslems. In four ivory chests the patriarch had collected the crosses, the images, the vases, and the relics of the holy place; they were seized by the conqueror, who was desirous of presenting the caliph with the trophies of Christian idolatry. He was persuaded, however, to intrust them to the patriarch and prince of Antioch; and the pious pledge was redeemed by Richard of England, at the expense of fifty-two thousand byzants of gold. [64]

[Footnote 63: Renaudot, Hist. Patriarch. Alex. p. 545.]

[Footnote 64: For the conquest of Jerusalem, Bohadin (p. 67—75) and Abulfeda (p. 40—43) are our Moslem witnesses. Of the Christian, Bernard Thesaurarius (c. 151—167) is the most copious and authentic; see likewise Matthew Paris, (p. 120—124.)]

The nations might fear and hope the immediate and final expulsion of the Latins from Syria; which was yet delayed above a century after the death of Saladin. [65] In the career of victory, he was first checked by the resistance of Tyre; the troops and garrisons, which had capitulated, were imprudently conducted to the same port: their numbers were adequate to the defence of the place; and the arrival of Conrad of Montferrat inspired the disorderly crowd with confidence and union. His father, a venerable pilgrim, had been made prisoner in the battle of Tiberias; but that disaster was unknown in Italy and Greece, when the son was urged by ambition and piety to visit the inheritance of his royal nephew, the infant Baldwin. The view of the Turkish banners warned him from the hostile coast of Jaffa; and Conrad was unanimously hailed as the prince and champion of Tyre, which was already besieged by the conqueror of Jerusalem. The firmness of his zeal, and perhaps his knowledge of a generous foe, enabled him to brave the threats of the sultan, and to declare, that should his aged parent be exposed before the walls, he himself would discharge the first arrow, and glory in his descent from a Christian martyr. [66] The Egyptian fleet was allowed to enter the harbor of Tyre; but the chain was suddenly drawn, and five galleys were either sunk or taken: a thousand Turks were slain in a sally; and Saladin, after burning his engines, concluded a glorious campaign by a disgraceful retreat to Damascus. He was soon assailed by a more formidable tempest. The pathetic narratives, and even the pictures, that represented in lively colors the servitude and profanation of Jerusalem, awakened the torpid sensibility of Europe: the emperor Frederic Barbarossa, and the kings of France and England, assumed the cross; and the tardy magnitude of their armaments was anticipated by the maritime states of the Mediterranean and the Ocean. The skilful and provident Italians first embarked in the ships of Genoa, Pisa, and Venice. They were speedily followed by the most eager pilgrims of France, Normandy, and the Western Isles. The powerful succor of Flanders, Frise, and Denmark, filled near a hundred vessels: and the Northern warriors were distinguished in the field by a lofty stature and a ponderous battle-axe. [67] Their increasing multitudes could no longer be confined within the walls of Tyre, or remain obedient to the voice of Conrad. They pitied the misfortunes, and revered the dignity, of Lusignan, who was released from prison, perhaps, to divide the army of the Franks. He proposed the recovery of Ptolemais, or Acre, thirty miles to the south of Tyre; and the place was first invested by two thousand horse and thirty thousand foot under his nominal command. I shall not expatiate on the story of this memorable siege; which lasted near two years, and consumed, in a narrow space, the forces of Europe and Asia. Never did the flame of enthusiasm burn with fiercer and more destructive rage; nor could the true believers, a common appellation, who consecrated their own martyrs, refuse some applause to the mistaken zeal and courage of their adversaries. At the sound of the holy trumpet, the Moslems of Egypt, Syria, Arabia, and the Oriental provinces, assembled under the servant of the prophet: [68] his camp was pitched and removed within a few miles of Acre; and he labored, night and day, for the relief of his brethren and the annoyance of the Franks. Nine battles, not unworthy of the name, were fought in the neighborhood of Mount Carmel, with such vicissitude of fortune, that in one attack, the sultan forced his way into the city; that in one sally, the Christians penetrated to the royal tent. By the means of divers and pigeons, a regular correspondence was maintained with the besieged; and, as often as the sea was left open, the exhausted garrison was withdrawn, and a fresh supply was poured into the place. The Latin camp was thinned by famine, the sword and the climate; but the tents of the dead were replenished with new pilgrims, who exaggerated the strength and speed of their approaching countrymen. The vulgar was astonished by the report, that the pope himself, with an innumerable crusade, was advanced as far as Constantinople. The march of the emperor filled the East with more serious alarms: the obstacles which he encountered in Asia, and perhaps in Greece, were raised by the policy of Saladin: his joy on the death of Barbarossa was measured by his esteem; and the Christians were rather dismayed than encouraged at the sight of the duke of Swabia and his way-worn remnant of five thousand Germans. At length, in the spring of the second year, the royal fleets of France and England cast anchor in the Bay of Acre, and the siege was more vigorously prosecuted by the youthful emulation of the two kings, Philip Augustus and Richard Plantagenet. After every resource had been tried, and every hope was exhausted, the defenders of Acre submitted to their fate; a capitulation was granted, but their lives and liberties were taxed at the hard conditions of a ransom of two hundred thousand pieces of gold, the deliverance of one hundred nobles, and fifteen hundred inferior captives, and the restoration of the wood of the holy cross. Some doubts in the agreement, and some delay in the execution, rekindled the fury of the Franks, and three thousand Moslems, almost in the sultan's view, were beheaded by the command of the sanguinary Richard. [69] By the conquest of Acre, the Latin powers acquired a strong town and a convenient harbor; but the advantage was most dearly purchased. The minister and historian of Saladin computes, from the report of the enemy, that their numbers, at different periods, amounted to five or six hundred thousand; that more than one hundred thousand Christians were slain; that a far greater number was lost by disease or shipwreck; and that a small portion of this mighty host could return in safety to their native countries. [70]

[Footnote 65: The sieges of Tyre and Acre are most copiously described by Bernard Thesaurarius, (de Acquisitione Terræ Sanctæ, c. 167—179,) the author of the Historia Hierosolymitana, (p. 1150—1172, in Bongarsius,) Abulfeda, (p. 43—50,) and Bohadin, (p. 75—179.)]

[Footnote 66: I have followed a moderate and probable representation of the fact; by Vertot, who adopts without reluctance a romantic tale the old marquis is actually exposed to the darts of the besieged.]

[Footnote 67: Northmanni et Gothi, et cæteri populi insularum quæ inter occidentem et septentrionem sitæ sunt, gentes bellicosæ, corporis proceri mortis intrepidæ, bipennibus armatæ, navibus rotundis, quæ Ysnachiæ dicuntur, advectæ.]

[Footnote 68: The historian of Jerusalem (p. 1108) adds the nations of the East from the Tigris to India, and the swarthy tribes of Moors and Getulians, so that Asia and Africa fought against Europe.]

[Footnote 69: Bohadin, p. 180; and this massacre is neither denied nor blamed by the Christian historians. Alacriter jussa complentes, (the English soldiers,) says Galfridus à Vinesauf, (l. iv. c. 4, p. 346,) who fixes at 2700 the number of victims; who are multiplied to 5000 by Roger Hoveden, (p. 697, 698.) The humanity or avarice of Philip Augustus was persuaded to ransom his prisoners, (Jacob à Vitriaco, l. i. c. 98, p. 1122.)]

[Footnote 70: Bohadin, p. 14. He quotes the judgment of Balianus, and the prince of Sidon, and adds, ex illo mundo quasi hominum paucissimi redierunt. Among the Christians who died before St. John d'Acre, I find the English names of De Ferrers earl of Derby, (Dugdale, Baronage, part i. p. 260,) Mowbray, (idem, p. 124,) De Mandevil, De Fiennes, St. John, Scrope, Bigot, Talbot, &c.]

## PART III

Philip Augustus, and Richard the First, are the only kings of France and England who have fought under the same banners; but the holy service in which they were enlisted was incessantly disturbed by their national jealousy; and the two factions, which they protected in Palestine, were more averse to each other than to the common enemy. In the eyes of the Orientals; the French monarch was superior in dignity and power; and, in the emperor's absence, the Latins revered him as their temporal chief. [71] His exploits were not adequate to his fame. Philip was brave, but the statesman predominated in his character; he was soon weary of sacrificing his health and interest on a barren coast: the surrender of Acre became the signal of his departure; nor could he justify this unpopular desertion, by leaving the duke of Burgundy with five hundred knights and ten thousand foot, for the service of the Holy Land. The king of England, though inferior in dignity, surpassed his rival in wealth and military renown; [72] and if heroism be confined to brutal and ferocious valor, Richard Plantagenet will stand high among the heroes of the age. The memory of Cur de Lion, of the lion-hearted prince, was long dear and glorious to his English subjects; and, at the distance of sixty years, it was celebrated in proverbial sayings by the grandsons of the Turks and Saracens, against whom he had fought: his tremendous name was employed by the Syrian mothers to silence their infants; and if a horse suddenly started from the way, his rider was wont to exclaim, "Dost thou think King Richard is in that bush?" [73] His cruelty to the Mahometans was the effect of temper and zeal; but I cannot believe that a soldier, so free and fearless in the use of his lance, would have descended to whet a dagger against his valiant brother Conrad of Montferrat, who was slain at Tyre by some secret assassins. [74] After the surrender of Acre, and the departure of Philip, the king of England led the crusaders to the recovery of the sea-coast; and the cities of Cæsarea and Jaffa were added to the fragments of the kingdom of Lusignan. A march of one hundred miles from Acre to Ascalon was a great and perpetual battle of eleven days. In the disorder of his troops, Saladin remained on the field with seventeen guards, without lowering his standard, or suspending the sound of his brazen kettle-drum: he again rallied and renewed the charge; and his preachers or heralds called aloud on the unitarians, manfully to stand up against the Christian idolaters. But the progress of these idolaters was irresistible; and it was only by demolishing the walls and buildings of Ascalon, that the sultan could prevent them from occupying an important fortress on the confines of Egypt. During a severe winter, the armies slept; but in the spring, the Franks advanced within a day's march of Jerusalem, under the leading standard of the English king; and his active spirit intercepted a convoy, or caravan, of seven thousand camels. Saladin [75] had fixed his station in the holy city; but the city was struck with consternation and discord: he fasted; he prayed; he preached; he offered to share the dangers of the siege; but his Mamalukes, who remembered the fate of their companions at Acre, pressed the sultan with loyal or seditious clamors, to reserve his person and their courage for the future defence of the religion and empire. [76] The Moslems were delivered by the sudden, or, as they deemed, the miraculous, retreat of the Christians; [77] and the laurels of Richard were blasted by the prudence, or envy, of his companions. The hero, ascending a hill, and veiling his face, exclaimed with an indignant voice, "Those who are unwilling to rescue, are unworthy to view, the sepulchre of Christ!" After his return to Acre, on the news that Jaffa was surprised by the sultan, he sailed with some merchant vessels, and leaped foremost on the beach: the castle was relieved by his presence; and sixty thousand Turks and Saracens fled before his arms. The discovery of his weakness, provoked them to return in the morning; and they found him carelessly encamped before the gates with only seventeen knights and three hundred archers. Without counting their numbers, he sustained their charge; and we learn from the evidence of his enemies, that the king of England, grasping his lance, rode furiously along their front, from the right to the left wing, without meeting an adversary who dared to encounter his career. [78] Am I writing the history of Orlando or Amadis?

[Footnote 71: Magnus hic apud eos, interque reges eorum tum virtute tum majestate eminens.... summus rerum arbiter, (Bohadin, p. 159.) He does not seem to have known the names either of Philip or Richard.]

[Footnote 72: Rex Angliæ, præstrenuus.... rege Gallorum minor apud eos censebatur ratione regni atque dignitatis; sed tum divitiis florentior, tum bellicâ virtute multo erat celebrior, (Bohadin, p. 161.) A stranger might admire those riches; the national historians will tell with what lawless and wasteful oppression they were collected.]

[Footnote 73: Joinville, p. 17. Cuides-tu que ce soit le roi Richart?]

[Footnote 74: Yet he was guilty in the opinion of the Moslems, who attest the confession of the assassins, that they were sent by the king of England, (Bohadin, p. 225;) and his only defence is an absurd and palpable forgery, (Hist. de l'Académie des Inscriptions, tom. xv. p. 155—163,) a pretended letter from the prince of the assassins, the Sheich, or old man of the mountain, who justified Richard, by assuming to himself the guilt or merit of the murder. Note: Von Hammer (Geschichte der Assassinen, p. 202) sums up against Richard, Wilken (vol. iv. p. 485) as strongly for acquittal. Michaud (vol. ii. p. 420) delivers no decided opinion. This crime was also attributed to Saladin, who is said, by an Oriental authority, (the continuator of Tabari,) to have employed the assassins to murder both Conrad and Richard. It is a melancholy admission, but it must be acknowledged, that such an act would be less inconsistent with the character of the Christian than of the Mahometan king—M.]

[Footnote 75: See the distress and pious firmness of Saladin, as they are described by Bohadin, (p. 7—9, 235—237,) who himself harangued the defenders of Jerusalem; their fears were not unknown to the enemy, (Jacob. à Vitriaco, l. i. c. 100, p. 1123. Vinisauf, l. v. c. 50, p. 399.)]

[Footnote 76: Yet unless the sultan, or an Ayoubite prince, remained in Jerusalem, nec Curdi Turcis, nec Turci essent obtemperaturi Curdis, (Bohadin, p. 236.) He draws aside a corner of the political curtain.]

[Footnote 77: Bohadin, (p. 237,) and even Jeffrey de Vinisauf, (l. vi. c. 1—8, p. 403—409,) ascribe the retreat to Richard himself; and Jacobus à Vitriaco observes, that in his impatience to depart, in alterum virum mutatus est, (p. 1123.) Yet Joinville, a French knight, accuses the envy of Hugh duke of Burgundy, (p. 116,) without supposing, like Matthew Paris, that he was bribed by Saladin.]

[Footnote 78: The expeditions to Ascalon, Jerusalem, and Jaffa, are related by Bohadin (p. 184—249) and Abulfeda, (p. 51, 52.) The author of the Itinerary, or the monk of St. Alban's, cannot exaggerate the cadhi's account of the prowess of Richard, (Vinisauf, l. vi. c. 14—24, p. 412—421. Hist. Major, p. 137—143;) and on the whole of this war there is a marvellous agreement between the Christian and Mahometan writers, who mutually praise the virtues of their enemies.]

During these hostilities, a languid and tedious negotiation [79] between the Franks and Moslems was started, and continued, and broken, and again resumed, and again broken. Some acts of royal courtesy, the gift of snow and fruit, the exchange of Norway hawks and Arabian horses, softened the asperity of religious war: from the vicissitude of success, the monarchs might learn to suspect that Heaven was neutral in the quarrel; nor, after the trial of each other, could either hope for a decisive victory. [80] The health both of Richard and Saladin appeared to be in a declining state; and they respectively suffered the evils of distant and domestic warfare: Plantagenet was impatient to punish a perfidious rival who had invaded Normandy in his absence; and the indefatigable sultan was subdued by the cries of the people, who was the victim, and of the soldiers, who were the instruments, of his martial zeal. The first demands of the king of England were the restitution of Jerusalem, Palestine, and the true cross; and he firmly declared, that himself and his brother pilgrims would end their lives in the pious labor, rather than return to Europe with ignominy and remorse. But the conscience of Saladin refused, without some weighty compensation, to restore the idols, or promote the idolatry, of the Christians; he asserted, with equal firmness, his religious and civil claim to the sovereignty of Palestine; descanted on the importance and sanctity of Jerusalem; and rejected all terms of the establishment, or partition of the Latins. The marriage which Richard proposed, of his sister with the sultan's brother, was defeated by the difference of faith; the princess abhorred the embraces of a Turk; and Adel, or Saphadin, would not easily renounce a plurality of wives. A personal interview was declined by Saladin, who alleged their mutual ignorance of each other's language; and the negotiation was managed with much art and delay by their interpreters and envoys. The final agreement was equally disapproved by the zealots of both parties, by the Roman pontiff and the caliph of Bagdad. It was stipulated that Jerusalem and the holy sepulchre should be open, without tribute or vexation, to the pilgrimage of the Latin Christians; that, after the demolition of Ascalon, they should inclusively possess the sea-coast from Jaffa to Tyre; that the count of Tripoli and the prince of Antioch should be comprised in the truce; and that, during three years and three months, all hostilities should cease. The principal chiefs of the two armies swore to the observance of the treaty; but the monarchs were satisfied with giving their word and their right hand; and the royal majesty was excused from an oath, which always implies some suspicion of falsehood and dishonor. Richard embarked for Europe, to seek a long captivity and a premature grave; and the space of a few months concluded the life and glories of Saladin. The Orientals describe his edifying death, which happened at Damascus; but they seem ignorant of the equal distribution of his alms among the three religions, [81] or of the display of a shroud, instead of a standard, to admonish the East of the instability of human greatness. The unity of empire was dissolved by his death; his sons were oppressed by the stronger arm of their uncle Saphadin; the hostile interests of the sultans of Egypt, Damascus, and Aleppo, [82] were again revived; and the Franks or Latins stood and breathed, and hoped, in their fortresses along the Syrian coast.

[Footnote 79: See the progress of negotiation and hostility in Bohadin, (p. 207—260,) who was himself an actor in the treaty. Richard declared his intention of returning with new armies to the conquest of the Holy Land; and Saladin answered the menace with a civil compliment, (Vinisauf l. vi. c. 28, p. 423.)]

[Footnote 80: The most copious and original account of this holy war is Galfridi à Vinisauf, Itinerarium Regis Anglorum Richardi et aliorum in Terram Hierosolymorum, in six books, published in the iid volume of Gale's Scriptores Hist. Anglicanæ, (p. 247—429.) Roger Hoveden and Matthew Paris afford likewise many valuable materials; and the former describes, with accuracy, the discipline and navigation of the English fleet.]

[Footnote 81: Even Vertot (tom. i. p. 251) adopts the foolish notion of the indifference of Saladin, who professed the Koran with his last breath.]

[Footnote 82: See the succession of the Ayoubites, in Abulpharagius, (Dynast. p. 277, &c.,) and the tables of M. De Guignes, l'Art de Vérifier les Dates, and the Bibliothèque Orientale.]

The noblest monument of a conqueror's fame, and of the terror which he inspired, is the Saladine tenth, a general tax which was imposed on the laity, and even the clergy, of the Latin church, for the service of the holy war. The practice was too lucrative to expire with the occasion: and this tribute became the foundation of all the tithes and tenths on ecclesiastical benefices, which have been granted by the Roman pontiffs to Catholic sovereigns, or reserved for the immediate use of the apostolic see. [83] This pecuniary emolument must have tended to increase the interest of the popes in the recovery of Palestine: after the death of Saladin, they preached the crusade, by their epistles, their legates, and their missionaries; and the accomplishment of the pious work might have been expected from the zeal and talents of Innocent the Third. [84] Under that young and ambitious priest, the successors of St. Peter attained the full meridian of their greatness: and in a reign of eighteen years, he exercised a despotic command over the emperors and kings, whom he raised and deposed; over the nations, whom an interdict of months or years deprived, for the offence of their rulers, of the exercise of Christian worship. In the council of the Lateran he acted as the ecclesiastical, almost as the temporal, sovereign of the East and West. It was at the feet of his legate that John of England surrendered his crown; and Innocent may boast of the two most signal triumphs over sense and humanity, the establishment of transubstantiation, and the origin of the inquisition. At his voice, two crusades, the fourth and the fifth, were undertaken; but, except a king of Hungary, the princes of the second order were at the head of the pilgrims: the forces were inadequate to the design; nor did the effects correspond with the hopes and wishes of the pope and the people. The fourth crusade was diverted from Syria to Constantinople; and the conquest of the Greek or Roman empire by the Latins will form the proper and important subject of the next chapter. In the fifth, [85] two hundred thousand Franks were landed at the eastern mouth of the Nile. They reasonably hoped that Palestine must be subdued in Egypt, the seat and storehouse of the sultan; and, after a siege of sixteen months, the Moslems deplored the loss of Damietta. But the Christian army was ruined by the pride and insolence of the legate Pelagius, who, in the pope's name, assumed the character of general: the sickly Franks were encompassed by the waters of the Nile and the Oriental forces; and it was by the evacuation of Damietta that they obtained a safe retreat, some concessions for the pilgrims, and the tardy restitution of the doubtful relic of the true cross. The failure may in some measure be ascribed to the abuse and multiplication of the crusades, which were preached at the same time against the Pagans of Livonia, the Moors of Spain, the Albigeois of France, and the kings of Sicily of the Imperial family. [86] In these meritorious services, the volunteers might acquire at home the same spiritual indulgence, and a larger measure of temporal rewards; and even the popes, in their zeal against a domestic enemy, were sometimes tempted to forget the distress of their Syrian brethren. From the last age of the crusades they derived the occasional command of an army and revenue; and some deep reasoners have suspected that the whole enterprise, from the first synod of Placentia, was contrived and executed by the policy of Rome. The suspicion is not founded, either in nature or in fact. The successors of St. Peter appear to have followed, rather than guided, the impulse of manners and prejudice; without much foresight of the seasons, or cultivation of the soil, they gathered the ripe and spontaneous fruits of the superstition of the times. They gathered these fruits without toil or personal danger: in the council of the Lateran, Innocent the Third declared an ambiguous resolution of animating the crusaders by his example; but the pilot of the sacred vessel could not abandon the helm; nor was Palestine ever blessed with the presence of a Roman pontiff. [87]

[Footnote 83: Thomassin (Discipline de l'Eglise, tom. iii. p. 311—374) has copiously treated of the origin, abuses, and restrictions of these tenths. A theory was started, but not pursued, that they were rightfully *due to the pope, a tenth of the Levite's tenth to the high priest, (Selden on Tithes; see his Works, vol. iii. p. ii. p. 1083.)]*

*[Footnote 84: See the Gesta Innocentii III. in Murat. Script. Rer. Ital., (tom. iii. p. 486—568.)]*

*[Footnote 85: See the vth crusade, and the siege of Damietta, in Jacobus à Vitriaco, (l. iii. p. 1125—1149, in the Gesta Dei of Bongarsius,) an eye-witness, Bernard Thesaurarius, (in Script. Muratori, tom. vii. p. 825—846, c. 190—207,) a contemporary, and Sanutus, (Secreta Fidel Crucis, l. iii. p. xi. c. 4—9,) a diligent compiler; and of the Arabians Abulpharagius, (Dynast. p. 294,) and the Extracts at the end of Joinville, (p. 533, 537, 540, 547, &c.)]*

*[Footnote 86: To those who took the cross against Mainfroy, the pope (A.D. 1255) granted plenissimam peccatorum remissionem. Fideles mirabantur quòd tantum eis promitteret pro sanguine Christianorum effundendo quantum pro cruore infidelium aliquando, (Matthew Paris p. 785.) A high flight for the reason of the xiiith century.]*

*[Footnote 87: This simple idea is agreeable to the good sense of Mosheim, (Institut. Hist. Ecclés. p. 332,) and the fine philosophy of Hume, (Hist. of England, vol. i. p. 330.)]*

The persons, the families, and estates of the pilgrims, were under the immediate protection of the popes; and these spiritual patrons soon claimed the prerogative of directing their operations, and enforcing, by commands and censures, the accomplishment of their vow. Frederic the Second, [88] the grandson of Barbarossa, was successively the pupil, the enemy, and the victim of the church. At the age of twenty-one years, and in obedience to his guardian Innocent the Third, he assumed the cross; the same promise was repeated at his royal and imperial coronations; and his marriage with the heiress of Jerusalem forever bound him to defend the kingdom of his son Conrad. But as Frederic advanced in age and authority, he repented of the rash engagements of his youth: his liberal sense and knowledge taught him to despise the phantoms of superstition and the crowns of Asia: he no longer entertained the same reverence for the successors of Innocent: and his ambition was occupied by the restoration of the Italian monarchy from Sicily to the Alps. But the success of this project would have reduced the popes to their primitive simplicity; and, after the delays and excuses of twelve years, they urged the emperor, with entreaties and threats, to fix the time and place of his departure for Palestine. In the harbors of Sicily and Apulia, he prepared a fleet of one hundred galleys, and of one hundred vessels, that were framed to transport and land two thousand five hundred knights, with their horses and attendants; his vassals of Naples and Germany formed a powerful army; and the number of English crusaders was magnified to sixty thousand by the report of fame. But the inevitable or affected slowness of these mighty preparations consumed the strength and provisions of the more indigent pilgrims: the multitude was thinned by sickness and desertion; and the sultry summer of Calabria anticipated the mischiefs of a Syrian campaign. At length the emperor hoisted sail at Brundusium, with a fleet and army of forty thousand men: but he kept the sea no more than three days; and his hasty retreat, which was ascribed by his friends to a grievous indisposition, was accused by his enemies as a voluntary and obstinate disobedience. For suspending his vow was Frederic excommunicated by Gregory the Ninth; for presuming, the next year, to accomplish his vow, he was again excommunicated by the same pope. [89] While he served under the banner of the cross, a crusade was preached against him in Italy; and after his return he was compelled to ask pardon for the injuries which he had suffered. The clergy and military orders of Palestine were previously instructed to renounce his communion and dispute his commands; and in his own kingdom, the emperor was forced to consent that the orders of the camp should be issued in the name of God and of the Christian republic. Frederic entered Jerusalem in triumph; and with his own hands (for no priest would perform the office) he took the crown from the altar of the holy sepulchre. But the patriarch cast an interdict on the church which his presence had profaned; and the knights of the hospital and temple informed the sultan how easily he might be surprised and slain in his unguarded visit to the River Jordan. In such a state of fanaticism and faction, victory was hopeless, and defence was difficult; but the conclusion of an advantageous peace may be imputed to the discord of the Mahometans, and their personal esteem for the character of Frederic. The enemy of the church is accused of maintaining with the miscreants an intercourse of hospitality and friendship unworthy of a Christian; of despising the barrenness of the land; and of indulging a profane thought, that if Jehovah had seen the kingdom of Naples he never would have selected Palestine for the inheritance of his chosen people. Yet Frederic obtained from the sultan the restitution of Jerusalem, of Bethlem and Nazareth, of Tyre and Sidon; the Latins were allowed to inhabit and fortify the city; an equal code of civil and religious freedom was ratified for the sectaries of Jesus and those of Mahomet; and, while the former worshipped at the holy sepulchre, the latter might pray and preach in the mosque of the temple, [90] from whence the prophet undertook his nocturnal journey to heaven. The clergy deplored this scandalous toleration; and the weaker Moslems were gradually expelled; but every rational object of the crusades was accomplished without bloodshed; the churches were restored, the monasteries were replenished; and, in the space of fifteen years, the Latins of Jerusalem exceeded the number of six thousand. This peace and prosperity, for which they were ungrateful to their benefactor, was terminated by the irruption of the strange and savage hordes of Carizmians. [91] Flying from the arms of the Moguls, those shepherds [91/1] of the Caspian rolled headlong on Syria; and the union of the Franks with the sultans of Aleppo, Hems, and Damascus, was insufficient to stem the violence of the torrent. Whatever stood against them was cut off by the sword, or dragged into captivity: the military orders were almost exterminated in a single battle; and in the pillage of the city, in the profanation of the holy sepulchre, the Latins confess and regret the modesty and discipline of the Turks and Saracens.

*[Footnote 88: The original materials for the crusade of Frederic II. may be drawn from Richard de St. Germano (in Muratori, Script. Rerum Ital. tom. vii. p. 1002—1013) and Matthew Paris, (p. 286, 291, 300, 302, 304.) The most rational moderns are Fleury, (Hist. Ecclés. tom. xvi.,) Vertot, (Chevaliers de Malthe, tom. i. l. iii.,) Giannone, (Istoria Civile di Napoli, tom. ii. l. xvi.,) and Muratori, (Annali d' Italia, tom. x.)]*

*[Footnote 89: Poor Muratori knows what to think, but knows not what to say: "Chino qui il capo," &c. p. 322.]*

*[Footnote 90: The clergy artfully confounded the mosque or church of the temple with the holy sepulchre, and their wilful error has deceived both Vertot and Muratori.]*

*[Footnote 91: The irruption of the Carizmians, or Corasmins, is related by Matthew Paris, (p. 546, 547,) and by Joinville, Nangis, and the Arabians, (p. 111, 112, 191, 192, 528, 530.)]*

*[Footnote 91/1: They were in alliance with Eyub, sultan of Syria. Wilken vol. vi. p. 630—M.]*

Of the seven crusades, the two last were undertaken by Louis the Ninth, king of France; who lost his liberty in Egypt, and his life on the coast of Africa. Twenty-eight years after his death, he was canonized at Rome; and sixty-five miracles were readily found, and solemnly attested, to justify the claim of the royal saint. [92] The voice of history renders a more honorable testimony, that he united the virtues of a king, a hero, and a man; that his martial spirit was tempered by the love of private and public justice; and that Louis was the father of his people, the friend of his neighbors, and the terror of the infidels. Superstition alone, in all the extent of her baleful influence, [93] corrupted his understanding and his heart: his devotion stooped to admire and imitate the begging friars of Francis and Dominic: he pursued with blind and cruel zeal the enemies of the faith; and the best of kings twice descended from his throne to seek the adventures of a spiritual knight-errant. A monkish historian would have been content to applaud the most despicable part of his character; but the noble and gallant Joinville, [94] who shared the friendship and captivity of Louis, has traced with the pencil of nature the free portrait of his virtues as well as of his failings. From this intimate knowledge we may learn to suspect the political views of depressing their great vassals, which are so often imputed to the royal authors of the crusades. Above all the princes of the middle ages, Louis the Ninth successfully labored to restore the prerogatives of the crown; but it was at home and not in the East, that he acquired for himself and his posterity: his vow was the result of enthusiasm and sickness; and if he were the promoter, he was likewise the victim, of his holy madness. For the invasion of Egypt, France was exhausted of her troops and treasures; he covered the sea of Cyprus with eighteen hundred sails; the most modest enumeration amounts to fifty thousand men; and, if we might trust his own confession, as it is reported by Oriental vanity, he disembarked nine thousand five hundred horse, and one hundred and thirty thousand foot, who performed their pilgrimage under the shadow of his power. [95]

*[Footnote 92: Read, if you can, the Life and Miracles of St. Louis, by the confessor of Queen Margaret, (p. 291—523. Joinville, du Louvre.)]*

*[Footnote 93: He believed all that mother church taught, (Joinville, p. 10,) but he cautioned Joinville against disputing with infidels. "L'omme lay (said he in his old language) quand il ot medire de la loi Crestienne, ne doit pas deffendre la loi Crestienne ne mais que de l'espée, dequoi il doit donner parmi le ventre dedens, tant comme elle y peut entrer" (p. 12.)]*

*[Footnote 94: I have two editions of Joinville, the one (Paris, 1668) most valuable for the observations of Ducange; the other (Paris, au Louvre, 1761) most precious for the pure and authentic text, a MS. of which has been recently discovered. The last edition proves that the history of St. Louis was finished A.D. 1309, without explaining, or even admiring, the age of the author, which must have exceeded ninety years, (Preface, p. x. Observations de Ducange, p. 17.)]*

*[Footnote 95: Joinville, p. 32. Arabic Extracts, p. 549. Note: Compare Wilken, vol. vii. p. 94—M.]*

In complete armor, the oriflamme waving before him, Louis leaped foremost on the beach; and the strong city of Damietta, which had cost his predecessors a siege of sixteen months, was abandoned on the first assault by the trembling Moslems. But Damietta was the first and the last of his conquests; and in the fifth and sixth crusades, the same causes, almost on the same ground, were productive of similar calamities. [96] After a ruinous delay, which introduced into the camp the seeds of an epidemic disease, the Franks advanced from the sea-coast towards the capital of Egypt, and strove to surmount the unseasonable inundation of the Nile, which opposed their progress. Under the eye of their intrepid monarch, the barons and knights of France displayed their invincible contempt of danger and discipline: his brother, the count of Artois, stormed with inconsiderate valor the town of Massoura; and the carrier pigeons announced to the inhabitants of Cairo that all was lost. But a soldier, who afterwards usurped the sceptre, rallied the flying troops: the main body of the Christians was far behind the vanguard; and Artois was overpowered and slain. A shower of Greek fire was incessantly poured on the invaders; the Nile was commanded by the Egyptian galleys, the open country by the Arabs; all provisions were intercepted; each day aggravated the sickness and famine; and about the same time a retreat was found to be necessary and impracticable. The Oriental writers confess, that Louis might have escaped, if he would have deserted his subjects; he was made prisoner, with the greatest part of his nobles; all who could not redeem their lives by service or ransom were inhumanly massacred; and the walls of Cairo were decorated with a circle of Christian heads. [97] The king of France was loaded with chains; but the generous victor, a great-grandson of the brother of Saladin, sent a robe of honor to his royal captive, and his deliverance, with that of his soldiers, was obtained by the restitution of Damietta [98] and the payment of four hundred thousand pieces of gold. In a soft and luxurious climate, the degenerate children of the companions of Noureddin and Saladin were incapable of resisting the flower of European chivalry: they triumphed by the arms of their slaves or Mamalukes, the hardy natives of Tartary, who at a tender age had been purchased of the Syrian merchants, and were educated in the camp and palace of the sultan. But Egypt soon afforded a new example of the danger of prætorian bands; and the rage of these ferocious animals, who had been let loose on the strangers, was provoked to devour their benefactor. In the pride of conquest, Touran Shaw, the last of his race, was murdered by his Mamalukes; and the most daring of the assassins entered the chamber of the captive king, with drawn cimeters, and their hands imbrued in the blood of their sultan. The firmness of Louis commanded their respect; [99] their avarice prevailed over cruelty and zeal; the treaty was accomplished; and the king of France, with the relics of his army, was permitted to embark for Palestine. He wasted four years within the walls of Acre, unable to visit Jerusalem, and unwilling to return without glory to his native country.

[Footnote 96: The last editors have enriched their Joinville with large and curious extracts from the Arabic historians, Macrizi, Abulfeda, &c. See likewise Abulpharagius, (Dynast. p. 322—325,) who calls him by the corrupt name of Redefrans. Matthew Paris (p. 683, 684) has described the rival folly of the French and English who fought and fell at Massoura.]

[Footnote 97: Savary, in his agreeable Letters sur L'Egypte, has given a description of Damietta, (tom. i. lettre xxiii. p. 274—290,) and a narrative of the exposition of St. Louis, (xxv. p. 306—350.)]

[Footnote 98: For the ransom of St. Louis, a million of byzants was asked and granted; but the sultan's generosity reduced that sum to 800,000 byzants, which are valued by Joinville at 400,000 French livres of his own time, and expressed by Matthew Paris by 100,000 marks of silver, (Ducange, Dissertation xx. sur Joinville.)]

[Footnote 99: The idea of the emirs to choose Louis for their sultan is seriously attested by Joinville, (p. 77, 78,) and does not appear to me so absurd as to M. de Voltaire, (Hist. Générale, tom. ii. p. 386, 387.) The Mamalukes themselves were strangers, rebels, and equals: they had felt his valor, they hoped his conversion; and such a motion, which was not seconded, might be made, perhaps by a secret Christian in their tumultuous assembly. Note: Wilken, vol. vii. p. 257, thinks the proposition could not have been made in earnest—M.]

The memory of his defeat excited Louis, after sixteen years of wisdom and repose, to undertake the seventh and last of the crusades. His finances were restored, his kingdom was enlarged; a new generation of warriors had arisen, and he advanced with fresh confidence at the head of six thousand horse and thirty thousand foot. The loss of Antioch had provoked the enterprise; a wild hope of baptizing the king of Tunis tempted him to steer for the African coast; and the report of an immense treasure reconciled his troops to the delay of their voyage to the Holy Land. Instead of a proselyte, he found a siege: the French panted and died on the burning sands: St. Louis expired in his tent; and no sooner had he closed his eyes, than his son and successor gave the signal of the retreat. [100] "It is thus," says a lively writer, "that a Christian king died near the ruins of Carthage, waging war against the sectaries of Mahomet, in a land to which Dido had introduced the deities of Syria." [101]

[Footnote 100: See the expedition in the annals of St. Louis, by William de Nangis, p. 270—287; and the Arabic extracts, p. 545, 555, of the Louvre edition of Joinville.]

[Footnote 101: Voltaire, Hist. Générale, tom. ii. p. 391.]

A more unjust and absurd constitution cannot be devised than that which condemns the natives of a country to perpetual servitude, under the arbitrary dominion of strangers and slaves. Yet such has been the state of Egypt above five hundred years. The most illustrious sultans of the Baharite and Borgite dynasties [102] were themselves promoted from the Tartar and Circassian bands; and the four-and-twenty beys, or military chiefs, have ever been succeeded, not by their sons, but by their servants. They produce the great charter of their liberties, the treaty of Selim the First with the republic: [103] and the Othman emperor still accepts from Egypt a slight acknowledgment of tribute and subjection. With some breathing intervals of peace and order, the two dynasties are marked as a period of rapine and bloodshed: [104] but their throne, however shaken, reposed on the two pillars of discipline and valor: their sway extended over Egypt, Nubia, Arabia, and Syria: their Mamalukes were multiplied from eight hundred to twenty-five thousand horse; and their numbers were increased by a provincial militia of one hundred and seven thousand foot, and the occasional aid of sixty-six thousand Arabs. [105] Princes of such power and spirit could not long endure on their coast a hostile and independent nation; and if the ruin of the Franks was postponed about forty years, they were indebted to the cares of an unsettled reign, to the invasion of the Moguls, and to the occasional aid of some warlike pilgrims. Among these, the English reader will observe the name of our first Edward, who assumed the cross in the lifetime of his father Henry. At the head of a thousand soldiers the future conqueror of Wales and Scotland delivered Acre from a siege; marched as far as Nazareth with an army of nine thousand men; emulated the fame of his uncle Richard; extorted, by his valor, a ten years' truce; [105/1] and escaped, with a dangerous wound, from the dagger of a fanatic assassin. [106] [106/1] Antioch, [107] whose situation had been less exposed to the calamities of the holy war, was finally occupied and ruined by Bondocdar, or Bibars, sultan of Egypt and Syria; the Latin principality was extinguished; and the first seat of the Christian name was dispeopled by the slaughter of seventeen, and the captivity of one hundred, thousand of her inhabitants. The maritime towns of Laodicea, Gabala, Tripoli, Berytus, Sidon, Tyre and Jaffa, and the stronger castles of the Hospitallers and Templars, successively fell; and the whole existence of the Franks was confined to the city and colony of St. John of Acre, which is sometimes described by the more classic title of Ptolemais.

[Footnote 102: The chronology of the two dynasties of Mamalukes, the Baharites, Turks or Tartars of Kipzak, and the Borgites, Circassians, is given by Pocock (Prolegom. ad Abulpharag. p. 6—31) and De Guignes (tom. i. p. 264—270;) their history from Abulfeda, Macrizi, &c., to the beginning of the xvth century, by the same M. De Guignes, (tom. iv. p. 110—328.)]

[Footnote 103: Savary, Lettres sur l'Egypte, tom. ii. lettre xv. p. 189—208. I much question the authenticity of this copy; yet it is true, that Sultan Selim concluded a treaty with the Circassians or Mamalukes of Egypt, and left them in possession of arms, riches, and power. See a new Abrégé de l'Histoire Ottomane, composed in Egypt, and translated by M. Digeon, (tom. i. p. 55—58, Paris, 1781,) a curious, authentic, and national history.]

[Footnote 104: Si totum quo regnum occupârunt tempus respicias, præsertim quod fini propius, reperies illud bellis, pugnis, injuriis, ac rapinis refertum, (Al Jannabi, apud Pocock, p. 31.) The reign of Mohammed (A.D. 1311—1341) affords a happy exception, (De Guignes, tom. iv. p. 208—210.)]

[Footnote 105: They are now reduced to 8500: but the expense of each Mamaluke may be rated at a hundred louis: and Egypt groans under the avarice and insolence of these strangers, (Voyages de Volney, tom. i. p. 89—187.)]

[Footnote 105/1: Gibbon colors rather highly the success of Edward. Wilken is more accurate vol. vii. p. 593, &c—M.]

[Footnote 106: See Carte's History of England, vol. ii. p. 165—175, and his original authors, Thomas Wikes and Walter Hemingford, (l. iii. c. 34, 35,) in Gale's Collection, (tom. ii. p. 97, 589—592.) They are both ignorant of the princess Eleanor's piety in sucking the poisoned wound, and saving her husband at the risk of her own life.]

[Footnote 106/1: The sultan Bibars was concerned in this attempt at assassination Wilken, vol. vii. p. 602. Ptolemæus Lucensis is the earliest authority for the devotion of Eleanora. Ibid. 605—M.]

[Footnote 107: Sanutus, Secret. Fidelium Crucis, 1. iii. p. xii. c. 9, and De Guignes, Hist. des Huns, tom. iv. p. 143, from the Arabic historians.]

After the loss of Jerusalem, Acre, [108] which is distant about seventy miles, became the metropolis of the Latin Christians, and was adorned with strong and stately buildings, with aqueducts, an artificial port, and a double wall. The population was increased by the incessant streams of pilgrims and fugitives: in the pauses of hostility the trade of the East and West was attracted to this convenient station; and the market could offer the produce of every clime and the interpreters of every tongue. But in this conflux of nations, every vice was propagated and practised: of all the disciples of Jesus and Mahomet, the male and female inhabitants of Acre were esteemed the most corrupt; nor could the abuse of religion be corrected by the discipline of law. The city had many sovereigns, and no government. The kings of Jerusalem and Cyprus, of the house of Lusignan, the princes of Antioch, the counts of Tripoli and Sidon, the great masters of the hospital, the temple, and the Teutonic order, the republics of Venice, Genoa, and Pisa, the pope's legate, the kings of France and England, assumed an independent command: seventeen tribunals exercised the power of life and death; every criminal was protected in the adjacent quarter; and the perpetual jealousy of the nations often burst forth in acts of violence and blood. Some adventurers, who disgraced the ensign of the cross, compensated their want of pay by the plunder of the Mahometan villages: nineteen Syrian merchants, who traded under the public faith, were despoiled and hanged by the Christians; and the denial of satisfaction justified the arms of the sultan Khalil. He marched against Acre, at the head of sixty thousand horse and one hundred and forty thousand foot: his train of artillery (if I may use the word) was numerous and weighty: the separate timbers of a single engine were transported in one hundred wagons; and the royal historian Abulfeda, who served with the troops of Hamah, was himself a spectator of the holy war. Whatever might be the vices of the Franks, their courage was rekindled by enthusiasm and despair; but they were torn by the discord of seventeen chiefs, and overwhelmed on all sides by the powers of the sultan. After a siege of thirty three days, the double wall was forced by the Moslems; the principal tower yielded to their engines; the Mamalukes made a general assault; the city was stormed; and death or slavery was the lot of sixty thousand Christians. The convent, or rather fortress, of the Templars resisted three days longer; but the great master was pierced with an arrow; and, of five hundred knights, only ten were left alive, less happy than the victims of the sword, if they lived to suffer on a scaffold, in the unjust and cruel proscription of the whole order. The king of Jerusalem, the patriarch and the great master of the hospital, effected their retreat to the shore; but the sea was rough, the vessels were insufficient; and great numbers of the fugitives were drowned before they could reach the Isle of Cyprus, which might comfort Lusignan for the loss of Palestine. By the command of the sultan, the churches and fortifications of the Latin cities were demolished: a motive of avarice or fear still opened the holy sepulchre to some devout and defenceless pilgrims; and a mournful and solitary silence prevailed along the coast which had so long resounded with the world's debate. [109]

[Footnote 108: *The state of Acre is represented in all the chronicles of te times, and most accurately in John Villani, l. vii. c. 144, in Muratori, Scriptores Rerum Italicarum, tom. xiii. 337, 338.*]

[Footnote 109: *See the final expulsion of the Franks, in Sanutus, l. iii. p. xii. c. 11—22; Abulfeda, Macrizi, &c., in De Guignes, tom. iv. p. 162, 164; and Vertot, tom. i. l. iii. p. 307—428. Note: after these chapters of Gibbon, the masterly prize composition, "Essai sur 'Influence des Croisades sur l'Europe," par A H. L. Heeren: traduit de l'Allemand par Charles Villars, Paris, 1808,' or the original German, in Heeren's "Vermischte Schriften," may be read with great advantage—M.]*

CHAPTER LX

THE FOURTH CRUSADE

PART I

SCHISM OF THE GREEKS AND LATINS—STATE OF CONSTANTINOPLE—REVOLT OF THE BULGARIANS—ISAAC DETHRONED BY HIS BROTHER ALEXIUS—ORIGIN OF THE FOURTH CRUSADE—ALLIANCE OF THE FRENCH AND VENETIANS WITH THE SON OF ISAAC—THEIR NAVAL EXPEDITION TO CONSTANTINOPLE—THE TWO SIEGES AND FINAL CONQUEST OF THE CITY BY THE LATINS

The restoration of the Western empire by Charlemagne was speedily followed by the separation of the Greek and Latin churches. [1] A religious and national animosity still divides the two largest communions of the Christian world; and the schism of Constantinople, by alienating her most useful allies, and provoking her most dangerous enemies, has precipitated the decline and fall of the Roman empire in the East.

[Footnote 1: *In the successive centuries, from the ixth to the xviiith, Mosheim traces the schism of the Greeks with learning, clearness, and impartiality; the filioque (Institut. Hist. Ecclés. p. 277,) Leo III. p. 303 Photius, p. 307, 308. Michael Cerularius, p. 370, 371, &c.]*

In the course of the present History, the aversion of the Greeks for the Latins has been often visible and conspicuous. It was originally derived from the disdain of servitude, inflamed, after the time of Constantine, by the pride of equality or dominion; and finally exasperated by the preference which their rebellious subjects had given to the alliance of the Franks. In every age the Greeks were proud of their superiority in profane and religious knowledge: they had first received the light of Christianity; they had pronounced the decrees of the seven general councils; they alone possessed the language of Scripture and philosophy; nor should the Barbarians, immersed in the darkness of the West, [2] presume to argue on the high and mysterious questions of theological science. Those Barbarians despised in then turn the restless and subtile levity of the Orientals, the authors of every heresy; and blessed their own simplicity, which was content to hold the tradition of the apostolic church. Yet in the seventh century, the synods of Spain, and afterwards of France, improved or corrupted the Nicene creed, on the mysterious subject of the third person of the Trinity. [3] In the long controversies of the East, the nature and generation of the Christ had been scrupulously defined; and the well-known relation of father and son seemed to convey a faint image to the human mind. The idea of birth was less analogous to the Holy Spirit, who, instead of a divine gift or attribute, was considered by the Catholics as a substance, a person, a god; he was not begotten, but in the orthodox style he proceeded. Did he proceed from the Father alone, perhaps by the Son? or from the Father and the Son? The first of these opinions was asserted by the Greeks, the second by the Latins; and the addition to the Nicene creed of the word filioque, kindled the flame of discord between the Oriental and the Gallic churches. In the origin of the disputes the Roman pontiffs affected a character of neutrality and moderation: [4] they condemned the innovation, but they acquiesced in the sentiment, of their Transalpine brethren: they seemed desirous of casting a veil of silence and charity over the superfluous research; and in the correspondence of Charlemagne and Leo the Third, the pope assumes the liberality of a statesman, and the prince descends to the passions and prejudices of a priest. [5] But the orthodoxy of Rome spontaneously obeyed the impulse of the temporal policy; and the filioque, which Leo wished to erase, was transcribed in the symbol and chanted in the liturgy of the Vatican. The Nicene and Athanasian creeds are held as the Catholic faith, without which none can be saved; and both Papists and Protestants must now sustain and return the anathemas of the Greeks, who deny the procession of the Holy Ghost from the Son, as well as from the Father. Such articles of faith are not susceptible of treaty; but the rules of discipline will vary in remote and independent churches; and the reason, even of divines, might allow, that the difference is inevitable and harmless. The craft or superstition of Rome has imposed on her priests and deacons the rigid obligation of celibacy; among the Greeks it is confined to the bishops; the loss is compensated by dignity or annihilated by age; and the parochial clergy, the papas, enjoy the conjugal society of the wives whom they have married before their entrance into holy orders. A question concerning the Azyms was fiercely debated in the eleventh century, and the essence of the Eucharist was supposed in the East and West to depend on the use of leavened or unleavened bread. Shall I mention in a serious history the furious reproaches that were urged against the Latins, who for a long while remained on the defensive? They neglected to abstain, according to the apostolical decree, from things strangled, and from blood: they fasted (a Jewish observance!) on the Saturday of each week: during the first week of Lent they permitted the use of milk and cheese; [6] their infirm monks were indulged in the taste of flesh; and animal grease was substituted for the want of vegetable oil: the holy chrism or unction in baptism was reserved to the episcopal order: the bishops, as the bridegrooms of their churches, were decorated with rings; their priests shaved their faces, and baptized by a single immersion. Such were the crimes which provoked the zeal of the patriarchs of Constantinople; and which were justified with equal zeal by the doctors of the Latin church. [7]

[Footnote 2: "AndreV dussebeiV kai apotropaioi, andreV ek sktouV anadunteV, thV gar 'Esperiou moiraV uphrcon gennhmata, (Phot. Epist. p. 47, edit. Montacut.) The Oriental patriarch continues to apply the images of thunder, earthquake, hail, wild boar, precursors of Antichrist, &c., &c.]

[Footnote 3: The mysterious subject of the procession of the Holy Ghost is discussed in the historical, theological, and controversial sense, or nonsense, by the Jesuit Petavius. (Dogmata Theologica, tom. ii. l. vii. p. 362—440.)]

[Footnote 4: Before the shrine of St. Peter he placed two shields of the weight of 94 1/2 pounds of pure silver; on which he inscribed the text of both creeds, (utroque symbolo,) pro amore et cautelâ orthodoxæ fidei, (Anastas. in Leon. III. in Muratori, tom. iii. pars. i. p. 208.) His language most clearly proves, that neither the filioque, nor the Athanasian creed were received at Rome about the year 830.]

[Footnote 5: The Missi of Charlemagne pressed him to declare, that all who rejected the filioque, or at least the doctrine, must be damned. All, replies the pope, are not capable of reaching the altiora mysteria qui potuerit, et non voluerit, salvus esse non potest, (Collect. Concil. tom. ix. p. 277—286.) The potuerit would leave a large loophole of salvation!]

[Footnote 6: In France, after some harsher laws, the ecclesiastical discipline is now relaxed: milk, cheese, and butter, are become a perpetual, and eggs an annual, indulgence in Lent, (Vie privée des François, tom. ii. p. 27—38.)]

[Footnote 7: The original monuments of the schism, of the charges of the Greeks against the Latins, are deposited in the epistles of Photius, (Epist Encyclica, ii. p. 47—61,) and of Michael Cerularius, (Canisii Antiq. Lectiones, tom. iii. p. i. p. 281—324, edit. Basnage, with the prolix answer of Cardinal Humbert.)]

Bigotry and national aversion are powerful magnifiers of every object of dispute; but the immediate cause of the schism of the Greeks may be traced in the emulation of the leading prelates, who maintained the supremacy of the old metropolis superior to all, and of the reigning capital, inferior to none, in the Christian world. About the middle of the ninth century, Photius, [8] an ambitious layman, the captain of the guards and principal secretary, was promoted by merit and favor to the more desirable office of patriarch of Constantinople. In science, even ecclesiastical science, he surpassed the clergy of the age; and the purity of his morals has never been impeached: but his ordination was hasty, his rise was irregular; and Ignatius, his abdicated predecessor, was yet supported by the public compassion and the obstinacy of his adherents. They appealed to the tribunal of Nicholas the First, one of the proudest and most aspiring of the Roman pontiffs, who embraced the welcome opportunity of judging and condemning his rival of the East. Their quarrel was embittered by a conflict of jurisdiction over the king and nation of the Bulgarians; nor was their recent conversion to Christianity of much avail to either prelate, unless he could number the proselytes among the subjects of his power. With the aid of his court the Greek patriarch was victorious; but in the furious contest he deposed in his turn the successor of St. Peter, and involved the Latin church in the reproach of heresy and schism. Photius sacrificed the peace of the world to a short and precarious reign: he fell with his patron, the Cæsar Bardas; and Basil the Macedonian performed an act of justice in the restoration of Ignatius, whose age and dignity had not been sufficiently respected. From his monastery, or prison, Photius solicited the favor of the emperor by pathetic complaints and artful flattery; and the eyes of his rival were scarcely closed, when he was again restored to the throne of Constantinople. After the death of Basil he experienced the vicissitudes of courts and the ingratitude of a royal pupil: the patriarch was again deposed, and in his last solitary hours he might regret the freedom of a secular and studious life. In each revolution, the breath, the nod, of the sovereign had been accepted by a submissive clergy; and a synod of three hundred bishops was always prepared to hail the triumph, or to stigmatize the fall, of the holy, or the execrable, Photius. [9] By a delusive promise of succor or reward, the popes were tempted to countenance these various proceedings; and the synods of Constantinople were ratified by their epistles or legates. But the court and the people, Ignatius and Photius, were equally adverse to their claims; their ministers were insulted or imprisoned; the procession of the Holy Ghost was forgotten; Bulgaria was forever annexed to the Byzantine throne; and the schism was prolonged by their rigid censure of all the multiplied ordinations of an irregular patriarch. The darkness and corruption of the tenth century suspended the intercourse, without reconciling the minds, of the two nations. But when the Norman sword restored the churches of Apulia to the jurisdiction of Rome, the departing flock was warned, by a petulant epistle of the Greek patriarch, to avoid and abhor the errors of the Latins. The rising majesty of Rome could no longer brook the insolence of a rebel; and Michael Cerularius was excommunicated in the heart of Constantinople by the pope's legates. Shaking the dust from their feet, they deposited on the altar of St. Sophia a direful anathema, [10] which enumerates the seven mortal heresies of the Greeks, and devotes the guilty teachers, and their unhappy sectaries, to the eternal society of the devil and his angels. According to the emergencies of the church and state, a friendly correspondence was some times resumed; the language of charity and concord was sometimes affected; but the Greeks have never recanted their errors; the popes have never repealed their sentence; and from this thunderbolt we may date the consummation of the schism. It was enlarged by each ambitious step of the Roman pontiffs: the emperors blushed and trembled at the ignominious fate of their royal brethren of Germany; and the people were scandalized by the temporal power and military life of the Latin clergy. [11]

[Footnote 8: The xth volume of the Venice edition of the Councils contains all the acts of the synods, and history of Photius: they are abridged, with a faint tinge of prejudice or prudence, by Dupin and Fleury.]

[Footnote 9: The synod of Constantinople, held in the year 869, is the viiith of the general councils, the last assembly of the East which is recognized by the Roman church. She rejects the synods of Constantinople of the years 867 and 879, which were, however, equally numerous and noisy; but they were favorable to Photius.]

[Footnote 10: See this anathema in the Councils, tom. xi. p. 1457—1460.]

[Footnote 11: Anna Comnena (Alexiad, l. i. p. 31—33) represents the abhorrence, not only of the church, but of the palace, for Gregory VII., the popes and the Latin communion. The style of Cinnamus and Nicetas is still more vehement. Yet how calm is the voice of history compared with that of polemics!]

The aversion of the Greeks and Latins was nourished and manifested in the three first expeditions to the Holy Land. Alexius Comnenus contrived the absence at least of the formidable pilgrims: his successors, Manuel and Isaac Angelus, conspired with the Moslems for the ruin of the greatest princes of the Franks; and their crooked and malignant policy was seconded by the active and voluntary obedience of every order of their subjects. Of this hostile temper, a large portion may doubtless be ascribed to the difference of language, dress, and manners, which severs and alienates the nations of the globe. The pride, as well as the prudence, of the sovereign was deeply wounded by the intrusion of foreign armies, that claimed a right of traversing his dominions, and passing under the walls of his capital: his subjects were insulted and plundered by the rude strangers of the West: and the hatred of the pusillanimous Greeks was sharpened by secret envy of the bold and pious enterprises of the Franks. But these profane causes of national enmity were fortified and inflamed by the venom of religious zeal. Instead of a kind embrace, a hospitable reception from their Christian brethren of the East, every tongue was taught to repeat the names of schismatic and heretic, more odious to an orthodox ear than those of pagan and infidel: instead of being loved for the general conformity of faith and worship, they were abhorred for some rules of discipline, some questions of theology, in which themselves or their teachers might differ from the Oriental church. In the crusade of Louis the Seventh, the Greek clergy washed and purified the altars which had been defiled by the sacrifice of a French priest. The companions of Frederic Barbarossa deplore the injuries which they endured, both in word and deed, from the peculiar rancor of the bishops and monks. Their prayers and sermons excited the people against the impious Barbarians; and the patriarch is accused of declaring, that the faithful might obtain the redemption of all their sins by the extirpation of the schismatics. [12] An enthusiast, named Dorotheus, alarmed the fears, and restored the confidence, of the emperor, by a prophetic assurance, that the German heretic, after assaulting the gate of Blachernes, would be made a signal example of the divine vengeance. The passage of these mighty armies were rare and perilous events; but the crusades introduced a frequent and familiar intercourse between the two nations, which enlarged their knowledge without abating their prejudices. The wealth and luxury of Constantinople demanded the productions of every climate these imports were balanced by the art and labor of her numerous inhabitants; her situation invites the commerce of the world; and, in every period of her existence, that commerce has been in the hands of foreigners. After the decline of Amalphi, the Venetians, Pisans, and Genoese, introduced their factories and settlements into the capital of the empire: their services were rewarded with honors and immunities; they acquired the possession of lands and houses; their families were multiplied by marriages with the natives; and, after the toleration of a Mahometan mosque, it was impossible to interdict the churches of the Roman rite. [13] The two wives of Manuel Comnenus [14] were of the race of the Franks: the first, a sister-in-law of the emperor Conrad; the second, a daughter of the prince of Antioch: he obtained for his son Alexius a daughter of Philip Augustus, king of France; and he bestowed his own daughter on a marquis of Montferrat, who was educated and dignified in the palace of Constantinople. The Greek encountered the arms, and aspired to the empire, of the West: he esteemed the valor, and trusted the fidelity, of the Franks; [15] their military talents were unfitly recompensed by the lucrative offices of judges and treasures; the policy of Manuel had solicited the alliance of the pope; and the popular voice accused him of a partial bias to the nation and religion of the Latins. [16] During his reign, and that of his successor Alexius, they were exposed at Constantinople to the reproach of foreigners, heretics, and favorites; and this triple guilt was severely expiated in the tumult, which announced the return and elevation of Andronicus. [17] The people rose in arms: from the Asiatic shore the tyrant despatched his troops and galleys to assist the national revenge; and the hopeless resistance of the strangers served only to justify the rage, and sharpen the daggers, of the assassins. Neither age, nor sex, nor the ties of friendship or kindred, could save the victims of national hatred, and avarice, and religious zeal; the Latins were slaughtered in their houses and in the streets; their quarter was reduced to ashes; the clergy were burnt in their churches, and the sick in their hospitals; and some estimate may be formed of the slain from the clemency which sold above four thousand Christians in perpetual slavery to the Turks. The priests and monks were the loudest and most active in the destruction of the schismatics; and they chanted a thanksgiving to the Lord, when the head of a Roman cardinal, the pope's legate, was severed from his body, fastened to the tail of a dog, and dragged, with savage mockery, through the city. The more diligent of the strangers had retreated, on the first alarm, to their vessels, and escaped through the Hellespont from the scene of blood. In their flight, they burnt and ravaged two hundred miles of the sea-coast; inflicted a severe revenge on the guiltless subjects of the empire; marked the priests and monks as their peculiar enemies; and compensated, by the accumulation of plunder, the loss of their property and friends. On their return, they exposed to Italy and Europe the wealth and weakness, the perfidy and malice, of the Greeks, whose vices were painted as the genuine characters of heresy and schism. The scruples of the first crusaders had neglected the fairest opportunities of securing, by the possession of Constantinople, the way to the Holy Land: domestic revolution invited, and almost compelled, the French and Venetians to achieve the conquest of the Roman empire of the East.

*[Footnote 12: His anonymous historian (de Expedit. Asiat. Fred. I. in Canisii Lection. Antiq. tom. iii. pars ii. p. 511, edit. Basnage) mentions the sermons of the Greek patriarch, quomodo Græcis injunxerat in remissionem peccatorum peregrinos occidere et delere de terra. Tagino observes, (in Scriptores Freher. tom. i. p. 409, edit. Struv.,) Græci hæreticos nos appellant: clerici et monachi dictis et factis persequuntur. We may add the declaration of the emperor Baldwin fifteen years afterwards: Hæc est (gens) quæ Latinos omnes non hominum nomine, sed canum dignabatur; quorum sanguinem effundere penè inter merita reputabant, (Gesta Innocent. III., c. 92, in Muratori, Script. Rerum Italicarum, tom. iii. pars i. p. 536.) There may be some exaggeration, but it was as effectual for the action and reaction of hatred.]*

[Footnote 13: See Anna Comnena, (Alexiad, l. vi. p. 161, 162,) and a remarkable passage of Nicetas, (in Manuel, l. v. c. 9,) who observes of the Venetians, kata smhnh kai jratriaV thn Kwnstantinou polin thV oikeiaV hllaxanto, &c.]

[Footnote 14: Ducange, Fam. Byzant. p. 186, 187.]

[Footnote 15: Nicetas in Manuel. l. vii. c. 2. Regnante enim (Manuele).... apud eum tantam Latinus populus repererat gratiam ut neglectis Græculis suis tanquam viris mollibus et effminatis,.... solis Latinis grandia committeret negotia.... erga eos profusâ liberalitate abundabat.... ex omni orbe ad eum tanquam ad benefactorem nobiles et ignobiles concurrebant. Willelm. Tyr. xxii. c. 10.]

[Footnote 16: The suspicions of the Greeks would have been confirmed, if they had seen the political epistles of Manuel to Pope Alexander III., the enemy of his enemy Frederic I., in which the emperor declares his wish of uniting the Greeks and Latins as one flock under one shepherd, &c (See Fleury, Hist. Ecclés. tom. xv. p. 187, 213, 243.)]

[Footnote 17: See the Greek and Latin narratives in Nicetas (in Alexio Comneno, c. 10) and William of Tyre, (l. xxii. c. 10, 11, 12, 13;) the first soft and concise, the second loud, copious, and tragical.]

In the series of the Byzantine princes, I have exhibited the hypocrisy and ambition, the tyranny and fall, of Andronicus, the last male of the Comnenian family who reigned at Constantinople. The revolution, which cast him headlong from the throne, saved and exalted Isaac Angelus, [18] who descended by the females from the same Imperial dynasty. The successor of a second Nero might have found it an easy task to deserve the esteem and affection of his subjects; they sometimes had reason to regret the administration of Andronicus. The sound and vigorous mind of the tyrant was capable of discerning the connection between his own and the public interest; and while he was feared by all who could inspire him with fear, the unsuspected people, and the remote provinces, might bless the inexorable justice of their master. But his successor was vain and jealous of the supreme power, which he wanted courage and abilities to exercise: his vices were pernicious, his virtues (if he possessed any virtues) were useless, to mankind; and the Greeks, who imputed their calamities to his negligence, denied him the merit of any transient or accidental benefits of the times. Isaac slept on the throne, and was awakened only by the sound of pleasure: his vacant hours were amused by comedians and buffoons, and even to these buffoons the emperor was an object of contempt: his feasts and buildings exceeded the examples of royal luxury: the number of his eunuchs and domestics amounted to twenty thousand; and a daily sum of four thousand pounds of silver would swell to four millions sterling the annual expense of his household and table. His poverty was relieved by oppression; and the public discontent was inflamed by equal abuses in the collection, and the application, of the revenue. While the Greeks numbered the days of their servitude, a flattering prophet, whom he rewarded with the dignity of patriarch, assured him of a long and victorious reign of thirty-two years; during which he should extend his sway to Mount Libanus, and his conquests beyond the Euphrates. But his only step towards the accomplishment of the prediction was a splendid and scandalous embassy to Saladin, [19] to demand the restitution of the holy sepulchre, and to propose an offensive and defensive league with the enemy of the Christian name. In these unworthy hands, of Isaac and his brother, the remains of the Greek empire crumbled into dust. The Island of Cyprus, whose name excites the ideas of elegance and pleasure, was usurped by his namesake, a Comnenian prince; and by a strange concatenation of events, the sword of our English Richard bestowed that kingdom on the house of Lusignan, a rich compensation for the loss of Jerusalem.

[Footnote 18: The history of the reign of Isaac Angelus is composed, in three books, by the senator Nicetas, (p. 228—290;) and his offices of logothete, or principal secretary, and judge of the veil or palace, could not bribe the impartiality of the historian. He wrote, it is true, after the fall and death of his benefactor.]

[Footnote 19: See Bohadin, Vit. Saladin. p. 129—131, 226, vers. Schultens. The ambassador of Isaac was equally versed in the Greek, French, and Arabic languages; a rare instance in those times. His embassies were received with honor, dismissed without effect, and reported with scandal in the West.]

The honor of the monarchy and the safety of the capital were deeply wounded by the revolt of the Bulgarians and Walachians. Since the victory of the second Basil, they had supported, above a hundred and seventy years, the loose dominion of the Byzantine princes; but no effectual measures had been adopted to impose the yoke of laws and manners on these savage tribes. By the command of Isaac, their sole means of subsistence, their flocks and herds, were driven away, to contribute towards the pomp of the royal nuptials; and their fierce warriors were exasperated by the denial of equal rank and pay in the military service. Peter and Asan, two powerful chiefs, of the race of the ancient kings, [20] asserted their own rights and the national freedom; their dæmoniac impostors proclaimed to the crowd, that their glorious patron St. Demetrius had forever deserted the cause of the Greeks; and the conflagration spread from the banks of the Danube to the hills of Macedonia and Thrace. After some faint efforts, Isaac Angelus and his brother acquiesced in their independence; and the Imperial troops were soon discouraged by the bones of their fellow-soldiers, that were scattered along the passes of Mount Hæmus. By the arms and policy of John or Joannices, the second kingdom of Bulgaria was firmly established. The subtle Barbarian sent an embassy to Innocent the Third, to acknowledge himself a genuine son of Rome in descent and religion, [21] and humbly received from the pope the license of coining money, the royal title, and a Latin archbishop or patriarch. The Vatican exulted in the spiritual conquest of Bulgaria, the first object of the schism; and if the Greeks could have preserved the prerogatives of the church, they would gladly have resigned the rights of the monarchy.

[Footnote 20: Ducange, Familiæ, Dalmaticæ, p. 318, 319, 320. The original correspondence of the Bulgarian king and the Roman pontiff is inscribed in the Gesta Innocent. III. c. 66—82, p. 513—525.]

[Footnote 21: The pope acknowledges his pedigree, a nobili urbis Romæ prosapiâ genitores tui originem traxerunt. This tradition, and the strong resemblance of the Latin and Walachian idioms, is explained by M. D'Anville, (Etats de l'Europe, p. 258—262.) The Italian colonies of the Dacia of Trajan were swept away by the tide of emigration from the Danube to the Volga, and brought back by another wave from the Volga to the Danube. Possible, but strange!]

The Bulgarians were malicious enough to pray for the long life of Isaac Angelus, the surest pledge of their freedom and prosperity. Yet their chiefs could involve in the same indiscriminate contempt the family and nation of the emperor. "In all the Greeks," said Asan to his troops, "the same climate, and character, and education, will be productive of the same fruits. Behold my lance," continued the warrior, "and the long streamers that float in the wind. They differ only in color; they are formed of the same silk, and fashioned by the same workman; nor has the stripe that is stained in purple any superior price or value above its fellows." [22] Several of these candidates for the purple successively rose and fell under the empire of Isaac; a general, who had repelled the fleets of Sicily, was driven to revolt and ruin by the ingratitude of the prince; and his luxurious repose was disturbed by secret conspiracies and popular insurrections. The emperor was saved by accident, or the merit of his servants: he was at length oppressed by an ambitious brother, who, for the hope of a precarious diadem, forgot the obligations of nature, of loyalty, and of friendship. [23] While Isaac in the Thracian valleys pursued the idle and solitary pleasures of the chase, his brother, Alexius Angelus, was invested with the purple, by the unanimous suffrage of the camp; the capital and the clergy subscribed to their choice; and the vanity of the new sovereign rejected the name of his fathers for the lofty and royal appellation of the Comnenian race. On the despicable character of Isaac I have exhausted the language of contempt, and can only add, that, in a reign of eight years, the baser Alexius [24] was supported by the masculine vices of his wife Euphrosyne. The first intelligence of his fall was conveyed to the late emperor by the hostile aspect and pursuit of the guards, no longer his own: he fled before them above fifty miles, as far as Stagyra, in Macedonia; but the fugitive, without an object or a follower, was arrested, brought back to Constantinople, deprived of his eyes, and confined in a lonesome tower, on a scanty allowance of bread and water. At the moment of the revolution, his son Alexius, whom he educated in the hope of empire, was twelve years of age. He was spared by the usurper, and reduced to attend his triumph both in peace and war; but as the army was encamped on the sea-shore, an Italian vessel facilitated the escape of the royal youth; and, in the disguise of a common sailor, he eluded the search of his enemies, passed the Hellespont, and found a secure refuge in the Isle of Sicily. After saluting the threshold of the apostles, and imploring the protection of Pope Innocent the Third, Alexius accepted the kind invitation of his sister Irene, the wife of Philip of Swabia, king of the Romans. But in his passage through Italy, he heard that the flower of Western chivalry was assembled at Venice for the deliverance of the Holy Land; and a ray of hope was kindled in his bosom, that their invincible swords might be employed in his father's restoration.

[Footnote 22: This parable is in the best savage style; but I wish the Walach had not introduced the classic name of Mysians, the experiment of the magnet or loadstone, and the passage of an old comic poet, (Nicetas in Alex. Comneno, l. i. p. 299, 300.)]

[Footnote 23: The Latins aggravate the ingratitude of Alexius, by supposing that he had been released by his brother Isaac from Turkish captivity This pathetic tale had doubtless been repeated at Venice and Zara but I do not readily discover its grounds in the Greek historians.]

[Footnote 24: See the reign of Alexius Angelus, or Comnenus, in the three books of Nicetas, p. 291—352.]

About ten or twelve years after the loss of Jerusalem, the nobles of France were again summoned to the holy war by the voice of a third prophet, less extravagant, perhaps, than Peter the hermit, but far below St. Bernard in the merit of an orator and a statesman. An illiterate priest of the neighborhood of Paris, Fulk of Neuilly, [25] forsook his parochial duty, to assume the more flattering character of a popular and itinerant missionary. The fame of his sanctity and miracles was spread over the land; he declaimed, with severity and vehemence, against the vices of the age; and his sermons, which he preached in the streets of Paris, converted the robbers, the usurers, the prostitutes, and even the doctors and scholars of the university. No sooner did Innocent the Third ascend the chair of St. Peter, than he proclaimed in Italy, Germany, and France, the obligation of a new crusade. [26] The eloquent pontiff described the ruin of Jerusalem, the triumph of the Pagans, and the shame of Christendom; his liberality proposed the redemption of sins, a plenary indulgence to all who should serve in Palestine, either a year in person, or two years by a substitute; [27] and among his legates and orators who blew the sacred trumpet, Fulk of Neuilly was the loudest and most successful. The situation of the principal monarchs was averse to the pious summons. The emperor Frederic the Second was a child; and his kingdom of Germany was disputed by the rival houses of Brunswick and Swabia, the memorable factions of the Guelphs and Ghibelines. Philip Augustus of France had performed, and could not be persuaded to renew, the perilous vow; but as he was not less ambitious of praise than of power, he cheerfully instituted a perpetual fund for the defence of the Holy Land Richard of England was satiated with the glory and misfortunes of his first adventure; and he presumed to deride the exhortations of Fulk of Neuilly, who was not abashed in the presence of kings. "You advise me," said Plantagenet, "to dismiss my three daughters, pride, avarice, and incontinence: I bequeath them to the most deserving; my pride to the knights templars, my avarice to the monks of Cisteaux, and my incontinence to the prelates." But the preacher was heard and obeyed by the great vassals, the princes of the second order; and Theobald, or Thibaut, count of Champagne, was the foremost in the holy race. The valiant youth, at the age of twenty-two years, was encouraged by the domestic examples of his father, who marched in the second crusade, and of his elder brother, who had ended his days in Palestine with the title of King of Jerusalem; two thousand two hundred knights owed service and homage to his peerage; [28] the nobles of Champagne excelled in all the exercises of war; [29] and, by his marriage with the heiress of Navarre, Thibaut could draw a band of hardy Gascons from either side of the Pyrenæan mountains. His companion in arms was Louis, count of Blois and Chartres; like himself of regal lineage, for both the princes were nephews, at the same time, of the kings of France and England. In a crowd of prelates and barons, who imitated their zeal, I distinguish the birth and merit of Matthew of Montmorency; the famous Simon of Montfort, the scourge of the Albigeois; and a valiant noble, Jeffrey of Villehardouin, [30] marshal of Champagne, [31] who has condescended, in the rude idiom of his age and country, [32] to write or dictate [33] an original narrative of the councils and actions in which he bore a memorable part. At the same time, Baldwin, count of Flanders, who had married the sister of Thibaut, assumed the cross at Bruges, with his brother Henry, and the principal knights and citizens of that rich and industrious province. [34] The vow which the chiefs had pronounced in churches, they ratified in tournaments; the operations of the war were debated in full and frequent assemblies; and it was resolved to seek the deliverance of Palestine in Egypt, a country, since Saladin's death, which was almost ruined by famine and civil war. But the fate of so many royal armies displayed the toils and perils of a land expedition; and if the Flemings dwelt along the ocean, the French barons were destitute of ships and ignorant of navigation. They embraced the wise resolution of choosing six deputies or representatives, of whom Villehardouin was one, with a discretionary trust to direct the motions, and to pledge the faith, of the whole confederacy. The maritime states of Italy were alone possessed of the means of transporting the holy warriors with their arms and horses; and the six deputies proceeded to Venice, to solicit, on motives of piety or interest, the aid of that powerful republic.

[Footnote 25: See Fleury, Hist. Ecclés. tom. xvi. p. 26, &c., and Villehardouin, No. 1, with the observations of Ducange, which I always mean to quote with the original text.]

[Footnote 26: The contemporary life of Pope Innocent III., published by Baluze and Muratori, (Scriptores Rerum Italicarum, tom. iii. pars i. p. 486—568), is most valuable for the important and original documents which are inserted in the text. The bull of the crusade may be read, c. 84, 85.]

[Footnote 27: Por-ce que cil pardon, fut issi gran, si s'en esmeurent mult li cuers des genz, et mult s'en croisierent, porce que li pardons ere si gran. Villehardouin, No. 1. Our philosophers may refine on the causes of the crusades, but such were the genuine feelings of a French knight.]

[Footnote 28: This number of fiefs (of which 1800 owed liege homage) was enrolled in the church of St. Stephen at Troyes, and attested A.D. 1213, by the marshal and butler of Champagne, (Ducange, Observ. p. 254.)]

[Footnote 29: Campania.... militiæ privilegio singularius excellit.... in tyrociniis.... prolusione armorum, &c., Duncage, p. 249, from the old Chronicle of Jerusalem, A.D. 1177—1199.]

[Footnote 30: The name of Villehardouin was taken from a village and castle in the diocese of Troyes, near the River Aube, between Bar and Arcis. The family was ancient and noble; the elder branch of our historian existed after the year 1400, the younger, which acquired the principality of Achaia, merged in the house of Savoy, (Ducange, p. 235—245.)]

[Footnote 31: This office was held by his father and his descendants; but Ducange has not hunted it with his usual sagacity. I find that, in the year 1356, it was in the family of Conflans; but these provincial have been long since eclipsed by the national marshals of France.]

[Footnote 32: This language, of which I shall produce some specimens, is explained by Vigenere and Ducange, in a version and glossary. The president Des Brosses (Méchanisme des Langues, tom. ii. p. 83) gives it as the example of a language which has ceased to be French, and is understood only by grammarians.]

[Footnote 33: His age, and his own expression, moi qui ceste uvre dicta, (No. 62, &c.,) may justify the suspicion (more probable than Mr. Wood's on Homer) that he could neither read nor write. Yet Champagne may boast of the two first historians, the noble authors of French prose, Villehardouin and Joinville.]

[Footnote 34: The crusade and reigns of the counts of Flanders, Baldwin and his brother Henry, are the subject of a particular history by the Jesuit Doutremens, (Constantinopolis Belgica; Turnaci, 1638, in 4to.,) which I have only seen with the eyes of Ducange.]

In the invasion of Italy by Attila, I have mentioned [35] the flight of the Venetians from the fallen cities of the continent, and their obscure shelter in the chain of islands that line the extremity of the Adriatic Gulf. In the midst of the waters, free, indigent, laborious, and inaccessible, they gradually coalesced into a republic: the first foundations of Venice were laid in the Island of Rialto; and the annual election of the twelve tribunes was superseded by the permanent office of a duke or doge. On the verge of the two empires, the Venetians exult in the belief of primitive and perpetual independence. [36] Against the Latins, their antique freedom has been asserted by the sword, and may be justified by the pen. Charlemagne himself resigned all claims of sovereignty to the islands of the Adriatic Gulf: his son Pepin was repulsed in the attacks of the lagunas or canals, too deep for the cavalry, and too shallow for the vessels; and in every age, under the German Cæsars, the lands of the republic have been clearly distinguished from the kingdom of Italy. But the inhabitants of Venice were considered by themselves, by strangers, and by their sovereigns, as an inalienable portion of the Greek empire: [37] in the ninth and tenth centuries, the proofs of their subjection are numerous and unquestionable; and the vain titles, the servile honors, of the Byzantine court, so ambitiously solicited by their dukes, would have degraded the magistrates of a free people. But the bands of this dependence, which was never absolute or rigid, were imperceptibly relaxed by the ambition of Venice and the weakness of Constantinople. Obedience was softened into respect, privilege ripened into prerogative, and the freedom of domestic government was fortified by the independence of foreign dominion. The maritime cities of Istria and Dalmatia bowed to the sovereigns of the Adriatic; and when they armed against the Normans in the cause of Alexius, the emperor applied, not to the duty of his subjects, but to the gratitude and generosity of his faithful allies. The sea was their patrimony: [38] the western parts of the Mediterranean, from Tuscany to Gibraltar, were indeed abandoned to their rivals of Pisa and Genoa; but the Venetians acquired an early and lucrative share of the commerce of Greece and Egypt. Their riches increased with the increasing demand of Europe; their manufactures of silk and glass, perhaps the institution of their bank, are of high antiquity; and they enjoyed the fruits of their industry in the magnificence of public and private life. To assert her flag, to avenge her injuries, to protect the freedom of navigation, the republic could launch and man a fleet of a hundred galleys; and the Greeks, the Saracens, and the Normans, were encountered by her naval arms. The Franks of Syria were assisted by the Venetians in the reduction of the sea coast; but their zeal was neither blind nor disinterested; and in the conquest of Tyre, they shared the sovereignty of a city, the first seat of the commerce of the world. The policy of Venice was marked by the avarice of a trading, and the insolence of a maritime, power; yet her ambition was prudent: nor did she often forget that if armed galleys were the effect and safeguard, merchant vessels were the cause and supply, of her greatness. In her religion, she avoided the schisms of the Greeks, without yielding a servile obedience to the Roman pontiff; and a free intercourse with the infidels of every clime appears to have allayed betimes the fever of superstition. Her primitive government was a loose mixture of democracy and monarchy; the doge was elected by the votes of the general assembly; as long as he was popular and successful, he reigned with the pomp and authority of a prince; but in the frequent revolutions of the state, he was deposed, or banished, or slain, by the justice or injustice of the multitude. The twelfth century produced the first rudiments of the wise and jealous aristocracy, which has reduced the doge to a pageant, and the people to a cipher. [39]

[Footnote 35: History, &c., vol. iii. p. 446, 447.]

[Footnote 36: The foundation and independence of Venice, and Pepin's invasion, are discussed by Pagi (Critica, tom. iii. A.D. 81, No. 4, &c.) and Beretti, (Dissert. Chorograph. Italiæ Medii Ævi, in Muratori, Script. tom. x. p. 153.) The two critics have a slight bias, the Frenchman adverse, the Italian favorable, to the republic.]

[Footnote 37: When the son of Charlemagne asserted his right of sovereignty, he was answered by the loyal Venetians, oti hmeiV douloi Jelomen einai tou 'RwmaiwnV basilewV, (Constantin. Porphyrogenit. de Administrat. Imperii, pars ii. c. 28, p. 85;) and the report of the ixth establishes the fact of the xth century, which is confirmed by the embassy of Liutprand of Cremona. The annual tribute, which the emperor allows them to pay to the king of Italy, alleviates, by doubling, their servitude; but the hateful word douloi must be translated, as in the charter of 827, (Laugier, Hist. de Venice, tom. i. p. 67, &c.,) by the softer appellation of subditi, or fideles.]

[Footnote 38: See the xxvth and xxxth dissertations of the Antiquitates Medii Ævi of Muratori. From Anderson's History of Commerce, I understand that the Venetians did not trade to England before the year 1323. The most flourishing state of their wealth and commerce, in the beginning of the xvth century, is agreeably described by the Abbé Dubos, (Hist. de la Ligue de Cambray, tom. ii. p. 443—480.)]

[Footnote 39: The Venetians have been slow in writing and publishing their history. Their most ancient monuments are, 1. The rude Chronicle (perhaps) of John Sagorninus, (Venezia, 1765, in octavo,) which represents the state and manners of Venice in the year 1008. 2. The larger history of the doge, (1342—1354,) Andrew Dandolo, published for the first time in the xiith tom. of Muratori, A.D. 1728. The History of Venice by the Abbé Laugier, (Paris, 1728,) is a work of some merit, which I have chiefly used for the constitutional part. Note: It is scarcely necessary to mention the valuable work of Count Daru, "History de Venise," of which I hear that an Italian translation has been published, with notes defensive of the ancient republic. I have not yet seen this work—M.]

## PART II

When the six ambassadors of the French pilgrims arrived at Venice, they were hospitably entertained in the palace of St. Mark, by the reigning duke; his name was Henry Dandolo; [40] and he shone in the last period of human life as one of the most illustrious characters of the times. Under the weight of years, and after the loss of his eyes, [41] Dandolo retained a sound understanding and a manly courage: the spirit of a hero, ambitious to signalize his reign by some memorable exploits; and the wisdom of a patriot, anxious to build his fame on the glory and advantage of his country. He praised the bold enthusiasm and liberal confidence of the barons and their deputies: in such a cause, and with such associates, he should aspire, were he a private man, to terminate his life; but he was the servant of the republic, and some delay was requisite to consult, on this arduous business, the judgment of his colleagues. The proposal of the French was first debated by the six sages who had been recently appointed to control the administration of the doge: it was next disclosed to the forty members of the council of state; and finally communicated to the legislative assembly of four hundred and fifty representatives, who were annually chosen in the six quarters of the city. In peace and war, the doge was still the chief of the republic; his legal authority was supported by the personal reputation of Dandolo: his arguments of public interest were balanced and approved; and he was authorized to inform the ambassadors of the following conditions of the treaty. [42] It was proposed that the crusaders should assemble at Venice, on the feast of St. John of the ensuing year; that flat-bottomed vessels should be prepared for four thousand five hundred horses, and nine thousand squires, with a number of ships sufficient for the embarkation of four thousand five hundred knights, and twenty thousand foot; that during a term of nine months they should be supplied with provisions, and transported to whatsoever coast the service of God and Christendom should require; and that the republic should join the armament with a squadron of fifty galleys. It was required, that the pilgrims should pay, before their departure, a sum of eighty-five thousand marks of silver; and that all conquests, by sea and land, should be equally divided between the confederates. The terms were hard; but the emergency was pressing, and the French barons were not less profuse of money than of blood. A general assembly was convened to ratify the treaty: the stately chapel and place of St. Mark were filled with ten thousand citizens; and the noble deputies were taught a new lesson of humbling themselves before the majesty of the people. "Illustrious Venetians," said the marshal of Champagne, "we are sent by the greatest and most powerful barons of France to implore the aid of the masters of the sea for the deliverance of Jerusalem. They have enjoined us to fall prostrate at your feet; nor will we rise from the ground till you have promised to avenge with us the injuries of Christ." The eloquence of their words and tears, [43] their martial aspect, and suppliant attitude, were applauded by a universal shout; as it were, says Jeffrey, by the sound of an earthquake. The venerable doge ascended the pulpit to urge their request by those motives of honor and virtue, which alone can be offered to a popular assembly: the treaty was transcribed on parchment, attested with oaths and seals, mutually accepted by the weeping and joyful representatives of France and Venice; and despatched to Rome for the approbation of Pope Innocent the Third. Two thousand marks were borrowed of the merchants for the first expenses of the armament. Of the six deputies, two repassed the Alps to announce their success, while their four companions made a fruitless trial of the zeal and emulation of the republics of Genoa and Pisa.

[Footnote 40: Henry Dandolo was eighty-four at his election, (A.D. 1192,) and ninety-seven at his death, (A.D. 1205.) See the Observations of Ducange sur Villehardouin, No. 204. But this extraordinary longevity is not observed by the original writers, nor does there exist another example of a hero near a hundred years of age. Theophrastus might afford an instance of a writer of ninety-nine; but instead of ennenhkonta, (Prom. ad Character.,)I am much inclined to read ebdomhkonta, with his last editor

Fischer, and the first thoughts of Casaubon. It is scarcely possible that the powers of the mind and body should support themselves till such a period of life.]

[Footnote 41: The modern Venetians (Laugier, tom. ii. p. 119) accuse the emperor Manuel; but the calumny is refuted by Villehardouin and the older writers, who suppose that Dandolo lost his eyes by a wound, (No. 31, and Ducange.) Note: The accounts differ, both as to the extent and the cause of his blindness According to Villehardouin and others, the sight was totally lost; according to the Chronicle of Andrew Dandolo. (Murat. tom. xii. p. 322,) he was vise debilis. See Wilken, vol. v. p. 143—M.]

[Footnote 42: See the original treaty in the Chronicle of Andrew Dandolo, p. 323—326.]

[Footnote 43: A reader of Villehardouin must observe the frequent tears of the marshal and his brother knights. Sachiez que la ot mainte lerme plorée de pitié, (No. 17;) mult plorant, (ibid.;) mainte lerme plorée, (No. 34;) si orent mult pitié et plorerent mult durement, (No. 60;) i ot mainte lerme plorée de pitié, (No. 202.) They weep on every occasion of grief, joy, or devotion.]

The execution of the treaty was still opposed by unforeseen difficulties and delays. The marshal, on his return to Troyes, was embraced and approved by Thibaut count of Champagne, who had been unanimously chosen general of the confederates. But the health of that valiant youth already declined, and soon became hopeless; and he deplored the untimely fate, which condemned him to expire, not in a field of battle, but on a bed of sickness. To his brave and numerous vassals, the dying prince distributed his treasures: they swore in his presence to accomplish his vow and their own; but some there were, says the marshal, who accepted his gifts and forfeited their words. The more resolute champions of the cross held a parliament at Soissons for the election of a new general; but such was the incapacity, or jealousy, or reluctance, of the princes of France, that none could be found both able and willing to assume the conduct of the enterprise. They acquiesced in the choice of a stranger, of Boniface marquis of Montferrat, descended of a race of heroes, and himself of conspicuous fame in the wars and negotiations of the times; [44] nor could the piety or ambition of the Italian chief decline this honorable invitation. After visiting the French court, where he was received as a friend and kinsman, the marquis, in the church of Soissons, was invested with the cross of a pilgrim and the staff of a general; and immediately repassed the Alps, to prepare for the distant expedition of the East. About the festival of the Pentecost he displayed his banner, and marched towards Venice at the head of the Italians: he was preceded or followed by the counts of Flanders and Blois, and the most respectable barons of France; and their numbers were swelled by the pilgrims of Germany, [45] whose object and motives were similar to their own. The Venetians had fulfilled, and even surpassed, their engagements: stables were constructed for the horses, and barracks for the troops: the magazines were abundantly replenished with forage and provisions; and the fleet of transports, ships, and galleys, was ready to hoist sail as soon as the republic had received the price of the freight and armament. But that price far exceeded the wealth of the crusaders who were assembled at Venice. The Flemings, whose obedience to their count was voluntary and precarious, had embarked in their vessels for the long navigation of the ocean and Mediterranean; and many of the French and Italians had preferred a cheaper and more convenient passage from Marseilles and Apulia to the Holy Land. Each pilgrim might complain, that after he had furnished his own contribution, he was made responsible for the deficiency of his absent brethren: the gold and silver plate of the chiefs, which they freely delivered to the treasury of St. Marks, was a generous but inadequate sacrifice; and after all their efforts, thirty-four thousand marks were still wanting to complete the stipulated sum. The obstacle was removed by the policy and patriotism of the doge, who proposed to the barons, that if they would join their arms in reducing some revolted cities of Dalmatia, he would expose his person in the holy war, and obtain from the republic a long indulgence, till some wealthy conquest should afford the means of satisfying the debt. After much scruple and hesitation, they chose rather to accept the offer than to relinquish the enterprise; and the first hostilities of the fleet and army were directed against Zara, [46] a strong city of the Sclavonian coast, which had renounced its allegiance to Venice, and implored the protection of the king of Hungary. [47] The crusaders burst the chain or boom of the harbor; landed their horses, troops, and military engines; and compelled the inhabitants, after a defence of five days, to surrender at discretion: their lives were spared, but the revolt was punished by the pillage of their houses and the demolition of their walls. The season was far advanced; the French and Venetians resolved to pass the winter in a secure harbor and plentiful country; but their repose was disturbed by national and tumultuous quarrels of the soldiers and mariners. The conquest of Zara had scattered the seeds of discord and scandal: the arms of the allies had been stained in their outset with the blood, not of infidels, but of Christians: the king of Hungary and his new subjects were themselves enlisted under the banner of the cross; and the scruples of the devout were magnified by the fear of lassitude of the reluctant pilgrims. The pope had excommunicated the false crusaders who had pillaged and massacred their brethren, [48] and only the marquis Boniface and Simon of Montfort [48/1] escaped these spiritual thunders; the one by his absence from the siege, the other by his final departure from the camp. Innocent might absolve the simple and submissive penitents of France; but he was provoked by the stubborn reason of the Venetians, who refused to confess their guilt, to accept their pardon, or to allow, in their temporal concerns, the interposition of a priest.

[Footnote 44: By a victory (A.D. 1191) over the citizens of Asti, by a crusade to Palestine, and by an embassy from the pope to the German princes, (Muratori, Annali d'Italia, tom. x. p. 163, 202.)]

[Footnote 45: See the crusade of the Germans in the Historia C. P. of Gunther, (Canisii Antiq. Lect. tom. iv. p. v—viii.,) who celebrates the pilgrimage of his abbot Martin, one of the preaching rivals of Fulk of Neuilly. His monastery, of the Cistercian order, was situate in the diocese of Basil.]

[Footnote 46: Jadera, now Zara, was a Roman colony, which acknowledged Augustus for its parent. It is now only two miles round, and contains five or six thousand inhabitants; but the fortifications are strong, and it is joined to the main land by a bridge. See the travels of the two companions, Spon and Wheeler, (Voyage de Dalmatie, de Grèce, &c., tom. i. p. 64—70. Journey into Greece, p. 8—14;) the last of whom, by mistaking Sestertia for Sestertii, values an arch with statues and columns at twelve pounds. If, in his time, there were no trees near Zara, the cherry-trees were not yet planted which produce our incomparable marasquin.]

[Footnote 47: Katona (Hist. Critica Reg. Hungariæ, Stirpis Arpad. tom. iv. p. 536—558) collects all the facts and testimonies most adverse to the conquerors of Zara.]

[Footnote 48: See the whole transaction, and the sentiments of the pope, in the Epistles of Innocent III. Gesta, c. 86, 87, 88.]

[Footnote 48/1: Montfort protested against the siege. Guido, the abbot of Vaux de Sernay, in the name of the pope, interdicted the attack on a Christian city; and the immediate surrender of the town was thus delayed for five days of fruitless resistance. Wilken, vol. v. p. 167. See likewise, at length, the history of the interdict issued by the pope. Ibid—M.]

The assembly of such formidable powers by sea and land had revived the hopes of young [49] Alexius; and both at Venice and Zara, he solicited the arms of the crusaders, for his own restoration and his father's [50] deliverance. The royal youth was recommended by Philip king of Germany: his prayers and presence excited the compassion of the camp; and his cause was embraced and pleaded by the marquis of Montferrat and the doge of Venice. A double alliance, and the dignity of Cæsar, had connected with the Imperial family the two elder brothers of Boniface: [51] he expected to derive a kingdom from the important service; and the more generous ambition of Dandolo was eager to secure the inestimable benefits of trade and dominion that might accrue to his country. [52] Their influence procured a favorable audience for the ambassadors of Alexius; and if the magnitude of his offers excited some suspicion, the motives and rewards which he displayed might justify the delay and diversion of those forces which had been consecrated to the deliverance of Jerusalem. He promised in his own and his father's name, that as soon as they should be seated on the throne of Constantinople, they would terminate the long schism of the Greeks, and submit themselves and their people to the lawful supremacy of the Roman church. He engaged to recompense the labors and merits of the crusaders, by the immediate payment of two hundred thousand marks of silver; to accompany them in person to Egypt; or, if it should be judged more advantageous, to maintain, during a year, ten thousand men, and, during his life, five hundred knights, for the service of the Holy Land. These tempting conditions were accepted by the republic of Venice; and the eloquence of the doge and marquis persuaded the counts of Flanders, Blois, and St. Pol, with eight barons of France, to join in the glorious enterprise. A treaty of offensive and defensive alliance was confirmed by their oaths and seals; and each individual, according to his situation and character, was swayed by the hope of public or private advantage; by the honor of restoring an exiled monarch; or by the sincere and probable opinion, that their efforts in Palestine would be fruitless and unavailing, and that the acquisition of Constantinople must precede and prepare the recovery of Jerusalem. But they were the chiefs or equals of a valiant band of freemen and volunteers, who thought and acted for themselves: the soldiers and clergy were divided; and, if a large majority subscribed to the alliance, the numbers and arguments of the dissidents were strong and respectable. [53] The boldest hearts were appalled by the report of the naval power and impregnable strength of Constantinople; and their apprehensions were disguised to the world, and perhaps to themselves, by the more decent objections of religion and duty. They alleged the sanctity of a vow, which had drawn them from their families and homes to the rescue of the holy sepulchre; nor should the dark and crooked counsels of human policy divert them from a pursuit, the event of which was in the hands of the Almighty. Their first offence, the attack of Zara, had been severely punished by the reproach of their conscience and the censures of the pope; nor would they again imbrue their hands in the blood of their fellow-Christians. The apostle of Rome had pronounced; nor would they usurp the right of avenging with the sword the schism of the Greeks and the doubtful usurpation of the Byzantine monarch. On these principles or pretences, many pilgrims, the most distinguished for their valor and piety, withdrew from the camp; and their retreat was less pernicious than the open or secret opposition of a discontented party, that labored, on every occasion, to separate the army and disappoint the enterprise.

*[Footnote 49: A modern reader is surprised to hear of the valet de Constantinople, as applied to young Alexius, on account of his youth, like the infants of Spain, and the nobilissimus puer of the Romans. The pages and valets of the knights were as noble as themselves, (Villehardouin and Ducange, No. 36.)]*

*[Footnote 50: The emperor Isaac is styled by Villehardouin, Sursac, (No. 35, &c.,) which may be derived from the French Sire, or the Greek Kur (kurioV?) melted into his proper name; the further corruptions of Tursac and Conserac will instruct us what license may have been used in the old dynasties of Assyria and Egypt.]*

[Footnote 51: Reinier and Conrad: the former married Maria, daughter of the emperor Manuel Comnenus; the latter was the husband of Theodora Angela, sister of the emperors Isaac and Alexius. Conrad abandoned the Greek court and princess for the glory of defending Tyre against Saladin, (Ducange, Fam. Byzant. p. 187, 203.)]

[Footnote 52: Nicetas (in Alexio Comneno, l. iii. c. 9) accuses the doge and Venetians as the first authors of the war against Constantinople, and considers only as a kuma epi kumati, the arrival and shameful offers of the royal exile. Note: He admits, however, that the Angeli had committed depredations on the Venetian trade, and the emperor himself had refused the payment of part of the stipulated compensation for the seizure of the Venetian merchandise by the emperor Manuel. Nicetas, in loc—M.]

[Footnote 53: Villehardouin and Gunther represent the sentiments of the two parties. The abbot Martin left the army at Zara, proceeded to Palestine, was sent ambassador to Constantinople, and became a reluctant witness of the second siege.]

Notwithstanding this defection, the departure of the fleet and army was vigorously pressed by the Venetians, whose zeal for the service of the royal youth concealed a just resentment to his nation and family. They were mortified by the recent preference which had been given to Pisa, the rival of their trade; they had a long arrear of debt and injury to liquidate with the Byzantine court; and Dandolo might not discourage the popular tale, that he had been deprived of his eyes by the emperor Manuel, who perfidiously violated the sanctity of an ambassador. A similar armament, for ages, had not rode the Adriatic: it was composed of one hundred and twenty flat-bottomed vessels or palanders for the horses; two hundred and forty transports filled with men and arms; seventy store-ships laden with provisions; and fifty stout galleys, well prepared for the encounter of an enemy. [54] While the wind was favorable, the sky serene, and the water smooth, every eye was fixed with wonder and delight on the scene of military and naval pomp which overspread the sea. [54/1] The shields of the knights and squires, at once an ornament and a defence, were arranged on either side of the ships; the banners of the nations and families were displayed from the stern; our modern artillery was supplied by three hundred engines for casting stones and darts: the fatigues of the way were cheered with the sound of music; and the spirits of the adventurers were raised by the mutual assurance, that forty thousand Christian heroes were equal to the conquest of the world. [55] In the navigation [56] from Venice and Zara, the fleet was successfully steered by the skill and experience of the Venetian pilots: at Durazzo, the confederates first landed on the territories of the Greek empire: the Isle of Corfu afforded a station and repose; they doubled, without accident, the perilous cape of Malea, the southern point of Peloponnesus or the Morea; made a descent in the islands of Negropont and Andros; and cast anchor at Abydus on the Asiatic side of the Hellespont. These preludes of conquest were easy and bloodless: the Greeks of the provinces, without patriotism or courage, were crushed by an irresistible force: the presence of the lawful heir might justify their obedience; and it was rewarded by the modesty and discipline of the Latins. As they penetrated through the Hellespont, the magnitude of their navy was compressed in a narrow channel, and the face of the waters was darkened with innumerable sails. They again expanded in the basin of the Propontis, and traversed that placid sea, till they approached the European shore, at the abbey of St. Stephen, three leagues to the west of Constantinople. The prudent doge dissuaded them from dispersing themselves in a populous and hostile land; and, as their stock of provisions was reduced, it was resolved, in the season of harvest, to replenish their store-ships in the fertile islands of the Propontis. With this resolution, they directed their course: but a strong gale, and their own impatience, drove them to the eastward; and so near did they run to the shore and the city, that some volleys of stones and darts were exchanged between the ships and the rampart. As they passed along, they gazed with admiration on the capital of the East, or, as it should seem, of the earth; rising from her seven hills, and towering over the continents of Europe and Asia. The swelling domes and lofty spires of five hundred palaces and churches were gilded by the sun and reflected in the waters: the walls were crowded with soldiers and spectators, whose numbers they beheld, of whose temper they were ignorant; and each heart was chilled by the reflection, that, since the beginning of the world, such an enterprise had never been undertaken by such a handful of warriors. But the momentary apprehension was dispelled by hope and valor; and every man, says the marshal of Champagne, glanced his eye on the sword or lance which he must speedily use in the glorious conflict. [57] The Latins cast anchor before Chalcedon; the mariners only were left in the vessels: the soldiers, horses, and arms, were safely landed; and, in the luxury of an Imperial palace, the barons tasted the first fruits of their success. On the third day, the fleet and army moved towards Scutari, the Asiatic suburb of Constantinople: a detachment of five hundred Greek horse was surprised and defeated by fourscore French knights; and in a halt of nine days, the camp was plentifully supplied with forage and provisions.

[Footnote 54: *The birth and dignity of Andrew Dandolo gave him the motive and the means of searching in the archives of Venice the memorable story of his ancestor. His brevity seems to accuse the copious and more recent narratives of Sanudo, (in Muratori, Script. Rerum Italicarum, tom. xxii.,) Blondus, Sabellicus, and Rhamnusius.*]

[Footnote 54/1: *This description rather belongs to the first setting sail of the expedition from Venice, before the siege of Zara. The armament did not return to Venice—M.*]

[Footnote 55: *Villehardouin, No. 62. His feelings and expressions are original: he often weeps, but he rejoices in the glories and perils of war with a spirit unknown to a sedentary writer.*]

[Footnote 56: *In this voyage, almost all the geographical names are corrupted by the Latins. The modern appellation of Chalcis, and all Euba, is derived from its Euripus, Evripo, Negri-po, Negropont, which dishonors our maps, (D'Anville, Géographie Ancienne, tom. i. p. 263.)*]

[Footnote 57: *Et sachiez que il ni ot si hardi cui le cuer ne fremist, (c. 66.).. Chascuns regardoit ses armes.... que par tems en arons mestier, (c. 67.) Such is the honesty of courage.*]

In relating the invasion of a great empire, it may seem strange that I have not described the obstacles which should have checked the progress of the strangers. The Greeks, in truth, were an unwarlike people; but they were rich, industrious, and subject to the will of a single man: had that man been capable of fear, when his enemies were at a distance, or of courage, when they approached his person. The first rumor of his nephew's alliance with the French and Venetians was despised by the usurper Alexius: his flatterers persuaded him, that in this contempt he was bold and sincere; and each evening, in the close of the banquet, he thrice discomfited the Barbarians of the West. These Barbarians had been justly terrified by the report of his naval power; and the sixteen hundred fishing boats of Constantinople [58] could have manned a fleet, to sink them in the Adriatic, or stop their entrance in the mouth of the Hellespont. But all force may be annihilated by the negligence of the prince and the venality of his ministers. The great duke, or admiral, made a scandalous, almost a public, auction of the sails, the masts, and the rigging: the royal forests were reserved for the more important purpose of the chase; and the trees, says Nicetas, were guarded by the eunuchs, like the groves of religious worship. [59] From his dream of pride, Alexius was awakened by the siege of Zara, and the rapid advances of the Latins; as soon as he saw the danger was real, he thought it inevitable, and his vain presumption was lost in abject despondency and despair. He suffered these contemptible Barbarians to pitch their camp in the sight of the palace; and his apprehensions were thinly disguised by the pomp and menace of a suppliant embassy. The sovereign of the Romans was astonished (his ambassadors were instructed to say) at the hostile appearance of the strangers. If these pilgrims were sincere in their vow for the deliverance of Jerusalem, his voice must applaud, and his treasures should assist, their pious design but should they dare to invade the sanctuary of empire, their numbers, were they ten times more considerable, should not protect them from his just resentment. The answer of the doge and barons was simple and magnanimous. "In the cause of honor and justice," they said, "we despise the usurper of Greece, his threats, and his offers. Our friendship and his allegiance are due to the lawful heir, to the young prince, who is seated among us, and to his father, the emperor Isaac, who has been deprived of his sceptre, his freedom, and his eyes, by the crime of an ungrateful brother. Let that brother confess his guilt, and implore forgiveness, and we ourselves will intercede, that he may be permitted to live in affluence and security. But let him not insult us by a second message; our reply will be made in arms, in the palace of Constantinople."

[Footnote 58: Eandem urbem plus in solis navibus piscatorum abundare, quam illos in toto navigio. Habebat enim mille et sexcentas piscatorias naves..... Bellicas autem sive mercatorias habebant infinitæ multitudinis et portum tutissimum. Gunther, Hist. C. P. c. 8, p. 10.]

[Footnote 59: Kaqaper iervn alsewn, eipein de kai Jeojuteutwn paradeiswn ejeid?onto toutwni. Nicetas in Alex. Comneno, l. iii. c. 9, p. 348.]

On the tenth day of their encampment at Scutari, the crusaders prepared themselves, as soldiers and as Catholics, for the passage of the Bosphorus. Perilous indeed was the adventure; the stream was broad and rapid: in a calm the current of the Euxine might drive down the liquid and unextinguishable fires of the Greeks; and the opposite shores of Europe were defended by seventy thousand horse and foot in formidable array. On this memorable day, which happened to be bright and pleasant, the Latins were distributed in six battles or divisions; the first, or vanguard, was led by the count of Flanders, one of the most powerful of the Christian princes in the skill and number of his crossbows. The four successive battles of the French were commanded by his brother Henry, the counts of St. Pol and Blois, and Matthew of Montmorency; the last of whom was honored by the voluntary service of the marshal and nobles of Champagne. The sixth division, the rear-guard and reserve of the army, was conducted by the marquis of Montferrat, at the head of the Germans and Lombards. The chargers, saddled, with their long comparisons dragging on the ground, were embarked in the flat palanders; [60] and the knights stood by the side of their horses, in complete armor, their helmets laced, and their lances in their hands. The numerous train of sergeants [61] and archers occupied the transports; and each transport was towed by the strength and swiftness of a galley. The six divisions traversed the Bosphorus, without encountering an enemy or an obstacle: to land the foremost was the wish, to conquer or die was the resolution, of every division and of every soldier. Jealous of the preeminence of danger, the knights in their heavy armor leaped into the sea, when it rose as high as their girdle; the sergeants and archers were animated by their valor; and the squires, letting down the draw-bridges of the palanders, led the horses to the shore. Before their squadrons could mount, and form, and couch their Lances, the seventy thousand Greeks had vanished from their sight: the timid Alexius gave the example to his troops; and it was only by the plunder of his rich pavilions that the Latins were informed that they had fought against an emperor. In the first consternation of the flying enemy, they resolved, by a double attack, to open the entrance of the harbor. The tower of Galata, [62] in the suburb of Pera, was attacked and stormed by the French, while the Venetians assumed the more difficult task of forcing the boom or chain that was stretched from that tower to the Byzantine shore. After some fruitless attempts, their intrepid perseverance prevailed: twenty ships of war, the relics of the Grecian navy, were either sunk or taken: the enormous and massy links of iron were cut asunder by the shears, or broken by the weight, of the galleys; [63] and the Venetian fleet, safe and triumphant, rode at anchor in the port of Constantinople. By these daring achievements, a remnant of twenty thousand Latins solicited the license of besieging a capital which contained above four hundred thousand inhabitants, [64] able, though not willing, to bear arms in defence of their country. Such an account would indeed suppose a population of near two millions; but whatever abatement may be required in the numbers of the Greeks, the belief of those numbers will equally exalt the fearless spirit of their assailants.

[Footnote 60: From the version of Vignere I adopt the well-sounding word palander, which is still used, I believe, in the Mediterranean. But had I written in French, I should have preserved the original and expressive denomination of vessiers or huissiers, from the huis or door which was let down as a drawbridge; but which, at sea, was closed into the side of the ship, (see Ducange au Villehardouin, No. 14, and Joinville. p. 27, 28, edit. du Louvre.)]

[Footnote 61: To avoid the vague expressions of followers, &c., I use, after Villehardouin, the word sergeants for all horsemen who were not knights. There were sergeants at arms, and sergeants at law; and if we visit the parade and Westminster Hall, we may observe the strange result of the distinction, (Ducange, Glossar. Latin, Servientes, &c., tom. vi. p. 226—231.)]

[Footnote 62: It is needless to observe, that on the subject of Galata, the chain, &c., Ducange is accurate and full. Consult likewise the proper chapters of the C. P. Christiana of the same author. The inhabitants of Galata were so vain and ignorant, that they applied to themselves St. Paul's Epistle to the Galatians.]

[Footnote 63: The vessel that broke the chain was named the Eagle, Aquila, (Dandolo, Chronicon, p. 322,) which Blondus (de Gestis Venet.) has changed into Aquilo, the north wind. Ducange (Observations, No. 83) maintains the latter reading; but he had not seen the respectable text of Dandolo, nor did he enough consider the topography of the harbor. The south-east would have been a more effectual wind. (Note to Wilken, vol. v. p. 215.)]

[Footnote 64: Quatre cens mil homes ou plus, (Villehardouin, No. 134,) must be understood of men of a military age. Le Beau (Hist. du. Bas Empire, tom. xx. p. 417) allows Constantinople a million of inhabitants, of whom 60,000 horse, and an infinite number of foot-soldiers. In its present decay, the capital of the Ottoman empire may contain 400,000 souls, (Bell's Travels, vol. ii. p. 401, 402;) but as the Turks keep no registers, and as circumstances are fallacious, it is impossible to ascertain (Niebuhr, Voyage en Arabie, tom. i. p. 18, 19) the real populousness of their cities.]

In the choice of the attack, the French and Venetians were divided by their habits of life and warfare. The former affirmed with truth, that Constantinople was most accessible on the side of the sea and the harbor. The latter might assert with honor, that they had long enough trusted their lives and fortunes to a frail bark and a precarious element, and loudly demanded a trial of knighthood, a firm ground, and a close onset, either on foot or on horseback. After a prudent compromise, of employing the two nations by sea and land, in the service best suited to their character, the fleet covering the army, they both proceeded from the entrance to the extremity of the harbor: the stone bridge of the river was hastily repaired; and the six battles of the French formed their encampment against the front of the capital, the basis of the triangle which runs about four miles from the port to the Propontis. [65] On the edge of a broad ditch, at the foot of a lofty rampart, they had leisure to contemplate the difficulties of their enterprise. The gates to the right and left of their narrow camp poured forth frequent sallies of cavalry and light-infantry, which cut off their stragglers, swept the country of provisions, sounded the alarm five or six times in the course of each day, and compelled them to plant a palisade, and sink an intrenchment, for their immediate safety. In the supplies and convoys the Venetians had been too sparing, or the Franks too voracious: the usual complaints of hunger and scarcity were heard, and perhaps felt their stock of flour would be exhausted in three weeks; and their disgust of salt meat tempted them to taste the flesh of their horses. The trembling usurper was supported by Theodore Lascaris, his son-in-law, a valiant youth, who aspired to save and to rule his country; the Greeks, regardless of that country, were awakened to the defence of their religion; but their firmest hope was in the strength and spirit of the Varangian guards, of the Danes and English, as they are named in the writers of the times. [66] After ten days' incessant labor, the ground was levelled, the ditch filled, the approaches of the besiegers were regularly made, and two hundred and fifty engines of assault exercised their various powers to clear the rampart, to batter the walls, and to sap the foundations. On the first appearance of a breach, the scaling-ladders were applied: the numbers that defended the vantage ground repulsed and oppressed the adventurous Latins; but they admired the resolution of fifteen knights and sergeants, who had gained the ascent, and maintained their perilous station till they were precipitated or made prisoners by the Imperial guards. On the side of the harbor the naval attack was more successfully conducted by the Venetians; and that industrious people employed every resource that was known and practiced before the invention of gunpowder. A double line, three bow-shots in front, was formed by the galleys and ships; and the swift motion of the former was supported by the weight and loftiness of the latter, whose decks, and poops, and turret, were the platforms of military engines, that discharged their shot over the heads of the first line. The soldiers, who leaped from the galleys on shore, immediately planted and ascended their scaling-ladders, while the large ships, advancing more slowly into the intervals, and lowering a draw-bridge, opened a way through the air from their masts to the rampart. In the midst of the conflict, the doge, a venerable and conspicuous form, stood aloft in complete armor on the prow of his galley. The great standard of St. Mark was displayed before him; his threats, promises, and exhortations, urged the diligence of the rowers; his vessel was the first that struck; and Dandolo was the first warrior on the shore. The nations admired the magnanimity of the blind old man, without reflecting that his age and infirmities diminished the price of life, and enhanced the value of immortal glory. On a sudden, by an invisible hand, (for the standard-bearer was probably slain,) the banner of the republic was fixed on the rampart: twenty-five towers were rapidly occupied; and, by the cruel expedient of fire, the Greeks were driven from the adjacent quarter. The doge had despatched the intelligence of his success, when he was checked by the danger of his confederates. Nobly declaring that he would rather die with the pilgrims than gain a victory by their destruction, Dandolo relinquished his advantage, recalled his troops, and hastened to the scene of action. He found the six weary diminutive battles of the French encompassed by sixty squadrons of the Greek cavalry, the least of which was more numerous than the largest of their divisions. Shame and despair had provoked Alexius to the last effort of a general sally; but he was awed by the firm order and manly aspect of the Latins; and, after skirmishing at a distance, withdrew his troops in the close of the evening. The silence or tumult of the night exasperated his fears; and the timid usurper, collecting a treasure of ten thousand pounds of gold, basely deserted his wife, his people, and his fortune; threw himself into a bark; stole through the Bosphorus; and landed in shameful safety in an obscure harbor of Thrace. As soon as they were apprised of his flight, the Greek nobles sought pardon and peace in the dungeon where the blind Isaac expected each hour the visit of the executioner. Again saved and exalted by the vicissitudes of fortune, the captive in his Imperial robes was replace on the throne, and surrounded with prostrate slaves, whose real terror and affected joy he was incapable of discerning. At the dawn of day, hostilities were suspended, and the Latin chiefs were surprised by a message from the lawful and reigning emperor, who was impatient to embrace his son, and to reward his generous deliverers. [67]

[Footnote 65: On the most correct plans of Constantinople, I know not how to measure more than 4000 paces. Yet Villehardouin computes the space at three leagues, (No. 86.) If his eye were not deceived, he must reckon by the old Gallic league of 1500 paces, which might still be used in Champagne.]

[Footnote 66: The guards, the Varangi, are styled by Villehardouin, (No. 89, 95) Englois et Danois avec leurs haches. Whatever had been their origin, a French pilgrim could not be mistaken in the nations of which they were at that time composed.]

[Footnote 67: For the first siege and conquest of Constantinople, we may read the original letter of the crusaders to Innocent III., Gesta, c. 91, p. 533, 534. Villehardouin, No. 75—99. Nicetas, in Alexio Comnen. l. iii. c. 10, p. 349—352. Dandolo, in Chron. p. 322. Gunther, and his abbot Martin, were not yet returned from their obstinate pilgrim age to Jerusalem, or St. John d'Acre, where the greatest part of the company had died of the plague.]

## PART III

But these generous deliverers were unwilling to release their hostage, till they had obtained from his father the payment, or at least the promise, of their recompense. They chose four ambassadors, Matthew of Montmorency, our historian the marshal of Champagne, and two Venetians, to congratulate the emperor. The gates were thrown open on their approach, the streets on both sides were lined with the battle axes of the Danish and English guard: the presence-chamber glittered with gold and jewels, the false substitute of virtue and power: by the side of the blind Isaac his wife was seated, the sister of the king of Hungary: and by her appearance, the noble matrons of Greece were drawn from their domestic retirement, and mingled with the circle of senators and soldiers. The Latins, by the mouth of the marshal, spoke like men conscious of their merits, but who respected the work of their own hands; and the emperor clearly understood, that his son's engagements with Venice and the pilgrims must be ratified without hesitation or delay. Withdrawing into a private chamber with the empress, a chamberlain, an interpreter, and the four ambassadors, the father of young Alexius inquired with some anxiety into the nature of his stipulations. The submission of the Eastern empire to the pope, the succor of the Holy Land, and a present contribution of two hundred thousand marks of silver—"These conditions are weighty," was his prudent reply: "they are hard to accept, and difficult to perform. But no conditions can exceed the measure of your services and deserts." After this satisfactory assurance, the barons mounted on horseback, and introduced the heir of Constantinople to the city and palace: his youth and marvellous adventures engaged every heart in his favor, and Alexius was solemnly crowned with his father in the dome of St. Sophia. In the first days of his reign, the people, already blessed with the restoration of plenty and peace, was delighted by the joyful catastrophe of the tragedy; and the discontent of the nobles, their regret, and their fears, were covered by the polished surface of pleasure and loyalty The mixture of two discordant nations in the same capital might have been pregnant with mischief and danger; and the suburb of Galata, or Pera, was assigned for the quarters of the French and Venetians. But the liberty of trade and familiar intercourse was allowed between the friendly nations: and each day the pilgrims were tempted by devotion or curiosity to visit the churches and palaces of Constantinople. Their rude minds, insensible perhaps of the finer arts, were astonished by the magnificent scenery: and the poverty of their native towns enhanced the populousness and riches of the first metropolis of Christendom. [68] Descending from his state, young Alexius was prompted by interest and gratitude to repeat his frequent and familiar visits to his Latin allies; and in the freedom of the table, the gay petulance of the French sometimes forgot the emperor of the East. [69] In their most serious conferences, it was agreed, that the reunion of the two churches must be the result of patience and time; but avarice was less tractable than zeal; and a larger sum was instantly disbursed to appease the wants, and silence the importunity, of the crusaders. [70] Alexius was alarmed by the approaching hour of their departure: their absence might have relieved him from the engagement which he was yet incapable of performing; but his friends would have left him, naked and alone, to the caprice and prejudice of a perfidious nation. He wished to bribe their stay, the delay of a year, by undertaking to defray their expense, and to satisfy, in their name, the freight of the Venetian vessels. The offer was agitated in the council of the barons; and, after a repetition of their debates and scruples, a majority of votes again acquiesced in the advice of the doge and the prayer of the young emperor. At the price of sixteen hundred pounds of gold, he prevailed on the marquis of Montferrat to lead him with an army round the provinces of Europe; to establish his authority, and pursue his uncle, while Constantinople was awed by the presence of Baldwin and his confederates of France and Flanders. The expedition was successful: the blind emperor exulted in the success of his arms, and listened to the predictions of his flatterers, that the same Providence which had raised him from the dungeon to the throne, would heal his gout, restore his sight, and watch over the long prosperity of his reign. Yet the mind of the suspicious old man was tormented by the rising glories of his son; nor could his pride conceal from his envy, that, while his own name was pronounced in faint and reluctant acclamations, the royal youth was the theme of spontaneous and universal praise. [71]

*[Footnote 68: Compare, in the rude energy of Villehardouin, (No. 66, 100,) the inside and outside views of Constantinople, and their impression on the minds of the pilgrims: cette ville (says he) que de toutes les autres ere souveraine. See the parallel passages of Fulcherius Carnotensis, Hist. Hierosol. l. i. c. 4, and Will. Tyr. ii. 3, xx. 26.]*

*[Footnote 69: As they played at dice, the Latins took off his diadem, and clapped on his head a woollen or hairy cap, to megaloprepeV kai pagkleiston katerrupainen onoma, (Nicetas, p. 358.) If these merry companions were Venetians, it was the insolence of trade and a commonwealth.]*

*[Footnote 70: Villehardouin, No. 101. Dandolo, p. 322. The doge affirms, that the Venetians were paid more slowly than the French; but he owns, that the histories of the two nations differed on that subject. Had he read Villehardouin? The Greeks complained, however, good totius Græciæ opes transtulisset, (Gunther, Hist. C. P. c 13) See the lamentations and invectives of Nicetas, (p. 355.)]*

*[Footnote 71: The reign of Alexius Comnenus occupies three books in Nicetas, p. 291—352. The short restoration of Isaac and his son is despatched in five chapters, p. 352—362.]*

By the recent invasion, the Greeks were awakened from a dream of nine centuries; from the vain presumption that the capital of the Roman empire was impregnable to foreign arms. The strangers of the West had violated the city, and bestowed the sceptre, of Constantine: their Imperial clients soon became as unpopular as themselves: the well-known vices of Isaac were rendered still more contemptible by his infirmities, and the young Alexius was hated as an apostate, who had renounced the manners and religion of his country. His secret covenant with the Latins was divulged or suspected; the people, and especially the clergy, were devoutly attached to their faith and superstition; and every convent, and every shop, resounded with the danger of the church and the tyranny of the pope. [72] An empty treasury could ill supply the demands of regal luxury and foreign extortion: the Greeks refused to avert, by a general tax, the impending evils of servitude and pillage; the oppression of the rich excited a more dangerous and personal resentment; and if the emperor melted the plate, and despoiled the images, of the sanctuary, he seemed to justify the complaints of heresy and sacrilege. During the absence of Marquis Boniface and his Imperial pupil, Constantinople was visited with a calamity which might be justly imputed to the zeal and indiscretion of the Flemish pilgrims. [73] In one of their visits to the city, they were scandalized by the aspect of a mosque or synagogue, in which one God was worshipped, without a partner or a son. Their effectual mode of controversy was to attack the infidels with the sword, and their habitation with fire: but the infidels, and some Christian neighbors, presumed to defend their lives and properties; and the flames which bigotry had kindled, consumed the most orthodox and innocent structures. During eight days and nights, the conflagration spread above a league in front, from the harbor to the Propontis, over the thickest and most populous regions of the city. It is not easy to count the stately churches and palaces that were reduced to a smoking ruin, to value the merchandise that perished in the trading streets, or to number the families that were involved in the common destruction. By this outrage, which the doge and the barons in vain affected to disclaim, the name of the Latins became still more unpopular; and the colony of that nation, above fifteen thousand persons, consulted their safety in a hasty retreat from the city to the protection of their standard in the suburb of Pera. The emperor returned in triumph; but the firmest and most dexterous policy would have been insufficient to steer him through the tempest, which overwhelmed the person and government of that unhappy youth. His own inclination, and his father's advice, attached him to his benefactors; but Alexius hesitated between gratitude and patriotism, between the fear of his subjects and of his allies. [74] By his feeble and fluctuating conduct he lost the esteem and confidence of both; and, while he invited the marquis of Monferrat to occupy the palace, he suffered the nobles to conspire, and the people to arm, for the deliverance of their country. Regardless of his painful situation, the Latin chiefs repeated their demands, resented his delays, suspected his intentions, and exacted a decisive answer of peace or war. The haughty summons was delivered by three French knights and three Venetian deputies, who girded their swords, mounted their horses, pierced through the angry multitude, and entered, with a fearful countenance, the palace and presence of the Greek emperor. In a peremptory tone, they recapitulated their services and his engagements; and boldly declared, that unless their just claims were fully and immediately satisfied, they should no longer hold him either as a sovereign or a friend. After this defiance, the first that had ever wounded an Imperial ear, they departed without betraying any symptoms of fear; but their escape from a servile palace and a furious city astonished the ambassadors themselves; and their return to the camp was the signal of mutual hostility.

[Footnote 72: When Nicetas reproaches Alexius for his impious league, he bestows the harshest names on the pope's new religion, meizon kai atopwtaton... parektrophn pistewV... tvn tou Papa pronomiwn kainismon,... metaqesin te kai metapoihsin tvn palaivn 'RwmaioiV?eqvn, (p. 348.) Such was the sincere language of every Greek to the last gasp of the empire.]

[Footnote 73: Nicetas (p. 355) is positive in the charge, and specifies the Flemings, (FlamioneV,) though he is wrong in supposing it an ancient name. Villehardouin (No. 107) exculpates the barons, and is ignorant (perhaps affectedly ignorant) of the names of the guilty.]

[Footnote 74: Compare the suspicions and complaints of Nicetas (p. 359—362) with the blunt charges of Baldwin of Flanders, (Gesta Innocent III. c. 92, p. 534,) cum patriarcha et mole nobilium, nobis promises perjurus et mendax.]

Among the Greeks, all authority and wisdom were overborne by the impetuous multitude, who mistook their rage for valor, their numbers for strength, and their fanaticism for the support and inspiration of Heaven. In the eyes of both nations Alexius was false and contemptible; the base and spurious race of the Angeli was rejected with clamorous disdain; and the people of Constantinople encompassed the senate, to demand at their hands a more worthy emperor. To every senator, conspicuous by his birth or dignity, they successively presented the purple: by each senator the deadly garment was repulsed: the contest lasted three days; and we may learn from the historian Nicetas, one of the members of the assembly, that fear and weaknesses were the guardians of their loyalty. A phantom, who vanished in oblivion, was forcibly proclaimed by the crowd: [75] but the author of the tumult, and the leader of the war, was a prince of the house of Ducas; and his common appellation of Alexius must be discriminated by the epithet of Mourzoufle, [76] which in the vulgar idiom expressed the close junction of his black and shaggy eyebrows. At once a patriot and a courtier, the perfidious Mourzoufle, who was not destitute of cunning and courage, opposed the Latins both in speech and action, inflamed the passions and prejudices of the Greeks, and insinuated himself into the favor and confidence of Alexius, who trusted him with the office of great chamberlain, and tinged his buskins with the colors of royalty. At the dead of night, he rushed into the bed-chamber with an affrighted aspect, exclaiming, that the palace was attacked by the people and betrayed by the guards. Starting from his couch, the unsuspecting prince threw himself into the arms of his enemy, who had contrived his escape by a private staircase. But that staircase terminated in a prison: Alexius was seized, stripped, and loaded with chains; and, after tasting some days the bitterness of death, he was poisoned, or strangled, or beaten with clubs, at the command, or in the presence, of the tyrant. The emperor Isaac Angelus soon followed his son to the grave; and Mourzoufle, perhaps, might spare the superfluous crime of hastening the extinction of impotence and blindness.

[Footnote 75: His name was Nicholas Canabus: he deserved the praise of Nicetas and the vengeance of Mourzoufle, (p. 362.)]

[Footnote 76: Villehardouin (No. 116) speaks of him as a favorite, without knowing that he was a prince of the blood, Angelus and Ducas. Ducange, who pries into every corner, believes him to be the son of Isaac Ducas Sebastocrator, and second cousin of young Alexius.]

The death of the emperors, and the usurpation of Mourzoufle, had changed the nature of the quarrel. It was no longer the disagreement of allies who overvalued their services, or neglected their obligations: the French and Venetians forgot their complaints against Alexius, dropped a tear on the untimely fate of their companion, and swore revenge against the perfidious nation who had crowned his assassin. Yet the prudent doge was still inclined to negotiate: he asked as a debt, a subsidy, or a fine, fifty thousand pounds of gold, about two millions sterling; nor would the conference have been abruptly broken, if the zeal, or policy, of Mourzoufle had not refused to sacrifice the Greek church to the safety of the state. [77] Amidst the invectives of his foreign and domestic enemies, we may discern, that he was not unworthy of the character which he had assumed, of the public champion: the second siege of Constantinople was far more laborious than the first; the treasury was replenished, and discipline was restored, by a severe inquisition into the abuses of the former reign; and Mourzoufle, an iron mace in his hand, visiting the posts, and affecting the port and aspect of a warrior, was an object of terror to his soldiers, at least, and to his kinsmen. Before and after the death of Alexius, the Greeks made two vigorous and well-conducted attempts to burn the navy in the harbor; but the skill and courage of the Venetians repulsed the fire-ships; and the vagrant flames wasted themselves without injury in the sea. [78] In a nocturnal sally the Greek emperor was vanquished by Henry, brother of the count of Flanders: the advantages of number and surprise aggravated the shame of his defeat: his buckler was found on the field of battle; and the Imperial standard, [79] a divine image of the Virgin, was presented, as a trophy and a relic to the Cistercian monks, the disciples of St. Bernard. Near three months, without excepting the holy season of Lent, were consumed in skirmishes and preparations, before the Latins were ready or resolved for a general assault. The land fortifications had been found impregnable; and the Venetian pilots represented, that, on the shore of the Propontis, the anchorage was unsafe, and the ships must be driven by the current far away to the straits of the Hellespont; a prospect not unpleasing to the reluctant pilgrims, who sought every opportunity of breaking the army. From the harbor, therefore, the assault was determined by the assailants, and expected by the besieged; and the emperor had placed his scarlet pavilions on a neighboring height, to direct and animate the efforts of his troops. A fearless spectator, whose mind could entertain the ideas of pomp and pleasure, might have admired the long array of two embattled armies, which extended above half a league, the one on the ships and galleys, the other on the walls and towers raised above the ordinary level by several stages of wooden turrets. Their first fury was spent in the discharge of darts, stones, and fire, from the engines; but the water was deep; the French were bold; the Venetians were skilful; they approached the walls; and a desperate conflict of swords, spears, and battle-axes, was fought on the trembling bridges that grappled the floating, to the stable, batteries. In more than a hundred places, the assault was urged, and the defence was sustained; till the superiority of ground and numbers finally prevailed, and the Latin trumpets sounded a retreat. On the ensuing days, the attack was renewed with equal vigor, and a similar event; and, in the night, the doge and the barons held a council, apprehensive only for the public danger: not a voice pronounced the words of escape or treaty; and each warrior, according to his temper, embraced the hope of victory, or the assurance of a glorious death. [80] By the experience of the former siege, the Greeks were instructed, but the Latins were animated; and the knowledge that Constantinople might be taken, was of more avail than the local precautions which that knowledge had inspired for its defence. In the third assault, two ships were linked together to double their strength; a strong north wind drove them on the shore; the bishops of Troyes and Soissons led the van; and the auspicious names of the pilgrim and the paradise resounded along the line. [81] The episcopal banners were displayed on the walls; a hundred marks of silver had been promised to the first adventurers; and if their reward was intercepted by death, their names have been immortalized by fame. [81/1] Four towers were scaled; three gates were burst open; and the French knights, who might tremble on the waves, felt themselves invincible on horseback on the solid ground. Shall I relate that the thousands who guarded the emperor's person fled on the approach, and before the lance, of a single warrior? Their ignominious flight is attested by their countryman Nicetas: an army of phantoms marched with the French hero, and he was magnified to a giant in the eyes of the Greeks. [82] While the fugitives deserted their posts and cast away their arms, the Latins entered the city under the banners of their leaders: the streets and gates opened for their passage; and either design or accident kindled a third conflagration, which consumed in a few hours the measure of three of the largest cities of France. [83] In the close of evening, the barons checked their troops, and fortified their stations: They were awed by the extent and populousness of the capital, which might yet require the labor of a month, if the churches and palaces were conscious of their internal strength. But in the morning, a suppliant procession, with crosses and images, announced the submission of the Greeks, and deprecated the wrath of the conquerors: the usurper escaped through the golden gate: the palaces of Blachernæ and Boucoleon were occupied by the count of Flanders and the marquis of Montferrat; and the empire, which still bore the name of Constantine, and the title of Roman, was subverted by the arms of the Latin pilgrims. [84]

*[Footnote 77: This negotiation, probable in itself, and attested by Nicetas, (p 65,) is omitted as scandalous by the delicacy of Dandolo and Villehardouin. Note: Wilken places it before the death of Alexius, vol. v. p. 276—M.]*

*[Footnote 78: Baldwin mentions both attempts to fire the fleet, (Gest. c. 92, p. 534, 535;) Villehardouin, (No. 113—15) only describes the first. It is remarkable that neither of these warriors observe any peculiar properties in the Greek fire.]*

[Footnote 79: Ducange (No. 119) pours forth a torrent of learning on the Gonfanon Imperial. This banner of the Virgin is shown at Venice as a trophy and relic: if it be genuine the pious doge must have cheated the monks of Citeaux.]

[Footnote 80: Villehardouin (No. 126) confesses, that mult ere grant peril; and Guntherus (Hist. C. P. c. 13) affirms, that nulla spes victoriæ arridere poterat. Yet the knight despises those who thought of flight, and the monk praises his countrymen who were resolved on death.]

[Footnote 81: Baldwin, and all the writers, honor the names of these two galleys, felici auspicio.]

[Footnote 81/1: Pietro Alberti, a Venetian noble and Andrew d'Amboise a French knight—M.]

[Footnote 82: With an allusion to Homer, Nicetas calls him enneorguioV, nine orgyæ, or eighteen yards high, a stature which would, indeed, have excused the terror of the Greek. On this occasion, the historian seems fonder of the marvellous than of his country, or perhaps of truth. Baldwin exclaims in the words of the psalmist, persequitur unus ex nobis centum alienos.]

[Footnote 83: Villehardouin (No. 130) is again ignorant of the authors of this more legitimate fire, which is ascribed by Gunther to a quidam comes Teutonicus, (c. 14.) They seem ashamed, the incendiaries!]

[Footnote 84: For the second siege and conquest of Constantinople, see Villehardouin (No. 113—132,) Baldwin's iid Epistle to Innocent III., (Gesta c. 92, p. 534—537,) with the whole reign of Mourzoufle, in Nicetas, (p 363—375;) and borrowed some hints from Dandolo (Chron. Venet. p. 323—330) and Gunther, (Hist. C. P. c. 14—18,) who added the decorations of prophecy and vision. The former produces an oracle of the Erythræan sibyl, of a great armament on the Adriatic, under a blind chief, against Byzantium, &c. Curious enough, were the prediction anterior to the fact.]

Constantinople had been taken by storm; and no restraints, except those of religion and humanity, were imposed on the conquerors by the laws of war. Boniface, marquis of Montferrat, still acted as their general; and the Greeks, who revered his name as that of their future sovereign, were heard to exclaim in a lamentable tone, "Holy marquis-king, have mercy upon us!" His prudence or compassion opened the gates of the city to the fugitives; and he exhorted the soldiers of the cross to spare the lives of their fellow-Christians. The streams of blood that flowed down the pages of Nicetas may be reduced to the slaughter of two thousand of his unresisting countrymen; [85] and the greater part was massacred, not by the strangers, but by the Latins, who had been driven from the city, and who exercised the revenge of a triumphant faction. Yet of these exiles, some were less mindful of injuries than of benefits; and Nicetas himself was indebted for his safety to the generosity of a Venetian merchant. Pope Innocent the Third accuses the pilgrims for respecting, in their lust, neither age nor sex, nor religious profession; and bitterly laments that the deeds of darkness, fornication, adultery, and incest, were perpetrated in open day; and that noble matrons and holy nuns were polluted by the grooms and peasants of the Catholic camp. [86] It is indeed probable that the license of victory prompted and covered a multitude of sins: but it is certain, that the capital of the East contained a stock of venal or willing beauty, sufficient to satiate the desires of twenty thousand pilgrims; and female prisoners were no longer subject to the right or abuse of domestic slavery. The marquis of Montferrat was the patron of discipline and decency; the count of Flanders was the mirror of chastity: they had forbidden, under pain of death, the rape of married women, or virgins, or nuns; and the proclamation was sometimes invoked by the vanquished [87] and respected by the victors. Their cruelty and lust were moderated by the authority of the chiefs, and feelings of the soldiers; for we are no longer describing an irruption of the northern savages; and however ferocious they might still appear, time, policy, and religion had civilized the manners of the French, and still more of the Italians. But a free scope was allowed to their avarice, which was glutted, even in the holy week, by the pillage of Constantinople. The right of victory, unshackled by any promise or treaty, had confiscated the public and private wealth of the Greeks; and every hand, according to its size and strength, might lawfully execute the sentence and seize the forfeiture. A portable and universal standard of exchange was found in the coined and uncoined metals of gold and silver, which each captor, at home or abroad, might convert into the possessions most suitable to his temper and situation. Of the treasures, which trade and luxury had accumulated, the silks, velvets, furs, the gems, spices, and rich movables, were the most precious, as they could not be procured for money in the ruder countries of Europe. An order of rapine was instituted; nor was the share of each individual abandoned to industry or chance. Under the tremendous penalties of perjury, excommunication, and death, the Latins were bound to deliver their plunder into the common stock: three churches were selected for the deposit and distribution of the spoil: a single share was allotted to a foot-soldier; two for a sergeant on horseback; four to a knight; and larger proportions according to the rank and merit of the barons and princes. For violating this sacred engagement, a knight belonging to the count of St. Paul was hanged with his shield and coat of arms round his neck; his example might render similar offenders more artful and discreet; but avarice was more powerful than fear; and it is generally believed that the secret far exceeded the acknowledged plunder. Yet the magnitude of the prize surpassed the largest scale of experience or expectation. [88] After the whole had been equally divided between the French and Venetians, fifty thousand marks were deducted to satisfy the debts of the former and the demands of the latter. The residue of the French amounted to four hundred thousand marks of silver, [89] about eight hundred thousand pounds sterling; nor can I better appreciate the value of that sum in the public and private transactions of the age, than by defining it as seven times the annual revenue of the kingdom of England. [90]

[Footnote 85: Ceciderunt tamen eâ die civium quasi duo millia, &c., (Gunther, c. 18.) Arithmetic is an excellent touchstone to try the amplifications of passion and rhetoric.]

[Footnote 86: Quidam (says Innocent III., Gesta, c. 94, p. 538) nec religioni, nec ætati, nec sexui pepercerunt: sed fornicationes, adulteria, et incestus in oculis omnium exercentes, non solûm maritatas et viduas, sed et matronas et virgines Deoque dicatas, exposuerunt spurcitiis garcionum. Villehardouin takes no notice of these common incidents.]

[Footnote 87: Nicetas saved, and afterwards married, a noble virgin, (p. 380,) whom a soldier, eti martusi polloiV onhdon epibrimwmenoV, had almost violated in spite of the entolai, entalmata eu gegonotwn.]

[Footnote 88: Of the general mass of wealth, Gunther observes, ut de pauperibus et advenis cives ditissimi redderentur, (Hist. C. P. c. 18; (Villehardouin, (No. 132,) that since the creation, ne fu tant gaaignié dans une ville; Baldwin, (Gesta, c. 92,) ut tantum tota non videatur possidere Latinitas.]

[Footnote 89: Villehardouin, No. 133—135. Instead of 400,000, there is a various reading of 500,000. The Venetians had offered to take the whole booty, and to give 400 marks to each knight, 200 to each priest and horseman, and 100 to each foot-soldier: they would have been great losers, (Le Beau, Hist. du. Bas Empire tom. xx. p. 506. I know not from whence.)]

[Footnote 90: At the council of Lyons (A.D. 1245) the English ambassadors stated the revenue of the crown as below that of the foreign clergy, which amounted to 60,000 marks a year, (Matthew Paris, p. 451 Hume's Hist. of England, vol. ii. p. 170.)]

In this great revolution we enjoy the singular felicity of comparing the narratives of Villehardouin and Nicetas, the opposite feelings of the marshal of Champagne and the Byzantine senator. [91] At the first view it should seem that the wealth of Constantinople was only transferred from one nation to another; and that the loss and sorrow of the Greeks is exactly balanced by the joy and advantage of the Latins. But in the miserable account of war, the gain is never equivalent to the loss, the pleasure to the pain; the smiles of the Latins were transient and fallacious; the Greeks forever wept over the ruins of their country; and their real calamities were aggravated by sacrilege and mockery. What benefits accrued to the conquerors from the three fires which annihilated so vast a portion of the buildings and riches of the city? What a stock of such things, as could neither be used nor transported, was maliciously or wantonly destroyed! How much treasure was idly wasted in gaming, debauchery, and riot! And what precious objects were bartered for a vile price by the impatience or ignorance of the soldiers, whose reward was stolen by the base industry of the last of the Greeks! These alone, who had nothing to lose, might derive some profit from the revolution; but the misery of the upper ranks of society is strongly painted in the personal adventures of Nicetas himself His stately palace had been reduced to ashes in the second conflagration; and the senator, with his family and friends, found an obscure shelter in another house which he possessed near the church of St. Sophia. It was the door of this mean habitation that his friend, the Venetian merchant, guarded in the disguise of a soldier, till Nicetas could save, by a precipitate flight, the relics of his fortune and the chastity of his daughter. In a cold, wintry season, these fugitives, nursed in the lap of prosperity, departed on foot; his wife was with child; the desertion of their slaves compelled them to carry their baggage on their own shoulders; and their women, whom they placed in the centre, were exhorted to conceal their beauty with dirt, instead of adorning it with paint and jewels Every step was exposed to insult and danger: the threats of the strangers were less painful than the taunts of the plebeians, with whom they were now levelled; nor did the exiles breathe in safety till their mournful pilgrimage was concluded at Selymbria, above forty miles from the capital. On the way they overtook the patriarch, without attendance and almost without apparel, riding on an ass, and reduced to a state of apostolical poverty, which, had it been voluntary, might perhaps have been meritorious. In the mean while, his desolate churches were profaned by the licentiousness and party zeal of the Latins. After stripping the gems and pearls, they converted the chalices into drinking-cups; their tables, on which they gamed and feasted, were covered with the pictures of Christ and the saints; and they trampled under foot the most venerable objects of the Christian worship. In the cathedral of St. Sophia, the ample veil of the sanctuary was rent asunder for the sake of the golden fringe; and the altar, a monument of art and riches, was broken in pieces and shared among the captors. Their mules and horses were laden with the wrought silver and gilt carvings, which they tore down from the doors and pulpit; and if the beasts stumbled under the burden, they were stabbed by their impatient drivers, and the holy pavement streamed with their impure blood. A prostitute was seated on the throne of the patriarch; and that daughter of Belial, as she is styled, sung and danced in the church, to ridicule the hymns and processions of the Orientals. Nor were the repositories of the royal dead secure from violation: in the church of the Apostles, the tombs of the emperors were rifled; and it is said, that after six centuries the corpse of Justinian was found without any signs of decay or putrefaction. In the streets, the French and Flemings clothed themselves and their horses in painted robes and flowing head-dresses of linen; and the coarse intemperance of their feasts [92] insulted the splendid sobriety of the East. To expose the arms of a people of scribes and scholars, they affected to display a pen, an inkhorn, and a sheet of paper, without discerning that the instruments of science and valor were alike feeble and useless in the hands of the modern Greeks.

*[Footnote 91: The disorders of the sack of Constantinople, and his own adventures, are feelingly described by Nicetas, p. 367—369, and in the Status Urb. C. P. p. 375—384. His complaints, even of*

sacrilege, are justified by Innocent III., (Gesta, c. 92;) but Villehardouin does not betray a symptom of pity or remorse.]

[Footnote 92: If I rightly apprehend the Greek of Nicetas's receipts, their favorite dishes were boiled buttocks of beef, salt pork and peas, and soup made of garlic and sharp or sour herbs, (p. 382.)]

Their reputation and their language encouraged them, however, to despise the ignorance and to overlook the progress of the Latins. [93] In the love of the arts, the national difference was still more obvious and real; the Greeks preserved with reverence the works of their ancestors, which they could not imitate; and, in the destruction of the statues of Constantinople, we are provoked to join in the complaints and invectives of the Byzantine historian. [94] We have seen how the rising city was adorned by the vanity and despotism of the Imperial founder: in the ruins of paganism, some gods and heroes were saved from the axe of superstition; and the forum and hippodrome were dignified with the relics of a better age. Several of these are described by Nicetas, [95] in a florid and affected style; and from his descriptions I shall select some interesting particulars. 1. The victorious charioteers were cast in bronze, at their own or the public charge, and fitly placed in the hippodrome: they stood aloft in their chariots, wheeling round the goal: the spectators could admire their attitude, and judge of the resemblance; and of these figures, the most perfect might have been transported from the Olympic stadium. 2. The sphinx, river-horse, and crocodile, denote the climate and manufacture of Egypt and the spoils of that ancient province. 3. The she-wolf suckling Romulus and Remus, a subject alike pleasing to the old and the new Romans, but which could really be treated before the decline of the Greek sculpture. 4. An eagle holding and tearing a serpent in his talons, a domestic monument of the Byzantines, which they ascribed, not to a human artist, but to the magic power of the philosopher Apollonius, who, by this talisman, delivered the city from such venomous reptiles. 5. An ass and his driver, which were erected by Augustus in his colony of Nicopolis, to commemorate a verbal omen of the victory of Actium. 6. An equestrian statue which passed, in the vulgar opinion, for Joshua, the Jewish conqueror, stretching out his hand to stop the course of the descending sun. A more classical tradition recognized the figures of Bellerophon and Pegasus; and the free attitude of the steed seemed to mark that he trod on air, rather than on the earth. 7. A square and lofty obelisk of brass; the sides were embossed with a variety of picturesque and rural scenes, birds singing; rustics laboring, or playing on their pipes; sheep bleating; lambs skipping; the sea, and a scene of fish and fishing; little naked cupids laughing, playing, and pelting each other with apples; and, on the summit, a female figure, turning with the slightest breath, and thence denominated the wind's attendant. 8. The Phrygian shepherd presenting to Venus the prize of beauty, the apple of discord. 9. The incomparable statue of Helen, which is delineated by Nicetas in the words of admiration and love: her well-turned feet, snowy arms, rosy lips, bewitching smiles, swimming eyes, arched eyebrows, the harmony of her shape, the lightness of her drapery, and her flowing locks that waved in the wind; a beauty that might have moved her Barbarian destroyers to pity and remorse. 10. The manly or divine form of Hercules, [96] as he was restored to life by the masterhand of Lysippus; of such magnitude, that his thumb was equal to his waist, his leg to the stature, of a common man: [97] his chest ample, his shoulders broad, his limbs strong and muscular, his hair curled, his aspect commanding. Without his bow, or quiver, or club, his lion's skin carelessly thrown over him, he was seated on an osier basket, his right leg and arm stretched to the utmost, his left knee bent, and supporting his elbow, his head reclining on his left hand, his countenance indignant and pensive. 11. A colossal statue of Juno, which had once adorned her temple of Samos, the enormous head by four yoke of oxen was laboriously drawn to the palace. 12. Another colossus, of Pallas or Minerva, thirty feet in height, and representing with admirable spirit the attributes and character of the martial maid. Before we accuse the Latins, it is just to remark, that this Pallas was destroyed after the first siege, by the fear and superstition of the Greeks themselves. [98] The other statues of brass which I have enumerated were broken and melted by the unfeeling avarice of the crusaders: the cost and labor were consumed in a moment; the soul of genius evaporated in smoke; and the remnant of base metal was coined into money for the payment of the troops. Bronze is not the most durable of monuments: from the marble forms of Phidias and Praxiteles, the Latins might turn aside with stupid contempt; [99] but unless they were crushed by some accidental injury, those useless stones stood secure on their pedestals. [100] The most enlightened of the strangers, above the gross and sensual pursuits of their countrymen, more piously exercised the right of conquest in the search and seizure of the relics of the saints. [101] Immense was the supply of heads and bones, crosses and images, that were scattered by this revolution over the churches of Europe; and such was the increase of pilgrimage and oblation, that no branch, perhaps, of more lucrative plunder was imported from the East. [102] Of the writings of antiquity, many that still existed in the twelfth century, are now lost. But the pilgrims were not solicitous to save or transport the volumes of an unknown tongue: the perishable substance of paper or parchment can only be preserved by the multiplicity of copies; the literature of the Greeks had almost centred in the metropolis; and, without computing the extent of our loss, we may drop a tear over the libraries that have perished in the triple fire of Constantinople. [103]

*[Footnote 93: Nicetas uses very harsh expressions, par agrammatoiV BarbaroiV, kai teleon analfabhtoiV, (Fragment, apud Fabric. Bibliot. Græc. tom. vi. p. 414.) This reproach, it is true, applies most strongly to their ignorance of Greek and of Homer. In their own language, the Latins of the xiith and xiiith centuries were not destitute of literature. See Harris's Philological Inquiries, p. iii. c. 9, 10, 11.]*

*[Footnote 94: Nicetas was of Chonæ in Phrygia, (the old Colossæ of St. Paul:) he raised himself to the honors of senator, judge of the veil, and great logothete; beheld the fall of the empire, retired to Nice, and composed an elaborate history from the death of Alexius Comnenus to the reign of Henry.]*

*[Footnote 95: A manuscript of Nicetas in the Bodleian library contains this curious fragment on the statues of Constantinople, which fraud, or shame, or rather carelessness, has dropped in the common editions. It is published by Fabricius, (Bibliot. Græc. tom. vi. p. 405—416,) and immoderately praised by the late ingenious Mr. Harris of Salisbury, (Philological Inquiries, p. iii. c. 5, p. 301—312.)]*

*[Footnote 96: To illustrate the statue of Hercules, Mr. Harris quotes a Greek epigram, and engraves a beautiful gem, which does not, however, copy the attitude of the statue: in the latter, Hercules had not his club, and his right leg and arm were extended.]*

*[Footnote 97: I transcribe these proportions, which appear to me inconsistent with each other; and may possibly show, that the boasted taste of Nicetas was no more than affectation and vanity.]*

*[Footnote 98: Nicetas in Isaaco Angelo et Alexio, c. 3, p. 359. The Latin editor very properly observes, that the historian, in his bombast style, produces ex pulice elephantem.]*

*[Footnote 99: In two passages of Nicetas (edit. Paris, p. 360. Fabric. p. 408) the Latins are branded with the lively reproach of oi tou kalou anerastoi barbaroi, and their avarice of brass is clearly expressed. Yet the Venetians had the merit of removing four bronze horses from Constantinople to the place of St. Mark, (Sanuto, Vite del Dogi, in Muratori, Script. Rerum Italicarum, tom. xxii. p. 534.)]*

*[Footnote 100: Winckelman, Hist. de l'Art. tom. iii. p. 269, 270.]*

[Footnote 101: See the pious robbery of the abbot Martin, who transferred a rich cargo to his monastery of Paris, diocese of Basil, (Gunther, Hist. C. P. c. 19, 23, 24.) Yet in secreting this booty, the saint incurred an excommunication, and perhaps broke his oath. (Compare Wilken vol. v. p. 308—M.)]

[Footnote 102: Fleury, Hist. Eccles tom. xvi. p. 139—145.]

[Footnote 103: I shall conclude this chapter with the notice of a modern history, which illustrates the taking of Constantinople by the Latins; but which has fallen somewhat late into my hands. Paolo Ramusio, the son of the compiler of Voyages, was directed by the senate of Venice to write the history of the conquest: and this order, which he received in his youth, he executed in a mature age, by an elegant Latin work, de Bello Constantinopolitano et Imperatoribus Comnenis per Gallos et Venetos restitutis, (Venet. 1635, in folio.) Ramusio, or Rhamnusus, transcribes and translates, sequitur ad unguem, a MS. of Villehardouin, which he possessed; but he enriches his narrative with Greek and Latin materials, and we are indebted to him for a correct state of the fleet, the names of the fifty Venetian nobles who commanded the galleys of the republic, and the patriot opposition of Pantaleon Barbus to the choice of the doge for emperor.]

CHAPTER LXI

PARTITION OF THE EMPIRE BY THE FRENCH AND VENETIANS

PART I

PARTITION OF THE EMPIRE BY THE FRENCH AND VENETIANS—FIVE LATIN EMPERORS OF THE HOUSES OF FLANDERS AND COURTENAY—THEIR WARS AGAINST THE BULGARIANS AND GREEKS—WEAKNESS AND POVERTY OF THE LATIN EMPIRE—RECOVERY OF CONSTANTINOPLE BY THE GREEKS—GENERAL CONSEQUENCES OF THE CRUSADES

After the death of the lawful princes, the French and Venetians, confident of justice and victory, agreed to divide and regulate their future possessions. [1] It was stipulated by treaty, that twelve electors, six of either nation, should be nominated; that a majority should choose the emperor of the East; and that, if the votes were equal, the decision of chance should ascertain the successful candidate. To him, with all the titles and prerogatives of the Byzantine throne, they assigned the two palaces of Boucoleon and Blachernæ, with a fourth part of the Greek monarchy. It was defined that the three remaining portions should be equally shared between the republic of Venice and the barons of France; that each feudatory, with an honorable exception for the doge, should acknowledge and perform the duties of homage and military service to the supreme head of the empire; that the nation which gave an emperor, should resign to their brethren the choice of a patriarch; and that the pilgrims, whatever might be their impatience to visit the Holy Land, should devote another year to the conquest and defence of the Greek provinces. After the conquest of Constantinople by the Latins, the treaty was confirmed and executed; and the first and most important step was the creation of an emperor. The six electors of the French nation were all ecclesiastics, the abbot of Loces, the archbishop elect of Acre in Palestine, and the bishops of Troyes, Soissons, Halberstadt, and Bethlehem, the last of whom exercised in the camp the office of pope's legate: their profession and knowledge were respectable; and as they could not be the objects, they were best qualified to be the authors of the choice. The six Venetians were the principal servants of the state, and in this list the noble families of Querini and Contarini are still proud to discover their ancestors. The twelve assembled in the chapel of the palace; and after the solemn invocation of the Holy Ghost, they proceeded to deliberate and vote. A just impulse of respect and gratitude prompted them to crown the virtues of the doge; his wisdom had inspired their enterprise; and the most youthful knights might envy and applaud the exploits of blindness and age. But the patriot Dandolo was devoid of all personal ambition, and fully satisfied that he had been judged worthy to reign. His nomination was overruled by the Venetians themselves: his countrymen, and perhaps his friends, [2] represented, with the eloquence of truth, the mischiefs that might arise to national freedom and the common cause, from the union of two incompatible characters, of the first magistrate of a republic and the emperor of the East. The exclusion of the doge left room for the more equal merits of Boniface and Baldwin; and at their names all meaner candidates respectfully withdrew. The marquis of Montferrat was recommended by his mature age and fair reputation, by the choice of the adventurers, and the wishes of the Greeks; nor can I believe that Venice, the mistress of the sea, could be seriously apprehensive of a petty lord at the foot of the Alps. [3] But the count of Flanders was the chief of a wealthy and warlike people: he was valiant, pious, and chaste; in the prime of life, since he was only thirty-two years of age; a descendant of Charlemagne, a cousin of the king of France, and a compeer of the prelates and barons who had yielded with reluctance to the command of a foreigner. Without the chapel, these barons, with the doge and marquis at their head, expected the decision of the twelve electors. It was announced by the bishop of Soissons, in the name of his colleagues: "Ye have sworn to obey the prince whom we should choose: by our unanimous suffrage, Baldwin count of Flanders and Hainault is now your sovereign, and the emperor of the East." He was saluted with loud applause, and the proclamation was reechoed through the city by the joy of the Latins, and the trembling adulation of the Greeks. Boniface was the first to kiss the hand of his rival, and to raise him on the buckler: and Baldwin was transported to the cathedral, and solemnly invested with the purple buskins. At the end of three weeks he was crowned by the legate, in the vacancy of the patriarch; but the Venetian clergy soon filled the chapter of St. Sophia, seated Thomas Morosini on the ecclesiastical throne, and employed every art to perpetuate in their own nation the honors and benefices of the Greek church. [4] Without delay the successor of Constantine instructed Palestine, France, and Rome, of this memorable revolution. To Palestine he sent, as a trophy, the gates of Constantinople, and the chain of the harbor; [5] and adopted, from the Assise of Jerusalem, the laws or customs best adapted to a French colony and conquest in the East. In his epistles, the natives of France are encouraged to swell that colony, and to secure that conquest, to people a magnificent city and a fertile land, which will reward the labors both of the priest and the soldier. He congratulates the Roman pontiff on the restoration of his authority in the East; invites him to extinguish the Greek schism by his presence in a general council; and implores his blessing and forgiveness for the disobedient pilgrims. Prudence and dignity are blended in the answer of Innocent. [6] In the subversion of the Byzantine empire, he arraigns the vices of man, and adores the providence of God; the conquerors will be absolved or condemned by their future conduct; the validity of their treaty depends on the judgment of St. Peter; but he inculcates their most sacred duty of establishing a just subordination of obedience and tribute, from the Greeks to the Latins, from the magistrate to the clergy, and from the clergy to the pope.

[Footnote 1: See the original treaty of partition, in the Venetian Chronicle of Andrew Dandolo, p. 326—330, and the subsequent election in Ville hardouin, No. 136—140, with Ducange in his Observations, and the book of his Histoire de Constantinople sous l'Empire des François.]

[Footnote 2: After mentioning the nomination of the doge by a French elector his kinsman Andrew Dandolo approves his exclusion, quidam Venetorum fidelis et nobilis senex, usus oratione satis probabili, &c., which has been embroidered by modern writers from Blondus to Le Beau.]

[Footnote 3: Nicetas, (p. 384,) with the vain ignorance of a Greek, describes the marquis of Montferrat as a maritime power. Dampardian de oikeisqai paralion. Was he deceived by the Byzantine theme of Lombardy which extended along the coast of Calabria?]

[Footnote 4: They exacted an oath from Thomas Morosini to appoint no canons of St. Sophia the lawful electors, except Venetians who had lived ten years at Venice, &c. But the foreign clergy was envious, the pope disapproved this national monopoly, and of the six Latin patriarchs of Constantinople, only the first and the last were Venetians.]

[Footnote 5: Nicetas, p. 383.]

[Footnote 6: The Epistles of Innocent III. are a rich fund for the ecclesiastical and civil institution of the Latin empire of Constantinople; and the most important of these epistles (of which the collection in 2 vols. in folio is published by Stephen Baluze) are inserted in his Gesta, in Muratori, Script. Rerum Italicarum, tom. iii. p. l. c. 94—105.]

In the division of the Greek provinces, [7] the share of the Venetians was more ample than that of the Latin emperor. No more than one fourth was appropriated to his domain; a clear moiety of the remainder was reserved for Venice; and the other moiety was distributed among the adventures of France and Lombardy. The venerable Dandolo was proclaimed despot of Romania, and invested after the Greek fashion with the purple buskins. He ended at Constantinople his long and glorious life; and if the prerogative was personal, the title was used by his successors till the middle of the fourteenth century, with the singular, though true, addition of lords of one fourth and a half of the Roman empire. [8] The doge, a slave of state, was seldom permitted to depart from the helm of the republic; but his place was supplied by the bail, or regent, who exercised a supreme jurisdiction over the colony of Venetians: they possessed three of the eight quarters of the city; and his independent tribunal was composed of six judges, four counsellors, two chamberlains two fiscal advocates, and a constable. Their long experience of the Eastern trade enabled them to select their portion with discernment: they had rashly accepted the dominion and defence of Adrianople; but it was the more reasonable aim of their policy to form a chain of factories, and cities, and islands, along the maritime coast, from the neighborhood of Ragusa to the Hellespont and the Bosphorus. The labor and cost of such extensive conquests exhausted their treasury: they abandoned their maxims of government, adopted a feudal system, and contented themselves with the homage of their nobles, [9] for the possessions which these private vassals undertook to reduce and maintain. And thus it was that the family of Sanut acquired the duchy of Naxos, which involved the greatest part of the archipelago. For the price of ten thousand marks, the republic purchased of the marquis of Montferrat the fertile Island of Crete or Candia, with the ruins of a hundred cities; [10] but its improvement was stinted by the proud and narrow spirit of an aristocracy; [11] and the wisest senators would confess that the sea, not the land, was the treasury of St. Mark. In the moiety of the adventurers the marquis Boniface might claim the most liberal reward; and, besides the Isle of Crete, his exclusion from the throne was compensated by the royal title and the provinces beyond the Hellespont. But he prudently exchanged that distant and difficult conquest for the kingdom of Thessalonica Macedonia, twelve days' journey from the capital, where he might be supported by the neighboring powers of his brother-in-law the king of Hungary. His progress was hailed by the voluntary or reluctant acclamations of the natives; and Greece, the proper and ancient Greece, again received a Latin conqueror, [12] who trod with indifference that classic ground. He viewed with a careless eye the beauties of the valley of Tempe; traversed with a cautious step the straits of Thermopylæ; occupied the unknown cities of Thebes, Athens, and Argos; and assaulted the fortifications of Corinth and Napoli, [13] which resisted his arms. The lots of the Latin pilgrims were regulated by chance, or choice, or subsequent exchange; and they abused, with intemperate joy, their triumph over the lives and fortunes of a great people. After a minute survey of the provinces, they weighed in the scales of avarice the revenue of each district, the advantage of the situation, and the ample on scanty supplies for the maintenance of soldiers and horses. Their presumption claimed and divided the long-lost dependencies of the Roman sceptre: the Nile and Euphrates rolled through their imaginary realms; and happy was the warrior who drew for his prize the palace of the Turkish sultan of Iconium. [14] I shall not descend to the pedigree of families and the rent-roll of estates, but I wish to specify that the counts of Blois and St. Pol were invested with the duchy of Nice and the lordship of Demotica: [15] the principal fiefs were held by the service of constable, chamberlain, cup-bearer, butler, and chief cook; and our historian, Jeffrey of Villehardouin, obtained a fair establishment on the banks of the Hebrus, and united the double office of marshal of Champagne and Romania. At the head of his knights and archers, each baron mounted on horseback to secure the possession of his share, and their first efforts were generally successful. But the public force was weakened by their dispersion; and a thousand quarrels must arise under a law, and among men, whose sole umpire was the sword. Within three months after the conquest of Constantinople, the emperor and the king of Thessalonica drew their hostile followers into the field; they were reconciled by the authority of the doge, the advice of the marshal, and the firm freedom of their peers. [16]

[Footnote 7: In the treaty of partition, most of the names are corrupted by the scribes: they might be restored, and a good map, suited to the last age of the Byzantine empire, would be an improvement of geography. But, alas D'Anville is no more!]

[Footnote 8: Their style was dominus quartæ partis et dimidiæ imperii Romani, till Giovanni Dolfino, who was elected doge in the year of 1356, (Sanuto, p. 530, 641.) For the government of Constantinople, see Ducange, Histoire de C. P. i. 37.]

[Footnote 9: Ducange (Hist. de C. P. ii. 6) has marked the conquests made by the state or nobles of Venice of the Islands of Candia, Corfu, Cephalonia, Zante, Naxos, Paros, Melos, Andros, Mycone, Syro, Cea, and Lemnos.]

[Footnote 10: Boniface sold the Isle of Candia, August 12, A.D. 1204. See the act in Sanuto, p. 533: but I cannot understand how it could be his mother's portion, or how she could be the daughter of an emperor Alexius.]

[Footnote 11: In the year 1212, the doge Peter Zani sent a colony to Candia, drawn from every quarter of Venice. But in their savage manners and frequent rebellions, the Candiots may be compared to the Corsicans under the yoke of Genoa; and when I compare the accounts of Belon and Tournefort, I cannot discern much difference between the Venetian and the Turkish island.]

[Footnote 12: Villehardouin (No. 159, 160, 173—177) and Nicetas (p. 387—394) describe the expedition into Greece of the marquis Boniface. The Choniate might derive his information from his brother Michael, archbishop of Athens, whom he paints as an orator, a statesman, and a saint. His encomium of Athens, and the description of Tempe, should be published from the Bodleian MS. of Nicetas, (Fabric. Bibliot. Græc. tom. vi. p. 405,) and would have deserved Mr. Harris's inquiries.]

[Footnote 13: Napoli de Romania, or Nauplia, the ancient seaport of Argos, is still a place of strength and consideration, situate on a rocky peninsula, with a good harbor, (Chandler's Travels into Greece, p. 227.)]

[Footnote 14: I have softened the expression of Nicetas, who strives to expose the presumption of the Franks. See the Rebus post C. P. expugnatam, p. 375—384.]

[Footnote 15: A city surrounded by the River Hebrus, and six leagues to the south of Adrianople, received from its double wall the Greek name of Didymoteichos, insensibly corrupted into Demotica and Dimot. I have preferred the more convenient and modern appellation of Demotica. This place was the last Turkish residence of Charles XII.]

[Footnote 16: Their quarrel is told by Villehardouin (No. 146—158) with the spirit of freedom. The merit and reputation of the marshal are so acknowledged by the Greek historian (p. 387) mega para touV tvn Dauinwn dunamenou strateumasi: unlike some modern heroes, whose exploits are only visible in their own memoirs. Note: William de Champlite, brother of the count of Dijon, assumed the title of Prince of Achaia: on the death of his brother, he returned, with regret, to France, to assume his paternal inheritance, and left Villehardouin his "bailli," on condition that if he did not return within a year Villehardouin was to retain an investiture. Brosset's Add. to Le Beau, vol. xvii. p. 200. M. Brosset adds, from the Greek chronicler edited by M. Buchon, the somewhat unknightly trick by which Villehardouin disembarrassed himself from the troublesome claim of Robert, the cousin of the count of Dijon. to the succession. He contrived that Robert should arrive just fifteen days too late; and with the general concurrence of the assembled knights was himself invested with the principality. Ibid. p. 283. M.]

Two fugitives, who had reigned at Constantinople, still asserted the title of emperor; and the subjects of their fallen throne might be moved to pity by the misfortunes of the elder Alexius, or excited to revenge by the spirit of Mourzoufle. A domestic alliance, a common interest, a similar guilt, and the merit of extinguishing his enemies, a brother and a nephew, induced the more recent usurper to unite with the former the relics of his power. Mourzoufle was received with smiles and honors in the camp of his father Alexius; but the wicked can never love, and should rarely trust, their fellow-criminals; he was seized in the bath, deprived of his eyes, stripped of his troops and treasures, and turned out to wander an object of horror and contempt to those who with more propriety could hate, and with more justice could punish, the assassin of the emperor Isaac and his son. As the tyrant, pursued by fear or remorse, was stealing over to Asia, he was seized by the Latins of Constantinople, and condemned, after an open trial, to an ignominious death. His judges debated the mode of his execution, the axe, the wheel, or the stake; and it was resolved that Mourzoufle [17] should ascend the Theodosian column, a pillar of white marble of one hundred and forty-seven feet in height. [18] From the summit he was cast down headlong, and dashed in pieces on the pavement, in the presence of innumerable spectators, who filled the forum of Taurus, and admired the accomplishment of an old prediction, which was explained by this singular event. [19] The fate of Alexius is less tragical: he was sent by the marquis a captive to Italy, and a gift to the king of the Romans; but he had not much to applaud his fortune, if the sentence of imprisonment and exile were changed from a fortress in the Alps to a monastery in Asia. But his daughter, before the national calamity, had been given in marriage to a young hero who continued the succession, and restored the throne, of the Greek princes. [20] The valor of Theodore Lascaris was signalized in the two sieges of Constantinople. After the flight of Mourzoufle, when the Latins were already in the city, he offered himself as their emperor to the soldiers and people; and his ambition, which might be virtuous, was undoubtedly brave. Could he have infused a soul into the multitude, they might have crushed the strangers under their feet: their abject despair refused his aid; and Theodore retired to breathe the air of freedom in Anatolia, beyond the immediate view and pursuit of the conquerors. Under the title, at first of despot, and afterwards of emperor, he drew to his standard the bolder spirits, who were fortified against slavery by the contempt of life; and as every means was lawful for the public safety implored without scruple the alliance of the Turkish sultan Nice, where Theodore established his residence, Prusa and Philadelphia, Smyrna and Ephesus, opened their gates to their deliverer: he derived strength and reputation from his victories, and even from his defeats; and the successor of Constantine preserved a fragment of the empire from the banks of the Mæander to the suburbs of Nicomedia, and at length of Constantinople. Another portion, distant and obscure, was possessed by the lineal heir of the Comneni, a son of the virtuous Manuel, a grandson of the tyrant Andronicus. His name was Alexius; and the epithet of great [20/1] was applied perhaps to his stature, rather than to his exploits. By the indulgence of the Angeli, he was appointed governor or duke of Trebizond: [21] [21/1] his birth gave him ambition, the revolution independence; and, without changing his title, he reigned in peace from Sinope to the Phasis, along the coast of the Black Sea. His nameless son and successor [21/2] is described as the vassal of the sultan, whom he served with two hundred lances: that Comnenian prince was no more than duke of Trebizond, and the title of emperor was first assumed by the pride and envy of the grandson of Alexius. In the West, a third fragment was saved from the common shipwreck by Michael, a bastard of the house of Angeli, who, before the revolution, had been known as a hostage, a soldier, and a rebel. His flight from the camp of the marquis Boniface secured his freedom; by his marriage with the governor's daughter, he commanded the important place of Durazzo, assumed the title of despot, and founded a strong and conspicuous principality in Epirus, Ætolia, and Thessaly, which have ever been peopled by a warlike race. The Greeks, who had offered their service to their new sovereigns, were excluded by the haughty Latins [22] from all civil and military honors, as a nation born to tremble and obey. Their resentment prompted them to show that they might have been useful friends, since they could be dangerous enemies: their nerves were braced by adversity: whatever was learned or holy, whatever was noble or valiant, rolled away into the independent states of Trebizond, Epirus, and Nice; and a single patrician is marked by the ambiguous praise of attachment and loyalty to the Franks. The vulgar herd of the cities and the country would have gladly submitted to a mild and regular servitude; and the transient disorders of war would have been obliterated by some years of industry and peace. But peace was banished, and industry was crushed, in the disorders of the feudal system. The Roman emperors of Constantinople, if they were endowed with abilities, were armed with power for the protection of their subjects: their laws were wise, and their administration was simple. The Latin throne was filled by a titular prince, the chief, and often the servant, of his licentious confederates; the fiefs of the empire, from a kingdom to a castle, were held and ruled by the sword of the barons; and their discord, poverty, and ignorance, extended the ramifications of tyranny to the most sequestered villages. The Greeks were oppressed by the double weight of the priest, who were invested with temporal power, and of the soldier, who was inflamed by fanatic hatred; and the insuperable bar of religion and language forever separated the stranger and the native. As long as the crusaders were united at Constantinople, the memory of their conquest, and the terror of their arms, imposed silence on the captive land: their dispersion betrayed the smallness of their numbers and the defects of their discipline; and some failures and mischances revealed the secret, that they were not invincible. As the fears of the Greeks abated, their hatred increased. They murdered; they conspired; and before a year of slavery had elapsed, they implored, or accepted, the succor of a Barbarian, whose power they had felt, and whose gratitude they trusted. [23]

[Footnote 17: See the fate of Mourzoufle in Nicetas, (p. 393,) Villehardouin, (No. 141—145, 163,) and Guntherus, (c. 20, 21.) Neither the marshal nor the monk afford a grain of pity for a tyrant or rebel, whose punishment, however, was more unexampled than his crime.]

[Footnote 18: The column of Arcadius, which represents in basso relievo his victories, or those of his father Theodosius, is still extant at Constantinople. It is described and measured, Gyllius, (Topograph. iv. 7,) Banduri, (ad l. i. Antiquit. C. P. p. 507, &c.,) and Tournefort, (Voyage du Levant, tom. ii. lettre xii. p. 231.) (Compare Wilken, note, vol. v p. 388—M.)]

[Footnote 19: The nonsense of Gunther and the modern Greeks concerning this *columna fatidica*, is unworthy of notice; but it is singular enough, that fifty years before the Latin conquest, the poet Tzetzes, (Chiliad, ix. 277) relates the dream of a matron, who saw an army in the forum, and a man sitting on the column, clapping his hands, and uttering a loud exclamation. Note: We read in the "Chronicle of the Conquest of Constantinople, and of the Establishment of the French in the Morea," translated by J A Buchon, Paris, 1825, p. 64 that Leo VI., called the Philosopher, had prophesied that a perfidious emperor should be precipitated from the top of this column. The crusaders considered themselves under an obligation to fulfil this prophecy. Brosset, note on Le Beau, vol. xvii. p. 180. M Brosset announces that a complete edition of this work, of which the original Greek of the first book only has been published by M. Buchon in preparation, to form part of the new series of the Byzantine historian—M.]

[Footnote 20: The dynasties of Nice, Trebizond, and Epirus (of which Nicetas saw the origin without much pleasure or hope) are learnedly explored, and clearly represented, in the Familiæ Byzantinæ of Ducange.]

[Footnote 20/1: This was a title, not a personal appellation. Joinville speaks of the "Grant Comnenie, et sire de Traffezzontes." Fallmerayer, p. 82—M.]

[Footnote 21: Except some facts in Pachymer and Nicephorus Gregoras, which will hereafter be used, the Byzantine writers disdain to speak of the empire of Trebizond, or principality of the Lazi; and among the Latins, it is conspicuous only in the romancers of the xivth or xvth centuries. Yet the indefatigable Ducange has dug out (Fam. Byz. p. 192) two authentic passages in Vincent of Beauvais (l. xxxi. c. 144) and the prothonotary Ogerius, (apud Wading, A.D. 1279, No. 4.)]

[Footnote 21/1: On the revolutions of Trebizond under the later empire down to this period, see Fallmerayer, Geschichte des Kaiserthums von Trapezunt, ch. iii. The wife of Manuel fled with her infant sons and her treasure from the relentless enmity of Isaac Angelus. Fallmerayer conjectures that her arrival enabled the Greeks of that region to make head against the formidable Thamar, the Georgian queen of Teflis, p. 42. They gradually formed a dominion on the banks of the Phasis, which the distracted government of the Angeli neglected or were unable to suppress. On the capture of Constantinople by the Latins, Alexius was joined by many noble fugitives from Constantinople. He had always retained the names of Cæsar and BasileuV. He now fixed the seat of his empire at Trebizond; but he had never abandoned his pretensions to the Byzantine throne, ch. iii. Fallmerayer appears to make out a triumphant case as to the assumption of the royal title by Alexius the First. Since the publication of M. Fallmerayer's work, (München, 1827,) M. Tafel has published, at the end of the opuscula of Eustathius, a curious chronicle of Trebizond by Michael Panaretas, (Frankfort, 1832.) It gives the succession of the emperors, and some other curious circumstances of their wars with the several Mahometan powers—M.]

[Footnote 21/2: The successor of Alexius was his son-in-law Andronicus I., of the Comnenian family, surnamed Gidon. There were five successions between Alexius and John, according to Fallmerayer, p. 103. The troops of Trebizond fought in the army of Dschelaleddin, the Karismian, against Alaleddin, the Seljukian sultan of Roum, but as allies rather than vassals, p. 107. It was after the defeat of Dschelaleddin that they furnished their contingent to Alai-eddin. Fallmerayer struggles in vain to mitigate this mark of the subjection of the Comneni to the sultan. p. 116—M.]

[Footnote 22: The portrait of the French Latins is drawn in Nicetas by the hand of prejudice and resentment: ouden tvn allwn eqnvn eiV "AreoV?rga parasumbeblhsqai sjisin hneiconto all' oude tiV tvn caritwn h tvn?mousvn para toiV barbaroiV toutoiV epexenizeto, kai para touto oimai thn jusin hsan anhmeroi, kai ton xolon eixon tou logou prstreconta. [P. 791 Ed. Bek.]

[Footnote 23: I here begin to use, with freedom and confidence, the eight books of the Histoire de C. P. sous l'Empire des François, which Ducange has given as a supplement to Villehardouin; and which, in a barbarous style, deserves the praise of an original and classic work.]

The Latin conquerors had been saluted with a solemn and early embassy from John, or Joannice, or Calo-John, the revolted chief of the Bulgarians and Walachians. He deemed himself their brother, as the votary of the Roman pontiff, from whom he had received the regal title and a holy banner; and in the subversion of the Greek monarchy, he might aspire to the name of their friend and accomplice. But Calo-John was astonished to find, that the Count of Flanders had assumed the pomp and pride of the successors of Constantine; and his ambassadors were dismissed with a haughty message, that the rebel must deserve a pardon, by touching with his forehead the footstool of the Imperial throne. His resentment [24] would have exhaled in acts of violence and blood: his cooler policy watched the rising discontent of the Greeks; affected a tender concern for their sufferings; and promised, that their first struggles for freedom should be supported by his person and kingdom. The conspiracy was propagated by national hatred, the firmest band of association and secrecy: the Greeks were impatient to sheathe their daggers in the breasts of the victorious strangers; but the execution was prudently delayed, till Henry, the emperor's brother, had transported the flower of his troops beyond the Hellespont. Most of the towns and villages of Thrace were true to the moment and the signal; and the Latins, without arms or suspicion, were slaughtered by the vile and merciless revenge of their slaves. From Demotica, the first scene of the massacre, the surviving vassals of the count of St. Pol escaped to Adrianople; but the French and Venetians, who occupied that city, were slain or expelled by the furious multitude: the garrisons that could effect their retreat fell back on each other towards the metropolis; and the fortresses, that separately stood against the rebels, were ignorant of each other's and of their sovereign's fate. The voice of fame and fear announced the revolt of the Greeks and the rapid approach of their Bulgarian ally; and Calo-John, not depending on the forces of his own kingdom, had drawn from the Scythian wilderness a body of fourteen thousand Comans, who drank, as it was said, the blood of their captives, and sacrificed the Christians on the altars of their gods. [25]

[Footnote 24: In Calo-John's answer to the pope we may find his claims and complaints, (Gesta Innocent III. c. 108, 109:) he was cherished at Rome as the prodigal son.]

[Footnote 25: The Comans were a Tartar or Turkman horde, which encamped in the xiith and xiiith centuries on the verge of Moldavia. The greater part were pagans, but some were Mahometans, and the whole horde was converted to Christianity (A.D. 1370) by Lewis, king of Hungary.]

Alarmed by this sudden and growing danger, the emperor despatched a swift messenger to recall Count Henry and his troops; and had Baldwin expected the return of his gallant brother, with a supply of twenty thousand Armenians, he might have encountered the invader with equal numbers and a decisive superiority of arms and discipline. But the spirit of chivalry could seldom discriminate caution from cowardice; and the emperor took the field with a hundred and forty knights, and their train of archers and sergeants. The marshal, who dissuaded and obeyed, led the vanguard in their march to Adrianople; the main body was commanded by the count of Blois; the aged doge of Venice followed with the rear; and their scanty numbers were increased from all sides by the fugitive Latins. They undertook to besiege the rebels of Adrianople; and such was the pious tendency of the crusades that they employed the holy week in pillaging the country for their subsistence, and in framing engines for the destruction of their fellow-Christians. But the Latins were soon interrupted and alarmed by the light cavalry of the Comans, who boldly skirmished to the edge of their imperfect lines: and a proclamation was issued by the marshal of Romania, that, on the trumpet's sound, the cavalry should mount and form; but that none, under pain of death, should abandon themselves to a desultory and dangerous pursuit. This wise injunction was first disobeyed by the count of Blois, who involved the emperor in his rashness and ruin. The Comans, of the Parthian or Tartar school, fled before their first charge; but after a career of two leagues, when the knights and their horses were almost breathless, they suddenly turned, rallied, and encompassed the heavy squadrons of the Franks. The count was slain on the field; the emperor was made prisoner; and if the one disdained to fly, if the other refused to yield, their personal bravery made a poor atonement for their ignorance, or neglect, of the duties of a general. [26]

[Footnote 26: Nicetas, from ignorance or malice, imputes the defeat to the cowardice of Dandolo, (p. 383;) but Villehardouin shares his own glory with his venerable friend, qui viels home ére et gote ne veoit, mais mult ére sages et preus et vigueros, (No. 193.) Note: Gibbon appears to me to have misapprehended the passage of Nicetas. He says, "that principal and subtlest mischief. that primary cause of all the horrible miseries suffered by the Romans," i. e. the Byzantines. It is an effusion of malicious triumph against the Venetians, to whom he always ascribes the capture of Constantinople—M.]

PART II

Proud of his victory and his royal prize, the Bulgarian advanced to relieve Adrianople and achieve the destruction of the Latins. They must inevitably have been destroyed, if the marshal of Romania had not displayed a cool courage and consummate skill; uncommon in all ages, but most uncommon in those times, when war was a passion, rather than a science. His grief and fears were poured into the firm and faithful bosom of the doge; but in the camp he diffused an assurance of safety, which could only be realized by the general belief. All day he maintained his perilous station between the city and the Barbarians: Villehardouin decamped in silence at the dead of night; and his masterly retreat of three days would have deserved the praise of Xenophon and the ten thousand. In the rear, the marshal supported the weight of the pursuit; in the front, he moderated the impatience of the fugitives; and wherever the Comans approached, they were repelled by a line of impenetrable spears. On the third day, the weary troops beheld the sea, the solitary town of Rodosta, [27] and their friends, who had landed from the Asiatic shore. They embraced, they wept; but they united their arms and counsels; and in his brother's absence, Count Henry assumed the regency of the empire, at once in a state of childhood and caducity. [28] If the Comans withdrew from the summer heats, seven thousand Latins, in the hour of danger, deserted Constantinople, their brethren, and their vows. Some partial success was overbalanced by the loss of one hundred and twenty knights in the field of Rusium; and of the Imperial domain, no more was left than the capital, with two or three adjacent fortresses on the shores of Europe and Asia. The king of Bulgaria was resistless and inexorable; and Calo-John respectfully eluded the demands of the pope, who conjured his new proselyte to restore peace and the emperor to the afflicted Latins. The deliverance of Baldwin was no longer, he said, in the power of man: that prince had died in prison; and the manner of his death is variously related by ignorance and credulity. The lovers of a tragic legend will be pleased to hear, that the royal captive was tempted by the amorous queen of the Bulgarians; that his chaste refusal exposed him to the falsehood of a woman and the jealousy of a savage; that his hands and feet were severed from his body; that his bleeding trunk was cast among the carcasses of dogs and horses; and that he breathed three days, before he was devoured by the birds of prey. [29] About twenty years afterwards, in a wood of the Netherlands, a hermit announced himself as the true Baldwin, the emperor of Constantinople, and lawful sovereign of Flanders. He related the wonders of his escape, his adventures, and his penance, among a people prone to believe and to rebel; and, in the first transport, Flanders acknowledged her long-lost sovereign. A short examination before the French court detected the impostor, who was punished with an ignominious death; but the Flemings still adhered to the pleasing error; and the countess Jane is accused by the gravest historians of sacrificing to her ambition the life of an unfortunate father. [30]

[Footnote 27: *The truth of geography, and the original text of Villehardouin, (No. 194,) place Rodosto three days' journey (trois journées) from Adrianople: but Vigenere, in his version, has most absurdly substituted trois heures; and this error, which is not corrected by Ducange has entrapped several moderns, whose names I shall spare.*]

[Footnote 28: *The reign and end of Baldwin are related by Villehardouin and Nicetas, (p. 386—416;) and their omissions are supplied by Ducange in his Observations, and to the end of his first book.*]

[Footnote 29: *After brushing away all doubtful and improbable circumstances, we may prove the death of Baldwin, 1. By the firm belief of the French barons, (Villehardouin, No. 230.) 2. By the declaration of Calo-John himself, who excuses his not releasing the captive emperor, quia debitum carnis exsolverat cum carcere teneretur, (Gesta Innocent III. c. 109.) Note: Compare Von Raumer. Geschichte der Hohenstaufen, vol. ii. p. 237. Petitot, in his preface to Villehardouin in the Collection des Mémoires, relatifs a l'Histoire de France, tom. i. p. 85, expresses his belief in the first part of the "tragic legend."—M.*]

[Footnote 30: *See the story of this impostor from the French and Flemish writers in Ducange, Hist. de C. P. iii. 9; and the ridiculous fables that were believed by the monks of St. Alban's, in Matthew Paris, Hist. Major, p. 271, 272.*]

In all civilized hostility, a treaty is established for the exchange or ransom of prisoners; and if their captivity be prolonged, their condition is known, and they are treated according to their rank with humanity or honor. But the savage Bulgarian was a stranger to the laws of war: his prisons were involved in darkness and silence; and above a year elapsed before the Latins could be assured of the death of Baldwin, before his brother, the regent Henry, would consent to assume the title of emperor. His moderation was applauded by the Greeks as an act of rare and inimitable virtue. Their light and perfidious ambition was eager to seize or anticipate the moment of a vacancy, while a law of succession, the guardian both of the prince and people, was gradually defined and confirmed in the hereditary monarchies of Europe. In the support of the Eastern empire, Henry was gradually left without an associate, as the heroes of the crusade retired from the world or from the war. The doge of Venice, the venerable Dandolo, in the fulness of years and glory, sunk into the grave. The marquis of Montferrat was slowly recalled from the Peloponnesian war to the revenge of Baldwin and the defence of Thessalonica. Some nice disputes of feudal homage and service were reconciled in a personal interview between the emperor and the king; they were firmly united by mutual esteem and the common danger; and their alliance was sealed by the nuptials of Henry with the daughter of the Italian prince. He soon deplored the loss of his friend and father. At the persuasion of some faithful Greeks, Boniface made a bold and successful inroad among the hills of Rhodope: the Bulgarians fled on his approach; they assembled to harass his retreat. On the intelligence that his rear was attacked, without waiting for any defensive armor, he leaped on horseback, couched his lance, and drove the enemies before him; but in the rash pursuit he was pierced with a mortal wound; and the head of the king of Thessalonica was presented to

Calo-John, who enjoyed the honors, without the merit, of victory. It is here, at this melancholy event, that the pen or the voice of Jeffrey of Villehardouin seems to drop or to expire; [31] and if he still exercised his military office of marshal of Romania, his subsequent exploits are buried in oblivion. [32] The character of Henry was not unequal to his arduous situation: in the siege of Constantinople, and beyond the Hellespont, he had deserved the fame of a valiant knight and a skilful commander; and his courage was tempered with a degree of prudence and mildness unknown to his impetuous brother. In the double war against the Greeks of Asia and the Bulgarians of Europe, he was ever the foremost on shipboard or on horseback; and though he cautiously provided for the success of his arms, the drooping Latins were often roused by his example to save and to second their fearless emperor. But such efforts, and some supplies of men and money from France, were of less avail than the errors, the cruelty, and death, of their most formidable adversary. When the despair of the Greek subjects invited Calo-John as their deliverer, they hoped that he would protect their liberty and adopt their laws: they were soon taught to compare the degrees of national ferocity, and to execrate the savage conqueror, who no longer dissembled his intention of dispeopling Thrace, of demolishing the cities, and of transplanting the inhabitants beyond the Danube. Many towns and villages of Thrace were already evacuated: a heap of ruins marked the place of Philippopolis, and a similar calamity was expected at Demotica and Adrianople, by the first authors of the revolt. They raised a cry of grief and repentance to the throne of Henry; the emperor alone had the magnanimity to forgive and trust them. No more than four hundred knights, with their sergeants and archers, could be assembled under his banner; and with this slender force he fought [32/1] and repulsed the Bulgarian, who, besides his infantry, was at the head of forty thousand horse. In this expedition, Henry felt the difference between a hostile and a friendly country: the remaining cities were preserved by his arms; and the savage, with shame and loss, was compelled to relinquish his prey. The siege of Thessalonica was the last of the evils which Calo-John inflicted or suffered: he was stabbed in the night in his tent; and the general, perhaps the assassin, who found him weltering in his blood, ascribed the blow, with general applause, to the lance of St. Demetrius. [33] After several victories, the prudence of Henry concluded an honorable peace with the successor of the tyrant, and with the Greek princes of Nice and Epirus. If he ceded some doubtful limits, an ample kingdom was reserved for himself and his feudatories; and his reign, which lasted only ten years, afforded a short interval of prosperity and peace. Far above the narrow policy of Baldwin and Boniface, he freely intrusted to the Greeks the most important offices of the state and army; and this liberality of sentiment and practice was the more seasonable, as the princes of Nice and Epirus had already learned to seduce and employ the mercenary valor of the Latins. It was the aim of Henry to unite and reward his deserving subjects, of every nation and language; but he appeared less solicitous to accomplish the impracticable union of the two churches. Pelagius, the pope's legate, who acted as the sovereign of Constantinople, had interdicted the worship of the Greeks, and sternly imposed the payment of tithes, the double procession of the Holy Ghost, and a blind obedience to the Roman pontiff. As the weaker party, they pleaded the duties of conscience, and implored the rights of toleration: "Our bodies," they said, "are Cæsar's, but our souls belong only to God." The persecution was checked by the firmness of the emperor: [34] and if we can believe that the same prince was poisoned by the Greeks themselves, we must entertain a contemptible idea of the sense and gratitude of mankind. His valor was a vulgar attribute, which he shared with ten thousand knights; but Henry possessed the superior courage to oppose, in a superstitious age, the pride and avarice of the clergy. In the cathedral of St. Sophia he presumed to place his throne on the right hand of the patriarch; and this presumption excited the sharpest censure of Pope Innocent the Third. By a salutary edict, one of the first examples of the laws of mortmain, he prohibited the alienation of fiefs: many of the Latins, desirous of returning to Europe, resigned their estates to the church for a spiritual or temporal reward; these holy lands were immediately discharged from military service, and a colony of soldiers would have been gradually transformed into a college of priests. [35]

[Footnote 31: Villehardouin, No. 257. I quote, with regret, this lamentable conclusion, where we lose at once the original history, and the rich illustrations of Ducange. The last pages may derive some light from Henry's two epistles to Innocent III., (Gesta, c. 106, 107.)]

[Footnote 32: The marshal was alive in 1212, but he probably died soon afterwards, without returning to France, (Ducange, Observations sur Villehardouin, p. 238.) His fief of Messinople, the gift of Boniface, was the ancient Maximianopolis, which flourished in the time of Ammianus Marcellinus, among the cities of Thrace, (No. 141.)]

[Footnote 32/1: There was no battle. On the advance of the Latins, John suddenly broke up his camp and retreated. The Latins considered this unexpected deliverance almost a miracle. Le Beau suggests the probability that the detection of the Comans, who usually quitted the camp during the heats of summer, may have caused the flight of the Bulgarians. Nicetas, c. 8 Villebardouin, c. 225. Le Beau, vol. xvii. p. 242—M.]

[Footnote 33: The church of this patron of Thessalonica was served by the canons of the holy sepulchre, and contained a divine ointment which distilled daily and stupendous miracles, (Ducange, Hist. de C. P. ii. 4.)]

[Footnote 34: Acropolita (c. 17) observes the persecution of the legate, and the toleration of Henry, ('Erh, as he calls him) kludwna katestorese. Note: Or rather 'ErrhV—M.]

[Footnote 35: See the reign of Henry, in Ducange, (Hist. de C. P. l. i. c. 35—41, l. ii. c. 1—22,) who is much indebted to the Epistles of the Popes. Le Beau (Hist. du Bas Empire, tom. xxi. p. 120—122) has found, perhaps in Doutreman, some laws of Henry, which determined the service of fiefs, and the prerogatives of the emperor.]

The virtuous Henry died at Thessalonica, in the defence of that kingdom, and of an infant, the son of his friend Boniface. In the two first emperors of Constantinople the male line of the counts of Flanders was extinct. But their sister Yolande was the wife of a French prince, the mother of a numerous progeny; and one of her daughters had married Andrew king of Hungary, a brave and pious champion of the cross. By seating him on the Byzantine throne, the barons of Romania would have acquired the forces of a neighboring and warlike kingdom; but the prudent Andrew revered the laws of succession; and the princess Yolande, with her husband Peter of Courtenay, count of Auxerre, was invited by the Latins to assume the empire of the East. The royal birth of his father, the noble origin of his mother, recommended to the barons of France the first cousin of their king. His reputation was fair, his possessions were ample, and in the bloody crusade against the Albigeois, the soldiers and the priests had been abundantly satisfied of his zeal and valor. Vanity might applaud the elevation of a French emperor of Constantinople; but prudence must pity, rather than envy, his treacherous and imaginary greatness. To assert and adorn his title, he was reduced to sell or mortgage the best of his patrimony. By these expedients, the liberality of his royal kinsman Philip Augustus, and the national spirit of chivalry, he was enabled to pass the Alps at the head of one hundred and forty knights, and five thousand five hundred sergeants and archers. After some hesitation, Pope Honorius the Third was persuaded to crown the successor of Constantine: but he performed the ceremony in a church without the walls, lest he should seem to imply or to bestow any right of sovereignty over the ancient capital of the empire. The Venetians had engaged to transport Peter and his forces beyond the Adriatic, and the empress, with her four children, to the Byzantine palace; but they required, as the price of their service, that he should recover Durazzo from the despot of Epirus. Michael Angelus, or Comnenus, the first of his dynasty, had bequeathed the succession of his power and ambition to Theodore, his legitimate brother, who already threatened and invaded the establishments of the Latins. After discharging his debt by a fruitless assault, the emperor raised the siege to prosecute a long and perilous journey over land from Durazzo to Thessalonica. He was soon lost in the mountains of Epirus: the passes were fortified; his provisions exhausted; he was delayed and deceived by a treacherous negotiation; and, after Peter of Courtenay and the Roman legate had been arrested in a banquet, the French troops, without leaders or hopes, were eager to exchange their arms for the delusive promise of mercy and bread. The Vatican thundered; and the impious Theodore was threatened with the vengeance of earth and heaven; but the captive emperor and his soldiers were forgotten, and the reproaches of the pope are confined to the imprisonment of his legate. No sooner was he satisfied by the deliverance of the priests and a promise of spiritual obedience, than he pardoned and protected the despot of Epirus. His peremptory commands suspended the ardor of the Venetians and the king of Hungary; and it was only by a natural or untimely death [36] that Peter of Courtenay was released from his hopeless captivity. [37]

[Footnote 36: Acropolita (c. 14) affirms, that Peter of Courtenay died by the sword, (ergon macairaV genesqai;) but from his dark expressions, I should conclude a previous captivity, wV pantaV ardhn desmwtaV poihsai sun pasi skeuesi. The Chronicle of Auxerre delays the emperor's death till the year 1219; and Auxerre is in the neighborhood of Courtenay. Note: Whatever may have been the fact, this can hardly be made out from the expressions of Acropolita—M.]

[Footnote 37: See the reign and death of Peter of Courtenay, in Ducange, (Hist. de C. P. l. ii. c. 22—28,) who feebly strives to excuse the neglect of the emperor by Honorius III.]

The long ignorance of his fate, and the presence of the lawful sovereign, of Yolande, his wife or widow, delayed the proclamation of a new emperor. Before her death, and in the midst of her grief, she was delivered of a son, who was named Baldwin, the last and most unfortunate of the Latin princes of Constantinople. His birth endeared him to the barons of Romania; but his childhood would have prolonged the troubles of a minority, and his claims were superseded by the elder claims of his brethren. The first of these, Philip of Courtenay, who derived from his mother the inheritance of Namur, had the wisdom to prefer the substance of a marquisate to the shadow of an empire; and on his refusal, Robert, the second of the sons of Peter and Yolande, was called to the throne of Constantinople. Warned by his father's mischance, he pursued his slow and secure journey through Germany and along the Danube: a passage was opened by his sister's marriage with the king of Hungary; and the emperor Robert was crowned by the patriarch in the cathedral of St. Sophia. But his reign was an æra of calamity and disgrace; and the colony, as it was styled, of New France yielded on all sides to the Greeks of Nice and Epirus. After a victory, which he owed to his perfidy rather than his courage, Theodore Angelus entered the kingdom of Thessalonica, expelled the feeble Demetrius, the son of the marquis Boniface, erected his standard on the walls of Adrianople; and added, by his vanity, a third or a fourth name to the list of rival emperors. The relics of the Asiatic province were swept away by John Vataces, the son-in-law and successor of Theodore Lascaris, and who, in a triumphant reign of thirty-three years, displayed the virtues both of peace and war. Under his discipline, the swords of the French mercenaries were the most effectual instruments of his conquests, and their desertion from the service of their country was at once a symptom and a cause of the rising ascendant of the Greeks. By the construction of a fleet, he obtained the command of the Hellespont, reduced the islands of Lesbos and Rhodes, attacked the Venetians of Candia, and intercepted the rare and parsimonious succors of the West. Once, and once only, the Latin emperor sent an army against Vataces; and in the defeat of that army, the veteran knights, the last of the original conquerors, were left on the field of battle. But the success of a foreign enemy was less painful to the pusillanimous Robert than the insolence of his Latin subjects, who confounded the weakness of the emperor and of the empire. His personal misfortunes will prove the anarchy of the government and the ferociousness of the times. The amorous youth had neglected his Greek bride, the daughter of Vataces, to introduce into the palace a beautiful maid, of a private, though noble family of Artois; and her mother had been tempted by the lustre of the purple to forfeit her engagements with a gentleman of Burgundy. His love was converted into rage; he assembled his friends, forced the palace gates, threw the mother into the sea, and inhumanly cut off the nose and lips of the wife or concubine of the emperor. Instead of punishing the offender, the barons avowed and applauded the savage deed, [38] which, as a prince and as a man, it was impossible that Robert should forgive. He escaped from the guilty city to implore the justice or compassion of the pope: the emperor was coolly exhorted to return to his station; before he could obey, he sunk under the weight of grief, shame, and impotent resentment. [39]

[Footnote 38: Marinus Sanutus (Secreta Fidelium Crucis, l. ii. p. 4, c. 18, p. 73) is so much delighted with this bloody deed, that he has transcribed it in his margin as a bonum exemplum. Yet he acknowledges the damsel for the lawful wife of Robert.]

[Footnote 39: See the reign of Robert, in Ducange, (Hist. de C. P. l. ii. c—12.)]

It was only in the age of chivalry, that valor could ascend from a private station to the thrones of Jerusalem and Constantinople. The titular kingdom of Jerusalem had devolved to Mary, the daughter of Isabella and Conrad of Montferrat, and the granddaughter of Almeric or Amaury. She was given to John of Brienne, of a noble family in Champagne, by the public voice, and the judgment of Philip Augustus, who named him as the most worthy champion of the Holy Land. [40] In the fifth crusade, he led a hundred thousand Latins to the conquest of Egypt: by him the siege of Damietta was achieved; and the subsequent failure was justly ascribed to the pride and avarice of the legate. After the marriage of his daughter with Frederic the Second, [41] he was provoked by the emperor's ingratitude to accept the command of the army of the church; and though advanced in life, and despoiled of royalty, the sword and spirit of John of Brienne were still ready for the service of Christendom. In the seven years of his brother's reign, Baldwin of Courtenay had not emerged from a state of childhood, and the barons of Romania felt the strong necessity of placing the sceptre in the hands of a man and a hero. The veteran king of Jerusalem might have disdained the name and office of regent; they agreed to invest him for his life with the title and prerogatives of emperor, on the sole condition that Baldwin should marry his second daughter, and succeed at a mature age to the throne of Constantinople. The expectation, both of the Greeks and Latins, was kindled by the renown, the choice, and the presence of John of Brienne; and they admired his martial aspect, his green and vigorous age of more than fourscore years, and his size and stature, which surpassed the common measure of mankind. [42] But avarice, and the love of ease, appear to have chilled the ardor of enterprise: [42/1] his troops were disbanded, and two years rolled away without action or honor, till he was awakened by the dangerous alliance of Vataces emperor of Nice, and of Azan king of Bulgaria. They besieged Constantinople by sea and land, with an army of one hundred thousand men, and a fleet of three hundred ships of war; while the entire force of the Latin emperor was reduced to one hundred and sixty knights, and a small addition of sergeants and archers. I tremble to relate, that instead of defending the city, the hero made a sally at the head of his cavalry; and that of forty-eight squadrons of the enemy, no more than three escaped from the edge of his invincible sword. Fired by his example, the infantry and the citizens boarded the vessels that anchored close to the walls; and twenty-five were dragged in triumph into the harbor of Constantinople. At the summons of the emperor, the vassals and allies armed in her defence; broke through every obstacle that opposed their passage; and, in the succeeding year, obtained a second victory over the same enemies. By the rude poets of the age, John of Brienne is compared to Hector, Roland, and Judas Machabæus: [43] but their credit, and his glory, receive some abatement from the silence of the Greeks. The empire was soon deprived of the last of her champions; and the dying monarch was ambitious to enter paradise in the habit of a Franciscan friar. [44]

[Footnote 40: Rex igitur Franciæ, deliberatione habitâ, respondit nuntiis, se daturum hominem Syriæ partibus aptum; in armis probum (preux) in bellis securum, in agendis providum, Johannem comitem Brennensem. Sanut. Secret. Fidelium, l. iii. p. xi. c. 4, p. 205 Matthew Paris, p. 159.]

[Footnote 41: Giannone (Istoria Civile, tom. ii. l. xvi. p. 380—385) discusses the marriage of Frederic II. with the daughter of John of Brienne, and the double union of the crowns of Naples and Jerusalem.]

[Footnote 42: Acropolita, c. 27. The historian was at that time a boy, and educated at Constantinople. In 1233, when he was eleven years old, his father broke the Latin chain, left a splendid fortune, and escaped to the Greek court of Nice, where his son was raised to the highest honors.]

[Footnote 42/1: John de Brienne, elected emperor 1229, wasted two years in preparations, and did not arrive at Constantinople till 1231. Two years more glided away in inglorious inaction; he then made some ineffective warlike expeditions. Constantinople was not besieged till 1234—M.]

[Footnote 43: Philip Mouskes, bishop of Tournay, (A.D. 1274—1282,) has composed a poem, or rather string of verses, in bad old Flemish French, on the Latin emperors of Constantinople, which Ducange has published at the end of Villehardouin; see p. 38, for the prowess of John of Brienne. N'Aie, Ector, Roll' ne Ogiers Ne Judas Machabeus li fiers Tant ne fit d'armes en estors Com fist li Rois Jehans cel jors Et il defors et il dedans La paru sa force et ses sens Et li hardiment qu'il avoit.]

[Footnote 44: See the reign of John de Brienne, in Ducange, Hist. de C. P. l. ii. c. 13—26.]

In the double victory of John of Brienne, I cannot discover the name or exploits of his pupil Baldwin, who had attained the age of military service, and who succeeded to the imperial dignity on the decease of his adoptive father. [45] The royal youth was employed on a commission more suitable to his temper; he was sent to visit the Western courts, of the pope more especially, and of the king of France; to excite their pity by the view of his innocence and distress; and to obtain some supplies of men or money for the relief of the sinking empire. He thrice repeated these mendicant visits, in which he seemed to prolong his stay and postpone his return; of the five-and-twenty years of his reign, a greater number were spent abroad than at home; and in no place did the emperor deem himself less free and secure than in his native country and his capital. On some public occasions, his vanity might be soothed by the title of Augustus, and by the honors of the purple; and at the general council of Lyons, when Frederic the Second was excommunicated and deposed, his Oriental colleague was enthroned on the right hand of the pope. But how often was the exile, the vagrant, the Imperial beggar, humbled with scorn, insulted with pity, and degraded in his own eyes and those of the nations! In his first visit to England, he was stopped at Dover by a severe reprimand, that he should presume, without leave, to enter an independent kingdom. After some delay, Baldwin, however, was permitted to pursue his journey, was entertained with cold civility, and thankfully departed with a present of seven hundred marks. [46] From the avarice of Rome he could only obtain the proclamation of a crusade, and a treasure of indulgences; a coin whose currency was depreciated by too frequent and indiscriminate abuse. His birth and misfortunes recommended him to the generosity of his cousin Louis the Ninth; but the martial zeal of the saint was diverted from Constantinople to Egypt and Palestine; and the public and private poverty of

Baldwin was alleviated, for a moment, by the alienation of the marquisate of Namur and the lordship of Courtenay, the last remains of his inheritance. [47] By such shameful or ruinous expedients, he once more returned to Romania, with an army of thirty thousand soldiers, whose numbers were doubled in the apprehension of the Greeks. His first despatches to France and England announced his victories and his hopes: he had reduced the country round the capital to the distance of three days' journey; and if he succeeded against an important, though nameless, city, (most probably Chiorli,) the frontier would be safe and the passage accessible. But these expectations (if Baldwin was sincere) quickly vanished like a dream: the troops and treasures of France melted away in his unskilful hands; and the throne of the Latin emperor was protected by a dishonorable alliance with the Turks and Comans. To secure the former, he consented to bestow his niece on the unbelieving sultan of Cogni; to please the latter, he complied with their Pagan rites; a dog was sacrificed between the two armies; and the contracting parties tasted each other's blood, as a pledge of their fidelity. [48] In the palace, or prison, of Constantinople, the successor of Augustus demolished the vacant houses for winter fuel, and stripped the lead from the churches for the daily expense of his family. Some usurious loans were dealt with a scanty hand by the merchants of Italy; and Philip, his son and heir, was pawned at Venice as the security for a debt. [49] Thirst, hunger, and nakedness, are positive evils: but wealth is relative; and a prince who would be rich in a private station, may be exposed by the increase of his wants to all the anxiety and bitterness of poverty.

[Footnote 45: See the reign of Baldwin II. till his expulsion from Constantinople, in Ducange, Hist. de C. P. l. iv. c. 1—34, the end l. v. c. 1—33.]

[Footnote 46: Matthew Paris relates the two visits of Baldwin II. to the English court, p. 396, 637; his return to Greece armatâ manû, p. 407 his letters of his nomen formidabile, &c., p. 481, (a passage which has escaped Ducange;) his expulsion, p. 850.]

[Footnote 47: Louis IX. disapproved and stopped the alienation of Courtenay (Ducange, l. iv. c. 23.) It is now annexed to the royal demesne but granted for a term (engagé) to the family of Boulainvilliers. Courtenay, in the election of Nemours in the Isle de France, is a town of 900 inhabitants, with the remains of a castle, (Mélanges tirés d'une Grande Bibliothèque, tom. xlv. p. 74—77.)]

[Footnote 48: Joinville, p. 104, edit. du Louvre. A Coman prince, who died without baptism, was buried at the gates of Constantinople with a live retinue of slaves and horses.]

[Footnote 49: Sanut. Secret. Fidel. Crucis, l. ii. p. iv. c. 18, p. 73.]


PART III

But in this abject distress, the emperor and empire were still possessed of an ideal treasure, which drew its fantastic value from the superstition of the Christian world. The merit of the true cross was somewhat impaired by its frequent division; and a long captivity among the infidels might shed some suspicion on the fragments that were produced in the East and West. But another relic of the Passion was preserved in the Imperial chapel of Constantinople; and the crown of thorns which had been placed on the head of Christ was equally precious and authentic. It had formerly been the practice of the Egyptian debtors to deposit, as a security, the mummies of their parents; and both their honor and religion were bound for the redemption of the pledge. In the same manner, and in the absence of the emperor, the barons of Romania borrowed the sum of thirteen thousand one hundred and thirty-four pieces of gold [50] on the credit of the holy crown: they failed in the performance of their contract; and a rich Venetian, Nicholas Querini, undertook to satisfy their impatient creditors, on condition that the relic should be lodged at Venice, to become his absolute property, if it were not redeemed within a short and definite term. The barons apprised their sovereign of the hard treaty and impending loss and as the empire could not afford a ransom of seven thousand pounds sterling, Baldwin was anxious to snatch the prize from the Venetians, and to vest it with more honor and emolument in the hands of the most Christian king. [51] Yet the negotiation was attended with some delicacy. In the purchase of relics, the saint would have started at the guilt of simony; but if the mode of expression were changed, he might lawfully repay the debt, accept the gift, and acknowledge the obligation. His ambassadors, two Dominicans, were despatched to Venice to redeem and receive the holy crown which had escaped the dangers of the sea and the galleys of Vataces. On opening a wooden box, they recognized the seals of the doge and barons, which were applied on a shrine of silver; and within this shrine the monument of the Passion was enclosed in a golden vase. The reluctant Venetians yielded to justice and power: the emperor Frederic granted a free and honorable passage; the court of France advanced as far as Troyes in Champagne, to meet with devotion this inestimable relic: it was borne in triumph through Paris by the king himself, barefoot, and in his shirt; and a free gift of ten thousand marks of silver reconciled Baldwin to his loss. The success of this transaction tempted the Latin emperor to offer with the same generosity the remaining furniture of his chapel; [52] a large and authentic portion of the true cross; the baby-linen of the Son of God, the lance, the sponge, and the chain, of his Passion; the rod of Moses, and part of the skull of St. John the Baptist. For the reception of these spiritual treasures, twenty thousand marks were expended by St. Louis on a stately foundation, the holy chapel of Paris, on which the muse of Boileau has bestowed a comic immortality. The truth of such remote and ancient relics, which cannot be proved by any human testimony, must be admitted by those who believe in the miracles which they have performed. About the middle of the last age, an inveterate ulcer was touched and cured by a holy prickle of the holy crown: [53] the prodigy is attested by the most pious and enlightened Christians of France; nor will the fact be easily disproved, except by those who are armed with a general antidote against religious credulity. [54]

[Footnote 50: Under the words Perparus, Perpera, Hyperperum, Ducange is short and vague: Monetæ genus. From a corrupt passage of Guntherus, (Hist. C. P. c. 8, p. 10,) I guess that the Perpera was the nummus aureus, the fourth part of a mark of silver, or about ten shillings sterling in value. In lead it would be too contemptible.]

[Footnote 51: For the translation of the holy crown, &c., from Constantinople to Paris, see Ducange (Hist. de C. P. l. iv. c. 11—14, 24, 35) and Fleury, (Hist. Ecclés. tom. xvii. p. 201—204.)]

[Footnote 52: Mélanges tirés d'une Grande Bibliothèque, tom. xliii. p. 201—205. The Lutrin of Boileau exhibits the inside, the soul and manners of the Sainte Chapelle; and many facts relative to the institution are collected and explained by his commentators, Brosset and De St. Marc.]

[Footnote 53: It was performed A.D. 1656, March 24, on the niece of Pascal; and that superior genius, with Arnauld, Nicole, &c., were on the spot, to believe and attest a miracle which confounded the Jesuits, and saved Port Royal, (uvres de Racine, tom. vi. p. 176—187, in his eloquent History of Port Royal.)]

[Footnote 54: Voltaire (Siécle de Louis XIV. c. 37, uvres, tom. ix. p. 178, 179) strives to invalidate the fact: but Hume, (Essays, vol. ii. p. 483, 484,) with more skill and success, seizes the battery, and turns the cannon against his enemies.]

The Latins of Constantinople [55] were on all sides encompassed and pressed; their sole hope, the last delay of their ruin, was in the division of their Greek and Bulgarian enemies; and of this hope they were deprived by the superior arms and policy of Vataces, emperor of Nice. From the Propontis to the rocky coast of Pamphylia, Asia was peaceful and prosperous under his reign; and the events of every campaign extended his influence in Europe. The strong cities of the hills of Macedonia and Thrace were rescued from the Bulgarians; and their kingdom was circumscribed by its present and proper limits, along the southern banks of the Danube. The sole emperor of the Romans could no longer brook that a lord of Epirus, a Comnenian prince of the West, should presume to dispute or share the honors of the purple; and the humble Demetrius changed the color of his buskins, and accepted with gratitude the appellation of despot. His own subjects were exasperated by his baseness and incapacity; they implored the protection of their supreme lord. After some resistance, the kingdom of Thessalonica was united to the empire of Nice; and Vataces reigned without a competitor from the Turkish borders to the Adriatic Gulf. The princes of Europe revered his merit and power; and had he subscribed an orthodox creed, it should seem that the pope would have abandoned without reluctance the Latin throne of Constantinople. But the death of Vataces, the short and busy reign of Theodore his son, and the helpless infancy of his grandson John, suspended the restoration of the Greeks. In the next chapter, I shall explain their domestic revolutions; in this place, it will be sufficient to observe, that the young prince was oppressed by the ambition of his guardian and colleague, Michael Palæologus, who displayed the virtues and vices that belong to the founder of a new dynasty. The emperor Baldwin had flattered himself, that he might recover some provinces or cities by an impotent negotiation. His ambassadors were dismissed from Nice with mockery and contempt. At every place which they named, Palæologus alleged some special reason, which rendered it dear and valuable in his eyes: in the one he was born; in another he had been first promoted to military command; and in a third he had enjoyed, and hoped long to enjoy, the pleasures of the chase. "And what then do you propose to give us?" said the astonished deputies. "Nothing," replied the Greek, "not a foot of land. If your master be desirous of peace, let him pay me, as an annual tribute, the sum which he receives from the trade and customs of Constantinople. On these terms, I may allow him to reign. If he refuses, it is war. I am not ignorant of the art of war, and I trust the event to God and my sword." [56] An expedition against the despot of Epirus was the first prelude of his arms. If a victory was followed by a defeat; if the race of the Comneni or Angeli survived in those mountains his efforts and his reign; the captivity of Villehardouin, prince of Achaia, deprived the Latins of the most active and powerful vassal of their expiring monarchy. The republics of Venice and Genoa disputed, in the first of their naval wars, the command of the sea and the commerce of the East. Pride and interest attached the Venetians to the defence of Constantinople; their rivals were tempted to promote the designs of her enemies, and the alliance of the Genoese with the schismatic conqueror provoked the indignation of the Latin church. [57]

[Footnote 55: The gradual losses of the Latins may be traced in the third fourth, and fifth books of the compilation of Ducange: but of the Greek conquests he has dropped many circumstances, which may be recovered from the larger history of George Acropolita, and the three first books of Nicephorus, Gregoras, two writers of the Byzantine series, who have had the good fortune to meet with learned editors Leo Allatius at Rome, and John Boivin in the Academy of Inscriptions of Paris.]

[Footnote 56: George Acropolita, c. 78, p. 89, 90. edit. Paris.]

[Footnote 57: The Greeks, ashamed of any foreign aid, disguise the alliance and succor of the Genoese: but the fact is proved by the testimony of J Villani (Chron. l. vi. c. 71, in Muratori, Script. Rerum

*Italicarum, tom. xiii. p. 202, 203) and William de Nangis, (Annales de St. Louis, p. 248 in the Louvre Joinville,) two impartial foreigners; and Urban IV threatened to deprive Genoa of her archbishop.]*

Intent on his great object, the emperor Michael visited in person and strengthened the troops and fortifications of Thrace. The remains of the Latins were driven from their last possessions: he assaulted without success the suburb of Galata; and corresponded with a perfidious baron, who proved unwilling, or unable, to open the gates of the metropolis. The next spring, his favorite general, Alexius Strategopulus, whom he had decorated with the title of Cæsar, passed the Hellespont with eight hundred horse and some infantry, [58] on a secret expedition. His instructions enjoined him to approach, to listen, to watch, but not to risk any doubtful or dangerous enterprise against the city. The adjacent territory between the Propontis and the Black Sea was cultivated by a hardy race of peasants and outlaws, exercised in arms, uncertain in their allegiance, but inclined by language, religion, and present advantage, to the party of the Greeks. They were styled the volunteers; [59] and by their free service the army of Alexius, with the regulars of Thrace and the Coman auxiliaries, [60] was augmented to the number of five-and-twenty thousand men. By the ardor of the volunteers, and by his own ambition, the Cæsar was stimulated to disobey the precise orders of his master, in the just confidence that success would plead his pardon and reward. The weakness of Constantinople, and the distress and terror of the Latins, were familiar to the observation of the volunteers; and they represented the present moment as the most propitious to surprise and conquest. A rash youth, the new governor of the Venetian colony, had sailed away with thirty galleys, and the best of the French knights, on a wild expedition to Daphnusia, a town on the Black Sea, at the distance of forty leagues; [60/1] and the remaining Latins were without strength or suspicion. They were informed that Alexius had passed the Hellespont; but their apprehensions were lulled by the smallness of his original numbers; and their imprudence had not watched the subsequent increase of his army. If he left his main body to second and support his operations, he might advance unperceived in the night with a chosen detachment. While some applied scaling-ladders to the lowest part of the walls, they were secure of an old Greek, who would introduce their companions through a subterraneous passage into his house; they could soon on the inside break an entrance through the golden gate, which had been long obstructed; and the conqueror would be in the heart of the city before the Latins were conscious of their danger. After some debate, the Cæsar resigned himself to the faith of the volunteers; they were trusty, bold, and successful; and in describing the plan, I have already related the execution and success. [61] But no sooner had Alexius passed the threshold of the golden gate, than he trembled at his own rashness; he paused, he deliberated; till the desperate volunteers urged him forwards, by the assurance that in retreat lay the greatest and most inevitable danger. Whilst the Cæsar kept his regulars in firm array, the Comans dispersed themselves on all sides; an alarm was sounded, and the threats of fire and pillage compelled the citizens to a decisive resolution. The Greeks of Constantinople remembered their native sovereigns; the Genoese merchants their recent alliance and Venetian foes; every quarter was in arms; and the air resounded with a general acclamation of "Long life and victory to Michael and John, the august emperors of the Romans!" Their rival, Baldwin, was awakened by the sound; but the most pressing danger could not prompt him to draw his sword in the defence of a city which he deserted, perhaps, with more pleasure than regret: he fled from the palace to the seashore, where he descried the welcome sails of the fleet returning from the vain and fruitless attempt on Daphnusia. Constantinople was irrecoverably lost; but the Latin emperor and the principal families embarked on board the Venetian galleys, and steered for the Isle of Euba, and afterwards for Italy, where the royal fugitive was entertained by the pope and Sicilian king with a mixture of contempt and pity. From the loss of Constantinople to his death, he consumed thirteen years, soliciting the Catholic powers to join in his restoration: the lesson had been familiar to his youth; nor was his last exile more indigent or shameful than his three former pilgrimages to the courts of Europe. His son Philip was the heir of an ideal empire;

and the pretensions of his daughter Catherine were transported by her marriage to Charles of Valois, the brother of Philip the Fair, king of France. The house of Courtenay was represented in the female line by successive alliances, till the title of emperor of Constantinople, too bulky and sonorous for a private name, modestly expired in silence and oblivion. [62]

[Footnote 58: Some precautions must be used in reconciling the discordant numbers; the 800 soldiers of Nicetas, the 25,000 of Spandugino, (apud Ducange, l. v. c. 24;) the Greeks and Scythians of Acropolita; and the numerous army of Michael, in the Epistles of Pope Urban IV. (i. 129.)]

[Footnote 59: Qelhmatarioi. They are described and named by Pachymer, (l. ii. c. 14.)]

[Footnote 60: It is needless to seek these Comans in the deserts of Tartary, or even of Moldavia. A part of the horde had submitted to John Vataces, and was probably settled as a nursery of soldiers on some waste lands of Thrace, (Cantacuzen. l. i. c. 2.)]

[Footnote 60/1: According to several authorities, particularly Abulfaradj. Chron. Arab. p. 336, this was a stratagem on the part of the Greeks to weaken the garrison of Constantinople. The Greek commander offered to surrender the town on the appearance of the Venetians—M.]

[Footnote 61: The loss of Constantinople is briefly told by the Latins: the conquest is described with more satisfaction by the Greeks; by Acropolita, (c. 85,) Pachymer, (l. ii. c. 26, 27,) Nicephorus Gregoras, (l. iv. c. 1, 2) See Ducange, Hist. de C. P. l. v. c. 19—27.]

[Footnote 62: See the three last books (l. v—viii.) and the genealogical tables of Ducange. In the year 1382, the titular emperor of Constantinople was James de Baux, duke of Andria in the kingdom of Naples, the son of Margaret, daughter of Catherine de Valois, daughter of Catharine, daughter of Philip, son of Baldwin II., (Ducange, l. viii. c. 37, 38.) It is uncertain whether he left any posterity.]

After this narrative of the expeditions of the Latins to Palestine and Constantinople, I cannot dismiss the subject without resolving the general consequences on the countries that were the scene, and on the nations that were the actors, of these memorable crusades. [63] As soon as the arms of the Franks were withdrawn, the impression, though not the memory, was erased in the Mahometan realms of Egypt and Syria. The faithful disciples of the prophet were never tempted by a profane desire to study the laws or language of the idolaters; nor did the simplicity of their primitive manners receive the slightest alteration from their intercourse in peace and war with the unknown strangers of the West. The Greeks, who thought themselves proud, but who were only vain, showed a disposition somewhat less inflexible. In the efforts for the recovery of their empire, they emulated the valor, discipline, and tactics of their antagonists. The modern literature of the West they might justly despise; but its free spirit would instruct them in the rights of man; and some institutions of public and private life were adopted from the French. The correspondence of Constantinople and Italy diffused the knowledge of the Latin tongue; and several of the fathers and classics were at length honored with a Greek version. [64] But the national and religious prejudices of the Orientals were inflamed by persecution, and the reign of the Latins confirmed the separation of the two churches.

[Footnote 63: Abulfeda, who saw the conclusion of the crusades, speaks of the kingdoms of the Franks, and those of the Negroes, as equally unknown, (Prolegom. ad Geograph.) Had he not disdained the Latin language, how easily might the Syrian prince have found books and interpreters!]

[Footnote 64: A short and superficial account of these versions from Latin into Greek is given by Huet, (de Interpretatione et de claris Interpretibus p. 131—135.) Maximus Planudes, a monk of Constantinople, (A.D. 1327—1353) has translated Cæsar's Commentaries, the Somnium Scipionis, the Metamorphoses and Heroides of Ovid, &c., (Fabric. Bib. Græc. tom. x. p. 533.)]

If we compare the æra of the crusades, the Latins of Europe with the Greeks and Arabians, their respective degrees of knowledge, industry, and art, our rude ancestors must be content with the third rank in the scale of nations. Their successive improvement and present superiority may be ascribed to a peculiar energy of character, to an active and imitative spirit, unknown to their more polished rivals, who at that time were in a stationary or retrograde state. With such a disposition, the Latins should have derived the most early and essential benefits from a series of events which opened to their eyes the prospect of the world, and introduced them to a long and frequent intercourse with the more cultivated regions of the East. The first and most obvious progress was in trade and manufactures, in the arts which are strongly prompted by the thirst of wealth, the calls of necessity, and the gratification of the sense or vanity. Among the crowd of unthinking fanatics, a captive or a pilgrim might sometimes observe the superior refinements of Cairo and Constantinople: the first importer of windmills [65] was the benefactor of nations; and if such blessings are enjoyed without any grateful remembrance, history has condescended to notice the more apparent luxuries of silk and sugar, which were transported into Italy from Greece and Egypt. But the intellectual wants of the Latins were more slowly felt and supplied; the ardor of studious curiosity was awakened in Europe by different causes and more recent events; and, in the age of the crusades, they viewed with careless indifference the literature of the Greeks and Arabians. Some rudiments of mathematical and medicinal knowledge might be imparted in practice and in figures; necessity might produce some interpreters for the grosser business of merchants and soldiers; but the commerce of the Orientals had not diffused the study and knowledge of their languages in the schools of Europe. [66] If a similar principle of religion repulsed the idiom of the Koran, it should have excited their patience and curiosity to understand the original text of the gospel; and the same grammar would have unfolded the sense of Plato and the beauties of Homer. Yet in a reign of sixty years, the Latins of Constantinople disdained the speech and learning of their subjects; and the manuscripts were the only treasures which the natives might enjoy without rapine or envy. Aristotle was indeed the oracle of the Western universities, but it was a barbarous Aristotle; and, instead of ascending to the fountain head, his Latin votaries humbly accepted a corrupt and remote version, from the Jews and Moors of Andalusia. The principle of the crusades was a savage fanaticism; and the most important effects were analogous to the cause. Each pilgrim was ambitious to return with his sacred spoils, the relics of Greece and Palestine; [67] and each relic was preceded and followed by a train of miracles and visions. The belief of the Catholics was corrupted by new legends, their practice by new superstitions; and the establishment of the inquisition, the mendicant orders of monks and friars, the last abuse of indulgences, and the final progress of idolatry, flowed from the baleful fountain of the holy war. The active spirit of the Latins preyed on the vitals of their reason and religion; and if the ninth and tenth centuries were the times of darkness, the thirteenth and fourteenth were the age of absurdity and fable.

[Footnote 65: Windmills, first invented in the dry country of Asia Minor, were used in Normandy as early as the year 1105, (Vie privée des François, tom. i. p. 42, 43. Ducange, Gloss. Latin. tom. iv. p. 474.)]

[Footnote 66: See the complaints of Roger Bacon, (Biographia Britannica, vol. i. p. 418, Kippis's edition.) If Bacon himself, or Gerbert, understood someGreek, they were prodigies, and owed nothing to the commerce of the East.]

*[Footnote 67: Such was the opinion of the great Leibnitz, (uvres de Fontenelle, tom. v. p. 458,) a master of the history of the middle ages. I shall only instance the pedigree of the Carmelites, and the flight of the house of Loretto, which were both derived from Palestine.]*

PART IV

In the profession of Christianity, in the cultivation of a fertile land, the northern conquerors of the Roman empire insensibly mingled with the provincials, and rekindled the embers of the arts of antiquity. Their settlements about the age of Charlemagne had acquired some degree of order and stability, when they were overwhelmed by new swarms of invaders, the Normans, Saracens, [68] and Hungarians, who replunged the western countries of Europe into their former state of anarchy and barbarism. About the eleventh century, the second tempest had subsided by the expulsion or conversion of the enemies of Christendom: the tide of civilization, which had so long ebbed, began to flow with a steady and accelerated course; and a fairer prospect was opened to the hopes and efforts of the rising generations. Great was the increase, and rapid the progress, during the two hundred years of the crusades; and some philosophers have applauded the propitious influence of these holy wars, which appear to me to have checked rather than forwarded the maturity of Europe. [69] The lives and labors of millions, which were buried in the East, would have been more profitably employed in the improvement of their native country: the accumulated stock of industry and wealth would have overflowed in navigation and trade; and the Latins would have been enriched and enlightened by a pure and friendly correspondence with the climates of the East. In one respect I can indeed perceive the accidental operation of the crusades, not so much in producing a benefit as in removing an evil. The larger portion of the inhabitants of Europe was chained to the soil, without freedom, or property, or knowledge; and the two orders of ecclesiastics and nobles, whose numbers were comparatively small, alone deserved the name of citizens and men. This oppressive system was supported by the arts of the clergy and the swords of the barons. The authority of the priests operated in the darker ages as a salutary antidote: they prevented the total extinction of letters, mitigated the fierceness of the times, sheltered the poor and defenceless, and preserved or revived the peace and order of civil society. But the independence, rapine, and discord of the feudal lords were unmixed with any semblance of good; and every hope of industry and improvement was crushed by the iron weight of the martial aristocracy. Among the causes that undermined that Gothic edifice, a conspicuous place must be allowed to the crusades. The estates of the barons were dissipated, and their race was often extinguished, in these costly and perilous expeditions. Their poverty extorted from their pride those charters of freedom which unlocked the fetters of the slave, secured the farm of the peasant and the shop of the artificer, and gradually restored a substance and a soul to the most numerous and useful part of the community. The conflagration which destroyed the tall and barren trees of the forest gave air and scope to the vegetation of the smaller and nutritive plants of the soil. [691]

*[Footnote 68: If I rank the Saracens with the Barbarians, it is only relative to their wars, or rather inroads, in Italy and France, where their sole purpose was to plunder and destroy.]*

*[Footnote 69: On this interesting subject, the progress of society in Europe, a strong ray of philosophical light has broke from Scotland in our own times; and it is with private, as well as public regard, that I repeat the names of Hume, Robertson, and Adam Smith.]*

[Footnote 691: *On the consequences of the crusades, compare the valuable Essay of Heeren, that of M. Choiseul d'Aillecourt, and a chapter of Mr. Forster's "Mahometanism Unveiled." I may admire this gentleman's learning and industry, without pledging myself to his wild theory of prophets interpretation—M.]*

Digression On The Family Of Courtenay.

The purple of three emperors, who have reigned at Constantinople, will authorize or excuse a digression on the origin and singular fortunes of the house of Courtenay, [70] in the three principal branches: I. Of Edessa; II. Of France; and III. Of England; of which the last only has survived the revolutions of eight hundred years.

[Footnote 70: *I have applied, but not confined, myself to A genealogical History of the noble and illustrious Family of Courtenay, by Ezra Cleaveland, Tutor to Sir William Courtenay, and Rector of Honiton; Exon. 1735, in folio. The first part is extracted from William of Tyre; the second from Bouchet's French history; and the third from various memorials, public, provincial, and private, of the Courtenays of Devonshire The rector of Honiton has more gratitude than industry, and more industry than criticism.]*

I. Before the introduction of trade, which scatters riches, and of knowledge, which dispels prejudice, the prerogative of birth is most strongly felt and most humbly acknowledged. In every age, the laws and manners of the Germans have discriminated the ranks of society; the dukes and counts, who shared the empire of Charlemagne, converted their office to an inheritance; and to his children, each feudal lord bequeathed his honor and his sword. The proudest families are content to lose, in the darkness of the middle ages, the tree of their pedigree, which, however deep and lofty, must ultimately rise from a plebeian root; and their historians must descend ten centuries below the Christian æra, before they can ascertain any lineal succession by the evidence of surnames, of arms, and of authentic records. With the first rays of light, [71] we discern the nobility and opulence of Atho, a French knight; his nobility, in the rank and title of a nameless father; his opulence, in the foundation of the castle of Courtenay in the district of Gatinois, about fifty-six miles to the south of Paris. From the reign of Robert, the son of Hugh Capet, the barons of Courtenay are conspicuous among the immediate vassals of the crown; and Joscelin, the grandson of Atho and a noble dame, is enrolled among the heroes of the first crusade. A domestic alliance (their mothers were sisters) attached him to the standard of Baldwin of Bruges, the second count of Edessa; a princely fief, which he was worthy to receive, and able to maintain, announces the number of his martial followers; and after the departure of his cousin, Joscelin himself was invested with the county of Edessa on both sides of the Euphrates. By economy in peace, his territories were replenished with Latin and Syrian subjects; his magazines with corn, wine, and oil; his castles with gold and silver, with arms and horses. In a holy warfare of thirty years, he was alternately a conqueror and a captive: but he died like a soldier, in a horse litter at the head of his troops; and his last glance beheld the flight of the Turkish invaders who had presumed on his age and infirmities. His son and successor, of the same name, was less deficient in valor than in vigilance; but he sometimes forgot that dominion is acquired and maintained by the same arms. He challenged the hostility of the Turks, without securing the friendship of the prince of Antioch; and, amidst the peaceful luxury of Turbessel, in Syria, [72] Joscelin neglected the defence of the Christian frontier beyond the Euphrates. In his absence, Zenghi, the first of the Atabeks, besieged and stormed his capital, Edessa, which was feebly defended by a timorous and disloyal crowd of Orientals: the Franks were oppressed in a bold attempt for its recovery, and Courtenay ended his days in the prison of Aleppo. He still left a fair and ample patrimony But the victorious Turks oppressed on all sides the weakness of a widow and orphan; and, for the equivalent of an annual pension, they resigned to the Greek emperor the charge of defending, and the shame of losing, the last relics of the Latin conquest. The countess-dowager of Edessa retired to Jerusalem with her two children; the daughter, Agnes, became the wife and mother of a king; the son, Joscelin the Third, accepted the office of seneschal, the first of the kingdom, and held his new estates in Palestine by the service of fifty knights. His name appears with honor in the transactions of peace and war; but he finally vanishes in the fall of Jerusalem; and the name of Courtenay, in this branch of Edessa, was lost by the marriage of his two daughters with a French and German baron. [73]

[Footnote 71: The primitive record of the family is a passage of the continuator of Aimoin, a monk of Fleury, who wrote in the xiith century. See his Chronicle, in the Historians of France, (tom. xi. p. 276.)]

[Footnote 72: Turbessel, or, as it is now styled, Telbesher, is fixed by D'Anville four-and-twenty miles from the great passage over the Euphrates at Zeugma.]

[Footnote 73: His possessions are distinguished in the Assises of Jerusalem (c. B26) among the feudal tenures of the kingdom, which must therefore have been collected between the years 1153 and 1187. His pedigree may be found in the Lignages d'Outremer, c. 16.]

II. While Joscelin reigned beyond the Euphrates, his elder brother Milo, the son of Joscelin, the son of Atho, continued, near the Seine, to possess the castle of their fathers, which was at length inherited by Rainaud, or Reginald, the youngest of his three sons. Examples of genius or virtue must be rare in the annals of the oldest families; and, in a remote age their pride will embrace a deed of rapine and violence; such, however, as could not be perpetrated without some superiority of courage, or, at least, of power. A descendant of Reginald of Courtenay may blush for the public robber, who stripped and imprisoned several merchants, after they had satisfied the king's duties at Sens and Orleans. He will glory in the offence, since the bold offender could not be compelled to obedience and restitution, till the regent and the count of Champagne prepared to march against him at the head of an army. [74] Reginald bestowed his estates on his eldest daughter, and his daughter on the seventh son of King Louis the Fat; and their marriage was crowned with a numerous offspring. We might expect that a private should have merged in a royal name; and that the descendants of Peter of France and Elizabeth of Courtenay would have enjoyed the titles and honors of princes of the blood. But this legitimate claim was long neglected, and finally denied; and the causes of their disgrace will represent the story of this second branch. 1. Of all the families now extant, the most ancient, doubtless, and the most illustrious, is the house of France, which has occupied the same throne above eight hundred years, and descends, in a clear and lineal series of males, from the middle of the ninth century. [75] In the age of the crusades, it was already revered both in the East and West. But from Hugh Capet to the marriage of Peter, no more than five reigns or generations had elapsed; and so precarious was their title, that the eldest sons, as a necessary precaution, were previously crowned during the lifetime of their fathers. The peers of France have long maintained their precedency before the younger branches of the royal line, nor had the princes of the blood, in the twelfth century, acquired that hereditary lustre which is now diffused over the most remote candidates for the succession. 2. The barons of Courtenay must have stood high in their own estimation, and in that of the world, since they could impose on the son of a king the obligation of adopting for himself and all his descendants the name and arms of their daughter and his wife. In the marriage of an heiress with her inferior or her equal, such exchange often required and allowed: but as they continued to diverge from the regal stem, the sons of Louis the Fat were insensibly confounded with their maternal ancestors; and the new Courtenays might deserve to forfeit the honors of their birth, which a motive of interest had tempted them to renounce. 3. The shame was far more permanent than the reward, and a momentary blaze was followed by a long darkness. The eldest son of these nuptials, Peter of Courtenay, had married, as I have already mentioned, the sister of the counts of

Flanders, the two first emperors of Constantinople: he rashly accepted the invitation of the barons of Romania; his two sons, Robert and Baldwin, successively held and lost the remains of the Latin empire in the East, and the granddaughter of Baldwin the Second again mingled her blood with the blood of France and of Valois. To support the expenses of a troubled and transitory reign, their patrimonial estates were mortgaged or sold: and the last emperors of Constantinople depended on the annual charity of Rome and Naples.

[Footnote 74: The rapine and satisfaction of Reginald de Courtenay, are preposterously arranged in the Epistles of the abbot and regent Suger, (cxiv. cxvi.,) the best memorials of the age, (Duchesne, Scriptores Hist. Franc. tom. iv. p. 530.)]

[Footnote 75: In the beginning of the xith century, after naming the father and grandfather of Hugh Capet, the monk Glaber is obliged to add, *cujus genus valde in-ante reperitur obscurum*. Yet we are assured that the great-grandfather of Hugh Capet was Robert the Strong count of Anjou, (A.D. 863—873,) a noble Frank of Neustria, Neustricus... *generosæ stirpis*, who was slain in the defence of his country against the Normans, *dum patriæ fines tuebatur*. Beyond Robert, all is conjecture or fable. It is a probable conjecture, that the third race descended from the second by Childebrand, the brother of Charles Martel. It is an absurd fable that the second was allied to the first by the marriage of Ansbert, a Roman senator and the ancestor of St. Arnoul, with Blitilde, a daughter of Clotaire I. The Saxon origin of the house of France is an ancient but incredible opinion. See a judicious memoir of M. de Foncemagne, (Mémoires de l'Académie des Inscriptions, tom. xx. p. 548—579.) He had promised to declare his own opinion in a second memoir, which has never appeared.]

While the elder brothers dissipated their wealth in romantic adventures, and the castle of Courtenay was profaned by a plebeian owner, the younger branches of that adopted name were propagated and multiplied. But their splendor was clouded by poverty and time: after the decease of Robert, great butler of France, they descended from princes to barons; the next generations were confounded with the simple gentry; the descendants of Hugh Capet could no longer be visible in the rural lords of Tanlay and of Champignelles. The more adventurous embraced without dishonor the profession of a soldier: the least active and opulent might sink, like their cousins of the branch of Dreux, into the condition of peasants. Their royal descent, in a dark period of four hundred years, became each day more obsolete and ambiguous; and their pedigree, instead of being enrolled in the annals of the kingdom, must be painfully searched by the minute diligence of heralds and genealogists. It was not till the end of the sixteenth century, on the accession of a family almost as remote as their own, that the princely spirit of the Courtenays again revived; and the question of the nobility provoked them to ascertain the royalty of their blood. They appealed to the justice and compassion of Henry the Fourth; obtained a favorable opinion from twenty lawyers of Italy and Germany, and modestly compared themselves to the descendants of King David, whose prerogatives were not impaired by the lapse of ages or the trade of a carpenter. [76] But every ear was deaf, and every circumstance was adverse, to their lawful claims. The Bourbon kings were justified by the neglect of the Valois; the princes of the blood, more recent and lofty, disdained the alliance of his humble kindred: the parliament, without denying their proofs, eluded a dangerous precedent by an arbitrary distinction, and established St. Louis as the first father of the royal line. [77] A repetition of complaints and protests was repeatedly disregarded; and the hopeless pursuit was terminated in the present century by the death of the last male of the family. [78] Their painful and anxious situation was alleviated by the pride of conscious virtue: they sternly rejected the temptations of fortune and favor; and a dying Courtenay would have sacrificed his son, if the youth could have renounced, for any temporal interest, the right and title of a legitimate prince of the blood of France. [79]

[Footnote 76: Of the various petitions, apologies, &c., published by the princes of Courtenay, I have seen the three following, all in octavo: 1. De Stirpe et Origine Domus de Courtenay: addita sunt Responsa celeberrimorum Europæ Jurisconsultorum; Paris, 1607. 2. Representation du Procedé tenû a l'instance faicte devant le Roi, par Messieurs de Courtenay, pour la conservation de l'Honneur et Dignité de leur Maison, branche de la royalle Maison de France; à Paris, 1613. 3. Representation du subject qui a porté Messieurs de Salles et de Fraville, de la Maison de Courtenay, à se retirer hors du Royaume, 1614. It was a homicide, for which the Courtenays expected to be pardoned, or tried, as princes of the blood.]

[Footnote 77: The sense of the parliaments is thus expressed by Thuanus Principis nomen nusquam in Galliâ tributum, nisi iis qui per mares e regibus nostris originem repetunt; qui nunc tantum a Ludovico none beatæ memoriæ numerantur; nam Cortini et Drocenses, a Ludovico crasso genus ducentes, hodie inter eos minime recensentur. A distinction of expediency rather than justice. The sanctity of Louis IX. could not invest him with any special prerogative, and all the descendants of Hugh Capet must be included in his original compact with the French nation.]

[Footnote 78: The last male of the Courtenays was Charles Roger, who died in the year 1730, without leaving any sons. The last female was Helene de Courtenay, who married Louis de Beaufremont. Her title of Princesse du Sang Royal de France was suppressed (February 7th, 1737) by an arrêt of the parliament of Paris.]

[Footnote 79: The singular anecdote to which I allude is related in the Recueil des Pieces interessantes et peu connues, (Maestricht, 1786, in 4 vols. 12mo.;) and the unknown editor quotes his author, who had received it from Helene de Courtenay, marquise de Beaufremont.]

III. According to the old register of Ford Abbey, the Courtenays of Devonshire are descended from Prince Florus, the second son of Peter, and the grandson of Louis the Fat. [80] This fable of the grateful or venal monks was too respectfully entertained by our antiquaries, Cambden [81] and Dugdale: [82] but it is so clearly repugnant to truth and time, that the rational pride of the family now refuses to accept this imaginary founder. Their most faithful historians believe, that, after giving his daughter to the king's son, Reginald of Courtenay abandoned his possessions in France, and obtained from the English monarch a second wife and a new inheritance. It is certain, at least, that Henry the Second distinguished in his camps and councils a Reginald, of the name and arms, and, as it may be fairly presumed, of the genuine race, of the Courtenays of France. The right of wardship enabled a feudal lord to reward his vassal with the marriage and estate of a noble heiress; and Reginald of Courtenay acquired a fair establishment in Devonshire, where his posterity has been seated above six hundred years. [83] From a Norman baron, Baldwin de Brioniis, who had been invested by the Conqueror, Hawise, the wife of Reginald, derived the honor of Okehampton, which was held by the service of ninety-three knights; and a female might claim the manly offices of hereditary viscount or sheriff, and of captain of the royal castle of Exeter. Their son Robert married the sister of the earl of Devon: at the end of a century, on the failure of the family of Rivers, [84] his great-grandson, Hugh the Second, succeeded to a title which was still considered as a territorial dignity; and twelve earls of Devonshire, of the name of Courtenay, have flourished in a period of two hundred and twenty years. They were ranked among the chief of the barons of the realm; nor was it till after a strenuous dispute, that they yielded to the fief of Arundel the first place in the parliament of England: their alliances were contracted with the noblest families, the Veres, Despensers, St. Johns, Talbots, Bohuns, and even the Plantagenets themselves; and in a contest with John of Lancaster, a Courtenay, bishop of London, and afterwards archbishop of Canterbury, might be accused of profane confidence in the strength and number of his kindred. In peace, the earls of Devon resided in their numerous castles and manors of the west; their ample revenue was appropriated to devotion and hospitality; and the epitaph of Edward, surnamed from his misfortune, the blind, from his virtues, the good, earl, inculcates with much ingenuity a moral sentence, which may, however, be abused by thoughtless generosity. After a grateful commemoration of the fifty-five years of union and happiness which he enjoyed with Mabe his wife, the good earl thus speaks from the tomb:—

"What we gave, we have;
What we spent, we had;
What we left, we lost." [85]

But their losses, in this sense, were far superior to their gifts and expenses; and their heirs, not less than the poor, were the objects of their paternal care. The sums which they paid for livery and seizin attest the greatness of their possessions; and several estates have remained in their family since the thirteenth and fourteenth centuries. In war, the Courtenays of England fulfilled the duties, and deserved the honors, of chivalry. They were often intrusted to levy and command the militia of Devonshire and Cornwall; they often attended their supreme lord to the borders of Scotland; and in foreign service, for a stipulated price, they sometimes maintained fourscore men-at-arms and as many archers. By sea and land they fought under the standard of the Edwards and Henries: their names are conspicuous in battles, in tournaments, and in the original list of the Order of the Garter; three brothers shared the Spanish victory of the Black Prince; and in the lapse of six generations, the English Courtenays had learned to despise the nation and country from which they derived their origin. In the quarrel of the two roses, the earls of Devon adhered to the house of Lancaster; and three brothers successively died either in the field or on the scaffold. Their honors and estates were restored by Henry the Seventh; a daughter of Edward the Fourth was not disgraced by the nuptials of a Courtenay; their son, who was created Marquis of Exeter, enjoyed the favor of his cousin Henry the Eighth; and in the camp of Cloth of Gold, he broke a lance against the French monarch. But the favor of Henry was the prelude of disgrace; his disgrace was the signal of death; and of the victims of the jealous tyrant, the marquis of Exeter is one of the most noble and guiltless. His son Edward lived a prisoner in the Tower, and died in exile at Padua; and the secret love of Queen Mary, whom he slighted, perhaps for the princess Elizabeth, has shed a romantic color on the story of this beautiful youth. The relics of his patrimony were conveyed into strange families by the marriages of his four aunts; and his personal honors, as if they had been legally extinct, were revived by the patents of succeeding princes. But there still survived a lineal descendant of Hugh, the first earl of Devon, a younger branch of the Courtenays, who have been seated at Powderham Castle above four hundred years, from the reign of Edward the Third to the present hour. Their estates have been increased by the grant and improvement of lands in Ireland, and they have been recently restored to the honors of the peerage. Yet the Courtenays still retain the plaintive motto, which asserts the innocence, and deplores the fall, of their ancient house. [86] While they sigh for past greatness, they are doubtless sensible of present blessings: in the long series of the Courtenay annals, the most splendid æra is likewise the most unfortunate; nor can an opulent peer of Britain be inclined to envy the emperors of Constantinople, who wandered over Europe to solicit alms for the support of their dignity and the defence of their capital.

[Footnote 80: Dugdale, Monasticon Anglicanum, vol. i. p. 786. Yet this fable must have been invented before the reign of Edward III. The profuse devotion of the three first generations to Ford Abbey was followed by oppression on one side and ingratitude on the other; and in the sixth generation, the monks ceased to register the births, actions, and deaths of their patrons.]

[Footnote 81: In his Britannia, in the list of the earls of Devonshire. His expression, e regio sanguine ortos, credunt, betrays, however, some doubt or suspicion.]

[Footnote 82: In his Baronage, P. i. p. 634, he refers to his own Monasticon. Should he not have corrected the register of Ford Abbey, and annihilated the phantom Florus, by the unquestionable evidence of the French historians?]

[Footnote 83: Besides the third and most valuable book of Cleaveland's History, I have consulted Dugdale, the father of our genealogical science, (Baronage, P. i. p. 634—643.)]

[Footnote 84: This great family, de Ripuariis, de Redvers, de Rivers, ended, in Edward the Fifth's time, in Isabella de Fortibus, a famous and potent dowager, who long survived her brother and husband, (Dugdale, Baronage, P i. p. 254—257.)]

[Footnote 85: Cleaveland p. 142. By some it is assigned to a Rivers earl of Devon; but the English denotes the xvth, rather than the xiiith century.]

[Footnote 86: Ubi lapsus! Quid feci? a motto which was probably adopted by the Powderham branch, after the loss of the earldom of Devonshire, &c. The primitive arms of the Courtenays were, Or, three torteaux, Gules, which seem to denote their affinity with Godfrey of Bouillon, and the ancient counts of Boulogne.]

CHAPTER LXII

GREEK EMPERORS OF NICE AND CONSTANTINOPLE

PART I

THE GREEK EMPERORS OF NICE AND CONSTANTINOPLE—ELEVATION AND REIGN OF MICHAEL PALÆOLOGUS—HIS FALSE UNION WITH THE POPE AND LATIN CHURCH—HOSTILE DESIGNS OF CHARLES OF ANJOU—REVOLT OF SICILY—WAR OF THE CATALANS IN ASIA AND GREECE—REVOLUTIONS AND PRESENT STATE OF ATHENS

The loss of Constantinople restored a momentary vigor to the Greeks. From their palaces, the princes and nobles were driven into the field; and the fragments of the falling monarchy were grasped by the hands of the most vigorous and the most skilful candidates. In the long and barren pages of the Byzantine annals, [1] it would not be an easy task to equal the two characters of Theodore Lascaris and John Ducas Vataces, [2] who replanted and upheld the Roman standard at Nice in Bithynia. The difference of their virtues was happily suited to the diversity of their situation. In his first efforts, the fugitive Lascaris commanded only three cities and two thousand soldiers: his reign was the season of generous and active despair: in every military operation he staked his life and crown; and his enemies of the Hellespont and the Mæander, were surprised by his celerity and subdued by his boldness. A victorious reign of eighteen years expanded the principality of Nice to the magnitude of an empire. The throne of his successor and son-in-law Vataces was founded on a more solid basis, a larger scope, and more plentiful resources; and it was the temper, as well as the interest, of Vataces to calculate the risk, to expect the moment, and to insure the success, of his ambitious designs. In the decline of the Latins, I have briefly exposed the progress of the Greeks; the prudent and gradual advances of a conqueror, who, in a reign of thirty-three years, rescued the provinces from national and foreign usurpers, till he pressed on all sides the Imperial city, a leafless and sapless trunk, which must full at the first stroke of the axe. But his interior and peaceful administration is still more deserving of notice and praise. [3] The calamities of the times had wasted the numbers and the substance of the Greeks; the motives and the means of agriculture were extirpated; and the most fertile lands were left without cultivation or inhabitants. A portion of this vacant property was occupied and improved by the command, and for the benefit, of the emperor: a powerful hand and a vigilant eye supplied and surpassed, by a skilful management, the minute diligence of a private farmer: the royal domain became the garden and granary of Asia; and without impoverishing the people, the sovereign acquired a fund of innocent and productive wealth. According to the nature of the soil, his lands were sown with corn or planted with vines; the pastures were filled with horses and oxen, with sheep and hogs; and when Vataces presented to the empress a crown of diamonds and pearls, he informed her, with a smile, that this precious ornament arose from the sale of the eggs of his innumerable poultry. The produce of his domain was applied to the maintenance of his palace and hospitals, the calls of dignity and benevolence: the lesson was still more useful than the revenue: the plough was restored to its ancient security and honor; and the nobles were taught to seek a sure and independent revenue from their estates, instead of adorning their splendid beggary by the oppression of the people, or (what is almost the same) by the favors of the court. The superfluous stock of corn and cattle was eagerly purchased by the Turks, with whom Vataces preserved a strict and sincere alliance; but he discouraged the importation of foreign manufactures, the costly silks of the East, and the curious labors of the Italian looms. "The demands of nature and necessity," was he accustomed to say, "are indispensable; but the influence of fashion may rise and sink at the breath of a monarch;" and both his precept and example recommended simplicity of manners and the use of domestic industry. The education of youth and the revival of learning were the most serious objects of his care; and, without deciding the precedency, he pronounced with truth, that a prince and a philosopher [4] are the two most eminent characters of human society. His first wife was Irene, the daughter of Theodore Lascaris, a woman more illustrious by her personal merit, the milder virtues of her sex, than by the blood of the Angeli and Comneni that flowed in her veins, and transmitted the inheritance of the empire. After her death he was contracted to Anne, or Constance, a natural daughter of the emperor Frederic [499] the Second; but as the bride had not attained the years of puberty, Vataces placed in his solitary bed an Italian damsel of her train; and his amorous weakness bestowed on the concubine the honors, though not the title, of a lawful empress. His frailty was censured as a flagitious and damnable sin by the monks; and their rude invectives exercised and displayed the patience of the royal lover. A philosophic age may excuse a single vice, which was redeemed by a crowd of virtues; and in the review of his faults, and the more intemperate passions of Lascaris, the judgment of their contemporaries was softened by gratitude to the second founders of the empire. [5] The slaves of the Latins, without law or peace, applauded the happiness of their brethren who had resumed their national freedom; and Vataces employed the laudable policy of convincing the Greeks of every dominion that it was their interest to be enrolled in the number of his subjects.

[Footnote 1: For the reigns of the Nicene emperors, more especially of John Vataces and his son, their minister, George Acropolita, is the only genuine contemporary; but George Pachymer returned to Constantinople with the Greeks at the age of nineteen, (Hanckius de Script. Byzant. c. 33, 34, p. 564—578. Fabric. Bibliot. Græc. tom. vi. p. 448—460.) Yet the history of Nicephorus Gregoras, though of the xivth century, is a valuable narrative from the taking of Constantinople by the Latins.]

[Footnote 2: Nicephorus Gregoras (l. ii. c. 1) distinguishes between the oxeia ormh of Lascaris, and the eustaqeia of Vataces. The two portraits are in a very good style.]

[Footnote 3: Pachymer, l. i. c. 23, 24. Nic. Greg. l. ii. c. 6. *The reader of the Byzantines must observe how rarely we are indulged with such precious details.*]

[Footnote 4: Monoi gar apantwn anqrwpwn onomastotatoi basileuV kai jilosojoV, (Greg. Acropol. c. 32.) *The emperor, in a familiar conversation, examined and encouraged the studies of his future logothete.*]

[Footnote 499: Sister of Manfred, afterwards king of Naples. Nic. Greg. p. 45—M.]

[Footnote 5: Compare Acropolita, (c. 18, 52,) and the two first books of Nicephorus Gregoras.]

A strong shade of degeneracy is visible between John Vataces and his son Theodore; between the founder who sustained the weight, and the heir who enjoyed the splendor, of the Imperial crown. [6] Yet the character of Theodore was not devoid of energy; he had been educated in the school of his father, in the exercise of war and hunting; Constantinople was yet spared; but in the three years of a short reign, he thrice led his armies into the heart of Bulgaria. His virtues were sullied by a choleric and suspicious temper: the first of these may be ascribed to the ignorance of control; and the second might naturally arise from a dark and imperfect view of the corruption of mankind. On a march in Bulgaria, he consulted on a question of policy his principal ministers; and the Greek logothete, George Acropolita, presumed to offend him by the declaration of a free and honest opinion. The emperor half unsheathed his cimeter; but his more deliberate rage reserved Acropolita for a baser punishment. One of the first officers of the empire was ordered to dismount, stripped of his robes, and extended on the ground in the presence of the prince and army. In this posture he was chastised with so many and such heavy blows from the clubs of two guards or executioners, that when Theodore commanded them to cease, the great logothete was scarcely able to rise and crawl away to his tent. After a seclusion of some days, he was recalled by a peremptory mandate to his seat in council; and so dead were the Greeks to the sense of honor and shame, that it is from the narrative of the sufferer himself that we acquire the knowledge of his disgrace. [7] The cruelty of the emperor was exasperated by the pangs of sickness, the approach of a premature end, and the suspicion of poison and magic. The lives and fortunes, the eyes and limbs, of his kinsmen and nobles, were sacrificed to each sally of passion; and before he died, the son of Vataces might deserve from the people, or at least from the court, the appellation of tyrant. A matron of the family of the Palæologi had provoked his anger by refusing to bestow her beauteous daughter on the vile plebeian who was recommended by his caprice. Without regard to her birth or age, her body, as high as the neck, was enclosed in a sack with several cats, who were pricked with pins to irritate their fury against their unfortunate fellow-captive. In his last hours the emperor testified a wish to forgive and be forgiven, a just anxiety for the fate of John his son and successor, who, at the age of eight years, was condemned to the dangers of a long minority. His last choice intrusted the office of guardian to the sanctity of the patriarch Arsenius, and to the courage of George Muzalon, the great domestic, who was equally distinguished by the royal favor and the public hatred. Since their connection with the Latins, the names and privileges of hereditary rank had insinuated themselves into the Greek monarchy; and the noble families [8] were provoked by the elevation of a worthless favorite, to whose influence they imputed the errors and calamities of the late reign. In the first council, after the emperor's death, Muzalon, from a lofty throne, pronounced a labored apology of his conduct and intentions: his modesty was subdued by a unanimous assurance of esteem and fidelity; and his most inveterate enemies were the loudest to salute him as the guardian and savior of the Romans. Eight days were sufficient to prepare the execution of the conspiracy. On the ninth, the obsequies of the deceased monarch were solemnized in the cathedral of Magnesia, [9] an Asiatic city, where he expired, on the banks of the Hermus, and at the foot of Mount Sipylus. The holy rites were interrupted by a sedition of the guards; Muzalon, his brothers, and his adherents, were massacred at the foot of the altar; and the absent patriarch was associated with a new colleague, with Michael Palæologus, the most illustrious, in birth and merit, of the Greek nobles. [10]

[Footnote 6: A Persian saying, that Cyrus was the father and Darius the master, of his subjects, was applied to Vataces and his son. But Pachymer (l. i. c. 23) has mistaken the mild Darius for the cruel Cambyses, despot or tyrant of his people. By the institution of taxes, Darius had incurred the less odious, but more contemptible, name of KaphloV, merchant or broker, (Herodotus, iii. 89.)]

[Footnote 7: Acropolita (c. 63) seems to admire his own firmness in sustaining a beating, and not returning to council till he was called. He relates the exploits of Theodore, and his own services, from c. 53 to c. 74 of his history. See the third book of Nicephorus Gregoras.]

[Footnote 8: Pachymer (l. i. c. 21) names and discriminates fifteen or twenty Greek families, kai osoi alloi, oiV h megalogenhV seira kai crush sugkekrothto. Does he mean, by this decoration, a figurative or a real golden chain? Perhaps, both.]

[Footnote 9: The old geographers, with Cellarius and D'Anville, and our travellers, particularly Pocock and Chandler, will teach us to distinguish the two Magnesias of Asia Minor, of the Mæander and of Sipylus. The latter, our present object, is still flourishing for a Turkish city, and lies eight hours, or leagues, to the north-east of Smyrna, (Tournefort, Voyage du Levant, tom. iii. lettre xxii. p. 365—370. Chandler's Travels into Asia Minor, p. 267.)]

[Footnote 10: See Acropolita, (c. 75, 76, &c.,) who lived too near the times; Pachymer, (l. i. c. 13—25,) Gregoras, (l. iii. c. 3, 4, 5.)]

Of those who are proud of their ancestors, the far greater part must be content with local or domestic renown; and few there are who dare trust the memorials of their family to the public annals of their country. As early as the middle of the eleventh century, the noble race of the Palæologi [11] stands high and conspicuous in the Byzantine history: it was the valiant George Palæologus who placed the father of the Comneni on the throne; and his kinsmen or descendants continue, in each generation, to lead the armies and councils of the state. The purple was not dishonored by their alliance, and had the law of succession, and female succession, been strictly observed, the wife of Theodore Lascaris must have yielded to her elder sister, the mother of Michael Palæologus, who afterwards raised his family to the throne. In his person, the splendor of birth was dignified by the merit of the soldier and statesman: in his early youth he was promoted to the office of constable or commander of the French mercenaries; the private expense of a day never exceeded three pieces of gold; but his ambition was rapacious and profuse; and his gifts were doubled by the graces of his conversation and manners. The love of the soldiers and people excited the jealousy of the court, and Michael thrice escaped from the dangers in which he was involved by his own imprudence or that of his friends. I. Under the reign of Justice and Vataces, a dispute arose [12] between two officers, one of whom accused the other of maintaining the hereditary right of the Palæologi The cause was decided, according to the new jurisprudence of the Latins, by single combat; the defendant was overthrown; but he persisted in declaring that himself alone was guilty; and that he had uttered these rash or treasonable speeches without the approbation or knowledge of his patron Yet a cloud of suspicion hung over the innocence of the constable; he was still pursued by the whispers of malevolence; and a subtle courtier, the archbishop of Philadelphia, urged him to accept the judgment of God in the fiery proof of the ordeal. [13] Three days before the trial, the patient's arm was enclosed in a bag, and secured by the royal signet; and it was incumbent on him to bear a red-hot ball of iron three times from the altar to the rails of the sanctuary, without artifice and without injury. Palæologus eluded the dangerous experiment with sense and pleasantry. "I am a soldier," said he, "and will boldly enter the lists with my accusers; but a layman, a sinner like myself, is not endowed with the gift of miracles. Your piety, most holy prelate, may deserve the interposition of Heaven, and from your hands I will receive the fiery globe, the pledge of my innocence." The archbishop started; the emperor smiled; and the absolution or pardon of Michael was approved by new rewards and new services. II. In the succeeding reign, as he held the government of Nice, he was secretly informed, that the mind of the absent prince was poisoned with jealousy; and that death, or blindness, would be his final reward. Instead of awaiting the return and sentence of Theodore, the constable, with some followers, escaped from the city and the empire; and though he was plundered by the Turkmans of the desert, he found a hospitable refuge in the court of the sultan. In the ambiguous state of an exile, Michael reconciled the duties of gratitude and loyalty: drawing his sword against the Tartars; admonishing the garrisons of the Roman limit; and promoting, by his influence, the restoration of peace, in which his pardon and recall were honorably included. III. While he guarded the West against the despot of Epirus, Michael was again suspected and condemned in the palace; and such was his loyalty or weakness, that he submitted to be led in chains above six hundred miles from Durazzo to Nice. The civility of the messenger alleviated his disgrace; the emperor's sickness dispelled his danger; and the last breath of Theodore, which recommended his infant son, at once acknowledged the innocence and the power of Palæologus.

[Footnote 11: The pedigree of Palæologus is explained by Ducange, (Famil. Byzant. p. 230, &c.:) the events of his private life are related by Pachymer (l. i. c. 7—12) and Gregoras (l. ii. 8, l. iii. 2, 4, l. iv. 1) with visible favor to the father of the reigning dynasty.]

[Footnote 12: Acropolita (c. 50) relates the circumstances of this curious adventure, which seem to have escaped the more recent writers.]

[Footnote 13: Pachymer, (l. i. c. 12,) who speaks with proper contempt of this barbarous trial, affirms, that he had seen in his youth many person who had sustained, without injury, the fiery ordeal. As a Greek, he is credulous; but the ingenuity of the Greeks might furnish some remedies of art or fraud against their own superstition, or that of their tyrant.]

But his innocence had been too unworthily treated, and his power was too strongly felt, to curb an aspiring subject in the fair field that was opened to his ambition. [14] In the council, after the death of Theodore, he was the first to pronounce, and the first to violate, the oath of allegiance to Muzalon; and so dexterous was his conduct, that he reaped the benefit, without incurring the guilt, or at least the reproach, of the subsequent massacre. In the choice of a regent, he balanced the interests and passions of the candidates; turned their envy and hatred from himself against each other, and forced every competitor to own, that after his own claims, those of Palæologus were best entitled to the preference. Under the title of great duke, he accepted or assumed, during a long minority, the active powers of government; the patriarch was a venerable name; and the factious nobles were seduced, or oppressed, by the ascendant of his genius. The fruits of the economy of Vataces were deposited in a strong castle on the banks of the Hermus, in the custody of the faithful Varangians: the constable retained his command or influence over the foreign troops; he employed the guards to possess the treasure, and the treasure to corrupt the guards; and whatsoever might be the abuse of the public money, his character was above the suspicion of private avarice. By himself, or by his emissaries, he strove to persuade every rank of subjects, that their own prosperity would rise in just proportion to the establishment of his authority. The weight of taxes was suspended, the perpetual theme of popular complaint; and he prohibited the trials by the ordeal and judicial combat. These Barbaric institutions were already abolished or undermined in France [15] and England; [16] and the appeal to the sword offended the sense of a civilized, [17] and the temper of an unwarlike, people. For the future maintenance of their wives and children, the veterans were grateful: the priests and the philosophers applauded his ardent zeal for the advancement of religion and learning; and his vague promise of rewarding merit was applied by every candidate to his own hopes. Conscious of the influence of the clergy, Michael successfully labored to secure the suffrage of that powerful order. Their expensive journey from Nice to Magnesia, afforded a decent and ample pretence: the leading prelates were tempted by the liberality of his nocturnal visits; and the incorruptible patriarch was flattered by the homage of his new colleague, who led his mule by the bridle into the town, and removed to a respectful distance the importunity of the crowd. Without renouncing his title by royal descent, Palæologus encouraged a free discussion into the advantages of elective monarchy; and his adherents asked, with the insolence of triumph, what patient would trust his health, or what merchant would abandon his vessel, to the hereditary skill of a physician or a pilot? The youth of the emperor, and the impending dangers of a minority, required the support of a mature and experienced guardian; of an associate raised above the envy of his equals, and invested with the name and prerogatives of royalty. For the interest of the prince and people, without any selfish views for himself or his family, the great duke consented to guard and instruct the son of Theodore; but he sighed for the happy moment when he might restore to his firmer hands the administration of his patrimony, and enjoy the blessings of a private station. He was first invested with the title and prerogatives of despot, which bestowed the purple ornaments and the second place in the Roman monarchy. It was afterwards agreed that John and Michael should be proclaimed as joint emperors, and raised on the buckler, but that the preeminence should be reserved for the birthright of the former. A mutual league of amity was pledged between the royal partners; and in case of a rupture, the subjects were bound, by their oath of allegiance, to declare themselves against the aggressor; an ambiguous name, the seed of discord and civil war. Palæologus was content; but, on the day of the coronation, and in the cathedral of Nice, his zealous adherents most vehemently urged the just priority of his age and merit. The unseasonable dispute was eluded by postponing to a more convenient opportunity the coronation of John Lascaris; and he walked with a slight diadem in the train of his guardian, who alone received the Imperial crown from the hands of the patriarch. It was not without extreme reluctance that Arsenius abandoned the cause of his pupil; out the Varangians brandished their battle-axes; a sign of assent was extorted from the trembling youth; and some voices were heard, that the life of a child should no longer impede the settlement of the nation. A full harvest of honors and employments was distributed among his friends by the grateful Palæologus. In his own family he created a despot and two sebastocrators; Alexius Strategopulus was decorated with the title of Cæsar; and that veteran commander soon repaid the obligation, by restoring Constantinople to the Greek emperor.

[Footnote 14: Without comparing Pachymer to Thucydides or Tacitus, I will praise his narrative, (l. i. c. 13—32, l. ii. c. 1—9,) which pursues the ascent of Palæologus with eloquence, perspicuity, and tolerable freedom. Acropolita is more cautious, and Gregoras more concise.]

[Footnote 15: The judicial combat was abolished by St. Louis in his own territories; and his example and authority were at length prevalent in France, (Esprit des Loix, l. xxviii. c. 29.)]

[Footnote 16: In civil cases Henry II. gave an option to the defendant: Glanville prefers the proof by evidence; and that by judicial combat is reprobated in the Fleta. Yet the trial by battle has never been abrogated in the English law, and it was ordered by the judges as late as the beginning of the last century. Note : And even demanded in the present—M.]

[Footnote 17: Yet an ingenious friend has urged to me in mitigation of this practice, 1. That in nations emerging from barbarism, it moderates the license of private war and arbitrary revenge. 2. That it is less absurd than the trials by the ordeal, or boiling water, or the cross, which it has contributed to abolish. 3. That it served at least as a test of personal courage; a quality so seldom united with a base disposition, that the danger of a trial might be some check to a malicious prosecutor, and a useful barrier against injustice supported by power. The gallant and unfortunate earl of Surrey might probably have escaped his unmerited fate, had not his demand of the combat against his accuser been overruled.]

It was in the second year of his reign, while he resided in the palace and gardens of Nymphæum, [18] near Smyrna, that the first messenger arrived at the dead of night; and the stupendous intelligence was imparted to Michael, after he had been gently waked by the tender precaution of his sister Eulogia. The man was unknown or obscure; he produced no letters from the victorious Cæsar; nor could it easily be credited, after the defeat of Vataces and the recent failure of Palæologus himself, that the capital had been surprised by a detachment of eight hundred soldiers. As a hostage, the doubtful author was confined, with the assurance of death or an ample recompense; and the court was left some hours in the anxiety of hope and fear, till the messengers of Alexius arrived with the authentic intelligence, and displayed the trophies of the conquest, the sword and sceptre, [19] the buskins and bonnet, [20] of the usurper Baldwin, which he had dropped in his precipitate flight. A general assembly of the bishops, senators, and nobles, was immediately convened, and never perhaps was an event received with more heartfelt and universal joy. In a studied oration, the new sovereign of Constantinople congratulated his own and the public fortune. "There was a time," said he, "a far distant time, when the Roman empire extended to the Adriatic, the Tigris, and the confines of Æthiopia. After the loss of the provinces, our capital itself, in these last and calamitous days, has been wrested from our hands by the Barbarians of the West. From the lowest ebb, the tide of prosperity has again returned in our favor; but our prosperity was that of fugitives and exiles: and when we were asked, which was the country of the Romans, we indicated with a blush the climate of the globe, and the quarter of the heavens. The divine Providence has now restored to our arms the city of Constantine, the sacred seat of religion and empire; and it will depend on our valor and conduct to render this important acquisition the pledge and omen of future victories." So eager was the impatience of the prince and people, that Michael made his triumphal entry into Constantinople only twenty days after the expulsion of the Latins. The golden gate was thrown open at his approach; the devout conqueror dismounted from his horse; and a miraculous image of Mary the Conductress was borne before him, that the divine Virgin in person might appear to conduct him to the temple of her Son, the cathedral of St. Sophia. But after the first transport of devotion and pride, he sighed at the dreary prospect of solitude and ruin. The palace was defiled with smoke and dirt, and the gross intemperance of the Franks; whole streets had been consumed by fire, or were decayed by the injuries of time; the sacred and profane edifices were stripped of their ornaments: and, as if they were conscious of their approaching exile, the industry of the Latins had been confined to the work of pillage and destruction. Trade had expired under the pressure of anarchy and distress, and the numbers of inhabitants had decreased with the opulence of the city. It was the first care of the Greek monarch to reinstate the nobles in the palaces of their fathers; and the houses or the ground which they occupied were restored to the families that could exhibit a legal right of inheritance. But the far greater part was extinct or lost; the vacant property had devolved to the lord; he repeopled Constantinople by a liberal invitation to the provinces; and the brave volunteers were seated in the capital which had been recovered by their arms. The French barons and the principal families had retired with their emperor; but the patient and humble crowd of Latins was attached to the country, and indifferent to the change of masters. Instead of banishing the factories of the Pisans, Venetians, and Genoese, the prudent conqueror accepted their oaths of allegiance, encouraged their industry, confirmed their privileges, and allowed them to live under the jurisdiction of their proper magistrates. Of these nations, the Pisans and

Venetians preserved their respective quarters in the city; but the services and power of the Genoese deserved at the same time the gratitude and the jealousy of the Greeks. Their independent colony was first planted at the seaport town of Heraclea in Thrace. They were speedily recalled, and settled in the exclusive possession of the suburb of Galata, an advantageous post, in which they revived the commerce, and insulted the majesty, of the Byzantine empire. [21]

[Footnote 18: The site of Nymphæum is not clearly defined in ancient or modern geography. But from the last hours of Vataces, (Acropolita, c. 52,) it is evident the palace and gardens of his favorite residence were in the neighborhood of Smyrna. Nymphæum might be loosely placed in Lydia, (Gregoras, l. vi. 6.)]

[Footnote 19: This sceptre, the emblem of justice and power, was a long staff, such as was used by the heroes in Homer. By the latter Greeks it was named Dicanice, and the Imperial sceptre was distinguished as usual by the red or purple color.]

[Footnote 20: Acropolita affirms (c. 87,) that this "Onnet" was after the French fashion; but from the ruby at the point or summit, Ducange (Hist. de C. P. l. v. c. 28, 29) believes that it was the high-crowned hat of the Greeks. Could Acropolita mistake the dress of his own court?]

[Footnote 21: See Pachymer, (l. ii. c. 28—33,) Acropolita, (c. 88,) Nicephorus Gregoras, (l. iv. 7,) and for the treatment of the subject Latins, Ducange, (l. v. c. 30, 31.)]

The recovery of Constantinople was celebrated as the æra of a new empire: the conqueror, alone, and by the right of the sword, renewed his coronation in the church of St. Sophia; and the name and honors of John Lascaris, his pupil and lawful sovereign, were insensibly abolished. But his claims still lived in the minds of the people; and the royal youth must speedily attain the years of manhood and ambition. By fear or conscience, Palæologus was restrained from dipping his hands in innocent and royal blood; but the anxiety of a usurper and a parent urged him to secure his throne by one of those imperfect crimes so familiar to the modern Greeks. The loss of sight incapacitated the young prince for the active business of the world; instead of the brutal violence of tearing out his eyes, the visual nerve was destroyed by the intense glare of a red-hot basin, [22] and John Lascaris was removed to a distant castle, where he spent many years in privacy and oblivion. Such cool and deliberate guilt may seem incompatible with remorse; but if Michael could trust the mercy of Heaven, he was not inaccessible to the reproaches and vengeance of mankind, which he had provoked by cruelty and treason. His cruelty imposed on a servile court the duties of applause or silence; but the clergy had a right to speak in the name of their invisible Master; and their holy legions were led by a prelate, whose character was above the temptations of hope or fear. After a short abdication of his dignity, Arsenius [23] had consented to ascend the ecclesiastical throne of Constantinople, and to preside in the restoration of the church. His pious simplicity was long deceived by the arts of Palæologus; and his patience and submission might soothe the usurper, and protect the safety of the young prince. On the news of his inhuman treatment, the patriarch unsheathed the spiritual sword; and superstition, on this occasion, was enlisted in the cause of humanity and justice. In a synod of bishops, who were stimulated by the example of his zeal, the patriarch pronounced a sentence of excommunication; though his prudence still repeated the name of Michael in the public prayers. The Eastern prelates had not adopted the dangerous maxims of ancient Rome; nor did they presume to enforce their censures, by deposing princes, or absolving nations from their oaths of allegiance. But the Christian, who had been separated from God and the church, became an object of horror; and, in a turbulent and fanatic capital, that horror might arm the hand of an assassin, or inflame a sedition of the people. Palæologus felt his danger, confessed his guilt, and deprecated his judge: the act was irretrievable; the prize was obtained; and the most rigorous penance, which he solicited, would have raised the sinner to the reputation of a saint. The unrelenting patriarch refused to announce any means of atonement or any hopes of mercy; and condescended only to pronounce, that for so great a crime, great indeed must be the satisfaction. "Do you require," said Michael, "that I should abdicate the empire?" and at these words, he offered, or seemed to offer, the sword of state. Arsenius eagerly grasped this pledge of sovereignty; but when he perceived that the emperor was unwilling to purchase absolution at so dear a rate, he indignantly escaped to his cell, and left the royal sinner kneeling and weeping before the door. [24]

*[Footnote 22: This milder invention for extinguishing the sight was tried by the philosopher Democritus on himself, when he sought to withdraw his mind from the visible world: a foolish story! The word abacinare, in Latin and Italian, has furnished Ducange (Gloss. Lat.) with an opportunity to review the various modes of blinding: the more violent were scooping, burning with an iron, or hot vinegar, and binding the head with a strong cord till the eyes burst from their sockets. Ingenious tyrants!]*

*[Footnote 23: See the first retreat and restoration of Arsenius, in Pachymer (l. ii. c. 15, l. iii. c. 1, 2) and Nicephorus Gregoras, (l. iii. c. 1, l. iv. c. 1.) Posterity justly accused the ajeleia and raqumia of Arsenius the virtues of a hermit, the vices of a minister, (l. xii. c. 2.)]*

*[Footnote 24: The crime and excommunication of Michael are fairly told by Pachymer (l. iii. c. 10, 14, 19, &c.) and Gregoras, (l. iv. c. 4.) His confession and penance restored their freedom.]*


PART II

The danger and scandal of this excommunication subsisted above three years, till the popular clamor was assuaged by time and repentance; till the brethren of Arsenius condemned his inflexible spirit, so repugnant to the unbounded forgiveness of the gospel. The emperor had artfully insinuated, that, if he were still rejected at home, he might seek, in the Roman pontiff, a more indulgent judge; but it was far more easy and effectual to find or to place that judge at the head of the Byzantine church. Arsenius was involved in a vague rumor of conspiracy and disaffection; [24/1] some irregular steps in his ordination and government were liable to censure; a synod deposed him from the episcopal office; and he was transported under a guard of soldiers to a small island of the Propontis. Before his exile, he sullenly requested that a strict account might be taken of the treasures of the church; boasted, that his sole riches, three pieces of gold, had been earned by transcribing the psalms; continued to assert the freedom of his mind; and denied, with his last breath, the pardon which was implored by the royal sinner. [25] After some delay, Gregory, [25/1] bishop of Adrianople, was translated to the Byzantine throne; but his authority was found insufficient to support the absolution of the emperor; and Joseph, a reverend monk, was substituted to that important function. This edifying scene was represented in the presence of the senate and the people; at the end of six years the humble penitent was restored to the communion of the faithful; and humanity will rejoice, that a milder treatment of the captive Lascaris was stipulated as a proof of his remorse. But the spirit of Arsenius still survived in a powerful faction of the monks and clergy, who persevered about forty-eight years in an obstinate schism. Their scruples were treated with tenderness and respect by Michael and his son; and the reconciliation of the Arsenites was the serious labor of the church and state. In the confidence of fanaticism, they had proposed to try their cause by a miracle; and when the two papers, that contained their own and the adverse cause, were cast into a fiery brazier, they expected that the Catholic verity would be respected by the flames. Alas! the two papers were indiscriminately consumed, and this unforeseen accident produced the union of a day, and renewed the quarrel of an age. [26] The final treaty displayed the victory of the Arsenites: the clergy abstained during forty days from all ecclesiastical functions; a slight penance was imposed on the laity; the body of Arsenius was deposited in the sanctuary; and, in the name of the departed saint, the prince and people were released from the sins of their fathers. [27]

[Footnote 24/1: Except the omission of a prayer for the emperor, the charges against Arsenius were of different nature: he was accused of having allowed the sultan of Iconium to bathe in vessels signed with the cross, and to have admitted him to the church, though unbaptized, during the service. It was pleaded, in favor of Arsenius, among other proofs of the sultan's Christianity, that he had offered to eat ham. Pachymer, l. iv. c. 4, p. 265. It was after his exile that he was involved in a charge of conspiracy—M.]

[Footnote 25: Pachymer relates the exile of Arsenius, (l. iv. c. 1—16:) he was one of the commissaries who visited him in the desert island. The last testament of the unforgiving patriarch is still extant, (Dupin, Bibliothèque Ecclésiastique, tom. x. p. 95.)]

[Footnote 25/1: Pachymer calls him Germanus—M.]

[Footnote 26: Pachymer (l. vii. c. 22) relates this miraculous trial like a philosopher, and treats with similar contempt a plot of the Arsenites, to hide a revelation in the coffin of some old saint, (l. vii. c. 13.) He compensates this incredulity by an image that weeps, another that bleeds, (l. vii. c. 30,) and the miraculous cures of a deaf and a mute patient, (l. xi. c. 32.)]

[Footnote 27: The story of the Arsenites is spread through the thirteen books of Pachymer. Their union and triumph are reserved for Nicephorus Gregoras, (l. vii. c. 9,) who neither loves nor esteems these sectaries.]

The establishment of his family was the motive, or at least the pretence, of the crime of Palæologus; and he was impatient to confirm the succession, by sharing with his eldest son the honors of the purple. Andronicus, afterwards surnamed the Elder, was proclaimed and crowned emperor of the Romans, in the fifteenth year of his age; and, from the first æra of a prolix and inglorious reign, he held that august title nine years as the colleague, and fifty as the successor, of his father. Michael himself, had he died in a private station, would have been thought more worthy of the empire; and the assaults of his temporal and spiritual enemies left him few moments to labor for his own fame or the happiness of his subjects. He wrested from the Franks several of the noblest islands of the Archipelago, Lesbos, Chios, and Rhodes: his brother Constantine was sent to command in Malvasia and Sparta; and the eastern side of the Morea, from Argos and Napoli to Cape Thinners, was repossessed by the Greeks. This effusion of Christian blood was loudly condemned by the patriarch; and the insolent priest presumed to interpose his fears and scruples between the arms of princes. But in the prosecution of these western conquests, the countries beyond the Hellespont were left naked to the Turks; and their depredations verified the prophecy of a dying senator, that the recovery of Constantinople would be the ruin of Asia. The victories of Michael were achieved by his lieutenants; his sword rusted in the palace; and, in the transactions of the emperor with the popes and the king of Naples, his political acts were stained with cruelty and fraud. [28]

[Footnote 28: Of the xiii books of Pachymer, the first six (as the ivth and vth of Nicephorus Gregoras) contain the reign of Michael, at the time of whose death he was forty years of age. Instead of breaking, *like his editor the Père Poussin, his history into two parts, I follow Ducange and Cousin, who number the xiii. books in one series.]*

I. The Vatican was the most natural refuge of a Latin emperor, who had been driven from his throne; and Pope Urban the Fourth appeared to pity the misfortunes, and vindicate the cause, of the fugitive Baldwin. A crusade, with plenary indulgence, was preached by his command against the schismatic Greeks: he excommunicated their allies and adherents; solicited Louis the Ninth in favor of his kinsman; and demanded a tenth of the ecclesiastical revenues of France and England for the service of the holy war. [29] The subtle Greek, who watched the rising tempest of the West, attempted to suspend or soothe the hostility of the pope, by suppliant embassies and respectful letters; but he insinuated that the establishment of peace must prepare the reconciliation and obedience of the Eastern church. The Roman court could not be deceived by so gross an artifice; and Michael was admonished, that the repentance of the son should precede the forgiveness of the father; and that faith (an ambiguous word) was the only basis of friendship and alliance. After a long and affected delay, the approach of danger, and the importunity of Gregory the Tenth, compelled him to enter on a more serious negotiation: he alleged the example of the great Vataces; and the Greek clergy, who understood the intentions of their prince, were not alarmed by the first steps of reconciliation and respect. But when he pressed the conclusion of the treaty, they strenuously declared, that the Latins, though not in name, were heretics in fact, and that they despised those strangers as the vilest and most despicable portion of the human race. [30] It was the task of the emperor to persuade, to corrupt, to intimidate the most popular ecclesiastics, to gain the vote of each individual, and alternately to urge the arguments of Christian charity and the public welfare. The texts of the fathers and the arms of the Franks were balanced in the theological and political scale; and without approving the addition to the Nicene creed, the most moderate were taught to confess, that the two hostile propositions of proceeding from the Father by the Son, and of proceeding from the Father and the Son, might be reduced to a safe and Catholic sense. [31] The supremacy of the pope was a doctrine more easy to conceive, but more painful to acknowledge: yet Michael represented to his monks and prelates, that they might submit to name the Roman bishop as the first of the patriarchs; and that their distance and discretion would guard the liberties of the Eastern church from the mischievous consequences of the right of appeal. He protested that he would sacrifice his life and empire rather than yield the smallest point of orthodox faith or national independence; and this declaration was sealed and ratified by a golden bull. The patriarch Joseph withdrew to a monastery, to resign or resume his throne, according to the event of the treaty: the letters of union and obedience were subscribed by the emperor, his son Andronicus, and thirty-five archbishops and metropolitans, with their respective synods; and the episcopal list was multiplied by many dioceses which were annihilated under the yoke of the infidels. An embassy was composed of some trusty ministers and prelates: they embarked for Italy, with rich ornaments and rare perfumes for the altar of St. Peter; and their secret orders authorized and recommended a boundless compliance. They were received in the general council of Lyons, by Pope Gregory the Tenth, at the head of five hundred bishops. [32] He embraced with tears his long-lost and repentant children; accepted the oath of the ambassadors, who abjured the schism in the name of the two emperors; adorned the prelates with the ring and mitre; chanted in Greek and Latin the Nicene creed with the addition of filioque; and rejoiced in the union of the East and West, which had been reserved for his reign. To consummate this pious work, the Byzantine deputies were speedily followed by the pope's nuncios; and their instruction discloses the policy of the Vatican, which could not be satisfied with the vain title of supremacy. After viewing the temper of the prince and people, they were enjoined to absolve the schismatic clergy, who should subscribe and swear their abjuration and obedience; to establish in all the churches the use of the perfect creed; to prepare the entrance of a cardinal legate, with the full powers and dignity of his office; and to instruct the emperor in the advantages which he might derive from the temporal protection of the Roman pontiff. [33]

[Footnote 29: Ducange, Hist. de C. P. l. v. c. 33, &c., from the Epistles of Urban IV.]

[Footnote 30: From their mercantile intercourse with the Venetians and Genoese, they branded the Latins as kaphloi and banausoi, (Pachymer, l. v. c. 10.) "Some are heretics in name; others, like the Latins, in fact," said the learned Veccus, (l. v. c. 12,) who soon afterwards became a convert (c. 15, 16) and a patriarch, (c. 24.)]

[Footnote 31: In this class we may place Pachymer himself, whose copious and candid narrative occupies the vth and vith books of his history. Yet the Greek is silent on the council of Lyons, and seems to believe that the popes always resided in Rome and Italy, (l. v. c. 17, 21.)]

[Footnote 32: See the acts of the council of Lyons in the year 1274. Fleury, Hist. Ecclésiastique, tom. xviii. p. 181—199. Dupin, Bibliot. Ecclés. tom. x. p. 135.]

[Footnote 33: This curious instruction, which has been drawn with more or less honesty by Wading and Leo Allatius from the archives of the Vatican, is given in an abstract or version by Fleury, (tom. xviii. p. 252—258.)]

But they found a country without a friend, a nation in which the names of Rome and Union were pronounced with abhorrence. The patriarch Joseph was indeed removed: his place was filled by Veccus, an ecclesiastic of learning and moderation; and the emperor was still urged by the same motives, to persevere in the same professions. But in his private language Palæologus affected to deplore the pride, and to blame the innovations, of the Latins; and while he debased his character by this double hypocrisy, he justified and punished the opposition of his subjects. By the joint suffrage of the new and the ancient Rome, a sentence of excommunication was pronounced against the obstinate schismatics; the censures of the church were executed by the sword of Michael; on the failure of persuasion, he tried the arguments of prison and exile, of whipping and mutilation; those touchstones, says an historian, of cowards and the brave. Two Greeks still reigned in Ætolia, Epirus, and Thessaly, with the appellation of despots: they had yielded to the sovereign of Constantinople, but they rejected the chains of the Roman pontiff, and supported their refusal by successful arms. Under their protection, the fugitive monks and bishops assembled in hostile synods; and retorted the name of heretic with the galling addition of apostate: the prince of Trebizond was tempted to assume the forfeit title of emperor; [33/1] and even the Latins of Negropont, Thebes, Athens, and the Morea, forgot the merits of the convert, to join, with open or clandestine aid, the enemies of Palæologus. His favorite generals, of his own blood, and family, successively deserted, or betrayed, the sacrilegious trust. His sister Eulogia, a niece, and two female cousins, conspired against him; another niece, Mary queen of Bulgaria, negotiated his ruin with the sultan of Egypt; and, in the public eye, their treason was consecrated as the most sublime virtue. [34] To the pope's nuncios, who urged the consummation of the work, Palæologus exposed a naked recital of all that he had done and suffered for their sake. They were assured that the guilty sectaries, of both sexes and every rank, had been deprived of their honors, their fortunes, and their liberty; a spreading list of confiscation and punishment, which involved many persons, the dearest to the emperor, or the best deserving of his favor. They were conducted to the prison, to behold four princes of the royal blood chained in the four corners, and shaking their fetters in an agony of grief and rage. Two of these captives were afterwards released; the one by submission, the other by death: but the obstinacy of their two companions was chastised by the loss of their eyes; and the Greeks, the least adverse to the union, deplored that cruel and inauspicious tragedy. [35] Persecutors must expect the hatred of those whom they oppress; but they commonly find some consolation in the testimony of their conscience, the applause of their party, and, perhaps, the success of their undertaking. But the hypocrisy of Michael, which was prompted only by political motives, must have forced him to hate himself, to despise his followers, and to esteem and envy the rebel champions by whom he was detested and despised. While his violence was abhorred at Constantinople, at Rome his slowness was arraigned, and his sincerity suspected; till at length Pope Martin the Fourth excluded the Greek emperor from the pale of a church, into which he was striving to reduce a schismatic people. No sooner had the tyrant expired, than the union was dissolved, and abjured by unanimous consent; the churches were purified; the penitents were reconciled; and his son Andronicus, after weeping the sins and errors of his youth most piously denied his father the burial of a prince and a Christian. [36]

[Footnote 33/1: According to Fallmarayer he had always maintained this title—M.]

[Footnote 34: This frank and authentic confession of Michael's distress is exhibited in barbarous Latin by Ogerius, who signs himself Protonotarius Interpretum, and transcribed by Wading from the MSS. of the Vatican, (A.D. 1278, No. 3.) His annals of the Franciscan order, the Fratres Minores, in xvii. volumes in folio, (Rome, 1741,) I have now accidentally seen among the waste paper of a bookseller.]

[Footnote 35: See the vith book of Pachymer, particularly the chapters 1, 11, 16, 18, 24—27. He is the more credible, as he speaks of this persecution with less anger than sorrow.]

[Footnote 36: Pachymer, l. vii. c. 1—ii. 17. The speech of Andronicus the Elder (lib. xii. c. 2) is a curious record, which proves that if the Greeks were the slaves of the emperor, the emperor was not less the slave of superstition and the clergy.]

II. In the distress of the Latins, the walls and towers of Constantinople had fallen to decay: they were restored and fortified by the policy of Michael, who deposited a plenteous store of corn and salt provisions, to sustain the siege which he might hourly expect from the resentment of the Western powers. Of these, the sovereign of the Two Sicilies was the most formidable neighbor: but as long as they were possessed by Mainfroy, the bastard of Frederic the Second, his monarchy was the bulwark, rather than the annoyance, of the Eastern empire. The usurper, though a brave and active prince, was sufficiently employed in the defence of his throne: his proscription by successive popes had separated Mainfroy from the common cause of the Latins; and the forces that might have besieged Constantinople were detained in a crusade against the domestic enemy of Rome. The prize of her avenger, the crown of the Two Sicilies, was won and worn by the brother of St Louis, by Charles count of Anjou and Provence, who led the chivalry of France on this holy expedition. [37] The disaffection of his Christian subjects compelled Mainfroy to enlist a colony of Saracens whom his father had planted in Apulia; and this odious succor will explain the defiance of the Catholic hero, who rejected all terms of accommodation. "Bear this message," said Charles, "to the sultan of Nocera, that God and the sword are umpire between us; and that he shall either send me to paradise, or I will send him to the pit of hell." The armies met: and though I am ignorant of Mainfroy's doom in the other world, in this he lost his friends, his kingdom, and his life, in the bloody battle of Benevento. Naples and Sicily were immediately peopled with a warlike race of French nobles; and their aspiring leader embraced the future conquest of Africa, Greece, and Palestine. The most specious reasons might point his first arms against the Byzantine empire; and Palæologus, diffident of his own strength, repeatedly appealed from the ambition of Charles to the humanity of St. Louis, who still preserved a just ascendant over the mind of his ferocious brother. For a while the attention of that brother was confined at home by the invasion of Conradin, the last heir to the imperial house of Swabia; but the hapless boy sunk in the unequal conflict; and his execution on a public scaffold taught the rivals of Charles to tremble for their heads as well as their dominions. A second respite was obtained by the last crusade of St. Louis to the African coast; and the double motive of interest and duty urged the king of Naples to assist, with his powers and his presence, the holy enterprise. The death of St. Louis released him from the importunity of a virtuous censor: the king of Tunis confessed himself the tributary and vassal of the crown of Sicily; and the boldest of the French knights were free to enlist under his banner against the Greek empire. A treaty and a marriage united his interest with the house of Courtenay; his daughter Beatrice was promised to Philip, son and heir of the emperor Baldwin; a pension of six hundred ounces of gold was allowed for his maintenance; and his generous father distributed among his aliens the kingdoms and provinces of the East, reserving only Constantinople, and one day's journey round the city for the imperial domain. [38] In this perilous moment, Palæologus was the most eager to subscribe the creed, and implore the protection, of the Roman pontiff, who assumed, with propriety and weight, the character of an angel of peace, the common father of the Christians. By his voice, the sword of Charles was chained in the scabbard; and the Greek ambassadors beheld him, in the pope's antechamber, biting his ivory sceptre in a transport of fury, and deeply resenting the refusal to enfranchise and consecrate his arms. He appears to have respected the disinterested mediation of Gregory the Tenth; but Charles was insensibly disgusted by the pride and partiality of Nicholas the Third; and his attachment to his kindred, the Ursini family, alienated the most strenuous champion from the service of the church. The hostile league against the Greeks, of Philip the Latin emperor, the king of the Two Sicilies, and the republic of Venice, was ripened into execution; and the election of Martin the Fourth, a French pope, gave a sanction to the cause. Of the allies, Philip supplied his name; Martin, a bull of excommunication; the Venetians, a squadron of forty galleys; and the formidable powers of Charles consisted of forty counts, ten thousand men at arms, a numerous body of infantry, and a fleet of more than three hundred ships and transports. A distant day was appointed for assembling this mighty force in the harbor of Brindisi; and a previous attempt was risked with a detachment of three hundred knights, who invaded Albania, and besieged the fortress of Belgrade. Their defeat might amuse with a triumph the vanity of Constantinople; but the more sagacious Michael, despairing of his arms, depended on the effects of a conspiracy; on the secret workings of a rat, who gnawed the bowstring [39] of the Sicilian tyrant.

[Footnote 37: The best accounts, the nearest the time, the most full and entertaining, of the conquest of Naples by Charles of Anjou, may be found in the Florentine Chronicles of Ricordano Malespina, (c. 175—193,) and Giovanni Villani, (l. vii. c. 1—10, 25—30,) which are published by Muratori in the viiith and xiiith volumes of the Historians of Italy. In his Annals (tom. xi. p. 56—72) he has abridged these great events which are likewise described in the Istoria Civile di Giannone. tom. l. xix. tom. iii. l. xx.]

[Footnote 38: Ducange, Hist. de C. P. l. v. c. 49—56, l. vi. c. 1—13. See Pachymer, l. iv. c. 29, l. v. c. 7—10, 25 l. vi. c. 30, 32, 33, and Nicephorus Gregoras, l. iv. 5, l. v. 1, 6.]

[Footnote 39: The reader of Herodotus will recollect how miraculously the Assyrian host of Sennacherib was disarmed and destroyed, (l. ii. c. 141.)]

Among the proscribed adherents of the house of Swabia, John of Procida forfeited a small island of that name in the Bay of Naples. His birth was noble, but his education was learned; and in the poverty of exile, he was relieved by the practice of physic, which he had studied in the school of Salerno. Fortune had left him nothing to lose, except life; and to despise life is the first qualification of a rebel. Procida was endowed with the art of negotiation, to enforce his reasons and disguise his motives; and in his various transactions with nations and men, he could persuade each party that he labored solely for their interest. The new kingdoms of Charles were afflicted by every species of fiscal and military oppression; [40] and the lives and fortunes of his Italian subjects were sacrificed to the greatness of their master and the licentiousness of his followers. The hatred of Naples was repressed by his presence; but the looser government of his vicegerents excited the contempt, as well as the aversion, of the Sicilians: the island was roused to a sense of freedom by the eloquence of Procida; and he displayed to every baron his private interest in the common cause. In the confidence of foreign aid, he successively visited the courts of the Greek emperor, and of Peter king of Arragon, [41] who possessed the maritime countries of Valentia and Catalonia. To the ambitious Peter a crown was presented, which he might justly claim by his marriage with the sister [41/2] of Mainfroy, and by the dying voice of Conradin, who from the scaffold had cast a ring to his heir and avenger. Palæologus was easily persuaded to divert his enemy from a foreign war by a rebellion at home; and a Greek subsidy of twenty-five thousand ounces of gold was most profitably applied to arm a Catalan fleet, which sailed under a holy banner to the specious attack of the Saracens of Africa. In the disguise of a monk or beggar, the indefatigable missionary of revolt flew from Constantinople to Rome, and from Sicily to Saragossa: the treaty was sealed with the signet of Pope Nicholas himself, the enemy of Charles; and his deed of gift transferred the fiefs of St. Peter from the house of Anjou to that of Arragon. So widely diffused and so freely circulated, the secret was preserved above two years with impenetrable discretion; and each of the conspirators imbibed the maxim of Peter, who declared that he would cut off his left hand if it were conscious of the intentions of his right. The mine was prepared with deep and dangerous artifice; but it may be questioned, whether the instant explosion of Palermo were the effect of accident or design.

*[Footnote 40: According to Sabas Malaspina, (Hist. Sicula, l. iii. c. 16, in Muratori, tom. viii. p. 832,) a zealous Guelph, the subjects of Charles, who had reviled Mainfroy as a wolf, began to regret him as a lamb; and he justifies their discontent by the oppressions of the French government, (l. vi. c. 2, 7.) See the Sicilian manifesto in Nicholas Specialis, (l. i. c. 11, in Muratori, tom. x. p. 930.)]*

*[Footnote 41: See the character and counsels of Peter, king of Arragon, in Mariana, (Hist. Hispan. l. xiv. c. 6, tom. ii. p. 133.) The reader forgives the Jesuit's defects, in favor, always of his style, and often of his sense.]*

*[Footnote 41/2: Daughter. See Hallam's Middle Ages, vol. i. p. 517—M.]*

On the vigil of Easter, a procession of the disarmed citizens visited a church without the walls; and a noble damsel was rudely insulted by a French soldier. [42] The ravisher was instantly punished with death; and if the people was at first scattered by a military force, their numbers and fury prevailed: the conspirators seized the opportunity; the flame spread over the island; and eight thousand French were exterminated in a promiscuous massacre, which has obtained the name of the Sicilian Vespers. [43] From every city the banners of freedom and the church were displayed: the revolt was inspired by the presence or the soul of Procida and Peter of Arragon, who sailed from the African coast to Palermo, was saluted as the king and savior of the isle. By the rebellion of a people on whom he had so long trampled with impunity, Charles was astonished and confounded; and in the first agony of grief and devotion, he was heard to exclaim, "O God! if thou hast decreed to humble me, grant me at least a gentle and gradual descent from the pinnacle of greatness!" His fleet and army, which already filled the seaports of Italy, were hastily recalled from the service of the Grecian war; and the situation of Messina exposed that town to the first storm of his revenge. Feeble in themselves, and yet hopeless of foreign succor, the citizens would have repented, and submitted on the assurance of full pardon and their ancient privileges. But the pride of the monarch was already rekindled; and the most fervent entreaties of the legate could extort no more than a promise, that he would forgive the remainder, after a chosen list of eight hundred rebels had been yielded to his discretion. The despair of the Messinese renewed their courage: Peter of Arragon approached to their relief; [44] and his rival was driven back by the failure of provision and the terrors of the equinox to the Calabrian shore. At the same moment, the Catalan admiral, the famous Roger de Loria, swept the channel with an invincible squadron: the French fleet, more numerous in transports than in galleys, was either burnt or destroyed; and the same blow assured the independence of Sicily and the safety of the Greek empire. A few days before his death, the emperor Michael rejoiced in the fall of an enemy whom he hated and esteemed; and perhaps he might be content with the popular judgment, that had they not been matched with each other, Constantinople and Italy must speedily have obeyed the same master. [45] From this disastrous moment, the life of Charles was a series of misfortunes: his capital was insulted, his son was made prisoner, and he sunk into the grave without recovering the Isle of Sicily, which, after a war of twenty years, was finally severed from the throne of Naples, and transferred, as an independent kingdom, to a younger branch of the house of Arragon. [46]

[Footnote 42: After enumerating the sufferings of his country, Nicholas Specialis adds, in the true spirit of Italian jealousy, Quæ omnia et graviora quidem, ut arbitror, patienti animo Siculi tolerassent, nisi (quod primum cunctis dominantibus cavendum est) alienas fminas invasissent, (l. i. c. 2, p. 924.)]

[Footnote 43: The French were long taught to remember this bloody lesson: "If I am provoked, (said Henry the Fourth,) I will breakfast at Milan, and dine at Naples." "Your majesty (replied the Spanish ambassador) may perhaps arrive in Sicily for vespers."]

[Footnote 44: This revolt, with the subsequent victory, are related by two national writers, Bartholemy à Neocastro (in Muratori, tom. xiii.,) and Nicholas Specialis (in Muratori, tom. x.,) the one a contemporary, the other of the next century. The patriot Specialis disclaims the name of rebellion, and all previous correspondence with Peter of Arragon, (nullo communicato consilio,) who happened to be with a fleet and army on the African coast, (l. i. c. 4, 9.)]

[Footnote 45: Nicephorus Gregoras (l. v. c. 6) admires the wisdom of Providence in this equal balance of states and princes. For the honor of Palæologus, I had rather this balance had been observed by an Italian writer.]

[Footnote 46: See the Chronicle of Villani, the xith volume of the Annali d'Italia of Muratori, and the xxth and xxist books of the Istoria Civile of Giannone.]


PART III

I shall not, I trust, be accused of superstition; but I must remark that, even in this world, the natural order of events will sometimes afford the strong appearances of moral retribution. The first Palæologus had saved his empire by involving the kingdoms of the West in rebellion and blood; and from these scenes of discord uprose a generation of iron men, who assaulted and endangered the empire of his son. In modern times our debts and taxes are the secret poison which still corrodes the bosom of peace: but in the weak and disorderly government of the middle ages, it was agitated by the present evil of the disbanded armies. Too idle to work, too proud to beg, the mercenaries were accustomed to a life of rapine: they could rob with more dignity and effect under a banner and a chief; and the sovereign, to whom their service was useless, and their presence importunate, endeavored to discharge the torrent on some neighboring countries. After the peace of Sicily, many thousands of Genoese, Catalans, [47] &c., who had fought, by sea and land, under the standard of Anjou or Arragon, were blended into one nation by the resemblance of their manners and interest. They heard that the Greek provinces of Asia were invaded by the Turks: they resolved to share the harvest of pay and plunder: and Frederic king of Sicily most liberally contributed the means of their departure. In a warfare of twenty years, a ship, or a camp, was become their country; arms were their sole profession and property; valor was the only virtue which they knew; their women had imbibed the fearless temper of their lovers and husbands: it was reported, that, with a stroke of their broadsword, the Catalans could cleave a horseman and a horse; and the report itself was a powerful weapon. Roger de Flor [47/1] was the most popular of their chiefs; and his personal merit overshadowed the dignity of his prouder rivals of Arragon. The offspring of a marriage between a German gentleman of the court of Frederic the Second and a damsel of Brindisi, Roger was successively a templar, an apostate, a pirate, and at length the richest and most powerful admiral of the Mediterranean. He sailed from Messina to Constantinople, with eighteen galleys, four great ships, and eight thousand adventurers; [47/2] and his previous treaty was faithfully accomplished by Andronicus the elder, who accepted with joy and terror this formidable succor. A palace was allotted for his reception, and a niece of the emperor was given in marriage to the valiant stranger, who was immediately created great duke or admiral of Romania. After a decent repose, he transported his troops over the Propontis, and boldly led them against the Turks: in two bloody battles thirty thousand of the Moslems were slain: he raised the siege of Philadelphia, and deserved the name of the deliverer of Asia. But after a short season of prosperity, the cloud of slavery and ruin again burst on that unhappy province. The inhabitants escaped (says a Greek historian) from the smoke into the flames; and the hostility of the Turks was less pernicious than the friendship of the Catalans. [47/3] The lives and fortunes which they had rescued they considered as their own: the willing or reluctant maid was saved from the race of circumcision for the embraces of a Christian soldier: the exaction of fines and supplies was enforced by licentious rapine and arbitrary executions; and, on the resistance of Magnesia, the great duke besieged a city of the Roman empire. [48] These disorders he excused by the wrongs and passions of a victorious army; nor would his own authority or person have been safe, had he dared to punish his faithful followers, who were defrauded of the just and covenanted price of their services. The threats and complaints of Andronicus disclosed the nakedness of the empire. His golden bull had invited no more than five hundred horse and a thousand foot soldiers; yet the crowds of volunteers, who migrated to the East, had been enlisted and fed by his spontaneous bounty. While his bravest allies were content with three byzants or pieces of gold, for their monthly pay, an ounce, or even two ounces, of gold were assigned to the Catalans, whose annual pension would thus amount to near a hundred pounds sterling: one of their chiefs had modestly rated at three hundred thousand crowns the value of his future merits; and above a million had been issued from the treasury for the maintenance of these costly mercenaries. A cruel tax had been imposed on the corn of the husbandman: one third was retrenched from the salaries of the public officers; and the standard of the coin was so shamefully debased, that of the four-and-twenty parts only five were of pure gold. [49] At the summons of the emperor, Roger evacuated a province which no longer supplied the materials of rapine; [49/1] but he refused to disperse his troops; and while his style was respectful, his conduct was independent and hostile. He protested, that if the emperor should march against him, he would advance forty paces to kiss the ground before him; but in rising from this prostrate attitude Roger had a life and sword at the service of his friends. The great duke of Romania condescended to accept the title and ornaments of Cæsar; but he rejected the new proposal of the government of Asia with a subsidy of corn and money, [49/2] on condition that he should reduce his troops to the harmless number of three thousand men. Assassination is the last resource of cowards. The Cæsar was tempted to visit the royal residence of Adrianople; in the apartment, and before the eyes, of the empress he was stabbed by the Alani guards; and though the deed was imputed to their private revenge, [49/3] his countrymen, who dwelt at

Constantinople in the security of peace, were involved in the same proscription by the prince or people. The loss of their leader intimidated the crowd of adventurers, who hoisted the sails of flight, and were soon scattered round the coasts of the Mediterranean. But a veteran band of fifteen hundred Catalans, or French, stood firm in the strong fortress of Gallipoli on the Hellespont, displayed the banners of Arragon, and offered to revenge and justify their chief, by an equal combat of ten or a hundred warriors. Instead of accepting this bold defiance, the emperor Michael, the son and colleague of Andronicus, resolved to oppress them with the weight of multitudes: every nerve was strained to form an army of thirteen thousand horse and thirty thousand foot; and the Propontis was covered with the ships of the Greeks and Genoese. In two battles by sea and land, these mighty forces were encountered and overthrown by the despair and discipline of the Catalans: the young emperor fled to the palace; and an insufficient guard of light-horse was left for the protection of the open country. Victory renewed the hopes and numbers of the adventures: every nation was blended under the name and standard of the great company; and three thousand Turkish proselytes deserted from the Imperial service to join this military association. In the possession of Gallipoli, [49/4] the Catalans intercepted the trade of Constantinople and the Black Sea, while they spread their devastation on either side of the Hellespont over the confines of Europe and Asia. To prevent their approach, the greatest part of the Byzantine territory was laid waste by the Greeks themselves: the peasants and their cattle retired into the city; and myriads of sheep and oxen, for which neither place nor food could be procured, were unprofitably slaughtered on the same day. Four times the emperor Andronicus sued for peace, and four times he was inflexibly repulsed, till the want of provisions, and the discord of the chiefs, compelled the Catalans to evacuate the banks of the Hellespont and the neighborhood of the capital. After their separation from the Turks, the remains of the great company pursued their march through Macedonia and Thessaly, to seek a new establishment in the heart of Greece. [50]

[Footnote 47: In this motley multitude, the Catalans and Spaniards, the bravest of the soldiery, were styled by themselves and the Greeks Amogavares. Moncada derives their origin from the Goths, and Pachymer (l. xi. c. 22) from the Arabs; and in spite of national and religious pride, I am afraid the latter is in the right.]

[Footnote 47/1: On Roger de Flor and his companions, see an historical fragment, detailed and interesting, entitled "The Spaniards of the Fourteenth Century," and inserted in "L'Espagne en 1808," a work translated from the German, vol. ii. p. 167. This narrative enables us to detect some slight errors which have crept into that of Gibbon—G.]

[Footnote 47/2: The troops of Roger de Flor, according to his companions Ramon de Montaner, were 1500 men at arms, 4000 Almogavares, and 1040 other foot, besides the sailors and mariners, vol. ii. p. 137—M.]

[Footnote 47/3: Ramon de Montaner suppresses the cruelties and oppressions of the Catalans, in which, perhaps, he shared—M.]

[Footnote 48: Some idea may be formed of the population of these cities, from the 36,000 inhabitants of Tralles, which, in the preceding reign, was rebuilt by the emperor, and ruined by the Turks. (Pachymer, l. vi. c. 20, 21.)]

[Footnote 49: I have collected these pecuniary circumstances from Pachymer, (l. xi. c. 21, l. xii. c. 4, 5, 8, 14, 19,) who describes the progressive degradation of the gold coin. Even in the prosperous times of John Ducas Vataces, the byzants were composed in equal proportions of the pure and the baser metal. The poverty of Michael Palæologus compelled him to strike a new coin, with nine parts, or carats, of gold, and fifteen of copper alloy. After his death, the standard rose to ten carats, till in the public distress it was reduced to the moiety. The prince was relieved for a moment, while credit and commerce were forever blasted. In France, the gold coin is of twenty-two carats, (one twelfth alloy,) and the standard of England and Holland is still higher.]

[Footnote 49/1]: Roger de Flor, according to Ramon de Montaner, was recalled from Natolia, on account of the war which had arisen on the death of Asan, king of Bulgaria. Andronicus claimed the kingdom for his nephew, the sons of Asan by his sister. Roger de Flor turned the tide of success in favor of the emperor of Constantinople and made peace—M.]

[Footnote 49/2: Andronicus paid the Catalans in the debased money, much to their indignation—M.]

[Footnote 49/3: According to Ramon de Montaner, he was murdered by order of Kyr (kurioV) Michael, son of the emperor. p. 170—M.]

[Footnote 49/4: Ramon de Montaner describes his sojourn at Gallipoli: Nous etions si riches, que nous ne semions, ni ne labourions, ni ne faisions enver des vins ni ne cultivions les vignes: et cependant tous les ans nous recucillions tour ce qu'il nous fallait, en vin, froment et avoine. p. 193. This lasted for five merry years. Ramon de Montaner is high authority, for he was "chancelier et maitre rational de l'armée," (commissary of rations.) He was left governor; all the scribes of the army remained with him, and with their aid he kept the books in which were registered the number of horse and foot employed on each expedition. According to this book the plunder was shared, of which he had a fifth for his trouble. p. 197—M.]

[Footnote 50: The Catalan war is most copiously related by Pachymer, in the xith, xiith, and xiiith books, till he breaks off in the year 1308. Nicephorus Gregoras (l. vii. 3—6) is more concise and complete. Ducange, who adopts these adventurers as French, has hunted their footsteps with his usual diligence, (Hist. de C. P. l. vi. c. 22—46.) He quotes an Arragonese history, which I have read with pleasure, and which the Spaniards extol as a model of style and composition, (Expedicion de los Catalanes y Arragoneses contra Turcos y Griegos: Barcelona, 1623 in quarto: Madrid, 1777, in octavo.) Don Francisco de Moncada Conde de Ossona, may imitate Cæsar or Sallust; he may transcribe the Greek or Italian contemporaries: but he never quotes his authorities, and I cannot discern any national records of the exploits of his countrymen. Note: Ramon de Montaner, one of the Catalans, who accompanied Roger de Flor, and who was governor of Gallipoli, has written, in Spanish, the history of this band of adventurers, to which he belonged, and from which he separated when it left the Thracian Chersonese to penetrate into Macedonia and Greece—G—The autobiography of Ramon de Montaner has been published in French by M. Buchon, in the great collection of Mémoires relatifs à l'Histoire de France. I quote this edition—M.]

After some ages of oblivion, Greece was awakened to new misfortunes by the arms of the Latins. In the two hundred and fifty years between the first and the last conquest of Constantinople, that venerable land was disputed by a multitude of petty tyrants; without the comforts of freedom and genius, her ancient cities were again plunged in foreign and intestine war; and, if servitude be preferable to anarchy, they might repose with joy under the Turkish yoke. I shall not pursue the obscure and various dynasties, that rose and fell on the continent or in the isles; but our silence on the fate of Athens [51] would argue a strange ingratitude to the first and purest school of liberal science and amusement. In the partition of the empire, the principality of Athens and Thebes was assigned to Otho de la Roche, a noble warrior of Burgundy, [52] with the title of great duke, [53] which the Latins understood in their own sense, and the Greeks more foolishly derived from the age of Constantine. [54] Otho followed the standard of the marquis of Montferrat: the ample state which he acquired by a miracle of conduct or fortune, [55] was peaceably inherited by his son and two grandsons, till the family, though not the nation, was changed, by the marriage of an heiress into the elder branch of the house of Brienne. The son of that marriage, Walter de Brienne, succeeded to the duchy of Athens; and, with the aid of some Catalan mercenaries, whom he invested with fiefs, reduced above thirty castles of the vassal or neighboring lords. But when he was informed of the approach and ambition of the great company, he collected a force of seven hundred knights, six thousand four hundred horse, and eight thousand foot, and boldly met them on the banks of the River Cephisus in Botia. The Catalans amounted to no more than three thousand five hundred horse, and four thousand foot; but the deficiency of numbers was compensated by stratagem and order. They formed round their camp an artificial inundation; the duke and his knights advanced without fear or precaution on the verdant meadow; their horses plunged into the bog; and he was cut in pieces, with the greatest part of the French cavalry. His family and nation were expelled; and his son Walter de Brienne, the titular duke of Athens, the tyrant of Florence, and the constable of France, lost his life in the field of Poitiers Attica and Botia were the rewards of the victorious Catalans; they married the widows and daughters of the slain; and during fourteen years, the great company was the terror of the Grecian states. Their factions drove them to acknowledge the sovereignty of the house of Arragon; and during the remainder of the fourteenth century, Athens, as a government or an appanage, was successively bestowed by the kings of Sicily. After the French and Catalans, the third dynasty was that of the Accaioli, a family, plebeian at Florence, potent at Naples, and sovereign in Greece. Athens, which they embellished with new buildings, became the capital of a state, that extended over Thebes, Argos, Corinth, Delphi, and a part of Thessaly; and their reign was finally determined by Mahomet the Second, who strangled the last duke, and educated his sons in the discipline and religion of the seraglio.

[Footnote 51: See the laborious history of Ducange, whose accurate table of the French dynasties recapitulates the thirty-five passages, in which he mentions the dukes of Athens.]

[Footnote 52: He is twice mentioned by Villehardouin with honor, (No. 151, 235;) and under the first passage, Ducange observes all that can be known of his person and family.]

[Footnote 53: From these Latin princes of the xivth century, Boccace, Chaucer. and Shakspeare, have borrowed their Theseus duke of Athens. An ignorant age transfers its own language and manners to the most distant times.]

[Footnote 54: The same Constantine gave to Sicily a king, to Russia the magnus dapifer of the empire, to Thebes the primicerius; and these absurd fables are properly lashed by Ducange, (ad Nicephor. Greg. l. vii. c. 5.) By the Latins, the lord of Thebes was styled, by corruption, the Megas Kurios, or Grand Sire!]

[Footnote 55: Quodam miraculo, says Alberic. He was probably received by Michael Choniates, the archbishop who had defended Athens against the tyrant Leo Sgurus, (Nicetas urbs capta, p. 805, ed. Bek.) Michael was the brother of the historian Nicetas; and his encomium of Athens is still extant in MS. in the Bodleian library, (Fabric. Bibliot. Græc tom. vi. p. 405.) Note: Nicetas says expressly that Michael surrendered the Acropolis to the marquis—M.]

Athens, [56] though no more than the shadow of her former self, still contains about eight or ten thousand inhabitants; of these, three fourths are Greeks in religion and language; and the Turks, who compose the remainder, have relaxed, in their intercourse with the citizens, somewhat of the pride and gravity of their national character. The olive-tree, the gift of Minerva, flourishes in Attica; nor has the honey of Mount Hymettus lost any part of its exquisite flavor: [57] but the languid trade is monopolized by strangers, and the agriculture of a barren land is abandoned to the vagrant Walachians. The Athenians are still distinguished by the subtlety and acuteness of their understandings; but these qualities, unless ennobled by freedom, and enlightened by study, will degenerate into a low and selfish cunning: and it is a proverbial saying of the country, "From the Jews of Thessalonica, the Turks of Negropont, and the Greeks of Athens, good Lord deliver us!" This artful people has eluded the tyranny of the Turkish bashaws, by an expedient which alleviates their servitude and aggravates their shame. About the middle of the last century, the Athenians chose for their protector the Kislar Aga, or chief black eunuch of the seraglio. This Æthiopian slave, who possesses the sultan's ear, condescends to accept the tribute of thirty thousand crowns: his lieutenant, the Waywode, whom he annually confirms, may reserve for his own about five or six thousand more; and such is the policy of the citizens, that they seldom fail to remove and punish an oppressive governor. Their private differences are decided by the archbishop, one of the richest prelates of the Greek church, since he possesses a revenue of one thousand pounds sterling; and by a tribunal of the eight geronti or elders, chosen in the eight quarters of the city: the noble families cannot trace their pedigree above three hundred years; but their principal members are distinguished by a grave demeanor, a fur cap, and the lofty appellation of archon. By some, who delight in the contrast, the modern language of Athens is represented as the most corrupt and barbarous of the seventy dialects of the vulgar Greek: [58] this picture is too darkly colored: but it would not be easy, in the country of Plato and Demosthenes, to find a reader or a copy of their works. The Athenians walk with supine indifference among the glorious ruins of antiquity; and such is the debasement of their character, that they are incapable of admiring the genius of their predecessors. [59]

[Footnote 56: The modern account of Athens, and the Athenians, is extracted from Spon, (Voyage en Grece, tom. ii. p. 79—199,) and Wheeler, (Travels into Greece, p. 337—414,) Stuart, (Antiquities of Athens, passim,) and Chandler, (Travels into Greece, p. 23—172.) The first of these travellers visited Greece in the year 1676; the last, 1765; and ninety years had not produced much difference in the tranquil scene.]

[Footnote 57: The ancients, or at least the Athenians, believed that all the bees in the world had been propagated from Mount Hymettus. They taught, that health might be preserved, and life prolonged, by the external use of oil, and the internal use of honey, (Geoponica, l. xv. c 7, p. 1089—1094, edit. Niclas.)]

[Footnote 58: Ducange, Glossar. Græc. Præfat. p. 8, who quotes for his author Theodosius Zygomalas, a modern grammarian. Yet Spon (tom. ii. p. 194) and Wheeler, (p. 355,) no incompetent judges, entertain a more favorable opinion of the Attic dialect.]

[Footnote 59: Yet we must not accuse them of corrupting the name of Athens, which they still call Athini. From the eiV thn 'Aqhnhn, we have formed our own barbarism of Setines. Note: Gibbon did not foresee a Bavarian prince on the throne of Greece, with Athens as his capital—M.]


CHAPTER LXIII

CIVIL WARS AND THE RUIN OF THE GREEK EMPIRE

PART I

CIVIL WARS AND THE RUIN OF THE GREEK EMPIRE—REIGNS OF ANDRONICUS, THE ELDER AND YOUNGER, AND JOHN PALÆOLOGUS—REGENCY, REVOLT, REIGN, AND ABDICATION OF JOHN CANTACUZENE—ESTABLISHMENT OF A GENOVESE COLONY AT PERA OR GALATA—THEIR WARS WITH THE EMPIRE AND CITY OF CONSTANTINOPLE

The long reign of Andronicus [1] the elder is chiefly memorable by the disputes of the Greek church, the invasion of the Catalans, and the rise of the Ottoman power. He is celebrated as the most learned and virtuous prince of the age; but such virtue, and such learning, contributed neither to the perfection of the individual, nor to the happiness of society A slave of the most abject superstition, he was surrounded on all sides by visible and invisible enemies; nor were the flames of hell less dreadful to his fancy, than those of a Catalan or Turkish war. Under the reign of the Palæologi, the choice of the patriarch was the most important business of the state; the heads of the Greek church were ambitious and fanatic monks; and their vices or virtues, their learning or ignorance, were equally mischievous or contemptible. By his intemperate discipline, the patriarch Athanasius [2] excited the hatred of the clergy and people: he was heard to declare, that the sinner should swallow the last dregs of the cup of penance; and the foolish tale was propagated of his punishing a sacrilegious ass that had tasted the lettuce of a convent garden. Driven from the throne by the universal clamor, Athanasius composed before his retreat two papers of a very opposite cast. His public testament was in the tone of charity and resignation; the private codicil breathed the direst anathemas against the authors of his disgrace, whom he excluded forever from the communion of the holy trinity, the angels, and the saints. This last paper he enclosed in an earthen pot, which was placed, by his order, on the top of one of the pillars, in the dome of St. Sophia, in the distant hope of discovery and revenge. At the end of four years, some youths, climbing by a ladder in search of pigeons' nests, detected the fatal secret; and, as Andronicus felt himself touched and bound by the excommunication, he trembled on the brink of the abyss which had been so treacherously dug under his feet. A synod of bishops was instantly convened to debate this important question: the rashness of these clandestine anathemas was generally condemned; but as the knot could be untied only by the same hand, as that hand was now deprived of the crosier, it appeared that this posthumous decree was irrevocable by any earthly power. Some faint testimonies of repentance and pardon were extorted from the author of the mischief; but the conscience of the emperor was still wounded, and he desired, with no less ardor than Athanasius himself, the restoration of a patriarch, by whom alone he could be healed. At the dead of night, a monk rudely knocked at the door of the royal bed-chamber, announcing a revelation of plague and famine, of inundations and earthquakes. Andronicus started from his bed, and spent the night in prayer, till he felt, or thought that he felt, a slight motion of the earth. The emperor on foot led the bishops and monks to the cell of Athanasius; and, after a proper resistance, the saint, from whom this message had been sent, consented to absolve the prince, and govern the church of Constantinople. Untamed by disgrace, and hardened by solitude, the shepherd was again odious to the flock, and his enemies contrived a singular, and as it proved, a successful, mode of revenge. In the night, they stole away the footstool or foot-cloth of his throne, which they secretly replaced with the decoration of a satirical picture. The emperor was painted with a bridle in his mouth, and Athanasius leading the tractable beast to the feet of Christ. The authors of the libel were detected and punished; but as their lives had been spared, the Christian priest in sullen indignation retired to his cell; and the eyes of Andronicus, which had been opened for a moment, were again closed by his successor.

[Footnote 1: Andronicus himself will justify our freedom in the invective, (Nicephorus Gregoras, l. i. c. i.,) which he pronounced against historic falsehood. It is true, that his censure is more pointedly urged against calumny than against adulation.]

[Footnote 2: For the anathema in the pigeon's nest, see Pachymer, (l. ix. c. 24,) who relates the general history of Athanasius, (l. viii. c. 13—16, 20, 24, l. x. c. 27—29, 31—36, l. xi. c. 1—3, 5, 6, l. xiii. c. 8, 10, 23, 35,) and is followed by Nicephorus Gregoras, (l. vi. c. 5, 7, l. vii. c. 1, 9,) who includes the second retreat of this second Chrysostom.]

If this transaction be one of the most curious and important of a reign of fifty years, I cannot at least accuse the brevity of my materials, since I reduce into some few pages the enormous folios of Pachymer, [3] Cantacuzene, [4] and Nicephorus Gregoras, [5] who have composed the prolix and languid story of the times. The name and situation of the emperor John Cantacuzene might inspire the most lively curiosity. His memorials of forty years extend from the revolt of the younger Andronicus to his own abdication of the empire; and it is observed, that, like Moses and Cæsar, he was the principal actor in the scenes which he describes. But in this eloquent work we should vainly seek the sincerity of a hero or a penitent. Retired in a cloister from the vices and passions of the world, he presents not a confession, but an apology, of the life of an ambitious statesman. Instead of unfolding the true counsels and characters of men, he displays the smooth and specious surface of events, highly varnished with his own praises and those of his friends. Their motives are always pure; their ends always legitimate: they conspire and rebel without any views of interest; and the violence which they inflict or suffer is celebrated as the spontaneous effect of reason and virtue.

[Footnote 3: Pachymer, in seven books, 377 folio pages, describes the first twenty-six years of Andronicus the Elder; and marks the date of his composition by the current news or lie of the day, (A.D. 1308.) Either death or disgust prevented him from resuming the pen.]

[Footnote 4: After an interval of twelve years, from the conclusion of Pachymer, Cantacuzenus takes up the pen; and his first book (c. 1—59, p. 9—150) relates the civil war, and the eight last years of the elder Andronicus. The ingenious comparison with Moses and Cæsar is fancied by his French translator, the president Cousin.]

[Footnote 5: Nicephorus Gregoras more briefly includes the entire life and reign of Andronicus the elder, (l. vi. c. 1, p. 96—291.) This is the part of which Cantacuzene complains as a false and malicious representation of his conduct.]

After the example of the first of the Palæologi, the elder Andronicus associated his son Michael to the honors of the purple; and from the age of eighteen to his premature death, that prince was acknowledged, above twenty-five years, as the second emperor of the Greeks. [6] At the head of an army, he excited neither the fears of the enemy, nor the jealousy of the court; his modesty and patience were never tempted to compute the years of his father; nor was that father compelled to repent of his liberality either by the virtues or vices of his son. The son of Michael was named Andronicus from his grandfather, to whose early favor he was introduced by that nominal resemblance. The blossoms of wit and beauty increased the fondness of the elder Andronicus; and, with the common vanity of age, he expected to realize in the second, the hope which had been disappointed in the first, generation. The boy was educated in the palace as an heir and a favorite; and in the oaths and acclamations of the people, the august triad was formed by the names of the father, the son, and the grandson. But the younger Andronicus was speedily corrupted by his infant greatness, while he beheld with puerile impatience the double obstacle that hung, and might long hang, over his rising ambition. It was not to acquire fame, or to diffuse happiness, that he so eagerly aspired: wealth and impunity were in his eyes the most precious attributes of a monarch; and his first indiscreet demand was the sovereignty of some rich and fertile island, where he might lead a life of independence and pleasure. The emperor was offended by the loud and frequent intemperance which disturbed his capital; the sums which his parsimony denied were supplied by the Genoese usurers of Pera; and the oppressive debt, which consolidated the interest of a faction, could be discharged only by a revolution. A beautiful female, a matron in rank, a prostitute in manners, had instructed the younger Andronicus in the rudiments of love; but he had reason to suspect the nocturnal visits of a rival; and a stranger passing through the street was pierced by the arrows of his guards, who were placed in ambush at her door. That stranger was his brother, Prince Manuel, who languished and died of his wound; and the emperor Michael, their common father, whose health was in a declining state, expired on the eighth day, lamenting the loss of both his children. [7] However guiltless in his intention, the younger Andronicus might impute a brother's and a father's death to the consequence of his own vices; and deep was the sigh of thinking and feeling men, when they perceived, instead of sorrow and repentance, his ill-dissembled joy on the removal of two odious competitors. By these melancholy events, and the increase of his disorders, the mind of the elder emperor was gradually alienated; and, after many fruitless reproofs, he transferred on another grandson [8] his hopes and affection. The change was announced by the new oath of allegiance to the reigning sovereign, and the person whom he should appoint for his successor; and the acknowledged heir, after a repetition of insults and complaints, was exposed to the indignity of a public trial. Before the sentence, which would probably have condemned him to a dungeon or a cell, the emperor was informed that the palace courts were filled with the armed followers of his grandson; the judgment was softened to a treaty of reconciliation; and the triumphant escape of the prince encouraged the ardor of the younger faction.

[Footnote 6: He was crowned May 21st, 1295, and died October 12th, 1320, (Ducange, Fam. Byz. p. 239.) His brother Theodore, by a second marriage, inherited the marquisate of Montferrat, apostatized to the religion and manners of the Latins, (oti kai gnwmh kai pistei kai schkati, kai geneiwn koura kai pasin eqesin DatinoV hn akraijnhV. Nic. Greg. l. ix. c. 1,) and founded a dynasty of Italian princes, which was extinguished A.D. 1533, (Ducange, Fam. Byz. p. 249—253.)]

[Footnote 7: We are indebted to Nicephorus Gregoras (l. viii. c. 1) for the knowledge of this tragic adventure; while Cantacuzene more discreetly conceals the vices of Andronicus the Younger, of which he was the witness and perhaps the associate, (l. i. c. 1, &c.)]

[Footnote 8: His destined heir was Michael Catharus, the bastard of Constantine his second son. In this project of excluding his grandson Andronicus, Nicephorus Gregoras (l. viii. c. 3) agrees with Cantacuzene, (l. i. c. 1, 2.)]

Yet the capital, the clergy, and the senate, adhered to the person, or at least to the government, of the old emperor; and it was only in the provinces, by flight, and revolt, and foreign succor, that the malecontents could hope to vindicate their cause and subvert his throne. The soul of the enterprise was the great domestic John Cantacuzene; the sally from Constantinople is the first date of his actions and memorials; and if his own pen be most descriptive of his patriotism, an unfriendly historian has not refused to celebrate the zeal and ability which he displayed in the service of the young emperor. [89] That prince escaped from the capital under the pretence of hunting; erected his standard at Adrianople; and, in a few days, assembled fifty thousand horse and foot, whom neither honor nor duty could have armed against the Barbarians. Such a force might have saved or commanded the empire; but their counsels were discordant, their motions were slow and doubtful, and their progress was checked by intrigue and negotiation. The quarrel of the two Andronici was protracted, and suspended, and renewed, during a ruinous period of seven years. In the first treaty, the relics of the Greek empire were divided: Constantinople, Thessalonica, and the islands, were left to the elder, while the younger acquired the sovereignty of the greatest part of Thrace, from Philippi to the Byzantine limit. By the second treaty, he stipulated the payment of his troops, his immediate coronation, and an adequate share of the power and revenue of the state. The third civil war was terminated by the surprise of Constantinople, the final retreat of the old emperor, and the sole reign of his victorious grandson. The reasons of this delay may be found in the characters of the men and of the times. When the heir of the monarchy first pleaded his wrongs and his apprehensions, he was heard with pity and applause: and his adherents repeated on all sides the inconsistent promise, that he would increase the pay of the soldiers and alleviate the burdens of the people. The grievances of forty years were mingled in his revolt; and the rising generation was fatigued by the endless prospect of a reign, whose favorites and maxims were of other times. The youth of Andronicus had been without spirit, his age was without reverence: his taxes produced an unusual revenue of five hundred thousand pounds; yet the richest of the sovereigns of Christendom was incapable of maintaining three thousand horse and twenty galleys, to resist the destructive progress of the Turks. [9] "How different," said the younger Andronicus, "is my situation from that of the son of Philip! Alexander might complain, that his father would leave him nothing to conquer: alas! my grandsire will leave me nothing to lose." But the Greeks were soon admonished, that the public disorders could not be healed by a civil war; and that their young favorite was not destined to be the savior of a falling empire. On the first repulse, his party was broken by his own levity, their intestine discord, and the intrigues of the ancient court, which tempted each malecontent to desert or betray the cause of the rebellion. Andronicus the younger was touched with remorse, or fatigued with business, or deceived by negotiation: pleasure rather than power was his aim; and the license of maintaining a thousand hounds, a thousand hawks, and a thousand huntsmen, was sufficient to sully his fame and disarm his ambition.

*[Footnote 8/1: The conduct of Cantacuzene, by his own showing, was inexplicable. He was unwilling to dethrone the old emperor, and dissuaded the immediate march on Constantinople. The young Andronicus, he says, entered into his views, and wrote to warn the emperor of his danger when the march was determined. Cantacuzenus, in Nov. Byz. Hist. Collect. vol. i. p. 104, &c—M.]*

*[Footnote 9: See Nicephorus Gregoras, l. viii. c. 6. The younger Andronicus complained, that in four years and four months a sum of 350,000 byzants of gold was due to him for the expenses of his household, (Cantacuzen l. i. c. 48.) Yet he would have remitted the debt, if he might have been allowed to squeeze the farmers of the revenue.]*

Let us now survey the catastrophe of this busy plot, and the final situation of the principal actors. [10] The age of Andronicus was consumed in civil discord; and, amidst the events of war and treaty, his power and reputation continually decayed, till the fatal night in which the gates of the city and palace were opened without resistance to his grandson. His principal commander scorned the repeated warnings of danger; and retiring to rest in the vain security of ignorance, abandoned the feeble monarch, with some priests and pages, to the terrors of a sleepless night. These terrors were quickly realized by the hostile shouts, which proclaimed the titles and victory of Andronicus the younger; and the aged emperor, falling prostrate before an image of the Virgin, despatched a suppliant message to resign the sceptre, and to obtain his life at the hands of the conqueror. The answer of his grandson was decent and pious; at the prayer of his friends, the younger Andronicus assumed the sole administration; but the elder still enjoyed the name and preeminence of the first emperor, the use of the great palace, and a pension of twenty-four thousand pieces of gold, one half of which was assigned on the royal treasury, and the other on the fishery of Constantinople. But his impotence was soon exposed to contempt and oblivion; the vast silence of the palace was disturbed only by the cattle and poultry of the neighborhood, [101] which roved with impunity through the solitary courts; and a reduced allowance of ten thousand pieces of gold [11] was all that he could ask, and more than he could hope. His calamities were imbittered by the gradual extinction of sight; his confinement was rendered each day more rigorous; and during the absence and sickness of his grandson, his inhuman keepers, by the threats of instant death, compelled him to exchange the purple for the monastic habit and profession. The monk Antony had renounced the pomp of the world; yet he had occasion for a coarse fur in the winter season, and as wine was forbidden by his confessor, and water by his physician, the sherbet of Egypt was his common drink. It was not without difficulty that the late emperor could procure three or four pieces to satisfy these simple wants; and if he bestowed the gold to relieve the more painful distress of a friend, the sacrifice is of some weight in the scale of humanity and religion. Four years after his abdication, Andronicus or Antony expired in a cell, in the seventy-fourth year of his age: and the last strain of adulation could only promise a more splendid crown of glory in heaven than he had enjoyed upon earth. [12] [12/1]

[Footnote 10: I follow the chronology of Nicephorus Gregoras, who is remarkably exact. It is proved that Cantacuzene has mistaken the dates of his own actions, or rather that his text has been corrupted by ignorant transcribers.]

[Footnote 101: And the washerwomen, according to Nic. Gregoras, p. 431—M.]

[Footnote 11: I have endeavored to reconcile the 24,000 pieces of Cantacuzene (l. ii. c. 1) with the 10,000 of Nicephorus Gregoras, (l. ix. c. 2;) the one of whom wished to soften, the other to magnify, the hardships of the old emperor.]

[Footnote 12: See Nicephorus Gregoras, (l. ix. 6, 7, 8, 10, 14, l. x. c. 1.) The historian had tasted of the prosperity, and shared the retreat, of his benefactor; and that friendship which "waits or to the scaffold or the cell," should not lightly be accused as "a hireling, a prostitute to praise." Note: But it may be accused of unparalleled absurdity. He compares the extinction of the feeble old man to that of the sun: his coffin is to be floated like Noah's ark by a deluge of tears—M.]

[Footnote 12/1: Prodigies (according to Nic. Gregoras, p. 460) announced the departure of the old and imbecile Imperial Monk from his earthly prison—M.]

Nor was the reign of the younger, more glorious or fortunate than that of the elder, Andronicus. [13] He gathered the fruits of ambition; but the taste was transient and bitter: in the supreme station he lost the remains of his early popularity; and the defects of his character became still more conspicuous to the world. The public reproach urged him to march in person against the Turks; nor did his courage fail in the hour of trial; but a defeat and a wound were the only trophies of his expedition in Asia, which confirmed the establishment of the Ottoman monarchy. The abuses of the civil government attained their full maturity and perfection: his neglect of forms, and the confusion of national dresses, are deplored by the Greeks as the fatal symptoms of the decay of the empire. Andronicus was old before his time; the intemperance of youth had accelerated the infirmities of age; and after being rescued from a dangerous malady by nature, or physic, or the Virgin, he was snatched away before he had accomplished his forty-fifth year. He was twice married; and, as the progress of the Latins in arms and arts had softened the prejudices of the Byzantine court, his two wives were chosen in the princely houses of Germany and Italy. The first, Agnes at home, Irene in Greece, was daughter of the duke of Brunswick. Her father [14] was a petty lord [15] in the poor and savage regions of the north of Germany: [16] yet he derived some revenue from his silver mines; [17] and his family is celebrated by the Greeks as the most ancient and noble of the Teutonic name. [18] After the death of this childish princess, Andronicus sought in marriage Jane, the sister of the count of Savoy; [19] and his suit was preferred to that of the French king. [20] The count respected in his sister the superior majesty of a Roman empress: her retinue was composed of knights and ladies; she was regenerated and crowned in St. Sophia, under the more orthodox appellation of Anne; and, at the nuptial feast, the Greeks and Italians vied with each other in the martial exercises of tilts and tournaments.

[Footnote 13: The sole reign of Andronicus the younger is described by Cantacuzene (l. ii. c. 1—40, p. 191—339) and Nicephorus Gregoras, (l. ix c. 7—l. xi. c. 11, p. 262—361.)]

[Footnote 14: Agnes, or Irene, was the daughter of Duke Henry the Wonderful, the chief of the house of Brunswick, and the fourth in descent from the famous Henry the Lion, duke of Saxony and Bavaria, and conqueror of the Sclavi on the Baltic coast. Her brother Henry was surnamed the Greek, from his two journeys into the East: but these journeys were subsequent to his sister's marriage; and I am ignorant how Agnes was discovered in the heart of Germany, and recommended to the Byzantine court. (Rimius, Memoirs of the House of Brunswick, p. 126—137.]

[Footnote 15: Henry the Wonderful was the founder of the branch of Grubenhagen, extinct in the year 1596, (Rimius, p. 287.) He resided in the castle of Wolfenbuttel, and possessed no more than a sixth part of the allodial estates of Brunswick and Luneburgh, which the Guelph family had saved from the confiscation of their great fiefs. The frequent partitions among brothers had almost ruined the princely houses of Germany, till that just, but pernicious, law was slowly superseded by the right of primogeniture. The principality of Grubenhagen, one of the last remains of the Hercynian forest, is a woody, mountainous, and barren tract, (Busching's Geography, vol. vi. p. 270—286, English translation.)]

[Footnote 16: The royal author of the Memoirs of Brandenburgh will teach us, how justly, in a much later period, the north of Germany deserved the epithets of poor and barbarous. (Essai sur les Murs, &c.) In the year 1306, in the woods of Luneburgh, some wild people of the Vened race were allowed to bury alive their infirm and useless parents. (Rimius, p. 136.)]

[Footnote 17: The assertion of Tacitus, that Germany was destitute of the precious metals, must be taken, even in his own time, with some limitation, (Germania, c. 5. Annal. xi. 20.) According to Spener, (Hist. Germaniæ Pragmatica, tom. i. p. 351,) Argentifodin in Hercyniis montibus, imperante Othone magno (A.D. 968) primum apertæ, largam etiam opes augendi dederunt copiam: but Rimius (p. 258, 259) defers till the year 1016 the discovery of the silver mines of Grubenhagen, or the Upper Hartz, which were productive in the beginning of the xivth century, and which still yield a considerable revenue to the house of Brunswick.]

[Footnote 18: Cantacuzene has given a most honorable testimony, hn d' ek Germanvn auth Jugathr doukoV nti Mprouzouhk, (the modern Greeks employ the nt for the d, and the mp for the b, and the whole will read in the Italian idiom di Brunzuic,) tou par autoiV epijanestatou, kai?iamprothti pantaV touV omojulouV uperballontoV. The praise is just in itself, and pleasing to an English ear.]

[Footnote 19: Anne, or Jane, was one of the four daughters of Amedée the Great, by a second marriage, and half-sister of his successor Edward count of Savoy. (Anderson's Tables, p. 650. See Cantacuzene, l. i. c. 40—42.)]

[Footnote 20: That king, if the fact be true, must have been Charles the Fair who in five years (1321—1326) was married to three wives, (Anderson, p. 628.) Anne of Savoy arrived at Constantinople in February, 1326.]

The empress Anne of Savoy survived her husband: their son, John Palæologus, was left an orphan and an emperor in the ninth year of his age; and his weakness was protected by the first and most deserving of the Greeks. The long and cordial friendship of his father for John Cantacuzene is alike honorable to the prince and the subject. It had been formed amidst the pleasures of their youth: their families were almost equally noble; [21] and the recent lustre of the purple was amply compensated by the energy of a private education. We have seen that the young emperor was saved by Cantacuzene from the power of his grandfather; and, after six years of civil war, the same favorite brought him back in triumph to the palace of Constantinople. Under the reign of Andronicus the younger, the great domestic ruled the emperor and the empire; and it was by his valor and conduct that the Isle of Lesbos and the principality of Ætolia were restored to their ancient allegiance. His enemies confess, that, among the public robbers, Cantacuzene alone was moderate and abstemious; and the free and voluntary account which he produces of his own wealth [22] may sustain the presumption that he was devolved by inheritance, and not accumulated by rapine. He does not indeed specify the value of his money, plate, and jewels; yet, after a voluntary gift of two hundred vases of silver, after much had been secreted by his friends and plundered by his foes, his forfeit treasures were sufficient for the equipment of a fleet of seventy galleys. He does not measure the size and number of his estates; but his granaries were heaped with an incredible store of wheat and barley; and the labor of a thousand yoke of oxen might cultivate, according to the practice of antiquity, about sixty-two thousand five hundred acres of arable land. [23] His pastures were stocked with two thousand five hundred brood mares, two hundred camels, three hundred mules, five hundred asses, five thousand horned cattle, fifty thousand hogs, and seventy thousand sheep: [24] a precious record of rural opulence, in the last period of the empire, and in a land, most probably in Thrace, so repeatedly wasted by foreign and domestic hostility. The favor of Cantacuzene was above his fortune. In the moments of familiarity, in the hour of sickness, the emperor was desirous to level the distance between them and pressed his friend to accept the diadem and purple. The virtue of the great domestic, which is attested by his own pen, resisted the dangerous proposal; but the last testament of Andronicus the younger named him the guardian of his son, and the regent of the empire.

[Footnote 21: The noble race of the Cantacuzeni (illustrious from the xith century in the Byzantine annals) was drawn from the Paladins of France, the heroes of those romances which, in the xiiith century, were translated and read by the Greeks, (Ducange, Fam. Byzant. p. 258.)]

[Footnote 22: See Cantacuzene, (l. iii. c. 24, 30, 36.)]

[Footnote 23: Saserna, in Gaul, and Columella, in Italy or Spain, allow two yoke of oxen, two drivers, and six laborers, for two hundred jugera (125 English acres) of arable land, and three more men must be added if there be much underwood, (Columella de Re Rustica, l. ii. c. 13, p 441, edit. Gesner.)]

[Footnote 24: In this enumeration (l. iii. c. 30) the French translation of the president Cousin is blotted with three palpable and essential errors. 1. He omits the 1000 yoke of working oxen. 2. He interprets the pentakosiai proV diaciliaiV, by the number of fifteen hundred. 3. He confounds myriads with chiliads, and gives Cantacuzene no more than 5000 hogs. Put not your trust in translations! Note: There seems to be another reading, ciliaiV. Niebuhr's edit. in loc—M.]

Had the regent found a suitable return of obedience and gratitude, perhaps he would have acted with pure and zealous fidelity in the service of his pupil. [25] A guard of five hundred soldiers watched over his person and the palace; the funeral of the late emperor was decently performed; the capital was silent and submissive; and five hundred letters, which Cantacuzene despatched in the first month, informed the provinces of their loss and their duty. The prospect of a tranquil minority was blasted by the great duke or admiral Apocaucus, and to exaggerate his perfidy, the Imperial historian is pleased to magnify his own imprudence, in raising him to that office against the advice of his more sagacious sovereign. Bold and subtle, rapacious and profuse, the avarice and ambition of Apocaucus were by turns subservient to each other; and his talents were applied to the ruin of his country. His arrogance was heightened by the command of a naval force and an impregnable castle, and under the mask of oaths and flattery he secretly conspired against his benefactor. The female court of the empress was bribed and directed; he encouraged Anne of Savoy to assert, by the law of nature, the tutelage of her son; the love of power was disguised by the anxiety of maternal tenderness: and the founder of the Palæologi had instructed his posterity to dread the example of a perfidious guardian. The patriarch John of Apri was a proud and feeble old man, encompassed by a numerous and hungry kindred. He produced an obsolete epistle of Andronicus, which bequeathed the prince and people to his pious care: the fate of his predecessor Arsenius prompted him to prevent, rather than punish, the crimes of a usurper; and Apocaucus smiled at the success of his own flattery, when he beheld the Byzantine priest assuming the state and temporal claims of the Roman pontiff. [26] Between three persons so different in their situation and character, a private league was concluded: a shadow of authority was restored to the senate; and the people was tempted by the name of freedom. By this powerful confederacy, the great domestic was assaulted at first with clandestine, at length with open, arms. His prerogatives were disputed; his opinions slighted; his friends persecuted; and his safety was threatened both in the camp and city. In his absence on the public service, he was accused of treason; proscribed as an enemy of the church and state; and delivered with all his adherents to the sword of justice, the vengeance of the people, and the power of the devil; his fortunes were confiscated; his aged mother was cast into prison; [26/1] all his past services were buried in oblivion; and he was driven by injustice to perpetrate the crime of which he was accused. [27] From the review of his preceding conduct, Cantacuzene appears to have been guiltless of any treasonable designs; and the only suspicion of his innocence must arise from the vehemence of his protestations, and the sublime purity which he ascribes to his own virtue. While the empress and the patriarch still affected the appearances of harmony, he repeatedly solicited the permission of retiring to a private, and even a monastic, life. After he had been declared a public enemy, it was his fervent wish to throw himself at the feet of the young emperor, and to receive without a murmur the stroke of the executioner: it was not without reluctance that he listened to the voice of reason, which inculcated the sacred duty of saving his family and friends, and proved that he could only save them by drawing the sword and assuming the Imperial title.

[Footnote 25: See the regency and reign of John Cantacuzenus, and the whole progress of the civil war, in his own history, (l. iii. c. 1—100, p. 348—700,) and in that of Nicephorus Gregoras, (l. xii. c. 1—l. xv. c. 9, p. 353—492.)]

[Footnote 26: He assumes the royal privilege of red shoes or buskins; placed on his head a mitre of silk and gold; subscribed his epistles with hyacinth or green ink, and claimed for the new, whatever Constantine had given to the ancient, Rome, (Cantacuzen. l. iii. c. 36. Nic. Gregoras, l. xiv. c. 3.)]

*[Footnote 26/1: She died there through persecution and neglect—M.]*

*[Footnote 27: Nic. Gregoras (l. xii. c. 5) confesses the innocence and virtues of Cantacuzenus, the guilt and flagitious vices of Apocaucus; nor does he dissemble the motive of his personal and religious enmity to the former; nun de dia kakian allwn, aitioV o praotatoV thV tvn olwn edoxaV? eioai jqoraV. Note: The alloi were the religious enemies and persecutors of Nicephorus—M.]*

PART II

In the strong city of Demotica, his peculiar domain, the emperor John Cantacuzenus was invested with the purple buskins: his right leg was clothed by his noble kinsmen, the left by the Latin chiefs, on whom he conferred the order of knighthood. But even in this act of revolt, he was still studious of loyalty; and the titles of John Palæologus and Anne of Savoy were proclaimed before his own name and that of his wife Irene. Such vain ceremony is a thin disguise of rebellion, nor are there perhaps any personal wrongs that can authorize a subject to take arms against his sovereign: but the want of preparation and success may confirm the assurance of the usurper, that this decisive step was the effect of necessity rather than of choice. Constantinople adhered to the young emperor; the king of Bulgaria was invited to the relief of Adrianople: the principal cities of Thrace and Macedonia, after some hesitation, renounced their obedience to the great domestic; and the leaders of the troops and provinces were induced, by their private interest, to prefer the loose dominion of a woman and a priest. [27/1] The army of Cantacuzene, in sixteen divisions, was stationed on the banks of the Melas to tempt or to intimidate the capital: it was dispersed by treachery or fear; and the officers, more especially the mercenary Latins, accepted the bribes, and embraced the service, of the Byzantine court. After this loss, the rebel emperor (he fluctuated between the two characters) took the road of Thessalonica with a chosen remnant; but he failed in his enterprise on that important place; and he was closely pursued by the great duke, his enemy Apocaucus, at the head of a superior power by sea and land. Driven from the coast, in his march, or rather flight, into the mountains of Servia, Cantacuzene assembled his troops to scrutinize those who were worthy and willing to accompany his broken fortunes. A base majority bowed and retired; and his trusty band was diminished to two thousand, and at last to five hundred, volunteers. The cral, [28] or despot of the Servians received him with general hospitality; but the ally was insensibly degraded to a suppliant, a hostage, a captive; and in this miserable dependence, he waited at the door of the Barbarian, who could dispose of the life and liberty of a Roman emperor. The most tempting offers could not persuade the cral to violate his trust; but he soon inclined to the stronger side; and his friend was dismissed without injury to a new vicissitude of hopes and perils. Near six years the flame of discord burnt with various success and unabated rage: the cities were distracted by the faction of the nobles and the plebeians; the Cantacuzeni and Palæologi: and the Bulgarians, the Servians, and the Turks, were invoked on both sides as the instruments of private ambition and the common ruin. The regent deplored the calamities, of which he was the author and victim: and his own experience might dictate a just and lively remark on the different nature of foreign and civil war. "The former," said he, "is the external warmth of summer, always tolerable, and often beneficial; the latter is the deadly heat of a fever, which consumes without a remedy the vitals of the constitution." [29]

*[Footnote 27/1: Cantacuzene asserts, that in all the cities, the populace were on the side of the emperor, the aristocracy on his. The populace took the opportunity of rising and plundering the wealthy as*

Cantacuzenites, vol. iii. c. 29 Ages of common oppression and ruin had not extinguished these republican factions—M.]

[Footnote 28: The princes of Servia (Ducange, Famil. Dalmaticæ, &c., c. 2, 3, 4, 9) were styled Despots in Greek, and Cral in their native idiom, (Ducange, Gloss. Græc. p. 751.) That title, the equivalent of king, appears to be of Sclavonic origin, from whence it has been borrowed by the Hungarians, the modern Greeks, and even by the Turks, (Leunclavius, Pandect. Turc. p. 422,) who reserve the name of Padishah for the emperor. To obtain the latter instead of the former is the ambition of the French at Constantinople, (Aversissement à l'Histoire de Timur Bec, p. 39.)]

[Footnote 29: Nic. Gregoras, l. xii. c. 14. It is surprising that Cantacuzene has not inserted this just and lively image in his own writings.]

The introduction of barbarians and savages into the contests of civilized nations, is a measure pregnant with shame and mischief; which the interest of the moment may compel, but which is reprobated by the best principles of humanity and reason. It is the practice of both sides to accuse their enemies of the guilt of the first alliances; and those who fail in their negotiations are loudest in their censure of the example which they envy and would gladly imitate. The Turks of Asia were less barbarous perhaps than the shepherds of Bulgaria and Servia; but their religion rendered them implacable foes of Rome and Christianity. To acquire the friendship of their emirs, the two factions vied with each other in baseness and profusion: the dexterity of Cantacuzene obtained the preference: but the succor and victory were dearly purchased by the marriage of his daughter with an infidel, the captivity of many thousand Christians, and the passage of the Ottomans into Europe, the last and fatal stroke in the fall of the Roman empire. The inclining scale was decided in his favor by the death of Apocaucus, the just though singular retribution of his crimes. A crowd of nobles or plebeians, whom he feared or hated, had been seized by his orders in the capital and the provinces; and the old palace of Constantine was assigned as the place of their confinement. Some alterations in raising the walls, and narrowing the cells, had been ingeniously contrived to prevent their escape, and aggravate their misery; and the work was incessantly pressed by the daily visits of the tyrant. His guards watched at the gate, and as he stood in the inner court to overlook the architects, without fear or suspicion, he was assaulted and laid breathless on the ground, by two [29/1] resolute prisoners of the Palæologian race, [30] who were armed with sticks, and animated by despair. On the rumor of revenge and liberty, the captive multitude broke their fetters, fortified their prison, and exposed from the battlements the tyrant's head, presuming on the favor of the people and the clemency of the empress. Anne of Savoy might rejoice in the fall of a haughty and ambitious minister, but while she delayed to resolve or to act, the populace, more especially the mariners, were excited by the widow of the great duke to a sedition, an assault, and a massacre. The prisoners (of whom the far greater part were guiltless or inglorious of the deed) escaped to a neighboring church: they were slaughtered at the foot of the altar; and in his death the monster was not less bloody and venomous than in his life. Yet his talents alone upheld the cause of the young emperor; and his surviving associates, suspicious of each other, abandoned the conduct of the war, and rejected the fairest terms of accommodation. In the beginning of the dispute, the empress felt, and complained, that she was deceived by the enemies of Cantacuzene: the patriarch was employed to preach against the forgiveness of injuries; and her promise of immortal hatred was sealed by an oath, under the penalty of excommunication. [31] But Anne soon learned to hate without a teacher: she beheld the misfortunes of the empire with the indifference of a stranger: her jealousy was exasperated by the competition of a rival empress; and on the first symptoms of a more yielding temper, she threatened the patriarch to convene a synod, and degrade him from his office. Their incapacity and discord would have afforded the most decisive advantage; but the civil war was protracted by the weakness of both parties; and the moderation of Cantacuzene has not escaped the reproach of timidity and indolence. He successively recovered the provinces and cities; and the realm of his pupil was measured by the walls of Constantinople; but the metropolis alone counterbalanced the rest of the empire; nor could he attempt that important conquest till he had secured in his favor the public voice and a private correspondence. An Italian, of the name of Facciolati, [32] had succeeded to the office of great duke: the ships, the guards, and the golden gate, were subject to his command; but his humble ambition was bribed to become the instrument of treachery; and the revolution was accomplished without danger or bloodshed. Destitute of the powers of resistance, or the hope of relief, the inflexible Anne would have still defended the palace, and have smiled to behold the capital in flames, rather than in the possession of a rival. She yielded to the prayers of her friends and enemies; and the treaty was dictated by the conqueror, who professed a loyal and zealous attachment to the son of his benefactor. The marriage of his daughter with John Palæologus was at length consummated: the hereditary right of the pupil was acknowledged; but the sole administration during ten years was vested in the guardian. Two emperors and three empresses were seated on the Byzantine throne; and a general amnesty quieted the apprehensions, and confirmed the property, of the most guilty subjects. The festival of the coronation and nuptials was celebrated with the appearances of concord and magnificence, and both were equally fallacious. During the late troubles, the treasures of the state, and even the furniture of the palace, had been alienated or embezzled; the royal banquet was served in pewter or earthenware; and such was the proud poverty of the times, that the absence of gold and jewels was supplied by the paltry artifices of glass and gilt-leather. [33]

[Footnote 29/1: Nicephorus says four, p.734.]

[Footnote 30: The two avengers were both Palæologi, who might resent, with royal indignation, the shame of their chains. The tragedy of Apocaucus may deserve a peculiar reference to Cantacuzene (l. iii. c. 86) and Nic. Gregoras, (l. xiv. c. 10.)]

[Footnote 31: Cantacuzene accuses the patriarch, and spares the empress, the mother of his sovereign, (l. iii. 33, 34,) against whom Nic. Gregoras expresses a particular animosity, (l. xiv. 10, 11, xv. 5.) It is true that they do not speak exactly of the same time.]

[Footnote 32: The traitor and treason are revealed by Nic. Gregoras, (l. xv. c. 8;) but the name is more discreetly suppressed by his great accomplice, (Cantacuzen. l. iii. c. 99.)]

[Footnote 33: Nic. Greg. l. xv. 11. There were, however, some true pearls, but very thinly sprinkled. The rest of the stones had only pantodaphn croian proV to diaugeV.]

I hasten to conclude the personal history of John Cantacuzene. [34] He triumphed and reigned; but his reign and triumph were clouded by the discontent of his own and the adverse faction. His followers might style the general amnesty an act of pardon for his enemies, and of oblivion for his friends: [35] in his cause their estates had been forfeited or plundered; and as they wandered naked and hungry through the streets, they cursed the selfish generosity of a leader, who, on the throne of the empire, might relinquish without merit his private inheritance. The adherents of the empress blushed to hold their lives and fortunes by the precarious favor of a usurper; and the thirst of revenge was concealed by a tender concern for the succession, and even the safety, of her son. They were justly alarmed by a petition of the friends of Cantacuzene, that they might be released from their oath of allegiance to the Palæologi, and intrusted with the defence of some cautionary towns; a measure supported with argument and eloquence; and which was rejected (says the Imperial historian) "by my sublime, and almost incredible virtue." His repose was disturbed by the sound of plots and seditions; and he trembled lest the lawful prince should be stolen away by some foreign or domestic enemy, who would inscribe his name and his wrongs in the banners of rebellion. As the son of Andronicus advanced in the years of manhood, he began to feel and to act for himself; and his rising ambition was rather stimulated than checked by the imitation of his father's vices. If we may trust his own professions, Cantacuzene labored with honest industry to correct these sordid and sensual appetites, and to raise the mind of the young prince to a level with his fortune. In the Servian expedition, the two emperors showed themselves in cordial harmony to the troops and provinces; and the younger colleague was initiated by the elder in the mysteries of war and government. After the conclusion of the peace, Palæologus was left at Thessalonica, a royal residence, and a frontier station, to secure by his absence the peace of Constantinople, and to withdraw his youth from the temptations of a luxurious capital. But the distance weakened the powers of control, and the son of Andronicus was surrounded with artful or unthinking companions, who taught him to hate his guardian, to deplore his exile, and to vindicate his rights. A private treaty with the cral or despot of Servia was soon followed by an open revolt; and Cantacuzene, on the throne of the elder Andronicus, defended the cause of age and prerogative, which in his youth he had so vigorously attacked. At his request the empress-mother undertook the voyage of Thessalonica, and the office of mediation: she returned without success; and unless Anne of Savoy was instructed by adversity, we may doubt the sincerity, or at least the fervor, of her zeal. While the regent grasped the sceptre with a firm and vigorous hand, she had been instructed to declare, that the ten years of his legal administration would soon elapse; and that, after a full trial of the vanity of the world, the emperor Cantacuzene sighed for the repose of a cloister, and was ambitious only of a heavenly crown. Had these sentiments been genuine, his voluntary abdication would have restored the peace of the empire, and his conscience would have been relieved by an act of justice. Palæologus alone was responsible for his future government; and whatever might be his vices, they were surely less formidable than the calamities of a civil war, in which the Barbarians and infidels were again invited to assist the Greeks in their mutual destruction. By the arms of the Turks, who now struck a deep and everlasting root in Europe, Cantacuzene prevailed in the third contest in which he had been involved; and the young emperor, driven from the sea and land, was compelled to take shelter among the Latins of the Isle of Tenedos. His insolence and obstinacy provoked the victor to a step which must render the quarrel irreconcilable; and the association of his son Matthew, whom he invested with the purple, established the succession in the family of the Cantacuzeni. But Constantinople was still attached to the blood of her ancient princes; and this last injury accelerated the restoration of the rightful heir. A noble Genoese espoused the cause of Palæologus, obtained a promise of his sister, and achieved the revolution with two galleys and two thousand five hundred auxiliaries. Under the pretence of distress, they were admitted into the lesser port; a gate was opened, and the Latin shout of, "Long life and victory to the emperor, John Palæologus!" was answered by a general rising in his favor. A numerous and loyal party yet adhered to the standard of Cantacuzene: but he asserts in his history (does he hope for belief?) that his tender conscience rejected the assurance of conquest; that, in free obedience to the voice of religion and philosophy, he descended from the throne and embraced with pleasure the monastic habit and profession. [36] So soon as he ceased to be a prince, his successor was not unwilling that he should be a saint: the remainder of his life was devoted to piety and learning; in the cells of Constantinople and Mount Athos, the monk Joasaph was respected as the temporal and spiritual father of the emperor; and if he issued from his retreat, it was as the minister of peace, to subdue the obstinacy, and solicit the pardon, of his rebellious son. [37]

[Footnote 34: From his return to Constantinople, Cantacuzene continues his history and that of the empire, one year beyond the abdication of his son Matthew, A.D. 1357, (l. iv. c. I—50, p. 705—911.) Nicephorus Gregoras ends with the synod of Constantinople, in the year 1351, (l. xxii. c. 3, p. 660; the rest, to the conclusion of the xxivth book, p. 717, is all controversy;) and his fourteen last books are still MSS. in the king of France's library.]

[Footnote 35: The emperor (Cantacuzen. l. iv. c. 1) represents his own virtues, and Nic. Gregoras (l. xv. c. 11) the complaints of his friends, who suffered by its effects. I have lent them the words of our poor cavaliers after the Restoration.]

[Footnote 36: The awkward apology of Cantacuzene, (l. iv. c. 39—42,) who relates, with visible confusion, his own downfall, may be supplied by the less accurate, but more honest, narratives of Matthew Villani (l. iv. c. 46, in the Script. Rerum Ital. tom. xiv. p. 268) and Ducas, (c 10, 11.)]

[Footnote 37: Cantacuzene, in the year 1375, was honored with a letter from the pope, (Fleury, Hist. Ecclés. tom. xx. p. 250.) His death is placed by a respectable authority on the 20th of November, 1411, (Ducange, Fam. Byzant. p. 260.) But if he were of the age of his companion Andronicus the Younger, he must have lived 116 years; a rare instance of longevity, which in so illustrious a person would have attracted universal notice.]

Yet in the cloister, the mind of Cantacuzene was still exercised by theological war. He sharpened a controversial pen against the Jews and Mahometans; [38] and in every state he defended with equal zeal the divine light of Mount Thabor, a memorable question which consummates the religious follies of the Greeks. The fakirs of India, [39] and the monks of the Oriental church, were alike persuaded, that in the total abstraction of the faculties of the mind and body, the purer spirit may ascend to the enjoyment and vision of the Deity. The opinion and practice of the monasteries of Mount Athos [40] will be best represented in the words of an abbot, who flourished in the eleventh century. "When thou art alone in thy cell," says the ascetic teacher, "shut thy door, and seat thyself in a corner: raise thy mind above all things vain and transitory; recline thy beard and chin on thy breast; turn thy eyes and thy thoughts toward the middle of thy belly, the region of the navel; and search the place of the heart, the seat of the soul. At first, all will be dark and comfortless; but if you persevere day and night, you will feel an ineffable joy; and no sooner has the soul discovered the place of the heart, than it is involved in a mystic and ethereal light." This light, the production of a distempered fancy, the creature of an empty stomach and an empty brain, was adored by the Quietists as the pure and perfect essence of God himself; and as long as the folly was confined to Mount Athos, the simple solitaries were not inquisitive how the divine essence could be a material substance, or how an immaterial substance could be perceived by the eyes of the body. But in the reign of the younger Andronicus, these monasteries were visited by Barlaam, [41] a Calabrian monk, who was equally skilled in philosophy and theology; who possessed the language of the Greeks and Latins; and whose versatile genius could maintain their opposite creeds, according to the interest of the moment. The indiscretion of an ascetic revealed to the curious traveller the secrets of mental prayer and Barlaam embraced the opportunity of ridiculing the Quietists, who placed the soul in the navel; of accusing the monks of Mount Athos of heresy and blasphemy. His attack compelled the more learned to renounce or dissemble the simple devotion of their brethren; and Gregory Palamas introduced a scholastic distinction between the essence and operation of God. His inaccessible essence dwells in the midst of an uncreated and eternal light; and this beatific vision of the saints had been manifested to the disciples on Mount Thabor, in the transfiguration of Christ. Yet this distinction could not escape the reproach of polytheism; the eternity of the light of Thabor was fiercely denied; and Barlaam still charged the Palamites with holding two eternal substances, a visible and an invisible God. From the rage of the monks of Mount Athos, who threatened his life, the Calabrian retired to Constantinople, where his smooth and specious manners introduced him to the favor of the great domestic and the emperor. The court and the city were involved in this theological dispute, which flamed amidst the civil war; but the doctrine of Barlaam was disgraced by his flight and apostasy: the Palamites triumphed; and their adversary, the patriarch John of Apri, was deposed by the consent of the adverse factions of the state. In the character of emperor and theologian, Cantacuzene presided in the synod of the Greek church, which established, as an article of faith, the uncreated light of Mount Thabor; and, after so many insults, the reason of mankind was slightly wounded by the addition of a single absurdity. Many rolls of paper or parchment have been blotted; and the impenitent sectaries, who refused to subscribe the orthodox creed, were deprived of the honors of Christian burial; but in the next age the question was forgotten; nor can I learn that the axe or the fagot were employed for the extirpation of the Barlaamite heresy. [42]

[Footnote 38: His four discourses, or books, were printed at Basil, 1543, (Fabric Bibliot. Græc. tom. vi. p. 473.) He composed them to satisfy a proselyte who was assaulted with letters from his friends of Ispahan. Cantacuzene had read the Koran; but I understand from Maracci that he adopts the vulgar prejudices and fables against Mahomet and his religion.]

[Footnote 39: See the Voyage de Bernier, tom. i. p. 127.]

[Footnote 40: Mosheim, Institut. Hist. Ecclés. p. 522, 523. Fleury, Hist. Ecclés. tom. xx. p. 22, 24, 107—114, &c. The former unfolds the causes with the judgment of a philosopher, the latter transcribes and transcribes and translates with the prejudices of a Catholic priest.]

[Footnote 41: Basnage (in Canisii Antiq. Lectiones, tom. iv. p. 363—368) has investigated the character and story of Barlaam. The duplicity of his opinions had inspired some doubts of the identity of his person. See likewise Fabricius, (Bibliot. Græc. tom. x. p. 427—432.)]

[Footnote 42: See Cantacuzene (l. ii. c. 39, 40, l. iv. c. 3, 23, 24, 25) and Nic. Gregoras, (l. xi. c. 10, l. xv. 3, 7, &c.,) whose last books, from the xixth to xxivth, are almost confined to a subject so interesting to the authors. Boivin, (in Vit. Nic. Gregoræ,) from the unpublished books, and Fabricius, (Bibliot. Græc. tom. x. p. 462—473,) or rather Montfaucon, from the MSS. of the Coislin library, have added some facts and documents.]

For the conclusion of this chapter, I have reserved the Genoese war, which shook the throne of Cantacuzene, and betrayed the debility of the Greek empire. The Genoese, who, after the recovery of Constantinople, were seated in the suburb of Pera or Galata, received that honorable fief from the bounty of the emperor. They were indulged in the use of their laws and magistrates; but they submitted to the duties of vassals and subjects; the forcible word of liegemen[43] was borrowed from the Latin jurisprudence; and their podesta, or chief, before he entered on his office, saluted the emperor with loyal acclamations and vows of fidelity. Genoa sealed a firm alliance with the Greeks; and, in case of a defensive war, a supply of fifty empty galleys and a succor of fifty galleys, completely armed and manned, was promised by the republic to the empire. In the revival of a naval force, it was the aim of Michael Palæologus to deliver himself from a foreign aid; and his vigorous government contained the Genoese of Galata within those limits which the insolence of wealth and freedom provoked them to exceed. A sailor threatened that they should soon be masters of Constantinople, and slew the Greek who resented this national affront; and an armed vessel, after refusing to salute the palace, was guilty of some acts of piracy in the Black Sea. Their countrymen threatened to support their cause; but the long and open village of Galata was instantly surrounded by the Imperial troops; till, in the moment of the assault, the prostrate Genoese implored the clemency of their sovereign. The defenceless situation which secured their obedience exposed them to the attack of their Venetian rivals, who, in the reign of the elder Andronicus, presumed to violate the majesty of the throne. On the approach of their fleets, the Genoese, with their families and effects, retired into the city: their empty habitations were reduced to ashes; and the feeble prince, who had viewed the destruction of his suburb, expressed his resentment, not by arms, but by ambassadors. This misfortune, however, was advantageous to the Genoese, who obtained, and imperceptibly abused, the dangerous license of surrounding Galata with a strong wall; of introducing into the ditch the waters of the sea; of erecting lofty turrets; and of mounting a train of military engines on the rampart. The narrow bounds in which they had been circumscribed were insufficient for the growing colony; each day they acquired some addition of landed property; and the adjacent hills were covered with their villas and castles, which they joined and protected by new fortifications. [44] The navigation and trade of the Euxine was the patrimony of the Greek emperors, who commanded the narrow entrance, the gates, as it were, of that inland sea. In the reign of Michael Palæologus, their prerogative was acknowledged by the sultan of Egypt, who solicited and obtained the liberty of sending an annual ship for the purchase of slaves in Circassia and the Lesser Tartary: a liberty pregnant with mischief to the Christian cause; since these youths were transformed by education and discipline into the formidable Mamalukes. [45] From the colony of Pera, the Genoese engaged with superior advantage in the lucrative trade of the Black Sea; and their industry supplied the Greeks with fish and corn; two articles of food almost equally important to a superstitious people. The spontaneous bounty of nature appears to have bestowed the harvests of Ukraine, the produce of a rude and savage husbandry; and the endless exportation of salt fish and caviare is annually renewed by the enormous sturgeons that are caught at the mouth of the Don or Tanais, in their last station of the rich mud and shallow water of the Mæotis. [46] The waters of the Oxus, the Caspian, the Volga, and the Don, opened a rare and laborious passage for the gems and spices of India; and after three months' march the caravans of Carizme met the Italian vessels in the harbors of Crimæa. [47] These various branches of trade were monopolized by the diligence and power of the Genoese. Their rivals of Venice and Pisa were forcibly expelled; the natives were awed by the castles and cities, which arose on the foundations of their humble factories; and their principal establishment of Caffa [48] was besieged without effect by the Tartar powers. Destitute of a navy, the Greeks were oppressed by these haughty merchants, who fed, or famished, Constantinople, according to their interest. They proceeded to usurp the customs, the fishery, and even the toll, of the Bosphorus; and while they derived from these objects a revenue of two hundred thousand pieces of gold, a remnant of thirty thousand was reluctantly allowed to the emperor. [49] The colony of Pera or Galata acted, in peace and war, as an independent state; and, as it will happen in distant settlements, the Genoese podesta too often forgot that he was the servant of his own masters.

[Footnote 43: Pachymer (l. v. c. 10) very properly explains liziouV (ligios) by?lidiouV. The use of these words in the Greek and Latin of the feudal times may be amply understood from the Glossaries of Ducange, (Græc. p. 811, 812. Latin. tom. iv. p. 109—111.)]

[Footnote 44: The establishment and progress of the Genoese at Pera, or Galata, is described by Ducange (C. P. Christiana, l. i. p. 68, 69) from the Byzantine historians, Pachymer, (l. ii. c. 35, l. v. c. 10, 30, l. ix. 15 l. xii. 6, 9,) Nicephorus Gregoras, (l. v. c. 4, l. vi. c. 11, l. ix. c. 5, l. ix. c. 1, l. xv. c. 1, 6,) and Cantacuzene, (l. i. c. 12, l. ii. c. 29, &c.)]

[Footnote 45: Both Pachymer (l. iii. c. 3, 4, 5) and Nic. Greg. (l. iv. c. 7) understand and deplore the effects of this dangerous indulgence. Bibars, sultan of Egypt, himself a Tartar, but a devout Mussulman, obtained from the children of Zingis the permission to build a stately mosque in the capital of Crimea, (De Guignes, Hist. des Huns, tom. iii. p. 343.)]

[Footnote 46: Chardin (Voyages en Perse, tom. i. p. 48) was assured at Caffa, that these fishes were sometimes twenty-four or twenty-six feet long, weighed eight or nine hundred pounds, and yielded three or four quintals of caviare. The corn of the Bosphorus had supplied the Athenians in the time of Demosthenes.]

[Footnote 47: De Guignes, Hist. des Huns, tom. iii. p. 343, 344. Viaggi di Ramusio, tom. i. fol. 400. But this land or water carriage could only be practicable when Tartary was united under a wise and powerful monarch.]

[Footnote 48: Nic. Gregoras (l. xiii. c. 12) is judicious and well informed on the trade and colonies of the Black Sea. Chardin describes the present ruins of Caffa, where, in forty days, he saw above 400 sail employed in the corn and fish trade, (Voyages en Perse, tom. i. p. 46—48.)]

[Footnote 49: See Nic. Gregoras, l. xvii. c. 1.]

These usurpations were encouraged by the weakness of the elder Andronicus, and by the civil wars that afflicted his age and the minority of his grandson. The talents of Cantacuzene were employed to the ruin, rather than the restoration, of the empire; and after his domestic victory, he was condemned to an ignominious trial, whether the Greeks or the Genoese should reign in Constantinople. The merchants of Pera were offended by his refusal of some contiguous land, some commanding heights, which they proposed to cover with new fortifications; and in the absence of the emperor, who was detained at Demotica by sickness, they ventured to brave the debility of a female reign. A Byzantine vessel, which had presumed to fish at the mouth of the harbor, was sunk by these audacious strangers; the fishermen were murdered. Instead of suing for pardon, the Genoese demanded satisfaction; required, in a haughty strain, that the Greeks should renounce the exercise of navigation; and encountered with regular arms the first sallies of the popular indignation. They instantly occupied the debatable land; and by the labor of a whole people, of either sex and of every age, the wall was raised, and the ditch was sunk, with incredible speed. At the same time, they attacked and burnt two Byzantine galleys; while the three others, the remainder of the Imperial navy, escaped from their hands: the habitations without the gates, or along the shore, were pillaged and destroyed; and the care of the regent, of the empress Irene, was confined to the preservation of the city. The return of Cantacuzene dispelled the public consternation: the emperor inclined to peaceful counsels; but he yielded to the obstinacy of his enemies, who rejected all reasonable terms, and to the ardor of his subjects, who threatened, in the style of Scripture, to break them in pieces like a potter's vessel. Yet they reluctantly paid the taxes, that he imposed for the construction of ships, and the expenses of the war; and as the two nations were masters, the one of the land, the other of the sea, Constantinople and Pera were pressed by the evils of a mutual siege. The merchants of the colony, who had believed that a few days would terminate the war, already murmured at their losses: the succors from their mother-country were delayed by the factions of Genoa; and the most cautious embraced the opportunity of a Rhodian vessel to remove their families and effects from the scene of hostility. In the spring, the Byzantine fleet, seven galleys and a train of smaller vessels, issued from the mouth of the harbor, and steered in a single line along the shore of Pera; unskilfully presenting their sides to the beaks of the adverse squadron. The crews were composed of peasants and mechanics; nor was their ignorance compensated by the native courage of Barbarians: the wind was strong, the waves were rough; and no sooner did the Greeks perceive a distant and inactive enemy, than they leaped headlong into the sea, from a doubtful, to an inevitable peril. The troops that marched to the attack of the lines of Pera were struck at the same moment with a similar panic; and the Genoese were astonished, and almost ashamed, at their double victory. Their triumphant vessels, crowned with flowers, and dragging after them the captive galleys, repeatedly passed and repassed before the palace:

the only virtue of the emperor was patience; and the hope of revenge his sole consolation. Yet the distress of both parties interposed a temporary agreement; and the shame of the empire was disguised by a thin veil of dignity and power. Summoning the chiefs of the colony, Cantacuzene affected to despise the trivial object of the debate; and, after a mild reproof, most liberally granted the lands, which had been previously resigned to the seeming custody of his officers. [50]

[Footnote 50: *The events of this war are related by Cantacuzene (l. iv. c. 11 with obscurity and confusion, and by Nic. Gregoras l. xvii. c. 1—7) in a clear and honest narrative. The priest was less responsible than the prince for the defeat of the fleet.*]

But the emperor was soon solicited to violate the treaty, and to join his arms with the Venetians, the perpetual enemies of Genoa and her colonies. While he compared the reasons of peace and war, his moderation was provoked by a wanton insult of the inhabitants of Pera, who discharged from their rampart a large stone that fell in the midst of Constantinople. On his just complaint, they coldly blamed the imprudence of their engineer; but the next day the insult was repeated; and they exulted in a second proof that the royal city was not beyond the reach of their artillery. Cantacuzene instantly signed his treaty with the Venetians; but the weight of the Roman empire was scarcely felt in the balance of these opulent and powerful republics. [51] From the Straits of Gibraltar to the mouth of the Tanais, their fleets encountered each other with various success; and a memorable battle was fought in the narrow sea, under the walls of Constantinople. It would not be an easy task to reconcile the accounts of the Greeks, the Venetians, and the Genoese; [52] and while I depend on the narrative of an impartial historian, [53] I shall borrow from each nation the facts that redound to their own disgrace, and the honor of their foes. The Venetians, with their allies the Catalans, had the advantage of number; and their fleet, with the poor addition of eight Byzantine galleys, amounted to seventy-five sail: the Genoese did not exceed sixty-four; but in those times their ships of war were distinguished by the superiority of their size and strength. The names and families of their naval commanders, Pisani and Doria, are illustrious in the annals of their country; but the personal merit of the former was eclipsed by the fame and abilities of his rival. They engaged in tempestuous weather; and the tumultuary conflict was continued from the dawn to the extinction of light. The enemies of the Genoese applaud their prowess; the friends of the Venetians are dissatisfied with their behavior; but all parties agree in praising the skill and boldness of the Catalans, [531] who, with many wounds, sustained the brunt of the action. On the separation of the fleets, the event might appear doubtful; but the thirteen Genoese galleys, that had been sunk or taken, were compensated by a double loss of the allies; of fourteen Venetians, ten Catalans, and two Greeks; [532] and even the grief of the conquerors expressed the assurance and habit of more decisive victories. Pisani confessed his defeat, by retiring into a fortified harbor, from whence, under the pretext of the orders of the senate, he steered with a broken and flying squadron for the Isle of Candia, and abandoned to his rivals the sovereignty of the sea. In a public epistle, [54] addressed to the doge and senate, Petrarch employs his eloquence to reconcile the maritime powers, the two luminaries of Italy. The orator celebrates the valor and victory of the Genoese, the first of men in the exercise of naval war: he drops a tear on the misfortunes of their Venetian brethren; but he exhorts them to pursue with fire and sword the base and perfidious Greeks; to purge the metropolis of the East from the heresy with which it was infected. Deserted by their friends, the Greeks were incapable of resistance; and three months after the battle, the emperor Cantacuzene solicited and subscribed a treaty, which forever banished the Venetians and Catalans, and granted to the Genoese a monopoly of trade, and almost a right of dominion. The Roman empire (I smile in transcribing the name) might soon have sunk into a province of Genoa, if the ambition of the republic had not been checked by the ruin of her freedom and naval power. A long contest of one hundred and thirty years was determined by the triumph of Venice; and the factions of the Genoese compelled them to seek for domestic peace under the protection of a foreign lord, the duke of Milan, or the French king. Yet the spirit of commerce survived that of conquest; and the colony of Pera still awed the capital and navigated the Euxine, till it was involved by the Turks in the final servitude of Constantinople itself.

[Footnote 51: The second war is darkly told by Cantacuzene, (l. iv. c. 18, p. 24, 25, 28—32,) who wishes to disguise what he dares not deny. I regret this part of Nic. Gregoras, which is still in MS. at Paris. Note: This part of Nicephorus Gregoras has not been printed in the new edition of the Byzantine Historians. The editor expresses a hope that it may be undertaken by Hase. I should join in the regret of Gibbon, if these books contain any historical information: if they are but a continuation of the controversies which fill the last books in our present copies, they may as well sleep their eternal sleep in MS. as in print—M.]

[Footnote 52: Muratori (Annali d' Italia, tom. xii. p. 144) refers to the most ancient Chronicles of Venice (Caresinus, the continuator of Andrew Dandulus, tom. xii. p. 421, 422) and Genoa, (George Stella Annales Genuenses, tom. xvii. p. 1091, 1092;) both which I have diligently consulted in his great Collection of the Historians of Italy.]

[Footnote 53: See the Chronicle of Matteo Villani of Florence, l. ii. c. 59, p. 145—147, c. 74, 75, p. 156, 157, in Muratori's Collection, tom. xiv.]

[Footnote 53/1: Cantacuzene praises their bravery, but imputes their losses to their ignorance of the seas: they suffered more by the breakers than by the enemy, vol. iii. p. 224—M.]

[Footnote 53/2: Cantacuzene says that the Genoese lost twenty-eight ships with their crews, autandroi; the Venetians and Catalans sixteen, the Imperials, none Cantacuzene accuses Pisani of cowardice, in not following up the victory, and destroying the Genoese. But Pisani's conduct, and indeed Cantacuzene's account of the battle, betray the superiority of the Genoese—M.]

[Footnote 54: The Abbé de Sade (Mémoires sur la Vie de Petrarque, tom. iii. p. 257—263) translates this letter, which he copied from a MS. in the king of France's library. Though a servant of the duke of Milan, Petrarch pours forth his astonishment and grief at the defeat and despair of the Genoese in the following year, (p. 323—332.)]

CHAPTER LXIV

MOGULS, OTTOMAN TURKS

PART I

CONQUESTS OF ZINGHIS KHAN AND THE MOGULS FROM CHINA TO POLAND—ESCAPE OF CONSTANTINOPLE AND THE GREEKS—ORIGIN OF THE OTTOMAN TURKS IN BITHYNIA—REIGNS AND VICTORIES OF OTHMAN, ORCHAN, AMURATH THE FIRST, AND BAJAZET THE FIRST—FOUNDATION AND PROGRESS OF THE TURKISH MONARCHY IN ASIA AND EUROPE—DANGER OFCONSTANTINOPLE AND THE GREEK EMPIRE

From the petty quarrels of a city and her suburbs, from the cowardice and discord of the falling Greeks, I shall now ascend to the victorious Turks; whose domestic slavery was ennobled by martial discipline, religious enthusiasm, and the energy of the national character. The rise and progress of the Ottomans, the present sovereigns of Constantinople, are connected with the most important scenes of modern history; but they are founded on a previous knowledge of the great eruption of the Moguls [100] and Tartars; whose rapid conquests may be compared with the primitive convulsions of nature, which have agitated and altered the surface of the globe. I have long since asserted my claim to introduce the nations, the immediate or remote authors of the fall of the Roman empire; nor can I refuse myself to those events, which, from their uncommon magnitude, will interest a philosophic mind in the history of blood. [1]

[Footnote 100: Mongol seems to approach the nearest to the proper name of this race. The Chinese call them Mong-kou; the Mondchoux, their neighbors, Monggo or Monggou. They called themselves also Beda. This fact seems to have been proved by M. Schmidt against the French Orientalists. See De Brosset. Note on Le Beau, tom. xxii p. 402.]

[Footnote 1: The reader is invited to review chapters xxii. to xxvi., and xxiii. to xxxviii., the manners of pastoral nations, the conquests of Attila and the Huns, which were composed at a time when I entertained the wish, rather than the hope, of concluding my history.]

From the spacious highlands between China, Siberia, and the Caspian Sea, the tide of emigration and war has repeatedly been poured. These ancient seats of the Huns and Turks were occupied in the twelfth century by many pastoral tribes, of the same descent and similar manners, which were united and led to conquest by the formidable Zingis. [101] In his ascent to greatness, that Barbarian (whose private appellation was Temugin) had trampled on the necks of his equals. His birth was noble; but it was the pride of victory, that the prince or people deduced his seventh ancestor from the immaculate conception of a virgin. His father had reigned over thirteen hordes, which composed about thirty or forty thousand families: above two thirds refused to pay tithes or obedience to his infant son; and at the age of thirteen, Temugin fought a battle against his rebellious subjects. The future conqueror of Asia was reduced to fly and to obey; but he rose superior to his fortune, and in his fortieth year he had established his fame and dominion over the circumjacent tribes. In a state of society, in which policy is rude and valor is universal, the ascendant of one man must be founded on his power and resolution to punish his enemies and recompense his friends. His first military league was ratified by the simple rites of sacrificing a horse and tasting of a running stream: Temugin pledged himself to divide with his followers the sweets and the bitters of life; and when he had shared among them his horses and apparel, he was rich in their gratitude and his own hopes. After his first victory, he placed seventy caldrons on the fire, and seventy of the most guilty rebels were cast headlong into the boiling water. The sphere of his attraction was continually enlarged by the ruin of the proud and the submission of the prudent; and the boldest chieftains might tremble, when they beheld, enchased in silver, the skull of the khan of Keraites; [2] who, under the name of Prester John, had corresponded with the Roman pontiff and the princes of Europe. The ambition of Temugin condescended to employ the arts of superstition; and it was from a naked prophet, who could ascend to heaven on a white horse, that he accepted the title of Zingis, [3] the most great; and a divine right to the conquest and dominion of the earth. In a general couroultai, or diet, he was seated on a felt, which was long afterwards revered as a relic, and solemnly proclaimed great khan, or emperor of the Moguls [4] and Tartars. [5] Of these kindred, though rival, names, the former had given birth to the imperial race; and the latter has been extended by accident or error over the spacious wilderness of the north.

[Footnote 101: On the traditions of the early life of Zingis, see D'Ohson, Hist des Mongols; Histoire des Mongols, Paris, 1824. Schmidt, Geschichte des Ost-Mongolen, p. 66, &c., and Notes—M.]

[Footnote 2: The khans of the Keraites were most probably incapable of reading the pompous epistles composed in their name by the Nestorian missionaries, who endowed them with the fabulous wonders of an Indian kingdom. Perhaps these Tartars (the Presbyter or Priest John) had submitted to the rites of baptism and ordination, (Asseman, Bibliot Orient tom. iii. p. ii. p. 487—503.)]

[Footnote 3: Since the history and tragedy of Voltaire, Gengis, at least in French, seems to be the more fashionable spelling; but Abulghazi Khan must have known the true name of his ancestor. His etymology appears just: Zin, in the Mogul tongue, signifies great, and gis is the superlative termination, (Hist. Généalogique des Tatars, part iii. p. 194, 195.) From the same idea of magnitude, the appellation of Zingis is bestowed on the ocean.]

[Footnote 4: The name of Moguls has prevailed among the Orientals, and still adheres to the titular sovereign, the Great Mogul of Hindastan. Note: M. Remusat (sur les Langues Tartares, p. 233) justly observes, that Timour was a Turk, not a Mogul, and, p. 242, that probably there was not Mogul in the army of Baber, who established the Indian throne of the "Great Mogul."—M.]

[Footnote 5: The Tartars (more properly Tatars) were descended from Tatar Khan, the brother of Mogul Khan, (see Abulghazi, part i. and ii.,) and once formed a horde of 70,000 families on the borders of Kitay, (p. 103—112.) In the great invasion of Europe (A.D. 1238) they seem to have led the vanguard; and the similitude of the name of Tartarei, recommended that of Tartars to the Latins, (Matt. Paris, p. 398, &c.) Note: This relationship, according to M. Klaproth, is fabulous, and invented by the Mahometan writers, who, from religious zeal, endeavored to connect the traditions of the nomads of Central Asia with those of the Old Testament, as preserved in the Koran. There is no trace of it in the Chinese writers. Tabl. de l'Asie, p. 156—M.]

The code of laws which Zingis dictated to his subjects was adapted to the preservation of a domestic peace, and the exercise of foreign hostility. The punishment of death was inflicted on the crimes of adultery, murder, perjury, and the capital thefts of a horse or ox; and the fiercest of men were mild and just in their intercourse with each other. The future election of the great khan was vested in the princes of his family and the heads of the tribes; and the regulations of the chase were essential to the pleasures and plenty of a Tartar camp. The victorious nation was held sacred from all servile labors, which were abandoned to slaves and strangers; and every labor was servile except the profession of arms. The service and discipline of the troops, who were armed with bows, cimeters, and iron maces, and divided by hundreds, thousands, and ten thousands, were the institutions of a veteran commander. Each officer and soldier was made responsible, under pain of death, for the safety and honor of his companions; and the spirit of conquest breathed in the law, that peace should never be granted unless to a vanquished and suppliant enemy. But it is the religion of Zingis that best deserves our wonder and applause. [501] The Catholic inquisitors of Europe, who defended nonsense by cruelty, might have been confounded by the example of a Barbarian, who anticipated the lessons of philosophy, [6] and established by his laws a system of pure theism and perfect toleration. His first and only article of faith was the existence of one God, the Author of all good; who fills by his presence the heavens and earth, which he has created by his power. The Tartars and Moguls were addicted to the idols of their peculiar tribes; and many of them had been converted by the foreign missionaries to the religions of Moses, of Mahomet, and of Christ. These various systems in freedom and concord were taught and practised within the precincts of the same camp; and the Bonze, the Imam, the Rabbi, the Nestorian, and the Latin priest, enjoyed the same honorable exemption from service and tribute: in the mosque of Bochara, the insolent victor might trample the Koran under his horse's feet, but the calm legislator respected the prophets and pontiffs of the most hostile sects. The reason of Zingis was not informed by books: the khan could neither read nor write; and, except the tribe of the Igours, the greatest part of the Moguls and Tartars were as illiterate as their sovereign. [601] The memory of their exploits was preserved by tradition: sixty-eight years after the death of Zingis, these traditions were collected and transcribed; [7] the brevity of their domestic annals may be supplied by the Chinese, [8] Persians, [9] Armenians, [10] Syrians, [11] Arabians, [12] Greeks, [13] Russians, [14] Poles, [15] Hungarians, [16] and Latins; [17] and each nation will deserve credit in the relation of their own disasters and defeats. [18]

[Footnote 501: Before his armies entered Thibet, he sent an embassy to Bogdosottnam-Dsimmo, a Lama high priest, with a letter to this effect: "I have chosen thee as high priest for myself and my empire. Repair then to me, and promote the present and future happiness of man: I will be thy supporter and protector: let us establish a system of religion, and unite it with the monarchy," &c. The high priest accepted the invitation; and the Mongol history literally terms this step the period of the first respect for religion; because the monarch, by his public profession, made it the religion of the state. Klaproth. "Travels in Caucasus," ch. 7, Eng. Trans. p. 92. Neither Dshingis nor his son and successor Oegodah had, on account of their continual wars, much leisure for the propagation of the religion of the Lama. By religion they understand a distinct, independent, sacred moral code, which has but one origin, one source, and one object. This notion they universally propagate, and even believe that the brutes, and all created beings, have a religion adapted to their sphere of action. The different forms of the various religions they ascribe to the difference of individuals, nations, and legislators. Never do you hear of their inveighing against any creed, even against the obviously absurd Schaman paganism, or of their persecuting others on that account. They themselves, on the other hand, endure every hardship, and even persecutions, with perfect resignation, and indulgently excuse the follies of others, nay, consider them as a motive for increased ardor in prayer, ch. ix. p. 109—M.]

[Footnote 6: A singular conformity may be found between the religious laws of Zingis Khan and of Mr. Locke, (Constitutions of Carolina, in his works, vol. iv. p. 535, 4to. edition, 1777.)]

[Footnote 601: See the notice on Tha-tha-toung-o, the Ouogour minister of Tchingis, in Abel Remusat's 2d series of Recherch. Asiat. vol. ii. p. 61. He taught the son of Tchingis to write: "He was the instructor of the Moguls in writing, of which they were before ignorant;" and hence the application of the Ouigour characters to the Mogul language cannot be placed earlier than the year 1204 or 1205, nor so late as the time of Pà-sse-pa, who lived under Khubilai. A new alphabet, approaching to that of Thibet, was introduced under Khubilai—M.]

[Footnote 7: In the year 1294, by the command of Cazan, khan of Persia, the fourth in descent from Zingis. From these traditions, his vizier Fadlallah composed a Mogul history in the Persian language, which has been used by Petit de la Croix, (Hist. de Genghizcan, p. 537—539.) The Histoire Généalogique des Tatars (à Leyde, 1726, in 12mo., 2 tomes) was translated by the Swedish prisoners in Siberia from the Mogul MS. of Abulgasi Bahadur Khan, a descendant of Zingis, who reigned over the Usbeks of Charasm, or Carizme, (A.D. 1644—1663.) He is of most value and credit for the names, pedigrees, and manners of his nation. Of his nine parts, the ist descends from Adam to Mogul Khan; the iid, from Mogul to Zingis; the iiid is the life of Zingis; the ivth, vth, vith, and viith, the general history of his four sons and their posterity; the viiith and ixth, the particular history of the descendants of Sheibani Khan, who reigned in Maurenahar and Charasm.]

[Footnote 8: Histoire de Gentchiscan, et de toute la Dinastie des Mongous ses Successeurs, Conquerans de la Chine; tirée de l'Histoire de la Chine par le R. P. Gaubil, de la Société de Jesus, Missionaire à Peking;

à Paris, 1739, in 4to. This translation is stamped with the Chinese character of domestic accuracy and foreign ignorance.]

[Footnote 9: See the Histoire du Grand Genghizcan, premier Empereur des Moguls et Tartares, par M. Petit de la Croix, à Paris, 1710, in 12mo.; a work of ten years' labor, chiefly drawn from the Persian writers, among whom Nisavi, the secretary of Sultan Gelaleddin, has the merit and prejudices of a contemporary. A slight air of romance is the fault of the originals, or the compiler. See likewise the articles of Genghizcan, Mohammed, Gelaleddin, &c., in the Bibliothèque Orientale of D'Herbelot. Note: The preface to the Hist. des Mongols, (Paris, 1824) gives a catalogue of the Arabic and Persian authorities— M.]

[Footnote 10: Haithonus, or Aithonus, an Armenian prince, and afterwards a monk of Premontré, (Fabric, Bibliot. Lat. Medii Ævi, tom. i. p. 34,) dictated in the French language, his book de Tartaris, his old fellow-soldiers. It was immediately translated into Latin, and is inserted in the Novus Orbis of Simon Grynæus, (Basil, 1555, in folio.) Note: A précis at the end of the new edition of Le Beau, Hist. des Empereurs, vol. xvii., by M. Brosset, gives large extracts from the accounts of the Armenian historians relating to the Mogul conquests—M.]

[Footnote 11: Zingis Khan, and his first successors, occupy the conclusion of the ixth Dynasty of Abulpharagius, (vers. Pocock, Oxon. 1663, in 4to.;) and his xth Dynasty is that of the Moguls of Persia. Assemannus (Bibliot. Orient. tom. ii.) has extracted some facts from his Syriac writings, and the lives of the Jacobite maphrians, or primates of the East.]

[Footnote 12: Among the Arabians, in language and religion, we may distinguish Abulfeda, sultan of Hamah in Syria, who fought in person, under the Mamaluke standard, against the Moguls.]

[Footnote 13: Nicephorus Gregoras (l. ii. c. 5, 6) has felt the necessity of connecting the Scythian and Byzantine histories. He describes with truth and elegance the settlement and manners of the Moguls of Persia, but he is ignorant of their origin, and corrupts the names of Zingis and his sons.]

[Footnote 14: M. Levesque (Histoire de Russie, tom. ii.) has described the conquest of Russia by the Tartars, from the patriarch Nicon, and the old chronicles.]

[Footnote 15: For Poland, I am content with the Sarmatia Asiatica et Europæa of Matthew à Michou, or De Michoviâ, a canon and physician of Cracow, (A.D. 1506,) inserted in the Novus Orbis of Grynæus. Fabric Bibliot. Latin. Mediæ et Infimæ Ætatis, tom. v. p. 56.]

[Footnote 16: I should quote Thuroczius, the oldest general historian (pars ii. c. 74, p. 150) in the 1st volume of the Scriptores Rerum Hungaricarum, did not the same volume contain the original narrative of a contemporary, an eye-witness, and a sufferer, (M. Rogerii, Hungari, Varadiensis Capituli Canonici, Carmen miserabile, seu Historia super Destructione Regni Hungariæ Temporibus Belæ IV. Regis per Tartaros facta, p. 292—321;) the best picture that I have ever seen of all the circumstances of a Barbaric invasion.]

[Footnote 17: Matthew Paris has represented, from authentic documents, the danger and distress of Europe, (consult the word Tartari in his copious Index.) From motives of zeal and curiosity, the court of the great khan in the xiiith century was visited by two friars, John de Plano Carpini, and William Rubruquis, and by Marco Polo, a Venetian gentleman. The Latin relations of the two former are inserted in the 1st volume of Hackluyt; the Italian original or version of the third (Fabric. Bibliot. Latin. Medii Ævi, tom. ii. p. 198, tom. v. p. 25) may be found in the second tome of Ramusio.]

[Footnote 18: In his great History of the Huns, M. de Guignes has most amply treated of Zingis Khan and his successors. See tom. iii. l. xv—xix., and in the collateral articles of the Seljukians of Roum, tom. ii. l. xi., the Carizmians, l. xiv., and the Mamalukes, tom. iv. l. xxi.; consult likewise the tables of the 1st volume. He is ever learned and accurate; yet I am only indebted to him for a general view, and some passages of Abulfeda, which are still latent in the Arabic text. Note: To this catalogue of the historians of the Moguls may be added D'Ohson, Histoire des Mongols; Histoire des Mongols, (from Arabic and Persian authorities,) Paris, 1824. Schmidt, Geschichte der Ost Mongolen, St. Petersburgh, 1829. This curious work, by Ssanang Ssetsen Chungtaidschi, published in the original Mongol, was written after the conversion of the nation to Buddhism: it is enriched with very valuable notes by the editor and translator; but, unfortunately, is very barren of information about the European and even the western Asiatic conquests of the Mongols—M.]

PART II

The arms of Zingis and his lieutenants successively reduced the hordes of the desert, who pitched their tents between the wall of China and the Volga; and the Mogul emperor became the monarch of the pastoral world, the lord of many millions of shepherds and soldiers, who felt their united strength, and were impatient to rush on the mild and wealthy climates of the south. His ancestors had been the tributaries of the Chinese emperors; and Temugin himself had been disgraced by a title of honor and servitude. The court of Pekin was astonished by an embassy from its former vassal, who, in the tone of the king of nations, exacted the tribute and obedience which he had paid, and who affected to treat the son of heaven as the most contemptible of mankind. A haughty answer disguised their secret apprehensions; and their fears were soon justified by the march of innumerable squadrons, who pierced on all sides the feeble rampart of the great wall. Ninety cities were stormed, or starved, by the Moguls; ten only escaped; and Zingis, from a knowledge of the filial piety of the Chinese, covered his vanguard with their captive parents; an unworthy, and by degrees a fruitless, abuse of the virtue of his enemies. His invasion was supported by the revolt of a hundred thousand Khitans, who guarded the frontier: yet he listened to a treaty; and a princess of China, three thousand horses, five hundred youths, and as many virgins, and a tribute of gold and silk, were the price of his retreat. In his second expedition, he compelled the Chinese emperor to retire beyond the yellow river to a more southern residence. The siege of Pekin [19] was long and laborious: the inhabitants were reduced by famine to decimate and devour their fellow-citizens; when their ammunition was spent, they discharged ingots of gold and silver from their engines; but the Moguls introduced a mine to the centre of the capital; and the conflagration of the palace burnt above thirty days. China was desolated by Tartar war and domestic faction; and the five northern provinces were added to the empire of Zingis.

[Footnote 19: More properly Yen-king, an ancient city, whose ruins still appear some furlongs to the south-east of the modern Pekin, which was built by Cublai Khan, (Gaubel, p. 146.) Pe-king and Nan-king are vague titles, the courts of the north and of the south. The identity and change of names perplex the most skilful readers of the Chinese geography, (p. 177.) Note: And likewise in Chinese history—see Abel Remusat, Mel. Asiat. 2d tom. ii. p. 5—M.]

In the West, he touched the dominions of Mohammed, sultan of Carizme, who reigned from the Persian Gulf to the borders of India and Turkestan; and who, in the proud imitation of Alexander the Great, forgot the servitude and ingratitude of his fathers to the house of Seljuk. It was the wish of Zingis to establish a friendly and commercial intercourse with the most powerful of the Moslem princes: nor could he be tempted by the secret solicitations of the caliph of Bagdad, who sacrificed to his personal wrongs the safety of the church and state. A rash and inhuman deed provoked and justified the Tartar arms in the invasion of the southern Asia. [19/1] A caravan of three ambassadors and one hundred and fifty merchants were arrested and murdered at Otrar, by the command of Mohammed; nor was it till after a demand and denial of justice, till he had prayed and fasted three nights on a mountain, that the Mogul emperor appealed to the judgment of God and his sword. Our European battles, says a philosophic writer, [20] are petty skirmishes, if compared to the numbers that have fought and fallen in the fields of Asia. Seven hundred thousand Moguls and Tartars are said to have marched under the standard of Zingis and his four sons. In the vast plains that extend to the north of the Sihon or Jaxartes, they were encountered by four hundred thousand soldiers of the sultan; and in the first battle, which was suspended by the night, one hundred and sixty thousand Carizmians were slain. Mohammed was astonished by the multitude and valor of his enemies: he withdrew from the scene of danger, and distributed his troops in the frontier towns; trusting that the Barbarians, invincible in the field, would be repulsed by the length and difficulty of so many regular sieges. But the prudence of Zingis had formed a body of Chinese engineers, skilled in the mechanic arts; informed perhaps of the secret of gunpowder, and capable, under his discipline, of attacking a foreign country with more vigor and success than they had defended their own. The Persian historians will relate the sieges and reduction of Otrar, Cogende, Bochara, Samarcand, Carizme, Herat, Merou, Nisabour, Balch, and Candahar; and the conquest of the rich and populous countries of Transoxiana, Carizme, and Chorazan. [20/1] The destructive hostilities of Attila and the Huns have long since been elucidated by the example of Zingis and the Moguls; and in this more proper place I shall be content to observe, that, from the Caspian to the Indus, they ruined a tract of many hundred miles, which was adorned with the habitations and labors of mankind, and that five centuries have not been sufficient to repair the ravages of four years. The Mogul emperor encouraged or indulged the fury of his troops: the hope of future possession was lost in the ardor of rapine and slaughter; and the cause of the war exasperated their native fierceness by the pretence of justice and revenge. The downfall and death of the sultan Mohammed, who expired, unpitied and alone, in a desert island of the Caspian Sea, is a poor atonement for the calamities of which he was the author. Could the Carizmian empire have been saved by a single hero, it would have been saved by his son Gelaleddin, whose active valor repeatedly checked the Moguls in the career of victory. Retreating, as he fought, to the banks of the Indus, he was oppressed by their innumerable host, till, in the last moment of despair, Gelaleddin spurred his horse into the waves, swam one of the broadest and most rapid rivers of Asia, and extorted the admiration and applause of Zingis himself. It was in this camp that the Mogul conqueror yielded with reluctance to the murmurs of his weary and wealthy troops, who sighed for the enjoyment of their native land. Eucumbered with the spoils of Asia, he slowly measured back his footsteps, betrayed some pity for the misery of the vanquished, and declared his intention of rebuilding the cities which had been swept away by the tempest of his arms. After he had repassed the Oxus and Jaxartes, he was joined by two generals, whom he had detached with thirty thousand horse, to subdue the western provinces of Persia. They had trampled on the nations which opposed their passage, penetrated through the gates of Derbent, traversed the Volga and the desert, and accomplished the circuit of the Caspian Sea, by an expedition which had never been attempted, and has never been repeated. The return of Zingis was signalized by the overthrow of the rebellious or independent kingdoms of Tartary; and he died in the fulness of years and glory, with his last breath exhorting and instructing his sons to achieve the conquest of the Chinese empire. [20/2]

[Footnote 19/1: See the particular account of this transaction, from the Kholauesut el Akbaur, in Price, vol. ii. p. 402—M.]

[Footnote 20: M. de Voltaire, Essai sur l'Histoire Générale, tom. iii. c. 60, p. 8. His account of Zingis and the Moguls contains, as usual, much general sense and truth, with some particular errors.]

[Footnote 20/1: Every where they massacred all classes, except the artisans, whom they made slaves. Hist. des Mongols—M.]

[Footnote 20/2: Their first duty, which he bequeathed to them, was to massacre the king of Tangcoute and all the inhabitants of Ninhia, the surrender of the city being already agreed upon, Hist. des Mongols. vol. i. p. 286—M.]

The harem of Zingis was composed of five hundred wives and concubines; and of his numerous progeny, four sons, illustrious by their birth and merit, exercised under their father the principal offices of peace and war. Toushi was his great huntsman, Zagatai [21] his judge, Octai his minister, and Tuli his general; and their names and actions are often conspicuous in the history of his conquests. Firmly united for their own and the public interest, the three brothers and their families were content with dependent sceptres; and Octai, by general consent, was proclaimed great khan, or emperor of the Moguls and Tartars. He was succeeded by his son Gayuk, after whose death the empire devolved to his cousins Mangou and Cublai, the sons of Tuli, and the grandsons of Zingis. In the sixty-eight years of his four first successors, the Mogul subdued almost all Asia, and a large portion of Europe. Without confining myself to the order of time, without expatiating on the detail of events, I shall present a general picture of the progress of their arms; I. In the East; II. In the South; III. In the West; and IV. In the North.

[Footnote 21: Zagatai gave his name to his dominions of Maurenahar, or Transoxiana; and the Moguls of Hindostan, who emigrated from that country, are styled Zagatais by the Persians. This certain etymology, and the similar example of Uzbek, Nogai, &c., may warn us not absolutely to reject the derivations of a national, from a personal, name. Note: See a curious anecdote of Tschagatai. Hist. des Mongols, p. 370—M.]

I. Before the invasion of Zingis, China was divided into two empires or dynasties of the North and South; [22] and the difference of origin and interest was smoothed by a general conformity of laws, language, and national manners. The Northern empire, which had been dismembered by Zingis, was finally subdued seven years after his death. After the loss of Pekin, the emperor had fixed his residence at Kaifong, a city many leagues in circumference, and which contained, according to the Chinese annals, fourteen hundred thousand families of inhabitants and fugitives. He escaped from thence with only seven horsemen, and made his last stand in a third capital, till at length the hopeless monarch, protesting his innocence and accusing his fortune, ascended a funeral pile, and gave orders, that, as soon as he had stabbed himself, the fire should be kindled by his attendants. The dynasty of the Song, the native and ancient sovereigns of the whole empire, survived about forty-five years the fall of the Northern usurpers; and the perfect conquest was reserved for the arms of Cublai. During this interval, the Moguls were often diverted by foreign wars; and, if the Chinese seldom dared to meet their victors in the field, their passive courage presented and endless succession of cities to storm and of millions to slaughter. In the attack and defence of places, the engines of antiquity and the Greek fire were alternately employed: the use of gunpowder in cannon and bombs appears as a familiar practice; [23] and the sieges were conducted by the Mahometans and Franks, who had been liberally invited into the service of Cublai. After passing the great river, the troops and artillery were conveyed along a series of canals, till they invested the royal residence of Hamcheu, or Quinsay, in the country of silk, the most delicious climate of China. The emperor, a defenceless youth, surrendered his person and sceptre; and before he was sent in exile into Tartary, he struck nine times the ground with his forehead, to adore in prayer or thanksgiving the mercy of the great khan. Yet the war (it was now styled a rebellion) was still maintained in the southern provinces from Hamcheu to Canton; and the obstinate remnant of independence and hostility was transported from the land to the sea. But when the fleet of the Song was surrounded and oppressed by a superior armament, their last champion leaped into the waves with his infant emperor in his arms. "It is more glorious," he cried, "to die a prince, than to live a slave." A hundred thousand Chinese imitated his example; and the whole empire, from Tonkin to the great wall, submitted to the dominion of Cublai. His boundless ambition aspired to the conquest of Japan: his fleet was twice shipwrecked; and the lives of a hundred thousand Moguls and Chinese were sacrificed in the fruitless expedition. But the circumjacent kingdoms, Corea, Tonkin, Cochinchina, Pegu, Bengal, and Thibet, were reduced in different degrees of tribute and obedience by the effort or terror of his arms. He explored the Indian Ocean with a fleet of a thousand ships: they sailed in sixty-eight days, most probably to the Isle of Borneo, under the equinoctial line; and though they returned not without spoil or glory, the emperor was dissatisfied that the savage king had escaped from their hands.

[Footnote 22: *In Marco Polo, and the Oriental geographers, the names of Cathay and Mangi distinguish the northern and southern empires, which, from A.D. 1234 to 1279, were those of the great khan, and of the Chinese. The search of Cathay, after China had been found, excited and misled our navigators of the sixteenth century, in their attempts to discover the north-east passage.*]

[Footnote 23: *I depend on the knowledge and fidelity of the Père Gaubil, who translates the Chinese text of the annals of the Moguls or Yuen, (p. 71, 93, 153;) but I am ignorant at what time these annals were composed and published. The two uncles of Marco Polo, who served as engineers at the siege of Siengyangfou, (l. ii. 61, in Ramusio, tom. ii. See Gaubil, p. 155, 157) must have felt and related the effects of this destructive powder, and their silence is a weighty, and almost decisive objection. I entertain a suspicion, that their recent discovery was carried from Europe to China by the caravans of the xvth century and falsely adopted as an old national discovery before the arrival of the Portuguese and Jesuits in the xvith. Yet the Père Gaubil affirms, that the use of gunpowder has been known to the Chinese above 1600 years. Note: Sou-houng-kian-lou. Abel Remusat—M. Note: La poudre à canon et d'autres compositions inflammantes, dont ils se servent pour construire des pièces d'artifice d'un effet suprenant, leur étaient connues depuis très long-temps, et l'on croit que des bombardes et des pierriers, dont ils avaient enseigné l'usage aux Tartares, ont pu donner en Europe l'idée d'artillerie, quoique la forme des fusils et des canons dont ils se servent actuellement, leur ait été apportée par les Francs, ainsi que l'attestent les noms mêmes qu'ils donnent à ces sortes d'armes. Abel Remusat, Mélanges Asiat. 2d ser. tom. i. p. 23—M.*]

II. The conquest of Hindostan by the Moguls was reserved in a later period for the house of Timour; but that of Iran, or Persia, was achieved by Holagou Khan, [23/1] the grandson of Zingis, the brother and lieutenant of the two successive emperors, Mangou and Cublai. I shall not enumerate the crowd of sultans, emirs, and atabeks, whom he trampled into dust; but the extirpation of the Assassins, or Ismaelians [24] of Persia, may be considered as a service to mankind. Among the hills to the south of the Caspian, these odious sectaries had reigned with impunity above a hundred and sixty years; and their prince, or Imam, established his lieutenant to lead and govern the colony of Mount Libanus, so famous and formidable in the history of the crusades. [25] With the fanaticism of the Koran the Ismaelians had blended the Indian transmigration, and the visions of their own prophets; and it was their first duty to devote their souls and bodies in blind obedience to the vicar of God. The daggers of his missionaries were felt both in the East and West: the Christians and the Moslems enumerate, and persons multiply, the illustrious victims that were sacrificed to the zeal, avarice, or resentment of the old man (as he was corruptly styled) of the mountain. But these daggers, his only arms, were broken by the sword of Holagou, and not a vestige is left of the enemies of mankind, except the word assassin, which, in the most odious sense, has been adopted in the languages of Europe. The extinction of the Abbassides cannot be indifferent to the spectators of their greatness and decline. Since the fall of their Seljukian tyrants the caliphs had recovered their lawful dominion of Bagdad and the Arabian Irak; but the city was distracted by theological factions, and the commander of the faithful was lost in a harem of seven hundred concubines. The invasion of the Moguls he encountered with feeble arms and haughty embassies. "On the divine decree," said the caliph Mostasem, "is founded the throne of the sons of Abbas: and their foes shall surely be destroyed in this world and in the next. Who is this Holagou that dares to rise against them? If he be desirous of peace, let him instantly depart from the sacred territory; and perhaps he may obtain from our clemency the pardon of his fault." This presumption was cherished by a perfidious vizier, who assured his master, that, even if the Barbarians had entered the city, the women and children, from the terraces, would be sufficient to overwhelm them with stones. But when Holagou touched the phantom, it instantly vanished into smoke. After a siege of two months, Bagdad was stormed and sacked by the Moguls; [* and their savage commander pronounced the death of the caliph Mostasem, the last of the temporal successors of Mahomet; whose noble kinsmen, of the race of Abbas, had reigned in Asia above five hundred years. Whatever might be the designs of the conqueror, the holy cities of Mecca and Medina [26] were protected by the Arabian desert; but the Moguls spread beyond the Tigris and Euphrates, pillaged Aleppo and Damascus, and threatened to join the Franks in the deliverance of Jerusalem. Egypt was lost, had she been defended only by her feeble offspring; but the Mamalukes had breathed in their infancy the keenness of a Scythian air: equal in valor, superior in discipline, they met the Moguls in many a well-fought field; and drove back the stream of hostility to the eastward of the Euphrates. [26/1] But it overflowed with resistless violence the kingdoms of Armenia [26/2] and Anatolia, of which the former was possessed by the Christians, and the latter by the Turks. The sultans of Iconium opposed some resistance to the Mogul arms, till Azzadin sought a refuge among the Greeks of Constantinople, and his feeble successors, the last of the Seljukian dynasty, were finally extirpated by the khans of Persia. [26/3]

[Footnote 23/1: See the curious account of the expedition of Holagou, translated from the Chinese, by M. Abel Remusat, Mélanges Asiat. 2d ser. tom. i. p. 171—M.]

[Footnote 24: All that can be known of the Assassins of Persia and Syria is poured from the copious, and even profuse, erudition of M. Falconet, in two Mémoires read before the Academy of Inscriptions, (tom. xvii. p. 127—170.) Note: Von Hammer's History of the Assassins has now thrown Falconet's Dissertation into the shade—M.]

[Footnote 25: The Ismaelians of Syria, 40,000 Assassins, had acquired or founded ten castles in the hills above Tortosa. About the year 1280, they were extirpated by the Mamalukes.]

[Footnote 251: Compare Von Hammer, Geschichte der Assassinen, p. 283, 307. Wilken, Geschichte der Kreuzzüge, vol. vii. p. 406. Price, Chronological Retrospect, vol. ii. p. 217—223—M.]

[Footnote 26: As a proof of the ignorance of the Chinese in foreign transactions, I must observe, that some of their historians extend the conquest of Zingis himself to Medina, the country of Mahomet, (Gaubil p. 42.)]

*[Footnote 26/1: Compare Wilken, vol. vii. p. 410—M.]*

*[Footnote 26/2: On the friendly relations of the Armenians with the Mongols see Wilken, Geschichte der Kreuzzüge, vol. vii. p. 402. They eagerly desired an alliance against the Mahometan powers—M.]*

*[Footnote 26/3: Trebizond escaped, apparently by the dexterous politics of the sovereign, but it acknowledged the Mogul supremacy. Falmerayer, p. 172—M.]*

III. No sooner had Octai subverted the northern empire of China, than he resolved to visit with his arms the most remote countries of the West. Fifteen hundred thousand Moguls and Tartars were inscribed on the military roll: of these the great khan selected a third, which he intrusted to the command of his nephew Batou, the son of Tuli; who reigned over his father's conquests to the north of the Caspian Sea. [264] After a festival of forty days, Batou set forwards on this great expedition; and such was the speed and ardor of his innumerable squadrons, than in less than six years they had measured a line of ninety degrees of longitude, a fourth part of the circumference of the globe. The great rivers of Asia and Europe, the Volga and Kama, the Don and Borysthenes, the Vistula and Danube, they either swam with their horses or passed on the ice, or traversed in leathern boats, which followed the camp, and transported their wagons and artillery. By the first victories of Batou, the remains of national freedom were eradicated in the immense plains of Turkestan and Kipzak. [27] In his rapid progress, he overran the kingdoms, as they are now styled, of Astracan and Cazan; and the troops which he detached towards Mount Caucasus explored the most secret recesses of Georgia and Circassia. The civil discord of the great dukes, or princes, of Russia, betrayed their country to the Tartars. They spread from Livonia to the Black Sea, and both Moscow and Kiow, the modern and the ancient capitals, were reduced to ashes; a temporary ruin, less fatal than the deep, and perhaps indelible, mark, which a servitude of two hundred years has imprinted on the character of the Russians. The Tartars ravaged with equal fury the countries which they hoped to possess, and those which they were hastening to leave. From the permanent conquest of Russia they made a deadly, though transient, inroad into the heart of Poland, and as far as the borders of Germany. The cities of Lublin and Cracow were obliterated: [27/1] they approached the shores of the Baltic; and in the battle of Lignitz they defeated the dukes of Silesia, the Polish palatines, and the great master of the Teutonic order, and filled nine sacks with the right ears of the slain. From Lignitz, the extreme point of their western march, they turned aside to the invasion of Hungary; and the presence or spirit of Batou inspired the host of five hundred thousand men: the Carpathian hills could not be long impervious to their divided columns; and their approach had been fondly disbelieved till it was irresistibly felt. The king, Bela the Fourth, assembled the military force of his counts and bishops; but he had alienated the nation by adopting a vagrant horde of forty thousand families of Comans, and these savage guests were provoked to revolt by the suspicion of treachery and the murder of their prince. The whole country north of the Danube was lost in a day, and depopulated in a summer; and the ruins of cities and churches were overspread with the bones of the natives, who expiated the sins of their Turkish ancestors. An ecclesiastic, who fled from the sack of Waradin, describes the calamities which he had seen, or suffered; and the sanguinary rage of sieges and battles is far less atrocious than the treatment of the fugitives, who had been allured from the woods under a promise of peace and pardon and who were coolly slaughtered as soon as they had performed the labors of the harvest and vintage. In the winter the Tartars passed the Danube on the ice, and advanced to Gran or Strigonium, a German colony, and the metropolis of the kingdom. Thirty engines were planted against the walls; the ditches were filled with sacks of earth and dead bodies; and after a promiscuous massacre, three hundred noble matrons were slain in the presence of the khan. Of all the cities and fortresses of Hungary, three alone survived the Tartar invasion, and the unfortunate Bata hid his head among the islands of the Adriatic.

[Footnote 264: See the curious extracts from the Mahometan writers, Hist. des Mongols, p. 707—M.]

[Footnote 27: The Dashté Kipzak, or plain of Kipzak, extends on either side of the Volga, in a boundless space towards the Jaik and Borysthenes, and is supposed to contain the primitive name and nation of the Cossacks.]

[Footnote 27/1: Olmutz was gallantly and successfully defended by Stenberg, Hist. des Mongols, p. 396—M.]

The Latin world was darkened by this cloud of savage hostility: a Russian fugitive carried the alarm to Sweden; and the remote nations of the Baltic and the ocean trembled at the approach of the Tartars, [28] whom their fear and ignorance were inclined to separate from the human species. Since the invasion of the Arabs in the eighth century, Europe had never been exposed to a similar calamity: and if the disciples of Mahomet would have oppressed her religion and liberty, it might be apprehended that the shepherds of Scythia would extinguish her cities, her arts, and all the institutions of civil society. The Roman pontiff attempted to appease and convert these invincible Pagans by a mission of Franciscan and Dominican friars; but he was astonished by the reply of the khan, that the sons of God and of Zingis were invested with a divine power to subdue or extirpate the nations; and that the pope would be involved in the universal destruction, unless he visited in person, and as a suppliant, the royal horde. The emperor Frederic the Second embraced a more generous mode of defence; and his letters to the kings of France and England, and the princes of Germany, represented the common danger, and urged them to arm their vassals in this just and rational crusade. [29] The Tartars themselves were awed by the fame and valor of the Franks; the town of Newstadt in Austria was bravely defended against them by fifty knights and twenty crossbows; and they raised the siege on the appearance of a German army. After wasting the adjacent kingdoms of Servia, Bosnia, and Bulgaria, Batou slowly retreated from the Danube to the Volga to enjoyed the rewards of victory in the city and palace of Serai, which started at his command from the midst of the desert. [291]

[Footnote 28: In the year 1238, the inhabitants of Gothia (Sweden) and Frise were prevented, by their fear of the Tartars, from sending, as usual, their ships to the herring fishery on the coast of England; and as there was no exportation, forty or fifty of these fish were sold for a shilling, (Matthew Paris, p. 396.) It is whimsical enough, that the orders of a Mogul khan, who reigned on the borders of China, should have lowered the price of herrings in the English market.]

[Footnote 29: I shall copy his characteristic or flattering epithets of the different countries of Europe: Furens ac fervens ad arma Germania, strenuæ militiæ genitrix et alumna Francia, bellicosa et audax Hispania, virtuosa viris et classe munita fertilis Anglia, impetuosis bellatoribus referta Alemannia, navalis Dacia, indomita Italia, pacis ignara Burgundia, inquieta Apulia, cum maris Græci, Adriatici et Tyrrheni insulis pyraticis et invictis, Cretâ, Cypro, Siciliâ, cum Oceano conterterminis insulis, et regionibus, cruenta Hybernia, cum agili Wallia palustris Scotia, glacialis Norwegia, suam electam militiam sub vexillo Crucis destinabunt, &c. (Matthew Paris, p. 498.)]

[Footnote 291: He was recalled by the death of Octai—M.]

IV. Even the poor and frozen regions of the north attracted the arms of the Moguls: Sheibani khan, the brother of the great Batou, led a horde of fifteen thousand families into the wilds of Siberia; and his descendants reigned at Tobolskoi above three centuries, till the Russian conquest. The spirit of enterprise which pursued the course of the Oby and Yenisei must have led to the discovery of the icy sea. After brushing away the monstrous fables, of men with dogs' heads and cloven feet, we shall find, that, fifteen years after the death of Zingis, the Moguls were informed of the name and manners of the Samoyedes in the neighborhood of the polar circle, who dwelt in subterraneous huts, and derived their furs and their food from the sole occupation of hunting. [30]

[Footnote 30: See Carpin's relation in Hackluyt, vol. i. p. 30. The pedigree of the khans of Siberia is given by Abulghazi, (part viii. p. 485—495.) Have the Russians found no Tartar chronicles at Tobolskoi? Note: See the account of the Mongol library in Bergman, Nomadische Streifereyen, vol. iii. p. 185, 205, and Remusat, Hist. des Langues Tartares, p. 327, and preface to Schmidt, Geschichte der Ost-Mongolen—M.]

While China, Syria, and Poland, were invaded at the same time by the Moguls and Tartars, the authors of the mighty mischief were content with the knowledge and declaration, that their word was the sword of death. Like the first caliphs, the first successors of Zingis seldom appeared in person at the head of their victorious armies. On the banks of the Onon and Selinga, the royal or golden horde exhibited the contrast of simplicity and greatness; of the roasted sheep and mare's milk which composed their banquets; and of a distribution in one day of five hundred wagons of gold and silver. The ambassadors and princes of Europe and Asia were compelled to undertake this distant and laborious pilgrimage; and the life and reign of the great dukes of Russia, the kings of Georgia and Armenia, the sultans of Iconium, and the emirs of Persia, were decided by the frown or smile of the great khan. The sons and grandsons of Zingis had been accustomed to the pastoral life; but the village of Caracorum [31] was gradually ennobled by their election and residence. A change of manners is implied in the removal of Octai and Mangou from a tent to a house; and their example was imitated by the princes of their family and the great officers of the empire. Instead of the boundless forest, the enclosure of a park afforded the more indolent pleasures of the chase; their new habitations were decorated with painting and sculpture; their superfluous treasures were cast in fountains, and basins, and statues of massy silver; and the artists of China and Paris vied with each other in the service of the great khan. [32] Caracorum contained two streets, the one of Chinese mechanics, the other of Mahometan traders; and the places of religious worship, one Nestorian church, two mosques, and twelve temples of various idols, may represent in some degree the number and division of inhabitants. Yet a French missionary declares, that the town of St. Denys, near Paris, was more considerable than the Tartar capital; and that the whole palace of Mangou was scarcely equal to a tenth part of that Benedictine abbey. The conquests of Russia and Syria might amuse the vanity of the great khans; but they were seated on the borders of China; the acquisition of that empire was the nearest and most interesting object; and they might learn from their pastoral economy, that it is for the advantage of the shepherd to protect and propagate his flock. I have already celebrated the wisdom and virtue of a Mandarin who prevented the desolation of five populous and cultivated provinces. In a spotless administration of thirty years, this friend of his country and of mankind continually labored to mitigate, or suspend, the havoc of war; to save the monuments, and to rekindle the flame, of science; to restrain the military commander by the restoration of civil magistrates; and to instil the love of peace and justice into the minds of the Moguls. He struggled with the barbarism of the first conquerors; but his salutary lessons produced a rich harvest in the second generation. [32/1] The northern, and by degrees the southern, empire acquiesced in the government of Cublai, the lieutenant, and afterwards the successor, of Mangou; and the nation was loyal to a prince who had been educated in the manners of China. He restored the forms of her venerable constitution; and the victors submitted to the laws, the fashions, and even the prejudices, of the vanquished people. This peaceful triumph, which has been more than once repeated, may be ascribed, in a great measure, to the numbers and servitude of the Chinese. The Mogul army was dissolved in a vast and populous country; and their emperors adopted with pleasure a political system, which gives to the prince the solid substance of despotism, and leaves to the subject the empty names of philosophy, freedom, and filial obedience. [32/2] Under the reign of Cublai, letters and commerce, peace and justice, were restored; the great canal, of five hundred miles, was opened from Nankin to the capital: he fixed his residence at Pekin; and displayed in his court the magnificence of the greatest monarch of Asia. Yet this learned prince declined from the pure and simple religion of his great ancestor: he sacrificed to the idol Fo; and his blind attachment to the lamas of Thibet and the bonzes of China [33] provoked the censure of the disciples of Confucius. His successors polluted the palace with a crowd of eunuchs, physicians, and astrologers, while thirteen millions of their subjects were consumed in the provinces by famine. One hundred and forty years after the death of Zingis, his degenerate race, the dynasty of the Yuen, was expelled by a revolt of the native Chinese; and the Mogul emperors were lost in the oblivion of the desert. Before this revolution, they had forfeited their supremacy over the dependent branches of their house, the khans of Kipzak and Russia, the khans of Zagatai, or Transoxiana, and the khans of Iran or Persia. By their distance and power, these royal lieutenants had soon been released from the duties of obedience; and after the death of Cublai, they scorned to accept a sceptre or a title from his unworthy successors. According to their respective situations, they maintained the simplicity of the pastoral life, or assumed the luxury of the cities of Asia; but the princes and their hordes were alike disposed for the reception of a foreign worship. After some hesitation between the Gospel and the Koran, they conformed to the religion of Mahomet; and while they adopted for their brethren the Arabs and Persians, they renounced all intercourse with the ancient Moguls, the idolaters of China.

[Footnote 31: *The Map of D'Anville and the Chinese Itineraries (De Guignes, tom. i. part ii. p. 57) seem to mark the position of Holin, or Caracorum, about six hundred miles to the north-west of Pekin. The distance between Selinginsky and Pekin is near 2000 Russian versts, between 1300 and 1400 English miles, (Bell's Travels, vol. ii. p. 67.)]*

[Footnote 32: *Rubruquis found at Caracorum his countryman Guillaume Boucher, orfevre de Paris, who had executed for the khan a silver tree supported by four lions, and ejecting four different liquors. Abulghazi (part iv. p. 366) mentions the painters of Kitay or China.]*

[Footnote 32/1: *See the interesting sketch of the life of this minister (Yelin-Thsouthsai) in the second volume of the second series of Recherches Asiatiques, par A Remusat, p. 64—M.]*

[Footnote 32/2: *Compare Hist. des Mongols, p. 616—M.]*

[Footnote 33: *The attachment of the khans, and the hatred of the mandarins, to the bonzes and lamas (Duhalde, Hist. de la Chine, tom. i. p. 502, 503) seems to represent them as the priests of the same god, of the Indian Fo, whose worship prevails among the sects of Hindostan Siam, Thibet, China, and Japan. But this mysterious subject is still lost in a cloud, which the researchers of our Asiatic Society may gradually dispel.]*

PART III

In this shipwreck of nations, some surprise may be excited by the escape of the Roman empire, whose relics, at the time of the Mogul invasion, were dismembered by the Greeks and Latins. Less potent than Alexander, they were pressed, like the Macedonian, both in Europe and Asia, by the shepherds of Scythia; and had the Tartars undertaken the siege, Constantinople must have yielded to the fate of

Pekin, Samarcand, and Bagdad. The glorious and voluntary retreat of Batou from the Danube was insulted by the vain triumph of the Franks and Greeks; [34] and in a second expedition death surprised him in full march to attack the capital of the Cæsars. His brother Borga carried the Tartar arms into Bulgaria and Thrace; but he was diverted from the Byzantine war by a visit to Novogorod, in the fifty-seventh degree of latitude, where he numbered the inhabitants and regulated the tributes of Russia. The Mogul khan formed an alliance with the Mamalukes against his brethren of Persia: three hundred thousand horse penetrated through the gates of Derbend; and the Greeks might rejoice in the first example of domestic war. After the recovery of Constantinople, Michael Palæologus, [35] at a distance from his court and army, was surprised and surrounded in a Thracian castle, by twenty thousand Tartars. But the object of their march was a private interest: they came to the deliverance of Azzadin, the Turkish sultan; and were content with his person and the treasure of the emperor. Their general Noga, whose name is perpetuated in the hordes of Astracan, raised a formidable rebellion against Mengo Timour, the third of the khans of Kipzak; obtained in marriage Maria, the natural daughter of Palæologus; and guarded the dominions of his friend and father. The subsequent invasions of a Scythian cast were those of outlaws and fugitives: and some thousands of Alani and Comans, who had been driven from their native seats, were reclaimed from a vagrant life, and enlisted in the service of the empire. Such was the influence in Europe of the invasion of the Moguls. The first terror of their arms secured, rather than disturbed, the peace of the Roman Asia. The sultan of Iconium solicited a personal interview with John Vataces; and his artful policy encouraged the Turks to defend their barrier against the common enemy. [36] That barrier indeed was soon overthrown; and the servitude and ruin of the Seljukians exposed the nakedness of the Greeks. The formidable Holagou threatened to march to Constantinople at the head of four hundred thousand men; and the groundless panic of the citizens of Nice will present an image of the terror which he had inspired. The accident of a procession, and the sound of a doleful litany, "From the fury of the Tartars, good Lord, deliver us," had scattered the hasty report of an assault and massacre. In the blind credulity of fear, the streets of Nice were crowded with thousands of both sexes, who knew not from what or to whom they fled; and some hours elapsed before the firmness of the military officers could relieve the city from this imaginary foe. But the ambition of Holagou and his successors was fortunately diverted by the conquest of Bagdad, and a long vicissitude of Syrian wars; their hostility to the Moslems inclined them to unite with the Greeks and Franks; [37] and their generosity or contempt had offered the kingdom of Anatolia as the reward of an Armenian vassal. The fragments of the Seljukian monarchy were disputed by the emirs who had occupied the cities or the mountains; but they all confessed the supremacy of the khans of Persia; and he often interposed his authority, and sometimes his arms, to check their depredations, and to preserve the peace and balance of his Turkish frontier. The death of Cazan, [38] one of the greatest and most accomplished princes of the house of Zingis, removed this salutary control; and the decline of the Moguls gave a free scope to the rise and progress of the Ottoman Empire. [39]

*[Footnote 34: Some repulse of the Moguls in Hungary (Matthew Paris, p. 545, 546) might propagate and color the report of the union and victory of the kings of the Franks on the confines of Bulgaria. Abulpharagius (Dynast. p. 310) after forty years, beyond the Tigris, might be easily deceived.]*

*[Footnote 35: See Pachymer, l. iii. c. 25, and l. ix. c. 26, 27; and the false alarm at Nice, l. iii. c. 27. Nicephorus Gregoras, l. iv. c. 6.]*

*[Footnote 36: G. Acropolita, p. 36, 37. Nic. Greg. l. ii. c. 6, l. iv. c. 5.]*

[Footnote 37: Abulpharagius, who wrote in the year 1284, declares that the Moguls, since the fabulous defeat of Batou, had not attacked either the Franks or Greeks; and of this he is a competent witness. Hayton likewise, the Armenian prince, celebrates their friendship for himself and his nation.]

[Footnote 38: Pachymer gives a splendid character of Cazan Khan, the rival of Cyrus and Alexander, (l. xii. c. 1.) In the conclusion of his history (l. xiii. c. 36) he hopes much from the arrival of 30,000 Tochars, or Tartars, who were ordered by the successor of Cazan to restrain the Turks of Bithynia, A.D. 1308.]

[Footnote 39: The origin of the Ottoman dynasty is illustrated by the critical learning of Mm. De Guignes (Hist. des Huns, tom. iv. p. 329—337) and D'Anville, (Empire Turc, p. 14—22,) two inhabitants of Paris, from whom the Orientals may learn the history and geography of their own country.  Note: They may be still more enlightened by the Geschichte des Osman Reiches, by M. von Hammer Purgstall of Vienna—M.]

After the retreat of Zingis, the sultan Gelaleddin of Carizme had returned from India to the possession and defence of his Persian kingdoms. In the space of eleven years, than hero fought in person fourteen battles; and such was his activity, that he led his cavalry in seventeen days from Teflis to Kerman, a march of a thousand miles. Yet he was oppressed by the jealousy of the Moslem princes, and the innumerable armies of the Moguls; and after his last defeat, Gelaleddin perished ignobly in the mountains of Curdistan. His death dissolved a veteran and adventurous army, which included under the name of Carizmians or Corasmins many Turkman hordes, that had attached themselves to the sultan's fortune. The bolder and more powerful chiefs invaded Syria, and violated the holy sepulchre of Jerusalem: the more humble engaged in the service of Aladin, sultan of Iconium; and among these were the obscure fathers of the Ottoman line. They had formerly pitched their tents near the southern banks of the Oxus, in the plains of Mahan and Nesa; and it is somewhat remarkable, that the same spot should have produced the first authors of the Parthian and Turkish empires. At the head, or in the rear, of a Carizmian army, Soliman Shah was drowned in the passage of the Euphrates: his son Orthogrul became the soldier and subject of Aladin, and established at Surgut, on the banks of the Sangar, a camp of four hundred families or tents, whom he governed fifty-two years both in peace and war. He was the father of Thaman, or Athman, whose Turkish name has been melted into the appellation of the caliph Othman; and if we describe that pastoral chief as a shepherd and a robber, we must separate from those characters all idea of ignominy and baseness. Othman possessed, and perhaps surpassed, the ordinary virtues of a soldier; and the circumstances of time and place were propitious to his independence and success. The Seljukian dynasty was no more; and the distance and decline of the Mogul khans soon enfranchised him from the control of a superior. He was situate on the verge of the Greek empire: the Koran sanctified his gazi, or holy war, against the infidels; and their political errors unlocked the passes of Mount Olympus, and invited him to descend into the plains of Bithynia. Till the reign of Palæologus, these passes had been vigilantly guarded by the militia of the country, who were repaid by their own safety and an exemption from taxes. The emperor abolished their privilege and assumed their office; but the tribute was rigorously collected, the custody of the passes was neglected, and the hardy mountaineers degenerated into a trembling crowd of peasants without spirit or discipline. It was on the twenty-seventh of July, in the year twelve hundred and ninety-nine of the Christian æra, that Othman first invaded the territory of Nicomedia; [40] and the singular accuracy of the date seems to disclose some foresight of the rapid and destructive growth of the monster. The annals of the twenty-seven years of his reign would exhibit a repetition of the same inroads; and his hereditary troops were multiplied in each campaign by the accession of captives and volunteers. Instead of retreating to the hills, he maintained the most useful and defensive posts; fortified the towns and castles which he had first pillaged; and renounced the pastoral life for the baths and palaces of his infant capitals. But it was not till Othman was oppressed by age and infirmities, that he received the welcome news of the conquest of Prusa, which had been surrendered by famine or treachery to the arms of his son Orchan. The glory of Othman is chiefly founded on that of his descendants; but the Turks have transcribed or composed a royal testament of his last counsels of justice and moderation. [41]

*[Footnote 40: See Pachymer, l. x. c. 25, 26, l. xiii. c. 33, 34, 36; and concerning the guard of the mountains, l. i. c. 3—6: Nicephorus Gregoras, l. vii. c. I., and the first book of Laonicus Chalcondyles, the Athenian.]*

*[Footnote 41: I am ignorant whether the Turks have any writers older than Mahomet II., nor can I reach beyond a meagre chronicle (Annales Turcici ad Annum 1550) translated by John Gaudier, and published by Leunclavius, (ad calcem Laonic. Chalcond. p. 311—350,) with copious pandects, or commentaries. The history of the Growth and Decay (A.D. 1300—1683) of the Othman empire was translated into English from the Latin MS. of Demetrius Cantemir, prince of Moldavia, (London, 1734, in folio.) The author is guilty of strange blunders in Oriental history; but he was conversant with the language, the annals, and institutions of the Turks. Cantemir partly draws his materials from the Synopsis of Saadi Effendi of Larissa, dedicated in the year 1696 to Sultan Mustapha, and a valuable abridgment of the original historians. In one of the Ramblers, Dr. Johnson praises Knolles (a General History of the Turks to the present Year. London, 1603) as the first of historians, unhappy only in the choice of his subject. Yet I much doubt whether a partial and verbose compilation from Latin writers, thirteen hundred folio pages of speeches and battles, can either instruct or amuse an enlightened age, which requires from the historian some tincture of philosophy and criticism. Note: We could have wished that M. von Hammer had given a more clear and distinct reply to this question of Gibbon. In a note, vol. i. p. 630. M. von Hammer shows that they had not only sheiks (religious writers) and learned lawyers, but poets and authors on medicine. But the inquiry of Gibbon obviously refers to historians. The oldest of their historical works, of which V. Hammer makes use, is the "Tarichi Aaschik Paschasade," i. e. the History of the Great Grandson of Aaschik Pasha, who was a dervis and celebrated ascetic poet in the reign of Murad (Amurath) I. Ahmed, the author of the work, lived during the reign of Bajazet II., but, he says, derived much information from the book of Scheik Jachshi, the son of Elias, who was Imaum to Sultan Orchan, (the second Ottoman king) and who related, from the lips of his father, the circumstances of the earliest Ottoman history. This book (having searched for it in vain for five-and-twenty years) our author found at length in the Vatican. All the other Turkish histories on his list, as indeed this, were written during the reign of Mahomet II. It does not appear whether any of the rest cite earlier authorities of equal value with that claimed by the "Tarichi Aaschik Paschasade."—M. (in Quarterly Review, vol. xlix. p. 292.)]*

From the conquest of Prusa, we may date the true æra of the Ottoman empire. The lives and possessions of the Christian subjects were redeemed by a tribute or ransom of thirty thousand crowns of gold; and the city, by the labors of Orchan, assumed the aspect of a Mahometan capital; Prusa was decorated with a mosque, a college, and a hospital, of royal foundation; the Seljukian coin was changed for the name and impression of the new dynasty: and the most skilful professors, of human and divine knowledge, attracted the Persian and Arabian students from the ancient schools of Oriental learning. The office of vizier was instituted for Aladin, the brother of Orchan; [41/1] and a different habit distinguished the citizens from the peasants, the Moslems from the infidels. All the troops of Othman had consisted of loose squadrons of Turkman cavalry; who served without pay and fought without discipline: but a regular body of infantry was first established and trained by the prudence of his son. A great number of volunteers was enrolled with a small stipend, but with the permission of living at home, unless they were summoned to the field: their rude manners, and seditious temper, disposed Orchan to educate his young captives as his soldiers and those of the prophet; but the Turkish peasants were still allowed to mount on horseback, and follow his standard, with the appellation and the hopes of freebooters. [41/2] By these arts he formed an army of twenty-five thousand Moslems: a train of battering engines was framed for the use of sieges; and the first successful experiment was made on the cities of Nice and Nicomedia. Orchan granted a safe-conduct to all who were desirous of departing with their families and effects; but the widows of the slain were given in marriage to the conquerors; and the sacrilegious plunder, the books, the vases, and the images, were sold or ransomed at Constantinople. The emperor Andronicus the Younger was vanquished and wounded by the son of Othman: [42] [42/1] he subdued the whole province or kingdom of Bithynia, as far as the shores of the Bosphorus and Hellespont; and the Christians confessed the justice and clemency of a reign which claimed the voluntary attachment of the Turks of Asia. Yet Orchan was content with the modest title of emir; and in the list of his compeers, the princes of Roum or Anatolia, [43] his military forces were surpassed by the emirs of Ghermian and Caramania, each of whom could bring into the field an army of forty thousand men. Their domains were situate in the heart of the Seljukian kingdom; but the holy warriors, though of inferior note, who formed new principalities on the Greek empire, are more conspicuous in the light of history. The maritime country from the Propontis to the Mæander and the Isle of Rhodes, so long threatened and so often pillaged, was finally lost about the thirteenth year of Andronicus the Elder. [44] Two Turkish chieftains, Sarukhan and Aidin, left their names to their conquests, and their conquests to their posterity. The captivity or ruin of the seven churches of Asia was consummated; and the barbarous lords of Ionia and Lydia still trample on the monuments of classic and Christian antiquity. In the loss of Ephesus, the Christians deplored the fall of the first angel, the extinction of the first candlestick, of the Revelations; [45] the desolation is complete; and the temple of Diana, or the church of Mary, will equally elude the search of the curious traveller. The circus and three stately theatres of Laodicea are now peopled with wolves and foxes; Sardes is reduced to a miserable village; the God of Mahomet, without a rival or a son, is invoked in the mosques of Thyatira and Pergamus; and the populousness of Smyrna is supported by the foreign trade of the Franks and Armenians. Philadelphia alone has been saved by prophecy, or courage. At a distance from the sea, forgotten by the emperors, encompassed on all sides by the Turks, her valiant citizens defended their religion and freedom above fourscore years; and at length capitulated with the proudest of the Ottomans. Among the Greek colonies and churches of Asia, Philadelphia is still erect; a column in a scene of ruins; a pleasing example, that the paths of honor and safety may sometimes be the same. The servitude of Rhodes was delayed about two centuries by the establishment of the knights of St. John of Jerusalem: [46] under the discipline of the order, that island emerged into fame and opulence; the noble and warlike monks were renowned by land and sea: and the bulwark of Christendom provoked, and repelled, the arms of the Turks and Saracens.

[Footnote 41/1: Von Hammer, Osm. Geschichte, vol. i. p. 82—M.]

[Footnote 41/2: Ibid. p. 91—M.]

[Footnote 42: Cantacuzene, though he relates the battle and heroic flight of the younger Andronicus, (l. ii. c. 6, 7, 8,) dissembles by his silence the loss of Prusa, Nice, and Nicomedia, which are fairly confessed by Nicephorus Gregoras, (l. viii. 15, ix. 9, 13, xi. 6.) It appears that Nice was taken by Orchan in 1330, and Nicomedia in 1339, which are somewhat different from the Turkish dates.]

[Footnote 42/1: For the conquests of Orchan over the ten pachaliks, or kingdoms of the Seljukians, in Asia Minor. see V. Hammer, vol. i. p. 112—M.]

[Footnote 43: The partition of the Turkish emirs is extracted from two contemporaries, the Greek Nicephorus Gregoras (l. vii. 1) and the Arabian Marakeschi, (De Guignes, tom. ii. P. ii. p. 76, 77.) See likewise the first book of Laonicus Chalcondyles.]

[Footnote 44: Pachymer, l. xiii. c. 13.]

[Footnote 45: See the Travels of Wheeler and Spon, of Pocock and Chandler, and more particularly Smith's Survey of the Seven Churches of Asia, p. 205—276. The more pious antiquaries labor to reconcile the promises and threats of the author of the Revelations with the present state of the seven cities. Perhaps it would be more prudent to confine his predictions to the characters and events of his own times.]

[Footnote 46: Consult the ivth book of the Histoire de l'Ordre de Malthe, par l'Abbé de Vertot. That pleasing writer betrays his ignorance, in supposing that Othman, a freebooter of the Bithynian hills, could besiege Rhodes by sea and land.]

The Greeks, by their intestine divisions, were the authors of their final ruin. During the civil wars of the elder and younger Andronicus, the son of Othman achieved, almost without resistance, the conquest of Bithynia; and the same disorders encouraged the Turkish emirs of Lydia and Ionia to build a fleet, and to pillage the adjacent islands and the sea-coast of Europe. In the defence of his life and honor, Cantacuzene was tempted to prevent, or imitate, his adversaries, by calling to his aid the public enemies of his religion and country. Amir, the son of Aidin, concealed under a Turkish garb the humanity and politeness of a Greek; he was united with the great domestic by mutual esteem and reciprocal services; and their friendship is compared, in the vain rhetoric of the times, to the perfect union of Orestes and Pylades. [47] On the report of the danger of his friend, who was persecuted by an ungrateful court, the prince of Ionia assembled at Smyrna a fleet of three hundred vessels, with an army of twenty-nine thousand men; sailed in the depth of winter, and cast anchor at the mouth of the Hebrus. From thence, with a chosen band of two thousand Turks, he marched along the banks of the river, and rescued the empress, who was besieged in Demotica by the wild Bulgarians. At that disastrous moment, the life or death of his beloved Cantacuzene was concealed by his flight into Servia: but the grateful Irene, impatient to behold her deliverer, invited him to enter the city, and accompanied her message with a present of rich apparel and a hundred horses. By a peculiar strain of delicacy, the Gentle Barbarian refused, in the absence of an unfortunate friend, to visit his wife, or to taste the luxuries of the palace; sustained in his tent the rigor of the winter; and rejected the hospitable gift, that he might share the hardships of two thousand companions, all as deserving as himself of that honor and distinction. Necessity and revenge might justify his predatory excursions by sea and land: he left nine thousand five hundred men for the guard of his fleet; and persevered in the fruitless search of Cantacuzene, till his embarkation was hastened by a fictitious letter, the severity of the season, the clamors of his independent troops, and the weight of his spoil and captives. In the prosecution of the civil war, the prince of Ionia twice returned to Europe; joined his arms with those of the emperor; besieged Thessalonica, and threatened Constantinople. Calumny might affix some reproach on his imperfect aid, his hasty departure, and a bribe of ten thousand crowns, which he accepted from the Byzantine court; but his friend was satisfied; and the conduct of Amir is excused by the more sacred duty of defending against the Latins his hereditary dominions. The maritime power of the Turks had united the pope, the king of Cyprus, the republic of Venice, and the order of St. John, in a laudable crusade; their galleys invaded the coast of Ionia; and Amir was slain with an arrow, in the attempt to wrest from the Rhodian knights the citadel of Smyrna. [48] Before his death, he generously recommended another ally of his own nation; not more sincere or zealous than himself, but more able to afford a prompt and powerful succor, by his situation along the Propontis and in the front of Constantinople. By the prospect of a more advantageous treaty, the Turkish prince of Bithynia was detached from his engagements with Anne of Savoy; and the pride of Orchan dictated the most solemn protestations, that if he could obtain the daughter of Cantacuzene, he would invariably fulfil the duties of a subject and a son. Parental tenderness was silenced by the voice of ambition: the Greek clergy connived at the marriage of a Christian princess with a sectary of Mahomet; and the father of Theodora describes, with shameful satisfaction, the dishonor of the purple. [49] A body of Turkish cavalry attended the ambassadors, who disembarked from thirty vessels, before his camp of Selybria. A stately pavilion was erected, in which the empress Irene passed the night with her daughters. In the morning, Theodora ascended a throne, which was surrounded with curtains of silk and gold: the troops were under arms; but the emperor alone was on horseback. At a signal the curtains were suddenly withdrawn to disclose the bride, or the victim, encircled by kneeling eunuchs and hymeneal torches: the sound of flutes and trumpets proclaimed the joyful event; and her pretended happiness was the theme of the nuptial song, which was chanted by such poets as the age could produce. Without the rites of the church, Theodora was delivered to her barbarous lord: but it had been stipulated, that she should preserve her religion in the harem of Bursa; and her father celebrates her charity and devotion in this ambiguous situation. After his peaceful establishment on the throne of Constantinople, the Greek emperor visited his Turkish ally, who with four sons, by various wives, expected him at Scutari, on the Asiatic shore. The two princes partook, with seeming cordiality, of the pleasures of the banquet and the chase; and Theodora was permitted to repass the Bosphorus, and to enjoy some days in the society of her mother. But the friendship of Orchan was subservient to his religion and interest; and in the Genoese war he joined without a blush the enemies of Cantacuzene.

[Footnote 47: Nicephorus Gregoras has expatiated with pleasure on this amiable character, (l. xii. 7, xiii. 4, 10, xiv. 1, 9, xvi. 6.) Cantacuzene speaks with honor and esteem of his ally, (l. iii. c. 56, 57, 63, 64, 66, 67, 68, 86, 89, 95, 96;) but he seems ignorant of his own sentimental passion for the Turks, and indirectly denies the possibility of such unnatural friendship, (l. iv. c. 40.)]

[Footnote 48: After the conquest of Smyrna by the Latins, the defence of this fortress was imposed by Pope Gregory XI. on the knights of Rhodes, (see Vertot, l. v.)]

[Footnote 49: See Cantacuzenus, l. iii. c. 95. Nicephorus Gregoras, who, for the light of Mount Thabor, brands the emperor with the names of tyrant and Herod, excuses, rather than blames, this Turkish marriage, and alleges the passion and power of Orchan, eggutatoV, kai th dunamo? touV kat' auton hdh PersikouV (Turkish) uperairwn SatrapaV, (l. xv. 5.) He afterwards celebrates his kingdom and armies. See his reign in Cantemir, p. 24—30.]

In the treaty with the empress Anne, the Ottoman prince had inserted a singular condition, that it should be lawful for him to sell his prisoners at Constantinople, or transport them into Asia. A naked crowd of Christians of both sexes and every age, of priests and monks, of matrons and virgins, was exposed in the public market; the whip was frequently used to quicken the charity of redemption; and the indigent Greeks deplored the fate of their brethren, who were led away to the worst evils of temporal and spiritual bondage [50] Cantacuzene was reduced to subscribe the same terms; and their execution must have been still more pernicious to the empire: a body of ten thousand Turks had been detached to the assistance of the empress Anne; but the entire forces of Orchan were exerted in the service of his father. Yet these calamities were of a transient nature; as soon as the storm had passed away, the fugitives might return to their habitations; and at the conclusion of the civil and foreign wars, Europe was completely evacuated by the Moslems of Asia. It was in his last quarrel with his pupil that

Cantacuzene inflicted the deep and deadly wound, which could never be healed by his successors, and which is poorly expiated by his theological dialogues against the prophet Mahomet. Ignorant of their own history, the modern Turks confound their first and their final passage of the Hellespont, [51] and describe the son of Orchan as a nocturnal robber, who, with eighty companions, explores by stratagem a hostile and unknown shore. Soliman, at the head of ten thousand horse, was transported in the vessels, and entertained as the friend, of the Greek emperor. In the civil wars of Romania, he performed some service and perpetrated more mischief; but the Chersonesus was insensibly filled with a Turkish colony; and the Byzantine court solicited in vain the restitution of the fortresses of Thrace. After some artful delays between the Ottoman prince and his son, their ransom was valued at sixty thousand crowns, and the first payment had been made when an earthquake shook the walls and cities of the provinces; the dismantled places were occupied by the Turks; and Gallipoli, the key of the Hellespont, was rebuilt and repeopled by the policy of Soliman. The abdication of Cantacuzene dissolved the feeble bands of domestic alliance; and his last advice admonished his countrymen to decline a rash contest, and to compare their own weakness with the numbers and valor, the discipline and enthusiasm, of the Moslems. His prudent counsels were despised by the headstrong vanity of youth, and soon justified by the victories of the Ottomans. But as he practised in the field the exercise of the jerid, Soliman was killed by a fall from his horse; and the aged Orchan wept and expired on the tomb of his valiant son. [511]

[Footnote 50: The most lively and concise picture of this captivity may be found in the history of Ducas, (c. 8,) who fairly describes what Cantacuzene confesses with a guilty blush!]

[Footnote 51: In this passage, and the first conquests in Europe, Cantemir (p. 27, &c.) gives a miserable idea of his Turkish guides; nor am I much better satisfied with Chalcondyles, (l. i. p. 12, &c.) They forget to consult the most authentic record, the ivth book of Cantacuzene. I likewise regret the last books, which are still manuscript, of Nicephorus Gregoras. Note: Von Hammer excuses the silence with which the Turkish historians pass over the earlier intercourse of the Ottomans with the European continent, of which he enumerates sixteen different occasions, as if they disdained those peaceful incursions by which they gained no conquest, and established no permanent footing on the Byzantine territory. Of the romantic account of Soliman's first expedition, he says, "As yet the prose of history had not asserted its right over the poetry of tradition." This defence would scarcely be accepted as satisfactory by the historian of the Decline and Fall—M. (in Quarterly Review, vol. xlix. p. 293.)]

[Footnote 51/1: In the 75th year of his age, the 35th of his reign. V. Hammer. M.]

PART IV

But the Greeks had not time to rejoice in the death of their enemies; and the Turkish cimeter was wielded with the same spirit by Amurath the First, the son of Orchan, and the brother of Soliman. By the pale and fainting light of the Byzantine annals, [52] we can discern, that he subdued without resistance the whole province of Romania or Thrace, from the Hellespont to Mount Hæmus, and the verge of the capital; and that Adrianople was chosen for the royal seat of his government and religion in Europe. Constantinople, whose decline is almost coeval with her foundation, had often, in the lapse of a thousand years, been assaulted by the Barbarians of the East and West; but never till this fatal hour had the Greeks been surrounded, both in Asia and Europe, by the arms of the same hostile monarchy. Yet the prudence or generosity of Amurath postponed for a while this easy conquest; and his pride was satisfied with the frequent and humble attendance of the emperor John Palæologus and his four sons, who followed at his summons the court and camp of the Ottoman prince. He marched against the Sclavonian nations between the Danube and the Adriatic, the Bulgarians, Servians, Bosnians, and Albanians; and these warlike tribes, who had so often insulted the majesty of the empire, were repeatedly broken by his destructive inroads. Their countries did not abound either in gold or silver; nor were their rustic hamlets and townships enriched by commerce or decorated by the arts of luxury. But the natives of the soil have been distinguished in every age by their hardiness of mind and body; and they were converted by a prudent institution into the firmest and most faithful supporters of the Ottoman greatness. [53] The vizier of Amurath reminded his sovereign that, according to the Mahometan law, he was entitled to a fifth part of the spoil and captives; and that the duty might easily be levied, if vigilant officers were stationed in Gallipoli, to watch the passage, and to select for his use the stoutest and most beautiful of the Christian youth. The advice was followed: the edict was proclaimed; many thousands of the European captives were educated in religion and arms; and the new militia was consecrated and named by a celebrated dervis. Standing in the front of their ranks, he stretched the sleeve of his gown over the head of the foremost soldier, and his blessing was delivered in these words: "Let them be called Janizaries, (Yengi cheri, or new soldiers;) may their countenance be ever bright! their hand victorious! their sword keen! may their spear always hang over the heads of their enemies! and wheresoever they go, may they return with a white face!" [54] [54/1] Such was the origin of these haughty troops, the terror of the nations, and sometimes of the sultans themselves. Their valor has declined, their discipline is relaxed, and their tumultuary array is incapable of contending with the order and weapons of modern tactics; but at the time of their institution, they possessed a decisive superiority in war; since a regular body of infantry, in constant exercise and pay, was not maintained by any of the princes of Christendom. The Janizaries fought with the zeal of proselytes against their idolatrous countrymen; and in the battle of Cossova, the league and independence of the Sclavonian tribes was finally crushed. As the conqueror walked over the field, he observed that the greatest part of the slain consisted of beardless youths; and listened to the flattering reply of his vizier, that age and wisdom would have taught them not to oppose his irresistible arms. But the sword of his Janizaries could not defend him from the dagger of despair; a Servian soldier started from the crowd of dead bodies, and Amurath was pierced in the belly with a mortal wound. [54/2] The grandson of Othman was mild in his temper, modest in his apparel, and a lover of learning and virtue; but the Moslems were scandalized at his absence from public worship; and he was corrected by the firmness of the mufti, who dared to reject his testimony in a civil cause: a mixture of servitude and freedom not unfrequent in Oriental history. [55]

[Footnote 52: After the conclusion of Cantacuzene and Gregoras, there follows a dark interval of a hundred years. George Phranza, Michael Ducas, and Laonicus Chalcondyles, all three wrote after the taking of Constantinople.]

[Footnote 53: See Cantemir, p. 37—41, with his own large and curious annotations.]

[Footnote 54: White and black face are common and proverbial expressions of praise and reproach in the Turkish language. Hic niger est, hunc tu Romane caveto, was likewise a Latin sentence.]

[Footnote 54/1: According to Von Hammer. vol. i. p. 90, Gibbon and the European writers assign too late a date to this enrolment of the Janizaries. It took place not in the reign of Amurath, but in that of his predecessor Orchan—M.]

[Footnote 54/2: Ducas has related this as a deliberate act of self-devotion on the part of a Servian noble who pretended to desert, and stabbed Amurath during a conference which he had requested. The Italian translator of Ducas, published by Bekker in the new edition of the Byzantines, has still further heightened the romance. See likewise in Von Hammer (Osmanische Geschichte, vol. i. p. 138) the popular Servian account, which resembles that of Ducas, and may have been the source of that of his Italian translator. The Turkish account agrees more nearly with Gibbon; but the Servian, (Milosch Kohilovisch) while he lay among the heap of the dead, pretended to have some secret to impart to Amurath, and stabbed him while he leaned over to listen—M.]

[Footnote 55: See the life and death of Morad, or Amurath I., in Cantemir, (p 33—45,) the first book of Chalcondyles, and the Annales Turcici of Leunclavius. According to another story, the sultan was stabbed by a Croat in his tent; and this accident was alleged to Busbequius (Epist i. p. 98) as an excuse for the unworthy precaution of pinioning, as if were, between two attendants, an ambassador's arms, when he is introduced to the royal presence.]

The character of Bajazet, the son and successor of Amurath, is strongly expressed in his surname of Ilderim, or the lightning; and he might glory in an epithet, which was drawn from the fiery energy of his soul and the rapidity of his destructive march. In the fourteen years of his reign, [56] he incessantly moved at the head of his armies, from Boursa to Adrianople, from the Danube to the Euphrates; and, though he strenuously labored for the propagation of the law, he invaded, with impartial ambition, the Christian and Mahometan princes of Europe and Asia. From Angora to Amasia and Erzeroum, the northern regions of Anatolia were reduced to his obedience: he stripped of their hereditary possessions his brother emirs of Ghermian and Caramania, of Aidin and Sarukhan; and after the conquest of Iconium the ancient kingdom of the Seljukians again revived in the Ottoman dynasty. Nor were the conquests of Bajazet less rapid or important in Europe. No sooner had he imposed a regular form of servitude on the Servians and Bulgarians, than he passed the Danube to seek new enemies and new subjects in the heart of Moldavia. [57] Whatever yet adhered to the Greek empire in Thrace, Macedonia, and Thessaly, acknowledged a Turkish master: an obsequious bishop led him through the gates of Thermopylæ into Greece; and we may observe, as a singular fact, that the widow of a Spanish chief, who possessed the ancient seat of the oracle of Delphi, deserved his favor by the sacrifice of a beauteous daughter. The Turkish communication between Europe and Asia had been dangerous and doubtful, till he stationed at Gallipoli a fleet of galleys, to command the Hellespont and intercept the Latin succors of Constantinople. While the monarch indulged his passions in a boundless range of injustice and cruelty, he imposed on his soldiers the most rigid laws of modesty and abstinence; and the harvest was peaceably reaped and sold within the precincts of his camp. Provoked by the loose and corrupt administration of justice, he collected in a house the judges and lawyers of his dominions, who expected that in a few moments the fire would be kindled to reduce them to ashes. His ministers trembled in silence: but an Æthiopian buffoon presumed to insinuate the true cause of the evil; and future venality was left without excuse, by annexing an adequate salary to the office of cadhi. [58] The humble title of emir was no longer suitable to the Ottoman greatness; and Bajazet condescended to accept a patent of sultan from the caliphs who served in Egypt under the yoke of the Mamalukes: [59] a last and frivolous homage that was yielded by force to opinion; by the Turkish conquerors to the house of Abbas and the successors of the Arabian prophet. The ambition of the sultan was inflamed by the obligation of deserving this august title; and he turned his arms against the kingdom of Hungary, the perpetual theatre of the Turkish victories and defeats. Sigismond, the Hungarian king, was the son and brother of the emperors of the West: his cause was that of Europe and the church; and, on the report of his danger, the bravest knights of France and Germany were eager to march under his standard and that of the cross. In the battle of Nicopolis, Bajazet defeated a confederate army of a hundred thousand Christians, who had proudly boasted, that if the sky should fall, they could uphold it on their lances. The far greater part were slain or driven into the Danube; and Sigismond, escaping to Constantinople by the river and the Black Sea, returned after a long circuit to his exhausted kingdom. [60] In the pride of victory, Bajazet threatened that he would besiege Buda; that he would subdue the adjacent countries of Germany and Italy, and that he would feed his horse with a bushel of oats on the altar of St. Peter at Rome. His progress was checked, not by the miraculous interposition of the apostle, not by a crusade of the Christian powers, but by a long and painful fit of the gout. The disorders of the moral, are sometimes corrected by those of the physical, world; and an acrimonious humor falling on a single fibre of one man, may prevent or suspend the misery of nations.

[Footnote 56: The reign of Bajazet I., or Ilderim Bayazid, is contained in Cantemir, (p. 46,) the iid book of Chalcondyles, and the Annales Turcici. The surname of Ilderim, or lightning, is an example, that the conquerors and poets of every age have felt the truth of a system which derives the sublime from the principle of terror.]

[Footnote 57: Cantemir, who celebrates the victories of the great Stephen over the Turks, (p. 47,) had composed the ancient and modern state of his principality of Moldavia, which has been long promised, and is still unpublished.]

[Footnote 58: Leunclav. Annal. Turcici, p. 318, 319. The venality of the cadhis has long been an object of scandal and satire; and if we distrust the observations of our travellers, we may consult the feeling of the Turks themselves, (D'Herbelot, Bibliot. Orientale, p. 216, 217, 229, 230.)]

[Footnote 59: The fact, which is attested by the Arabic history of Ben Schounah, a contemporary Syrian, (De Guignes Hist. des Huns. tom. iv. p. 336.) destroys the testimony of Saad Effendi and Cantemir, (p. 14, 15,) of the election of Othman to the dignity of sultan.]

[Footnote 60: See the Decades Rerum Hungaricarum (Dec. iii. l. ii. p. 379) of Bonfinius, an Italian, who, in the xvth century, was invited into Hungary to compose an eloquent history of that kingdom. Yet, if it be extant and accessible, I should give the preference to some homely chronicle of the time and country.]

Such is the general idea of the Hungarian war; but the disastrous adventure of the French has procured us some memorials which illustrate the victory and character of Bajazet. [61] The duke of Burgundy, sovereign of Flanders, and uncle of Charles the Sixth, yielded to the ardor of his son, John count of Nevers; and the fearless youth was accompanied by four princes, his cousins, and those of the French monarch. Their inexperience was guided by the Sire de Coucy, one of the best and oldest captain of Christendom; [62] but the constable, admiral, and marshal of France [63] commanded an army which did not exceed the number of a thousand knights and squires. [63/1] These splendid names were the source of presumption and the bane of discipline. So many might aspire to command, that none were willing to obey; their national spirit despised both their enemies and their allies; and in the persuasion that Bajazet would fly, or must fall, they began to compute how soon they should visit Constantinople and deliver the holy sepulchre. When their scouts announced the approach of the Turks, the gay and thoughtless youths were at table, already heated with wine; they instantly clasped their armor, mounted their horses, rode full speed to the vanguard, and resented as an affront the advice of Sigismond, which would have deprived them of the right and honor of the foremost attack. The battle of Nicopolis would not have been lost, if the French would have obeyed the prudence of the Hungarians; but it might have been gloriously won, had the Hungarians imitated the valor of the French. They dispersed the first line, consisting of the troops of Asia; forced a rampart of stakes, which had been planted against the cavalry; broke, after a bloody conflict, the Janizaries themselves; and were at length overwhelmed by the numerous squadrons that issued from the woods, and charged on all sides this handful of intrepid warriors. In the speed and secrecy of his march, in the order and evolutions of the battle, his enemies felt and admired the military talents of Bajazet. They accuse his cruelty in the use of victory. After reserving the count of Nevers, and four-and-twenty lords, [63/2] whose birth and riches were attested by his Latin interpreters, the remainder of the French captives, who had survived the slaughter of the day, were led before his throne; and, as they refused to abjure their faith, were successively beheaded in his presence. The sultan was exasperated by the loss of his bravest Janizaries; and if it be true, that, on the eve of the engagement, the French had massacred their Turkish prisoners, [64] they might impute to themselves the consequences of a just retaliation. [64/1] A knight, whose life had been spared, was permitted to return to Paris, that he might relate the deplorable tale, and solicit the ransom of the noble captives. In the mean while, the count of Nevers, with the princes and barons of France, were dragged along in the marches of the Turkish camp, exposed as a grateful trophy to the Moslems of Europe and Asia, and strictly confined at Boursa, as often as Bajazet resided in his capital. The sultan was pressed each day to expiate with their blood the blood of his martyrs; but he had pronounced that they should live, and either for mercy or destruction his word was irrevocable. He was assured of their value and importance by the return of the messenger, and the gifts and intercessions of the kings of France and of Cyprus. Lusignan presented him with a gold saltcellar of curious workmanship, and of the price of ten thousand ducats; and Charles the Sixth despatched by the way of Hungary a cast of Norwegian hawks, and six horse-loads of scarlet cloth, of fine linen of Rheims, and of Arras tapestry, representing the battles of the great Alexander. After much delay, the effect of distance rather than of art, Bajazet agreed to accept a ransom of two hundred thousand ducats for the count of Nevers and the surviving princes and barons: the marshal Boucicault, a famous warrior, was of the number of the fortunate; but the admiral of France had been slain in battle; and the constable, with the Sire de Coucy, died in the prison of Boursa. This heavy demand, which was doubled by incidental costs, fell chiefly on the duke of Burgundy, or rather on his Flemish subjects, who were bound by the feudal laws to contribute for the knighthood and captivity of the eldest son of their lord. For the faithful discharge of the debt, some merchants of Genoa gave security to the amount of five times the sum; a lesson to those warlike times, that commerce and credit are the links of the society of nations. It had been stipulated in the treaty, that the French captives should swear never to bear arms against the person of their conqueror; but the ungenerous restraint was abolished by Bajazet himself. "I despise," said he to the heir of Burgundy, "thy oaths and thy arms. Thou art young, and mayest be ambitious of effacing the disgrace or misfortune of thy first chivalry. Assemble thy powers, proclaim thy design, and be assured that Bajazet will rejoice to meet thee a second time in a field of battle." Before their departure, they were indulged in the freedom and hospitality of the court of Boursa. The French princes admired the magnificence of the Ottoman, whose hunting and hawking equipage was composed of seven thousand huntsmen and seven thousand falconers. [65] In their presence, and at his command, the belly of one of his chamberlains was cut open, on a complaint against him for drinking the goat's milk of a poor woman. The strangers were astonished by this act of justice; but it was the justice of a sultan who disdains to balance the weight of evidence, or to measure the degrees of guilt.

[Footnote 61: I should not complain of the labor of this work, if my materials were always derived from such books as the chronicle of honest Froissard, (vol. iv. c. 67, 72, 74, 79—83, 85, 87, 89,) who read little, inquired much, and believed all. The original Mémoires of the Maréchal de Boucicault (Partie i. c. 22—28) add some facts, but they are dry and deficient, if compared with the pleasant garrulity of Froissard.]

[Footnote 62: An accurate Memoir on the Life of Enguerrand VII., Sire de Coucy, has been given by the Baron de Zurlauben, (Hist. de l'Académie des Inscriptions, tom. xxv.) His rank and possessions were equally considerable in France and England; and, in 1375, he led an army of adventurers into

Switzerland, to recover a large patrimony which he claimed in right of his grandmother, the daughter of the emperor Albert I. of Austria, (Sinner, Voyage dans la Suisse Occidentale, tom. i. p. 118—124.)]

[Footnote 63: That military office, so respectable at present, was still more conspicuous when it was divided between two persons, (Daniel, Hist. de la Milice Françoise, tom. ii. p. 5.) One of these, the marshal of the crusade, was the famous Boucicault, who afterwards defended Constantinople, governed Genoa, invaded the coast of Asia, and died in the field of Azincour.]

[Footnote 63/1: Daru, Hist. de Venice, vol. ii. p. 104, makes the whole French army amount to 10,000 men, of whom 1000 were knights. The curious volume of Schiltberger, a German of Munich, who was taken prisoner in the battle, (edit. Munich, 1813,) and which V. Hammer receives as authentic, gives the whole number at 6000. See Schiltberger. Reise in dem Orient. and V. Hammer, note, p. 610—M.]

[Footnote 63/2: According to Schiltberger there were only twelve French lords granted to the prayer of the "duke of Burgundy," and "Herr Stephan Synther, and Johann von Bodem." Schiltberger, p. 13—M.]

[Footnote 64: For this odious fact, the Abbé de Vertot quotes the Hist. Anonyme de St. Denys, l. xvi. c. 10, 11. (Ordre de Malthe, tom. ii. p. 310.)]

[Footnote 64/1: See Schiltberger's very graphic account of the massacre. He was led out to be slaughtered in cold blood with the rest f the Christian prisoners, amounting to 10,000. He was spared at the intercession of the son of Bajazet, with a few others, on account of their extreme youth. No one under 20 years of age was put to death. The "duke of Burgundy" was obliged to be a spectator of this butchery which lasted from early in the morning till four o'clock, P. M. It ceased only at the supplication of the leaders of Bajazet's army. Schiltberger, p. 14—M.]

[Footnote 65: Sherefeddin Ali (Hist. de Timour Bec, l. v. c. 13) allows Bajazet a round number of 12,000 officers and servants of the chase. A part of his spoils was afterwards displayed in a hunting-match of Timour, l. hounds with satin housings; 2. leopards with collars set with jewels; 3. Grecian greyhounds; and 4, dogs from Europe, as strong as African lions, (idem, l. vi. c. 15.) Bajazet was particularly fond of flying his hawks at cranes, (Chalcondyles, l. ii. p. 85.)]

After his enfranchisement from an oppressive guardian, John Palæologus remained thirty-six years, the helpless, and, as it should seem, the careless spectator of the public ruin. [66] Love, or rather lust, was his only vigorous passion; and in the embraces of the wives and virgins of the city, the Turkish slave forgot the dishonor of the emperor of the Romans Andronicus, his eldest son, had formed, at Adrianople, an intimate and guilty friendship with Sauzes, the son of Amurath; and the two youths conspired against the authority and lives of their parents. The presence of Amurath in Europe soon discovered and dissipated their rash counsels; and, after depriving Sauzes of his sight, the Ottoman threatened his vassal with the treatment of an accomplice and an enemy, unless he inflicted a similar punishment on his own son. Palæologus trembled and obeyed; and a cruel precaution involved in the same sentence the childhood and innocence of John, the son of the criminal. But the operation was so mildly, or so unskilfully, performed, that the one retained the sight of an eye, and the other was afflicted only with the infirmity of squinting. Thus excluded from the succession, the two princes were confined in the tower of Anema; and the piety of Manuel, the second son of the reigning monarch, was rewarded with the gift of the Imperial crown. But at the end of two years, the turbulence of the Latins and the levity of the Greeks, produced a revolution; [66/1] and the two emperors were buried in the tower from whence the two prisoners were exalted to the throne. Another period of two years afforded Palæologus and Manuel the means of escape: it was contrived by the magic or subtlety of a monk, who was alternately named the angel or the devil: they fled to Scutari; their adherents armed in their cause; and the two Byzantine factions displayed the ambition and animosity with which Cæsar and Pompey had disputed the empire of the world. The Roman world was now contracted to a corner of Thrace, between the Propontis and the Black Sea, about fifty miles in length and thirty in breadth; a space of ground not more extensive than the lesser principalities of Germany or Italy, if the remains of Constantinople had not still represented the wealth and populousness of a kingdom. To restore the public peace, it was found necessary to divide this fragment of the empire; and while Palæologus and Manuel were left in possession of the capital, almost all that lay without the walls was ceded to the blind princes, who fixed their residence at Rhodosto and Selybria. In the tranquil slumber of royalty, the passions of John Palæologus survived his reason and his strength: he deprived his favorite and heir of a blooming princess of Trebizond; and while the feeble emperor labored to consummate his nuptials, Manuel, with a hundred of the noblest Greeks, was sent on a peremptory summons to the Ottoman porte. They served with honor in the wars of Bajazet; but a plan of fortifying Constantinople excited his jealousy: he threatened their lives; the new works were instantly demolished; and we shall bestow a praise, perhaps above the merit of Palæologus, if we impute this last humiliation as the cause of his death.

[Footnote 66: For the reigns of John Palæologus and his son Manuel, from 1354 to 1402, see Ducas, c. 9—15, Phranza, l. i. c. 16—21, and the ist and iid books of Chalcondyles, whose proper subject is drowned in a sea of episode.]

[Footnote 66/1: According to Von Hammer it was the power of Bajazet, vol. i. p. 218.]

The earliest intelligence of that event was communicated to Manuel, who escaped with speed and secrecy from the palace of Boursa to the Byzantine throne. Bajazet affected a proud indifference at the loss of this valuable pledge; and while he pursued his conquests in Europe and Asia, he left the emperor to struggle with his blind cousin John of Selybria, who, in eight years of civil war, asserted his right of primogeniture. At length, the ambition of the victorious sultan pointed to the conquest of Constantinople; but he listened to the advice of his vizier, who represented that such an enterprise might unite the powers of Christendom in a second and more formidable crusade. His epistle to the emperor was conceived in these words: "By the divine clemency, our invincible cimeter has reduced to our obedience almost all Asia, with many and large countries in Europe, excepting only the city of Constantinople; for beyond the walls thou hast nothing left. Resign that city; stipulate thy reward; or tremble, for thyself and thy unhappy people, at the consequences of a rash refusal." But his ambassadors were instructed to soften their tone, and to propose a treaty, which was subscribed with submission and gratitude. A truce of ten years was purchased by an annual tribute of thirty thousand crowns of gold; the Greeks deplored the public toleration of the law of Mahomet, and Bajazet enjoyed the glory of establishing a Turkish cadhi, and founding a royal mosque in the metropolis of the Eastern church. [67] Yet this truce was soon violated by the restless sultan: in the cause of the prince of Selybria, the lawful emperor, an army of Ottomans again threatened Constantinople; and the distress of Manuel implored the protection of the king of France. His plaintive embassy obtained much pity and some relief; and the conduct of the succor was intrusted to the marshal Boucicault, [68] whose religious chivalry was inflamed by the desire of revenging his captivity on the infidels. He sailed with four ships of war, from Aiguesmortes to the Hellespont; forced the passage, which was guarded by seventeen Turkish galleys; landed at Constantinople a supply of six hundred men-at-arms and sixteen hundred archers; and reviewed them in the adjacent plain, without condescending to number or array the multitude of Greeks. By his presence, the blockade was raised both by sea and land; the flying squadrons of Bajazet were driven to a more respectful distance; and several castles in Europe and Asia were stormed by the emperor and the marshal, who fought with equal valor by each other's side. But the Ottomans soon returned with an increase of numbers; and the intrepid Boucicault, after a year's struggle, resolved to evacuate a country which could no longer afford either pay or provisions for his soldiers. The marshal offered to conduct Manuel to the French court, where he might solicit in person a supply of men and money; and advised, in the mean while, that, to extinguish all domestic discord, he should leave his blind competitor on the throne. The proposal was embraced: the prince of Selybria was introduced to the capital; and such was the public misery, that the lot of the exile seemed more fortunate than that of the sovereign. Instead of applauding the success of his vassal, the Turkish sultan claimed the city as his own; and on the refusal of the emperor John, Constantinople was more closely pressed by the calamities of war and famine. Against such an enemy prayers and resistance were alike unavailing; and the savage would have devoured his prey, if, in the fatal moment, he had not been overthrown by another savage stronger than himself. By the victory of Timour or Tamerlane, the fall of Constantinople was delayed about fifty years; and this important, though accidental, service may justly introduce the life and character of the Mogul conqueror.

[Footnote 67: Cantemir, p. 50—53. Of the Greeks, Ducas alone (c. 13, 15) acknowledges the Turkish cadhi at Constantinople. Yet even Ducas dissembles the mosque.]

[Footnote 68: Mémoires du bon Messire Jean le Maingre, dit Boucicault, Maréchal de France, partie ire c. 30, 35.]

CHAPTER LXV

ELEVATION OF TIMOUR OR TAMERLANE, AND HIS DEATH

PART I

ELEVATION OF TIMOUR OR TAMERLANE TO THE THRONE OF SAMARCAND—HIS CONQUESTS IN PERSIA, GEORGIA, TARTARY RUSSIA, INDIA, SYRIA, AND ANATOLIA—HIS TURKISH WAR—DEFEAT AND CAPTIVITY OF BAJAZET—DEATH OF TIMOUR—CIVIL WAR OF THE SONS OF BAJAZET—RESTORATION OF THE TURKISH MONARCHY BY MAHOMET THE FIRST—SIEGE OF CONSTANTINOPLE BY AMURATH THE SECOND

The conquest and monarchy of the world was the first object of the ambition of Timour. To live in the memory and esteem of future ages was the second wish of his magnanimous spirit. All the civil and military transactions of his reign were diligently recorded in the journals of his secretaries: [1] the authentic narrative was revised by the persons best informed of each particular transaction; and it is believed in the empire and family of Timour, that the monarch himself composed the commentaries [2] of his life, and the institutions [3] of his government. [4] But these cares were ineffectual for the preservation of his fame, and these precious memorials in the Mogul or Persian language were concealed from the world, or, at least, from the knowledge of Europe. The nations which he vanquished exercised a base and impotent revenge; and ignorance has long repeated the tale of calumny, [5] which had disfigured the birth and character, the person, and even the name, of Tamerlane. [6] Yet his real merit would be enhanced, rather than debased, by the elevation of a peasant to the throne of Asia; nor can his lameness be a theme of reproach, unless he had the weakness to blush at a natural, or perhaps an honorable, infirmity. [606]

[Footnote 1: These journals were communicated to Sherefeddin, or Cherefeddin Ali, a native of Yezd, who composed in the Persian language a history of Timour Beg, which has been translated into French by M. Petit de la Croix, (Paris, 1722, in 4 vols. 12 mo.,) and has always been my faithful guide. His geography and chronology are wonderfully accurate; and he may be trusted for public facts, though he servilely praises the virtue and fortune of the hero. Timour's attention to procure intelligence from his own and foreign countries may be seen in the Institutions, p. 215, 217, 349, 351.]

[Footnote 2: These Commentaries are yet unknown in Europe: but Mr. White gives some hope that they may be imported and translated by his friend Major Davy, who had read in the East this "minute and faithful narrative of an interesting and eventful period." Note: The manuscript of Major Davy has been translated by Major Stewart, and published by the Oriental Translation Committee of London. It contains the life of Timour, from his birth to his forty-first year; but the last thirty years of western war and conquest are wanting. Major Stewart intimates that two manuscripts exist in this country containing the whole work, but excuses himself, on account of his age, from undertaking the laborious task of completing the translation. It is to be hoped that the European public will be soon enabled to judge of the value and authenticity of the Commentaries of the Cæsar of the East. Major Stewart's work commences with the Book of Dreams and Omens—a wild, but characteristic, chronicle of Visions and Sortes Koranicæ. Strange that a life of Timour should awaken a reminiscence of the diary of Archbishop Laud! The early dawn and the gradual expression of his not less splendid but more real visions of ambition are touched with the simplicity of truth and nature. But we long to escape from the petty feuds of the pastoral chieftain, to the triumphs and the legislation of the conqueror of the world—M.]

[Footnote 3: I am ignorant whether the original institution, in the Turki or Mogul language, be still extant. The Persic version, with an English translation, and most valuable index, was published (Oxford, 1783, in 4to.) by the joint labors of Major Davy and Mr. White, the Arabic professor. This work has been since translated from the Persic into French, (Paris, 1787,) by M. Langlès, a learned Orientalist, who has added the life of Timour, and many curious notes.]

[Footnote 4: Shaw Allum, the present Mogul, reads, values, but cannot imitate, the institutions of his great ancestor. The English translator relies on their internal evidence; but if any suspicions should arise of fraud and fiction, they will not be dispelled by Major Davy's letter. The Orientals have never cultivated the art of criticism; the patronage of a prince, less honorable, perhaps, is not less lucrative than that of a bookseller; nor can it be deemed incredible that a Persian, the real author, should renounce the credit, to raise the value and price, of the work.]

[Footnote 5: The original of the tale is found in the following work, which is much esteemed for its florid elegance of style: Ahmedis Arabsiad (Ahmed Ebn Arabshah) Vitæ et Rerum gestarum Timuri. Arabice et Latine. Edidit Samuel Henricus Manger. Franequer, 1767, 2 tom. in 4to. This Syrian author is ever a malicious, and often an ignorant enemy: the very titles of his chapters are injurious; as how the wicked, as how the impious, as how the viper, &c. The copious article of Timur, in Bibliothèque Orientale, is of a mixed nature, as D'Herbelot indifferently draws his materials (p. 877—888) from Khondemir Ebn Schounah, and the Lebtarikh.]

[Footnote 6: Demir or Timour signifies in the Turkish language, Iron; and it is the appellation of a lord or prince. By the change of a letter or accent, it is changed into Lenc, or Lame; and a European corruption confounds the two words in the name of Tamerlane. Note: According to the memoirs he was so called by a Shaikh, who, when visited by his mother on his birth, was reading the verse of the Koran, 'Are you sure *that he who dwelleth in heaven will not cause the earth to swallow you up, and behold it shall shake, Tamûrn." The Shaikh then stopped and said, "We have named your son Timûr," p. 21—M.]*

*[Footnote 606: He was lamed by a wound at the siege of the capital of Sistan. Sherefeddin, lib. iii. c. 17. p. 136. See Von Hammer, vol. i. p. 260—M.]*

In the eyes of the Moguls, who held the indefeasible succession of the house of Zingis, he was doubtless a rebel subject; yet he sprang from the noble tribe of Berlass: his fifth ancestor, Carashar Nevian, had been the vizier [607] of Zagatai, in his new realm of Transoxiana; and in the ascent of some generations, the branch of Timour is confounded, at least by the females, [7] with the Imperial stem. [8] He was born forty miles to the south of Samarcand in the village of Sebzar, in the fruitful territory of Cash, of which his fathers were the hereditary chiefs, as well as of a toman of ten thousand horse. [9] His birth [10] was cast on one of those periods of anarchy, which announce the fall of the Asiatic dynasties, and open a new field to adventurous ambition. The khans of Zagatai were extinct; the emirs aspired to independence; and their domestic feuds could only be suspended by the conquest and tyranny of the khans of Kashgar, who, with an army of Getes or Calmucks, [11] invaded the Transoxian kingdom. From the twelfth year of his age, Timour had entered the field of action; in the twenty-fifth [11/1] he stood forth as the deliverer of his country; and the eyes and wishes of the people were turned towards a hero who suffered in their cause. The chiefs of the law and of the army had pledged their salvation to support him with their lives and fortunes; but in the hour of danger they were silent and afraid; and, after waiting seven days on the hills of Samarcand, he retreated to the desert with only sixty horsemen. The fugitives were overtaken by a thousand Getes, whom he repulsed with incredible slaughter, and his enemies were forced to exclaim, "Timour is a wonderful man: fortune and the divine favor are with him." But in this bloody action his own followers were reduced to ten, a number which was soon diminished by the desertion of three Carizmians. [11/2] He wandered in the desert with his wife, seven companions, and four horses; and sixty-two days was he plunged in a loathsome dungeon, from whence he escaped by his own courage and the remorse of the oppressor. After swimming the broad and rapid steam of the Jihoon, or Oxus, he led, during some months, the life of a vagrant and outlaw, on the borders of the adjacent states. But his fame shone brighter in adversity; he learned to distinguish the friends of his person, the associates of his fortune, and to apply the various characters of men for their advantage, and, above all, for his own. On his return to his native country, Timour was successively joined by the parties of his confederates, who anxiously sought him in the desert; nor can I refuse to describe, in his pathetic simplicity, one of their fortunate encounters. He presented himself as a guide to three chiefs, who were at the head of seventy horse. "When their eyes fell upon me," says Timour, "they were overwhelmed with joy; and they alighted from their horses; and they came and kneeled; and they kissed my stirrup. I also came down from my horse, and took each of them in my arms. And I put my turban on the head of the first chief; and my girdle, rich in jewels and wrought with gold, I bound on the loins of the second; and the third I clothed in my own coat. And they wept, and I wept also; and the hour of prayer was arrived, and we prayed. And we mounted our horses, and came to my dwelling; and I collected my people, and made a feast." His trusty bands were soon increased by the bravest of the tribes; he led them against a superior foe; and, after some vicissitudes of war the Getes were finally driven from the kingdom of Transoxiana. He had done much for his own glory; but much remained to be done, much art to be exerted, and some blood to be spilt, before he could teach his equals to obey him as their master. The birth and power of emir Houssein compelled him to accept a vicious and unworthy colleague, whose sister was the best beloved of his wives. Their union was short and jealous; but the policy of Timour, in their frequent quarrels, exposed his rival to the reproach of injustice and perfidy; and, after a final defeat, Houssein was slain by some sagacious friends, who presumed, for the last time, to disobey the commands of their lord. [11/3] At the age of thirty-four, [12] and in a general diet or couroultai, he was invested with Imperial command, but he affected to revere the house of Zingis; and while the emir Timour reigned over Zagatai and the East, a nominal khan served as a private officer in the armies of his servant. A fertile kingdom, five hundred miles in length and in breadth, might have satisfied the ambition of a subject; but Timour aspired to the dominion of the world; and before his death, the crown of Zagatai was one of the twenty-seven crowns which he had placed on his head. Without expatiating on the victories of thirty-five campaigns; without describing the lines of march, which he repeatedly traced over the continent of Asia; I shall briefly represent his conquests in, I. Persia, II. Tartary, and, III. India, [13] and from thence proceed to the more interesting narrative of his Ottoman war.

[Footnote 607: In the memoirs, the title Gurgân is in one place (p. 23) interpreted the son-in-law; in another (p. 28) as Kurkan, great prince, generalissimo, and prime minister of Jagtai—M.]

[Footnote 7: After relating some false and foolish tales of Timour Lenc, Arabshah is compelled to speak truth, and to own him for a kinsman of Zingis, per mulieres, (as he peevishly adds,) laqueos Satanæ, (pars i. c. i. p. 25.) The testimony of Abulghazi Khan (P. ii. c. 5, P. v. c. 4) is clear, unquestionable, and decisive.]

[Footnote 8: According to one of the pedigrees, the fourth ancestor of Zingis, and the ninth of Timour, were brothers; and they agreed, that the posterity of the elder should succeed to the dignity of khan, and that the descendants of the younger should fill the office of their minister and general. This tradition was at least convenient to justify the first steps of Timour's ambition, (Institutions, p. 24, 25, from the MS. fragments of Timour's History.)]

[Footnote 9: See the preface of Sherefeddin, and Abulfeda's Geography, (Chorasmiæ, &c., Descriptio, p. 60, 61,) in the iiid volume of Hudson's Minor Greek Geographers.]

[Footnote 10: See his nativity in Dr. Hyde, (Syntagma Dissertat. tom. ii. p. 466,) as it was cast by the astrologers of his grandson Ulugh Beg. He was born, A.D. 1336, April 9, 11º 57'. p. m., lat. 36. I know not whether they can prove the great conjunction of the planets from whence, like other conquerors and prophets, Timour derived the surname of Saheb Keran, or master of the conjunctions, (Bibliot. Orient. p. 878.)]

[Footnote 11: In the Institutions of Timour, these subjects of the khan of Kashgar are most improperly styled Ouzbegs, or Usbeks, a name which belongs to another branch and country of Tartars, (Abulghazi, P. v. c. v. P. vii. c. 5.) Could I be sure that this word is in the Turkish original, I would boldly pronounce, that the Institutions were framed a century after the death of Timour, since the establishment of the Usbeks in Transoxiana. Note: Col. Stewart observes, that the Persian translator has sometimes made use of the name Uzbek by anticipation. He observes, likewise, that these Jits (Getes) are not to be confounded with the ancient Getæ: they were unconverted Turks. Col. Tod (History of Rajasthan, vol. i. p. 166) would identify the Jits with the ancient race—M.]

[Footnote 11/1: He was twenty-seven before he served his first wars under the emir Houssein, who ruled over Khorasan and Mawerainnehr. Von Hammer, vol. i. p. 262. Neither of these statements agrees with the Memoirs. At twelve he was a boy. "I fancied that I perceived in myself all the signs of greatness and wisdom, and whoever came to visit me, I received with great hauteur and dignity." At seventeen he undertook the management of the flocks and herds of the family, (p. 24.) At nineteen he became religious, and "left off playing chess," made a kind of Budhist vow never to injure living thing and felt his foot paralyzed from having accidentally trod upon an ant, (p. 30.) At twenty, thoughts of rebellion and greatness rose in his mind; at twenty-one, he seems to have performed his first feat of arms. He was a practised warrior when he served, in his twenty-seventh year, under Emir Houssein.]

[Footnote 11/2: Compare Memoirs, page 61. The imprisonment is there stated at fifty-three days. "At this time I made a vow to God that I would never keep any person, whether guilty or innocent, for any length of time, in prison or in chains." p. 63—M.]

[Footnote 11/3: Timour, on one occasion, sent him this message: "He who wishes to embrace the bride of royalty must kiss her across the edge of the sharp sword," p. 83. The scene of the trial of Houssein, the resistance of Timour gradually becoming more feeble, the vengeance of the chiefs becoming proportionably more determined, is strikingly portrayed. Mem. p 130—M.]

[Footnote 12: The ist book of Sherefeddin is employed on the private life of the hero: and he himself, or his secretary, (Institutions, p. 3—77,) enlarges with pleasure on the thirteen designs and enterprises which most truly constitute his personal merit. It even shines through the dark coloring of Arabshah, (P. i. c. 1—12.)]

[Footnote 13: The conquests of Persia, Tartary, and India, are represented in the iid and iiid books of Sherefeddin, and by Arabshah, (c. 13—55.) Consult the excellent Indexes to the Institutions. Note: Compare the seventh book of Von Hammer, Geschichte des Osmanischen Reiches—M.]

I. For every war, a motive of safety or revenge, of honor or zeal, of right or convenience, may be readily found in the jurisprudence of conquerors. No sooner had Timour reunited to the patrimony of Zagatai the dependent countries of Carizme and Candahar, than he turned his eyes towards the kingdoms of Iran or Persia. From the Oxus to the Tigris, that extensive country was left without a lawful sovereign since the death of Abousaid, the last of the descendants of the great Holacou. Peace and justice had been banished from the land above forty years; and the Mogul invader might seem to listen to the cries of an oppressed people. Their petty tyrants might have opposed him with confederate arms: they separately stood, and successively fell; and the difference of their fate was only marked by the promptitude of submission or the obstinacy of resistance. Ibrahim, prince of Shirwan, or Albania, kissed the footstool of the Imperial throne. His peace-offerings of silks, horses, and jewels, were composed, according to the Tartar fashion, each article of nine pieces; but a critical spectator observed, that there were only eight slaves. "I myself am the ninth," replied Ibrahim, who was prepared for the remark; and his flattery was rewarded by the smile of Timour. [14] Shah Mansour, prince of Fars, or the proper Persia, was one of the least powerful, but most dangerous, of his enemies. In a battle under the walls of Shiraz, he broke, with three or four thousand soldiers, the coul or main body of thirty thousand horse, where the emperor fought in person. No more than fourteen or fifteen guards remained near the standard of Timour: he stood firm as a rock, and received on his helmet two weighty strokes of a cimeter: [15] the Moguls rallied; the head of Mansour was thrown at his feet; and he declared his esteem of the valor of a foe, by extirpating all the males of so intrepid a race. From Shiraz, his troops advanced to the Persian Gulf; and the richness and weakness of Ormuz [16] were displayed in an annual tribute of six hundred thousand dinars of gold. Bagdad was no longer the city of peace, the seat of the caliphs; but the noblest conquest of Holacou could not be overlooked by his ambitious successor. The whole course of the Tigris and Euphrates, from the mouth to the sources of those rivers, was reduced to his obedience: he entered Edessa; and the Turkmans of the black sheep were chastised for the sacrilegious pillage of a caravan of Mecca. In the mountains of Georgia, the native Christians still braved the law and the sword of Mahomet, by three expeditions he obtained the merit of the gazie, or holy war; and the prince of Teflis became his proselyte and friend.

[Footnote 14: The reverence of the Tartars for the mysterious number of nine is declared by Abulghazi Khan, who, for that reason, divides his Genealogical History into nine parts.]

[Footnote 15: According to Arabshah, (P. i. c. 28, p. 183,) the coward Timour ran away to his tent, and hid himself from the pursuit of Shah Mansour under the women's garments. Perhaps Sherefeddin (l. iii. c. 25) has magnified his courage.]

[Footnote 16: The history of Ormuz is not unlike that of Tyre. The old city, on the continent, was destroyed by the Tartars, and renewed in a neighboring island, without fresh water or vegetation. The kings of Ormuz, rich in the Indian trade and the pearl fishery, possessed large territories both in Persia and Arabia; but they were at first the tributaries of the sultans of Kerman, and at last were delivered (A.D. 1505) by the Portuguese tyrants from the tyranny of their own viziers, (Marco Polo, l. i. c. 15, 16, fol. 7, 8. Abulfeda, Geograph. tabul. xi. p. 261, 262, an original Chronicle of Ormuz, in Texeira, or Stevens's History of Persia, p. 376—416, and the Itineraries inserted in the ist volume of Ramusio, of Ludovico Barthema, (1503,) fol. 167, of Andrea Corsali, (1517) fol. 202, 203, and of Odoardo Barbessa, (in 1516,) fol. 313—318.)]

II. A just retaliation might be urged for the invasion of Turkestan, or the Eastern Tartary. The dignity of Timour could not endure the impunity of the Getes: he passed the Sihoon, subdued the kingdom of Kashgar, and marched seven times into the heart of their country. His most distant camp was two months' journey, or four hundred and eighty leagues to the north-east of Samarcand; and his emirs, who traversed the River Irtish, engraved in the forests of Siberia a rude memorial of their exploits. The conquest of Kipzak, or the Western Tartary, [17] was founded on the double motive of aiding the distressed, and chastising the ungrateful. Toctamish, a fugitive prince, was entertained and protected in his court: the ambassadors of Auruss Khan were dismissed with a haughty denial, and followed on the same day by the armies of Zagatai; and their success established Toctamish in the Mogul empire of the North. But, after a reign of ten years, the new khan forgot the merits and the strength of his benefactor; the base usurper, as he deemed him, of the sacred rights of the house of Zingis. Through the gates of Derbend, he entered Persia at the head of ninety thousand horse: with the innumerable forces of Kipzak, Bulgaria, Circassia, and Russia, he passed the Sihoon, burnt the palaces of Timour, and compelled him, amidst the winter snows, to contend for Samarcand and his life. After a mild expostulation, and a glorious victory, the emperor resolved on revenge; and by the east, and the west, of the Caspian, and the Volga, he twice invaded Kipzak with such mighty powers, that thirteen miles were measured from his right to his left wing. In a march of five months, they rarely beheld the footsteps of man; and their daily subsistence was often trusted to the fortune of the chase. At length the armies encountered each other; but the treachery of the standard-bearer, who, in the heat of action, reversed the Imperial standard of Kipzak, determined the victory of the Zagatais; and Toctamish (I peak the language of the Institutions) gave the tribe of Toushi to the wind of desolation. [18] He fled to the Christian duke of Lithuania; again returned to the banks of the Volga; and, after fifteen battles with a domestic rival, at last perished in the wilds of Siberia. The pursuit of a flying enemy carried Timour into the tributary provinces of Russia: a duke of the reigning family was made prisoner amidst the ruins of his capital; and Yeletz, by the pride and ignorance of the Orientals, might easily be confounded with the genuine metropolis of the nation. Moscow trembled at the approach of the Tartar, and the resistance would have been feeble, since the hopes of the Russians were placed in a miraculous image of the Virgin, to whose protection they ascribed the casual and voluntary retreat of the conqueror. Ambition and prudence recalled him to the South, the desolate country was exhausted, and the Mogul soldiers were enriched with an immense spoil of precious furs, of linen of Antioch, [19] and of ingots of gold and silver. [20] On the banks of the Don, or Tanais, he received an humble deputation from the consuls and merchants of Egypt, [21] Venice, Genoa, Catalonia, and Biscay, who occupied the commerce and city of Tana, or Azoph, at the mouth of the river. They offered their gifts, admired his magnificence, and trusted his royal word. But the peaceful visit of an emir, who explored the state of the magazines and harbor, was speedily followed by the destructive presence of the Tartars. The city was reduced to ashes; the Moslems were pillaged and dismissed; but all the Christians, who had not fled to their ships, were condemned either to death or slavery. [22] Revenge prompted him to burn the cities of Serai and Astrachan, the monuments of rising civilization; and his vanity proclaimed, that he had penetrated to the region of perpetual daylight, a strange phenomenon, which authorized his Mahometan doctors to dispense with the obligation of evening prayer. [23]

[Footnote 17: Arabshah had travelled into Kipzak, and acquired a singular knowledge of the geography, cities, and revolutions, of that northern region, (P. i. c. 45—49.)]

[Footnote 18: Institutions of Timour, p. 123, 125. Mr. White, the editor, bestows some animadversion on the superficial account of Sherefeddin, (l. iii. c. 12, 13, 14,) who was ignorant of the designs of Timour, and the true springs of action.]

[Footnote 19: The furs of Russia are more credible than the ingots. But the linen of Antioch has never been famous: and Antioch was in ruins. I suspect that it was some manufacture of Europe, which the Hanse merchants had imported by the way of Novogorod.]

[Footnote 20: M. Levesque (Hist. de Russie, tom. ii. p. 247. Vie de Timour, p. 64—67, before the French version of the Institutes) has corrected the error of Sherefeddin, and marked the true limit of Timour's conquests. His arguments are superfluous; and a simple appeal to the Russian annals is sufficient to prove that Moscow, which six years before had been taken by Toctamish, escaped the arms of a more formidable invader.]

[Footnote 21: An Egyptian consul from Grand Cairo is mentioned in Barbaro's voyage to Tana in 1436, after the city had been rebuilt, (Ramusio, tom. ii. fol. 92.)]

[Footnote 22: The sack of Azoph is described by Sherefeddin, (l. iii. c. 55,) and much more particularly by the author of an Italian chronicle, (Andreas de Redusiis de Quero, in Chron. Tarvisiano, in Muratori, Script. Rerum Italicarum, tom. xix. p. 802—805.) He had conversed with the Mianis, two Venetian brothers, one of whom had been sent a deputy to the camp of Timour, and the other had lost at Azoph three sons and 12,000 ducats.]

[Footnote 23: Sherefeddin only says (l. iii. c. 13) that the rays of the setting, and those of the rising sun, were scarcely separated by any interval; a problem which may be solved in the latitude of Moscow, (the 56th degree,) with the aid of the Aurora Borealis, and a long summer twilight. But a day of forty days (Khondemir apud D'Herbelot, p. 880) would rigorously confine us within the polar circle.]

III. When Timour first proposed to his princes and emirs the invasion of India or Hindostan, [24] he was answered by a murmur of discontent: "The rivers! and the mountains and deserts! and the soldiers clad in armor! and the elephants, destroyers of men!" But the displeasure of the emperor was more dreadful than all these terrors; and his superior reason was convinced, that an enterprise of such tremendous aspect was safe and easy in the execution. He was informed by his spies of the weakness and anarchy of Hindostan: the soubahs of the provinces had erected the standard of rebellion; and the perpetual infancy of Sultan Mahmoud was despised even in the harem of Delhi. The Mogul army moved in three great divisions; and Timour observes with pleasure, that the ninety-two squadrons of a thousand horse most fortunately corresponded with the ninety-two names or epithets of the prophet Mahomet. [24/1] Between the Jihoon and the Indus they crossed one of the ridges of mountains, which are styled by the Arabian geographers The Stony Girdles of the Earth. The highland robbers were subdued or extirpated; but great numbers of men and horses perished in the snow; the emperor himself was let down a precipice on a portable scaffold—the ropes were one hundred and fifty cubits in length; and before he could reach the bottom, this dangerous operation was five times repeated. Timour crossed the Indus at the ordinary passage of Attok; and successively traversed, in the footsteps of Alexander, the Punjab, or five rivers, [25] that fall into the master stream. From Attok to Delhi, the high road measures no more than six hundred miles; but the two conquerors deviated to the south-east; and the motive of Timour was to join his grandson, who had achieved by his command the conquest of Moultan. On the eastern bank of the Hyphasis, on the edge of the desert, the Macedonian hero halted and wept: the Mogul entered the desert, reduced the fortress of Batmir, and stood in arms before the gates of Delhi, a great and flourishing city, which had subsisted three centuries under the dominion of the Mahometan kings. [25/1] The siege, more especially of the castle, might have been a work of time; but he tempted, by the appearance of weakness, the sultan Mahmoud and his vizier to descend into the plain, with ten thousand cuirassiers, forty thousand of his foot-guards, and one hundred and twenty elephants, whose tusks are said to have been armed with sharp and poisoned daggers. Against these monsters, or rather against the imagination of his troops, he condescended to use some extraordinary precautions of fire and a ditch, of iron spikes and a rampart of bucklers; but the event taught the Moguls to smile at their own fears; and as soon as these unwieldy animals were routed, the inferior species (the men of India) disappeared from the field. Timour made his triumphal entry into the capital of Hindostan; and admired, with a view to imitate, the architecture of the stately mosque; but the order or license of a general pillage and massacre polluted the festival of his victory. He resolved to purify his soldiers in the blood of the idolaters, or Gentoos, who still surpass, in the proportion of ten to one, the numbers of the Moslems. [25/2] In this pious design, he advanced one hundred miles to the north-east of Delhi, passed the Ganges, fought several battles by land and water, and penetrated to the famous rock of Coupele, the statue of the cow, [25/3] that seems to discharge the mighty river, whose source is far distant among the mountains of Thibet. [26] His return was along the skirts of the northern hills; nor could this rapid campaign of one year justify the strange foresight of his emirs, that their children in a warm climate would degenerate into a race of Hindoos.

[Footnote 24: For the Indian war, see the Institutions, (p. 129—139,) the fourth book of Sherefeddin, and the history of Ferishta, (in Dow, vol. ii. p. 1—20,) which throws a general light on the affairs of Hindostan.]

[Footnote 24/1: Gibbon (observes M. von Hammer) is mistaken in the correspondence of the ninety-two squadrons of his army with the ninety-two names of God: the names of God are ninety-nine. and Allah is the hundredth, p. 286, note. But Gibbon speaks of the names or epithets of Mahomet, not of God—M.]

[Footnote 25: The rivers of the Punjab, the five eastern branches of the Indus, have been laid down for the first time with truth and accuracy in Major Rennel's incomparable map of Hindostan. In this Critical Memoir he illustrates with judgment and learning the marches of Alexander and Timour. Note See vol. i. ch. ii. note 1—M.]

[Footnote 25/1: They took, on their march, 100,000 slaves, Guebers they were all murdered. V. Hammer, vol. i. p. 286. They are called idolaters. Briggs's Ferishta, vol. i. p. 491—M.]

*[Footnote 25/2: See a curious passage on the destruction of the Hindoo idols, Memoirs, p. 15—M.]*

*[Footnote 25/3: Consult the very striking description of the Cow's Mouth by Captain Hodgson, Asiat. Res. vol. xiv. p. 117. "A most wonderful scene. The B'hagiratha or Ganges issues from under a very low arch at the foot of the grand snow bed. My guide, an illiterate mountaineer compared the pendent icicles to Mahodeva's hair." (Compare Poems, Quarterly Rev. vol. xiv. p. 37, and at the end of my translation of Nala.) "Hindoos of research may formerly have been here; and if so, I cannot think of any place to which they might more aptly give the name of a cow's mouth than to this extraordinary debouche."—M.]*

*[Footnote 26: The two great rivers, the Ganges and Burrampooter, rise in Thibet, from the opposite ridges of the same hills, separate from each other to the distance of 1200 miles, and, after a winding course of 2000 miles, again meet in one point near the Gulf of Bengal. Yet so capricious is Fame, that the Burrampooter is a late discovery, while his brother Ganges has been the theme of ancient and modern story Coupele, the scene of Timour's last victory, must be situate near Loldong, 1100 miles from Calcutta; and in 1774, a British camp! (Rennel's Memoir, p. 7, 59, 90, 91, 99.)]*

It was on the banks of the Ganges that Timour was informed, by his speedy messengers, of the disturbances which had arisen on the confines of Georgia and Anatolia, of the revolt of the Christians, and the ambitious designs of the sultan Bajazet. His vigor of mind and body was not impaired by sixty-three years, and innumerable fatigues; and, after enjoying some tranquil months in the palace of Samarcand, he proclaimed a new expedition of seven years into the western countries of Asia. [27] To the soldiers who had served in the Indian war he granted the choice of remaining at home, or following their prince; but the troops of all the provinces and kingdoms of Persia were commanded to assemble at Ispahan, and wait the arrival of the Imperial standard. It was first directed against the Christians of Georgia, who were strong only in their rocks, their castles, and the winter season; but these obstacles were overcome by the zeal and perseverance of Timour: the rebels submitted to the tribute or the Koran; and if both religions boasted of their martyrs, that name is more justly due to the Christian prisoners, who were offered the choice of abjuration or death. On his descent from the hills, the emperor gave audience to the first ambassadors of Bajazet, and opened the hostile correspondence of complaints and menaces, which fermented two years before the final explosion. Between two jealous and haughty neighbors, the motives of quarrel will seldom be wanting. The Mogul and Ottoman conquests now touched each other in the neighborhood of Erzeroum, and the Euphrates; nor had the doubtful limit been ascertained by time and treaty. Each of these ambitious monarchs might accuse his rival of violating his territory, of threatening his vassals, and protecting his rebels; and, by the name of rebels, each understood the fugitive princes, whose kingdoms he had usurped, and whose life or liberty he implacably pursued. The resemblance of character was still more dangerous than the opposition of interest; and in their victorious career, Timour was impatient of an equal, and Bajazet was ignorant of a superior. The first epistle [28] of the Mogul emperor must have provoked, instead of reconciling, the Turkish sultan, whose family and nation he affected to despise. [29] "Dost thou not know, that the greatest part of Asia is subject to our arms and our laws? that our invincible forces extend from one sea to the other? that the potentates of the earth form a line before our gate? and that we have compelled Fortune herself to watch over the prosperity of our empire. What is the foundation of thy insolence and folly? Thou hast fought some battles in the woods of Anatolia; contemptible trophies! Thou hast obtained some victories over the Christians of Europe; thy sword was blessed by the apostle of God; and thy obedience to the precept of the Koran, in waging war against the infidels, is the sole consideration that prevents us from destroying thy country, the frontier and bulwark of the Moslem world. Be wise in time; reflect; repent; and avert the thunder of our vengeance, which is yet suspended over thy head.

Thou art no more than a pismire; why wilt thou seek to provoke the elephants? Alas! they will trample thee under their feet." In his replies, Bajazet poured forth the indignation of a soul which was deeply stung by such unusual contempt. After retorting the basest reproaches on the thief and rebel of the desert, the Ottoman recapitulates his boasted victories in Iran, Touran, and the Indies; and labors to prove, that Timour had never triumphed unless by his own perfidy and the vices of his foes. "Thy armies are innumerable: be they so; but what are the arrows of the flying Tartar against the cimeters and battle-axes of my firm and invincible Janizaries? I will guard the princes who have implored my protection: seek them in my tents. The cities of Arzingan and Erzeroum are mine; and unless the tribute be duly paid, I will demand the arrears under the walls of Tauris and Sultania." The ungovernable rage of the sultan at length betrayed him to an insult of a more domestic kind. "If I fly from thy arms," said he, "may my wives be thrice divorced from my bed: but if thou hast not courage to meet me in the field, mayest thou again receive thy wives after they have thrice endured the embraces of a stranger." [30] Any violation by word or deed of the secrecy of the harem is an unpardonable offence among the Turkish nations; [31] and the political quarrel of the two monarchs was imbittered by private and personal resentment. Yet in his first expedition, Timour was satisfied with the siege and destruction of Siwas or Sebaste, a strong city on the borders of Anatolia; and he revenged the indiscretion of the Ottoman, on a garrison of four thousand Armenians, who were buried alive for the brave and faithful discharge of their duty. [31/1] As a Mussulman, he seemed to respect the pious occupation of Bajazet, who was still engaged in the blockade of Constantinople; and after this salutary lesson, the Mogul conqueror checked his pursuit, and turned aside to the invasion of Syria and Egypt. In these transactions, the Ottoman prince, by the Orientals, and even by Timour, is styled the Kaissar of Roum, the Cæsar of the Romans; a title which, by a small anticipation, might be given to a monarch who possessed the provinces, and threatened the city, of the successors of Constantine. [32]

[Footnote 27: See the Institutions, p. 141, to the end of the 1st book, and Sherefeddin, (l. v. c. 1—16,) to the entrance of Timour into Syria.]

[Footnote 28: We have three copies of these hostile epistles in the Institutions, (p. 147,) in Sherefeddin, (l. v. c. 14,) and in Arabshah, (tom. ii. c. 19 p. 183—201;) which agree with each other in the spirit and substance rather than in the style. It is probable, that they have been translated, with various latitude, from the Turkish original into the Arabic and Persian tongues. Note: Von Hammer considers the letter which Gibbon inserted in the text to be spurious. On the various copies of these letters, see his note, p 116—M.]

[Footnote 29: The Mogul emir distinguishes himself and his countrymen by the name of Turks, and stigmatizes the race and nation of Bajazet with the less honorable epithet of Turkmans. Yet I do not understand how the Ottomans could be descended from a Turkman sailor; those inland shepherds were so remote from the sea, and all maritime affairs. Note: Price translated the word pilot or boatman—M.]

[Footnote 30: According to the Koran, (c. ii. p. 27, and Sale's Discourses, p. 134,) Mussulman who had thrice divorced his wife, (who had thrice repeated the words of a divorce,) could not take her again, till after she had been married to, and repudiated by, another husband; an ignominious transaction, which it is needless to aggravate, by supposing that the first husband must see her enjoyed by a second before his face, (Rycaut's State of the Ottoman Empire, l. ii. c. 21.)]

[Footnote 31: The common delicacy of the Orientals, in never speaking of their women, is ascribed in a much higher degree by Arabshah to the Turkish nations; and it is remarkable enough, that Chalcondyles *(l. ii. p. 55) had some knowledge of the prejudice and the insult. Note: See Von Hammer, p. 308, and note, p. 621—M.]*

*[Footnote 31/1: Still worse barbarities were perpetrated on these brave men. Von Hammer, vol. i. p. 295—M.]*

*[Footnote 32: For the style of the Moguls, see the Institutions, (p. 131, 147,) and for the Persians, the Bibliothèque Orientale, (p. 882;) but I do not find that the title of Cæsar has been applied by the Arabians, or assumed by the Ottomans themselves.]*

PART II

The military republic of the Mamalukes still reigned in Egypt and Syria: but the dynasty of the Turks was overthrown by that of the Circassians; [33] and their favorite Barkok, from a slave and a prisoner, was raised and restored to the throne. In the midst of rebellion and discord, he braved the menaces, corresponded with the enemies, and detained the ambassadors, of the Mogul, who patiently expected his decease, to revenge the crimes of the father on the feeble reign of his son Farage. The Syrian emirs [34] were assembled at Aleppo to repel the invasion: they confided in the fame and discipline of the Mamalukes, in the temper of their swords and lances of the purest steel of Damascus, in the strength of their walled cities, and in the populousness of sixty thousand villages; and instead of sustaining a siege, they threw open their gates, and arrayed their forces in the plain. But these forces were not cemented by virtue and union; and some powerful emirs had been seduced to desert or betray their more loyal companions. Timour's front was covered with a line of Indian elephants, whose turrets were filled with archers and Greek fire: the rapid evolutions of his cavalry completed the dismay and disorder; the Syrian crowds fell back on each other: many thousands were stifled or slaughtered in the entrance of the great street; the Moguls entered with the fugitives; and after a short defence, the citadel, the impregnable citadel of Aleppo, was surrendered by cowardice or treachery. Among the suppliants and captives, Timour distinguished the doctors of the law, whom he invited to the dangerous honor of a personal conference. [35] The Mogul prince was a zealous Mussulman; but his Persian schools had taught him to revere the memory of Ali and Hosein; and he had imbibed a deep prejudice against the Syrians, as the enemies of the son of the daughter of the apostle of God. To these doctors he proposed a captious question, which the casuists of Bochara, Samarcand, and Herat, were incapable of resolving. "Who are the true martyrs, of those who are slain on my side, or on that of my enemies?" But he was silenced, or satisfied, by the dexterity of one of the cadhis of Aleppo, who replied in the words of Mahomet himself, that the motive, not the ensign, constitutes the martyr; and that the Moslems of either party, who fight only for the glory of God, may deserve that sacred appellation. The true succession of the caliphs was a controversy of a still more delicate nature; and the frankness of a doctor, too honest for his situation, provoked the emperor to exclaim, "Ye are as false as those of Damascus: Moawiyah was a usurper, Yezid a tyrant, and Ali alone is the lawful successor of the prophet." A prudent explanation restored his tranquillity; and he passed to a more familiar topic of conversation. "What is your age?" said he to the cadhi. "Fifty years."—"It would be the age of my eldest son: you see me here (continued Timour) a poor lame, decrepit mortal. Yet by my arm has the Almighty been pleased to subdue the kingdoms of Iran, Touran, and the Indies. I am not a man of blood; and God is my witness, that in all my wars I have never been the aggressor, and that my enemies have always been the authors of their own calamity." During this peaceful conversation the streets of Aleppo streamed with blood, and reechoed with the cries of mothers and children, with the shrieks of violated virgins. The rich plunder that was abandoned to his soldiers might stimulate their avarice; but their cruelty was enforced by the peremptory command of producing an adequate number of heads, which, according to his custom, were curiously piled in columns and pyramids: the Moguls celebrated the feast of victory, while the surviving Moslems passed the night in tears and in chains. I shall not dwell on the march of the destroyer from Aleppo to Damascus, where he was rudely encountered, and almost overthrown, by the armies of Egypt. A retrograde motion was imputed to his distress and despair: one of his nephews deserted to the enemy; and Syria rejoiced in the tale of his defeat, when the sultan was driven by the revolt of the Mamalukes to escape with precipitation and shame to his palace of Cairo. Abandoned by their prince, the inhabitants of Damascus still defended their walls; and Timour consented to raise the siege, if they would adorn his retreat with a gift or ransom; each article of nine pieces. But no sooner had he introduced himself into the city, under color of a truce, than he perfidiously violated the treaty; imposed a contribution of ten millions of gold; and animated his troops to chastise the posterity of those Syrians who had executed, or approved, the murder of the grandson of Mahomet. A family which had given honorable burial to the head of Hosein, and a colony of artificers, whom he sent to labor at Samarcand, were alone reserved in the general massacre, and after a period of seven centuries, Damascus was reduced to ashes, because a Tartar was moved by religious zeal to avenge the blood of an Arab. The losses and fatigues of the campaign obliged Timour to renounce the conquest of Palestine and Egypt; but in his return to the Euphrates he delivered Aleppo to the flames; and justified his pious motive by the pardon and reward of two thousand sectaries of Ali, who were desirous to visit the tomb of his son. I have expatiated on the personal anecdotes which mark the character of the Mogul hero; but I shall briefly mention, [36] that he erected on the ruins of Bagdad a pyramid of ninety thousand heads; again visited Georgia; encamped on the banks of Araxes; and proclaimed his resolution of marching against the Ottoman emperor. Conscious of the importance of the war, he collected his forces from every province: eight hundred thousand men were enrolled on his military list; [37] but the splendid commands of five, and ten, thousand horse, may be rather expressive of the rank and pension of the chiefs, than of the genuine number of effective soldiers. [38] In the pillage of Syria, the Moguls had acquired immense riches: but the delivery of their pay and arrears for seven years more firmly attached them to the Imperial standard.

[Footnote 33: See the reigns of Barkok and Pharadge, in M. De Guignes, (tom. iv. l. xxii.,) who, from the Arabic texts of Aboulmahasen, Ebn (Schounah, and Aintabi, has added some facts to our common stock of materials.)]

[Footnote 34: For these recent and domestic transactions, Arabshah, though a partial, is a credible, witness, (tom. i. c. 64—68, tom. ii. c. 1—14.) Timour must have been odious to a Syrian; but the notoriety of facts would have obliged him, in some measure, to respect his enemy and himself. His bitters may correct the luscious sweets of Sherefeddin, (l. v. c. 17—29.)]

[Footnote 35: These interesting conversations appear to have been copied by Arabshah (tom. i. c. 68, p. 625—645) from the cadhi and historian Ebn Schounah, a principal actor. Yet how could he be alive seventy-five years afterwards? (D'Herbelot, p. 792.)]

[Footnote 36: The marches and occupations of Timour between the Syrian and Ottoman wars are represented by Sherefeddin (l. v. c. 29—43) and Arabshah, (tom. ii. c. 15—18.)]

[Footnote 37: This number of 800,000 was extracted by Arabshah, or rather by Ebn Schounah, ex rationario Timuri, on the faith of a Carizmian officer, (tom. i. c. 68, p. 617;) and it is remarkable enough, that a Greek historian (Phranza, l. i. c. 29) adds no more than 20,000 men. Poggius reckons 1,000,000;

another Latin contemporary (Chron. Tarvisianum, apud Muratori, tom. xix. p. 800) 1,100,000; and the enormous sum of 1,600,000 is attested by a German soldier, who was present at the battle of Angora, (Leunclav. ad Chalcondyl. l. iii. p. 82.) Timour, in his Institutions, has not deigned to calculate his troops, his subjects, or his revenues.]

[Footnote 38: A wide latitude of non-effectives was allowed by the Great Mogul for his own pride and the benefit of his officers. Bernier's patron was Penge-Hazari, commander of 5000 horse; of which he maintained no more than 500, (Voyages, tom. i. p. 288, 289.)]

During this diversion of the Mogul arms, Bajazet had two years to collect his forces for a more serious encounter. They consisted of four hundred thousand horse and foot, [39] whose merit and fidelity were of an unequal complexion. We may discriminate the Janizaries, who have been gradually raised to an establishment of forty thousand men; a national cavalry, the Spahis of modern times; twenty thousand cuirassiers of Europe, clad in black and impenetrable armor; the troops of Anatolia, whose princes had taken refuge in the camp of Timour, and a colony of Tartars, whom he had driven from Kipzak, and to whom Bajazet had assigned a settlement in the plains of Adrianople. The fearless confidence of the sultan urged him to meet his antagonist; and, as if he had chosen that spot for revenge, he displayed his banner near the ruins of the unfortunate Suvas. In the mean while, Timour moved from the Araxes through the countries of Armenia and Anatolia: his boldness was secured by the wisest precautions; his speed was guided by order and discipline; and the woods, the mountains, and the rivers, were diligently explored by the flying squadrons, who marked his road and preceded his standard. Firm in his plan of fighting in the heart of the Ottoman kingdom, he avoided their camp; dexterously inclined to the left; occupied Cæsarea; traversed the salt desert and the River Halys; and invested Angora: while the sultan, immovable and ignorant in his post, compared the Tartar swiftness to the crawling of a snail; [40] he returned on the wings of indignation to the relief of Angora: and as both generals were alike impatient for action, the plains round that city were the scene of a memorable battle, which has immortalized the glory of Timour and the shame of Bajazet. For this signal victory the Mogul emperor was indebted to himself, to the genius of the moment, and the discipline of thirty years. He had improved the tactics, without violating the manners, of his nation, [41] whose force still consisted in the missile weapons, and rapid evolutions, of a numerous cavalry. From a single troop to a great army, the mode of attack was the same: a foremost line first advanced to the charge, and was supported in a just order by the squadrons of the great vanguard. The general's eye watched over the field, and at his command the front and rear of the right and left wings successively moved forwards in their several divisions, and in a direct or oblique line: the enemy was pressed by eighteen or twenty attacks; and each attack afforded a chance of victory. If they all proved fruitless or unsuccessful, the occasion was worthy of the emperor himself, who gave the signal of advancing to the standard and main body, which he led in person. [42] But in the battle of Angora, the main body itself was supported, on the flanks and in the rear, by the bravest squadrons of the reserve, commanded by the sons and grandsons of Timour. The conqueror of Hindostan ostentatiously showed a line of elephants, the trophies, rather than the instruments, of victory; the use of the Greek fire was familiar to the Moguls and Ottomans; but had they borrowed from Europe the recent invention of gunpowder and cannon, the artificial thunder, in the hands of either nation, must have turned the fortune of the day. [43] In that day Bajazet displayed the qualities of a soldier and a chief: but his genius sunk under a stronger ascendant; and, from various motives, the greatest part of his troops failed him in the decisive moment. His rigor and avarice [43/1] had provoked a mutiny among the Turks; and even his son Soliman too hastily withdrew from the field. The forces of Anatolia, loyal in their revolt, were drawn away to the banners of their lawful princes. His Tartar allies had been tempted by the letters and emissaries of Timour; [44] who reproached their ignoble servitude under the slaves of their fathers; and offered to their hopes the dominion of their new, or the liberty of their ancient, country. In the right wing of Bajazet the cuirassiers of Europe charged, with faithful hearts and irresistible arms: but these men of iron were soon broken by an artful flight and headlong pursuit; and the Janizaries, alone, without cavalry or missile weapons, were encompassed by the circle of the Mogul hunters. Their valor was at length oppressed by heat, thirst, and the weight of numbers; and the unfortunate sultan, afflicted with the gout in his hands and feet, was transported from the field on the fleetest of his horses. He was pursued and taken by the titular khan of Zagatai; and, after his capture, and the defeat of the Ottoman powers, the kingdom of Anatolia submitted to the conqueror, who planted his standard at Kiotahia, and dispersed on all sides the ministers of rapine and destruction. Mirza Mehemmed Sultan, the eldest and best beloved of his grandsons, was despatched to Boursa, with thirty thousand horse; and such was his youthful ardor, that he arrived with only four thousand at the gates of the capital, after performing in five days a march of two hundred and thirty miles. Yet fear is still more rapid in its course; and Soliman, the son of Bajazet, had already passed over to Europe with the royal treasure. The spoil, however, of the palace and city was immense: the inhabitants had escaped; but the buildings, for the most part of wood, were reduced to ashes From Boursa, the grandson of Timour advanced to Nice, ever yet a fair and flourishing city; and the Mogul squadrons were only stopped by the waves of the Propontis. The same success attended the other mirzas and emirs in their excursions; and Smyrna, defended by the zeal and courage of the Rhodian knights, alone deserved the presence of the emperor himself. After an obstinate defence, the place was taken by storm: all that breathed was put to the sword; and the heads of the Christian heroes were launched from the engines, on board of two carracks, or great ships of Europe, that rode at anchor in the harbor. The Moslems of Asia rejoiced in their deliverance from a dangerous and domestic foe; and a parallel was drawn between the two rivals, by observing that Timour, in fourteen days, had reduced a fortress which had sustained seven years the siege, or at least the blockade, of Bajazet. [45]

[Footnote 39: Timour himself fixes at 400,000 men the Ottoman army, (Institutions, p. 153,) which is reduced to 150,000 by Phranza, (l. i. c. 29,) and swelled by the German soldier to 1,400,000. It is evident that the Moguls were the more numerous.]

[Footnote 40: It may not be useless to mark the distances between Angora and the neighboring cities, by the journeys of the caravans, each of twenty or twenty-five miles; to Smyrna xx., to Kiotahia x., to Boursa x., to Cæsarea, viii., to Sinope x., to Nicomedia ix., to Constantinople xii. or xiii., (see Tournefort, Voyage au Levant, tom. ii. lettre xxi.)]

[Footnote 41: See the Systems of Tactics in the Institutions, which the English editors have illustrated with elaborate plans, (p. 373—407.)]

[Footnote 42: The sultan himself (says Timour) must then put the foot of courage into the stirrup of patience. A Tartar metaphor, which is lost in the English, but preserved in the French, version of the Institutes, (p. 156, 157.)]

[Footnote 43: The Greek fire, on Timour's side, is attested by Sherefeddin, (l. v. c. 47;) but Voltaire's strange suspicion, that some cannon, inscribed with strange characters, must have been sent by that monarch to Delhi, is refuted by the universal silence of contemporaries.]

[Footnote 43/1: See V. Hammer, vol. i. p. 310, for the singular hints which were conveyed to him of the wisdom of unlocking his hoarded treasures—M.]

[Footnote 44: Timour has dissembled this secret and important negotiation with the Tartars, which is indisputably proved by the joint evidence of the Arabian, (tom. i. c. 47, p. 391,) Turkish, (Annal. Leunclav. p. 321,) and Persian historians, (Khondemir, apud d'Herbelot, p. 882.)]

[Footnote 45: For the war of Anatolia or Roum, I add some hints in the Institutions, to the copious narratives of Sherefeddin (l. v. c. 44—65) and Arabshah, (tom. ii. c. 20—35.) On this part only of Timour's history it is lawful to quote the Turks, (Cantemir, p. 53—55, Annal. Leunclav. p. 320—322,) and the Greeks, (Phranza, l. i. c. 59, Ducas, c. 15—17, Chalcondyles, l. iii.)]

The iron cage in which Bajazet was imprisoned by Tamerlane, so long and so often repeated as a moral lesson, is now rejected as a fable by the modern writers, who smile at the vulgar credulity. [46] They appeal with confidence to the Persian history of Sherefeddin Ali, which has been given to our curiosity in a French version, and from which I shall collect and abridge a more specious narrative of this memorable transaction. No sooner was Timour informed that the captive Ottoman was at the door of his tent, than he graciously stepped forwards to receive him, seated him by his side, and mingled with just reproaches a soothing pity for his rank and misfortune. "Alas!" said the emperor, "the decree of fate is now accomplished by your own fault; it is the web which you have woven, the thorns of the tree which yourself have planted. I wished to spare, and even to assist, the champion of the Moslems; you braved our threats; you despised our friendship; you forced us to enter your kingdom with our invincible armies. Behold the event. Had you vanquished, I am not ignorant of the fate which you reserved for myself and my troops. But I disdain to retaliate: your life and honor are secure; and I shall express my gratitude to God by my clemency to man." The royal captive showed some signs of repentance, accepted the humiliation of a robe of honor, and embraced with tears his son Mousa, who, at his request, was sought and found among the captives of the field. The Ottoman princes were lodged in a splendid pavilion; and the respect of the guards could be surpassed only by their vigilance. On the arrival of the harem from Boursa, Timour restored the queen Despina and her daughter to their father and husband; but he piously required, that the Servian princess, who had hitherto been indulged in the profession of Christianity, should embrace without delay the religion of the prophet. In the feast of victory, to which Bajazet was invited, the Mogul emperor placed a crown on his head and a sceptre in his hand, with a solemn assurance of restoring him with an increase of glory to the throne of his ancestors. But the effect of his promise was disappointed by the sultan's untimely death: amidst the care of the most skilful physicians, he expired of an apoplexy at Akshehr, the Antioch of Pisidia, about nine months after his defeat. The victor dropped a tear over his grave: his body, with royal pomp, was conveyed to the mausoleum which he had erected at Boursa; and his son Mousa, after receiving a rich present of gold and jewels, of horses and arms, was invested by a patent in red ink with the kingdom of Anatolia.

[Footnote 46: The scepticism of Voltaire (Essai sur l'Histoire Générale, c. 88) is ready on this, as on every occasion, to reject a popular tale, and to diminish the magnitude of vice and virtue; and on most occasions his incredulity is reasonable.]

Such is the portrait of a generous conqueror, which has been extracted from his own memorials, and dedicated to his son and grandson, nineteen years after his decease; [47] and, at a time when the truth was remembered by thousands, a manifest falsehood would have implied a satire on his real conduct. Weighty indeed is this evidence, adopted by all the Persian histories; [48] yet flattery, more especially in the East, is base and audacious; and the harsh and ignominious treatment of Bajazet is attested by a chain of witnesses, some of whom shall be produced in the order of their time and country. 1. The reader has not forgot the garrison of French, whom the marshal Boucicault left behind him for the defence of Constantinople. They were on the spot to receive the earliest and most faithful intelligence of the overthrow of their great adversary; and it is more than probable, that some of them accompanied the Greek embassy to the camp of Tamerlane. From their account, the hardships of the prison and death of Bajazet are affirmed by the marshal's servant and historian, within the distance of seven years. [49] 2. The name of Poggius the Italian [50] is deservedly famous among the revivers of learning in the fifteenth century. His elegant dialogue on the vicissitudes of fortune [51] was composed in his fiftieth year, twenty-eight years after the Turkish victory of Tamerlane; [52] whom he celebrates as not inferior to the illustrious Barbarians of antiquity. Of his exploits and discipline Poggius was informed by several ocular witnesses; nor does he forget an example so apposite to his theme as the Ottoman monarch, whom the Scythian confined like a wild beast in an iron cage, and exhibited a spectacle to Asia. I might add the authority of two Italian chronicles, perhaps of an earlier date, which would prove at least that the same story, whether false or true, was imported into Europe with the first tidings of the revolution. [53] 3. At the time when Poggius flourished at Rome, Ahmed Ebn Arabshah composed at Damascus the florid and malevolent history of Timour, for which he had collected materials in his journeys over Turkey and Tartary. [54] Without any possible correspondence between the Latin and the Arabian writer, they agree in the fact of the iron cage; and their agreement is a striking proof of their common veracity. Ahmed Arabshah likewise relates another outrage, which Bajazet endured, of a more domestic and tender nature. His indiscreet mention of women and divorces was deeply resented by the jealous Tartar: in the feast of victory the wine was served by female cupbearers, and the sultan beheld his own concubines and wives confounded among the slaves, and exposed without a veil to the eyes of intemperance. To escape a similar indignity, it is said that his successors, except in a single instance, have abstained from legitimate nuptials; and the Ottoman practice and belief, at least in the sixteenth century, is asserted by the observing Busbequius, [55] ambassador from the court of Vienna to the great Soliman. 4. Such is the separation of language, that the testimony of a Greek is not less independent than that of a Latin or an Arab. I suppress the names of Chalcondyles and Ducas, who flourished in the latter period, and who speak in a less positive tone; but more attention is due to George Phranza, [56] protovestiare of the last emperors, and who was born a year before the battle of Angora. Twenty-two years after that event, he was sent ambassador to Amurath the Second; and the historian might converse with some veteran Janizaries, who had been made prisoners with the sultan, and had themselves seen him in his iron cage. 5. The last evidence, in every sense, is that of the Turkish annals, which have been consulted or transcribed by Leunclavius, Pocock, and Cantemir. [57] They unanimously deplore the captivity of the iron cage; and some credit may be allowed to national historians, who cannot stigmatize the Tartar without uncovering the shame of their king and country.

[Footnote 47: See the History of Sherefeddin, (l. v. c. 49, 52, 53, 59, 60.) This work was finished at Shiraz, in the year 1424, and dedicated to Sultan Ibrahim, the son of Sharokh, the son of Timour, who reigned in Farsistan in his father's lifetime.]

[Footnote 48: After the perusal of Khondemir, Ebn Schounah, &c., the learned D'Herbelot (Bibliot. Orientale, p. 882) may affirm, that this fable is not mentioned in the most authentic histories; but his denial of the visible testimony of Arabshah leaves some room to suspect his accuracy.]

[Footnote 49: Et fut lui-même (Bajazet) pris, et mené en prison, en laquelle mourut de dure mort! Mémoires de Boucicault, P. i. c. 37. These Memoirs were composed while the marshal was still governor of Genoa, from whence he was expelled in the year 1409, by a popular insurrection, (Muratori, Annali d'Italia, tom. xii. p. 473, 474.)]

[Footnote 50: The reader will find a satisfactory account of the life and writings of Poggius in the Poggiana, an entertaining work of M. Lenfant, and in the Bibliotheca Latina Mediæ et Infimæ Ætatis of Fabricius, (tom. v. p. 305—308.) Poggius was born in the year 1380, and died in 1459.]

[Footnote 51: The dialogue de Varietate Fortunæ, (of which a complete and elegant edition has been published at Paris in 1723, in 4to.,) was composed a short time before the death of Pope Martin V., (p. 5,) and consequently about the end of the year 1430.]

[Footnote 52: See a splendid and eloquent encomium of Tamerlane, p. 36—39 ipse enim novi (says Poggius) qui fuere in ejus castris.... Regem vivum cepit, caveâque in modum feræ inclusum per omnem Asian circumtulit egregium admirandumque spectaculum fortunæ.]

[Footnote 53: The Chronicon Tarvisianum, (in Muratori, Script. Rerum Italicarum tom. xix. p. 800,) and the Annales Estenses, (tom. xviii. p. 974.) The two authors, Andrea de Redusiis de Quero, and James de Delayto, were both contemporaries, and both chancellors, the one of Trevigi, the other of Ferrara. The evidence of the former is the most positive.]

[Footnote 54: See Arabshah, tom. ii. c. 28, 34. He travelled in regiones Rumæas, A. H. 839, (A.D. 1435, July 27,) tom. i. c. 2, p. 13.]

[Footnote 55: Busbequius in Legatione Turcicâ, epist. i. p. 52. Yet his respectable authority is somewhat shaken by the subsequent marriages of Amurath II. with a Servian, and of Mahomet II. with an Asiatic, princess, (Cantemir, p. 83, 93.)]

[Footnote 56: See the testimony of George Phranza, (l. i. c. 29,) and his life in Hanckius (de Script. Byzant. P. i. c. 40.) Chalcondyles and Ducas speak in general terms of Bajazet's chains.]

[Footnote 57: Annales Leunclav. p. 321. Pocock, Prolegomen. ad Abulpharag Dynast. Cantemir, p. 55. Note: Von Hammer, p. 318, cites several authorities unknown to Gibbon—M.]

From these opposite premises, a fair and moderate conclusion may be deduced. I am satisfied that Sherefeddin Ali has faithfully described the first ostentatious interview, in which the conqueror, whose spirits were harmonized by success, affected the character of generosity. But his mind was insensibly alienated by the unseasonable arrogance of Bajazet; the complaints of his enemies, the Anatolian princes, were just and vehement; and Timour betrayed a design of leading his royal captive in triumph to Samarcand. An attempt to facilitate his escape, by digging a mine under the tent, provoked the Mogul emperor to impose a harsher restraint; and in his perpetual marches, an iron cage on a wagon might be invented, not as a wanton insult, but as a rigorous precaution. Timour had read in some fabulous history a similar treatment of one of his predecessors, a king of Persia; and Bajazet was condemned to represent the person, and expiate the guilt, of the Roman Cæsar [58] [58/1] But the strength of his mind and body fainted under the trial, and his premature death might, without injustice, be ascribed to the severity of Timour. He warred not with the dead: a tear and a sepulchre were all that he could bestow on a captive who was delivered from his power; and if Mousa, the son of Bajazet, was permitted to reign over the ruins of Boursa, the greatest part of the province of Anatolia had been restored by the conqueror to their lawful sovereigns.

[Footnote 58: Sapor, king of Persia, had been made prisoner, and enclosed in the figure of a cow's hide by Maximian or Galerius Cæsar. Such is the fable related by Eutychius, (Annal. tom. i. p. 421, vers.

Pocock). *The recollection of the true history (Decline and Fall, &c., vol. ii. p 140—152) will teach us to appreciate the knowledge of the Orientals of the ages which precede the Hegira.]*

*[Footnote 58/1: Von Hammer's explanation of this contested point is both simple and satisfactory. It originates in a mistake in the meaning of the Turkish word kafe, which means a covered litter or palanquin drawn by two horses, and is generally used to convey the harem of an Eastern monarch. In such a litter, with the lattice-work made of iron, Bajazet either chose or was constrained to travel. This was either mistaken for, or transformed by, ignorant relaters into a cage. The European Schiltberger, the two oldest of the Turkish historians, and the most valuable of the later compilers, Seadeddin, describe this litter. Seadeddin discusses the question with some degree of historical criticism, and ascribes the choice of such a vehicle to the indignant state of Bajazet's mind, which would not brook the sight of his Tartar conquerors. Von Hammer, p. 320—M.]*

From the Irtish and Volga to the Persian Gulf, and from the Ganges to Damascus and the Archipelago, Asia was in the hand of Timour: his armies were invincible, his ambition was boundless, and his zeal might aspire to conquer and convert the Christian kingdoms of the West, which already trembled at his name. He touched the utmost verge of the land; but an insuperable, though narrow, sea rolled between the two continents of Europe and Asia; [59] and the lord of so many tomans, or myriads, of horse, was not master of a single galley. The two passages of the Bosphorus and Hellespont, of Constantinople and Gallipoli, were possessed, the one by the Christians, the other by the Turks. On this great occasion, they forgot the difference of religion, to act with union and firmness in the common cause: the double straits were guarded with ships and fortifications; and they separately withheld the transports which Timour demanded of either nation, under the pretence of attacking their enemy. At the same time, they soothed his pride with tributary gifts and suppliant embassies, and prudently tempted him to retreat with the honors of victory. Soliman, the son of Bajazet, implored his clemency for his father and himself; accepted, by a red patent, the investiture of the kingdom of Romania, which he already held by the sword; and reiterated his ardent wish, of casting himself in person at the feet of the king of the world. The Greek emperor [60] (either John or Manuel) submitted to pay the same tribute which he had stipulated with the Turkish sultan, and ratified the treaty by an oath of allegiance, from which he could absolve his conscience so soon as the Mogul arms had retired from Anatolia. But the fears and fancy of nations ascribed to the ambitious Tamerlane a new design of vast and romantic compass; a design of subduing Egypt and Africa, marching from the Nile to the Atlantic Ocean, entering Europe by the Straits of Gibraltar, and, after imposing his yoke on the kingdoms of Christendom, of returning home by the deserts of Russia and Tartary. This remote, and perhaps imaginary, danger was averted by the submission of the sultan of Egypt: the honors of the prayer and the coin attested at Cairo the supremacy of Timour; and a rare gift of a giraffe, or camelopard, and nine ostriches, represented at Samarcand the tribute of the African world. Our imagination is not less astonished by the portrait of a Mogul, who, in his camp before Smyrna, meditates, and almost accomplishes, the invasion of the Chinese empire. [61] Timour was urged to this enterprise by national honor and religious zeal. The torrents which he had shed of Mussulman blood could be expiated only by an equal destruction of the infidels; and as he now stood at the gates of paradise, he might best secure his glorious entrance by demolishing the idols of China, founding mosques in every city, and establishing the profession of faith in one God, and his prophet Mahomet. The recent expulsion of the house of Zingis was an insult on the Mogul name; and the disorders of the empire afforded the fairest opportunity for revenge. The illustrious Hongvou, founder of the dynasty of Ming, died four years before the battle of Angora; and his grandson, a weak and unfortunate youth, was burnt in his palace, after a million of Chinese had perished in the civil war. [62] Before he evacuated Anatolia, Timour despatched beyond the Sihoon a numerous army, or rather colony, of his old and new subjects, to open the road, to subdue the Pagan Calmucks and Mungals, and to found cities and magazines in the desert; and, by the diligence of his lieutenant, he soon received a perfect map and description of the unknown regions, from the source of the Irtish to the wall of China. During these preparations, the emperor achieved the final conquest of Georgia; passed the winter on the banks of the Araxes; appeased the troubles of Persia; and slowly returned to his capital, after a campaign of four years and nine months.

[Footnote 59: Arabshah (tom. ii. c. 25) describes, like a curious traveller, the Straits of Gallipoli and Constantinople. To acquire a just idea of these events, I have compared the narratives and prejudices of the Moguls, Turks, Greeks, and Arabians. The Spanish ambassador mentions this hostile union of the Christians and Ottomans, (Vie de Timour, p. 96.)]

[Footnote 60: Since the name of Cæsar had been transferred to the sultans of Roum, the Greek princes of Constantinople (Sherefeddin, l. v. c. 54) were confounded with the Christian lords of Gallipoli, Thessalonica, &c. under the title of Tekkur, which is derived by corruption from the genitive tou kuriou, (Cantemir, p. 51.)]

[Footnote 61: See Sherefeddin, l. v. c. 4, who marks, in a just itinerary, the road to China, which Arabshah (tom. ii. c. 33) paints in vague and rhetorical colors.]

[Footnote 62: Synopsis Hist. Sinicæ, p. 74—76, (in the ivth part of the Relations de Thevenot,) Duhalde, Hist. de la Chine, (tom. i. p. 507, 508, folio edition;) and for the Chronology of the Chinese emperors, De Guignes, Hist. des Huns, (tom. i. p. 71, 72.)]


PART III

On the throne of Samarcand, [63] he displayed, in a short repose, his magnificence and power; listened to the complaints of the people; distributed a just measure of rewards and punishments; employed his riches in the architecture of palaces and temples; and gave audience to the ambassadors of Egypt, Arabia, India, Tartary, Russia, and Spain, the last of whom presented a suit of tapestry which eclipsed the pencil of the Oriental artists. The marriage of six of the emperor's grandsons was esteemed an act of religion as well as of paternal tenderness; and the pomp of the ancient caliphs was revived in their nuptials. They were celebrated in the gardens of Canighul, decorated with innumerable tents and pavilions, which displayed the luxury of a great city and the spoils of a victorious camp. Whole forests were cut down to supply fuel for the kitchens; the plain was spread with pyramids of meat, and vases of every liquor, to which thousands of guests were courteously invited: the orders of the state, and the nations of the earth, were marshalled at the royal banquet; nor were the ambassadors of Europe (says the haughty Persian) excluded from the feast; since even the casses, the smallest of fish, find their place in the ocean. [64] The public joy was testified by illuminations and masquerades; the trades of Samarcand passed in review; and every trade was emulous to execute some quaint device, some marvellous pageant, with the materials of their peculiar art. After the marriage contracts had been ratified by the cadhis, the bride-grooms and their brides retired to the nuptial chambers: nine times, according to the Asiatic fashion, they were dressed and undressed; and at each change of apparel, pearls and rubies were showered on their heads, and contemptuously abandoned to their attendants. A general indulgence was proclaimed: every law was relaxed, every pleasure was allowed; the people was free, the sovereign was idle; and the historian of Timour may remark, that, after devoting fifty years to the attainment of empire, the only happy period of his life were the two months in which he ceased to exercise his power. But he was soon awakened to the cares of government and war. The standard was unfurled for the invasion of China: the emirs made their report of two hundred thousand, the select and veteran soldiers of Iran and Touran: their baggage and provisions were transported by five hundred great wagons, and an immense train of horses and camels; and the troops might prepare for a long absence, since more than six months were employed in the tranquil journey of a caravan from Samarcand to Pekin. Neither age, nor the severity of the winter, could retard the impatience of Timour; he mounted on horseback, passed the Sihoon on the ice, marched seventy-six parasangs, three hundred miles, from his capital, and pitched his last camp in the neighborhood of Otrar, where he was expected by the angel of death. Fatigue, and the indiscreet use of iced water, accelerated the progress of his fever; and the conqueror of Asia expired in the seventieth year of his age, thirty-five years after he had ascended the throne of Zagatai. His designs were lost; his armies were disbanded; China was saved; and fourteen years after his decease, the most powerful of his children sent an embassy of friendship and commerce to the court of Pekin. [65]

[Footnote 63: For the return, triumph, and death of Timour, see Sherefeddin (l. vi. c. 1—30) and Arabshah, (tom. ii. c. 36—47.)]

[Footnote 64: Sherefeddin (l. vi. c. 24) mentions the ambassadors of one of the most potent sovereigns of Europe. We know that it was Henry III. king of Castile; and the curious relation of his two embassies is still extant, (Mariana, Hist. Hispan. l. xix. c. 11, tom. ii. p. 329, 330. Avertissement à l'Hist. de Timur Bec, p. 28—33.) There appears likewise to have been some correspondence between the Mogul emperor and the court of Charles VII. king of France, (Histoire de France, par Velly et Villaret, tom. xii. p. 336.)]

[Footnote 65: See the translation of the Persian account of their embassy, a curious and original piece, (in the ivth part of the Relations de Thevenot.) They presented the emperor of China with an old horse which Timour had formerly rode. It was in the year 1419 that they departed from the court of Herat, to which place they returned in 1422 from Pekin.]

The fame of Timour has pervaded the East and West: his posterity is still invested with the Imperial title; and the admiration of his subjects, who revered him almost as a deity, may be justified in some degree by the praise or confession of his bitterest enemies. [66] Although he was lame of a hand and foot, his form and stature were not unworthy of his rank; and his vigorous health, so essential to himself and to the world, was corroborated by temperance and exercise. In his familiar discourse he was grave and modest, and if he was ignorant of the Arabic language, he spoke with fluency and elegance the Persian and Turkish idioms. It was his delight to converse with the learned on topics of history and science; and the amusement of his leisure hours was the game of chess, which he improved or corrupted with new refinements. [67] In his religion he was a zealous, though not perhaps an orthodox, Mussulman; [68] but his sound understanding may tempt us to believe, that a superstitious reverence for omens and prophecies, for saints and astrologers, was only affected as an instrument of policy. In the government of a vast empire, he stood alone and absolute, without a rebel to oppose his power, a favorite to seduce his affections, or a minister to mislead his judgment. It was his firmest maxim, that whatever might be the consequence, the word of the prince should never be disputed or recalled; but his foes have maliciously observed, that the commands of anger and destruction were more strictly executed than those of beneficence and favor. His sons and grandsons, of whom Timour left six-and-thirty at his decease, were his first and most submissive subjects; and whenever they deviated from their duty, they were corrected, according to the laws of Zingis, with the bastinade, and afterwards restored to honor and command. Perhaps his heart was not devoid of the social virtues; perhaps he was not incapable of loving his friends and pardoning his enemies; but the rules of morality are founded on the public interest; and it may be sufficient to applaud the wisdom of a monarch, for the liberality by which he is not impoverished, and for the justice by which he is strengthened and enriched. To maintain the harmony of authority and obedience, to chastise the proud, to protect the weak, to reward the deserving, to banish vice and idleness from his dominions, to secure the traveller and merchant, to restrain the depredations of the soldier, to cherish the labors of the husbandman, to encourage industry and learning, and, by an equal and moderate assessment, to increase the revenue, without increasing the taxes, are indeed the duties of a prince; but, in the discharge of these duties, he finds an ample and immediate recompense. Timour might boast, that, at his accession to the throne, Asia was the prey of anarchy and rapine, whilst under his prosperous monarchy a child, fearless and unhurt, might carry a purse of gold from the East to the West. Such was his confidence of merit, that from this reformation he derived an excuse for his victories, and a title to universal dominion. The four following observations will serve to appreciate his claim to the public gratitude; and perhaps we shall conclude, that the Mogul emperor was rather the scourge than the benefactor of mankind. 1. If some partial disorders, some local oppressions, were healed by the sword of Timour, the remedy was far more pernicious than the disease. By their rapine, cruelty, and discord, the petty tyrants of Persia might afflict their subjects; but whole nations were crushed under the footsteps of the reformer. The ground which had been occupied by flourishing cities was often marked by his abominable trophies, by columns, or pyramids, of human heads. Astracan, Carizme, Delhi, Ispahan, Bagdad, Aleppo, Damascus, Boursa, Smyrna, and a thousand others, were sacked, or burnt, or utterly destroyed, in his presence, and by his troops: and perhaps his conscience would have been startled, if a priest or philosopher had dared to number the millions of victims whom he had sacrificed to the establishment of peace and order. [69] 2. His most destructive wars were rather inroads than conquests. He invaded Turkestan, Kipzak, Russia, Hindostan, Syria, Anatolia, Armenia, and Georgia, without a hope or a desire of preserving those distant provinces. From thence he departed laden with spoil; but he left behind him neither troops to awe the contumacious, nor magistrates to protect the obedient, natives. When he had broken the fabric of their ancient government, he abandoned them to the evils which his invasion had aggravated or caused; nor were these evils compensated by any present or possible benefits. 3. The kingdoms of Transoxiana and Persia were the proper field which he labored to cultivate and adorn, as the perpetual inheritance of his family. But his peaceful labors were often interrupted, and sometimes blasted, by the absence of the conqueror. While he triumphed on the Volga or the Ganges, his servants, and even his sons, forgot their master and their duty. The public and private injuries were poorly redressed by the tardy rigor of inquiry and punishment; and we must be content to praise the Institutions of Timour, as the specious idea of a perfect monarchy. 4. Whatsoever might be the blessings of his administration, they evaporated with his life. To reign, rather than to govern, was the ambition of his children and grandchildren; [70] the enemies of each other and of the people. A fragment of the empire was upheld with some glory by Sharokh, his youngest son; but after his decease, the scene was again involved in darkness and blood; and before the end of a century, Transoxiana and Persia were trampled by the Uzbeks from the north, and the Turkmans of the black and white sheep. The race of Timour would have been extinct, if a hero, his descendant in the fifth degree, had not fled before the Uzbek arms to the conquest of Hindostan. His successors (the great Moguls [71]) extended their sway from the mountains of Cashmir to Cape Comorin, and from Candahar to the Gulf of Bengal. Since the reign of Aurungzebe, their empire had been dissolved; their treasures of Delhi have been rifled by a Persian robber; and the richest of their kingdoms is now possessed by a company of Christian merchants, of a remote island in the Northern Ocean.

[Footnote 66: From Arabshah, tom. ii. c. 96. The bright or softer colors are borrowed from Sherefeddin, D'Herbelot, and the Institutions.]

[Footnote 67: His new system was multiplied from 32 pieces and 64 squares to 56 pieces and 110 or 130 squares; but, except in his court, the old game has been thought sufficiently elaborate. The Mogul emperor was rather pleased than hurt with the victory of a subject: a chess player will feel the value of this encomium!]

[Footnote 68: See Sherefeddin, (l. v. c. 15, 25. Arabshah tom. ii. c. 96, p. 801, 803) approves the impiety of Timour and the Moguls, who almost preferred to the Koran the Yacsa, or Law of Zingis, (cui Deus maledicat;) nor will he believe that Sharokh had abolished the use and authority of that Pagan code.]

[Footnote 69: Besides the bloody passages of this narrative, I must refer to an anticipation in the third volume of the Decline and Fall, which in a single note (p. 234, note 25) accumulates nearly 300,000 heads of the monuments of his cruelty. Except in Rowe's play on the fifth of November, I did not expect to hear of Timour's amiable moderation (White's preface, p. 7.) Yet I can excuse a generous enthusiasm in the reader, and still more in the editor, of the Institutions.]

[Footnote 70: Consult the last chapters of Sherefeddin and Arabshah, and M. De Guignes, (Hist. des Huns, tom. iv. l. xx.) Fraser's History of Nadir Shah, (p. 1—62.) The story of Timour's descendants is imperfectly told; and the second and third parts of Sherefeddin are unknown.]

[Footnote 71: Shah Allum, the present Mogul, is in the fourteenth degree from Timour, by Miran Shah, his third son. See the second volume of Dow's History of Hindostan.]

Far different was the fate of the Ottoman monarchy. The massy trunk was bent to the ground, but no sooner did the hurricane pass away, than it again rose with fresh vigor and more lively vegetation. When Timour, in every sense, had evacuated Anatolia, he left the cities without a palace, a treasure, or a king. The open country was overspread with hordes of shepherds and robbers of Tartar or Turkman origin; the recent conquests of Bajazet were restored to the emirs, one of whom, in base revenge, demolished his sepulchre; and his five sons were eager, by civil discord, to consume the remnant of their patrimony. I shall enumerate their names in the order of their age and actions. [72] 1. It is doubtful, whether I relate the story of the true Mustapha, or of an impostor who personated that lost prince. He fought by his father's side in the battle of Angora: but when the captive sultan was permitted to inquire for his children, Mousa alone could be found; and the Turkish historians, the slaves of the triumphant faction, are persuaded that his brother was confounded among the slain. If Mustapha escaped from that disastrous field, he was concealed twelve years from his friends and enemies; till he emerged in Thessaly, and was hailed by a numerous party, as the son and successor of Bajazet. His first defeat would have been his last, had not the true, or false, Mustapha been saved by the Greeks, and restored, after the decease of his brother Mahomet, to liberty and empire. A degenerate mind seemed to argue his spurious birth; and if, on the throne of Adrianople, he was adored as the Ottoman sultan, his flight, his fetters, and an ignominious gibbet, delivered the impostor to popular contempt. A similar character and claim was asserted by several rival pretenders: thirty persons are said to have suffered under the name of Mustapha; and these frequent executions may perhaps insinuate, that the Turkish court was not perfectly secure of the death of the lawful prince. 2. After his father's captivity, Isa [73] reigned for some time in the neighborhood of Angora, Sinope, and the Black Sea; and his ambassadors were dismissed from the presence of Timour with fair promises and honorable gifts. But their master was soon deprived of his province and life, by a jealous brother, the sovereign of Amasia; and the final event suggested a pious allusion, that the law of Moses and Jesus, of Isa and Mousa, had been abrogated by the greater Mahomet. 3. Soliman is not numbered in the list of the Turkish emperors: yet he checked the victorious progress of the Moguls; and after their departure, united for a while the thrones of

Adrianople and Boursa. In war he was brave, active, and fortunate; his courage was softened by clemency; but it was likewise inflamed by presumption, and corrupted by intemperance and idleness. He relaxed the nerves of discipline, in a government where either the subject or the sovereign must continually tremble: his vices alienated the chiefs of the army and the law; and his daily drunkenness, so contemptible in a prince and a man, was doubly odious in a disciple of the prophet. In the slumber of intoxication he was surprised by his brother Mousa; and as he fled from Adrianople towards the Byzantine capital, Soliman was overtaken and slain in a bath, [731] after a reign of seven years and ten months. 4. The investiture of Mousa degraded him as the slave of the Moguls: his tributary kingdom of Anatolia was confined within a narrow limit, nor could his broken militia and empty treasury contend with the hardy and veteran bands of the sovereign of Romania. Mousa fled in disguise from the palace of Boursa; traversed the Propontis in an open boat; wandered over the Walachian and Servian hills; and after some vain attempts, ascended the throne of Adrianople, so recently stained with the blood of Soliman. In a reign of three years and a half, his troops were victorious against the Christians of Hungary and the Morea; but Mousa was ruined by his timorous disposition and unseasonable clemency. After resigning the sovereignty of Anatolia, he fell a victim to the perfidy of his ministers, and the superior ascendant of his brother Mahomet. 5.The final victory of Mahomet was the just recompense of his prudence and moderation. Before his father's captivity, the royal youth had been intrusted with the government of Amasia, thirty days' journey from Constantinople, and the Turkish frontier against the Christians of Trebizond and Georgia. The castle, in Asiatic warfare, was esteemed impregnable; and the city of Amasia, [74] which is equally divided by the River Iris, rises on either side in the form of an amphitheatre, and represents on a smaller scale the image of Bagdad. In his rapid career, Timour appears to have overlooked this obscure and contumacious angle of Anatolia; and Mahomet, without provoking the conqueror, maintained his silent independence, and chased from the province the last stragglers of the Tartar host. [741] He relieved himself from the dangerous neighborhood of Isa; but in the contests of their more powerful brethren his firm neutrality was respected; till, after the triumph of Mousa, he stood forth the heir and avenger of the unfortunate Soliman. Mahomet obtained Anatolia by treaty, and Romania by arms; and the soldier who presented him with the head of Mousa was rewarded as the benefactor of his king and country. The eight years of his sole and peaceful reign were usefully employed in banishing the vices of civil discord, and restoring on a firmer basis the fabric of the Ottoman monarchy. His last care was the choice of two viziers, Bajazet and Ibrahim, [75] who might guide the youth of his son Amurath; and such was their union and prudence, that they concealed above forty days the emperor's death, till the arrival of his successor in the palace of Boursa. A new war was kindled in Europe by the prince, or impostor, Mustapha; the first vizier lost his army and his head; but the more fortunate Ibrahim, whose name and family are still revered, extinguished the last pretender to the throne of Bajazet, and closed the scene of domestic hostility.

[Footnote 72: *The civil wars, from the death of Bajazet to that of Mustapha, are related, according to the Turks, by Demetrius Cantemir, (p. 58—82.) Of the Greeks, Chalcondyles, (l. iv. and v.,) Phranza, (l. i. c. 30—32,) and Ducas, (c. 18—27,) the last is the most copious and best informed.*]

[Footnote 73: *Arabshah, (tom. ii. c. 26,) whose testimony on this occasion is weighty and valuable. The existence of Isa (unknown to the Turks) is likewise confirmed by Sherefeddin, (l. v. c. 57.)*]

[Footnote 73/1: *He escaped from the bath, and fled towards Constantinople. Five mothers from a village, Dugundschi, whose inhabitants had suffered severely from the exactions of his officers, recognized and followed him. Soliman shot two of them, the others discharged their arrows in their turn the sultan fell and his head was cut off. V. Hammer, vol. i. p. 349—M.*]

[Footnote 74: Arabshah, loc. citat. Abulfeda, Geograph. tab. xvii. p. 302. Busbequius, epist. i. p. 96, 97, in Itinere C. P. et Amasiano.]

[Footnote 74/1: See his nine battles. V. Hammer, p. 339—M.]

[Footnote 75: The virtues of Ibrahim are praised by a contemporary Greek, (Ducas, c. 25.) His descendants are the sole nobles in Turkey: they content themselves with the administration of his pious foundations, are excused from public offices, and receive two annual visits from the sultan, (Cantemir, p. 76.)]

In these conflicts, the wisest Turks, and indeed the body of the nation, were strongly attached to the unity of the empire; and Romania and Anatolia, so often torn asunder by private ambition, were animated by a strong and invincible tendency of cohesion. Their efforts might have instructed the Christian powers; and had they occupied, with a confederate fleet, the Straits of Gallipoli, the Ottomans, at least in Europe, must have been speedily annihilated. But the schism of the West, and the factions and wars of France and England, diverted the Latins from this generous enterprise: they enjoyed the present respite, without a thought of futurity; and were often tempted by a momentary interest to serve the common enemy of their religion. A colony of Genoese, [76] which had been planted at Phocæa [77] on the Ionian coast, was enriched by the lucrative monopoly of alum; [78] and their tranquillity, under the Turkish empire, was secured by the annual payment of tribute. In the last civil war of the Ottomans, the Genoese governor, Adorno, a bold and ambitious youth, embraced the party of Amurath; and undertook, with seven stout galleys, to transport him from Asia to Europe. The sultan and five hundred guards embarked on board the admiral's ship; which was manned by eight hundred of the bravest Franks. His life and liberty were in their hands; nor can we, without reluctance, applaud the fidelity of Adorno, who, in the midst of the passage, knelt before him, and gratefully accepted a discharge of his arrears of tribute. They landed in sight of Mustapha and Gallipoli; two thousand Italians, armed with lances and battle-axes, attended Amurath to the conquest of Adrianople; and this venal service was soon repaid by the ruin of the commerce and colony of Phocæa.

[Footnote 76: See Pachymer, (l. v. c. 29,) Nicephorus Gregoras, (l. ii. c. 1,) Sherefeddin, (l. v. c. 57,) and Ducas, (c. 25.) The last of these, a curious and careful observer, is entitled, from his birth and station, to particular credit in all that concerns Ionia and the islands. Among the nations that resorted to New Phocæa, he mentions the English; ('Igglhnoi;) an early evidence of Mediterranean trade.]

[Footnote 77: For the spirit of navigation, and freedom of ancient Phocæa, or rather the Phocæans, consult the first book of Herodotus, and the Geographical Index of his last and learned French translator, M. Larcher (tom. vii. p. 299.)]

[Footnote 78: Phocæa is not enumerated by Pliny (Hist. Nat. xxxv. 52) among the places productive of alum: he reckons Egypt as the first, and for the second the Isle of Melos, whose alum mines are described by Tournefort, (tom. i. lettre iv.,) a traveller and a naturalist. After the loss of Phocæa, the Genoese, in 1459, found that useful mineral in the Isle of Ischia, (Ismael. Bouillaud, ad Ducam, c. 25.)]

If Timour had generously marched at the request, and to the relief, of the Greek emperor, he might be entitled to the praise and gratitude of the Christians. [79] But a Mussulman, who carried into Georgia the sword of persecution, and respected the holy warfare of Bajazet, was not disposed to pity or succor the idolaters of Europe. The Tartar followed the impulse of ambition; and the deliverance of Constantinople was the accidental consequence. When Manuel abdicated the government, it was his prayer, rather than his hope, that the ruin of the church and state might be delayed beyond his unhappy days; and after his return from a western pilgrimage, he expected every hour the news of the sad catastrophe. On a sudden, he was astonished and rejoiced by the intelligence of the retreat, the overthrow, and the captivity of the Ottoman. Manuel [80] immediately sailed from Modon in the Morea; ascended the throne of Constantinople, and dismissed his blind competitor to an easy exile in the Isle of Lesbos. The ambassadors of the son of Bajazet were soon introduced to his presence; but their pride was fallen, their tone was modest: they were awed by the just apprehension, lest the Greeks should open to the Moguls the gates of Europe. Soliman saluted the emperor by the name of father; solicited at his hands the government or gift of Romania; and promised to deserve his favor by inviolable friendship, and the restitution of Thessalonica, with the most important places along the Strymon, the Propontis, and the Black Sea. The alliance of Soliman exposed the emperor to the enmity and revenge of Mousa: the Turks appeared in arms before the gates of Constantinople; but they were repulsed by sea and land; and unless the city was guarded by some foreign mercenaries, the Greeks must have wondered at their own triumph. But, instead of prolonging the division of the Ottoman powers, the policy or passion of Manuel was tempted to assist the most formidable of the sons of Bajazet. He concluded a treaty with Mahomet, whose progress was checked by the insuperable barrier of Gallipoli: the sultan and his troops were transported over the Bosphorus; he was hospitably entertained in the capital; and his successful sally was the first step to the conquest of Romania. The ruin was suspended by the prudence and moderation of the conqueror: he faithfully discharged his own obligations and those of Soliman, respected the laws of gratitude and peace; and left the emperor guardian of his two younger sons, in the vain hope of saving them from the jealous cruelty of their brother Amurath. But the execution of his last testament would have offended the national honor and religion; and the divan unanimously pronounced, that the royal youths should never be abandoned to the custody and education of a Christian dog. On this refusal, the Byzantine councils were divided; but the age and caution of Manuel yielded to the presumption of his son John; and they unsheathed a dangerous weapon of revenge, by dismissing the true or false Mustapha, who had long been detained as a captive and hostage, and for whose maintenance they received an annual pension of three hundred thousand aspers. [81] At the door of his prison, Mustapha subscribed to every proposal; and the keys of Gallipoli, or rather of Europe, were stipulated as the price of his deliverance. But no sooner was he seated on the throne of Romania, than he dismissed the Greek ambassadors with a smile of contempt, declaring, in a pious tone, that, at the day of judgment, he would rather answer for the violation of an oath, than for the surrender of a Mussulman city into the hands of the infidels. The emperor was at once the enemy of the two rivals; from whom he had sustained, and to whom he had offered, an injury; and the victory of Amurath was followed, in the ensuing spring, by the siege of Constantinople. [82]

*[Footnote 79: The writer who has the most abused this fabulous generosity, is our ingenious Sir William Temple, (his Works, vol. iii. p. 349, 350, octavo edition,) that lover of exotic virtue. After the conquest of Russia, &c., and the passage of the Danube, his Tartar hero relieves, visits, admires, and refuses the city of Constantine. His flattering pencil deviates in every line from the truth of history; yet his pleasing fictions are more excusable than the gross errors of Cantemir.]*

*[Footnote 80: For the reigns of Manuel and John, of Mahomet I. and Amurath II., see the Othman history of Cantemir, (p. 70—95,) and the three Greeks, Chalcondyles, Phranza, and Ducas, who is still superior to his rivals.]*

*[Footnote 81: The Turkish asper (from the Greek asproV) is, or was, a piece of white or silver money, at present much debased, but which was formerly equivalent to the 54th part, at least, of a Venetian ducat or sequin; and the 300,000 aspers, a princely allowance or royal tribute, may be computed at 2500l.*

sterling, (Leunclav. Pandect. Turc. p. 406—408.) Note: According to Von Hammer, this calculation is much too low. The asper was a century before the time of which writes, the tenth part of a ducat; for the same tribute which the Byzantine writers state at 300,000 aspers the Ottomans state at 30,000 ducats, about 15000l Note, vol. p. 636—M.]

[Footnote 82: For the siege of Constantinople in 1422, see the particular and contemporary narrative of John Cananus, published by Leo Allatius, at the end of his edition of Acropolita, (p. 188—199.)]

The religious merit of subduing the city of the Cæsars attracted from Asia a crowd of volunteers, who aspired to the crown of martyrdom: their military ardor was inflamed by the promise of rich spoils and beautiful females; and the sultan's ambition was consecrated by the presence and prediction of Seid Bechar, a descendant of the prophet, [83] who arrived in the camp, on a mule, with a venerable train of five hundred disciples. But he might blush, if a fanatic could blush, at the failure of his assurances. The strength of the walls resisted an army of two hundred thousand Turks; their assaults were repelled by the sallies of the Greeks and their foreign mercenaries; the old resources of defence were opposed to the new engines of attack; and the enthusiasm of the dervis, who was snatched to heaven in visionary converse with Mahomet, was answered by the credulity of the Christians, who beheld the Virgin Mary, in a violet garment, walking on the rampart and animating their courage. [84] After a siege of two months, Amurath was recalled to Boursa by a domestic revolt, which had been kindled by Greek treachery, and was soon extinguished by the death of a guiltless brother. While he led his Janizaries to new conquests in Europe and Asia, the Byzantine empire was indulged in a servile and precarious respite of thirty years. Manuel sank into the grave; and John Palæologus was permitted to reign, for an annual tribute of three hundred thousand aspers, and the dereliction of almost all that he held beyond the suburbs of Constantinople.

[Footnote 83: Cantemir, p. 80. Cananus, who describes Seid Bechar, without naming him, supposes that the friend of Mahomet assumed in his amours the privilege of a prophet, and that the fairest of the Greek nuns were promised to the saint and his disciples.]

[Footnote 84: For this miraculous apparition, Cananus appeals to the Mussulman saint; but who will bear testimony for Seid Bechar?]

In the establishment and restoration of the Turkish empire, the first merit must doubtless be assigned to the personal qualities of the sultans; since, in human life, the most important scenes will depend on the character of a single actor. By some shades of wisdom and virtue, they may be discriminated from each other; but, except in a single instance, a period of nine reigns, and two hundred and sixty-five years, is occupied, from the elevation of Othman to the death of Soliman, by a rare series of warlike and active princes, who impressed their subjects with obedience and their enemies with terror. Instead of the slothful luxury of the seraglio, the heirs of royalty were educated in the council and the field: from early youth they were intrusted by their fathers with the command of provinces and armies; and this manly institution, which was often productive of civil war, must have essentially contributed to the discipline and vigor of the monarchy. The Ottomans cannot style themselves, like the Arabian caliphs, the descendants or successors of the apostle of God; and the kindred which they claim with the Tartar khans of the house of Zingis appears to be founded in flattery rather than in truth. [85] Their origin is obscure; but their sacred and indefeasible right, which no time can erase, and no violence can infringe, was soon and unalterably implanted in the minds of their subjects. A weak or vicious sultan may be deposed and strangled; but his inheritance devolves to an infant or an idiot: nor has the most daring rebel presumed to ascend the throne of his lawful sovereign. [86]

[Footnote 85: See Ricaut, (l. i. c. 13.) The Turkish sultans assume the title of khan. Yet Abulghazi is ignorant of his Ottoman cousins.]

[Footnote 86: The third grand vizier of the name of Kiuperli, who was slain at the battle of Salankanen in 1691, (Cantemir, p. 382,) presumed to say that all the successors of Soliman had been fools or tyrants, and that it was time to abolish the race, (Marsigli Stato Militaire, &c., p. 28.) This political heretic was a good Whig, and justified against the French ambassador the revolution of England, (Mignot, Hist. des Ottomans, tom. iii. p. 434.) His presumption condemns the singular exception of continuing offices in the same family.]

While the transient dynasties of Asia have been continually subverted by a crafty vizier in the palace, or a victorious general in the camp, the Ottoman succession has been confirmed by the practice of five centuries, and is now incorporated with the vital principle of the Turkish nation.

To the spirit and constitution of that nation, a strong and singular influence may, however, be ascribed. The primitive subjects of Othman were the four hundred families of wandering Turkmans, who had followed his ancestors from the Oxus to the Sangar; and the plains of Anatolia are still covered with the white and black tents of their rustic brethren. But this original drop was dissolved in the mass of voluntary and vanquished subjects, who, under the name of Turks, are united by the common ties of religion, language, and manners. In the cities, from Erzeroum to Belgrade, that national appellation is common to all the Moslems, the first and most honorable inhabitants; but they have abandoned, at least in Romania, the villages, and the cultivation of the land, to the Christian peasants. In the vigorous age of the Ottoman government, the Turks were themselves excluded from all civil and military honors; and a servile class, an artificial people, was raised by the discipline of education to obey, to conquer, and to command. [87] From the time of Orchan and the first Amurath, the sultans were persuaded that a government of the sword must be renewed in each generation with new soldiers; and that such soldiers must be sought, not in effeminate Asia, but among the hardy and warlike natives of Europe. The provinces of Thrace, Macedonia, Albania, Bulgaria, and Servia, became the perpetual seminary of the Turkish army; and when the royal fifth of the captives was diminished by conquest, an inhuman tax of the fifth child, or of every fifth year, was rigorously levied on the Christian families. At the age of twelve or fourteen years, the most robust youths were torn from their parents; their names were enrolled in a book; and from that moment they were clothed, taught, and maintained, for the public service. According to the promise of their appearance, they were selected for the royal schools of Boursa, Pera, and Adrianople, intrusted to the care of the bashaws, or dispersed in the houses of the Anatolian peasantry. It was the first care of their masters to instruct them in the Turkish language: their bodies were exercised by every labor that could fortify their strength; they learned to wrestle, to leap, to run, to shoot with the bow, and afterwards with the musket; till they were drafted into the chambers and companies of the Janizaries, and severely trained in the military or monastic discipline of the order. The youths most conspicuous for birth, talents, and beauty, were admitted into the inferior class of Agiamoglans, or the more liberal rank of Ichoglans, of whom the former were attached to the palace, and the latter to the person, of the prince. In four successive schools, under the rod of the white eunuchs, the arts of horsemanship and of darting the javelin were their daily exercise, while those of a more studious cast applied themselves to the study of the Koran, and the knowledge of the Arabic and Persian tongues. As they advanced in seniority and merit, they were gradually dismissed to military, civil, and even ecclesiastical employments: the longer their stay, the higher was their expectation; till, at a mature period, they were admitted into the number of the forty agas, who stood before the sultan, and were promoted by his choice to the government of provinces and the first honors of the empire. [88]

Such a mode of institution was admirably adapted to the form and spirit of a despotic monarchy. The ministers and generals were, in the strictest sense, the slaves of the emperor, to whose bounty they were indebted for their instruction and support. When they left the seraglio, and suffered their beards to grow as the symbol of enfranchisement, they found themselves in an important office, without faction or friendship, without parents and without heirs, dependent on the hand which had raised them from the dust, and which, on the slightest displeasure, could break in pieces these statues of glass, as they were aptly termed by the Turkish proverb. [89] In the slow and painful steps of education, their characters and talents were unfolded to a discerning eye: the man, naked and alone, was reduced to the standard of his personal merit; and, if the sovereign had wisdom to choose, he possessed a pure and boundless liberty of choice. The Ottoman candidates were trained by the virtues of abstinence to those of action; by the habits of submission to those of command. A similar spirit was diffused among the troops; and their silence and sobriety, their patience and modesty, have extorted the reluctant praise of their Christian enemies. [90] Nor can the victory appear doubtful, if we compare the discipline and exercise of the Janizaries with the pride of birth, the independence of chivalry, the ignorance of the new levies, the mutinous temper of the veterans, and the vices of intemperance and disorder, which so long contaminated the armies of Europe.

[Footnote 87: Chalcondyles (l. v.) and Ducas (c. 23) exhibit the rude lineament of the Ottoman policy, and the transmutation of Christian children into Turkish soldiers.]

[Footnote 88: This sketch of the Turkish education and discipline is chiefly borrowed from Ricaut's State of the Ottoman Empire, the Stato Militaire del' Imperio Ottomano of Count Marsigli, (in Haya, 1732, in folio,) and a description of the Seraglio, approved by Mr. Greaves himself, a curious traveller, and inserted in the second volume of his works.]

[Footnote 89: From the series of cxv. viziers, till the siege of Vienna, (Marsigli, p. 13,) their place may be valued at three years and a half purchase.]

[Footnote 90: See the entertaining and judicious letters of Busbequius.]

The only hope of salvation for the Greek empire, and the adjacent kingdoms, would have been some more powerful weapon, some discovery in the art of war, that would give them a decisive superiority over their Turkish foes. Such a weapon was in their hands; such a discovery had been made in the critical moment of their fate. The chemists of China or Europe had found, by casual or elaborate experiments, that a mixture of saltpetre, sulphur, and charcoal, produces, with a spark of fire, a tremendous explosion. It was soon observed, that if the expansive force were compressed in a strong tube, a ball of stone or iron might be expelled with irresistible and destructive velocity. The precise æra of the invention and application of gunpowder [91] is involved in doubtful traditions and equivocal language; yet we may clearly discern, that it was known before the middle of the fourteenth century; and that before the end of the same, the use of artillery in battles and sieges, by sea and land, was familiar to the states of Germany, Italy, Spain, France, and England. [92] The priority of nations is of small account; none could derive any exclusive benefit from their previous or superior knowledge; and in the common improvement, they stood on the same level of relative power and military science. Nor was it possible to circumscribe the secret within the pale of the church; it was disclosed to the Turks by the treachery of apostates and the selfish policy of rivals; and the sultans had sense to adopt, and wealth to reward, the talents of a Christian engineer. The Genoese, who transported Amurath into Europe, must be accused as his preceptors; and it was probably by their hands that his cannon was cast and directed at the siege of Constantinople. [93] The first attempt was indeed unsuccessful; but in the general warfare of the age, the advantage was on their side, who were most commonly the assailants: for a while the proportion of the attack and defence was suspended; and this thundering artillery was pointed against the walls and towers which had been erected only to resist the less potent engines of antiquity. By the Venetians, the use of gunpowder was communicated without reproach to the sultans of Egypt and Persia, their allies against the Ottoman power; the secret was soon propagated to the extremities of Asia; and the advantage of the European was confined to his easy victories over the savages of the new world. If we contrast the rapid progress of this mischievous discovery with the slow and laborious advances of reason, science, and the arts of peace, a philosopher, according to his temper, will laugh or weep at the folly of mankind.

[Footnote 91: The first and second volumes of Dr. Watson's Chemical Essays contain two valuable discourses on the discovery and composition of gunpowder.]

[Footnote 92: On this subject modern testimonies cannot be trusted. The original passages are collected by Ducange, (Gloss. Latin. tom. i. p. 675, Bombarda.) But in the early doubtful twilight, the name, sound, fire, and effect, that seem to express our artillery, may be fairly interpreted of the old engines and the Greek fire. For the English cannon at Crecy, the authority of John Villani (Chron. l. xii. c. 65) must be weighed against the silence of Froissard. Yet Muratori (Antiquit. Italiæ Medii Ævi, tom. ii. Dissert. xxvi. p. 514, 515) has produced a decisive passage from Petrarch, (De Remediis utriusque Fortunæ Dialog.,) who, before the year 1344, execrates this terrestrial thunder, nuper rara, nunc communis. Note: Mr. Hallam makes the following observation on the objection thrown our by Gibbon: "The positive testimony of Villani, who died within two years afterwards, and had manifestly obtained much information as to the great events passing in France, cannot be rejected. He ascribes a material effect to the cannon of Edward, Colpi delle bombarde, which I suspect, from his strong expressions, had not been employed before, except against stone walls. It seems, he says, as if God thundered con grande uccisione di genti e efondamento di cavalli." Middle Ages, vol. i. p. 510—M.]

[Footnote 93: The Turkish cannon, which Ducas (c. 30) first introduces before Belgrade, (A.D. 1436,) is mentioned by Chalcondyles (l. v. p. 123) in 1422, at the siege of Constantinople.]

CHAPTER LXVI

UNION OF THE GREEK AND LATIN CHURCHES

PART I

APPLICATIONS OF THE EASTERN EMPERORS TO THE POPES—VISITS TO THE WEST, OF JOHN THE FIRST, MANUEL, AND JOHN THE SECOND PALÆOLOGUS—UNION OF THE GREEK AND LATIN CHURCHES, PROMOTED BY THE COUNCIL OF BASIL, AND CONCLUDED AT FERRARA AND FLORENCE—STATE OF LITERATURE AT CONSTANTINOPLE—ITS REVIVAL IN ITALY BY THE GREEK FUGITIVES—CURIOSITY AND EMULATION OF THE LATINS

In the four last centuries of the Greek emperors, their friendly or hostile aspect towards the pope and the Latins may be observed as the thermometer of their prosperity or distress; as the scale of the rise and fall of the Barbarian dynasties. When the Turks of the house of Seljuk pervaded Asia, and threatened Constantinople, we have seen, at the council of Placentia, the suppliant ambassadors of

Alexius imploring the protection of the common father of the Christians. No sooner had the arms of the French pilgrims removed the sultan from Nice to Iconium, than the Greek princes resumed, or avowed, their genuine hatred and contempt for the schismatics of the West, which precipitated the first downfall of their empire. The date of the Mogul invasion is marked in the soft and charitable language of John Vataces. After the recovery of Constantinople, the throne of the first Palæologus was encompassed by foreign and domestic enemies; as long as the sword of Charles was suspended over his head, he basely courted the favor of the Roman pontiff; and sacrificed to the present danger his faith, his virtue, and the affection of his subjects. On the decease of Michael, the prince and people asserted the independence of their church, and the purity of their creed: the elder Andronicus neither feared nor loved the Latins; in his last distress, pride was the safeguard of superstition; nor could he decently retract in his age the firm and orthodox declarations of his youth. His grandson, the younger Andronicus, was less a slave in his temper and situation; and the conquest of Bithynia by the Turks admonished him to seek a temporal and spiritual alliance with the Western princes. After a separation and silence of fifty years, a secret agent, the monk Barlaam, was despatched to Pope Benedict the Twelfth; and his artful instructions appear to have been drawn by the master-hand of the great domestic. [1] "Most holy father," was he commissioned to say, "the emperor is not less desirous than yourself of a union between the two churches: but in this delicate transaction, he is obliged to respect his own dignity and the prejudices of his subjects. The ways of union are twofold; force and persuasion. Of force, the inefficacy has been already tried; since the Latins have subdued the empire, without subduing the minds, of the Greeks. The method of persuasion, though slow, is sure and permanent. A deputation of thirty or forty of our doctors would probably agree with those of the Vatican, in the love of truth and the unity of belief; but on their return, what would be the use, the recompense, of such an agreement? the scorn of their brethren, and the reproaches of a blind and obstinate nation. Yet that nation is accustomed to reverence the general councils, which have fixed the articles of our faith; and if they reprobate the decrees of Lyons, it is because the Eastern churches were neither heard nor represented in that arbitrary meeting. For this salutary end, it will be expedient, and even necessary, that a well-chosen legate should be sent into Greece, to convene the patriarchs of Constantinople, Alexandria, Antioch, and Jerusalem; and, with their aid, to prepare a free and universal synod. But at this moment," continued the subtle agent, "the empire is assaulted and endangered by the Turks, who have occupied four of the greatest cities of Anatolia. The Christian inhabitants have expressed a wish of returning to their allegiance and religion; but the forces and revenues of the emperor are insufficient for their deliverance: and the Roman legate must be accompanied, or preceded, by an army of Franks, to expel the infidels, and open a way to the holy sepulchre." If the suspicious Latins should require some pledge, some previous effect of the sincerity of the Greeks, the answers of Barlaam were perspicuous and rational. "1. A general synod can alone consummate the union of the churches; nor can such a synod be held till the three Oriental patriarchs, and a great number of bishops, are enfranchised from the Mahometan yoke. 2. The Greeks are alienated by a long series of oppression and injury: they must be reconciled by some act of brotherly love, some effectual succor, which may fortify the authority and arguments of the emperor, and the friends of the union. 3. If some difference of faith or ceremonies should be found incurable, the Greeks, however, are the disciples of Christ; and the Turks are the common enemies of the Christian name. The Armenians, Cyprians, and Rhodians, are equally attacked; and it will become the piety of the French princes to draw their swords in the general defence of religion. 4. Should the subjects of Andronicus be treated as the worst of schismatics, of heretics, of pagans, a judicious policy may yet instruct the powers of the West to embrace a useful ally, to uphold a sinking empire, to guard the confines of Europe; and rather to join the Greeks against the Turks, than to expect the union of the Turkish arms with the troops and treasures of captive Greece." The reasons, the offers, and the demands, of Andronicus were eluded with cold and stately indifference. The kings of France and Naples declined the dangers and glory of a crusade; the pope refused to call a new synod to determine old articles of faith; and his regard for the obsolete claims of the Latin emperor and clergy engaged him to use an offensive superscription,—"To the moderator [2] of the Greeks, and the persons who style themselves the patriarchs of the Eastern churches." For such an embassy, a time and character less propitious could not easily have been found. Benedict the Twelfth [3] was a dull peasant, perplexed with scruples, and immersed in sloth and wine: his pride might enrich with a third crown the papal tiara, but he was alike unfit for the regal and the pastoral office.

*[Footnote 1: This curious instruction was transcribed (I believe) from the Vatican archives, by Odoricus Raynaldus, in his Continuation of the Annals of Baronius, (Romæ, 1646—1677, in x. volumes in folio.) I have contented myself with the Abbé Fleury, (Hist. Ecclésiastique. tom. xx. p. 1—8,) whose abstracts I have always found to be clear, accurate, and impartial.]*

*[Footnote 2: The ambiguity of this title is happy or ingenious; and moderator, as synonymous to rector, gubernator, is a word of classical, and even Ciceronian, Latinity, which may be found, not in the Glossary of Ducange, but in the Thesaurus of Robert Stephens.]*

*[Footnote 3: The first epistle (sine titulo) of Petrarch exposes the danger of the bark, and the incapacity of the pilot. Hæc inter, vino madidus, ævo gravis, ac soporifero rore perfusus, jamjam nutitat, dormitat, jam somno præceps, atque (utinam solus) ruit..... Heu quanto felicius patrio terram sulcasset aratro, quam scalmum piscatorium ascendisset! This satire engages his biographer to weigh the virtues and vices of Benedict XII. which have been exaggerated by Guelphs and Ghibe lines, by Papists and Protestants, (see Mémoires sur la Vie de Pétrarque, tom. i. p. 259, ii. not. xv. p. 13—16.) He gave occasion to the saying, Bibamus papaliter.]*

After the decease of Andronicus, while the Greeks were distracted by intestine war, they could not presume to agitate a general union of the Christians. But as soon as Cantacuzene had subdued and pardoned his enemies, he was anxious to justify, or at least to extenuate, the introduction of the Turks into Europe, and the nuptials of his daughter with a Mussulman prince. Two officers of state, with a Latin interpreter, were sent in his name to the Roman court, which was transplanted to Avignon, on the banks of the Rhône, during a period of seventy years: they represented the hard necessity which had urged him to embrace the alliance of the miscreants, and pronounced by his command the specious and edifying sounds of union and crusade. Pope Clement the Sixth, [4] the successor of Benedict, received them with hospitality and honor, acknowledged the innocence of their sovereign, excused his distress, applauded his magnanimity, and displayed a clear knowledge of the state and revolutions of the Greek empire, which he had imbibed from the honest accounts of a Savoyard lady, an attendant of the empress Anne. [5] If Clement was ill endowed with the virtues of a priest, he possessed, however, the spirit and magnificence of a prince, whose liberal hand distributed benefices and kingdoms with equal facility. Under his reign Avignon was the seat of pomp and pleasure: in his youth he had surpassed the licentiousness of a baron; and the palace, nay, the bed-chamber of the pope, was adorned, or polluted, by the visits of his female favorites. The wars of France and England were adverse to the holy enterprise; but his vanity was amused by the splendid idea; and the Greek ambassadors returned with two Latin bishops, the ministers of the pontiff. On their arrival at Constantinople, the emperor and the nuncios admired each other's piety and eloquence; and their frequent conferences were filled with mutual praises and promises, by which both parties were amused, and neither could be deceived. "I am delighted," said the devout Cantacuzene, "with the project of our holy war, which must redound to my personal glory, as well as to the public benefit of Christendom. My dominions will give a free passage to the armies of France: my troops, my galleys, my treasures, shall be consecrated to the common cause; and happy would be my fate, could I deserve and obtain the crown of martyrdom. Words are insufficient to express the ardor with which I sigh for the reunion of the scattered members of Christ. If my death could avail, I would gladly present my sword and my neck: if the spiritual phnix could arise from my ashes, I would erect the pile, and kindle the flame with my own hands." Yet the Greek emperor presumed to observe, that the articles of faith which divided the two churches had been introduced by the pride and precipitation of the Latins: he disclaimed the servile and arbitrary steps of the first Palæologus; and firmly declared, that he would never submit his conscience unless to the decrees of a free and universal synod. "The situation of the times," continued he, "will not allow the pope and myself to meet either at Rome or Constantinople; but some maritime city may be chosen on the verge of the two empires, to unite the bishops, and to instruct the faithful, of the East and West." The nuncios seemed content with the proposition; and Cantacuzene affects to deplore the failure of his hopes, which were soon overthrown by the death of Clement, and the different temper of his successor. His own life was prolonged, but it was prolonged in a cloister; and, except by his prayers, the humble monk was incapable of directing the counsels of his pupil or the state. [6]

[Footnote 4: See the original Lives of Clement VI. in Muratori, (Script. Rerum Italicarum, tom. iii. P. ii. p. 550—589;) Matteo Villani, (Chron. l. iii. c. 43, in Muratori, tom. xiv. p. 186,) who styles him, molto cavallaresco, poco religioso; Fleury, (Hist. Ecclés. tom. xx. p. 126;) and the Vie de Pétrarque, (tom. ii. p. 42—45.) The abbé de Sade treats him with the most indulgence; but he is a gentleman as well as a priest.]

[Footnote 5: Her name (most probably corrupted) was Zampea. She had accompanied, and alone remained with her mistress at Constantinople, where her prudence, erudition, and politeness deserved the praises of the Greeks themselves, (Cantacuzen. l. i. c. 42.)]

[Footnote 6: See this whole negotiation in Cantacuzene, (l. iv. c. 9,) who, amidst the praises and virtues which he bestows on himself, reveals the uneasiness of a guilty conscience.]

Yet of all the Byzantine princes, that pupil, John Palæologus, was the best disposed to embrace, to believe, and to obey, the shepherd of the West. His mother, Anne of Savoy, was baptized in the bosom of the Latin church: her marriage with Andronicus imposed a change of name, of apparel, and of worship, but her heart was still faithful to her country and religion: she had formed the infancy of her son, and she governed the emperor, after his mind, or at least his stature, was enlarged to the size of man. In the first year of his deliverance and restoration, the Turks were still masters of the Hellespont; the son of Cantacuzene was in arms at Adrianople; and Palæologus could depend neither on himself nor on his people. By his mother's advice, and in the hope of foreign aid, he abjured the rights both of the church and state; and the act of slavery, [7] subscribed in purple ink, and sealed with the golden bull, was privately intrusted to an Italian agent. The first article of the treaty is an oath of fidelity and obedience to Innocent the Sixth and his successors, the supreme pontiffs of the Roman and Catholic church. The emperor promises to entertain with due reverence their legates and nuncios; to assign a palace for their residence, and a temple for their worship; and to deliver his second son Manuel as the hostage of his faith. For these condescensions he requires a prompt succor of fifteen galleys, with five hundred men at arms, and a thousand archers, to serve against his Christian and Mussulman enemies. Palæologus engages to impose on his clergy and people the same spiritual yoke; but as the resistance of the Greeks might be justly foreseen, he adopts the two effectual methods of corruption and education. The legate was empowered to distribute the vacant benefices among the ecclesiastics who should subscribe the creed of the Vatican: three schools were instituted to instruct the youth of Constantinople in the language and doctrine of the Latins; and the name of Andronicus, the heir of the empire, was enrolled as the first student. Should he fail in the measures of persuasion or force, Palæologus declares himself unworthy to reign; transferred to the pope all regal and paternal authority; and invests Innocent with full power to regulate the family, the government, and the marriage, of his son and successor. But this treaty was neither executed nor published: the Roman galleys were as vain and imaginary as the submission of the Greeks; and it was only by the secrecy that their sovereign escaped the dishonor of this fruitless humiliation.

[Footnote 7: See this ignominious treaty in Fleury, (Hist. Ecclés. p. 151—154,) from Raynaldus, who drew it from the Vatican archives. It was not worth the trouble of a pious forgery.]

The tempest of the Turkish arms soon burst on his head; and after the loss of Adrianople and Romania, he was enclosed in his capital, the vassal of the haughty Amurath, with the miserable hope of being the last devoured by the savage. In this abject state, Palæologus embraced the resolution of embarking for Venice, and casting himself at the feet of the pope: he was the first of the Byzantine princes who had ever visited the unknown regions of the West, yet in them alone he could seek consolation or relief; and with less violation of his dignity he might appear in the sacred college than at the Ottoman Porte. After a long absence, the Roman pontiffs were returning from Avignon to the banks of the Tyber: Urban the Fifth, [8] of a mild and virtuous character, encouraged or allowed the pilgrimage of the Greek prince; and, within the same year, enjoyed the glory of receiving in the Vatican the two Imperial shadows who represented the majesty of Constantine and Charlemagne. In this suppliant visit, the emperor of Constantinople, whose vanity was lost in his distress, gave more than could be expected of empty sounds and formal submissions. A previous trial was imposed; and, in the presence of four cardinals, he acknowledged, as a true Catholic, the supremacy of the pope, and the double procession of the Holy Ghost. After this purification, he was introduced to a public audience in the church of St. Peter: Urban, in the midst of the cardinals, was seated on his throne; the Greek monarch, after three genuflections, devoutly kissed the feet, the hands, and at length the mouth, of the holy father, who celebrated high mass in his presence, allowed him to lead the bridle of his mule, and treated him with a sumptuous banquet in the Vatican. The entertainment of Palæologus was friendly and honorable; yet some difference was observed between the emperors of the East and West; [9] nor could the former be entitled to the rare privilege of chanting the gospel in the rank of a deacon. [10] In favor of his proselyte, Urban strove to rekindle the zeal of the French king and the other powers of the West; but he found them cold in the general cause, and active only in their domestic quarrels. The last hope of the emperor was in an English mercenary, John Hawkwood, [11] or Acuto, who, with a band of adventurers, the white brotherhood, had ravaged Italy from the Alps to Calabria; sold his services to the hostile states; and incurred a just excommunication by shooting his arrows against the papal residence. A special license was granted to negotiate with the outlaw, but the forces, or the spirit, of Hawkwood, were unequal to the enterprise: and it was for the advantage, perhaps, of Palæologus to be disappointed of succor, that must have been costly, that could not be effectual, and which might have been dangerous. [12] The disconsolate Greek [13] prepared for his return, but even his return was impeded by a most ignominious obstacle. On his arrival at Venice, he had borrowed large sums at exorbitant usury; but his coffers were empty, his creditors were impatient, and his person was detained as the best security for the payment. His eldest son, Andronicus, the regent of Constantinople, was repeatedly urged to exhaust every resource; and even by stripping the churches, to extricate his father from captivity and disgrace. But the unnatural youth was insensible of the disgrace, and secretly pleased with the captivity of the emperor: the state was poor, the clergy were obstinate; nor could some religious scruple be wanting to excuse the guilt of his indifference and delay. Such undutiful neglect was severely reproved by the piety of his brother Manuel, who instantly sold or mortgaged all that he possessed, embarked for Venice, relieved his father, and pledged his own freedom to be responsible for the debt. On his return to Constantinople, the parent and king distinguished his two sons with suitable rewards; but the faith and manners of the slothful Palæologus had not been improved by his Roman pilgrimage; and his apostasy or conversion, devoid of any spiritual or temporal effects, was speedily forgotten by the Greeks and Latins. [14]

[Footnote 8: See the two first original Lives of Urban V., (in Muratori, Script. Rerum Italicarum, tom. iii. P. ii. p. 623, 635,) and the Ecclesiastical Annals of Spondanus, (tom. i. p. 573, A.D. 1369, No. 7,) and Raynaldus, (Fleury, Hist. Ecclés. tom. xx. p. 223, 224.) Yet, from some variations, I suspect the papal writers of slightly magnifying the genuflections of Palæologus.]

[Footnote 9: Paullo minus quam si fuisset Imperator Romanorum. Yet his title of Imperator Græcorum was no longer disputed, (Vit. Urban V. p. 623.)]

[Footnote 10: It was confined to the successors of Charlemagne, and to them only on Christmas-day. On all other festivals these Imperial deacons were content to serve the pope, as he said mass, with the book and the corporale. Yet the abbé de Sade generously thinks that the merits of Charles IV. might have entitled him, though not on the proper day, (A.D. 1368, November 1,) to the whole privilege. He seems to affix a just value on the privilege and the man, (Vie de Petrarque, tom. iii. p. 735.)]

[Footnote 11: Through some Italian corruptions, the etymology of Falcone in bosco, (Matteo Villani, l. xi. c. 79, in Muratori, tom. xv. p. 746,) suggests the English word Hawkwood, the true name of our adventurous countryman, (Thomas Walsingham, Hist. Anglican. inter Scriptores Camdeni, p. 184.) After two-and-twenty victories, and one defeat, he died, in 1394, general of the Florentines, and was buried with such honors as the republic has not paid to Dante or Petrarch, (Muratori, Annali d'Italia, tom. xii. p. 212—371.)]

[Footnote 12: This torrent of English (by birth or service) overflowed from France into Italy after the peace of Bretigny in 1630. Yet the exclamation of Muratori (Annali, tom. xii. p. 197) is rather true than civil. "Ci mancava ancor questo, che dopo essere calpestrata l'Italia da tanti masnadieri Tedeschi ed Ungheri, venissero fin dall' Inghliterra nuovi cani a finire di divorarla."]

[Footnote 13: Chalcondyles, l. i. p. 25, 26. The Greek supposes his journey to the king of France, which is sufficiently refuted by the silence of the national historians. Nor am I much more inclined to believe, that Palæologus departed from Italy, valde bene consolatus et contentus, (Vit. Urban V. p. 623.)]

[Footnote 14: His return in 1370, and the coronation of Manuel, Sept. 25, 1373, (Ducange, Fam. Byzant. p. 241,) leaves some intermediate æra for the conspiracy and punishment of Andronicus.]

Thirty years after the return of Palæologus, his son and successor, Manuel, from a similar motive, but on a larger scale, again visited the countries of the West. In a preceding chapter I have related his treaty with Bajazet, the violation of that treaty, the siege or blockade of Constantinople, and the French succor under the command of the gallant Boucicault. [15] By his ambassadors, Manuel had solicited the Latin powers; but it was thought that the presence of a distressed monarch would draw tears and supplies from the hardest Barbarians; [16] and the marshal who advised the journey prepared the reception of the Byzantine prince. The land was occupied by the Turks; but the navigation of Venice was safe and open: Italy received him as the first, or, at least, as the second, of the Christian princes; Manuel was pitied as the champion and confessor of the faith; and the dignity of his behavior prevented that pity from sinking into contempt. From Venice he proceeded to Padua and Pavia; and even the duke of Milan, a secret ally of Bajazet, gave him safe and honorable conduct to the verge of his dominions. [17] On the confines of France [18] the royal officers undertook the care of his person, journey, and expenses; and two thousand of the richest citizens, in arms and on horseback, came forth to meet him as far as Charenton, in the neighborhood of the capital. At the gates of Paris, he was saluted by the chancellor and the parliament; and Charles the Sixth, attended by his princes and nobles, welcomed his brother with a cordial embrace. The successor of Constantine was clothed in a robe of white silk, and mounted on a milk-white steed, a circumstance, in the French ceremonial, of singular importance: the white color is considered as the symbol of sovereignty; and, in a late visit, the German emperor, after a haughty demand and a peevish refusal, had been reduced to content himself with a black courser. Manuel was lodged in the Louvre; a succession of feasts and balls, the pleasures of the banquet and the chase, were ingeniously varied by the politeness of the French, to display their magnificence, and amuse his grief: he was indulged in the liberty of his chapel; and the doctors of the Sorbonne were astonished, and possibly scandalized, by the language, the rites, and the vestments, of his Greek clergy. But the slightest glance on the state of the kingdom must teach him to despair of any effectual assistance. The unfortunate Charles, though he enjoyed some lucid intervals, continually relapsed into furious or stupid insanity: the reins of government were alternately seized by his brother and uncle, the dukes of Orleans and Burgundy, whose factious competition prepared the miseries of civil war. The former was a gay youth, dissolved in luxury and love: the latter was the father of John count of Nevers, who had so lately been ransomed from Turkish captivity; and, if the fearless son was ardent to revenge his defeat, the more prudent Burgundy was content with the cost and peril of the first experiment. When Manuel had satiated the curiosity, and perhaps fatigued the patience, of the French, he resolved on a visit to the adjacent island. In his progress from Dover, he was entertained at Canterbury with due reverence by the prior and monks of St. Austin; and, on Blackheath, King Henry the Fourth, with the English court, saluted the Greek hero, (I copy our old historian,) who, during many days, was lodged and treated in London as emperor of the East. [19] But the state of England was still more adverse to the design of the holy war. In the same year, the hereditary sovereign had been deposed and murdered: the reigning prince was a successful usurper, whose ambition was punished by jealousy and remorse: nor could Henry of Lancaster withdraw his person or forces from the defence of a throne incessantly shaken by conspiracy and rebellion. He pitied, he praised, he feasted, the emperor of Constantinople; but if the English monarch assumed the cross, it was only to appease his people, and perhaps his conscience, by the merit or semblance of his pious intention. [20] Satisfied, however, with gifts and honors, Manuel returned to Paris; and, after a residence of two years in the West, shaped his course through Germany and Italy, embarked at Venice, and patiently expected, in the Morea, the moment of his ruin or deliverance. Yet he had escaped the ignominious necessity of offering his religion to public or private sale. The Latin church was distracted by the great schism; the kings, the nations, the universities, of Europe were divided in their obedience between the popes of Rome and Avignon; and the emperor, anxious to conciliate the friendship of both parties, abstained from any correspondence with the indigent and unpopular rivals. His journey coincided with the year of the jubilee; but he passed through Italy without desiring, or deserving, the plenary indulgence which abolished the guilt or penance of the sins of the faithful. The Roman pope was offended by this neglect; accused him of irreverence to an image of Christ; and exhorted the princes of Italy to reject and abandon the obstinate schismatic. [21]

*[Footnote 15: Mémoires de Boucicault, P. i. c. 35, 36.]*

*[Footnote 16: His journey into the west of Europe is slightly, and I believe reluctantly, noticed by Chalcondyles (l. ii. c. 44—50) and Ducas, (c. 14.)]*

[Footnote 17: Muratori, Annali d'Italia, tom. xii. p. 406. John Galeazzo was the first and most powerful duke of Milan. His connection with Bajazet is attested by Froissard; and he contributed to save and deliver the French captives of Nicopolis.]

[Footnote 18: For the reception of Manuel at Paris, see Spondanus, (Annal. Ecclés. tom. i. p. 676, 677, A.D. 1400, No. 5,) who quotes Juvenal des Ursins and the monk of St. Denys; and Villaret, (Hist. de France, tom. xii. p. 331—334,) who quotes nobody according to the last fashion of the French writers.]

[Footnote 19: A short note of Manuel in England is extracted by Dr. Hody from a MS. at Lambeth, (de Græcis illustribus, p. 14,) C. P. Imperator, diu variisque et horrendis Paganorum insultibus coarctatus, ut pro eisdem resistentiam triumphalem perquireret, Anglorum Regem visitare decrevit, &c. Rex (says Walsingham, p. 364) nobili apparatû... suscepit (ut decuit) tantum Heroa, duxitque Londonias, et per multos dies exhibuit gloriose, pro expensis hospitii sui solvens, et eum respiciens tanto fastigio donativis. He repeats the same in his Upodigma Neustriæ, (p. 556.)]

[Footnote 20: Shakspeare begins and ends the play of Henry IV. with that prince's vow of a crusade, and his belief that he should die in Jerusalem.]

[Footnote 21: This fact is preserved in the Historia Politica, A.D. 1391—1478, published by Martin Crusius, (Turco Græcia, p. 1—43.) The image of Christ, which the Greek emperor refused to worship, was probably a work of sculpture.]

PART II

During the period of the crusades, the Greeks beheld with astonishment and terror the perpetual stream of emigration that flowed, and continued to flow, from the unknown climates of their West. The visits of their last emperors removed the veil of separation, and they disclosed to their eyes the powerful nations of Europe, whom they no longer presumed to brand with the name of Barbarians. The observations of Manuel, and his more inquisitive followers, have been preserved by a Byzantine historian of the times: [22] his scattered ideas I shall collect and abridge; and it may be amusing enough, perhaps instructive, to contemplate the rude pictures of Germany, France, and England, whose ancient and modern state are so familiar to our minds. I. Germany (says the Greek Chalcondyles) is of ample latitude from Vienna to the ocean; and it stretches (a strange geography) from Prague in Bohemia to the River Tartessus, and the Pyrenæan Mountains. [23] The soil, except in figs and olives, is sufficiently fruitful; the air is salubrious; the bodies of the natives are robust and healthy; and these cold regions are seldom visited with the calamities of pestilence, or earthquakes. After the Scythians or Tartars, the Germans are the most numerous of nations: they are brave and patient; and were they united under a single head, their force would be irresistible. By the gift of the pope, they have acquired the privilege of choosing the Roman emperor; [24] nor is any people more devoutly attached to the faith and obedience of the Latin patriarch. The greatest part of the country is divided among the princes and prelates; but Strasburg, Cologne, Hamburgh, and more than two hundred free cities, are governed by sage and equal laws, according to the will, and for the advantage, of the whole community. The use of duels, or single combats on foot, prevails among them in peace and war: their industry excels in all the mechanic arts; and the Germans may boast of the invention of gunpowder and cannon, which is now diffused over the greatest part of the world. II. The kingdom of France is spread above fifteen or twenty days' journey from Germany to Spain, and from the Alps to the British Ocean; containing many flourishing cities, and among these Paris, the seat of the king, which surpasses the rest in riches and luxury. Many princes and lords alternately wait in his palace, and acknowledge him as their sovereign: the most powerful are the dukes of Bretagne and Burgundy; of whom the latter possesses the wealthy province of Flanders, whose harbors are frequented by the ships and merchants of our own, and the more remote, seas. The French are an ancient and opulent people; and their language and manners, though somewhat different, are not dissimilar from those of the Italians. Vain of the Imperial dignity of Charlemagne, of their victories over the Saracens, and of the exploits of their heroes, Oliver and Rowland, [25] they esteem themselves the first of the western nations; but this foolish arrogance has been recently humbled by the unfortunate events of their wars against the English, the inhabitants of the British island. III. Britain, in the ocean, and opposite to the shores of Flanders, may be considered either as one, or as three islands; but the whole is united by a common interest, by the same manners, and by a similar government. The measure of its circumference is five thousand stadia: the land is overspread with towns and villages: though destitute of wine, and not abounding in fruit-trees, it is fertile in wheat and barley; in honey and wool; and much cloth is manufactured by the inhabitants. In populousness and power, in richness and luxury, London, [26] the metropolis of the isle, may claim a preeminence over all the cities of the West. It is situate on the Thames, a broad and rapid river, which at the distance of thirty miles falls into the Gallic Sea; and the daily flow and ebb of the tide affords a safe entrance and departure to the vessels of commerce. The king is head of a powerful and turbulent aristocracy: his principal vassals hold their estates by a free and unalterable tenure; and the laws define the limits of his authority and their obedience. The kingdom has been often afflicted by foreign conquest and domestic sedition: but the natives are bold and hardy, renowned in arms and victorious in war. The form of their shields or targets is derived from the Italians, that of their swords from the Greeks; the use of the long bow is the peculiar and decisive advantage of the English. Their language bears no affinity to the idioms of the Continent: in the habits of domestic life, they are not easily distinguished from their neighbors of France: but the most singular circumstance of their manners is their disregard of conjugal honor and of female chastity. In their mutual visits, as the first act of hospitality, the guest is welcomed in the embraces of their wives and daughters: among friends they are lent and borrowed without shame; nor are the islanders offended at this strange commerce, and its inevitable consequences. [27] Informed as we are of the customs of Old England and assured of the virtue of our mothers, we may smile at the credulity, or resent the injustice, of the Greek, who must have confounded a modest salute [28] with a criminal embrace. But his credulity and injustice may teach an important lesson; to distrust the accounts of foreign and remote nations, and to suspend our belief of every tale that deviates from the laws of nature and the character of man. [29]

[Footnote 22: The Greek and Turkish history of Laonicus Chalcondyles ends with the winter of 1463; and the abrupt conclusion seems to mark, that he laid down his pen in the same year. We know that he was an Athenian, and that some contemporaries of the same name contributed to the revival of the Greek language in Italy. But in his numerous digressions, the modest historian has never introduced himself; and his editor Leunclavius, as well as Fabricius, (Bibliot. Græc. tom. vi. p. 474,) seems ignorant of his life and character. For his descriptions of Germany, France, and England, see l. ii. p. 36, 37, 44—50.]

[Footnote 23: I shall not animadvert on the geographical errors of Chalcondyles. In this instance, he perhaps followed, and mistook, Herodotus, (l. ii. c. 33,) whose text may be explained, (Herodote de Larcher, tom. ii. p. 219, 220,) or whose ignorance may be excused. Had these modern Greeks never read Strabo, or any of their lesser geographers?]

[Footnote 24: A citizen of new Rome, while new Rome survived, would have scorned to dignify the German 'Rhx with titles of BasileuV or Autokratwr 'Rwmaiwn: but all pride was extinct in the bosom of

Chalcondyles; and he describes the Byzantine prince, and his subject, by the proper, though humble, names of "EllhneV and BasileuV 'Ellhnwn.]

[Footnote 25: Most of the old romances were translated in the xivth century into French prose, and soon became the favorite amusement of the knights and ladies in the court of Charles VI. If a Greek believed in the exploits of Rowland and Oliver, he may surely be excused, since the monks of St. Denys, the national historians, have inserted the fables of Archbishop Turpin in their Chronicles of France.]

[Footnote 26: Londinh.... de te poliV dunamei te proecousa tvn en th nhsw tauth pasvn polewn, olbw te kai th allh eudaimonia oudemiaV tvn peoV esperan leipomenh. Even since the time of Fitzstephen, (the xiith century,) London appears to have maintained this preeminence of wealth and magnitude; and her gradual increase has, at least, kept pace with the general improvement of Europe.]

[Footnote 27: If the double sense of the verb Kuw (osculor, and in utero gero) be equivocal, the context and pious horror of Chalcondyles can leave no doubt of his meaning and mistake, (p. 49.)

Note: I can discover no "pious horror" in the plain manner in which Chalcondyles relates this strange usage. He says, oude aiscunun tovto feoei eautoiV kuesqai taV te gunaikaV autvn kai taV qugateraV, yet these are expression beyond what would be used, if the ambiguous word kuesqai were taken in its more innocent sense. Nor can the phrase parecontai taV eautvn gunaikaV en toiV epithdeioiV well bear a less coarse interpretation. Gibbon is possibly right as to the origin of this extraordinary mistake—M.]

[Footnote 28: Erasmus (Epist. Fausto Andrelino) has a pretty passage on the English fashion of kissing strangers on their arrival and departure, from whence, however, he draws no scandalous inferences.]

[Footnote 29: Perhaps we may apply this remark to the community of wives among the old Britons, as it is supposed by Cæsar and Dion, (Dion Cassius, l. lxii. tom. ii. p. 1007,) with Reimar's judicious annotation. The Arreoy of Otaheite, so certain at first, is become less visible and scandalous, in proportion as we have studied the manners of that gentle and amorous people.]

After his return, and the victory of Timour, Manuel reigned many years in prosperity and peace. As long as the sons of Bajazet solicited his friendship and spared his dominions, he was satisfied with the national religion; and his leisure was employed in composing twenty theological dialogues for its defence. The appearance of the Byzantine ambassadors at the council of Constance, [30] announces the restoration of the Turkish power, as well as of the Latin church: the conquest of the sultans, Mahomet and Amurath, reconciled the emperor to the Vatican; and the siege of Constantinople almost tempted him to acquiesce in the double procession of the Holy Ghost. When Martin the Fifth ascended without a rival the chair of St. Peter, a friendly intercourse of letters and embassies was revived between the East and West. Ambition on one side, and distress on the other, dictated the same decent language of charity and peace: the artful Greek expressed a desire of marrying his six sons to Italian princesses; and the Roman, not less artful, despatched the daughter of the marquis of Montferrat, with a company of noble virgins, to soften, by their charms, the obstinacy of the schismatics. Yet under this mask of zeal, a discerning eye will perceive that all was hollow and insincere in the court and church of Constantinople. According to the vicissitudes of danger and repose, the emperor advanced or retreated; alternately instructed and disavowed his ministers; and escaped from the importunate pressure by urging the duty of inquiry, the obligation of collecting the sense of his patriarchs and bishops, and the impossibility of convening them at a time when the Turkish arms were at the gates of his capital. From a review of the public transactions it will appear that the Greeks insisted on three successive measures, a succor, a council, and a final reunion, while the Latins eluded the second, and only promised the first, as a consequential and voluntary reward of the third. But we have an opportunity of unfolding the most secret intentions of Manuel, as he explained them in a private conversation without artifice or disguise. In his declining age, the emperor had associated John Palæologus, the second of the name, and the eldest of his sons, on whom he devolved the greatest part of the authority and weight of government. One day, in the presence only of the historian Phranza, [31] his favorite chamberlain, he opened to his colleague and successor the true principle of his negotiations with the pope. [32] "Our last resource," said Manuel, against the Turks, "is their fear of our union with the Latins, of the warlike nations of the West, who may arm for our relief and for their destruction. As often as you are threatened by the miscreants, present this danger before their eyes. Propose a council; consult on the means; but ever delay and avoid the convocation of an assembly, which cannot tend either to our spiritual or temporal emolument. The Latins are proud; the Greeks are obstinate; neither party will recede or retract; and the attempt of a perfect union will confirm the schism, alienate the churches, and leave us, without hope or defence, at the mercy of the Barbarians." Impatient of this salutary lesson, the royal youth arose from his seat, and departed in silence; and the wise monarch (continued Phranza) casting his eyes on me, thus resumed his discourse: "My son deems himself a great and heroic prince; but, alas! our miserable age does not afford scope for heroism or greatness. His daring spirit might have suited the happier times of our ancestors; but the present state requires not an emperor, but a cautious steward of the last relics of our fortunes. Well do I remember the lofty expectations which he built on our alliance with Mustapha; and much do I fear, that this rash courage will urge the ruin of our house, and that even religion may precipitate our downfall." Yet the experience and authority of Manuel preserved the peace, and eluded the council; till, in the seventy-eighth year of his age, and in the habit of a monk, he terminated his career, dividing his precious movables among his children and the poor, his physicians and his favorite servants. Of his six sons, [33] Andronicus the Second was invested with the principality of Thessalonica, and died of a leprosy soon after the sale of that city to the Venetians and its final conquest by the Turks. Some fortunate incidents had restored Peloponnesus, or the Morea, to the empire; and in his more prosperous days, Manuel had fortified the narrow isthmus of six miles [34] with a stone wall and one hundred and fifty-three towers. The wall was overthrown by the first blast of the Ottomans; the fertile peninsula might have been sufficient for the four younger brothers, Theodore and Constantine, Demetrius and Thomas; but they wasted in domestic contests the remains of their strength; and the least successful of the rivals were reduced to a life of dependence in the Byzantine palace.

[Footnote 30: See Lenfant, Hist. du Concile de Constance, tom. ii. p. 576; and or the ecclesiastical history of the times, the Annals of Spondanus the Bibliothèque of Dupin, tom. xii., and xxist and xxiid volumes of the History, or rather the Continuation, of Fleury.]

[Footnote 31: From his early youth, George Phranza, or Phranzes, was employed in the service of the state and palace; and Hanckius (de Script. Byzant. P. i. c. 40) has collected his life from his own writings. He was no more than four-and-twenty years of age at the death of Manuel, who recommended him in the strongest terms to his successor: Imprimis vero hunc Phranzen tibi commendo, qui ministravit mihi fideliter et diligenter (Phranzes, l. ii. c. i.) Yet the emperor John was cold, and he preferred the service of the despots of Peloponnesus.]

[Footnote 32: See Phranzes, l. ii. c. 13. While so many manuscripts of the Greek original are extant in the libraries of Rome, Milan, the Escurial, &c., it is a matter of shame and reproach, that we should be reduced to the Latin version, or abstract, of James Pontanus, (ad calcem Theophylact, Simocattæ: Ingolstadt, 1604,) so deficient in accuracy and elegance, (Fabric. Bibliot. Græc. tom. vi. p. 615—620.)

*Note: The Greek text of Phranzes was edited by F. C. Alter Vindobonæ, 1796. It has been re-edited by Bekker for the new edition of the Byzantines, Bonn, 1838—M.]*

*[Footnote 33: See Ducange, Fam. Byzant. p. 243—248.]*

*[Footnote 34: The exact measure of the Hexamilion, from sea to sea, was 3800 orgyiæ, or toises, of six Greek feet, (Phranzes, l. i. c. 38,) which would produce a Greek mile, still smaller than that of 660 French toises, which is assigned by D'Anville, as still in use in Turkey. Five miles are commonly reckoned for the breadth of the isthmus. See the Travels of Spon, Wheeler and Chandler.]*

The eldest of the sons of Manuel, John Palæologus the Second, was acknowledged, after his father's death, as the sole emperor of the Greeks. He immediately proceeded to repudiate his wife, and to contract a new marriage with the princess of Trebizond: beauty was in his eyes the first qualification of an empress; and the clergy had yielded to his firm assurance, that unless he might be indulged in a divorce, he would retire to a cloister, and leave the throne to his brother Constantine. The first, and in truth the only, victory of Palæologus, was over a Jew, [35] whom, after a long and learned dispute, he converted to the Christian faith; and this momentous conquest is carefully recorded in the history of the times. But he soon resumed the design of uniting the East and West; and, regardless of his father's advice, listened, as it should seem with sincerity, to the proposal of meeting the pope in a general council beyond the Adriatic. This dangerous project was encouraged by Martin the Fifth, and coldly entertained by his successor Eugenius, till, after a tedious negotiation, the emperor received a summons from the Latin assembly of a new character, the independent prelates of Basil, who styled themselves the representatives and judges of the Catholic church.

*[Footnote 35: The first objection of the Jews is on the death of Christ: if it were voluntary, Christ was a suicide; which the emperor parries with a mystery. They then dispute on the conception of the Virgin, the sense of the prophecies, &c., (Phranzes, l. ii. c. 12, a whole chapter.)]*

The Roman pontiff had fought and conquered in the cause of ecclesiastical freedom; but the victorious clergy were soon exposed to the tyranny of their deliverer; and his sacred character was invulnerable to those arms which they found so keen and effectual against the civil magistrate. Their great charter, the right of election, was annihilated by appeals, evaded by trusts or commendams, disappointed by reversionary grants, and superseded by previous and arbitrary reservations. [36] A public auction was instituted in the court of Rome: the cardinals and favorites were enriched with the spoils of nations; and every country might complain that the most important and valuable benefices were accumulated on the heads of aliens and absentees. During their residence at Avignon, the ambition of the popes subsided in the meaner passions of avarice [37] and luxury: they rigorously imposed on the clergy the tributes of first-fruits and tenths; but they freely tolerated the impunity of vice, disorder, and corruption. These manifold scandals were aggravated by the great schism of the West, which continued above fifty years. In the furious conflicts of Rome and Avignon, the vices of the rivals were mutually exposed; and their precarious situation degraded their authority, relaxed their discipline, and multiplied their wants and exactions. To heal the wounds, and restore the monarchy, of the church, the synods of Pisa and Constance [38] were successively convened; but these great assemblies, conscious of their strength, resolved to vindicate the privileges of the Christian aristocracy. From a personal sentence against two pontiffs, whom they rejected, and a third, their acknowledged sovereign, whom they deposed, the fathers of Constance proceeded to examine the nature and limits of the Roman supremacy; nor did they separate till they had established the authority, above the pope, of a general council. It was enacted, that, for the government and reformation of the church, such assemblies should be held at regular intervals; and that each synod, before its dissolution, should appoint the time and place of the subsequent meeting. By the influence of the court of Rome, the next convocation at Sienna was easily eluded; but the bold and vigorous proceedings of the council of Basil [39] had almost been fatal to the reigning pontiff, Eugenius the Fourth. A just suspicion of his design prompted the fathers to hasten the promulgation of their first decree, that the representatives of the church-militant on earth were invested with a divine and spiritual jurisdiction over all Christians, without excepting the pope; and that a general council could not be dissolved, prorogued, or transferred, unless by their free deliberation and consent. On the notice that Eugenius had fulminated a bull for that purpose, they ventured to summon, to admonish, to threaten, to censure the contumacious successor of St. Peter. After many delays, to allow time for repentance, they finally declared, that, unless he submitted within the term of sixty days, he was suspended from the exercise of all temporal and ecclesiastical authority. And to mark their jurisdiction over the prince as well as the priest, they assumed the government of Avignon, annulled the alienation of the sacred patrimony, and protected Rome from the imposition of new taxes. Their boldness was justified, not only by the general opinion of the clergy, but by the support and power of the first monarchs of Christendom: the emperor Sigismond declared himself the servant and protector of the synod; Germany and France adhered to their cause; the duke of Milan was the enemy of Eugenius; and he was driven from the Vatican by an insurrection of the Roman people. Rejected at the same time by temporal and spiritual subjects, submission was his only choice: by a most humiliating bull, the pope repealed his own acts, and ratified those of the council; incorporated his legates and cardinals with that venerable body; and seemed to resign himself to the decrees of the supreme legislature. Their fame pervaded the countries of the East: and it was in their presence that Sigismond received the ambassadors of the Turkish sultan, [40] who laid at his feet twelve large vases, filled with robes of silk and pieces of gold. The fathers of Basil aspired to the glory of reducing the Greeks, as well as the Bohemians, within the pale of the church; and their deputies invited the emperor and patriarch of Constantinople to unite with an assembly which possessed the confidence of the Western nations. Palæologus was not averse to the proposal; and his ambassadors were introduced with due honors into the Catholic senate. But the choice of the place appeared to be an insuperable obstacle, since he refused to pass the Alps, or the sea of Sicily, and positively required that the synod should be adjourned to some convenient city in Italy, or at least on the Danube. The other articles of this treaty were more readily stipulated: it was agreed to defray the travelling expenses of the emperor, with a train of seven hundred persons, [41] to remit an immediate sum of eight thousand ducats [42] for the accommodation of the Greek clergy; and in his absence to grant a supply of ten thousand ducats, with three hundred archers and some galleys, for the protection of Constantinople. The city of Avignon advanced the funds for the preliminary expenses; and the embarkation was prepared at Marseilles with some difficulty and delay.

[Footnote 36: In the treatise delle Materie Beneficiarie of Fra Paolo, (in the ivth volume of the last, and best, edition of his works,) the papal system is deeply studied and freely described. Should Rome and her religion be annihilated, this golden volume may still survive, a philosophical history, and a salutary warning.]

[Footnote 37: Pope John XXII. (in 1334) left behind him, at Avignon, eighteen millions of gold florins, and the value of seven millions more in plate and jewels. See the Chronicle of John Villani, (l. xi. c. 20, in Muratori's Collection, tom. xiii. p. 765,) whose brother received the account from the papal treasurers. A treasure of six or eight millions sterling in the xivth century is enormous, and almost incredible.]

[Footnote 38: A learned and liberal Protestant, M. Lenfant, has given a fair history of the councils of Pisa, Constance, and Basil, in six volumes in quarto; but the last part is the most hasty and imperfect, except in the account of the troubles of Bohemia.]

[Footnote 39: The original acts or minutes of the council of Basil are preserved in the public library, in twelve volumes in folio. Basil was a free city, conveniently situate on the Rhine, and guarded by the arms of the neighboring and confederate Swiss. In 1459, the university was founded by Pope Pius II., (Æneas Sylvius,) who had been secretary to the council. But what is a council, or a university, to the presses o Froben and the studies of Erasmus?]

[Footnote 40: This Turkish embassy, attested only by Crantzius, is related with some doubt by the annalist Spondanus, A.D. 1433, No. 25, tom. i. p. 824.]

[Footnote 41: Syropulus, p. 19. In this list, the Greeks appear to have exceeded the real numbers of the clergy and laity which afterwards attended the emperor and patriarch, but which are not clearly specified by the great ecclesiarch. The 75,000 florins which they asked in this negotiation of the pope, (p. 9,) were more than they could hope or want.]

[Footnote 42: I use indifferently the words ducat and florin, which derive their names, the former from the dukes of Milan, the latter from the republic of Florence. These gold pieces, the first that were coined in Italy, perhaps in the Latin world, may be compared in weight and value to one third of the English guinea.]

In his distress, the friendship of Palæologus was disputed by the ecclesiastical powers of the West; but the dexterous activity of a monarch prevailed over the slow debates and inflexible temper of a republic. The decrees of Basil continually tended to circumscribe the despotism of the pope, and to erect a supreme and perpetual tribunal in the church. Eugenius was impatient of the yoke; and the union of the Greeks might afford a decent pretence for translating a rebellious synod from the Rhine to the Po. The independence of the fathers was lost if they passed the Alps: Savoy or Avignon, to which they acceded with reluctance, were described at Constantinople as situate far beyond the pillars of Hercules; [43] the emperor and his clergy were apprehensive of the dangers of a long navigation; they were offended by a haughty declaration, that after suppressing the new heresy of the Bohemians, the council would soon eradicate the old heresy of the Greeks. [44] On the side of Eugenius, all was smooth, and yielding, and respectful; and he invited the Byzantine monarch to heal by his presence the schism of the Latin, as well as of the Eastern, church. Ferrara, near the coast of the Adriatic, was proposed for their amicable interview; and with some indulgence of forgery and theft, a surreptitious decree was procured, which transferred the synod, with its own consent, to that Italian city. Nine galleys were equipped for the service at Venice, and in the Isle of Candia; their diligence anticipated the slower vessels of Basil: the Roman admiral was commissioned to burn, sink, and destroy; [45] and these priestly squadrons might have encountered each other in the same seas where Athens and Sparta had formerly contended for the preeminence of glory. Assaulted by the importunity of the factions, who were ready to fight for the possession of his person, Palæologus hesitated before he left his palace and country on a perilous experiment. His father's advice still dwelt on his memory; and reason must suggest, that since the Latins were divided among themselves, they could never unite in a foreign cause. Sigismond dissuaded the unreasonable adventure; his advice was impartial, since he adhered to the council; and it was enforced by the strange belief, that the German Cæsar would nominate a Greek his heir and successor in the empire of the West. [46] Even the Turkish sultan was a counsellor whom it might be unsafe to trust, but whom it was dangerous to offend. Amurath was unskilled in the disputes, but he was apprehensive of the union, of the Christians. From his own treasures, he offered to relieve the wants of the Byzantine court; yet he declared with seeming magnanimity, that Constantinople should be secure and inviolate, in the absence of her sovereign. [47] The resolution of Palæologus was decided by the most splendid gifts and the most specious promises: he wished to escape for a while from a scene of danger and distress and after dismissing with an ambiguous answer the messengers of the council, he declared his intention of embarking in the Roman galleys. The age of the patriarch Joseph was more susceptible of fear than of hope; he trembled at the perils of the sea, and expressed his apprehension, that his feeble voice, with thirty perhaps of his orthodox brethren, would be oppressed in a foreign land by the power and numbers of a Latin synod. He yielded to the royal mandate, to the flattering assurance, that he would be heard as the oracle of nations, and to the secret wish of learning from his brother of the West, to deliver the church from the yoke of kings. [48] The five cross-bearers, or dignitaries, of St. Sophia, were bound to attend his person; and one of these, the great ecclesiarch or preacher, Sylvester Syropulus, [49] has composed a free and curious history [50] of the false union. [51] Of the clergy that reluctantly obeyed the summons of the emperor and the patriarch, submission was the first duty, and patience the most useful virtue. In a chosen list of twenty bishops, we discover the metropolitan titles of Heracleæ and Cyzicus, Nice and Nicomedia, Ephesus and Trebizond, and the personal merit of Mark and Bessarion who, in the confidence of their learning and eloquence, were promoted to the episcopal rank. Some monks and philosophers were named to display the science and sanctity of the Greek church; and the service of the choir was performed by a select band of singers and musicians. The patriarchs of Alexandria, Antioch, and Jerusalem, appeared by their genuine or fictitious deputies; the primate of Russia represented a national church, and the Greeks might contend with the Latins in the extent of their spiritual empire. The precious vases of St. Sophia were exposed to the winds and waves, that the patriarch might officiate with becoming splendor: whatever gold the emperor could procure, was expended in the massy ornaments of his bed and chariot; [52] and while they affected to maintain the prosperity of their ancient fortune, they quarrelled for the division of fifteen thousand ducats, the first alms of the Roman pontiff. After the necessary preparations, John Palæologus, with a numerous train, accompanied by his brother Demetrius, and the most respectable persons of the church and state, embarked in eight vessels with sails and oars which steered through the Turkish Straits of Gallipoli to the Archipelago, the Morea, and the Adriatic Gulf. [53]

[Footnote 43: At the end of the Latin version of Phranzes, we read a long Greek epistle or declamation of George of Trebizond, who advises the emperor to prefer Eugenius and Italy. He treats with contempt the schismatic assembly of Basil, the Barbarians of Gaul and Germany, who had conspired to transport the chair of St. Peter beyond the Alps; oi aqlioi (says he) se kai thn meta sou sunodon exw tvn 'Hrakleiwn sthlwn kai pera Gadhrwn exaxousi. Was Constantinople unprovided with a map?]

[Footnote 44: Syropulus (p. 26—31) attests his own indignation, and that of his countrymen; and the Basil deputies, who excused the rash declaration, could neither deny nor alter an act of the council.]

[Footnote 45: Condolmieri, the pope's nephew and admiral, expressly declared, oti orismon eceipara tou Papa ina polemhsh opou an eurh ta katerga thV Sunodou, kai ei dunhqh, katadush, kai ajanish. The naval orders of the synod were less peremptory, and, till the hostile squadrons appeared, both parties tried to conceal their quarrel from the Greeks.]

[Footnote 46: Syropulus mentions the hopes of Palæologus, (p. 36,) and the last advice of Sigismond,(p. 57.) At Corfu, the Greek emperor was informed of his friend's death; had he known it sooner, he would have returned home,(p. 79.)]

[Footnote 47: Phranzes himself, though from different motives, was of the advice of Amurath, (l. ii. c. 13.) Utinam ne synodus ista unquam fuisset, si tantes offensiones et detrimenta paritura erat. This Turkish embassy is likewise mentioned by Syropulus, (p. 58;) and Amurath kept his word. He might threaten, (p. 125, 219,) but he never attacked, the city.]

[Footnote 48: The reader will smile at the simplicity with which he imparted these hopes to his favorites: toiauthn plhrojorian schsein hlpize kai dia tou Papa eqarrei eleuqervdai thn ekklhsian apo thV apoteqeishV autou douleiaV para tou basilewV, (p. 92.) Yet it would have been difficult for him to have practised the lessons of Gregory VII.]

[Footnote 49: The Christian name of Sylvester is borrowed from the Latin calendar. In modern Greek, pouloV, as a diminutive, is added to the end of words: nor can any reasoning of Creyghton, the editor, excuse his changing into Sguropulus, (Sguros, fuscus,) the Syropulus of his own manuscript, whose name is subscribed with his own hand in the acts of the council of Florence. Why might not the author be of Syrian extraction?]

[Footnote 50: From the conclusion of the history, I should fix the date to the year 1444, four years after the synod, when great ecclesiarch had abdicated his office, (section xii. p. 330—350.) His passions were cooled by time and retirement; and, although Syropulus is often partial, he is never intemperate.]

[Footnote 51: Vera historia unionis non ver inter Græcos et Latinos, (Haga Comitis, 1660, in folio,) was first published with a loose and florid version, by Robert Creyghton, chaplain to Charles II. in his exile. The zeal of the editor has prefixed a polemic title, for the beginning of the original is wanting. Syropulus may be ranked with the best of the Byzantine writers for the merit of his narration, and even of his style; but he is excluded from the orthodox collections of the councils.]

[Footnote 52: Syropulus (p. 63) simply expresses his intention in' outw pompawn en' 'ItaloiV megaV basileuV par ekeinvn nomizoito; and the Latin of Creyghton may afford a specimen of his florid paraphrase. Ut pompâ circumductus noster Imperator Italiæ populis aliquis deauratus Jupiter crederetur, aut Crsus ex opulenta Lydia.]

[Footnote 53: Although I cannot stop to quote Syropulus for every fact, I will observe that the navigation of the Greeks from Constantinople to Venice and Ferrara is contained in the ivth section, (p. 67—100,) and that the historian has the uncommon talent of placing each scene before the reader's eye.]

PART III

After a tedious and troublesome navigation of seventy-seven days, this religious squadron cast anchor before Venice; and their reception proclaimed the joy and magnificence of that powerful republic. In the command of the world, the modest Augustus had never claimed such honors from his subjects as were paid to his feeble successor by an independent state. Seated on the poop on a lofty throne, he received the visit, or, in the Greek style, the adoration of the doge and senators. [54] They sailed in the Bucentaur, which was accompanied by twelve stately galleys: the sea was overspread with innumerable gondolas of pomp and pleasure; the air resounded with music and acclamations; the mariners, and even the vessels, were dressed in silk and gold; and in all the emblems and pageants, the Roman eagles were blended with the lions of St. Mark. The triumphal procession, ascending the great canal, passed under the bridge of the Rialto; and the Eastern strangers gazed with admiration on the palaces, the churches, and the populousness of a city, that seems to float on the bosom of the waves. [55] They sighed to behold the spoils and trophies with which it had been decorated after the sack of Constantinople. After a hospitable entertainment of fifteen days, Palæologus pursued his journey by land and water from Venice to Ferrara; and on this occasion the pride of the Vatican was tempered by policy to indulge the ancient dignity of the emperor of the East. He made his entry on a black horse; but a milk-white steed, whose trappings were embroidered with golden eagles, was led before him; and the canopy was borne over his head by the princes of Este, the sons or kinsmen of Nicholas, marquis of the city, and a sovereign more powerful than himself. [56] Palæologus did not alight till he reached the bottom of the staircase: the pope advanced to the door of the apartment; refused his proffered genuflection; and, after a paternal embrace, conducted the emperor to a seat on his left hand. Nor would the patriarch descend from his galley, till a ceremony almost equal, had been stipulated between the bishops of Rome and Constantinople. The latter was saluted by his brother with a kiss of union and charity; nor would any of the Greek ecclesiastics submit to kiss the feet of the Western primate. On the opening of the synod, the place of honor in the centre was claimed by the temporal and ecclesiastical chiefs; and it was only by alleging that his predecessors had not assisted in person at Nice or Chalcedon, that Eugenius could evade the ancient precedents of Constantine and Marcian. After much debate, it was agreed that the right and left sides of the church should be occupied by the two nations; that the solitary chair of St. Peter should be raised the first of the Latin line; and that the throne of the Greek emperor, at the head of his clergy, should be equal and opposite to the second place, the vacant seat of the emperor of the West. [57]

*[Footnote 54: At the time of the synod, Phranzes was in Peloponnesus: but he received from the despot Demetrius a faithful account of the honorable reception of the emperor and patriarch both at Venice and Ferrara, (Dux.... sedentem Imperatorem adorat,) which are more slightly mentioned by the Latins, (l. ii. c. 14, 15, 16.)]*

*[Footnote 55: The astonishment of a Greek prince and a French ambassador (Mémoires de Philippe de Comines, l. vii. c. 18,) at the sight of Venice, abundantly proves that in the xvth century it was the first and most splendid of the Christian cities. For the spoils of Constantinople at Venice, see Syropulus, (p. 87.)]*

*[Footnote 56: Nicholas III. of Este reigned forty-eight years, (A.D. 1393—1441,) and was lord of Ferrara, Modena, Reggio, Parma, Rovigo, and Commachio. See his Life in Muratori, (Antichità Estense, tom. ii. p. 159—201.)]*

*[Footnote 57: The Latin vulgar was provoked to laughter at the strange dresses of the Greeks, and especially the length of their garments, their sleeves, and their beards; nor was the emperor distinguished, except by the purple color, and his diadem or tiara, with a jewel on the top, (Hody de Græcis Illustribus, p. 31.) Yet another spectator confesses that the Greek fashion was piu grave e piu degna than the Italian. (Vespasiano in Vit. Eugen. IV. in Muratori, tom. xxv. p. 261.)]*

But as soon as festivity and form had given place to a more serious treaty, the Greeks were dissatisfied with their journey, with themselves, and with the pope. The artful pencil of his emissaries had painted him in a prosperous state; at the head of the princes and prelates of Europe, obedient at his voice, to believe and to arm. The thin appearance of the universal synod of Ferrara betrayed his weakness: and the Latins opened the first session with only five archbishops, eighteen bishops, and ten abbots, the greatest part of whom were the subjects or countrymen of the Italian pontiff. Except the duke of

Burgundy, none of the potentates of the West condescended to appear in person, or by their ambassadors; nor was it possible to suppress the judicial acts of Basil against the dignity and person of Eugenius, which were finally concluded by a new election. Under these circumstances, a truce or delay was asked and granted, till Palæologus could expect from the consent of the Latins some temporal reward for an unpopular union; and after the first session, the public proceedings were adjourned above six months. The emperor, with a chosen band of his favorites and Janizaries, fixed his summer residence at a pleasant, spacious monastery, six miles from Ferrara; forgot, in the pleasures of the chase, the distress of the church and state; and persisted in destroying the game, without listening to the just complaints of the marquis or the husbandman. [58] In the mean while, his unfortunate Greeks were exposed to all the miseries of exile and poverty; for the support of each stranger, a monthly allowance was assigned of three or four gold florins; and although the entire sum did not amount to seven hundred florins, a long arrear was repeatedly incurred by the indigence or policy of the Roman court. [59] They sighed for a speedy deliverance, but their escape was prevented by a triple chain: a passport from their superiors was required at the gates of Ferrara; the government of Venice had engaged to arrest and send back the fugitives; and inevitable punishment awaited them at Constantinople; excommunication, fines, and a sentence, which did not respect the sacerdotal dignity, that they should be stripped naked and publicly whipped. [60] It was only by the alternative of hunger or dispute that the Greeks could be persuaded to open the first conference; and they yielded with extreme reluctance to attend from Ferrara to Florence the rear of a flying synod. This new translation was urged by inevitable necessity: the city was visited by the plague; the fidelity of the marquis might be suspected; the mercenary troops of the duke of Milan were at the gates; and as they occupied Romagna, it was not without difficulty and danger that the pope, the emperor, and the bishops, explored their way through the unfrequented paths of the Apennine. [61]

[Footnote 58: For the emperor's hunting, see Syropulus, (p. 143, 144, 191.) The pope had sent him eleven miserable hacks; but he bought a strong and swift horse that came from Russia. The name of Janizaries may surprise; but the name, rather than the institution, had passed from the Ottoman, to the Byzantine, court, and is often used in the last age of the empire.]

[Footnote 59: The Greeks obtained, with much difficulty, that instead of provisions, money should be distributed, four florins per month to the persons of honorable rank, and three florins to their servants, with an addition of thirty more to the emperor, twenty-five to the patriarch, and twenty to the prince, or despot, Demetrius. The payment of the first month amounted to 691 florins, a sum which will not allow us to reckon above 200 Greeks of every condition. (Syropulus, p. 104, 105.) On the 20th October, 1438, there was an arrear of four months; in April, 1439, of three; and of five and a half in July, at the time of the union, (p. 172, 225, 271.)]

[Footnote 60: Syropulus (p. 141, 142, 204, 221) deplores the imprisonment of the Greeks, and the tyranny of the emperor and patriarch.]

[Footnote 61: The wars of Italy are most clearly represented in the xiiith vol. of the Annals of Muratori. The schismatic Greek, Syropulus, (p. 145,) appears to have exaggerated the fear and disorder of the pope in his retreat from Ferrara to Florence, which is proved by the acts to have been somewhat more decent and deliberate.]

Yet all these obstacles were surmounted by time and policy. The violence of the fathers of Basil rather promoted than injured the cause of Eugenius; the nations of Europe abhorred the schism, and disowned the election, of Felix the Fifth, who was successively a duke of Savoy, a hermit, and a pope; and the great princes were gradually reclaimed by his competitor to a favorable neutrality and a firm attachment. The legates, with some respectable members, deserted to the Roman army, which insensibly rose in numbers and reputation; the council of Basil was reduced to thirty-nine bishops, and three hundred of the inferior clergy; [62] while the Latins of Florence could produce the subscriptions of the pope himself, eight cardinals, two patriarchs, eight archbishops, fifty two bishops, and forty-five abbots, or chiefs of religious orders. After the labor of nine months, and the debates of twenty-five sessions, they attained the advantage and glory of the reunion of the Greeks. Four principal questions had been agitated between the two churches; 1. The use of unleavened bread in the communion of Christ's body. 2. The nature of purgatory. 3. The supremacy of the pope. And, 4. The single or double procession of the Holy Ghost. The cause of either nation was managed by ten theological champions: the Latins were supported by the inexhaustible eloquence of Cardinal Julian; and Mark of Ephesus and Bessarion of Nice were the bold and able leaders of the Greek forces. We may bestow some praise on the progress of human reason, by observing that the first of these questions was now treated as an immaterial rite, which might innocently vary with the fashion of the age and country. With regard to the second, both parties were agreed in the belief of an intermediate state of purgation for the venial sins of the faithful; and whether their souls were purified by elemental fire was a doubtful point, which in a few years might be conveniently settled on the spot by the disputants. The claims of supremacy appeared of a more weighty and substantial kind; yet by the Orientals the Roman bishop had ever been respected as the first of the five patriarchs; nor did they scruple to admit, that his jurisdiction should be exercised agreeably to the holy canons; a vague allowance, which might be defined or eluded by occasional convenience. The procession of the Holy Ghost from the Father alone, or from the Father and the Son, was an article of faith which had sunk much deeper into the minds of men; and in the sessions of Ferrara and Florence, the Latin addition of filioque was subdivided into two questions, whether it were legal, and whether it were orthodox. Perhaps it may not be necessary to boast on this subject of my own impartial indifference; but I must think that the Greeks were strongly supported by the prohibition of the council of Chalcedon, against adding any article whatsoever to the creed of Nice, or rather of Constantinople. [63] In earthly affairs, it is not easy to conceive how an assembly equal of legislators can bind their successors invested with powers equal to their own. But the dictates of inspiration must be true and unchangeable; nor should a private bishop, or a provincial synod, have presumed to innovate against the judgment of the Catholic church. On the substance of the doctrine, the controversy was equal and endless: reason is confounded by the procession of a deity: the gospel, which lay on the altar, was silent; the various texts of the fathers might be corrupted by fraud or entangled by sophistry; and the Greeks were ignorant of the characters and writings of the Latin saints. [64] Of this at least we may be sure, that neither side could be convinced by the arguments of their opponents. Prejudice may be enlightened by reason, and a superficial glance may be rectified by a clear and more perfect view of an object adapted to our faculties. But the bishops and monks had been taught from their infancy to repeat a form of mysterious words: their national and personal honor depended on the repetition of the same sounds; and their narrow minds were hardened and inflamed by the acrimony of a public dispute.

[Footnote 62: Syropulus is pleased to reckon seven hundred prelates in the council of Basil. The error is manifest, and perhaps voluntary. That extravagant number could not be supplied by all the ecclesiastics of every degree who were present at the council, nor by all the absent bishops of the West, who, expressly or tacitly, might adhere to its decrees.]

[Footnote 63: The Greeks, who disliked the union, were unwilling to sally from this strong fortress, (p. 178, 193, 195, 202, of Syropulus.) The shame of the Latins was aggravated by their producing an old MS. of the second council of Nice, with filioque in the Nicene creed. A palpable forgery! (p. 173.)]

[Footnote 64: 'WV egw (said an eminent Greek) otan eiV naon eiselqw Datinwn ou proskunv tina tvn ekeise agiwn, epei oude gnwrizw tina, (Syropulus, p. 109.) See the perplexity of the Greeks, (p. 217, 218, 252, 253, 273.)]

While they were most in a cloud of dust and darkness, the Pope and emperor were desirous of a seeming union, which could alone accomplish the purposes of their interview; and the obstinacy of public dispute was softened by the arts of private and personal negotiation. The patriarch Joseph had sunk under the weight of age and infirmities; his dying voice breathed the counsels of charity and concord, and his vacant benefice might tempt the hopes of the ambitious clergy. The ready and active obedience of the archbishops of Russia and Nice, of Isidore and Bessarion, was prompted and recompensed by their speedy promotion to the dignity of cardinals. Bessarion, in the first debates, had stood forth the most strenuous and eloquent champion of the Greek church; and if the apostate, the bastard, was reprobated by his country, [65] he appears in ecclesiastical story a rare example of a patriot who was recommended to court favor by loud opposition and well-timed compliance. With the aid of his two spiritual coadjutors, the emperor applied his arguments to the general situation and personal characters of the bishops, and each was successively moved by authority and example. Their revenues were in the hands of the Turks, their persons in those of the Latins: an episcopal treasure, three robes and forty ducats, was soon exhausted: [66] the hopes of their return still depended on the ships of Venice and the alms of Rome; and such was their indigence, that their arrears, the payment of a debt, would be accepted as a favor, and might operate as a bribe. [67] The danger and relief of Constantinople might excuse some prudent and pious dissimulation; and it was insinuated, that the obstinate heretics who should resist the consent of the East and West would be abandoned in a hostile land to the revenge or justice of the Roman pontiff. [68] In the first private assembly of the Greeks, the formulary of union was approved by twenty-four, and rejected by twelve, members; but the five cross-bearers of St. Sophia, who aspired to represent the patriarch, were disqualified by ancient discipline; and their right of voting was transferred to the obsequious train of monks, grammarians, and profane laymen. The will of the monarch produced a false and servile unanimity, and no more than two patriots had courage to speak their own sentiments and those of their country. Demetrius, the emperor's brother, retired to Venice, that he might not be witness of the union; and Mark of Ephesus, mistaking perhaps his pride for his conscience, disclaimed all communion with the Latin heretics, and avowed himself the champion and confessor of the orthodox creed. [69] In the treaty between the two nations, several forms of consent were proposed, such as might satisfy the Latins, without dishonoring the Greeks; and they weighed the scruples of words and syllables, till the theological balance trembled with a slight preponderance in favor of the Vatican. It was agreed (I must entreat the attention of the reader) that the Holy Ghost proceeds from the Father and the Son, as from one principle and one substance; that he proceeds by the Son, being of the same nature and substance, and that he proceeds from the Father and the Son, by one spiration and production. It is less difficult to understand the articles of the preliminary treaty; that the pope should defray all the expenses of the Greeks in their return home; that he should annually maintain two galleys and three hundred soldiers for the defence of Constantinople: that all the ships which transported pilgrims to Jerusalem should be obliged to touch at that port; that as often as they were required, the pope should furnish ten galleys for a year, or twenty for six months; and that he should powerfully solicit the princes of Europe, if the emperor had occasion for land forces.

[Footnote 65: See the polite altercation of Marc and Bessarion in Syropulus, (p. 257,) who never dissembles the vices of his own party, and fairly praises the virtues of the Latins.]

[Footnote 66: For the poverty of the Greek bishops, see a remarkable passage of Ducas, (c. 31.) One had possessed, for his whole property, three old gowns, &c. By teaching one-and-twenty years in his monastery, Bessarion himself had collected forty gold florins; but of these, the archbishop had expended twenty-eight in his voyage from Peloponnesus, and the remainder at Constantinople, (Syropulus, p. 127.)]

[Footnote 67: Syropulus denies that the Greeks received any money before they had subscribed the art of union, (p. 283:) yet he relates some suspicious circumstances; and their bribery and corruption are positively affirmed by the historian Ducas.]

[Footnote 68: The Greeks most piteously express their own fears of exile and perpetual slavery, (Syropul. p. 196;) and they were strongly moved by the emperor's threats, (p. 260.)]

[Footnote 69: I had forgot another popular and orthodox protester: a favorite bound, who usually lay quiet on the foot-cloth of the emperor's throne but who barked most furiously while the act of union was reading without being silenced by the soothing or the lashes of the royal attendants, (Syropul. p. 265, 266.)]

The same year, and almost the same day, were marked by the deposition of Eugenius at Basil; and, at Florence, by his reunion of the Greeks and Latins. In the former synod, (which he styled indeed an assembly of dæmons,) the pope was branded with the guilt of simony, perjury, tyranny, heresy, and schism; [70] and declared to be incorrigible in his vices, unworthy of any title, and incapable of holding any ecclesiastical office. In the latter, he was revered as the true and holy vicar of Christ, who, after a separation of six hundred years, had reconciled the Catholics of the East and West in one fold, and under one shepherd. The act of union was subscribed by the pope, the emperor, and the principal members of both churches; even by those who, like Syropulus, [71] had been deprived of the right of voting. Two copies might have sufficed for the East and West; but Eugenius was not satisfied, unless four authentic and similar transcripts were signed and attested as the monuments of his victory. [72] On a memorable day, the sixth of July, the successors of St. Peter and Constantine ascended their thrones the two nations assembled in the cathedral of Florence; their representatives, Cardinal Julian and Bessarion archbishop of Nice, appeared in the pulpit, and, after reading in their respective tongues the act of union, they mutually embraced, in the name and the presence of their applauding brethren. The pope and his ministers then officiated according to the Roman liturgy; the creed was chanted with the addition of filioque; the acquiescence of the Greeks was poorly excused by their ignorance of the harmonious, but inarticulate sounds; [73] and the more scrupulous Latins refused any public celebration of the Byzantine rite. Yet the emperor and his clergy were not totally unmindful of national honor. The treaty was ratified by their consent: it was tacitly agreed that no innovation should be attempted in their creed or ceremonies: they spared, and secretly respected, the generous firmness of Mark of Ephesus; and, on the decease of the patriarch, they refused to elect his successor, except in the cathedral of St. Sophia. In the distribution of public and private rewards, the liberal pontiff exceeded his hopes and his promises: the Greeks, with less pomp and pride, returned by the same road of Ferrara and Venice; and their reception at Constantinople was such as will be described in the following chapter. [74] The success of the first trial encouraged Eugenius to repeat the same edifying scenes; and the deputies of the Armenians, the Maronites, the Jacobites of Syria and Egypt, the Nestorians and the Æthiopians, were successively introduced, to kiss the feet of the Roman pontiff, and to announce the obedience and the orthodoxy of the East. These Oriental embassies, unknown in the countries which they presumed to represent, [75] diffused over the West the fame of Eugenius; and a clamor was artfully propagated against the remnant of a schism in Switzerland and Savoy, which alone impeded the harmony of the Christian world. The vigor of opposition was succeeded by the lassitude of despair: the council of Basil was silently dissolved; and Felix, renouncing the tiara, again withdrew to the devout or delicious hermitage of Ripaille. [76] A general peace was secured by mutual acts of oblivion and indemnity: all ideas of reformation subsided; the popes continued to exercise and abuse their ecclesiastical despotism; nor has Rome been since disturbed by the mischiefs of a contested election. [77]

[Footnote 70: From the original Lives of the Popes, in Muratori's Collection, (tom. iii. p. ii. tom. xxv.,) the manners of Eugenius IV. appear to have been decent, and even exemplary. His situation, exposed to the world and to his enemies, was a restraint, and is a pledge.]

[Footnote 71: Syropulus, rather than subscribe, would have assisted, as the least evil, at the ceremony of the union. He was compelled to do both; and the great ecclesiarch poorly excuses his submission to the emperor, (p. 290—292.)]

[Footnote 72: None of these original acts of union can at present be produced. Of the ten MSS. that are preserved, (five at Rome, and the remainder at Florence, Bologna, Venice, Paris, and London,) nine have been examined by an accurate critic, (M. de Brequigny,) who condemns them for the variety and imperfections of the Greek signatures. Yet several of these may be esteemed as authentic copies, which were subscribed at Florence, before (26th of August, 1439) the final separation of the pope and emperor, (Mémoires de l'Académie des Inscriptions, tom. xliii. p. 287—311.)]

[Footnote 73: Hmin de wV ashmoi edokoun jwnai, (Syropul. p. 297.)]

[Footnote 74: In their return, the Greeks conversed at Bologna with the ambassadors of England: and after some questions and answers, these impartial strangers laughed at the pretended union of Florence, (Syropul. p. 307.)]

[Footnote 75: So nugatory, or rather so fabulous, are these reunions of the Nestorians, Jacobites, &c., that I have turned over, without success, the Bibliotheca Orientalis of Assemannus, a faithful slave of the Vatican.]

[Footnote 76: Ripaille is situate near Thonon in Savoy, on the southern side of the Lake of Geneva. It is now a Carthusian abbey; and Mr. Addison (Travels into Italy, vol. ii. p. 147, 148, of Baskerville's edition of his works) has celebrated the place and the founder. Æneas Sylvius, and the fathers of Basil, applaud the austere life of the ducal hermit; but the French and Italian proverbs most unluckily attest the popular opinion of his luxury.]

[Footnote 77: In this account of the councils of Basil, Ferrara, and Florence, I have consulted the original acts, which fill the xviith and xviiith tome of the edition of Venice, and are closed by the perspicuous, though partial, history of Augustin Patricius, an Italian of the xvth century. They are digested and abridged by Dupin, (Bibliothèque Ecclés. tom. xii.,) and the continuator of Fleury, (tom. xxii.;) and the respect of the Gallican church for the adverse parties confines their members to an awkward moderation.]

The journeys of three emperors were unavailing for their temporal, or perhaps their spiritual, salvation; but they were productive of a beneficial consequence—the revival of the Greek learning in Italy, from whence it was propagated to the last nations of the West and North. In their lowest servitude and depression, the subjects of the Byzantine throne were still possessed of a golden key that could unlock the treasures of antiquity; of a musical and prolific language, that gives a soul to the objects of sense, and a body to the abstractions of philosophy. Since the barriers of the monarchy, and even of the capital, had been trampled under foot, the various Barbarians had doubtless corrupted the form and substance of the national dialect; and ample glossaries have been composed, to interpret a multitude of words, of Arabic, Turkish, Sclavonian, Latin, or French origin. [78] But a purer idiom was spoken in the court and taught in the college; and the flourishing state of the language is described, and perhaps embellished, by a learned Italian, [79] who, by a long residence and noble marriage, [80] was naturalized at Constantinople about thirty years before the Turkish conquest. "The vulgar speech," says Philelphus, [81] "has been depraved by the people, and infected by the multitude of strangers and merchants, who every day flock to the city and mingle with the inhabitants. It is from the disciples of such a school that the Latin language received the versions of Aristotle and Plato; so obscure in sense, and in spirit so poor. But the Greeks who have escaped the contagion, are those whom we follow; and they alone are worthy of our imitation. In familiar discourse, they still speak the tongue of Aristophanes and Euripides, of the historians and philosophers of Athens; and the style of their writings is still more elaborate and correct. The persons who, by their birth and offices, are attached to the Byzantine court, are those who maintain, with the least alloy, the ancient standard of elegance and purity; and the native graces of language most conspicuously shine among the noble matrons, who are excluded from all intercourse with foreigners. With foreigners do I say? They live retired and sequestered from the eyes of their fellow-citizens. Seldom are they seen in the streets; and when they leave their houses, it is in the dusk of evening, on visits to the churches and their nearest kindred. On these occasions, they are on horseback, covered with a veil, and encompassed by their parents, their husbands, or their servants." [82]

[Footnote 78: In the first attempt, Meursius collected 3600 Græco-barbarous words, to which, in a second edition, he subjoined 1800 more; yet what plenteous gleanings did he leave to Portius, Ducange, Fabrotti, the Bollandists, &c.! (Fabric. Bibliot. Græc. tom. x. p. 101, &c.) Some Persic words may be found in Xenophon, and some Latin ones in Plutarch; and such is the inevitable effect of war and commerce; but the form and substance of the language were not affected by this slight alloy.]

[Footnote 79: The life of Francis Philelphus, a sophist, proud, restless, and rapacious, has been diligently composed by Lancelot (Mémoires de l'Académie des Inscriptions, tom. x. p. 691—751) (Istoria della Letteratura Italiana, tom. vii. p. 282—294,) for the most part from his own letters. His elaborate writings, and those of his contemporaries, are forgotten; but their familiar epistles still describe the men and the times.]

[Footnote 80: He married, and had perhaps debauched, the daughter of John, and the granddaughter of Manuel Chrysoloras. She was young, beautiful, and wealthy; and her noble family was allied to the Dorias of Genoa and the emperors of Constantinople.]

[Footnote 81: Græci quibus lingua depravata non sit.... ita loquuntur vulgo hâc etiam tempestate ut Aristophanes comicus, aut Euripides tragicus, ut oratores omnes, ut historiographi, ut philosophi.... litterati autem homines et doctius et emendatius.... Nam viri aulici veterem sermonis dignitatem atque elegantiam retinebant in primisque ipsæ nobiles mulieres; quibus cum nullum esset omnino cum viris peregrinis commercium, merus ille ac purus Græcorum sermo servabatur intactus, (Philelph. Epist. ad ann. 1451, apud Hodium, p. 188, 189.) He observes in another passage, uxor illa mea Theodora locutione erat admodum moderatâ et suavi et maxime Atticâ.]

[Footnote 82: Philelphus, absurdly enough, derives this Greek or Oriental jealousy from the manners of ancient Rome.]

Among the Greeks a numerous and opulent clergy was dedicated to the service of religion: their monks and bishops have ever been distinguished by the gravity and austerity of their manners; nor were they diverted, like the Latin priests, by the pursuits and pleasures of a secular, and even military, life. After a large deduction for the time and talent that were lost in the devotion, the laziness, and the discord, of the church and cloister, the more inquisitive and ambitious minds would explore the sacred and profane erudition of their native language. The ecclesiastics presided over the education of youth; the schools of philosophy and eloquence were perpetuated till the fall of the empire; and it may be affirmed, that more books and more knowledge were included within the walls of Constantinople, than could be dispersed over the extensive countries of the West. [83] But an important distinction has been already noticed: the Greeks were stationary or retrograde, while the Latins were advancing with a rapid and progressive motion. The nations were excited by the spirit of independence and emulation; and even the little world of the Italian states contained more people and industry than the decreasing circle of the Byzantine empire. In Europe, the lower ranks of society were relieved from the yoke of feudal servitude; and freedom is the first step to curiosity and knowledge. The use, however rude and corrupt, of the Latin tongue had been preserved by superstition; the universities, from Bologna to Oxford, [84] were peopled with thousands of scholars; and their misguided ardor might be directed to more liberal and manly studies. In the resurrection of science, Italy was the first that cast away her shroud; and the eloquent Petrarch, by his lessons and his example, may justly be applauded as the first harbinger of day. A purer style of composition, a more generous and rational strain of sentiment, flowed from the study and imitation of the writers of ancient Rome; and the disciples of Cicero and Virgil approached, with reverence and love, the sanctuary of their Grecian masters. In the sack of Constantinople, the French, and even the Venetians, had despised and destroyed the works of Lysippus and Homer: the monuments of art may be annihilated by a single blow; but the immortal mind is renewed and multiplied by the copies of the pen; and such copies it was the ambition of Petrarch and his friends to possess and understand. The arms of the Turks undoubtedly pressed the flight of the Muses; yet we may tremble at the thought, that Greece might have been overwhelmed, with her schools and libraries, before Europe had emerged from the deluge of barbarism; that the seeds of science might have been scattered by the winds, before the Italian soil was prepared for their cultivation.

[Footnote 83: See the state of learning in the xiiith and xivth centuries, in the learned and judicious Mosheim, (Instit. Hist. Ecclés. p. 434—440, 490—494.)]

[Footnote 84: At the end of the xvth century, there existed in Europe about fifty universities, and of these the foundation of ten or twelve is prior to the year 1300. They were crowded in proportion to their scarcity. Bologna contained 10,000 students, chiefly of the civil law. In the year 1357 the number at Oxford had decreased from 30,000 to 6000 scholars, (Henry's History of Great Britain, vol. iv. p. 478.) Yet even this decrease is much superior to the present list of the members of the university.]

PART IV

The most learned Italians of the fifteenth century have confessed and applauded the restoration of Greek literature, after a long oblivion of many hundred years. [85] Yet in that country, and beyond the Alps, some names are quoted; some profound scholars, who in the darker ages were honorably distinguished by their knowledge of the Greek tongue; and national vanity has been loud in the praise of such rare examples of erudition. Without scrutinizing the merit of individuals, truth must observe, that their science is without a cause, and without an effect; that it was easy for them to satisfy themselves and their more ignorant contemporaries; and that the idiom, which they had so marvellously acquired was transcribed in few manuscripts, and was not taught in any university of the West. In a corner of Italy, it faintly existed as the popular, or at least as the ecclesiastical dialect. [86] The first impression of the Doric and Ionic colonies has never been completely erased: the Calabrian churches were long attached to the throne of Constantinople: and the monks of St. Basil pursued their studies in Mount Athos and the schools of the East. Calabria was the native country of Barlaam, who has already appeared as a sectary and an ambassador; and Barlaam was the first who revived, beyond the Alps, the memory, or at least the writings, of Homer. [87] He is described, by Petrarch and Boccace, [88] as a man of diminutive stature, though truly great in the measure of learning and genius; of a piercing discernment, though of a slow and painful elocution. For many ages (as they affirm) Greece had not produced his equal in the knowledge of history, grammar, and philosophy; and his merit was celebrated in the attestations of the princes and doctors of Constantinople. One of these attestations is still extant; and the emperor Cantacuzene, the protector of his adversaries, is forced to allow, that Euclid, Aristotle, and Plato, were familiar to that profound and subtle logician. [89] In the court of Avignon, he formed an intimate connection with Petrarch, [90] the first of the Latin scholars; and the desire of mutual instruction was the principle of their literary commerce. The Tuscan applied himself with eager curiosity and assiduous diligence to the study of the Greek language; and in a laborious struggle with the dryness and difficulty of the first rudiments, he began to reach the sense, and to feel the spirit, of poets and philosophers, whose minds were congenial to his own. But he was soon deprived of the society and lessons of this useful assistant: Barlaam relinquished his fruitless embassy; and, on his return to Greece, he rashly provoked the swarms of fanatic monks, by attempting to substitute the light of reason to that of their navel. After a separation of three years, the two friends again met in the court of Naples: but the generous pupil renounced the fairest occasion of improvement; and by his recommendation Barlaam was finally settled in a small bishopric of his native Calabria. [91] The manifold avocations of Petrarch, love and friendship, his various correspondence and frequent journeys, the Roman laurel, and his elaborate compositions in prose and verse, in Latin and Italian, diverted him from a foreign idiom; and as he advanced in life, the attainment of the Greek language was the object of his wishes rather than of his hopes. When he was about fifty years of age, a Byzantine ambassador, his friend, and a master of both tongues, presented him with a copy of Homer; and the answer of Petrarch is at one expressive of his eloquence, gratitude, and regret. After celebrating the generosity of the donor, and the value of a gift more precious in his estimation than gold or rubies, he thus proceeds: "Your present of the genuine and original text of the divine poet, the fountain of all inventions, is worthy of yourself and of me: you have fulfilled your promise, and satisfied my desires. Yet your liberality is still imperfect: with Homer you should have given me yourself; a guide, who could lead me into the fields of light, and disclose to my wondering eyes the spacious miracles of the Iliad and Odyssey. But, alas! Homer is dumb, or I am deaf; nor is it in my power to enjoy the beauty which I possess. I have seated him by the side of Plato, the prince of poets near the prince of philosophers; and I glory in the sight of my illustrious guests. Of their immortal writings, whatever had been translated into the Latin idiom, I had already acquired; but, if there be no profit, there is some pleasure, in beholding these venerable Greeks in their proper and national habit. I am delighted with the aspect of Homer; and as often as I embrace the silent volume, I exclaim with a sigh, Illustrious bard! with what pleasure should I listen to thy song, if my sense of hearing were not obstructed and lost by the death of one friend, and in the much-lamented absence of another. Nor do I yet despair; and the example of Cato suggests some comfort and hope, since it was in the last period of age that he attained the knowledge of the Greek letters." [92]

*[Footnote 85: Of those writers who professedly treat of the restoration of the Greek learning in Italy, the two principal are Hodius, Dr. Humphrey Hody, (de Græcis Illustribus, Linguæ Græcæ Literarumque humaniorum Instauratoribus; Londini, 1742, in large octavo,) and Tiraboschi, (Istoria della Letteratura*

Italiana, tom. v. p. 364—377, tom. vii. p. 112—143.) The Oxford professor is a laborious scholar, but the librarian of Modena enjoys the superiority of a modern and national historian.]

[Footnote 86: In Calabria quæ olim magna Græcia dicebatur, coloniis Græcis repleta, remansit quædam linguæ veteris, cognitio, (Hodius, p. 2.) If it were eradicated by the Romans, it was revived and perpetuated by the monks of St. Basil, who possessed seven convents at Rossano alone, (Giannone, Istoria di Napoli, tom. i. p. 520.)]

[Footnote 87: Ii Barbari (says Petrarch, the French and Germans) vix, non dicam libros sed nomen Homeri audiverunt. Perhaps, in that respect, the xiiith century was less happy than the age of Charlemagne.]

[Footnote 88: See the character of Barlaam, in Boccace de Genealog. Deorum, l. xv. c. 6.]

[Footnote 89: Cantacuzen. l. ii. c. 36.]

[Footnote 90: For the connection of Petrarch and Barlaam, and the two interviews at Avignon in 1339, and at Naples in 1342, see the excellent Mémoires sur la Vie de Pétrarque, tom. i. p. 406—410, tom. ii. p. 74—77.]

[Footnote 91: The bishopric to which Barlaam retired, was the old Locri, in the middle ages. Scta. Cyriaca, and by corruption Hieracium, Gerace, (Dissert. Chorographica Italiæ Medii Ævi, p. 312.) The dives opum of the Norman times soon lapsed into poverty, since even the church was poor: yet the town still contains 3000 inhabitants, (Swinburne, p. 340.)]

[Footnote 92: I will transcribe a passage from this epistle of Petrarch, (Famil. ix. 2;) Donasti Homerum non in alienum sermonem violento alveâ?? derivatum, sed ex ipsis Græci eloquii scatebris, et qualis divino illi profluxit ingenio.... Sine tuâ voce Homerus tuus apud me mutus, immo vero ego apud illum surdus sum. Gaudeo tamen vel adspectû solo, ac sæpe illum amplexus atque suspirans dico, O magne vir, &c.]

The prize which eluded the efforts of Petrarch, was obtained by the fortune and industry of his friend Boccace, [93] the father of the Tuscan prose. That popular writer, who derives his reputation from the Decameron, a hundred novels of pleasantry and love, may aspire to the more serious praise of restoring in Italy the study of the Greek language. In the year one thousand three hundred and sixty, a disciple of Barlaam, whose name was Leo, or Leontius Pilatus, was detained in his way to Avignon by the advice and hospitality of Boccace, who lodged the stranger in his house, prevailed on the republic of Florence to allow him an annual stipend, and devoted his leisure to the first Greek professor, who taught this language in the Western countries of Europe. The appearance of Leo might disgust the most eager disciple, he was clothed in the mantle of a philosopher, or a mendicant; his countenance was hideous; his face was overshadowed with black hair; his beard long an uncombed; his deportment rustic; his temper gloomy and inconstant; nor could he grace his discourse with the ornaments, or even the perspicuity, of Latin elocution. But his mind was stored with a treasure of Greek learning: history and fable, philosophy and grammar, were alike at his command; and he read the poems of Homer in the schools of Florence. It was from his explanation that Boccace composed [* and transcribed a literal prose version of the Iliad and Odyssey, which satisfied the thirst of his friend Petrarch, and which, perhaps, in the succeeding century, was clandestinely used by Laurentius Valla, the Latin interpreter. It was from his narratives that the same Boccace collected the materials for his treatise on the genealogy of the heathen gods, a work, in that age, of stupendous erudition, and which he ostentatiously sprinkled with Greek characters and passages, to excite the wonder and applause of his more ignorant readers. [94] The first steps of learning are slow and laborious; no more than ten votaries of Homer could be enumerated in all Italy; and neither Rome, nor Venice, nor Naples, could add a single name to this studious catalogue. But their numbers would have multiplied, their progress would have been accelerated, if the inconstant Leo, at the end of three years, had not relinquished an honorable and beneficial station. In his passage, Petrarch entertained him at Padua a short time: he enjoyed the scholar, but was justly offended with the gloomy and unsocial temper of the man. Discontented with the world and with himself, Leo depreciated his present enjoyments, while absent persons and objects were dear to his imagination. In Italy he was a Thessalian, in Greece a native of Calabria: in the company of the Latins he disdained their language, religion, and manners: no sooner was he landed at Constantinople, than he again sighed for the wealth of Venice and the elegance of Florence. His Italian friends were deaf to his importunity: he depended on their curiosity and indulgence, and embarked on a second voyage; but on his entrance into the Adriatic, the ship was assailed by a tempest, and the unfortunate teacher, who like Ulysses had fastened himself to the mast, was struck dead by a flash of lightning. The humane Petrarch dropped a tear on his disaster; but he was most anxious to learn whether some copy of Euripides or Sophocles might not be saved from the hands of the mariners. [95]

[Footnote 93: For the life and writings of Boccace, who was born in 1313, and died in 1375, Fabricius (Bibliot. Latin. Medii Ævi, tom. i. p. 248, &c.) and Tiraboschi (tom. v. p. 83, 439—451) may be consulted. The editions, versions, imitations of his novels, are innumerable. Yet he was ashamed to communicate that trifling, and perhaps scandalous, work to Petrarch, his respectable friend, in whose letters and memoirs he conspicuously appears.]

[Footnote *: This translation of Homer was by Pilatus, not by Boccacio. See Hallam, Hist. of Lit. vol. i. p. 132—M.]

[Footnote 94: Boccace indulges an honest vanity: Ostentationis causâ Græca carmina adscripsi.... jure utor meo; meum est hoc decus, mea gloria scilicet inter Etruscos Græcis uti carminibus. Nonne ego fui qui Leontium Pilatum, &c., (de Genealogia Deorum, l. xv. c. 7, a work which, though now forgotten, has run through thirteen or fourteen editions.)]

[Footnote 95: Leontius, or Leo Pilatus, is sufficiently made known by Hody, (p. 2—11,) and the abbé de Sade, (Vie de Pétrarque, tom. iii. p. 625—634, 670—673,) who has very happily caught the lively and dramatic manner of his original.]

But the faint rudiments of Greek learning, which Petrarch had encouraged and Boccace had planted, soon withered and expired. The succeeding generation was content for a while with the improvement of Latin eloquence; nor was it before the end of the fourteenth century that a new and perpetual flame was rekindled in Italy. [96] Previous to his own journey the emperor Manuel despatched his envoys and orators to implore the compassion of the Western princes. Of these envoys, the most conspicuous, or the most learned, was Manuel Chrysoloras, [97] of noble birth, and whose Roman ancestors are supposed to have migrated with the great Constantine. After visiting the courts of France and England, where he obtained some contributions and more promises, the envoy was invited to assume the office of a professor; and Florence had again the honor of this second invitation. By his knowledge, not only of the Greek, but of the Latin tongue, Chrysoloras deserved the stipend, and surpassed the expectation, of the republic. His school was frequented by a crowd of disciples of every rank and age; and one of these, in a general history, has described his motives and his success. "At that time," says Leonard Aretin, [98] "I was a student of the civil law; but my soul was inflamed with the love of letters; and I bestowed some application on the sciences of logic and rhetoric. On the arrival of Manuel, I hesitated whether I should desert my legal studies, or relinquish this golden opportunity; and thus, in the ardor of youth, I communed with my own mind—Wilt thou be wanting to thyself and thy fortune? Wilt thou refuse to be introduced to a familiar converse with Homer, Plato, and Demosthenes; with those poets, philosophers, and orators, of whom such wonders are related, and who are celebrated by every age as the great masters of human science? Of professors and scholars in civil law, a sufficient supply will always be found in our universities; but a teacher, and such a teacher, of the Greek language, if he once be suffered to escape, may never afterwards be retrieved. Convinced by these reasons, I gave myself to Chrysoloras; and so strong was my passion, that the lessons which I had imbibed in the day were the constant object of my nightly dreams." [99] At the same time and place, the Latin classics were explained by John of Ravenna, the domestic pupil of Petrarch; [100] the Italians, who illustrated their age and country, were formed in this double school; and Florence became the fruitful seminary of Greek and Roman erudition. [101] The presence of the emperor recalled Chrysoloras from the college to the court; but he afterwards taught at Pavia and Rome with equal industry and applause. The remainder of his life, about fifteen years, was divided between Italy and Constantinople, between embassies and lessons. In the noble office of enlightening a foreign nation, the grammarian was not unmindful of a more sacred duty to his prince and country; and Emanuel Chrysoloras died at Constance on a public mission from the emperor to the council.

[Footnote 96: Dr. Hody (p. 54) is angry with Leonard Aretin, Guarinus, Paulus Jovius, &c., for affirming, that the Greek letters were restored in Italy post septingentos annos; as if, says he, they had flourished till the end of the viith century. These writers most probably reckoned from the last period of the exarchate; and the presence of the Greek magistrates and troops at Ravenna and Rome must have preserved, in some degree, the use of their native tongue.]

[Footnote 97: See the article of Emanuel, or Manuel Chrysoloras, in Hody (p 12—54) and Tiraboschi, (tom. vii. p. 113—118.) The precise date of his arrival floats between the years 1390 and 1400, and is only confined by the reign of Boniface IX.]

[Footnote 98: The name of Aretinus has been assumed by five or six natives of Arezzo in Tuscany, of whom the most famous and the most worthless lived in the xvith century. Leonardus Brunus Aretinus, the disciple of Chrysoloras, was a linguist, an orator, and an historian, the secretary of four successive popes, and the chancellor of the republic of Florence, where he died A.D. 1444, at the age of seventy-five, (Fabric. Bibliot. Medii Ævi, tom. i. p. 190 &c. Tiraboschi, tom. vii. p. 33—38.)]

[Footnote 99: See the passage in Aretin. Commentario Rerum suo Tempore in Italia gestarum, apud Hodium, p. 28—30.]

[Footnote 100: In this domestic discipline, Petrarch, who loved the youth, often complains of the eager curiosity, restless temper, and proud feelings, which announce the genius and glory of a riper age, (Mémoires sur Pétrarque, tom. iii. p. 700—709.)]

[Footnote 101: Hinc Græcæ Latinæque scholæ exortæ sunt, Guarino Philelpho, Leonardo Aretino, Caroloque, ac plerisque aliis tanquam ex equo Trojano prodeuntibus, quorum emulatione multa ingenia deinceps ad laudem excitata sunt, (Platina in Bonifacio IX.) Another Italian writer adds the names of Paulus Petrus Vergerius, Omnibonus Vincentius, Poggius, Franciscus Barbarus, &c. But I question whether a rigid chronology would allow Chrysoloras all these eminent scholars, (Hodius, p. 25—27, &c.)]

After his example, the restoration of the Greek letters in Italy was prosecuted by a series of emigrants, who were destitute of fortune, and endowed with learning, or at least with language. From the terror or oppression of the Turkish arms, the natives of Thessalonica and Constantinople escaped to a land of freedom, curiosity, and wealth. The synod introduced into Florence the lights of the Greek church, and the oracles of the Platonic philosophy; and the fugitives who adhered to the union, had the double merit of renouncing their country, not only for the Christian, but for the catholic cause. A patriot, who sacrifices his party and conscience to the allurements of favor, may be possessed, however, of the private and social virtues: he no longer hears the reproachful epithets of slave and apostate; and the consideration which he acquires among his new associates will restore in his own eyes the dignity of his character. The prudent conformity of Bessarion was rewarded with the Roman purple: he fixed his residence in Italy; and the Greek cardinal, the titular patriarch of Constantinople, was respected as the chief and protector of his nation: [102] his abilities were exercised in the legations of Bologna, Venice, Germany, and France; and his election to the chair of St. Peter floated for a moment on the uncertain breath of a conclave. [103] His ecclesiastical honors diffused a splendor and preeminence over his literary merit and service: his palace was a school; as often as the cardinal visited the Vatican, he was attended by a learned train of both nations; [104] of men applauded by themselves and the public; and whose writings, now overspread with dust, were popular and useful in their own times. I shall not attempt to enumerate the restorers of Grecian literature in the fifteenth century; and it may be sufficient to mention with gratitude the names of Theodore Gaza, of George of Trebizond, of John Argyropulus, and Demetrius Chalcocondyles, who taught their native language in the schools of Florence and Rome. Their labors were not inferior to those of Bessarion, whose purple they revered, and whose fortune was the secret object of their envy. But the lives of these grammarians were humble and obscure: they had declined the lucrative paths of the church; their dress and manners secluded them from the commerce of the world; and since they were confined to the merit, they might be content with the rewards, of learning. From this character, Janus Lascaris [105] will deserve an exception. His eloquence, politeness, and Imperial descent, recommended him to the French monarch; and in the same cities he was alternately employed to teach and to negotiate. Duty and interest prompted them to cultivate the study of the Latin language; and the most successful attained the faculty of writing and speaking with fluency and elegance in a foreign idiom. But they ever retained the inveterate vanity of their country: their praise, or at least their esteem, was reserved for the national writers, to whom they owed their fame and subsistence; and they sometimes betrayed their contempt in licentious criticism or satire on Virgil's poetry, and the oratory of Tully. [106] The superiority of these masters arose from the familiar use of a living language; and their first disciples were incapable of discerning how far they had degenerated from the knowledge, and even the practice of their ancestors. A vicious pronunciation, [107] which they introduced, was banished from the schools by the reason of the succeeding age. Of the power of the Greek accents they were ignorant; and those musical notes, which, from an Attic tongue, and to an Attic ear, must have been the secret soul of harmony, were to their eyes, as to our own, no more than minute and unmeaning marks, in prose superfluous and troublesome in verse. The art of grammar they truly possessed; the valuable fragments of Apollonius and Herodian were transfused into their lessons; and their treatises of syntax and etymology, though devoid of philosophic spirit, are still useful to the Greek student. In the shipwreck of the Byzantine libraries, each fugitive seized a fragment of treasure, a copy of some author, who without his industry might have perished: the transcripts were multiplied by an assiduous, and sometimes an elegant pen; and the text was corrected and explained by their own comments, or those of the elder scholiasts. The sense, though not the spirit, of the Greek classics, was interpreted to the Latin world: the beauties of style evaporate in a version; but the judgment of Theodore Gaza selected the more solid works of Aristotle and Theophrastus, and their natural histories of animals and plants opened a rich fund of genuine and experimental science.

[Footnote 102: See in Hody the article of Bessarion, (p. 136—177.) Theodore Gaza, George of Trebizond, and the rest of the Greeks whom I have named or omitted, are inserted in their proper chapters of his learned work. See likewise Tiraboschi, in the 1st and 2d parts of the vith tome.]

[Footnote 103: The cardinals knocked at his door, but his conclavist refused to interrupt the studies of Bessarion: "Nicholas," said he, "thy respect has cost thee a hat, and me the tiara."

Note: Roscoe (Life of Lorenzo de Medici, vol. i. p. 75) considers that Hody has refuted this "idle tale."— M.]

[Footnote 104: Such as George of Trebizond, Theodore Gaza, Argyropulus, Andronicus of Thessalonica, Philelphus, Poggius, Blondus, Nicholas Perrot, Valla, Campanus, Platina, &c. Viri (says Hody, with the pious zeal of a scholar) (nullo ævo perituri, p. 156.)]

[Footnote 105: He was born before the taking of Constantinople, but his honorable life was stretched far into the xvith century, (A.D. 1535.) Leo X. and Francis I. were his noblest patrons, under whose auspices he founded the Greek colleges of Rome and Paris, (Hody, p. 247—275.) He left posterity in France; but the counts de Vintimille, and their numerous branches, derive the name of Lascaris from a doubtful marriage in the xiiith century with the daughter of a Greek emperor (Ducange, Fam. Byzant. p. 224—230.)]

[Footnote 106: Two of his epigrams against Virgil, and three against Tully, are preserved and refuted by Franciscus Floridus, who can find no better names than Græculus ineptus et impudens, (Hody, p. 274.) In our own times, an English critic has accused the Æneid of containing multa languida, nugatoria, spiritû et majestate carminis heroici defecta; many such verses as he, the said Jeremiah Markland, would have been ashamed of owning, (præfat. ad Statii Sylvas, p. 21, 22.)]

[Footnote 107: Emanuel Chrysoloras, and his colleagues, are accused of ignorance, envy, or avarice, (Sylloge, &c., tom. ii. p. 235.) The modern Greeks pronounce the b as a V consonant, and confound three vowels, (h i u,) and several diphthongs. Such was the vulgar pronunciation which the stern Gardiner maintained by penal statutes in the university of Cambridge: but the monosyllable bh represented to an Attic ear the bleating of sheep, and a bellwether is better evidence than a bishop or a chancellor. The treatises of those scholars, particularly Erasmus, who asserted a more classical pronunciation, are collected in the Sylloge of Havercamp, (2 vols. in octavo, Lugd. Bat. 1736, 1740:) but it is difficult to paint sounds by words: and in their reference to modern use, they can be understood only by their respective countrymen. We may observe, that our peculiar pronunciation of the O, th, is approved by Erasmus, (tom. ii. p. 130.)]

Yet the fleeting shadows of metaphysics were pursued with more curiosity and ardor. After a long oblivion, Plato was revived in Italy by a venerable Greek, [108] who taught in the house of Cosmo of Medicis. While the synod of Florence was involved in theological debate, some beneficial consequences might flow from the study of his elegant philosophy: his style is the purest standard of the Attic dialect, and his sublime thoughts are sometimes adapted to familiar conversation, and sometimes adorned with the richest colors of poetry and eloquence. The dialogues of Plato are a dramatic picture of the life and death of a sage; and, as often as he descends from the clouds, his moral system inculcates the love of truth, of our country, and of mankind. The precept and example of Socrates recommended a modest doubt and liberal inquiry; and if the Platonists, with blind devotion, adored the visions and errors of their divine master, their enthusiasm might correct the dry, dogmatic method of the Peripatetic school.

So equal, yet so opposite, are the merits of Plato and Aristotle, that they may be balanced in endless controversy; but some spark of freedom may be produced by the collision of adverse servitude. The modern Greeks were divided between the two sects: with more fury than skill they fought under the banner of their leaders; and the field of battle was removed in their flight from Constantinople to Rome. But this philosophical debate soon degenerated into an angry and personal quarrel of grammarians; and Bessarion, though an advocate for Plato, protected the national honor, by interposing the advice and authority of a mediator. In the gardens of the Medici, the academical doctrine was enjoyed by the polite and learned: but their philosophic society was quickly dissolved; and if the writings of the Attic sage were perused in the closet, the more powerful Stagyrite continued to reign, the oracle of the church and school. [109]

[Footnote 108: George Gemistus Pletho, a various and voluminous writer, the master of Bessarion, and all the Platonists of the times. He visited Italy in his old age, and soon returned to end his days in Peloponnesus. See the curious Diatribe of Leo Allatius de Georgiis, in Fabricius. (Bibliot. Græc. tom. x. p. 739—756.)]

[Footnote 109: The state of the Platonic philosophy in Italy is illustrated by Boivin, (Mém. de l'Acad. des Inscriptions, tom. ii. p. 715—729,) and Tiraboschi, (tom. vi. P. i. p. 259—288.)]

I have fairly represented the literary merits of the Greeks; yet it must be confessed, that they were seconded and surpassed by the ardor of the Latins. Italy was divided into many independent states; and at that time it was the ambition of princes and republics to vie with each other in the encouragement and reward of literature. The fame of Nicholas the Fifth [110] has not been adequate to his merits. From a plebeian origin he raised himself by his virtue and learning: the character of the man prevailed over the interest of the pope; and he sharpened those weapons which were soon pointed against the Roman church. [111] He had been the friend of the most eminent scholars of the age: he became their patron; and such was the humility of his manners, that the change was scarcely discernible either to them or to himself. If he pressed the acceptance of a liberal gift, it was not as the measure of desert, but as the proof of benevolence; and when modest merit declined his bounty, "Accept it," would he say, with a consciousness of his own worth: "ye will not always have a Nicholas among you." The influence of the holy see pervaded Christendom; and he exerted that influence in the search, not of benefices, but of books. From the ruins of the Byzantine libraries, from the darkest monasteries of Germany and Britain, he collected the dusty manuscripts of the writers of antiquity; and wherever the original could not be removed, a faithful copy was transcribed and transmitted for his use. The Vatican, the old repository for bulls and legends, for superstition and forgery, was daily replenished with more precious furniture; and such was the industry of Nicholas, that in a reign of eight years he formed a library of five thousand volumes. To his munificence the Latin world was indebted for the versions of Xenophon, Diodorus, Polybius, Thucydides, Herodotus, and Appian; of Strabo's Geography, of the Iliad, of the most valuable works of Plato and Aristotle, of Ptolemy and Theophrastus, and of the fathers of the Greek church. The example of the Roman pontiff was preceded or imitated by a Florentine merchant, who governed the republic without arms and without a title. Cosmo of Medicis [112] was the father of a line of princes, whose name and age are almost synonymous with the restoration of learning: his credit was ennobled into fame; his riches were dedicated to the service of mankind; he corresponded at once with Cairo and London: and a cargo of Indian spices and Greek books was often imported in the same vessel. The genius and education of his grandson Lorenzo rendered him not only a patron, but a judge and candidate, in the literary race. In his palace, distress was entitled to relief, and merit to reward: his leisure hours were delightfully spent in the Platonic academy; he encouraged the emulation of Demetrius Chalcocondyles and Angelo Politian; and his active missionary Janus Lascaris returned from the East with a treasure of two hundred manuscripts, fourscore of which were as yet unknown in the libraries of Europe. [113] The rest of Italy was animated by a similar spirit, and the progress of the nation repaid the liberality of their princes. The Latins held the exclusive property of their own literature; and these disciples of Greece were soon capable of transmitting and improving the lessons which they had imbibed. After a short succession of foreign teachers, the tide of emigration subsided; but the language of Constantinople was spread beyond the Alps and the natives of France, Germany, and England, [114] imparted to their country the sacred fire which they had kindled in the schools of Florence and Rome. [115] In the productions of the mind, as in those of the soil, the gifts of nature are excelled by industry and skill: the Greek authors, forgotten on the banks of the Ilissus, have been illustrated on those of the Elbe and the Thames: and Bessarion or Gaza might have envied the superior science of the Barbarians; the accuracy of Budæus, the taste of Erasmus, the copiousness of Stephens, the erudition of Scaliger, the discernment of Reiske, or of Bentley. On the side of the Latins, the discovery of printing was a casual advantage: but this useful art has been applied by Aldus, and his innumerable successors, to perpetuate and multiply the works of antiquity. [116] A single manuscript imported from Greece is revived in ten thousand copies; and each copy is fairer than the original. In this form, Homer and Plato would peruse with more satisfaction their own writings; and their scholiasts must resign the prize to the labors of our Western editors.

[Footnote 110: See the Life of Nicholas V. by two contemporary authors, Janottus Manettus, (tom. iii. P. ii. p. 905—962,) and Vespasian of Florence, (tom. xxv. p. 267—290,) in the collection of Muratori; and consult Tiraboschi, (tom. vi. P. i. p. 46—52, 109,) and Hody in the articles of Theodore Gaza, George of Trebizond, &c.]

[Footnote 111: Lord Bolingbroke observes, with truth and spirit, that the popes in this instance, were worse politicians than the muftis, and that the charm which had bound mankind for so many ages was broken by the magicians themselves, (Letters on the Study of History, l. vi. p. 165, 166, octavo edition, 1779.)]

[Footnote 112: See the literary history of Cosmo and Lorenzo of Medicis, in Tiraboschi, (tom. vi. P. i. l. i. c. 2,) who bestows a due measure of praise on Alphonso of Arragon, king of Naples, the dukes of Milan, Ferrara Urbino, &c. The republic of Venice has deserved the least from the gratitude of scholars.]

[Footnote 113: Tiraboschi, (tom. vi. P. i. p. 104,) from the preface of Janus Lascaris to the Greek Anthology, printed at Florence, 1494. Latebant (says Aldus in his preface to the Greek orators, apud Hodium, p. 249) in Atho Thraciæ monte. Eas Lascaris.... in Italiam reportavit. Miserat enim ipsum Laurentius ille Medices in Græciam ad inquirendos simul, et quantovis emendos pretio bonos libros. It is remarkable enough, that the research was facilitated by Sultan Bajazet II.]

[Footnote 114: The Greek language was introduced into the university of Oxford in the last years of the xvth century, by Grocyn, Linacer, and Latimer, who had all studied at Florence under Demetrius Chalcocondyles. See Dr. Knight's curious Life of Erasmus. Although a stout academical patriot, he is forced to acknowledge that Erasmus learned Greek at Oxford, and taught it at Cambridge.]

[Footnote 115: The jealous Italians were desirous of keeping a monopoly of Greek learning. When Aldus was about to publish the Greek scholiasts on Sophocles and Euripides, Cave, (said they,) cave hoc facias, ne Barbari istis adjuti domi maneant, et pauciores in Italiam ventitent, (Dr. Knight, in his Life of Erasmus, p. 365, from Beatus Rhemanus.)]

[Footnote 116: The press of Aldus Manutius, a Roman, was established at Venice about the year 1494: he printed above sixty considerable works of Greek literature, almost all for the first time; several containing different treatises and authors, and of several authors, two, three, or four editions, (Fabric. Bibliot. Græc. tom. xiii. p. 605, &c.) Yet his glory must not tempt us to forget, that the first Greek book, the Grammar of Constantine Lascaris, was printed at Milan in 1476; and that the Florence Homer of 1488 displays all the luxury of the typographical art. See the Annales Typographical of Mattaire, and the Bibliographie Instructive of De Bure, a knowing bookseller of Paris.]

Before the revival of classic literature, the Barbarians in Europe were immersed in ignorance; and their vulgar tongues were marked with the rudeness and poverty of their manners. The students of the more perfect idioms of Rome and Greece were introduced to a new world of light and science; to the society of the free and polished nations of antiquity; and to a familiar converse with those immortal men who spoke the sublime language of eloquence and reason. Such an intercourse must tend to refine the taste, and to elevate the genius, of the moderns; and yet, from the first experiments, it might appear that the study of the ancients had given fetters, rather than wings, to the human mind. However laudable, the spirit of imitation is of a servile cast; and the first disciples of the Greeks and Romans were a colony of strangers in the midst of their age and country. The minute and laborious diligence which explored the antiquities of remote times might have improved or adorned the present state of society, the critic and metaphysician were the slaves of Aristotle; the poets, historians, and orators, were proud to repeat the thoughts and words of the Augustan age: the works of nature were observed with the eyes of Pliny and Theophrastus; and some Pagan votaries professed a secret devotion to the gods of Homer and Plato. [117] The Italians were oppressed by the strength and number of their ancient auxiliaries: the century after the deaths of Petrarch and Boccace was filled with a crowd of Latin imitators, who decently repose on our shelves; but in that æra of learning it will not be easy to discern a real discovery of science, a work of invention or eloquence, in the popular language of the country. [118] But as soon as it had been deeply saturated with the celestial dew, the soil was quickened into vegetation and life; the modern idioms were refined; the classics of Athens and Rome inspired a pure taste and a generous emulation; and in Italy, as afterwards in France and England, the pleasing reign of poetry and fiction was succeeded by the light of speculative and experimental philosophy. Genius may anticipate the season of maturity; but in the education of a people, as in that of an individual, memory must be exercised, before the powers of reason and fancy can be expanded: nor may the artist hope to equal or surpass, till he has learned to imitate, the works of his predecessors.

[Footnote 117: I will select three singular examples of this classic enthusiasm. I. At the synod of Florence, Gemistus Pletho said, in familiar conversation to George of Trebizond, that in a short time mankind would unanimously renounce the Gospel and the Koran, for a religion similar to that of the Gentiles, (Leo Allatius, apud Fabricium, tom. x. p. 751.) 2. Paul II. persecuted the Roman academy, which had been founded by Pomponius Lætus; and the principal members were accused of heresy, impiety, and paganism, (Tiraboschi, tom. vi. P. i. p. 81, 82.) 3. In the next century, some scholars and poets in France celebrated the success of Jodelle's tragedy of Cleopatra, by a festival of Bacchus, and, as it is said, by the sacrifice of a goat, (Bayle, Dictionnaire, Jodelle. Fontenelle, tom. iii. p. 56—61.) Yet the spirit of bigotry might often discern a serious impiety in the sportive play of fancy and learning.]

[Footnote 118: The survivor Boccace died in the year 1375; and we cannot place before 1480 the composition of the Morgante Maggiore of Pulci and the Orlando Innamorato of Boyardo, (Tiraboschi, tom. vi. P. ii. p. 174—177.)]

# CHAPTER LXVII

## SCHISM OF THE GREEKS AND LATINS

### PART I

SCHISM OF THE GREEKS AND LATINS—REIGN AND CHARACTER OF AMURATH THE SECOND—CRUSADE OF LADISLAUS, KING OF HUNGARY—HIS DEFEAT AND DEATH—JOHN HUNIADES—SCANDERBEG—CONSTANTINE PALÆOLOGUS, LAST EMPEROR OF THE EAST

The respective merits of Rome and Constantinople are compared and celebrated by an eloquent Greek, the father of the Italian schools. [1] The view of the ancient capital, the seat of his ancestors, surpassed the most sanguine expectations of Emanuel Chrysoloras; and he no longer blamed the exclamation of an old sophist, that Rome was the habitation, not of men, but of gods. Those gods, and those men, had long since vanished; but to the eye of liberal enthusiasm, the majesty of ruin restored the image of her ancient prosperity. The monuments of the consuls and Cæsars, of the martyrs and apostles, engaged on all sides the curiosity of the philosopher and the Christian; and he confessed that in every age the arms and the religion of Rome were destined to reign over the earth. While Chrysoloras admired the venerable beauties of the mother, he was not forgetful of his native country, her fairest daughter, her Imperial colony; and the Byzantine patriot expatiates with zeal and truth on the eternal advantages of nature, and the more transitory glories of art and dominion, which adorned, or had adorned, the city of Constantine. Yet the perfection of the copy still redounds (as he modestly observes) to the honor of the original, and parents are delighted to be renewed, and even excelled, by the superior merit of their children. "Constantinople," says the orator, "is situate on a commanding point, between Europe and Asia, between the Archipelago and the Euxine. By her interposition, the two seas, and the two continents, are united for the common benefit of nations; and the gates of commerce may be shut or opened at her command. The harbor, encompassed on all sides by the sea, and the continent, is the most secure and capacious in the world. The walls and gates of Constantinople may be compared with those of Babylon: the towers many; each tower is a solid and lofty structure; and the second wall, the outer fortification, would be sufficient for the defence and dignity of an ordinary capital. A broad and rapid stream may be introduced into the ditches and the artificial island may be encompassed, like Athens, [2] by land or water." Two strong and natural causes are alleged for the perfection of the model of new Rome. The royal founder reigned over the most illustrious nations of the globe; and in the accomplishment of his designs, the power of the Romans was combined with the art and science of the Greeks. Other cities have been reared to maturity by accident and time: their beauties are mingled with disorder and deformity; and the inhabitants, unwilling to remove from their natal spot, are incapable of correcting the errors of their ancestors, and the original vices of situation or climate. But the free idea of Constantinople was formed and executed by a single mind; and the primitive model was improved by the obedient zeal of the subjects and successors of the first monarch. The adjacent isles were stored with an inexhaustible supply of marble; but the various materials were transported from the most remote shores of Europe and Asia; and the public and private buildings, the palaces, churches, aqueducts, cisterns, porticos, columns, baths, and hippodromes, were adapted to the greatness of the capital of the East. The superfluity of wealth was spread along the shores of Europe and Asia; and the Byzantine territory, as far as the Euxine, the Hellespont, and the long wall, might be considered as a populous suburb and a perpetual garden. In this flattering picture, the past and the present, the times of prosperity and decay, are art fully confounded; but a sigh and a confession escape, from the orator, that his wretched country was the shadow and sepulchre of its former self. The works of ancient sculpture had been defaced by Christian zeal or Barbaric violence; the fairest structures were demolished; and the marbles of Paros or Numidia were burnt for lime, or applied to the meanest uses. Of many a statue, the place was marked by an empty pedestal; of many a column, the size was determined by a broken capital; the tombs of the emperors were scattered on the ground; the stroke of time was accelerated by storms and earthquakes; and the vacant space was adorned, by vulgar tradition, with fabulous monuments of gold and silver. From these wonders, which lived only in memory or belief, he distinguishes, however, the porphyry pillar, the column and colossus of Justinian, [3] and the church, more especially the dome, of St. Sophia; the best conclusion, since it could not be described according to its merits, and after it no other object could deserve to be mentioned. But he forgets that, a century before, the trembling fabrics of the colossus and the church had been saved and supported by the timely care of Andronicus the Elder. Thirty years after the emperor had fortified St. Sophia with two new buttresses or pyramids, the eastern hemisphere suddenly gave way: and the images, the altars, and the sanctuary, were crushed by the falling ruin. The mischief indeed was speedily repaired; the rubbish was cleared by the incessant labor of every rank and age; and the poor remains of riches and industry were consecrated by the Greeks to the most stately and venerable temple of the East. [4]

[Footnote 1: The epistle of Emanuel Chrysoloras to the emperor John Palæologus will not offend the eye or ear of a classical student, (ad calcem Codini de Antiquitatibus C. P. p. 107—126.) The superscription suggests a chronological remark, that John Palæologus II. was associated in the empire before the year 1414, the date of Chrysoloras's death. A still earlier date, at least 1408, is deduced from the age of his youngest sons, Demetrius and Thomas, who were both Porphyrogeniti (Ducange, Fam. Byzant. p. 244, 247.)]

[Footnote 2: Somebody observed that the city of Athens might be circumnavigated, (tiV eipen tin polin tvn Aqhnaiwn dunasqai kai paraplein kai periplein.) But what may be true in a rhetorical sense of Constantinople, cannot be applied to the situation of Athens, five miles from the sea, and not intersected or surrounded by any navigable streams.]

[Footnote 3: Nicephorus Gregoras has described the Colossus of Justinian, (l. vii. 12:) but his measures are false and inconsistent. The editor Boivin consulted his friend Girardon; and the sculptor gave him the true proportions of an equestrian statue. That of Justinian was still visible to Peter Gyllius, not on the column, but in the outward court of the seraglio; and he was at Constantinople when it was melted down, and cast into a brass cannon, (de Topograph. C. P. l. ii. c. 17.)]

[Footnote 4: See the decay and repairs of St. Sophia, in Nicephorus Gregoras (l. vii. 12, l. xv. 2.) The building was propped by Andronicus in 1317, the eastern hemisphere fell in 1345. The Greeks, in their pompous rhetoric, exalt the beauty and holiness of the church, an earthly heaven the abode of angels, and of God himself, &c.]

The last hope of the falling city and empire was placed in the harmony of the mother and daughter, in the maternal tenderness of Rome, and the filial obedience of Constantinople. In the synod of Florence, the Greeks and Latins had embraced, and subscribed, and promised; but these signs of friendship were perfidious or fruitless; [5] and the baseless fabric of the union vanished like a dream. [6] The emperor and his prelates returned home in the Venetian galleys; but as they touched at the Morea and the Isles of Corfu and Lesbos, the subjects of the Latins complained that the pretended union would be an instrument of oppression. No sooner did they land on the Byzantine shore, than they were saluted, or rather assailed, with a general murmur of zeal and discontent. During their absence, above two years, the capital had been deprived of its civil and ecclesiastical rulers; fanaticism fermented in anarchy; the most furious monks reigned over the conscience of women and bigots; and the hatred of the Latin name was the first principle of nature and religion. Before his departure for Italy, the emperor had flattered the city with the assurance of a prompt relief and a powerful succor; and the clergy, confident in their orthodoxy and science, had promised themselves and their flocks an easy victory over the blind shepherds of the West. The double disappointment exasperated the Greeks; the conscience of the subscribing prelates was awakened; the hour of temptation was past; and they had more to dread from the public resentment, than they could hope from the favor of the emperor or the pope. Instead of justifying their conduct, they deplored their weakness, professed their contrition, and cast themselves on the mercy of God and of their brethren. To the reproachful question, what had been the event or the use of their Italian synod? they answered with sighs and tears, "Alas! we have made a new faith; we have exchanged piety for impiety; we have betrayed the immaculate sacrifice; and we are become Azymites." (The Azymites were those who celebrated the communion with unleavened bread; and I must retract or qualify the praise which I have bestowed on the growing philosophy of the times.) "Alas! we have been seduced by distress, by fraud, and by the hopes and fears of a transitory life. The hand that has signed the union should be cut off; and the tongue that has pronounced the Latin creed deserves to be torn from the root." The best proof of their repentance was an increase of zeal for the most trivial rites and the most incomprehensible doctrines; and an absolute separation from all, without excepting their prince, who preserved some regard for honor and consistency. After the decease of the patriarch Joseph, the archbishops of Heraclea and Trebizond had courage to refuse the vacant office; and Cardinal Bessarion preferred the warm and comfortable shelter of the Vatican. The choice of the emperor and his clergy was confined to Metrophanes of Cyzicus: he was consecrated in St. Sophia, but the temple was vacant. The cross-bearers abdicated their service; the infection spread from the city to the villages; and Metrophanes discharged, without effect, some ecclesiastical thunders against a nation of schismatics. The eyes of the Greeks were directed to Mark of Ephesus, the champion of his country; and the sufferings of the holy confessor were repaid with a tribute of admiration and applause. His example and writings propagated the flame of religious discord; age and infirmity soon removed him from the world; but the gospel of Mark was not a law of forgiveness; and he requested with his dying breath, that none of the adherents of Rome might attend his obsequies or pray for his soul.

[Footnote 5: The genuine and original narrative of Syropulus (p. 312—351) opens the schism from the first office of the Greeks at Venice to the general opposition at Constantinople, of the clergy and people.]

[Footnote 6: On the schism of Constantinople, see Phranza, (l. ii. c. 17,) Laonicus Chalcondyles, (l. vi. p. 155, 156,) and Ducas, (c. 31;) the last of whom writes with truth and freedom. Among the moderns we may distinguish the continuator of Fleury, (tom. xxii. p. 338, &c., 401, 420, &c.,) and Spondanus, (A.D. 1440—50.) The sense of the latter is drowned in prejudice and passion, as soon as Rome and religion are concerned.]

The schism was not confined to the narrow limits of the Byzantine empire. Secure under the Mamaluke sceptre, the three patriarchs of Alexandria, Antioch, and Jerusalem, assembled a numerous synod; disowned their representatives at Ferrara and Florence; condemned the creed and council of the Latins; and threatened the emperor of Constantinople with the censures of the Eastern church. Of the sectaries of the Greek communion, the Russians were the most powerful, ignorant, and superstitious. Their primate, the cardinal Isidore, hastened from Florence to Moscow, [7] to reduce the independent nation under the Roman yoke. But the Russian bishops had been educated at Mount Athos; and the prince and people embraced the theology of their priests. They were scandalized by the title, the pomp, the Latin cross of the legate, the friend of those impious men who shaved their beards, and performed the divine office with gloves on their hands and rings on their fingers: Isidore was condemned by a synod; his person was imprisoned in a monastery; and it was with extreme difficulty that the cardinal could escape from the hands of a fierce and fanatic people. [8] The Russians refused a passage to the missionaries of Rome who aspired to convert the Pagans beyond the Tanais; [9] and their refusal was justified by the maxim, that the guilt of idolatry is less damnable than that of schism. The errors of the Bohemians were excused by their abhorrence for the pope; and a deputation of the Greek clergy solicited the friendship of those sanguinary enthusiasts. [10] While Eugenius triumphed in the union and orthodoxy of the Greeks, his party was contracted to the walls, or rather to the palace of Constantinople. The zeal of Palæologus had been excited by interest; it was soon cooled by opposition: an attempt to violate the national belief might endanger his life and crown; not could the pious rebels be destitute of foreign and domestic aid. The sword of his brother Demetrius, who in Italy had maintained a prudent and popular silence, was half unsheathed in the cause of religion; and Amurath, the Turkish sultan, was displeased and alarmed by the seeming friendship of the Greeks and Latins.

[Footnote 7: *Isidore was metropolitan of Kiow, but the Greeks subject to Poland have removed that see from the ruins of Kiow to Lemberg, or Leopold, (Herbestein, in Ramusio, tom. ii. p. 127.) On the other hand, the Russians transferred their spiritual obedience to the archbishop, who became, in 1588, the patriarch, of Moscow, (Levesque Hist. de Russie, tom. iii. p. 188, 190, from a Greek MS. at Turin, Iter et labores Archiepiscopi Arsenii.)*]

[Footnote 8: *The curious narrative of Levesque (Hist. de Russie, tom. ii. p. 242—247) is extracted from the patriarchal archives. The scenes of Ferrara and Florence are described by ignorance and passion; but the Russians are credible in the account of their own prejudices.*]

[Footnote 9: *The Shamanism, the ancient religion of the Samanæans and Gymnosophists, has been driven by the more popular Bramins from India into the northern deserts: the naked philosophers were compelled to wrap themselves in fur; but they insensibly sunk into wizards and physicians. The Mordvans and Tcheremisses in the European Russia adhere to this religion, which is formed on the earthly model of one king or God, his ministers or angels, and the rebellious spirits who oppose his government. As these tribes of the Volga have no images, they might more justly retort on the Latin missionaries the name of idolaters, (Levesque, Hist. des Peuples soumis à la Domination des Russes, tom. i. p. 194—237, 423—460.)*]

[Footnote 10: *Spondanus, Annal. Eccles. tom ii. A.D. 1451, No. 13. The epistle of the Greeks with a Latin version, is extant in the college library at Prague.*]

"Sultan Murad, or Amurath, lived forty-nine, and reigned thirty years, six months, and eight days. He was a just and valiant prince, of a great soul, patient of labors, learned, merciful, religious, charitable; a lover and encourager of the studious, and of all who excelled in any art or science; a good emperor and a great general. No man obtained more or greater victories than Amurath; Belgrade alone withstood his attacks. [101] Under his reign, the soldier was ever victorious, the citizen rich and secure. If he subdued any country, his first care was to build mosques and caravansaras, hospitals, and colleges. Every year he gave a thousand pieces of gold to the sons of the Prophet; and sent two thousand five hundred to the religious persons of Mecca, Medina, and Jerusalem." [11] This portrait is transcribed from the historian of the Othman empire: but the applause of a servile and superstitious people has been lavished on the worst of tyrants; and the virtues of a sultan are often the vices most useful to himself, or most agreeable to his subjects. A nation ignorant of the equal benefits of liberty and law, must be awed by the flashes of arbitrary power: the cruelty of a despot will assume the character of justice; his profusion, of liberality; his obstinacy, of firmness. If the most reasonable excuse be rejected, few acts of obedience will be found impossible; and guilt must tremble, where innocence cannot always be secure. The tranquillity of the people, and the discipline of the troops, were best maintained by perpetual action in the field; war was the trade of the Janizaries; and those who survived the peril, and divided the spoil, applauded the generous ambition of their sovereign. To propagate the true religion, was the duty of a faithful Mussulman: the unbelievers were his enemies, and those of the Prophet; and, in the hands of the Turks, the cimeter was the only instrument of conversion. Under these circumstances, however, the justice and moderation of Amurath are attested by his conduct, and acknowledged by the Christians themselves; who consider a prosperous reign and a peaceful death as the reward of his singular merits. In the vigor of his age and military power, he seldom engaged in war till he was justified by a previous and adequate provocation: the victorious sultan was disarmed by submission; and in the observance of treaties, his word was inviolate and sacred. [12] The Hungarians were commonly the aggressors; he was provoked by the revolt of Scanderbeg; and the perfidious Caramanian was twice vanquished, and twice pardoned, by the Ottoman monarch. Before he invaded the Morea, Thebes had been surprised by the despot: in the conquest of Thessalonica, the grandson of Bajazet might dispute the recent purchase of the Venetians; and after the first siege of Constantinople, the sultan was never tempted, by the distress, the absence, or the injuries of Palæologus, to extinguish the dying light of the Byzantine empire.

*[Footnote 101: See the siege and massacre at Thessalonica. Von Hammer vol. i p. 433—M.]*

*[Footnote 11: See Cantemir, History of the Othman Empire, p. 94. Murad, or Morad, may be more correct: but I have preferred the popular name to that obscure diligence which is rarely successful in translating an Oriental, into the Roman, alphabet.]*

*[Footnote 12: See Chalcondyles, (l. vii. p. 186, 198,) Ducas, (c. 33,) and Marinus Barletius, (in Vit. Scanderbeg, p. 145, 146.) In his good faith towards the garrison of Sfetigrade, he was a lesson and example to his son Mahomet.]*

But the most striking feature in the life and character of Amurath is the double abdication of the Turkish throne; and, were not his motives debased by an alloy of superstition, we must praise the royal philosopher, [13] who at the age of forty could discern the vanity of human greatness. Resigning the sceptre to his son, he retired to the pleasant residence of Magnesia; but he retired to the society of saints and hermits. It was not till the fourth century of the Hegira, that the religion of Mahomet had been corrupted by an institution so adverse to his genius; but in the age of the crusades, the various orders of Dervises were multiplied by the example of the Christian, and even the Latin, monks. [14] The lord of nations submitted to fast, and pray, and turn round [14/1] in endless rotation with the fanatics, who mistook the giddiness of the head for the illumination of the spirit. [15] But he was soon awakened from his dreams of enthusiasm by the Hungarian invasion; and his obedient son was the foremost to urge the public danger and the wishes of the people. Under the banner of their veteran leader, the Janizaries fought and conquered but he withdrew from the field of Varna, again to pray, to fast, and to turn round with his Magnesian brethren. These pious occupations were again interrupted by the danger of the state. A victorious army disdained the inexperience of their youthful ruler: the city of Adrianople was abandoned to rapine and slaughter; and the unanimous divan implored his presence to appease the tumult, and prevent the rebellion, of the Janizaries. At the well-known voice of their master, they trembled and obeyed; and the reluctant sultan was compelled to support his splendid servitude, till at the end of four years, he was relieved by the angel of death. Age or disease, misfortune or caprice, have tempted several princes to descend from the throne; and they have had leisure to repent of their irretrievable step. But Amurath alone, in the full liberty of choice, after the trial of empire and solitude, has repeated his preference of a private life.

[Footnote 13: Voltaire (Essai sur l'Histoire Générale, c. 89, p. 283, 284) admires le Philosophe Turc: would he have bestowed the same praise on a Christian prince for retiring to a monastery? In his way, Voltaire was a bigot, an intolerant bigot.]

[Footnote 14: See the articles Dervische, Fakir, Nasser, Rohbaniat, in D'Herbelot's Bibliothèque Orientale. Yet the subject is superficially treated from the Persian and Arabian writers. It is among the Turks that these orders have principally flourished.]

[Footnote 14/1: Gibbon has fallen into a remarkable error. The unmonastic retreat of Amurath was that of an epicurean rather than of a dervis; more like that of Sardanapalus than of Charles the Fifth. Profane, not divine, love was its chief occupation: the only dance, that described by Horace as belonging to the country, motus doceri gaudet Ionicos. See Von Hammer note, p. 652—M.]

[Footnote 15: Ricaut (in the Present State of the Ottoman Empire, p. 242—268) affords much information, which he drew from his personal conversation with the heads of the dervises, most of whom ascribed their origin to the time of Orchan. He does not mention the Zichid of Chalcondyles, (l. vii. p. 286,) among whom Amurath retired: the Seids of that author are the descendants of Mahomet.]

After the departure of his Greek brethren, Eugenius had not been unmindful of their temporal interest; and his tender regard for the Byzantine empire was animated by a just apprehension of the Turks, who approached, and might soon invade, the borders of Italy. But the spirit of the crusades had expired; and the coldness of the Franks was not less unreasonable than their headlong passion. In the eleventh century, a fanatic monk could precipitate Europe on Asia for the recovery of the holy sepulchre; but in the fifteenth, the most pressing motives of religion and policy were insufficient to unite the Latins in the defence of Christendom. Germany was an inexhaustible storehouse of men and arms: [16] but that complex and languid body required the impulse of a vigorous hand; and Frederic the Third was alike impotent in his personal character and his Imperial dignity. A long war had impaired the strength, without satiating the animosity, of France and England: [17] but Philip duke of Burgundy was a vain and magnificent prince; and he enjoyed, without danger or expense, the adventurous piety of his subjects, who sailed, in a gallant fleet, from the coast of Flanders to the Hellespont. The maritime republics of Venice and Genoa were less remote from the scene of action; and their hostile fleets were associated under the standard of St. Peter. The kingdoms of Hungary and Poland, which covered as it were the interior pale of the Latin church, were the most nearly concerned to oppose the progress of the Turks. Arms were the patrimony of the Scythians and Sarmatians; and these nations might appear equal to the contest, could they point, against the common foe, those swords that were so wantonly drawn in bloody and domestic quarrels. But the same spirit was adverse to concord and obedience: a poor country and a limited monarch are incapable of maintaining a standing force; and the loose bodies of Polish and Hungarian horse were not armed with the sentiments and weapons which, on some occasions, have given irresistible weight to the French chivalry. Yet, on this side, the designs of the Roman pontiff, and the eloquence of Cardinal Julian, his legate, were promoted by the circumstances of the times: [18] by the union of the two crowns on the head of Ladislaus, [19] a young and ambitious soldier; by the valor of a hero, whose name, the name of John Huniades, was already popular among the Christians, and formidable to the Turks. An endless treasure of pardons and indulgences was scattered by the legate; many private warriors of France and Germany enlisted under the holy banner; and the crusade derived some strength, or at least some reputation, from the new allies both of Europe and Asia. A fugitive despot of Servia exaggerated the distress and ardor of the Christians beyond the Danube, who would unanimously rise to vindicate their religion and liberty. The Greek emperor, [20] with a spirit unknown to his fathers, engaged to guard the Bosphorus, and to sally from Constantinople at the head of his national and mercenary troops. The sultan of Caramania [21] announced the retreat of Amurath, and a powerful diversion in the heart of Anatolia; and if the fleets of the West could occupy at the same moment the Straits of the Hellespont, the Ottoman monarchy would be dissevered and destroyed. Heaven and earth must rejoice in the perdition of the miscreants; and the legate, with prudent ambiguity, instilled the opinion of the invisible, perhaps the visible, aid of the Son of God, and his divine mother.

[Footnote 16: In the year 1431, Germany raised 40,000 horse, men-at-arms, against the Hussites of Bohemia, (Lenfant, Hist. du Concile de Basle, tom. i. p. 318.) At the siege of Nuys, on the Rhine, in 1474, the princes, prelates, and cities, sent their respective quotas; and the bishop of Munster (qui n'est pas des plus grands) furnished 1400 horse, 6000 foot, all in green, with 1200 wagons. The united armies of the king of England and the duke of Burgundy scarcely equalled one third of this German host, (Mémoires de Philippe de Comines, l. iv. c. 2.) At present, six or seven hundred thousand men are maintained in constant pay and admirable discipline by the powers of Germany.]

[Footnote 17: It was not till the year 1444, that France and England could agree on a truce of some months. (See Rymer's Fdera, and the chronicles of both nations.)]

[Footnote 18: In the Hungarian crusade, Spondanus (Annal. Ecclés. A.D. 1443, 1444) has been my leading guide. He has diligently read, and critically compared, the Greek and Turkish materials, the historians of Hungary, Poland, and the West. His narrative is perspicuous and where he can be free from a religious bias, the judgment of Spondanus is not contemptible.]

[Footnote 19: I have curtailed the harsh letter (Wladislaus) which most writers affix to his name, either in compliance with the Polish pronunciation, or to distinguish him from his rival the infant Ladislaus of Austria. Their competition for the crown of Hungary is described by Callimachus, (l. i. ii. p. 447—486,) Bonfinius, (Decad. iii. l. iv.,) Spondanus, and Lenfant.]

[Footnote 20: The Greek historians, Phranza, Chalcondyles, and Ducas, do not ascribe to their prince a very active part in this crusade, which he seems to have promoted by his wishes, and injured by his fears.]

[Footnote 21: Cantemir (p. 88) ascribes to his policy the original plan, and transcribes his animating epistle to the king of Hungary. But the Mahometan powers are seldom it formed of the state of Christendom and the situation and correspondence of the knights of Rhodes must connect them with the sultan of Caramania.]

Of the Polish and Hungarian diets, a religious war was the unanimous cry; and Ladislaus, after passing the Danube, led an army of his confederate subjects as far as Sophia, the capital of the Bulgarian kingdom. In this expedition they obtained two signal victories, which were justly ascribed to the valor and conduct of Huniades. In the first, with a vanguard of ten thousand men, he surprised the Turkish camp; in the second, he vanquished and made prisoner the most renowned of their generals, who possessed the double advantage of ground and numbers. The approach of winter, and the natural and artificial obstacles of Mount Hæmus, arrested the progress of the hero, who measured a narrow interval of six days' march from the foot of the mountains to the hostile towers of Adrianople, and the friendly capital of the Greek empire. The retreat was undisturbed; and the entrance into Buda was at once a military and religious triumph. An ecclesiastical procession was followed by the king and his warriors on foot: he nicely balanced the merits and rewards of the two nations; and the pride of conquest was blended with the humble temper of Christianity. Thirteen bashaws, nine standards, and four thousand captives, were unquestionable trophies; and as all were willing to believe, and none were present to contradict, the crusaders multiplied, with unblushing confidence, the myriads of Turks whom they had left on the field of battle. [22] The most solid proof, and the most salutary consequence, of victory, was a deputation from the divan to solicit peace, to restore Servia, to ransom the prisoners, and to evacuate the Hungarian frontier. By this treaty, the rational objects of the war were obtained: the king, the despot, and Huniades himself, in the diet of Segedin, were satisfied with public and private emolument; a truce of ten years was concluded; and the followers of Jesus and Mahomet, who swore on the Gospel and the Koran, attested the word of God as the guardian of truth and the avenger of perfidy. In the place of the Gospel, the Turkish ministers had proposed to substitute the Eucharist, the real presence of the Catholic deity; but the Christians refused to profane their holy mysteries; and a superstitious conscience is less forcibly bound by the spiritual energy, than by the outward and visible symbols of an oath. [23]

[Footnote 22: In their letters to the emperor Frederic III. the Hungarians slay 80,000 Turks in one battle; but the modest Julian reduces the slaughter to 6000 or even 2000 infidels, (Æneas Sylvius in Europ. c. 5, and epist. 44, 81, apud Spondanum.)]

[Footnote 23: See the origin of the Turkish war, and the first expedition of Ladislaus, in the vth and vith books of the iiid decad of Bonfinius, who, in his division and style, copies Livy with tolerable success Callimachus (l. ii p. 487—496) is still more pure and authentic.]

During the whole transaction, the cardinal legate had observed a sullen silence, unwilling to approve, and unable to oppose, the consent of the king and people. But the diet was not dissolved before Julian was fortified by the welcome intelligence, that Anatolia was invaded by the Caramanian, and Thrace by the Greek emperor; that the fleets of Genoa, Venice, and Burgundy, were masters of the Hellespont; and that the allies, informed of the victory, and ignorant of the treaty, of Ladislaus, impatiently waited for the return of his victorious army. "And is it thus," exclaimed the cardinal, [24] "that you will desert their expectations and your own fortune? It is to them, to your God, and your fellow-Christians, that you have pledged your faith; and that prior obligation annihilates a rash and sacrilegious oath to the enemies of Christ. His vicar on earth is the Roman pontiff; without whose sanction you can neither promise nor perform. In his name I absolve your perjury and sanctify your arms: follow my footsteps in the paths of glory and salvation; and if still ye have scruples, devolve on my head the punishment and the sin." This mischievous casuistry was seconded by his respectable character, and the levity of popular assemblies: war was resolved, on the same spot where peace had so lately been sworn; and, in the execution of the treaty, the Turks were assaulted by the Christians; to whom, with some reason, they might apply the epithet of Infidels. The falsehood of Ladislaus to his word and oath was palliated by the religion of the times: the most perfect, or at least the most popular, excuse would have been the success of his arms and the deliverance of the Eastern church. But the same treaty which should have bound his conscience had diminished his strength. On the proclamation of the peace, the French and German volunteers departed with indignant murmurs: the Poles were exhausted by distant warfare, and perhaps disgusted with foreign command; and their palatines accepted the first license, and hastily retired to their provinces and castles. Even Hungary was divided by faction, or restrained by a laudable scruple; and the relics of the crusade that marched in the second expedition were reduced to an inadequate force of twenty thousand men. A Walachian chief, who joined the royal standard with his vassals, presumed to remark that their numbers did not exceed the hunting retinue that sometimes attended the sultan; and the gift of two horses of matchless speed might admonish Ladislaus of his secret foresight of the event. But the despot of Servia, after the restoration of his country and children, was tempted by the promise of new realms; and the inexperience of the king, the enthusiasm of the legate, and the martial presumption of Huniades himself, were persuaded that every obstacle must yield to the invincible virtue of the sword and the cross. After the passage of the Danube, two roads might lead to Constantinople and the Hellespont: the one direct, abrupt, and difficult through the mountains of Hæmus; the other more tedious and secure, over a level country, and along the shores of the Euxine; in which their flanks, according to the Scythian discipline, might always be covered by a movable fortification of wagons. The latter was judiciously preferred: the Catholics marched through the plains of Bulgaria, burning, with wanton cruelty, the churches and villages of the Christian natives; and their last station was at Warna, near the sea-shore; on which the defeat and death of Ladislaus have bestowed a memorable name. [25]

[Footnote 24: I do not pretend to warrant the literal accuracy of Julian's speech, which is variously worded by Callimachus, (l. iii. p. 505—507,) Bonfinius, (dec. iii. l. vi. p. 457, 458,) and other historians, who might indulge their own eloquence, while they represent one of the orators of the age. But they all agree in the advice and arguments for perjury, which in the field of controversy are fiercely attacked by the Protestants, and feebly defended by the Catholics. The latter are discouraged by the misfortune of Warna.]

[Footnote 25: Warna, under the Grecian name of Odessus, was a colony of the Milesians, which they denominated from the hero Ulysses, (Cellarius, tom. i. p. 374. D'Anville, tom. i. p. 312.) According to Arrian's Periplus of the Euxine, (p. 24, 25, in the first volume of Hudson's Geographers,) it was situate 1740 stadia, or furlongs, from the mouth of the Danube, 2140 from Byzantium, and 360 to the north of a ridge of promontory of Mount Hæmus, which advances into the sea.]

PART II

It was on this fatal spot, that, instead of finding a confederate fleet to second their operations, they were alarmed by the approach of Amurath himself, who had issued from his Magnesian solitude, and transported the forces of Asia to the defence of Europe. According to some writers, the Greek emperor had been awed, or seduced, to grant the passage of the Bosphorus; and an indelible stain of corruption is fixed on the Genoese, or the pope's nephew, the Catholic admiral, whose mercenary connivance betrayed the guard of the Hellespont. From Adrianople, the sultan advanced by hasty marches, at the head of sixty thousand men; and when the cardinal, and Huniades, had taken a nearer survey of the numbers and order of the Turks, these ardent warriors proposed the tardy and impracticable measure of a retreat. The king alone was resolved to conquer or die; and his resolution had almost been crowned with a glorious and salutary victory. The princes were opposite to each other in the centre; and the Beglerbegs, or generals of Anatolia and Romania, commanded on the right and left, against the adverse divisions of the despot and Huniades. The Turkish wings were broken on the first onset: but the advantage was fatal; and the rash victors, in the heat of the pursuit, were carried away far from the annoyance of the enemy, or the support of their friends. When Amurath beheld the flight of his squadrons, he despaired of his fortune and that of the empire: a veteran Janizary seized his horse's bridle; and he had magnanimity to pardon and reward the soldier who dared to perceive the terror, and arrest the flight, of his sovereign. A copy of the treaty, the monument of Christian perfidy, had been displayed in the front of battle; and it is said, that the sultan in his distress, lifting his eyes and his hands to heaven, implored the protection of the God of truth; and called on the prophet Jesus himself to avenge the impious mockery of his name and religion. [26] With inferior numbers and disordered ranks, the king of Hungary rushed forward in the confidence of victory, till his career was stopped by the impenetrable phalanx of the Janizaries. If we may credit the Ottoman annals, his horse was pierced by the javelin of Amurath; [27] he fell among the spears of the infantry; and a Turkish soldier proclaimed with a loud voice, "Hungarians, behold the head of your king!" The death of Ladislaus was the signal of their defeat. On his return from an intemperate pursuit, Huniades deplored his error, and the public loss; he strove to rescue the royal body, till he was overwhelmed by the tumultuous crowd of the victors and vanquished; and the last efforts of his courage and conduct were exerted to save the remnant of his Walachian cavalry. Ten thousand Christians were slain in the disastrous battle of Warna: the loss of the Turks, more considerable in numbers, bore a smaller proportion to their total strength; yet the philosophic sultan was not ashamed to confess, that his ruin must be the consequence of a second and similar victory. [271] At his command a column was erected on the spot where Ladislaus had fallen; but the modest inscription, instead of accusing the rashness, recorded the valor, and bewailed the misfortune, of the Hungarian youth. [28]

[Footnote 26: Some Christian writers affirm, that he drew from his bosom the host or wafer on which the treaty had not been sworn. The Moslems suppose, with more simplicity, an appeal to God and his prophet Jesus, which is likewise insinuated by Callimachus, (l. iii. p. 516. Spondan. A.D. 1444, No. 8.)]

[Footnote 27: A critic will always distrust these spolia opima of a victorious general, so difficult for valor to obtain, so easy for flattery to invent, (Cantemir, p. 90, 91.) Callimachus (l. iii. p. 517) more simply and probably affirms, supervenitibus Janizaris, telorum multitudine, non jam confossus est, quam obrutus.]

[Footnote 27/1: Compare Von Hammer, p. 463—M.]

[Footnote 28: Besides some valuable hints from Æneas Sylvius, which are diligently collected by Spondanus, our best authorities are three historians of the xvth century, Philippus Callimachus, (de Rebus a Vladislao Polonorum atque Hungarorum Rege gestis, libri iii. in Bel. Script. Rerum Hungaricarum, tom. i. p. 433—518,) Bonfinius, (decad. iii. l. v. p. 460—467,) and Chalcondyles, (l. vii. p. 165—179.) The two first were Italians, but they passed their lives in Poland and Hungary, (Fabric. Bibliot. Latin. Med. et Infimæ Ætatis, tom. i. p. 324. Vossius, de Hist. Latin. l. iii. c. 8, 11. Bayle, Dictionnaire, Bonfinius.) A small tract of Fælix Petancius, chancellor of Segnia, (ad calcem Cuspinian. de Cæsaribus, p. 716—722,) represents the theatre of the war in the xvth century.]

Before I lose sight of the field of Warna, I am tempted to pause on the character and story of two principal actors, the cardinal Julian and John Huniades. Julian [29] Cæsarini was born of a noble family of Rome: his studies had embraced both the Latin and Greek learning, both the sciences of divinity and law; and his versatile genius was equally adapted to the schools, the camp, and the court. No sooner had he been invested with the Roman purple, than he was sent into Germany to arm the empire against the rebels and heretics of Bohemia. The spirit of persecution is unworthy of a Christian; the military profession ill becomes a priest; but the former is excused by the times; and the latter was ennobled by the courage of Julian, who stood dauntless and alone in the disgraceful flight of the German host. As the pope's legate, he opened the council of Basil; but the president soon appeared the most strenuous champion of ecclesiastical freedom; and an opposition of seven years was conducted by his ability and zeal. After promoting the strongest measures against the authority and person of Eugenius, some secret motive of interest or conscience engaged him to desert on a sudden the popular party. The cardinal withdrew himself from Basil to Ferrara; and, in the debates of the Greeks and Latins, the two nations admired the dexterity of his arguments and the depth of his theological erudition. [30] In his Hungarian embassy, we have already seen the mischievous effects of his sophistry and eloquence, of which Julian himself was the first victim. The cardinal, who performed the duties of a priest and a soldier, was lost in the defeat of Warna. The circumstances of his death are variously related; but it is believed, that a weighty encumbrance of gold impeded his flight, and tempted the cruel avarice of some Christian fugitives.

[Footnote 29: M. Lenfant has described the origin (Hist. du Concile de Basle, tom. i. p. 247, &c.) and Bohemian campaign (p. 315, &c.) of Cardinal Julian. His services at Basil and Ferrara, and his unfortunate end, are occasionally related by Spondanus, and the continuator of Fleury.]

[Footnote 30: Syropulus honorably praises the talent of an enemy, (p. 117:) toiauta tina eipen o IoulianoV peplatusmenwV agan kai logikwV, kai met episthmhV kai deinothtoV 'RhtprikhV.]

From an humble, or at least a doubtful origin, the merit of John Huniades promoted him to the command of the Hungarian armies. His father was a Walachian, his mother a Greek: her unknown race might possibly ascend to the emperors of Constantinople; and the claims of the Walachians, with the surname of Corvinus, from the place of his nativity, might suggest a thin pretence for mingling his blood with the patricians of ancient Rome. [31] In his youth he served in the wars of Italy, and was retained, with twelve horsemen, by the bishop of Zagrab: the valor of the white knight [32] was soon conspicuous; he increased his fortunes by a noble and wealthy marriage; and in the defence of the Hungarian borders he won in the same year three battles against the Turks. By his influence, Ladislaus of Poland obtained the crown of Hungary; and the important service was rewarded by the title and office of Waivod of Transylvania. The first of Julian's crusades added two Turkish laurels on his brow; and in the public distress the fatal errors of Warna were forgotten. During the absence and minority of Ladislaus of Austria, the titular king, Huniades was elected supreme captain and governor of Hungary; and if envy at first was silenced by terror, a reign of twelve years supposes the arts of policy as well as of war. Yet the idea of a consummate general is not delineated in his campaigns; the white knight fought with the hand rather than the head, as the chief of desultory Barbarians, who attack without fear and fly without shame; and his military life is composed of a romantic alternative of victories and escapes. By the Turks, who employed his name to frighten their perverse children, he was corruptly denominated Jancus Lain, or the Wicked: their hatred is the proof of their esteem; the kingdom which he guarded was inaccessible to their arms; and they felt him most daring and formidable, when they fondly believed the captain and his country irrecoverably lost. Instead of confining himself to a defensive war, four years after the defeat of Warna he again penetrated into the heart of Bulgaria, and in the plain of Cossova, sustained, till the third day, the shock of the Ottoman army, four times more numerous than his own. As he fled alone through the woods of Walachia, the hero was surprised by two robbers; but while they disputed a gold chain that hung at his neck, he recovered his sword, slew the one, terrified the other, and, after new perils of captivity or death, consoled by his presence an afflicted kingdom. But the last and most glorious action of his life was the defence of Belgrade against the powers of Mahomet the Second in person. After a siege of forty days, the Turks, who had already entered the town, were compelled to retreat; and the joyful nations celebrated Huniades and Belgrade as the bulwarks of Christendom. [33] About a month after this great deliverance, the champion expired; and his most splendid epitaph is the regret of the Ottoman prince, who sighed that he could no longer hope for revenge against the single antagonist who had triumphed over his arms. On the first vacancy of the throne, Matthias Corvinus, a youth of eighteen years of age, was elected and crowned by the grateful Hungarians. His reign was prosperous and long: Matthias aspired to the glory of a conqueror and a saint: but his purest merit is the encouragement of learning; and the Latin orators and historians, who were invited from Italy by the son, have shed the lustre of their eloquence on the father's character. [34]

[Footnote 31: See Bonfinius, decad. iii. l. iv. p. 423. Could the Italian historian pronounce, or the king of Hungary hear, without a blush, the absurd flattery which confounded the name of a Walachian village with the casual, though glorious, epithet of a single branch of the Valerian family at Rome?]

[Footnote 32: Philip de Comines, (Mémoires, l. vi. c. 13,) from the tradition of the times, mentions him with high encomiums, but under the whimsical name of the Chevalier Blanc de Valaigne, (Valachia.) The Greek Chalcondyles, and the Turkish annals of Leunclavius, presume to accuse his fidelity or valor.]

[Footnote 33: See Bonfinius (decad. iii. l. viii. p. 492) and Spondanus, (A.D. 456, No. 1—7.) Huniades shared the glory of the defence of Belgrade with Capistran, a Franciscan friar; and in their respective narratives, neither the saint nor the hero condescend to take notice of his rival's merit.]

[Footnote 34: See Bonfinius, decad. iii. l. viii—decad. iv. l. viii. The observations of Spondanus on the life and character of Matthias Corvinus are curious and critical, (A.D. 1464, No. 1, 1475, No. 6, 1476, No. 14—16, 1490, No. 4, 5.) Italian fame was the object of his vanity. His actions are celebrated in the Epitome Rerum Hungaricarum (p. 322—412) of Peter Ranzanus, a Sicilian. His wise and facetious sayings are registered by Galestus Martius of Narni, (528—568,) and we have a particular narrative of his wedding and coronation. These three tracts are all contained in the first vol. of Bel's Scriptores Rerum Hungaricarum.]

In the list of heroes, John Huniades and Scanderbeg are commonly associated; [35] and they are both entitled to our notice, since their occupation of the Ottoman arms delayed the ruin of the Greek empire. John Castriot, the father of Scanderbeg, [36] was the hereditary prince of a small district of Epirus or Albania, between the mountains and the Adriatic Sea. Unable to contend with the sultan's power, Castriot submitted to the hard conditions of peace and tribute: he delivered his four sons as the pledges of his fidelity; and the Christian youths, after receiving the mark of circumcision, were instructed in the Mahometan religion, and trained in the arms and arts of Turkish policy. [37] The three elder brothers were confounded in the crowd of slaves; and the poison to which their deaths are ascribed cannot be verified or disproved by any positive evidence. Yet the suspicion is in a great measure removed by the kind and paternal treatment of George Castriot, the fourth brother, who, from his tender youth, displayed the strength and spirit of a soldier. The successive overthrow of a Tartar and two Persians, who carried a proud defiance to the Turkish court, recommended him to the favor of Amurath, and his Turkish appellation of Scanderbeg, (Iskender beg,) or the lord Alexander, is an indelible memorial of his glory and servitude. His father's principality was reduced into a province; but the loss was compensated by the rank and title of Sanjiak, a command of five thousand horse, and the prospect of the first dignities of the empire. He served with honor in the wars of Europe and Asia; and we may smile at the art or credulity of the historian, who supposes, that in every encounter he spared the Christians, while he fell with a thundering arm on his Mussulman foes. The glory of Huniades is without reproach: he fought in the defence of his religion and country; but the enemies who applaud the patriot, have branded his rival with the name of traitor and apostate. In the eyes of the Christian, the rebellion of Scanderbeg is justified by his father's wrongs, the ambiguous death of his three brothers, his own degradation, and the slavery of his country; and they adore the generous, though tardy, zeal, with which he asserted the faith and independence of his ancestors. But he had imbibed from his ninth year the doctrines of the Koran; he was ignorant of the Gospel; the religion of a soldier is determined by authority and habit; nor is it easy to conceive what new illumination at the age of forty [38] could be poured into his soul. His motives would be less exposed to the suspicion of interest or revenge, had he broken his chain from the moment that he was sensible of its weight: but a long oblivion had surely impaired his original right; and every year of obedience and reward had cemented the mutual bond of the sultan and his subject. If Scanderbeg had long harbored the belief of Christianity and the intention of revolt, a worthy mind must condemn the base dissimulation, that could serve only to betray, that could promise only to be forsworn, that could actively join in the temporal and spiritual perdition of so many thousands of his unhappy brethren. Shall we praise a secret correspondence with Huniades, while he commanded the vanguard of the Turkish army? shall we excuse the desertion of his standard, a treacherous desertion which abandoned the victory to the enemies of his benefactor? In the confusion of a defeat, the eye of Scanderbeg was fixed on the Reis Effendi or principal secretary: with the dagger at his breast, he extorted a firman or patent for the government of Albania; and the murder of the guiltless scribe and his train prevented the consequences of an immediate discovery. With some bold companions, to whom he had revealed his design he escaped in the night, by rapid marches, from the field or battle to his paternal mountains. The gates of Croya were opened to the royal mandate; and no sooner did he command the fortress, than George Castriot dropped the mask of dissimulation; abjured the prophet and the sultan, and proclaimed himself the avenger of his family and country. The names of religion and liberty provoked a general revolt: the Albanians, a martial race, were unanimous to live and die with their hereditary prince; and the Ottoman garrisons were indulged in the choice of martyrdom or baptism. In the assembly of the states of Epirus, Scanderbeg was elected general of the Turkish war; and each of the allies engaged to furnish his respective proportion of men and money. From these contributions, from his patrimonial estate, and from the valuable salt-pits of Selina, he drew an annual revenue of two hundred thousand ducats; [39] and the entire sum, exempt from the demands of luxury, was strictly appropriated to the public use. His manners were popular; but his discipline was severe; and every superfluous vice was banished from his camp: his example strengthened his command; and under his conduct, the Albanians were invincible in their own opinion and that of their enemies. The bravest adventurers of France and Germany were allured by his fame and retained in his service: his standing militia consisted of eight thousand horse and seven thousand foot; the horses were small, the men were active; but he viewed with a discerning eye the difficulties and resources of the mountains; and, at the blaze of the beacons, the whole nation was distributed in the strongest posts. With such unequal arms Scanderbeg resisted twenty-three years the powers of the Ottoman empire; and two conquerors, Amurath the Second, and his greater son, were repeatedly baffled by a rebel, whom they pursued with seeming contempt and implacable resentment. At the head of sixty thousand horse and forty thousand Janizaries, Amurath entered Albania: he might ravage the open country, occupy the defenceless towns, convert the churches into mosques, circumcise the Christian youths, and punish with death his adult and obstinate captives: but the conquests of the sultan were confined to the petty fortress of Sfetigrade; and the garrison, invincible to his arms, was oppressed by a paltry artifice and a superstitious scruple. [40] Amurath retired with shame and loss from the walls of Croya, the castle and residence of the Castriots; the march, the siege, the retreat, were harassed by a vexatious, and almost invisible, adversary; [41] and the disappointment might tend to imbitter, perhaps to shorten, the last days of the sultan. [42] In the fulness of conquest, Mahomet the Second still felt at his bosom this domestic thorn: his lieutenants were permitted to negotiate a truce; and the Albanian prince may justly be praised as a firm and able champion of his national independence. The enthusiasm of chivalry and religion has ranked him with the names of Alexander and Pyrrhus; nor would they blush to acknowledge their intrepid countryman: but his narrow dominion, and slender powers, must leave him at an humble distance below the heroes of antiquity, who triumphed over the East and the Roman legions. His splendid achievements, the bashaws whom he encountered, the armies that he discomfited, and the three thousand Turks who were slain by his single hand, must be weighed in the scales of suspicious criticism. Against an illiterate enemy, and in the dark solitude of Epirus, his partial biographers may safely indulge the latitude of romance: but their fictions are exposed by the light of Italian history; and they afford a strong presumption against their own truth, by a fabulous tale of his exploits, when he passed the Adriatic with eight hundred horse to the succor of the king of Naples. [43] Without disparagement to his fame, they might have owned, that he was finally oppressed by the Ottoman powers: in his extreme danger he applied to Pope Pius the Second for a refuge in the ecclesiastical state; and his resources were almost exhausted, since Scanderbeg died a fugitive at Lissus, on the Venetian territory. [44] His sepulchre was soon violated by the Turkish conquerors; but the Janizaries, who wore his bones enchased in a bracelet, declared by this superstitious amulet their involuntary reverence for his valor. The instant ruin of his country may redound to the hero's glory; yet, had he balanced the consequences of submission and resistance, a patriot perhaps would have declined the unequal contest which must depend on the life and genius of one man. Scanderbeg might indeed be supported by the rational, though fallacious, hope, that the pope, the king of Naples, and the Venetian republic, would join in the defence of a free and Christian people, who guarded the sea-coast of the Adriatic, and the narrow passage from Greece to Italy. His infant son was saved from the national shipwreck; the Castriots [45] were invested with a Neapolitan dukedom, and their blood continues to flow in the noblest families of the realm. A colony of Albanian fugitives obtained a settlement in Calabria, and they preserve at this day the language and manners of their ancestors. [46]

*[Footnote 35: They are ranked by Sir William Temple, in his pleasing Essay on Heroic Virtue, (Works, vol. iii. p. 385,) among the seven chiefs who have deserved without wearing, a royal crown; Belisarius, Narses, Gonsalvo of Cordova, William first prince of Orange, Alexander duke of Parma, John Huniades, and George Castriot, or Scanderbeg.]*

*[Footnote 36: I could wish for some simple authentic memoirs of a friend of Scanderbeg, which would introduce me to the man, the time, and the place. In the old and national history of Marinus Barletius, a priest of Scodra, (de Vita. Moribus, et Rebus gestis Georgii Castrioti, &c. libri xiii. p. 367. Argentorat. 1537, in fol.,) his gaudy and cumbersome robes are stuck with many false jewels. See likewise Chalcondyles, l vii. p. 185, l. viii. p. 229.]*

*[Footnote 37: His circumcision, education, &c., are marked by Marinus with brevity and reluctance, (l. i. p. 6, 7.)]*

*[Footnote 38: Since Scanderbeg died A.D. 1466, in the lxiiid year of his age, (Marinus, l. xiii. p. 370,) he was born in 1403; since he was torn from his parents by the Turks, when he was novennis, (Marinus, l. i. p. 1, 6,) that event must have happened in 1412, nine years before the accession of Amurath II., who must have inherited, not acquired the Albanian slave. Spondanus has remarked this inconsistency, A.D. 1431, No. 31, 1443, No. 14.]*

*[Footnote 39: His revenue and forces are luckily given by Marinus, (l. ii. p. 44.)]*

*[Footnote 40: There were two Dibras, the upper and lower, the Bulgarian and Albanian: the former, 70 miles from Croya, (l. i. p. 17,) was contiguous to the fortress of Sfetigrade, whose inhabitants refused to drink from a well into which a dead dog had traitorously been cast, (l. v. p. 139, 140.) We want a good map of Epirus.]*

*[Footnote 41: Compare the Turkish narrative of Cantemir (p. 92) with the pompous and prolix declamation in the ivth, vth, and vith books of the Albanian priest, who has been copied by the tribe of strangers and moderns.]*

[Footnote 42: In honor of his hero, Barletius (l. vi. p. 188—192) kills the sultan by disease indeed, under the walls of Croya. But this audacious fiction is disproved by the Greeks and Turks, who agree in the time and manner of Amurath's death at Adrianople.]

[Footnote 43: See the marvels of his Calabrian expedition in the ixth and xth books of Marinus Barletius, which may be rectified by the testimony or silence of Muratori, (Annali d'Italia, tom. xiii. p. 291,) and his original authors, (Joh. Simonetta de Rebus Francisci Sfortiæ, in Muratori, Script. Rerum Ital. tom. xxi. p. 728, et alios.) The Albanian cavalry, under the name of Stradiots, soon became famous in the wars of Italy, (Mémoires de Comines, l. viii. c. 5.)]

[Footnote 44: Spondanus, from the best evidence, and the most rational criticism, has reduced the giant Scanderbeg to the human size, (A.D. 1461, No. 20, 1463, No. 9, 1465, No. 12, 13, 1467, No. 1.) His own letter to the pope, and the testimony of Phranza, (l. iii. c. 28,) a refugee in the neighboring isle of Corfu, demonstrate his last distress, which is awkwardly concealed by Marinus Barletius, (l. x.)]

[Footnote 45: See the family of the Castriots, in Ducange, (Fam. Dalmaticæ, &c, xviii. p. 348—350.)]

[Footnote 46: This colony of Albanese is mentioned by Mr. Swinburne, (Travels into the Two Sicilies, vol. i. p. 350—354.)]

In the long career of the decline and fall of the Roman empire, I have reached at length the last reign of the princes of Constantinople, who so feebly sustained the name and majesty of the Cæsars. On the decease of John Palæologus, who survived about four years the Hungarian crusade, [47] the royal family, by the death of Andronicus and the monastic profession of Isidore, was reduced to three princes, Constantine, Demetrius, and Thomas, the surviving sons of the emperor Manuel. Of these the first and the last were far distant in the Morea; but Demetrius, who possessed the domain of Selybria, was in the suburbs, at the head of a party: his ambition was not chilled by the public distress; and his conspiracy with the Turks and the schismatics had already disturbed the peace of his country. The funeral of the late emperor was accelerated with singular and even suspicious haste: the claim of Demetrius to the vacant throne was justified by a trite and flimsy sophism, that he was born in the purple, the eldest son of his father's reign. But the empress-mother, the senate and soldiers, the clergy and people, were unanimous in the cause of the lawful successor: and the despot Thomas, who, ignorant of the change, accidentally returned to the capital, asserted with becoming zeal the interest of his absent brother. An ambassador, the historian Phranza, was immediately despatched to the court of Adrianople. Amurath received him with honor and dismissed him with gifts; but the gracious approbation of the Turkish sultan announced his supremacy, and the approaching downfall of the Eastern empire. By the hands of two illustrious deputies, the Imperial crown was placed at Sparta on the head of Constantine. In the spring he sailed from the Morea, escaped the encounter of a Turkish squadron, enjoyed the acclamations of his subjects, celebrated the festival of a new reign, and exhausted by his donatives the treasure, or rather the indigence, of the state. The emperor immediately resigned to his brothers the possession of the Morea; and the brittle friendship of the two princes, Demetrius and Thomas, was confirmed in their mother's presence by the frail security of oaths and embraces. His next occupation was the choice of a consort. A daughter of the doge of Venice had been proposed; but the Byzantine nobles objected the distance between an hereditary monarch and an elective magistrate; and in their subsequent distress, the chief of that powerful republic was not unmindful of the affront. Constantine afterwards hesitated between the royal families of Trebizond and Georgia; and the embassy of Phranza represents in his public and private life the last days of the Byzantine empire. [48]

*[Footnote 47: The Chronology of Phranza is clear and authentic; but instead of four years and seven months, Spondanus (A.D. 1445, No. 7,) assigns seven or eight years to the reign of the last Constantine which he deduces from a spurious epistle of Eugenius IV. to the king of Æthiopia.]*

*[Footnote 48: Phranza (l. iii. c. 1—6) deserves credit and esteem.]*

The protovestiare, or great chamberlain, Phranza sailed from Constantinople as the minister of a bridegroom; and the relics of wealth and luxury were applied to his pompous appearance. His numerous retinue consisted of nobles and guards, of physicians and monks: he was attended by a band of music; and the term of his costly embassy was protracted above two years. On his arrival in Georgia or Iberia, the natives from the towns and villages flocked around the strangers; and such was their simplicity, that they were delighted with the effects, without understanding the cause, of musical harmony. Among the crowd was an old man, above a hundred years of age, who had formerly been carried away a captive by the Barbarians, [49] and who amused his hearers with a tale of the wonders of India, [50] from whence he had returned to Portugal by an unknown sea. [51] From this hospitable land, Phranza proceeded to the court of Trebizond, where he was informed by the Greek prince of the recent decease of Amurath. Instead of rejoicing in the deliverance, the experienced statesman expressed his apprehension, that an ambitious youth would not long adhere to the sage and pacific system of his father. After the sultan's decease, his Christian wife, Maria, [52] the daughter of the Servian despot, had been honorably restored to her parents; on the fame of her beauty and merit, she was recommended by the ambassador as the most worthy object of the royal choice; and Phranza recapitulates and refutes the specious objections that might be raised against the proposal. The majesty of the purple would ennoble an unequal alliance; the bar of affinity might be removed by liberal alms and the dispensation of the church; the disgrace of Turkish nuptials had been repeatedly overlooked; and, though the fair Maria was nearly fifty years of age, she might yet hope to give an heir to the empire. Constantine listened to the advice, which was transmitted in the first ship that sailed from Trebizond; but the factions of the court opposed his marriage; and it was finally prevented by the pious vow of the sultana, who ended her days in the monastic profession. Reduced to the first alternative, the choice of Phranza was decided in favor of a Georgian princess; and the vanity of her father was dazzled by the glorious alliance. Instead of demanding, according to the primitive and national custom, a price for his daughter, [53] he offered a portion of fifty-six thousand, with an annual pension of five thousand, ducats; and the services of the ambassador were repaid by an assurance, that, as his son had been adopted in baptism by the emperor, the establishment of his daughter should be the peculiar care of the empress of Constantinople. On the return of Phranza, the treaty was ratified by the Greek monarch, who with his own hand impressed three vermilion crosses on the golden bull, and assured the Georgian envoy that in the spring his galleys should conduct the bride to her Imperial palace. But Constantine embraced his faithful servant, not with the cold approbation of a sovereign, but with the warm confidence of a friend, who, after a long absence, is impatient to pour his secrets into the bosom of his friend. "Since the death of my mother and of Cantacuzene, who alone advised me without interest or passion, [54] I am surrounded," said the emperor, "by men whom I can neither love nor trust, nor esteem. You are not a stranger to Lucas Notaras, the great admiral; obstinately attached to his own sentiments, he declares, both in private and public, that his sentiments are the absolute measure of my thoughts and actions. The rest of the courtiers are swayed by their personal or factious views; and how can I consult the monks on questions of policy and marriage? I have yet much employment for your diligence and fidelity. In the spring you shall engage one of my brothers to solicit the succor of the Western powers; from the Morea you shall sail to Cyprus on a particular commission; and from thence proceed to Georgia to receive and conduct the future empress."—"Your commands," replied Phranza, "are irresistible; but deign, great sir," he added, with a serious smile, "to consider, that if I am thus perpetually absent from my family, my wife may be tempted either to seek another husband, or to throw herself into a monastery." After laughing at his apprehensions, the emperor more gravely consoled him by the pleasing assurance that this should be his last service abroad, and that he destined for his son a wealthy and noble heiress; for himself, the important office of great logothete, or principal minister of state. The marriage was immediately stipulated: but the office, however incompatible with his own, had been usurped by the ambition of the admiral. Some delay was requisite to negotiate a consent and an equivalent; and the nomination of Phranza was half declared, and half suppressed, lest it might be displeasing to an insolent and powerful favorite. The winter was spent in the preparations of his embassy; and Phranza had resolved, that the youth his son should embrace this opportunity of foreign travel, and be left, on the appearance of danger, with his maternal kindred of the Morea. Such were the private and public designs, which were interrupted by a Turkish war, and finally buried in the ruins of the empire.

[Footnote 49: Suppose him to have been captured in 1394, in Timour's first war in Georgia, (Sherefeddin, l. iii. c. 50;) he might follow his Tartar master into Hindostan in 1398, and from thence sail to the spice islands.]

[Footnote 50: The happy and pious Indians lived a hundred and fifty years, and enjoyed the most perfect productions of the vegetable and mineral kingdoms. The animals were on a large scale: dragons seventy cubits, ants (the formica Indica) nine inches long, sheep like elephants, elephants like sheep. Quidlibet audendi, &c.]

[Footnote 51: He sailed in a country vessel from the spice islands to one of the ports of the exterior India; invenitque navem grandem Ibericam quâ in Portugalliam est delatus. This passage, composed in 1477, (Phranza, l. iii. c. 30,) twenty years before the discovery of the Cape of Good Hope, is spurious or wonderful. But this new geography is sullied by the old and incompatible error which places the source of the Nile in India.]

[Footnote 52: Cantemir, (p. 83,) who styles her the daughter of Lazarus Ogli, and the Helen of the Servians, places her marriage with Amurath in the year 1424. It will not easily be believed, that in six-and-twenty years' cohabitation, the sultan corpus ejus non tetigit. After the taking of Constantinople, she fled to Mahomet II., (Phranza, l. iii. c. 22.)]

[Footnote 53: The classical reader will recollect the offers of Agamemnon, (Iliad, c. v. 144,) and the general practice of antiquity.]

[Footnote 54: Cantacuzene (I am ignorant of his relation to the emperor of that name) was great domestic, a firm assertor of the Greek creed, and a brother of the queen of Servia, whom he visited with the character of ambassador, (Syropulus, p. 37, 38, 45.)]

CHAPTER LXVIII

REIGN OF MAHOMET THE SECOND, EXTINCTION OF THE EASTERN EMPIRE

PART I

REIGN AND CHARACTER OF MAHOMET THE SECOND—SIEGE, ASSAULT, AND FINAL CONQUEST, OF CONSTANTINOPLE BY THE TURKS—DEATH OF CONSTANTINE PALÆOLOGUS—SERVITUDE OF THE GREEKS—EXTINCTION OF THE ROMAN EMPIRE IN THE EAST—CONSTERNATION OF EUROPE— CONQUESTS AND DEATH OF MAHOMET THE SECOND

The siege of Constantinople by the Turks attracts our first attention to the person and character of the great destroyer. Mahomet the Second [1] was the son of the second Amurath; and though his mother has been decorated with the titles of Christian and princess, she is more probably confounded with the numerous concubines who peopled from every climate the harem of the sultan. His first education and sentiments were those of a devout Mussulman; and as often as he conversed with an infidel, he purified his hands and face by the legal rites of ablution. Age and empire appear to have relaxed this narrow bigotry: his aspiring genius disdained to acknowledge a power above his own; and in his looser hours he presumed (it is said) to brand the prophet of Mecca as a robber and impostor. Yet the sultan persevered in a decent reverence for the doctrine and discipline of the Koran: [2] his private indiscretion must have been sacred from the vulgar ear; and we should suspect the credulity of strangers and sectaries, so prone to believe that a mind which is hardened against truth must be armed with superior contempt for absurdity and error. Under the tuition of the most skilful masters, Mahomet advanced with an early and rapid progress in the paths of knowledge; and besides his native tongue it is affirmed that he spoke or understood five languages, [3] the Arabic, the Persian, the Chaldæan or Hebrew, the Latin, and the Greek. The Persian might indeed contribute to his amusement, and the Arabic to his edification; and such studies are familiar to the Oriental youth. In the intercourse of the Greeks and Turks, a conqueror might wish to converse with the people over which he was ambitious to reign: his own praises in Latin poetry [4] or prose [5] might find a passage to the royal ear; but what use or merit could recommend to the statesman or the scholar the uncouth dialect of his Hebrew slaves? The history and geography of the world were familiar to his memory: the lives of the heroes of the East, perhaps of the West, [6] excited his emulation: his skill in astrology is excused by the folly of the times, and supposes some rudiments of mathematical science; and a profane taste for the arts is betrayed in his liberal invitation and reward of the painters of Italy. [7] But the influence of religion and learning were employed without effect on his savage and licentious nature. I will not transcribe, nor do I firmly believe, the stories of his fourteen pages, whose bellies were ripped open in search of a stolen melon; or of the beauteous slave, whose head he severed from her body, to convince the Janizaries that their master was not the votary of love. [701] His sobriety is attested by the silence of the Turkish annals, which accuse three, and three only, of the Ottoman line of the vice of drunkenness. [8] But it cannot be denied that his passions were at once furious and inexorable; that in the palace, as in the field, a torrent of blood was spilt on the slightest provocation; and that the noblest of the captive youth were often dishonored by his unnatural lust. In the Albanian war he studied the lessons, and soon surpassed the example, of his father; and the conquest of two empires, twelve kingdoms, and two hundred cities, a vain and flattering account, is ascribed to his invincible sword. He was doubtless a soldier, and possibly a general; Constantinople has sealed his glory; but if we compare the means, the obstacles, and the achievements, Mahomet the Second must blush to sustain a parallel with Alexander or Timour. Under his command, the Ottoman forces were always more numerous than their enemies; yet their progress was bounded by the Euphrates and the Adriatic; and his arms were checked by Huniades and Scanderbeg, by the Rhodian knights and by the Persian king.

[Footnote 1: For the character of Mahomet II. it is dangerous to trust either the Turks or the Christians. The most moderate picture appears to be drawn by Phranza, (l. i. c. 33,) whose resentment had cooled in age and solitude; see likewise Spondanus, (A.D. 1451, No. 11,) and the continuator of Fleury, (tom. xxii. p.

552,) the Elogia of Paulus Jovius, (l. iii. p. 164—166,) and the Dictionnaire de Bayle, (tom. iii. p. 273—279.)]

[Footnote 2: Cantemir, (p. 115.) and the mosques which he founded, attest his public regard for religion. Mahomet freely disputed with the Gennadius on the two religions, (Spond. A.D. 1453, No. 22.)]

[Footnote 3: Quinque linguas præter suam noverat, Græcam, Latinam, Chaldaicam, Persicam. The Latin translator of Phranza has dropped the Arabic, which the Koran must recommend to every Mussulman. Note: It appears in the original Greek text, p. 95, edit. Bonn—M.]

[Footnote 4: Philelphus, by a Latin ode, requested and obtained the liberty of his wife's mother and sisters from the conqueror of Constantinople. It was delivered into the sultan's hands by the envoys of the duke of Milan. Philelphus himself was suspected of a design of retiring to Constantinople; yet the orator often sounded the trumpet of holy war, (see his Life by M. Lancelot, in the Mémoires de l'Académie des Inscriptions, tom. x. p. 718, 724, &c.)]

[Footnote 5: Robert Valturio published at Verona, in 1483, his xii. books de Re Militari, in which he first mentions the use of bombs. By his patron Sigismund Malatesta, prince of Rimini, it had been addressed with a Latin epistle to Mahomet II.]

[Footnote 6: According to Phranza, he assiduously studied the lives and actions of Alexander, Augustus, Constantine, and Theodosius. I have read somewhere, that Plutarch's Lives were translated by his orders into the Turkish language. If the sultan himself understood Greek, it must have been for the benefit of his subjects. Yet these lives are a school of freedom as well as of valor.  Note: Von Hammer disdainfully rejects this fable of Mahomet's knowledge of languages. Knolles adds, that he delighted in reading the history of Alexander the Great, and of Julius Cæsar. The former, no doubt, was the Persian legend, which, it is remarkable, came back to Europe, and was popular throughout the middle ages as the "Romaunt of Alexander." The founder of the Imperial dynasty of Rome, according to M. Von Hammer, is altogether unknown in the East. Mahomet was a great patron of Turkish literature: the romantic poems of Persia were translated, or imitated, under his patronage. Von Hammer vol ii. p. 268—M.]

[Footnote 7: The famous Gentile Bellino, whom he had invited from Venice, was dismissed with a chain and collar of gold, and a purse of 3000 ducats. With Voltaire I laugh at the foolish story of a slave purposely beheaded to instruct the painter in the action of the muscles.]

[Footnote 701: This story, the subject of Johnson's Irene, is rejected by M. Von Hammer, vol. ii. p. 208. The German historian's general estimate of Mahomet's character agrees in its more marked features with Gibbon's—M.]

[Footnote 8: These Imperial drunkards were Soliman I., Selim II., and Amurath IV., (Cantemir, p. 61.) The sophis of Persia can produce a more regular succession; and in the last age, our European travellers were the witnesses and companions of their revels.]

In the reign of Amurath, he twice tasted of royalty, and twice descended from the throne: his tender age was incapable of opposing his father's restoration, but never could he forgive the viziers who had recommended that salutary measure. His nuptials were celebrated with the daughter of a Turkman emir; and, after a festival of two months, he departed from Adrianople with his bride, to reside in the government of Magnesia. Before the end of six weeks, he was recalled by a sudden message from the divan, which announced the decease of Amurath, and the mutinous spirit of the Janizaries. His speed and vigor commanded their obedience: he passed the Hellespont with a chosen guard: and at the distance of a mile from Adrianople, the viziers and emirs, the imams and cadhis, the soldiers and the people, fell prostrate before the new sultan. They affected to weep, they affected to rejoice: he ascended the throne at the age of twenty-one years, and removed the cause of sedition by the death, the inevitable death, of his infant brothers. [9] [901] The ambassadors of Europe and Asia soon appeared to congratulate his accession and solicit his friendship; and to all he spoke the language of moderation and peace. The confidence of the Greek emperor was revived by the solemn oaths and fair assurances with which he sealed the ratification of the treaty: and a rich domain on the banks of the Strymon was assigned for the annual payment of three hundred thousand aspers, the pension of an Ottoman prince, who was detained at his request in the Byzantine court. Yet the neighbors of Mahomet might tremble at the severity with which a youthful monarch reformed the pomp of his father's household: the expenses of luxury were applied to those of ambition, and a useless train of seven thousand falconers was either dismissed from his service, or enlisted in his troops. [902] In the first summer of his reign, he visited with an army the Asiatic provinces; but after humbling the pride, Mahomet accepted the submission, of the Caramanian, that he might not be diverted by the smallest obstacle from the execution of his great design. [10]

[Footnote 9: Calapin, one of these royal infants, was saved from his cruel brother, and baptized at Rome under the name of Callistus Othomannus. The emperor Frederic III. presented him with an estate in Austria, where he ended his life; and Cuspinian, who in his youth conversed with the aged prince at Vienna, applauds his piety and wisdom, (de Cæsaribus, p. 672, 673.)]

[Footnote 901: Ahmed, the son of a Greek princess, was the object of his especial jealousy. Von Hammer, p. 501—M.]

[Footnote 902: The Janizaries obtained, for the first time, a gift on the accession of a new sovereign, p. 504—M.]

[Footnote 10: See the accession of Mahomet II. in Ducas, (c. 33,) Phranza, (l. i. c. 33, l. iii. c. 2,) Chalcondyles, (l. vii. p. 199,) and Cantemir, (p. 96.)]

The Mahometan, and more especially the Turkish casuists, have pronounced that no promise can bind the faithful against the interest and duty of their religion; and that the sultan may abrogate his own treaties and those of his predecessors. The justice and magnanimity of Amurath had scorned this immoral privilege; but his son, though the proudest of men, could stoop from ambition to the basest arts of dissimulation and deceit. Peace was on his lips, while war was in his heart: he incessantly sighed for the possession of Constantinople; and the Greeks, by their own indiscretion, afforded the first pretence of the fatal rupture. [11] Instead of laboring to be forgotten, their ambassadors pursued his camp, to demand the payment, and even the increase, of their annual stipend: the divan was importuned by their complaints, and the vizier, a secret friend of the Christians, was constrained to deliver the sense of his brethren. "Ye foolish and miserable Romans," said Calil, "we know your devices, and ye are ignorant of your own danger! The scrupulous Amurath is no more; his throne is occupied by a young conqueror, whom no laws can bind, and no obstacles can resist: and if you escape from his hands, give praise to the divine clemency, which yet delays the chastisement of your sins. Why do ye seek to affright us by vain and indirect menaces? Release the fugitive Orchan, crown him sultan of Romania; call the Hungarians from beyond the Danube; arm against us the nations of the West; and be assured, that you will only provoke and precipitate your ruin." But if the fears of the ambassadors were alarmed by the stern language of the vizier, they were soothed by the courteous audience and friendly speeches of the Ottoman prince; and Mahomet assured them that on his return to Adrianople he would redress the grievances, and consult the true interests, of the Greeks. No sooner had he repassed the Hellespont, than he issued a mandate to suppress their pension, and to expel their officers from the banks of the Strymon: in this measure he betrayed a hostile mind; and the second order announced, and in some degree commenced, the siege of Constantinople. In the narrow pass of the Bosphorus, an Asiatic fortress had formerly been raised by his grandfather; in the opposite situation, on the European side, he resolved to erect a more formidable castle; and a thousand masons were commanded to assemble in the spring on a spot named Asomaton, about five miles from the Greek metropolis. [12] Persuasion is the resource of the feeble; and the feeble can seldom persuade: the ambassadors of the emperor attempted, without success, to divert Mahomet from the execution of his design. They represented, that his grandfather had solicited the permission of Manuel to build a castle on his own territories; but that this double fortification, which would command the strait, could only tend to violate the alliance of the nations; to intercept the Latins who traded in the Black Sea, and perhaps to annihilate the subsistence of the city. "I form the enterprise," replied the perfidious sultan, "against the city; but the empire of Constantinople is measured by her walls. Have you forgot the distress to which my father was reduced when you formed a league with the Hungarians; when they invaded our country by land, and the Hellespont was occupied by the French galleys? Amurath was compelled to force the passage of the Bosphorus; and your strength was not equal to your malevolence. I was then a child at Adrianople; the Moslems trembled; and, for a while, the Gabours [13] insulted our disgrace. But when my father had triumphed in the field of Warna, he vowed to erect a fort on the western shore, and that vow it is my duty to accomplish. Have ye the right, have ye the power, to control my actions on my own ground? For that ground is my own: as far as the shores of the Bosphorus, Asia is inhabited by the Turks, and Europe is deserted by the Romans. Return, and inform your king, that the present Ottoman is far different from his predecessors; that his resolutions surpass their wishes; and that he performs more than they could resolve. Return in safety—but the next who delivers a similar message may expect to be flayed alive." After this declaration, Constantine, the first of the Greeks in spirit as in rank, [14] had determined to unsheathe the sword, and to resist the approach and establishment of the Turks on the Bosphorus. He was disarmed by the advice of his civil and ecclesiastical ministers, who recommended a system less generous, and even less prudent, than his own, to approve their patience and long-suffering, to brand the Ottoman with the name and guilt of an aggressor, and to depend on chance and time for their own safety, and the destruction of a fort which could not long be maintained in the neighborhood of a great and populous city. Amidst hope and fear, the fears of the wise, and the hopes of the credulous, the winter rolled away; the proper business of each man, and each hour, was postponed; and the Greeks shut their eyes against the impending danger, till the arrival of the spring and the sultan decide the assurance of their ruin.

[Footnote 11: Before I enter on the siege of Constantinople, I shall observe, that except the short hints of Cantemir and Leunclavius, I have not been able to obtain any Turkish account of this conquest; such an account as we possess of the siege of Rhodes by Soliman II., (Mémoires de l'Académie des Inscriptions, tom. xxvi. p. 723—769.) I must therefore depend on the Greeks, whose prejudices, in some degree, are subdued by their distress. Our standard texts ar those of Ducas, (c. 34—42,) Phranza, (l. iii. c. 7—20,) Chalcondyles, (l. viii. p. 201—214,) and Leonardus Chiensis, (Historia C. P. a Turco expugnatæ. Norimberghæ, 1544, in 4to., 20 leaves.) The last of these narratives is the earliest in date, since it was composed in the Isle of Chios, the 16th of August, 1453, only seventy-nine days after the loss of the city, and in the first confusion of ideas and passions. Some hints may be added from an epistle of Cardinal Isidore (in Farragine Rerum Turcicarum, ad calcem Chalcondyl. Clauseri, Basil, 1556) to Pope Nicholas V., and a tract of Theodosius Zygomala, which he addressed in the year 1581 to Martin Crucius, (Turco-

Græcia, l. i. p. 74—98, Basil, 1584.) The various facts and materials are briefly, though critically, reviewed by Spondanus, (A.D. 1453, No. 1—27.) The hearsay relations of Monstrelet and the distant Latins I shall take leave to disregard. Note: M. Von Hammer has added little new information on the siege of Constantinople, and, by his general agreement, has borne an honorable testimony to the truth, and by his close imitation to the graphic spirit and boldness, of Gibbon—M.]

[Footnote 12: The situation of the fortress, and the topography of the Bosphorus, are best learned from Peter Gyllius, (de Bosphoro Thracio, l. ii. c. 13,) Leunclavius, (Pandect. p. 445,) and Tournefort, (Voyage dans le Levant, tom. ii. lettre xv. p. 443, 444;) but I must regret the map or plan which Tournefort sent to the French minister of the marine. The reader may turn back to chap. xvii. of this History.]

[Footnote 13: The opprobrious name which the Turks bestow on the infidels, is expressed Kabour by Ducas, and Giaour by Leunclavius and the moderns. The former term is derived by Ducange (Gloss. Græc tom. i. p. 530) from Kabouron, in vulgar Greek, a tortoise, as denoting a retrograde motion from the faith. But alas! Gabour is no more than Gheber, which was transferred from the Persian to the Turkish language, from the worshippers of fire to those of the crucifix, (D'Herbelot, Bibliot. Orient. p. 375.)]

[Footnote 14: Phranza does justice to his master's sense and courage. Calliditatem hominis non ignorans Imperator prior arma movere constituit, and stigmatizes the folly of the cum sacri tum profani proceres, which he had heard, amentes spe vanâ pasci. Ducas was not a privy-counsellor.]

Of a master who never forgives, the orders are seldom disobeyed. On the twenty-sixth of March, the appointed spot of Asomaton was covered with an active swarm of Turkish artificers; and the materials by sea and land were diligently transported from Europe and Asia. [15] The lime had been burnt in Cataphrygia; the timber was cut down in the woods of Heraclea and Nicomedia; and the stones were dug from the Anatolian quarries. Each of the thousand masons was assisted by two workmen; and a measure of two cubits was marked for their daily task. The fortress [16] was built in a triangular form; each angle was flanked by a strong and massy tower; one on the declivity of the hill, two along the sea-shore: a thickness of twenty-two feet was assigned for the walls, thirty for the towers; and the whole building was covered with a solid platform of lead. Mahomet himself pressed and directed the work with indefatigable ardor: his three viziers claimed the honor of finishing their respective towers; the zeal of the cadhis emulated that of the Janizaries; the meanest labor was ennobled by the service of God and the sultan; and the diligence of the multitude was quickened by the eye of a despot, whose smile was the hope of fortune, and whose frown was the messenger of death. The Greek emperor beheld with terror the irresistible progress of the work; and vainly strove, by flattery and gifts, to assuage an implacable foe, who sought, and secretly fomented, the slightest occasion of a quarrel. Such occasions must soon and inevitably be found. The ruins of stately churches, and even the marble columns which had been consecrated to Saint Michael the archangel, were employed without scruple by the profane and rapacious Moslems; and some Christians, who presumed to oppose the removal, received from their hands the crown of martyrdom. Constantine had solicited a Turkish guard to protect the fields and harvests of his subjects: the guard was fixed; but their first order was to allow free pasture to the mules and horses of the camp, and to defend their brethren if they should be molested by the natives. The retinue of an Ottoman chief had left their horses to pass the night among the ripe corn; the damage was felt; the insult was resented; and several of both nations were slain in a tumultuous conflict. Mahomet listened with joy to the complaint; and a detachment was commanded to exterminate the guilty village: the guilty had fled; but forty innocent and unsuspecting reapers were massacred by the soldiers. Till this provocation, Constantinople had been opened to the visits of commerce and curiosity: on the first alarm, the gates were shut; but the emperor, still anxious for peace, released on the third day his

Turkish captives; [17] and expressed, in a last message, the firm resignation of a Christian and a soldier. "Since neither oaths, nor treaty, nor submission, can secure peace, pursue," said he to Mahomet, "your impious warfare. My trust is in God alone; if it should please him to mollify your heart, I shall rejoice in the happy change; if he delivers the city into your hands, I submit without a murmur to his holy will. But until the Judge of the earth shall pronounce between us, it is my duty to live and die in the defence of my people." The sultan's answer was hostile and decisive: his fortifications were completed; and before his departure for Adrianople, he stationed a vigilant Aga and four hundred Janizaries, to levy a tribute on the ships of every nation that should pass within the reach of their cannon. A Venetian vessel, refusing obedience to the new lords of the Bosphorus, was sunk with a single bullet. [171] The master and thirty sailors escaped in the boat; but they were dragged in chains to the Porte: the chief was impaled; his companions were beheaded; and the historian Ducas [18] beheld, at Demotica, their bodies exposed to the wild beasts. The siege of Constantinople was deferred till the ensuing spring; but an Ottoman army marched into the Morea to divert the force of the brothers of Constantine. At this æra of calamity, one of these princes, the despot Thomas, was blessed or afflicted with the birth of a son; "the last heir," says the plaintive Phranza, "of the last spark of the Roman empire." [19]

[Footnote 15: Instead of this clear and consistent account, the Turkish Annals (Cantemir, p. 97) revived the foolish tale of the ox's hide, and Dido's stratagem in the foundation of Carthage. These annals (unless we are swayed by an anti-Christian prejudice) are far less valuable than the Greek historians.]

[Footnote 16: In the dimensions of this fortress, the old castle of Europe, Phranza does not exactly agree with Chalcondyles, whose description has been verified on the spot by his editor Leunclavius.]

[Footnote 17: Among these were some pages of Mahomet, so conscious of his inexorable rigor, that they begged to lose their heads in the city unless they could return before sunset.]

[Footnote 171: This was from a model cannon cast by Urban the Hungarian. See p. 291. Von Hammer. p. 510—M.]

[Footnote 18: Ducas, c. 35. Phranza, (l. iii. c. 3,) who had sailed in his vessel, commemorates the Venetian pilot as a martyr.]

[Footnote 19: Auctum est Palæologorum genus, et Imperii successor, parvæque Romanorum scintillæ hæres natus, Andreas, &c., (Phranza, l. iii. c. 7.) The strong expression was inspired by his feelings.]

The Greeks and the Turks passed an anxious and sleepless winter: the former were kept awake by their fears, the latter by their hopes; both by the preparations of defence and attack; and the two emperors, who had the most to lose or to gain, were the most deeply affected by the national sentiment. In Mahomet, that sentiment was inflamed by the ardor of his youth and temper: he amused his leisure with building at Adrianople [20] the lofty palace of Jehan Numa, (the watchtower of the world;) but his serious thoughts were irrevocably bent on the conquest of the city of Cæsar. At the dead of night, about the second watch, he started from his bed, and commanded the instant attendance of his prime vizier. The message, the hour, the prince, and his own situation, alarmed the guilty conscience of Calil Basha; who had possessed the confidence, and advised the restoration, of Amurath. On the accession of the son, the vizier was confirmed in his office and the appearances of favor; but the veteran statesman was not insensible that he trod on a thin and slippery ice, which might break under his footsteps, and plunge him in the abyss. His friendship for the Christians, which might be innocent under the late reign, had stigmatized him with the name of Gabour Ortachi, or foster-brother of the infidels; [21] and his avarice entertained a venal and treasonable correspondence, which was detected and punished after the conclusion of the war. On receiving the royal mandate, he embraced, perhaps for the last time, his wife and children; filled a cup with pieces of gold, hastened to the palace, adored the sultan, and offered, according to the Oriental custom, the slight tribute of his duty and gratitude. [22] "It is not my wish," said Mahomet, "to resume my gifts, but rather to heap and multiply them on thy head. In my turn, I ask a present far more valuable and important;—Constantinople." As soon as the vizier had recovered from his surprise, "The same God," said he, "who has already given thee so large a portion of the Roman empire, will not deny the remnant, and the capital. His providence, and thy power, assure thy success; and myself, with the rest of thy faithful slaves, will sacrifice our lives and fortunes."—"Lala," [23] (or preceptor,) continued the sultan, "do you see this pillow? All the night, in my agitation, I have pulled it on one side and the other; I have risen from my bed, again have I lain down; yet sleep has not visited these weary eyes. Beware of the gold and silver of the Romans: in arms we are superior; and with the aid of God, and the prayers of the prophet, we shall speedily become masters of Constantinople." To sound the disposition of his soldiers, he often wandered through the streets alone, and in disguise; and it was fatal to discover the sultan, when he wished to escape from the vulgar eye. His hours were spent in delineating the plan of the hostile city; in debating with his generals and engineers, on what spot he should erect his batteries; on which side he should assault the walls; where he should spring his mines; to what place he should apply his scaling-ladders: and the exercises of the day repeated and proved the lucubrations of the night.

[Footnote 20: Cantemir, p. 97, 98. The sultan was either doubtful of his conquest, or ignorant of the superior merits of Constantinople. A city or a kingdom may sometimes be ruined by the Imperial fortune of their sovereign.]

[Footnote 21: SuntrojoV, by the president Cousin, is translated père nourricier, most correctly indeed from the Latin version; but in his haste he has overlooked the note by which Ishmæl Boillaud (ad Ducam, c. 35) acknowledges and rectifies his own error.]

[Footnote 22: The Oriental custom of never appearing without gifts before a sovereign or a superior is of high antiquity, and seems analogous with the idea of sacrifice, still more ancient and universal. See the examples of such Persian gifts, Ælian, Hist. Var. l. i. c. 31, 32, 33.]

[Footnote 23: The Lala of the Turks (Cantemir, p. 34) and the Tata of the Greeks (Ducas, c. 35) are derived from the natural language of children; and it may be observed, that all such primitive words which denote their parents, are the simple repetition of one syllable, composed of a labial or a dental consonant and an open vowel, (Des Brosses, Méchanisme des Langues, tom. i. p. 231—247.)]

PART II

Among the implements of destruction, he studied with peculiar care the recent and tremendous discovery of the Latins; and his artillery surpassed whatever had yet appeared in the world. A founder of cannon, a Dane [23/1] or Hungarian, who had been almost starved in the Greek service, deserted to the Moslems, and was liberally entertained by the Turkish sultan. Mahomet was satisfied with the answer to his first question, which he eagerly pressed on the artist. "Am I able to cast a cannon capable of throwing a ball or stone of sufficient size to batter the walls of Constantinople? I am not ignorant of their strength; but were they more solid than those of Babylon, I could oppose an engine of superior power: the position and management of that engine must be left to your engineers." On this assurance, a foundry was established at Adrianople: the metal was prepared; and at the end of three months, Urban produced a piece of brass ordnance of stupendous, and almost incredible magnitude; a measure of twelve palms is assigned to the bore; and the stone bullet weighed above six hundred pounds. [24] [241] A vacant place before the new palace was chosen for the first experiment; but to prevent the sudden and mischievous effects of astonishment and fear, a proclamation was issued, that the cannon would be discharged the ensuing day. The explosion was felt or heard in a circuit of a hundred furlongs: the ball, by the force of gunpowder, was driven above a mile; and on the spot where it fell, it buried itself a fathom deep in the ground. For the conveyance of this destructive engine, a frame or carriage of thirty wagons was linked together and drawn along by a team of sixty oxen: two hundred men on both sides were stationed, to poise and support the rolling weight; two hundred and fifty workmen marched before to smooth the way and repair the bridges; and near two months were employed in a laborious journey of one hundred and fifty miles. A lively philosopher [25] derides on this occasion the credulity of the Greeks, and observes, with much reason, that we should always distrust the exaggerations of a vanquished people. He calculates, that a ball, even o two hundred pounds, would require a charge of one hundred and fifty pounds of powder; and that the stroke would be feeble and impotent, since not a fifteenth part of the mass could be inflamed at the same moment. A stranger as I am to the art of destruction, I can discern that the modern improvements of artillery prefer the number of pieces to the weight of metal; the quickness of the fire to the sound, or even the consequence, of a single explosion. Yet I dare not reject the positive and unanimous evidence of contemporary writers; nor can it seem improbable, that the first artists, in their rude and ambitious efforts, should have transgressed the standard of moderation. A Turkish cannon, more enormous than that of Mahomet, still guards the entrance of the Dardanelles; and if the use be inconvenient, it has been found on a late trial that the effect was far from contemptible. A stone bullet of eleven hundred pounds' weight was once discharged with three hundred and thirty pounds of powder: at the distance of six hundred yards it shivered into three rocky fragments; traversed the strait; and leaving the waters in a foam, again rose and bounded against the opposite hill. [26]

[Footnote 23/1: Gibbon has written Dane by mistake for Dace, or Dacian. Lax ti kinoV?. Chalcondyles, Von Hammer, p. 510—M.]

[Footnote 24: The Attic talent weighed about sixty minæ, or avoirdupois pounds (see Hooper on Ancient Weights, Measures, &c.;) but among the modern Greeks, that classic appellation was extended to a weight of one hundred, or one hundred and twenty-five pounds, (Ducange, talanton.) Leonardus Chiensis measured the ball or stone of the second cannon Lapidem, qui palmis undecim ex meis ambibat in gyro.]

[Footnote 24/1: 1200, according to Leonardus Chiensis. Von Hammer states that he had himself seen the great cannon of the Dardanelles, in which a tailor who had run away from his creditors, had concealed himself several days Von Hammer had measured balls twelve spans round. Note. p. 666—M.]

[Footnote 25: See Voltaire, (Hist. Générale, c. xci. p. 294, 295.) He was ambitious of universal monarchy; and the poet frequently aspires to the name and style of an astronomer, a chemist, &c.]

[Footnote 26: The Baron de Tott, (tom. iii. p. 85—89,) who fortified the Dardanelles against the Russians, describes in a lively, and even comic, strain his own prowess, and the consternation of the Turks. But that adventurous traveller does not possess the art of gaining our confidence.]

While Mahomet threatened the capital of the East, the Greek emperor implored with fervent prayers the assistance of earth and heaven. But the invisible powers were deaf to his supplications; and Christendom beheld with indifference the fall of Constantinople, while she derived at least some promise of supply from the jealous and temporal policy of the sultan of Egypt. Some states were too weak, and others too remote; by some the danger was considered as imaginary by others as inevitable: the Western princes were involved in their endless and domestic quarrels; and the Roman pontiff was exasperated by the falsehood or obstinacy of the Greeks. Instead of employing in their favor the arms and treasures of Italy, Nicholas the Fifth had foretold their approaching ruin; and his honor was engaged in the accomplishment of his prophecy. [261] Perhaps he was softened by the last extremity o their distress; but his compassion was tardy; his efforts were faint and unavailing; and Constantinople had fallen, before the squadrons of Genoa and Venice could sail from their harbors. [27] Even the princes of the Morea and of the Greek islands affected a cold neutrality: the Genoese colony of Galata negotiated a private treaty; and the sultan indulged them in the delusive hope, that by his clemency they might survive the ruin of the empire. A plebeian crowd, and some Byzantine nobles basely withdrew from the danger of their country; and the avarice of the rich denied the emperor, and reserved for the Turks, the secret treasures which might have raised in their defence whole armies of mercenaries. [28] The indigent and solitary prince prepared, however, to sustain his formidable adversary; but if his courage were equal to the peril, his strength was inadequate to the contest. In the beginning of the spring, the Turkish vanguard swept the towns and villages as far as the gates of Constantinople: submission was spared and protected; whatever presumed to resist was exterminated with fire and sword. The Greek places on the Black Sea, Mesembria, Acheloum, and Bizon, surrendered on the first summons; Selybria alone deserved the honors of a siege or blockade; and the bold inhabitants, while they were invested by land, launched their boats, pillaged the opposite coast of Cyzicus, and sold their captives in the public market. But on the approach of Mahomet himself all was silent and prostrate: he first halted at the distance of five miles; and from thence advancing in battle array, planted before the gates of St. Romanus the Imperial standard; and on the sixth day of April formed the memorable siege of Constantinople.

[Footnote 26/1: See the curious Christian and Mahometan predictions of the fall of Constantinople, Von Hammer, p. 518—M.]

[Footnote 27: Non audivit, indignum ducens, says the honest Antoninus; but as the Roman court was afterwards grieved and ashamed, we find the more courtly expression of Platina, in animo fuisse pontifici juvare Græcos, and the positive assertion of Æneas Sylvius, structam classem &c. (Spond. A.D. 1453, No. 3.)]

[Footnote 28: Antonin. in Proem—Epist. Cardinal. Isidor. apud Spondanum and Dr. Johnson, in the tragedy of Irene, has happily seized this characteristic circumstance:— The groaning Greeks dig up the golden caverns. The accumulated wealth of hoarding ages; That wealth which, granted to their weeping prince, Had ranged embattled nations at their gates.]

The troops of Asia and Europe extended on the right and left from the Propontis to the harbor; the Janizaries in the front were stationed before the sultan's tent; the Ottoman line was covered by a deep intrenchment; and a subordinate army enclosed the suburb of Galata, and watched the doubtful faith of the Genoese. The inquisitive Philelphus, who resided in Greece about thirty years before the siege, is confident, that all the Turkish forces of any name or value could not exceed the number of sixty thousand horse and twenty thousand foot; and he upbraids the pusillanimity of the nations, who had tamely yielded to a handful of Barbarians. Such indeed might be the regular establishment of the

Capiculi, [29] the troops of the Porte who marched with the prince, and were paid from his royal treasury. But the bashaws, in their respective governments, maintained or levied a provincial militia; many lands were held by a military tenure; many volunteers were attracted by the hope of spoil and the sound of the holy trumpet invited a swarm of hungry and fearless fanatics, who might contribute at least to multiply the terrors, and in a first attack to blunt the swords, of the Christians. The whole mass of the Turkish powers is magnified by Ducas, Chalcondyles, and Leonard of Chios, to the amount of three or four hundred thousand men; but Phranza was a less remote and more accurate judge; and his precise definition of two hundred and fifty-eight thousand does not exceed the measure of experience and probability. [30] The navy of the besiegers was less formidable: the Propontis was overspread with three hundred and twenty sail; but of these no more than eighteen could be rated as galleys of war; and the far greater part must be degraded to the condition of store-ships and transports, which poured into the camp fresh supplies of men, ammunition, and provisions. In her last decay, Constantinople was still peopled with more than a hundred thousand inhabitants; but these numbers are found in the accounts, not of war, but of captivity; and they mostly consisted of mechanics, of priests, of women, and of men devoid of that spirit which even women have sometimes exerted for the common safety. I can suppose, I could almost excuse, the reluctance of subjects to serve on a distant frontier, at the will of a tyrant; but the man who dares not expose his life in the defence of his children and his property, has lost in society the first and most active energies of nature. By the emperor's command, a particular inquiry had been made through the streets and houses, how many of the citizens, or even of the monks, were able and willing to bear arms for their country. The lists were intrusted to Phranza; [31] and, after a diligent addition, he informed his master, with grief and surprise, that the national defence was reduced to four thousand nine hundred and seventy Romans. Between Constantine and his faithful minister this comfortless secret was preserved; and a sufficient proportion of shields, cross-bows, and muskets, were distributed from the arsenal to the city bands. They derived some accession from a body of two thousand strangers, under the command of John Justiniani, a noble Genoese; a liberal donative was advanced to these auxiliaries; and a princely recompense, the Isle of Lemnos, was promised to the valor and victory of their chief. A strong chain was drawn across the mouth of the harbor: it was supported by some Greek and Italian vessels of war and merchandise; and the ships of every Christian nation, that successively arrived from Candia and the Black Sea, were detained for the public service. Against the powers of the Ottoman empire, a city of the extent of thirteen, perhaps of sixteen, miles was defended by a scanty garrison of seven or eight thousand soldiers. Europe and Asia were open to the besiegers; but the strength and provisions of the Greeks must sustain a daily decrease; nor could they indulge the expectation of any foreign succor or supply.

[Footnote 29: The palatine troops are styled Capiculi, the provincials, Seratculi; and most of the names and institutions of the Turkish militia existed before the Canon Nameh of Soliman II, from which, and his own experience, Count Marsigli has composed his military state of the Ottoman empire.]

[Footnote 30: The observation of Philelphus is approved by Cuspinian in the year 1508, (de Cæsaribus, in Epilog. de Militiâ Turcicâ, p. 697.) Marsigli proves, that the effective armies of the Turks are much less numerous than they appear. In the army that besieged Constantinople Leonardus Chiensis reckons no more than 15,000 Janizaries.]

[Footnote 31: Ego, eidem (Imp.) tabellas extribui non absque dolore et mstitia, mansitque apud nos duos aliis occultus numerus, (Phranza, l. iii. c. 8.) With some indulgence for national prejudices, we cannot desire a more authentic witness, not only of public facts, but of private counsels.]

The primitive Romans would have drawn their swords in the resolution of death or conquest. The primitive Christians might have embraced each other, and awaited in patience and charity the stroke of martyrdom. But the Greeks of Constantinople were animated only by the spirit of religion, and that spirit was productive only of animosity and discord. Before his death, the emperor John Palæologus had renounced the unpopular measure of a union with the Latins; nor was the idea revived, till the distress of his brother Constantine imposed a last trial of flattery and dissimulation. [32] With the demand of temporal aid, his ambassadors were instructed to mingle the assurance of spiritual obedience: his neglect of the church was excused by the urgent cares of the state; and his orthodox wishes solicited the presence of a Roman legate. The Vatican had been too often deluded; yet the signs of repentance could not decently be overlooked; a legate was more easily granted than an army; and about six months before the final destruction, the cardinal Isidore of Russia appeared in that character with a retinue of priests and soldiers. The emperor saluted him as a friend and father; respectfully listened to his public and private sermons; and with the most obsequious of the clergy and laymen subscribed the act of union, as it had been ratified in the council of Florence. On the twelfth of December, the two nations, in the church of St. Sophia, joined in the communion of sacrifice and prayer; and the names of the two pontiffs were solemnly commemorated; the names of Nicholas the Fifth, the vicar of Christ, and of the patriarch Gregory, who had been driven into exile by a rebellious people.

*[Footnote 32: In Spondanus, the narrative of the union is not only partial, but imperfect. The bishop of Pamiers died in 1642, and the history of Ducas, which represents these scenes (c. 36, 37) with such truth and spirit, was not printed till the year 1649.]*

But the dress and language of the Latin priest who officiated at the altar were an object of scandal; and it was observed with horror, that he consecrated a cake or wafer of unleavened bread, and poured cold water into the cup of the sacrament. A national historian acknowledges with a blush, that none of his countrymen, not the emperor himself, were sincere in this occasional conformity. [33] Their hasty and unconditional submission was palliated by a promise of future revisal; but the best, or the worst, of their excuses was the confession of their own perjury. When they were pressed by the reproaches of their honest brethren, "Have patience," they whispered, "have patience till God shall have delivered the city from the great dragon who seeks to devour us. You shall then perceive whether we are truly reconciled with the Azymites." But patience is not the attribute of zeal; nor can the arts of a court be adapted to the freedom and violence of popular enthusiasm. From the dome of St. Sophia the inhabitants of either sex, and of every degree, rushed in crowds to the cell of the monk Gennadius, [34] to consult the oracle of the church. The holy man was invisible; entranced, as it should seem, in deep meditation, or divine rapture: but he had exposed on the door of his cell a speaking tablet; and they successively withdrew, after reading those tremendous words: "O miserable Romans, why will ye abandon the truth? and why, instead of confiding in God, will ye put your trust in the Italians? In losing your faith you will lose your city. Have mercy on me, O Lord! I protest in thy presence that I am innocent of the crime. O miserable Romans, consider, pause, and repent. At the same moment that you renounce the religion of your fathers, by embracing impiety, you submit to a foreign servitude." According to the advice of Gennadius, the religious virgins, as pure as angels, and as proud as dæmons, rejected the act of union, and abjured all communion with the present and future associates of the Latins; and their example was applauded and imitated by the greatest part of the clergy and people. From the monastery, the devout Greeks dispersed themselves in the taverns; drank confusion to the slaves of the pope; emptied their glasses in honor of the image of the holy Virgin; and besought her to defend against Mahomet the city which she had formerly saved from Chosroes and the Chagan. In the double intoxication of zeal and wine, they valiantly exclaimed, "What occasion have we for succor, or union, or Latins? Far from us be the worship of the Azymites!" During the winter that preceded the Turkish conquest, the nation was distracted by this epidemical frenzy; and the season of Lent, the approach of Easter, instead of breathing charity and love, served only to fortify the obstinacy and influence of the zealots. The confessors scrutinized and alarmed the conscience of their votaries, and a rigorous penance was imposed on those who had received the communion from a priest who had given an express or tacit consent to the union. His service at the altar propagated the infection to the mute and simple spectators of the ceremony: they forfeited, by the impure spectacle, the virtue of the sacerdotal character; nor was it lawful, even in danger of sudden death, to invoke the assistance of their prayers or absolution. No sooner had the church of St. Sophia been polluted by the Latin sacrifice, than it was deserted as a Jewish synagogue, or a heathen temple, by the clergy and people; and a vast and gloomy silence prevailed in that venerable dome, which had so often smoked with a cloud of incense, blazed with innumerable lights, and resounded with the voice of prayer and thanksgiving. The Latins were the most odious of heretics and infidels; and the first minister of the empire, the great duke, was heard to declare, that he had rather behold in Constantinople the turban of Mahomet, than the pope's tiara or a cardinal's hat. [35] A sentiment so unworthy of Christians and patriots was familiar and fatal to the Greeks: the emperor was deprived of the affection and support of his subjects; and their native cowardice was sanctified by resignation to the divine decree, or the visionary hope of a miraculous deliverance.

[Footnote 33: Phranza, one of the conforming Greeks, acknowledges that the measure was adopted only propter spem auxilii; he affirms with pleasure, that those who refused to perform their devotions in St. Sophia, extra culpam et in pace essent, (l. iii. c. 20.)]

[Footnote 34: His primitive and secular name was George Scholarius, which he changed for that of Gennadius, either when he became a monk or a patriarch. His defence, at Florence, of the same union, which he so furiously attacked at Constantinople, has tempted Leo Allatius (Diatrib. de Georgiis, in Fabric. Bibliot. Græc. tom. x. p. 760—786) to divide him into two men; but Renaudot (p. 343—383) has restored the identity of his person and the duplicity of his character.]

[Footnote 35: Fakiolion, kaluptra, may be fairly translated a cardinal's hat. The difference of the Greek and Latin habits imbittered the schism.]

Of the triangle which composes the figure of Constantinople, the two sides along the sea were made inaccessible to an enemy; the Propontis by nature, and the harbor by art. Between the two waters, the basis of the triangle, the land side was protected by a double wall, and a deep ditch of the depth of one hundred feet. Against this line of fortification, which Phranza, an eye-witness, prolongs to the measure of six miles, [36] the Ottomans directed their principal attack; and the emperor, after distributing the service and command of the most perilous stations, undertook the defence of the external wall. In the first days of the siege the Greek soldiers descended into the ditch, or sallied into the field; but they soon discovered, that, in the proportion of their numbers, one Christian was of more value than twenty Turks: and, after these bold preludes, they were prudently content to maintain the rampart with their missile weapons. Nor should this prudence be accused of pusillanimity. The nation was indeed pusillanimous and base; but the last Constantine deserves the name of a hero: his noble band of volunteers was inspired with Roman virtue; and the foreign auxiliaries supported the honor of the Western chivalry. The incessant volleys of lances and arrows were accompanied with the smoke, the sound, and the fire, of their musketry and cannon. Their small arms discharged at the same time either five, or even ten, balls of lead, of the size of a walnut; and, according to the closeness of the ranks and the force of the powder, several breastplates and bodies were transpierced by the same shot. But the Turkish approaches were soon sunk in trenches, or covered with ruins. Each day added to the science of the Christians; but their inadequate stock of gunpowder was wasted in the operations of each day. Their ordnance was not powerful, either in size or number; and if they possessed some heavy cannon, they feared to plant them on the walls, lest the aged structure should be shaken and overthrown by the explosion. [37] The same destructive secret had been revealed to the Moslems; by whom it was employed with the superior energy of zeal, riches, and despotism. The great cannon of Mahomet has been separately noticed; an important and visible object in the history of the times: but that enormous engine was flanked by two fellows almost of equal magnitude: [38] the long order of the Turkish artillery was pointed against the walls; fourteen batteries thundered at once on the most accessible places; and of one of these it is ambiguously expressed, that it was mounted with one hundred and thirty guns, or that it discharged one hundred and thirty bullets. Yet in the power and activity of the sultan, we may discern the infancy of the new science. Under a master who counted the moments, the great cannon could be loaded and fired no more than seven times in one day. [39] The heated metal unfortunately burst; several workmen were destroyed; and the skill of an artist [391] was admired who bethought himself of preventing the danger and the accident, by pouring oil, after each explosion, into the mouth of the cannon.

[Footnote 36: We are obliged to reduce the Greek miles to the smallest measure which is preserved in the wersts of Russia, of 547 French toises, and of 104 2/5 to a degree. The six miles of Phranza do not exceed four English miles, (D'Anville, Mesures Itineraires, p. 61, 123, &c.)]

[Footnote 37: At indies doctiores nostri facti paravere contra hostes machinamenta, quæ tamen avare dabantur. Pulvis erat nitri modica exigua; tela modica; bombardæ, si aderant incommoditate loci primum hostes offendere, maceriebus alveisque tectos, non poterant. Nam si quæ magnæ erant, ne murus concuteretur noster, quiescebant. This passage of Leonardus Chiensis is curious and important.]

[Footnote 38: According to Chalcondyles and Phranza, the great cannon burst; an incident which, according to Ducas, was prevented by the artist's skill. It is evident that they do not speak of the same gun. Note: They speak, one of a Byzantine, one of a Turkish, gun. Von Hammer note, p. 669.]

[Footnote 39: Near a hundred years after the siege of Constantinople, the French and English fleets in the Channel were proud of firing 300 shot in an engagement of two hours, (Mémoires de Martin du Bellay, l. x., in the Collection Générale, tom. xxi. p. 239.)]

[Footnote 39/1: The founder of the gun. Von Hammer, p. 526.]

The first random shots were productive of more sound than effect; and it was by the advice of a Christian, that the engineers were taught to level their aim against the two opposite sides of the salient angles of a bastion. However imperfect, the weight and repetition of the fire made some impression on the walls; and the Turks, pushing their approaches to the edge of the ditch, attempted to fill the enormous chasm, and to build a road to the assault. [40] Innumerable fascines, and hogsheads, and trunks of trees, were heaped on each other; and such was the impetuosity of the throng, that the foremost and the weakest were pushed headlong down the precipice, and instantly buried under the accumulated mass. To fill the ditch was the toil of the besiegers; to clear away the rubbish was the safety of the besieged; and after a long and bloody conflict, the web that had been woven in the day was still unravelled in the night. The next resource of Mahomet was the practice of mines; but the soil was rocky; in every attempt he was stopped and undermined by the Christian engineers; nor had the art been yet invented of replenishing those subterraneous passages with gunpowder, and blowing whole towers and cities into the air. [41] A circumstance that distinguishes the siege of Constantinople is the reunion of the ancient and modern artillery. The cannon were intermingled with the mechanical engines for casting stones and darts; the bullet and the battering-ram [41/1] were directed against the same walls: nor had the discovery of gunpowder superseded the use of the liquid and unextinguishable fire. A wooden turret of the largest size was advanced on rollers this portable magazine of ammunition and fascines was protected by a threefold covering of bulls' hides: incessant volleys were securely discharged from the loop-holes; in the front, three doors were contrived for the alternate sally and retreat of the soldiers and workmen. They ascended by a staircase to the upper platform, and, as high as the level of that platform, a scaling-ladder could be raised by pulleys to form a bridge, and grapple with the adverse rampart. By these various arts of annoyance, some as new as they were pernicious to the Greeks, the tower of St. Romanus was at length overturned: after a severe struggle, the Turks were repulsed from the breach, and interrupted by darkness; but they trusted that with the return of light they should renew the attack with fresh vigor and decisive success. Of this pause of action, this interval of hope, each moment was improved, by the activity of the emperor and Justiniani, who passed the night on the spot, and urged the labors which involved the safety of the church and city. At the dawn of day, the impatient sultan perceived, with astonishment and grief, that his wooden turret had been reduced to ashes: the ditch was cleared and restored; and the tower of St. Romanus was again strong and entire. He deplored the failure of his design; and uttered a profane exclamation, that the word of the thirty-seven thousand prophets should not have compelled him to believe that such a work, in so short a time, could have been accomplished by the infidels.

[Footnote 40: I have selected some curious facts, without striving to emulate the bloody and obstinate eloquence of the abbé de Vertot, in his prolix descriptions of the sieges of Rhodes, Malta, &c. But that agreeable historian had a turn for romance; and as he wrote to please the order he had adopted the same spirit of enthusiasm and chivalry.]

[Footnote 41: The first theory of mines with gunpowder appears in 1480 in a MS. of George of Sienna, (Tiraboschi, tom. vi. P. i. p. 324.) They were first practised by Sarzanella, in 1487; but the honor and improvement in 1503 is ascribed to Peter of Navarre, who used them with success in the wars of Italy, (Hist. de la Ligue de Cambray, tom. ii. p. 93—97.)]

[Footnote 41/1: The battering-ram according to Von Hammer, (p. 670,) was not used—M.]


PART III

The generosity of the Christian princes was cold and tardy; but in the first apprehension of a siege, Constantine had negotiated, in the isles of the Archipelago, the Morea, and Sicily, the most indispensable supplies. As early as the beginning of April, five [42] great ships, equipped for merchandise and war, would have sailed from the harbor of Chios, had not the wind blown obstinately from the north. [43] One of these ships bore the Imperial flag; the remaining four belonged to the Genoese; and they were laden with wheat and barley, with wine, oil, and vegetables, and, above all, with soldiers and mariners for the service of the capital. After a tedious delay, a gentle breeze, and, on the second day, a strong gale from the south, carried them through the Hellespont and the Propontis: but the city was already invested by sea and land; and the Turkish fleet, at the entrance of the Bosphorus, was stretched from shore to shore, in the form of a crescent, to intercept, or at least to repel, these bold auxiliaries. The reader who has present to his mind the geographical picture of Constantinople, will conceive and admire the greatness of the spectacle. The five Christian ships continued to advance with joyful shouts, and a full press both of sails and oars, against a hostile fleet of three hundred vessels; and the rampart, the camp, the coasts of Europe and Asia, were lined with innumerable spectators, who anxiously awaited the event of this momentous succor. At the first view that event could not appear doubtful; the superiority of the Moslems was beyond all measure or account: and, in a calm, their numbers and valor must inevitably have prevailed. But their hasty and imperfect navy had been created, not by the genius of the people, but by the will of the sultan: in the height of their prosperity, the Turks have acknowledged, that if God had given them the earth, he had left the sea to the infidels; [44] and a series of defeats, a rapid progress of decay, has established the truth of their modest confession. Except eighteen galleys of some force, the rest of their fleet consisted of open boats, rudely constructed and awkwardly managed, crowded with troops, and destitute of cannon; and since courage arises in a great measure from the consciousness of strength, the bravest of the Janizaries might tremble on a new element. In the Christian squadron, five stout and lofty ships were guided by skilful pilots, and manned with the veterans of Italy and Greece, long practised in the arts and perils of the sea. Their weight was directed to sink or scatter the weak obstacles that impeded their passage: their artillery swept the waters: their liquid fire was poured on the heads of the adversaries, who, with the design of boarding, presumed to approach them; and the winds and waves are always on the side of the ablest navigators. In this conflict, the Imperial vessel, which had been almost overpowered, was rescued by the Genoese; but the Turks, in a distant and closer attack, were twice repulsed with considerable loss. Mahomet himself sat on horseback on the beach to encourage their valor by his voice and presence, by the promise of reward, and by fear more potent than the fear of the enemy. The passions of his soul, and even the gestures of his body, [45] seemed to imitate the actions of the combatants; and, as if he had been the lord of nature, he spurred his horse with a fearless and impotent effort into the sea. His loud reproaches, and the clamors of the camp, urged the Ottomans to a third attack, more fatal and bloody than the two former; and I must repeat, though I cannot credit, the evidence of Phranza, who affirms, from their own mouth, that they lost above twelve thousand men in the slaughter of the day. They fled in disorder to the shores of Europe and Asia, while the Christian squadron, triumphant and unhurt, steered along the Bosphorus, and securely anchored within the chain of the harbor. In the confidence of victory, they boasted that the whole Turkish power must have yielded to their arms; but the admiral, or captain bashaw, found some consolation for a painful wound in his eye, by representing that accident as the cause of his defeat. Balthi Ogli was a renegade of the race of the Bulgarian princes: his military character was tainted with the unpopular vice of avarice; and under the despotism of the prince or people, misfortune is a sufficient evidence of guilt. [451] His rank and services were annihilated by the displeasure of Mahomet. In the royal presence, the captain bashaw was extended on the ground by four slaves, and received one hundred strokes with a golden rod: [46] his death had been pronounced; and he adored the clemency of the sultan, who was satisfied with the milder punishment of confiscation and exile. The introduction of this supply revived the hopes of the Greeks, and accused the supineness of their Western allies. Amidst the deserts of Anatolia and the rocks of Palestine, the millions of the crusades had buried themselves in a voluntary and inevitable grave; but the situation of the Imperial city was strong against her enemies, and accessible to her friends; and a rational and moderate armament of the marine states might have saved the relics of the Roman name, and maintained a Christian fortress in the heart of the Ottoman empire. Yet this was the sole and feeble attempt for the deliverance of Constantinople: the more distant powers were insensible of its danger; and the ambassador of Hungary, or at least of Huniades, resided in the Turkish camp, to remove the fears, and to direct the operations, of the sultan. [47]

*[Footnote 42: It is singular that the Greeks should not agree in the number of these illustrious vessels; the five of Ducas, the four of Phranza and Leonardus, and the two of Chalcondyles, must be extended to the smaller, or confined to the larger, size. Voltaire, in giving one of these ships to Frederic III., confounds the emperors of the East and West.]*

[Footnote 43: In bold defiance, or rather in gross ignorance, of language and geography, the president Cousin detains them in Chios with a south, and wafts them to Constantinople with a north, wind.]

[Footnote 44: The perpetual decay and weakness of the Turkish navy may be observed in Ricaut, (State of the Ottoman Empire, p. 372—378,) Thevenot, (Voyages, P. i. p. 229—242, and Tott), (Mémoires, tom. iii;) the last of whom is always solicitous to amuse and amaze his reader.]

[Footnote 45: I must confess that I have before my eyes the living picture which Thucydides (l. vii. c. 71) has drawn of the passions and gestures of the Athenians in a naval engagement in the great harbor of Syracuse.]

[Footnote 451: According to Ducas, one of the Afabi beat out his eye with a stone Compare Von Hammer—M.]

[Footnote 46: According to the exaggeration or corrupt text of Ducas, (c. 38,) this golden bar was of the enormous or incredible weight of 500 libræ, or pounds. Bouillaud's reading of 500 drachms, or five pounds, is sufficient to exercise the arm of Mahomet, and bruise the back of his admiral.]

[Footnote 47: Ducas, who confesses himself ill informed of the affairs of Hungary assigns a motive of superstition, a fatal belief that Constantinople would be the term of the Turkish conquests. See Phranza (l. iii. c. 20) and Spondanus.]

It was difficult for the Greeks to penetrate the secret of the divan; yet the Greeks are persuaded, that a resistance so obstinate and surprising, had fatigued the perseverance of Mahomet. He began to meditate a retreat; and the siege would have been speedily raised, if the ambition and jealousy of the second vizier had not opposed the perfidious advice of Calil Bashaw, who still maintained a secret correspondence with the Byzantine court. The reduction of the city appeared to be hopeless, unless a double attack could be made from the harbor as well as from the land; but the harbor was inaccessible: an impenetrable chain was now defended by eight large ships, more than twenty of a smaller size, with several galleys and sloops; and, instead of forcing this barrier, the Turks might apprehend a naval sally, and a second encounter in the open sea. In this perplexity, the genius of Mahomet conceived and executed a plan of a bold and marvellous cast, of transporting by land his lighter vessels and military stores from the Bosphorus into the higher part of the harbor. The distance is about ten [471] miles; the ground is uneven, and was overspread with thickets; and, as the road must be opened behind the suburb of Galata, their free passage or total destruction must depend on the option of the Genoese. But these selfish merchants were ambitious of the favor of being the last devoured; and the deficiency of art was supplied by the strength of obedient myriads. A level way was covered with a broad platform of strong and solid planks; and to render them more slippery and smooth, they were anointed with the fat of sheep and oxen. Fourscore light galleys and brigantines, of fifty and thirty oars, were disembarked on the Bosphorus shore; arranged successively on rollers; and drawn forwards by the power of men and pulleys. Two guides or pilots were stationed at the helm, and the prow, of each vessel: the sails were unfurled to the winds; and the labor was cheered by song and acclamation. In the course of a single night, this Turkish fleet painfully climbed the hill, steered over the plain, and was launched from the declivity into the shallow waters of the harbor, far above the molestation of the deeper vessels of the Greeks. The real importance of this operation was magnified by the consternation and confidence which it inspired: but the notorious, unquestionable fact was displayed before the eyes, and is recorded by the pens, of the two nations. [48] A similar stratagem had been repeatedly practised by the ancients; [49] the Ottoman galleys (I must again repeat) should be considered as large boats; and, if we compare the magnitude and the distance, the obstacles and the means, the boasted miracle [50] has perhaps been equalled by the industry of our own times. [51] As soon as Mahomet had occupied the upper harbor with a fleet and army, he constructed, in the narrowest part, a bridge, or rather mole, of fifty cubits in breadth, and one hundred in length: it was formed of casks and hogsheads; joined with rafters, linked with iron, and covered with a solid floor. On this floating battery he planted one of his largest cannon, while the fourscore galleys, with troops and scaling ladders, approached the most accessible side, which had formerly been stormed by the Latin conquerors. The indolence of the Christians has been accused for not destroying these unfinished works; [51/1] but their fire, by a superior fire, was controlled and silenced; nor were they wanting in a nocturnal attempt to burn the vessels as well as the bridge of the sultan. His vigilance prevented their approach; their foremost galiots were sunk or taken; forty youths, the bravest of Italy and Greece, were inhumanly massacred at his command; nor could the emperor's grief be assuaged by the just though cruel retaliation, of exposing from the walls the heads of two hundred and sixty Mussulman captives. After a siege of forty days, the fate of Constantinople could no longer be averted. The diminutive garrison was exhausted by a double attack: the fortifications, which had stood for ages against hostile violence, were dismantled on all sides by the Ottoman cannon: many breaches were opened; and near the gate of St. Romanus, four towers had been levelled with the ground. For the payment of his feeble and mutinous troops, Constantine was compelled to despoil the churches with the promise of a fourfold restitution; and his sacrilege offered a new reproach to the enemies of the union. A spirit of discord impaired the remnant of the Christian strength; the Genoese and Venetian auxiliaries asserted the preeminence of their respective service; and Justiniani and the great duke, whose ambition was not extinguished by the common danger, accused each other of treachery and cowardice.

[Footnote 471: Six miles. Von Hammer—M.]?

[Footnote 48: The unanimous testimony of the four Greeks is confirmed by Cantemir (p. 96) from the Turkish annals; but I could wish to contract the distance of ten miles, and to prolong the term of one night. Note: Six miles. Von Hammer—M.]

[Footnote 49: Phranza relates two examples of a similar transportation over the six miles of the Isthmus of Corinth; the one fabulous, of Augustus after the battle of Actium; the other true, of Nicetas, a Greek general in the xth century. To these he might have added a bold enterprise of Hannibal, to introduce his vessels into the harbor of Tarentum, (Polybius, l. viii. p. 749, edit. Gronov. Note: Von Hammer gives a longer list of such transportations, p. 533. Dion Cassius distinctly relates the occurrence treated as fabulous by Gibbon—M.]

[Footnote 50: A Greek of Candia, who had served the Venetians in a similar undertaking, (Spond. A.D. 1438, No. 37,) might possibly be the adviser and agent of Mahomet.]

[Footnote 51: I particularly allude to our own embarkations on the lakes of Canada in the years 1776 and 1777, so great in the labor, so fruitless in the event.]

[Footnote 51/1: They were betrayed, according to some accounts, by the Genoese of Galata. Von Hammer, p. 536—M.]

During the siege of Constantinople, the words of peace and capitulation had been sometimes pronounced; and several embassies had passed between the camp and the city. [52] The Greek emperor was humbled by adversity; and would have yielded to any terms compatible with religion and royalty.

The Turkish sultan was desirous of sparing the blood of his soldiers; still more desirous of securing for his own use the Byzantine treasures: and he accomplished a sacred duty in presenting to the Gabours the choice of circumcision, of tribute, or of death. The avarice of Mahomet might have been satisfied with an annual sum of one hundred thousand ducats; but his ambition grasped the capital of the East: to the prince he offered a rich equivalent, to the people a free toleration, or a safe departure: but after some fruitless treaty, he declared his resolution of finding either a throne, or a grave, under the walls of Constantinople. A sense of honor, and the fear of universal reproach, forbade Palæologus to resign the city into the hands of the Ottomans; and he determined to abide the last extremities of war. Several days were employed by the sultan in the preparations of the assault; and a respite was granted by his favorite science of astrology, which had fixed on the twenty-ninth of May, as the fortunate and fatal hour. On the evening of the twenty-seventh, he issued his final orders; assembled in his presence the military chiefs, and dispersed his heralds through the camp to proclaim the duty, and the motives, of the perilous enterprise. Fear is the first principle of a despotic government; and his menaces were expressed in the Oriental style, that the fugitives and deserters, had they the wings of a bird, [53] should not escape from his inexorable justice. The greatest part of his bashaws and Janizaries were the offspring of Christian parents: but the glories of the Turkish name were perpetuated by successive adoption; and in the gradual change of individuals, the spirit of a legion, a regiment, or an oda, is kept alive by imitation and discipline. In this holy warfare, the Moslems were exhorted to purify their minds with prayer, their bodies with seven ablutions; and to abstain from food till the close of the ensuing day. A crowd of dervises visited the tents, to instil the desire of martyrdom, and the assurance of spending an immortal youth amidst the rivers and gardens of paradise, and in the embraces of the black-eyed virgins. Yet Mahomet principally trusted to the efficacy of temporal and visible rewards. A double pay was promised to the victorious troops: "The city and the buildings," said Mahomet, "are mine; but I resign to your valor the captives and the spoil, the treasures of gold and beauty; be rich and be happy. Many are the provinces of my empire: the intrepid soldier who first ascends the walls of Constantinople shall be rewarded with the government of the fairest and most wealthy; and my gratitude shall accumulate his honors and fortunes above the measure of his own hopes." Such various and potent motives diffused among the Turks a general ardor, regardless of life and impatient for action: the camp reechoed with the Moslem shouts of "God is God: there is but one God, and Mahomet is the apostle of God;" [54] and the sea and land, from Galata to the seven towers, were illuminated by the blaze of their nocturnal fires. [541]

[Footnote 52: Chalcondyles and Ducas differ in the time and circumstances of the negotiation; and as it was neither glorious nor salutary, the faithful Phranza spares his prince even the thought of a surrender.]

[Footnote 53: These wings (Chalcondyles, l. viii. p. 208) are no more than an Oriental figure: but in the tragedy of Irene, Mahomet's passion soars above sense and reason:— Should the fierce North, upon his frozen wings. Bear him aloft above the wondering clouds, And seat him in the Pleiads' golden chariot— Then should my fury drag him down to tortures.

Besides the extravagance of the rant, I must observe, 1. That the operation of the winds must be confined to the lower region of the air. 2. That the name, etymology, and fable of the Pleiads are purely Greek, (Scholiast ad Homer, S. 686. Eudocia in Ioniâ, p. 399. Apollodor. l. iii. c. 10. Heyne, p. 229, Not. 682,) and had no affinity with the astronomy of the East, (Hyde ad Ulugbeg, Tabul. in Syntagma Dissert. tom. i. p. 40, 42. Goguet, Origine des Arts, &c., tom. vi. p. 73—78. Gebelin, Hist. du Calendrier, p. 73,) which Mahomet had studied. 3. The golden chariot does not exist either in science or fiction; but I much fear Dr. Johnson has confounded the Pleiads with the great bear or wagon, the zodiac with a northern constellation:— "Ark-on q' hn kai amaxan epiklhsin kaleouein. Il. S. 487.]

[Footnote 54: Phranza quarrels with these Moslem acclamations, not for the name of God, but for that of the prophet: the pious zeal of Voltaire is excessive, and even ridiculous.]

[Footnote 54/1: The picture is heightened by the addition of the wailing cries of Kyris, which were heard from the dark interior of the city. Von Hammer p. 539—M.]

Far different was the state of the Christians; who, with loud and impotent complaints, deplored the guilt, or the punishment, of their sins. The celestial image of the Virgin had been exposed in solemn procession; but their divine patroness was deaf to their entreaties: they accused the obstinacy of the emperor for refusing a timely surrender; anticipated the horrors of their fate; and sighed for the repose and security of Turkish servitude. The noblest of the Greeks, and the bravest of the allies, were summoned to the palace, to prepare them, on the evening of the twenty-eighth, for the duties and dangers of the general assault. The last speech of Palæologus was the funeral oration of the Roman empire: [55] he promised, he conjured, and he vainly attempted to infuse the hope which was extinguished in his own mind. In this world all was comfortless and gloomy; and neither the gospel nor the church have proposed any conspicuous recompense to the heroes who fall in the service of their country. But the example of their prince, and the confinement of a siege, had armed these warriors with the courage of despair, and the pathetic scene is described by the feelings of the historian Phranza, who was himself present at this mournful assembly. They wept, they embraced; regardless of their families and fortunes, they devoted their lives; and each commander, departing to his station, maintained all night a vigilant and anxious watch on the rampart. The emperor, and some faithful companions, entered the dome of St. Sophia, which in a few hours was to be converted into a mosque; and devoutly received, with tears and prayers, the sacrament of the holy communion. He reposed some moments in the palace, which resounded with cries and lamentations; solicited the pardon of all whom he might have injured; [56] and mounted on horseback to visit the guards, and explore the motions of the enemy. The distress and fall of the last Constantine are more glorious than the long prosperity of the Byzantine Cæsars. [561]

[Footnote 55: I am afraid that this discourse was composed by Phranza himself; and it smells so grossly of the sermon and the convent, that I almost doubt whether it was pronounced by Constantine. Leonardus assigns him another speech, in which he addresses himself more respectfully to the Latin auxiliaries.]

[Footnote 56: This abasement, which devotion has sometimes extorted from dying princes, is an improvement of the gospel doctrine of the forgiveness of injuries: it is more easy to forgive 490 times, than once to ask pardon of an inferior.]

[Footnote 561: Compare the very curious Armenian elegy on the fall of Constantinople, translated by M. Boré, in the Journal Asiatique for March, 1835; and by M. Brosset, in the new edition of Le Beau, (tom. xxi. p. 308.) The author thus ends his poem: "I, Abraham, loaded with sins, have composed this elegy with the most lively sorrow; for I have seen Constantinople in the days of its glory."—M.]

In the confusion of darkness, an assailant may sometimes succeed; out in this great and general attack, the military judgment and astrological knowledge of Mahomet advised him to expect the morning, the memorable twenty-ninth of May, in the fourteen hundred and fifty-third year of the Christian æra. The preceding night had been strenuously employed: the troops, the cannons, and the fascines, were advanced to the edge of the ditch, which in many parts presented a smooth and level passage to the breach; and his fourscore galleys almost touched, with the prows and their scaling-ladders, the less defensible walls of the harbor. Under pain of death, silence was enjoined: but the physical laws of motion and sound are not obedient to discipline or fear; each individual might suppress his voice and measure his footsteps; but the march and labor of thousands must inevitably produce a strange confusion of dissonant clamors, which reached the ears of the watchmen of the towers. At daybreak, without the customary signal of the morning gun, the Turks assaulted the city by sea and land; and the similitude of a twined or twisted thread has been applied to the closeness and continuity of their line of attack. [57] The foremost ranks consisted of the refuse of the host, a voluntary crowd who fought without order or command; of the feebleness of age or childhood, of peasants and vagrants, and of all who had joined the camp in the blind hope of plunder and martyrdom. The common impulse drove them onwards to the wall; the most audacious to climb were instantly precipitated; and not a dart, not a bullet, of the Christians, was idly wasted on the accumulated throng. But their strength and ammunition were exhausted in this laborious defence: the ditch was filled with the bodies of the slain; they supported the footsteps of their companions; and of this devoted vanguard the death was more serviceable than the life. Under their respective bashaws and sanjaks, the troops of Anatolia and Romania were successively led to the charge: their progress was various and doubtful; but, after a conflict of two hours, the Greeks still maintained, and improved their advantage; and the voice of the emperor was heard, encouraging his soldiers to achieve, by a last effort, the deliverance of their country. In that fatal moment, the Janizaries arose, fresh, vigorous, and invincible. The sultan himself on horseback, with an iron mace in his hand, was the spectator and judge of their valor: he was surrounded by ten thousand of his domestic troops, whom he reserved for the decisive occasion; and the tide of battle was directed and impelled by his voice and eye. His numerous ministers of justice were posted behind the line, to urge, to restrain, and to punish; and if danger was in the front, shame and inevitable death were in the rear, of the fugitives. The cries of fear and of pain were drowned in the martial music of drums, trumpets, and attaballs; and experience has proved, that the mechanical operation of sounds, by quickening the circulation of the blood and spirits, will act on the human machine more forcibly than the eloquence of reason and honor. From the lines, the galleys, and the bridge, the Ottoman artillery thundered on all sides; and the camp and city, the Greeks and the Turks, were involved in a cloud of smoke which could only be dispelled by the final deliverance or destruction of the Roman empire. The single combats of the heroes of history or fable amuse our fancy and engage our affections: the skilful evolutions of war may inform the mind, and improve a necessary, though pernicious, science. But in the uniform and odious pictures of a general assault, all is blood, and horror, and confusion nor shall I strive, at the distance of three centuries, and a thousand miles, to delineate a scene of which there could be no spectators, and of which the actors themselves were incapable of forming any just or adequate idea.

[Footnote 57: Besides the 10,000 guards, and the sailors and the marines, Ducas numbers in this general assault 250,000 Turks, both horse and foot.]

The immediate loss of Constantinople may be ascribed to the bullet, or arrow, which pierced the gauntlet of John Justiniani. The sight of his blood, and the exquisite pain, appalled the courage of the chief, whose arms and counsels were the firmest rampart of the city. As he withdrew from his station in quest of a surgeon, his flight was perceived and stopped by the indefatigable emperor. "Your wound," exclaimed Palæologus, "is slight; the danger is pressing: your presence is necessary; and whither will you retire?"—"I will retire," said the trembling Genoese, "by the same road which God has opened to the Turks;" and at these words he hastily passed through one of the breaches of the inner wall. By this pusillanimous act he stained the honors of a military life; and the few days which he survived in Galata, or the Isle of Chios, were embittered by his own and the public reproach. [58] His example was imitated by the greatest part of the Latin auxiliaries, and the defence began to slacken when the attack was pressed with redoubled vigor. The number of the Ottomans was fifty, perhaps a hundred, times superior to that of the Christians; the double walls were reduced by the cannon to a heap of ruins: in a circuit of several miles, some places must be found more easy of access, or more feebly guarded; and if the besiegers could penetrate in a single point, the whole city was irrecoverably lost. The first who deserved the sultan's reward was Hassan the Janizary, of gigantic stature and strength. With his cimeter in one hand and his buckler in the other, he ascended the outward fortification: of the thirty Janizaries, who were emulous of his valor, eighteen perished in the bold adventure. Hassan and his twelve companions had reached the summit: the giant was precipitated from the rampart: he rose on one knee, and was again oppressed by a shower of darts and stones. But his success had proved that the achievement was possible: the walls and towers were instantly covered with a swarm of Turks; and the Greeks, now driven from the vantage ground, were overwhelmed by increasing multitudes. Amidst these multitudes, the emperor, [59] who accomplished all the duties of a general and a soldier, was long seen and finally lost. The nobles, who fought round his person, sustained, till their last breath, the honorable names of Palæologus and Cantacuzene: his mournful exclamation was heard, "Cannot there be found a Christian to cut off my head?" [60] and his last fear was that of falling alive into the hands of the infidels. [61] The prudent despair of Constantine cast away the purple: amidst the tumult he fell by an unknown hand, and his body was buried under a mountain of the slain. After his death, resistance and order were no more: the Greeks fled towards the city; and many were pressed and stifled in the narrow pass of the gate of St. Romanus. The victorious Turks rushed through the breaches of the inner wall; and as they advanced into the streets, they were soon joined by their brethren, who had forced the gate Phenar on the side of the harbor. [62] In the first heat of the pursuit, about two thousand Christians were put to the sword; but avarice soon prevailed over cruelty; and the victors acknowledged, that they should immediately have given quarter if the valor of the emperor and his chosen bands had not prepared them for a similar opposition in every part of the capital. It was thus, after a siege of fifty-three days, that Constantinople, which had defied the power of Chosroes, the Chagan, and the caliphs, was irretrievably subdued by the arms of Mahomet the Second. Her empire only had been subverted by the Latins: her religion was trampled in the dust by the Moslem conquerors. [63]

[Footnote 58: In the severe censure of the flight of Justiniani, Phranza expresses his own feelings and those of the public. For some private reasons, he is treated with more lenity and respect by Ducas; but the words of Leonardus Chiensis express his strong and recent indignation, gloriæ salutis suique oblitus. In the whole series of their Eastern policy, his countrymen, the Genoese, were always suspected, and often guilty. Note: M. Brosset has given some extracts from the Georgian account of the siege of Constantinople, in which Justiniani's wound in the left foot is represented as more serious. With charitable ambiguity the chronicler adds that his soldiers carried him away with them in their vessel—M.]

[Footnote 59: Ducas kills him with two blows of Turkish soldiers; Chalcondyles wounds him in the shoulder, and then tramples him in the gate. The grief of Phranza, carrying him among the enemy, escapes from the precise image of his death; but we may, without flattery, apply these noble lines of Dryden:— As to Sebastian, let them search the field; And where they find a mountain of the slain, Send one to climb, and looking down beneath, There they will find him at his manly length, With his face up to heaven, in that red monument Which his good sword had digged.]

[Footnote 60: Spondanus, (A.D. 1453, No. 10,) who has hopes of his salvation, wishes to absolve this demand from the guilt of suicide.]

[Footnote 61: Leonardus Chiensis very properly observes, that the Turks, had they known the emperor, would have labored to save and secure a captive so acceptable to the sultan.]

[Footnote 62: Cantemir, p. 96. The Christian ships in the mouth of the harbor had flanked and retarded this naval attack.]

[Footnote 63: Chalcondyles most absurdly supposes, that Constantinople was sacked by the Asiatics in revenge for the ancient calamities of Troy; and the grammarians of the xvth century are happy to melt down the uncouth appellation of Turks into the more classical name of Teucri.]

The tidings of misfortune fly with a rapid wing; yet such was the extent of Constantinople, that the more distant quarters might prolong, some moments, the happy ignorance of their ruin. [64] But in the general consternation, in the feelings of selfish or social anxiety, in the tumult and thunder of the assault, a sleepless night and morning [641] must have elapsed; nor can I believe that many Grecian ladies were awakened by the Janizaries from a sound and tranquil slumber. On the assurance of the public calamity, the houses and convents were instantly deserted; and the trembling inhabitants flocked together in the streets, like a herd of timid animals, as if accumulated weakness could be productive of strength, or in the vain hope, that amid the crowd each individual might be safe and invisible. From every part of the capital, they flowed into the church of St. Sophia: in the space of an hour, the sanctuary, the choir, the nave, the upper and lower galleries, were filled with the multitudes of fathers and husbands, of women and children, of priests, monks, and religious virgins: the doors were barred on the inside, and they sought protection from the sacred dome, which they had so lately abhorred as a profane and polluted edifice. Their confidence was founded on the prophecy of an enthusiast or impostor; that one day the Turks would enter Constantinople, and pursue the Romans as far as the column of Constantine in the square before St. Sophia: but that this would be the term of their calamities: that an angel would descend from heaven, with a sword in his hand, and would deliver the empire, with that celestial weapon, to a poor man seated at the foot of the column. "Take this sword," would he say, "and avenge the people of the Lord." At these animating words, the Turks would instantly fly, and the victorious Romans would drive them from the West, and from all Anatolia as far as the frontiers of Persia. It is on this occasion that Ducas, with some fancy and much truth, upbraids the discord and obstinacy of the Greeks. "Had that angel appeared," exclaims the historian, "had he offered to exterminate your foes if you would consent to the union of the church, even event then, in that fatal moment, you would have rejected your safety, or have deceived your God." [65]

[Footnote 64: When Cyrus suppressed Babylon during the celebration of a festival, so vast was the city, and so careless were the inhabitants, that much time elapsed before the distant quarters knew that they were captives. Herodotus, (l. i. c. 191,) and Usher, (Annal. p. 78,) who has quoted from the prophet Jeremiah a passage of similar import.]

[Footnote 641: This refers to an expression in Ducas, who, to heighten the effect of his description, speaks of the "sweet morning sleep resting on the eyes of youths and maidens," p. 288. Edit. Bekker—M.]

[Footnote 65: This lively description is extracted from Ducas, (c. 39,) who two years afterwards was sent ambassador from the prince of Lesbos to the sultan, (c. 44.) Till Lesbos was subdued in 1463, (Phranza, l. iii. c. 27,) that island must have been full of the fugitives of Constantinople, who delighted to repeat, perhaps to adorn, the tale of their misery.]

PART IV

While they expected the descent of the tardy angel, the doors were broken with axes; and as the Turks encountered no resistance, their bloodless hands were employed in selecting and securing the multitude of their prisoners. Youth, beauty, and the appearance of wealth, attracted their choice; and the right of property was decided among themselves by a prior seizure, by personal strength, and by the authority of command. In the space of an hour, the male captives were bound with cords, the females with their veils and girdles. The senators were linked with their slaves; the prelates, with the porters of the church; and young men of the plebeian class, with noble maids, whose faces had been invisible to the sun and their nearest kindred. In this common captivity, the ranks of society were confounded; the ties of nature were cut asunder; and the inexorable soldier was careless of the father's groans, the tears of the mother, and the lamentations of the children. The loudest in their wailings were the nuns, who were torn from the altar with naked bosoms, outstretched hands, and dishevelled hair; and we should piously believe that few could be tempted to prefer the vigils of the harem to those of the monastery. Of these unfortunate Greeks, of these domestic animals, whole strings were rudely driven through the streets; and as the conquerors were eager to return for more prey, their trembling pace was quickened with menaces and blows. At the same hour, a similar rapine was exercised in all the churches and monasteries, in all the palaces and habitations, of the capital; nor could any place, however sacred or sequestered, protect the persons or the property of the Greeks. Above sixty thousand of this devoted people were transported from the city to the camp and fleet; exchanged or sold according to the caprice or interest of their masters, and dispersed in remote servitude through the provinces of the Ottoman empire. Among these we may notice some remarkable characters. The historian Phranza, first chamberlain and principal secretary, was involved with his family in the common lot. After suffering four months the hardships of slavery, he recovered his freedom: in the ensuing winter he ventured to Adrianople, and ransomed his wife from the mir bashi, or master of the horse; but his two children, in the flower of youth and beauty, had been seized for the use of Mahomet himself. The daughter of Phranza died in the seraglio, perhaps a virgin: his son, in the fifteenth year of his age, preferred death to infamy, and was stabbed by the hand of the royal lover. [66] A deed thus inhuman cannot surely be expiated by the taste and liberality with which he released a Grecian matron and her two daughters, on receiving a Latin doe From ode from Philelphus, who had chosen a wife in that noble family. [67] The pride or cruelty of Mahomet would have been most sensibly gratified by the capture of a Roman legate; but the dexterity of Cardinal Isidore eluded the search, and he escaped from Galata in a plebeian habit. [68] The chain and entrance of the outward harbor was still occupied by the Italian ships of merchandise and war. They had signalized their valor in the siege: they embraced the moment of retreat, while the Turkish mariners were dissipated in the pillage of the city. When they hoisted sail, the beach was covered with a suppliant and lamentable crowd; but the means of transportation were scanty: the Venetians and Genoese selected their countrymen; and, notwithstanding the fairest promises of the sultan, the inhabitants of Galata evacuated their houses, and embarked with their most precious effects.

*[Footnote 66: See Phranza, l. iii. c. 20, 21. His expressions are positive: Ameras suâ manû jugulavit.... volebat enim eo turpiter et nefarie abuti. Me miserum et infelicem! Yet he could only learn from report the bloody or impure scenes that were acted in the dark recesses of the seraglio.]*

*[Footnote 67: See Tiraboschi (tom. vi. P. i. p. 290) and Lancelot, (Mém. de l'Académie des Inscriptions, tom. x. p. 718.) I should be curious to learn how he could praise the public enemy, whom he so often reviles as the most corrupt and inhuman of tyrants.]*

[Footnote 68: *The commentaries of Pius II. suppose that he craftily placed his cardinal's hat on the head of a corpse which was cut off and exposed in triumph, while the legate himself was bought and delivered as a captive of no value. The great Belgic Chronicle adorns his escape with new adventures, which he suppressed (says Spondanus, A.D. 1453, No. 15) in his own letters, lest he should lose the merit and reward of suffering for Christ. Note: He was sold as a slave in Galata, according to Von Hammer, p. 175. See the somewhat vague and declamatory letter of Cardinal Isidore, in the appendix to Clarke's Travels, vol. ii. p. 653—M.*]

In the fall and the sack of great cities, an historian is condemned to repeat the tale of uniform calamity: the same effects must be produced by the same passions; and when those passions may be indulged without control, small, alas! is the difference between civilized and savage man. Amidst the vague exclamations of bigotry and hatred, the Turks are not accused of a wanton or immoderate effusion of Christian blood: but according to their maxims, (the maxims of antiquity,) the lives of the vanquished were forfeited; and the legitimate reward of the conqueror was derived from the service, the sale, or the ransom, of his captives of both sexes. [69] The wealth of Constantinople had been granted by the sultan to his victorious troops; and the rapine of an hour is more productive than the industry of years. But as no regular division was attempted of the spoil, the respective shares were not determined by merit; and the rewards of valor were stolen away by the followers of the camp, who had declined the toil and danger of the battle. The narrative of their depredations could not afford either amusement or instruction: the total amount, in the last poverty of the empire, has been valued at four millions of ducats; [70] and of this sum a small part was the property of the Venetians, the Genoese, the Florentines, and the merchants of Ancona. Of these foreigners, the stock was improved in quick and perpetual circulation: but the riches of the Greeks were displayed in the idle ostentation of palaces and wardrobes, or deeply buried in treasures of ingots and old coin, lest it should be demanded at their hands for the defence of their country. The profanation and plunder of the monasteries and churches excited the most tragic complaints. The dome of St. Sophia itself, the earthly heaven, the second firmament, the vehicle of the cherubim, the throne of the glory of God, [71] was despoiled of the oblation of ages; and the gold and silver, the pearls and jewels, the vases and sacerdotal ornaments, were most wickedly converted to the service of mankind. After the divine images had been stripped of all that could be valuable to a profane eye, the canvas, or the wood, was torn, or broken, or burnt, or trod under foot, or applied, in the stables or the kitchen, to the vilest uses. The example of sacrilege was imitated, however, from the Latin conquerors of Constantinople; and the treatment which Christ, the Virgin, and the saints, had sustained from the guilty Catholic, might be inflicted by the zealous Mussulman on the monuments of idolatry. Perhaps, instead of joining the public clamor, a philosopher will observe, that in the decline of the arts the workmanship could not be more valuable than the work, and that a fresh supply of visions and miracles would speedily be renewed by the craft of the priests and the credulity of the people. He will more seriously deplore the loss of the Byzantine libraries, which were destroyed or scattered in the general confusion: one hundred and twenty thousand manuscripts are said to have disappeared; [72] ten volumes might be purchased for a single ducat; and the same ignominious price, too high perhaps for a shelf of theology, included the whole works of Aristotle and Homer, the noblest productions of the science and literature of ancient Greece. We may reflect with pleasure that an inestimable portion of our classic treasures was safely deposited in Italy; and that the mechanics of a German town had invented an art which derides the havoc of time and barbarism.

[Footnote 69: *Busbequius expatiates with pleasure and applause on the rights of war, and the use of slavery, among the ancients and the Turks, (de Legat. Turcicâ, epist. iii. p. 161.)*]

[Footnote 70: This sum is specified in a marginal note of Leunclavius, (Chalcondyles, l. viii. p. 211,) but in the distribution to Venice, Genoa, Florence, and Ancona, of 50, 20, and 15,000 ducats, I suspect that a figure has been dropped. Even with the restitution, the foreign property would scarcely exceed one fourth.]

[Footnote 71: See the enthusiastic praises and lamentations of Phranza, (l. iii. c. 17.)]

[Footnote 72: See Ducas, (c. 43,) and an epistle, July 15th, 1453, from Laurus Quirinus to Pope Nicholas V., (Hody de Græcis, p. 192, from a MS. in the Cotton library.)]

From the first hour [73] of the memorable twenty-ninth of May, disorder and rapine prevailed in Constantinople, till the eighth hour of the same day; when the sultan himself passed in triumph through the gate of St. Romanus. He was attended by his viziers, bashaws, and guards, each of whom (says a Byzantine historian) was robust as Hercules, dexterous as Apollo, and equal in battle to any ten of the race of ordinary mortals. The conqueror [74] gazed with satisfaction and wonder on the strange, though splendid, appearance of the domes and palaces, so dissimilar from the style of Oriental architecture. In the hippodrome, or atmeidan, his eye was attracted by the twisted column of the three serpents; and, as a trial of his strength, he shattered with his iron mace or battle-axe the under jaw of one of these monsters, [75] which in the eyes of the Turks were the idols or talismans of the city. [75/1] At the principal door of St. Sophia, he alighted from his horse, and entered the dome; and such was his jealous regard for that monument of his glory, that on observing a zealous Mussulman in the act of breaking the marble pavement, he admonished him with his cimeter, that, if the spoil and captives were granted to the soldiers, the public and private buildings had been reserved for the prince. By his command the metropolis of the Eastern church was transformed into a mosque: the rich and portable instruments of superstition had been removed; the crosses were thrown down; and the walls, which were covered with images and mosaics, were washed and purified, and restored to a state of naked simplicity. On the same day, or on the ensuing Friday, the muezin, or crier, ascended the most lofty turret, and proclaimed the ezan, or public invitation in the name of God and his prophet; the imam preached; and Mahomet and Second performed the namaz of prayer and thanksgiving on the great altar, where the Christian mysteries had so lately been celebrated before the last of the Cæsars. [76] From St. Sophia he proceeded to the august, but desolate mansion of a hundred successors of the great Constantine, but which in a few hours had been stripped of the pomp of royalty. A melancholy reflection on the vicissitudes of human greatness forced itself on his mind; and he repeated an elegant distich of Persian poetry: "The spider has wove his web in the Imperial palace; and the owl hath sung her watch-song on the towers of Afrasiab." [77]

[Footnote 73: The Julian Calendar, which reckons the days and hours from midnight, was used at Constantinople. But Ducas seems to understand the natural hours from sunrise.]

[Footnote 74: See the Turkish Annals, p. 329, and the Pandects of Leunclavius, p. 448.]

[Footnote 75: I have had occasion (vol. ii. p. 100) to mention this curious relic of Grecian antiquity.]

[Footnote 75/1: Von Hammer passes over this circumstance, which is treated by Dr. Clarke (Travels, vol. ii. p. 58, 4to. edit,) as a fiction of Thevenot. Chishull states that the monument was broken by some attendants of the Polish ambassador—M.]

[Footnote 76: We are obliged to Cantemir (p. 102) for the Turkish account of the conversion of St. Sophia, so bitterly deplored by Phranza and Ducas. It is amusing enough to observe, in what opposite lights the same object appears to a Mussulman and a Christian eye.]

[Footnote 77: This distich, which Cantemir gives in the original, derives new beauties from the application. It was thus that Scipio repeated, in the sack of Carthage, the famous prophecy of Homer. The same generous feeling carried the mind of the conqueror to the past or the future.]

Yet his mind was not satisfied, nor did the victory seem complete, till he was informed of the fate of Constantine; whether he had escaped, or been made prisoner, or had fallen in the battle. Two Janizaries claimed the honor and reward of his death: the body, under a heap of slain, was discovered by the golden eagles embroidered on his shoes; the Greeks acknowledged, with tears, the head of their late emperor; and, after exposing the bloody trophy, [78] Mahomet bestowed on his rival the honors of a decent funeral. After his decease, Lucas Notaras, great duke, [79] and first minister of the empire, was the most important prisoner. When he offered his person and his treasures at the foot of the throne, "And why," said the indignant sultan, "did you not employ these treasures in the defence of your prince and country?"—"They were yours," answered the slave; "God had reserved them for your hands."—"If he reserved them for me," replied the despot, "how have you presumed to withhold them so long by a fruitless and fatal resistance?" The great duke alleged the obstinacy of the strangers, and some secret encouragement from the Turkish vizier; and from this perilous interview he was at length dismissed with the assurance of pardon and protection. Mahomet condescended to visit his wife, a venerable princess oppressed with sickness and grief; and his consolation for her misfortunes was in the most tender strain of humanity and filial reverence. A similar clemency was extended to the principal officers of state, of whom several were ransomed at his expense; and during some days he declared himself the friend and father of the vanquished people. But the scene was soon changed; and before his departure, the hippodrome streamed with the blood of his noblest captives. His perfidious cruelty is execrated by the Christians: they adorn with the colors of heroic martyrdom the execution of the great duke and his two sons; and his death is ascribed to the generous refusal of delivering his children to the tyrant's lust. [791] Yet a Byzantine historian has dropped an unguarded word of conspiracy, deliverance, and Italian succor: such treason may be glorious; but the rebel who bravely ventures, has justly forfeited his life; nor should we blame a conqueror for destroying the enemies whom he can no longer trust. On the eighteenth of June the victorious sultan returned to Adrianople; and smiled at the base and hollow embassies of the Christian princes, who viewed their approaching ruin in the fall of the Eastern empire.

[Footnote 78: I cannot believe with Ducas (see Spondanus, A.D. 1453, No. 13) that Mahomet sent round Persia, Arabia, &c., the head of the Greek emperor: he would surely content himself with a trophy less inhuman.]

[Footnote 79: Phranza was the personal enemy of the great duke; nor could time, or death, or his own retreat to a monastery, extort a feeling of sympathy or forgiveness. Ducas is inclined to praise and pity the martyr; Chalcondyles is neuter, but we are indebted to him for the hint of the Greek conspiracy.]

[Footnote 79/1: Von Hammer relates this undoubtingly, apparently on good authority, p. 559—M.]

Constantinople had been left naked and desolate, without a prince or a people. But she could not be despoiled of the incomparable situation which marks her for the metropolis of a great empire; and the genius of the place will ever triumph over the accidents of time and fortune. Boursa and Adrianople, the ancient seats of the Ottomans, sunk into provincial towns; and Mahomet the Second established his own residence, and that of his successors, on the same commanding spot which had been chosen by Constantine. [80] The fortifications of Galata, which might afford a shelter to the Latins, were prudently destroyed; but the damage of the Turkish cannon was soon repaired; and before the month of August, great quantities of lime had been burnt for the restoration of the walls of the capital. As the entire property of the soil and buildings, whether public or private, or profane or sacred, was now transferred to the conqueror, he first separated a space of eight furlongs from the point of the triangle for the establishment of his seraglio or palace. It is here, in the bosom of luxury, that the Grand Signor (as he has been emphatically named by the Italians) appears to reign over Europe and Asia; but his person on the shores of the Bosphorus may not always be secure from the insults of a hostile navy. In the new character of a mosque, the cathedral of St. Sophia was endowed with an ample revenue, crowned with lofty minarets, and surrounded with groves and fountains, for the devotion and refreshment of the Moslems. The same model was imitated in the jami, or royal mosques; and the first of these was built, by Mahomet himself, on the ruins of the church of the holy apostles, and the tombs of the Greek emperors. On the third day after the conquest, the grave of Abu Ayub, or Job, who had fallen in the first siege of the Arabs, was revealed in a vision; and it is before the sepulchre of the martyr that the new sultans are girded with the sword of empire. [81] Constantinople no longer appertains to the Roman historian; nor shall I enumerate the civil and religious edifices that were profaned or erected by its Turkish masters: the population was speedily renewed; and before the end of September, five thousand families of Anatolia and Romania had obeyed the royal mandate, which enjoined them, under pain of death, to occupy their new habitations in the capital. The throne of Mahomet was guarded by the numbers and fidelity of his Moslem subjects: but his rational policy aspired to collect the remnant of the Greeks; and they returned in crowds, as soon as they were assured of their lives, their liberties, and the free exercise of their religion. In the election and investiture of a patriarch, the ceremonial of the Byzantine court was revived and imitated. With a mixture of satisfaction and horror, they beheld the sultan on his throne; who delivered into the hands of Gennadius the crosier or pastoral staff, the symbol of his ecclesiastical office; who conducted the patriarch to the gate of the seraglio, presented him with a horse richly caparisoned, and directed the viziers and bashaws to lead him to the palace which had been allotted for his residence. [82] The churches of Constantinople were shared between the two religions: their limits were marked; and, till it was infringed by Selim, the grandson of Mahomet, the Greeks [83] enjoyed above sixty years the benefit of this equal partition. Encouraged by the ministers of the divan, who wished to elude the fanaticism of the sultan, the Christian advocates presumed to allege that this division had been an act, not of generosity, but of justice; not a concession, but a compact; and that if one half of the city had been taken by storm, the other moiety had surrendered on the faith of a sacred capitulation. The original grant had indeed been consumed by fire: but the loss was supplied by the testimony of three aged Janizaries who remembered the transaction; and their venal oaths are of more weight in the opinion of Cantemir, than the positive and unanimous consent of the history of the times. [84]

[Footnote 80: *For the restitution of Constantinople and the Turkish foundations, see Cantemir, (p. 102—109,) Ducas, (c. 42,) with Thevenot, Tournefort, and the rest of our modern travellers. From a gigantic picture of the greatness, population, &c., of Constantinople and the Ottoman empire, (Abrégé de l'Histoire Ottomane, tom. i. p. 16—21,) we may learn, that in the year 1586 the Moslems were less numerous in the capital than the Christians, or even the Jews.*]

[Footnote 81: *The Turbé, or sepulchral monument of Abu Ayub, is described and engraved in the Tableau Générale de l'Empire Ottoman, (Paris 1787, in large folio,) a work of less use, perhaps, than magnificence, (tom. i. p. 305, 306.)*]

[Footnote 82: Phranza (l. iii. c. 19) relates the ceremony, which has possibly been adorned in the Greek reports to each other, and to the Latins. The fact is confirmed by Emanuel Malaxus, who wrote, in vulgar Greek, the History of the Patriarchs after the taking of Constantinople, inserted in the Turco-Græcia of Crusius, (l. v. p. 106—184.) But the most patient reader will not believe that Mahomet adopted the Catholic form, "Sancta Trinitas quæ mihi donavit imperium te in patriarcham novæ Romæ deligit."]

[Footnote 83: From the Turco-Græcia of Crusius, &c. Spondanus (A.D. 1453, No. 21, 1458, No. 16) describes the slavery and domestic quarrels of the Greek church. The patriarch who succeeded Gennadius threw himself in despair into a well.]

[Footnote 84: Cantemir (p. 101—105) insists on the unanimous consent of the Turkish historians, ancient as well as modern, and argues, that they would not have violated the truth to diminish their national glory, since it is esteemed more honorable to take a city by force than by composition. But, 1. I doubt this consent, since he quotes no particular historian, and the Turkish Annals of Leunclavius affirm, without exception, that Mahomet took Constantinople per vim, (p. 329.) 2 The same argument may be turned in favor of the Greeks of the times, who would not have forgotten this honorable and salutary treaty. Voltaire, as usual, prefers the Turks to the Christians.]

The remaining fragments of the Greek kingdom in Europe and Asia I shall abandon to the Turkish arms; but the final extinction of the two last dynasties [85] which have reigned in Constantinople should terminate the decline and fall of the Roman empire in the East. The despots of the Morea, Demetrius and Thomas, [86] the two surviving brothers of the name of Palæologus, were astonished by the death of the emperor Constantine, and the ruin of the monarchy. Hopeless of defence, they prepared, with the noble Greeks who adhered to their fortune, to seek a refuge in Italy, beyond the reach of the Ottoman thunder. Their first apprehensions were dispelled by the victorious sultan, who contented himself with a tribute of twelve thousand ducats; and while his ambition explored the continent and the islands, in search of prey, he indulged the Morea in a respite of seven years. But this respite was a period of grief, discord, and misery. The hexamilion, the rampart of the Isthmus, so often raised and so often subverted, could not long be defended by three hundred Italian archers: the keys of Corinth were seized by the Turks: they returned from their summer excursions with a train of captives and spoil; and the complaints of the injured Greeks were heard with indifference and disdain. The Albanians, a vagrant tribe of shepherds and robbers, filled the peninsula with rapine and murder: the two despots implored the dangerous and humiliating aid of a neighboring bashaw; and when he had quelled the revolt, his lessons inculcated the rule of their future conduct. Neither the ties of blood, nor the oaths which they repeatedly pledged in the communion and before the altar, nor the stronger pressure of necessity, could reconcile or suspend their domestic quarrels. They ravaged each other's patrimony with fire and sword: the alms and succors of the West were consumed in civil hostility; and their power was only exerted in savage and arbitrary executions. The distress and revenge of the weaker rival invoked their supreme lord; and, in the season of maturity and revenge, Mahomet declared himself the friend of Demetrius, and marched into the Morea with an irresistible force. When he had taken possession of Sparta, "You are too weak," said the sultan, "to control this turbulent province: I will take your daughter to my bed; and you shall pass the remainder of your life in security and honor." Demetrius sighed and obeyed; surrendered his daughter and his castles; followed to Adrianople his sovereign and his son; and received for his own maintenance, and that of his followers, a city in Thrace and the adjacent isles of Imbros, Lemnos, and Samothrace. He was joined the next year by a companion [86/1] of misfortune, the last of the Comnenian race, who, after the taking of Constantinople by the Latins, had founded a new empire on the coast of the Black Sea. [87] In the progress of his Anatolian conquest, Mahomet invested with a fleet and army the capital of David, who presumed to style himself emperor of Trebizond; [88] and the negotiation was comprised in a short and peremptory question, "Will you secure your life and treasures by resigning your kingdom? or had you rather forfeit your kingdom, your treasures, and your life?" The feeble Comnenus was subdued by his own fears, [88/1] and the example of a Mussulman neighbor, the prince of Sinope, [89] who, on a similar summons, had yielded a fortified city, with four hundred cannon and ten or twelve thousand soldiers. The capitulation of Trebizond was faithfully performed: [89/1] and the emperor, with his family, was transported to a castle in Romania; but on a slight suspicion of corresponding with the Persian king, David, and the whole Comnenian race, were sacrificed to the jealousy or avarice of the conqueror. [89/2] Nor could the name of father long protect the unfortunate Demetrius from exile and confiscation; his abject submission moved the pity and contempt of the sultan; his followers were transplanted to Constantinople; and his poverty was alleviated by a pension of fifty thousand aspers, till a monastic habit and a tardy death released Palæologus from an earthly master. It is not easy to pronounce whether the servitude of Demetrius, or the exile of his brother Thomas, [90] be the most inglorious. On the conquest of the Morea, the despot escaped to Corfu, and from thence to Italy, with some naked adherents: his name, his sufferings, and the head of the apostle St. Andrew, entitled him to the hospitality of the Vatican; and his misery was prolonged by a pension of six thousand ducats from the pope and cardinals. His two sons, Andrew and Manuel, were educated in Italy; but the eldest, contemptible to his enemies and burdensome to his friends, was degraded by the baseness of his life and marriage. A title was his sole inheritance; and that inheritance he successively sold to the kings of France and Arragon. [91] During his transient prosperity, Charles the Eighth was ambitious of joining the empire of the East with the kingdom of Naples: in a public festival, he assumed the appellation and the purple of Augustus: the Greeks rejoiced and the Ottoman already trembled, at the approach of the French chivalry. [92] Manuel Palæologus, the second son, was tempted to revisit his native country: his return might be grateful, and could not be dangerous, to the Porte: he was maintained at Constantinople in safety and ease; and an honorable train of Christians and Moslems attended him to the grave. If there be some animals of so generous a nature that they refuse to propagate in a domestic state, the last of the Imperial race must be ascribed to an inferior kind: he accepted from the sultan's liberality two beautiful females; and his surviving son was lost in the habit and religion of a Turkish slave.

[Footnote 85: For the genealogy and fall of the Comneni of Trebizond, see Ducange, (Fam. Byzant. p. 195;) for the last Palæologi, the same accurate antiquarian, (p. 244, 247, 248.) The Palæologi of Montferrat were not extinct till the next century; but they had forgotten their Greek origin and kindred.]

[Footnote 86: In the worthless story of the disputes and misfortunes of the two brothers, Phranza (l. iii. c. 21—30) is too partial on the side of Thomas Ducas (c. 44, 45) is too brief, and Chalcondyles (l. viii. ix. x.) too diffuse and digressive.]

[Footnote 86/1]: Kalo-Johannes, the predecessor of David his brother, the last emperor of Trebizond, had attempted to organize a confederacy against Mahomet it comprehended Hassan Bei, sultan of Mesopotamia, the Christian princes of Georgia and Iberia, the emir of Sinope, and the sultan of Caramania. The negotiations were interrupted by his sudden death, A.D. 1458. Fallmerayer, p. 257—260—M.]

[Footnote 87: See the loss or conquest of Trebizond in Chalcondyles, (l. ix. p. 263—266,) Ducas, (c. 45,) Phranza, (l. iii. c. 27,) and Cantemir, (p. 107.)]

[Footnote 88: Though Tournefort (tom. iii. lettre xvii. p. 179) speaks of Trebizond as mal peuplée, Peysonnel, the latest and most accurate observer, can find 100,000 inhabitants, (Commerce de la Mer Noire, tom. ii. p. 72, and for the province, p. 53—90.) Its prosperity and trade are perpetually disturbed by the factious quarrels of two odas of Janizaries, in one which 30,000 Lazi are commonly enrolled, (Mémoires de Tott, tom. iii. p. 16, 17.)]

[Footnote 88/1: According to the Georgian account of these transactions, (translated by M. Brosset, additions to Le Beau, vol. xxi. p. 325,) the emperor of Trebizond humbly entreated the sultan to have the goodness to marry one of his daughters—M.]

[Footnote 89: Ismael Beg, prince of Sinope or Sinople, was possessed (chiefly from his copper mines) of a revenue of 200,000 ducats, (Chalcond. l. ix. p. 258, 259.) Peysonnel (Commerce de la Mer Noire, tom. ii. p. 100) ascribes to the modern city 60,000 inhabitants. This account seems enormous; yet it is by trading with people that we become acquainted with their wealth and numbers.]

[Footnote 89/1: M. Boissonade has published, in the fifth volume of his Anecdota Græca (p. 387, 401.) a very interesting letter from George Amiroutzes, protovestiarius of Trebizond, to Bessarion, describing the surrender of Trebizond, and the fate of its chief inhabitants—M.]

[Footnote 89/2: See in Von Hammer, vol. ii. p. 60, the striking account of the mother, the empress Helena the Cantacuzene, who, in defiance of the edict, like that of Creon in the Greek tragedy, dug the grave for her murdered children with her own hand, and sank into it herself—M.]

[Footnote 90: Spondanus (from Gobelin Comment. Pii II. l. v.) relates the arrival and reception of the despot Thomas at Rome,. (A.D. 1461 No. NO. 3.)]

[Footnote 91: By an act dated A.D. 1494, Sept. 6, and lately transmitted from the archives of the Capitol to the royal library of Paris, the despot Andrew Palæologus, reserving the Morea, and stipulating some private advantages, conveys to Charles VIII., king of France, the empires of Constantinople and Trebizond, (Spondanus, A.D. 1495, No. 2.) M. D. Foncemagne (Mém. de l'Académie des Inscriptions, tom. xvii. p. 539—578) has bestowed a dissertation on his national title, of which he had obtained a copy from Rome.]

[Footnote 92: See Philippe de Comines, (l. vii. c. 14,) who reckons with pleasure the number of Greeks who were prepared to rise, 60 miles of an easy navigation, eighteen days' journey from Valona to Constantinople, &c. On this occasion the Turkish empire was saved by the policy of Venice.]

The importance of Constantinople was felt and magnified in its loss: the pontificate of Nicholas the Fifth, however peaceful and prosperous, was dishonored by the fall of the Eastern empire; and the grief and terror of the Latins revived, or seemed to revive, the old enthusiasm of the crusades. In one of the most distant countries of the West, Philip duke of Burgundy entertained, at Lisle in Flanders, an assembly of his nobles; and the pompous pageants of the feast were skilfully adapted to their fancy and feelings. [93] In the midst of the banquet a gigantic Saracen entered the hall, leading a fictitious elephant with a castle on his back: a matron in a mourning robe, the symbol of religion, was seen to issue from the castle: she deplored her oppression, and accused the slowness of her champions: the principal herald of the golden fleece advanced, bearing on his fist a live pheasant, which, according to the rites of chivalry, he presented to the duke. At this extraordinary summons, Philip, a wise and aged prince, engaged his person and powers in the holy war against the Turks: his example was imitated by the barons and knights of the assembly: they swore to God, the Virgin, the ladies and the pheasant; and their particular vows were not less extravagant than the general sanction of their oath. But the performance was made to depend on some future and foreign contingency; and during twelve years, till the last hour of his life, the duke of Burgundy might be scrupulously, and perhaps sincerely, on the eve of his departure. Had every breast glowed with the same ardor; had the union of the Christians corresponded with their bravery; had every country, from Sweden [94] to Naples, supplied a just proportion of cavalry and infantry, of men and money, it is indeed probable that Constantinople would have been delivered, and that the Turks might have been chased beyond the Hellespont or the Euphrates. But the secretary of the emperor, who composed every epistle, and attended every meeting, Æneas Sylvius, [95] a statesman and orator, describes from his own experience the repugnant state and spirit of Christendom. "It is a body," says he, "without a head; a republic without laws or magistrates. The pope and the emperor may shine as lofty titles, as splendid images; but they are unable to command, and none are willing to obey: every state has a separate prince, and every prince has a separate interest. What eloquence could unite so many discordant and hostile powers under the same standard? Could they be assembled in arms, who would dare to assume the office of general? What order could be maintained?—what military discipline? Who would undertake to feed such an enormous multitude? Who would understand their various languages, or direct their stranger and incompatible manners? What mortal could reconcile the English with the French, Genoa with Arragon the Germans with the natives of Hungary and Bohemia? If a small number enlisted in the holy war, they must be overthrown by the infidels; if many, by their own weight and confusion." Yet the same Æneas, when he was raised to the papal throne, under the name of Pius the Second, devoted his life to the prosecution of the Turkish war. In the council of Mantua he excited some sparks of a false or feeble enthusiasm; but when the pontiff appeared at Ancona, to embark in person with the troops, engagements vanished in excuses; a precise day was adjourned to an indefinite term; and his effective army consisted of some German pilgrims, whom he was obliged to disband with indulgences and arms. Regardless of futurity, his successors and the powers of Italy were involved in the schemes of present and domestic ambition; and the distance or proximity of each object determined in their eyes its apparent magnitude. A more enlarged view of their interest would have taught them to maintain a defensive and naval war against the common enemy; and the support of Scanderbeg and his brave Albanians might have prevented the subsequent invasion of the kingdom of Naples. The siege and sack of Otranto by the Turks diffused a general consternation; and Pope Sixtus was preparing to fly beyond the Alps, when the storm was instantly dispelled by the death of Mahomet the Second, in the fifty-first year of his age. [96] His lofty genius aspired to the conquest of Italy: he was possessed of a strong city and a capacious harbor; and the same reign might have been decorated with the trophies of the New and the Ancient Rome. [97]

[Footnote 93: See the original feast in Olivier de la Marche, (Mémoires, P. i. c. 29, 30,) with the abstract and observations of M. de Ste. Palaye, (Mémoires sur la Chevalerie, tom. i. P. iii. p. 182—185.) The peacock and the pheasant were distinguished as royal birds.]

[Footnote 94: It was found by an actual enumeration, that Sweden, Gothland, and Finland, contained 1,800,000 fighting men, and consequently were far more populous than at present.]

[Footnote 95: In the year 1454, Spondanus has given, from Æneas Sylvius, a view of the state of Europe, enriched with his own observations. That valuable annalist, and the Italian Muratori, will continue the series of events from the year 1453 to 1481, the end of Mahomet's life, and of this chapter.]

[Footnote 96: Besides the two annalists, the reader may consult Giannone (Istoria Civile, tom. iii. p. 449—455) for the Turkish invasion of the kingdom of Naples. For the reign and conquests of Mahomet II., I have occasionally used the Memorie Istoriche de Monarchi Ottomanni di Giovanni Sagredo, (Venezia, 1677, in 4to.) In peace and war, the Turks have ever engaged the attention of the republic of Venice. All her despatches and archives were open to a procurator of St. Mark, and Sagredo is not contemptible either in sense or style. Yet he too bitterly hates the infidels: he is ignorant of their language and manners; and his narrative, which allows only 70 pages to Mahomet II., (p. 69—140,) becomes more copious and authentic as he approaches the years 1640 and 1644, the term of the historic labors of John Sagredo.]

[Footnote 97: As I am now taking an everlasting farewell of the Greek empire, I shall briefly mention the great collection of Byzantine writers whose names and testimonies have been successively repeated in this work. The Greeks presses of Aldus and the Italians were confined to the classics of a better age; and the first rude editions of Procopius, Agathias, Cedrenus, Zonaras, &c., were published by the learned diligence of the Germans. The whole Byzantine series (xxxvi. volumes in folio) has gradually issued (A.D. 1648, &c.) from the royal press of the Louvre, with some collateral aid from Rome and Leipsic; but the Venetian edition, (A.D. 1729,) though cheaper and more copious, is not less inferior in correctness than in magnificence to that of Paris. The merits of the French editors are various; but the value of Anna Comnena, Cinnamus, Villehardouin, &c., is enhanced by the historical notes of Charles de Fresne du Cange. His supplemental works, the Greek Glossary, the Constantinopolis Christiana, the Familiæ Byzantinæ, diffuse a steady light over the darkness of the Lower Empire. Note: The new edition of the Byzantines, projected by Niebuhr, and continued under the patronage of the Prussian government, is the most convenient in size, and contains some authors (Leo Diaconus, Johannes Lydus, Corippus, the new fragment of Dexippus, Eunapius, &c., discovered by Mai) which could not be comprised in the former collections; but the names of such editors as Bekker, the Dindorfs, &c., raised hopes of something more than the mere republication of the text, and the notes of former editors. Little, I regret to say, has been added of annotation, and in some cases, the old incorrect versions have been retained—M.]

CHAPTER LXIX

STATE OF ROME FROM THE TWELFTH CENTURY

PART I

STATE OF ROME FROM THE TWELFTH CENTURY—TEMPORAL DOMINION OF THE POPES—SEDITIONS OF THE CITY—POLITICAL HERESY OF ARNOLD OF BRESCIA—RESTORATION OF THE REPUBLIC—THE SENATORS—PRIDE OF THE ROMANS—THEIR WARS—THEY ARE DEPRIVED OF THE ELECTION AND PRESENCE OF THE POPES, WHO RETIRE TO AVIGNON—THE JUBILEE—NOBLE FAMILIES OF ROME—FEUD OF THE COLONNA AND URSINI

In the first ages of the decline and fall of the Roman empire, our eye is invariably fixed on the royal city, which had given laws to the fairest portion of the globe. We contemplate her fortunes, at first with admiration, at length with pity, always with attention, and when that attention is diverted from the capital to the provinces, they are considered as so many branches which have been successively severed from the Imperial trunk. The foundation of a second Rome, on the shores of the Bosphorus, has compelled the historian to follow the successors of Constantine; and our curiosity has been tempted to visit the most remote countries of Europe and Asia, to explore the causes and the authors of the long decay of the Byzantine monarchy. By the conquest of Justinian, we have been recalled to the banks of the Tyber, to the deliverance of the ancient metropolis; but that deliverance was a change, or perhaps an aggravation, of servitude. Rome had been already stripped of her trophies, her gods, and her Cæsars; nor was the Gothic dominion more inglorious and oppressive than the tyranny of the Greeks. In the eighth century of the Christian æra, a religious quarrel, the worship of images, provoked the Romans to assert their independence: their bishop became the temporal, as well as the spiritual, father of a free people; and of the Western empire, which was restored by Charlemagne, the title and image still decorate the singular constitution of modern Germany. The name of Rome must yet command our involuntary respect: the climate (whatsoever may be its influence) was no longer the same: [1] the purity of blood had been contaminated through a thousand channels; but the venerable aspect of her ruins, and the memory of past greatness, rekindled a spark of the national character. The darkness of the middle ages exhibits some scenes not unworthy of our notice. Nor shall I dismiss the present work till I have reviewed the state and revolutions of the Roman City, which acquiesced under the absolute dominion of the popes, about the same time that Constantinople was enslaved by the Turkish arms.

*[Footnote 1: The abbé Dubos, who, with less genius than his successor Montesquieu, has asserted and magnified the influence of climate, objects to himself the degeneracy of the Romans and Batavians. To the first of these examples he replies, 1. That the change is less real than apparent, and that the modern Romans prudently conceal in themselves the virtues of their ancestors. 2. That the air, the soil, and the climate of Rome have suffered a great and visible alteration, (Réflexions sur la Poësie et sur la Peinture, part ii. sect. 16.) Note: This question is discussed at considerable length in Dr. Arnold's History of Rome, ch. xxiii. See likewise Bunsen's Dissertation on the Aria Cattiva Roms Beschreibung, pp. 82, 108—M.]*

In the beginning of the twelfth century, [2] the æra of the first crusade, Rome was revered by the Latins, as the metropolis of the world, as the throne of the pope and the emperor, who, from the eternal city, derived their title, their honors, and the right or exercise of temporal dominion. After so long an interruption, it may not be useless to repeat that the successors of Charlemagne and the Othos were chosen beyond the Rhine in a national diet; but that these princes were content with the humble names of kings of Germany and Italy, till they had passed the Alps and the Apennine, to seek their Imperial crown on the banks of the Tyber. [3] At some distance from the city, their approach was saluted by a long procession of the clergy and people with palms and crosses; and the terrific emblems of wolves and lions, of dragons and eagles, that floated in the military banners, represented the departed legions and cohorts of the republic. The royal path to maintain the liberties of Rome was thrice reiterated, at the bridge, the gate, and on the stairs of the Vatican; and the distribution of a customary donative feebly imitated the magnificence of the first Cæsars. In the church of St. Peter, the coronation was performed by his successor: the voice of God was confounded with that of the people; and the public consent was declared in the acclamations of "Long life and victory to our lord the pope! long life and victory to our lord the emperor! long life and victory to the Roman and Teutonic armies!" [4] The names of Cæsar and Augustus, the laws of Constantine and Justinian, the example of Charlemagne and Otho, established the supreme dominion of the emperors: their title and image was engraved on the papal coins; [5] and their jurisdiction was marked by the sword of justice, which they delivered to the præfect of the city. But every Roman prejudice was awakened by the name, the language, and the manners, of a Barbarian lord. The Cæsars of Saxony or Franconia were the chiefs of a feudal aristocracy; nor could they exercise the discipline of civil and military power, which alone secures the obedience of a distant people, impatient of servitude, though perhaps incapable of freedom. Once, and once only, in his life, each emperor, with an army of Teutonic vassals, descended from the Alps. I have described the peaceful order of his entry and coronation; but that order was commonly disturbed by the clamor and sedition of the Romans, who encountered their sovereign as a foreign invader: his departure was always speedy, and often shameful; and, in the absence of a long reign, his authority was insulted, and his name was forgotten. The progress of independence in Germany and Italy undermined the foundations of the Imperial sovereignty, and the triumph of the popes was the deliverance of Rome.

[Footnote 2: The reader has been so long absent from Rome, that I would advise him to recollect or review the xlixth chapter of this History.]

[Footnote 3: The coronation of the German emperors at Rome, more especially in the xith century, is best represented from the original monuments by Muratori (Antiquitat. Italiæ Medii Ævi, tom. i. dissertat. ii. p. 99, &c.) and Cenni, (Monument. Domin. Pontif. tom. ii. diss. vi. p. 261,) the latter of whom I only know from the copious extract of Schmidt, (Hist. des Allemands tom. iii. p. 255—266.)]

[Footnote 4: Exercitui Romano et Teutonico! The latter was both seen and felt; but the former was no more than magni nominis umbra.]

[Footnote 5: Muratori has given the series of the papal coins, (Antiquitat. tom. ii. diss. xxvii. p. 548—554.) He finds only two more early than the year 800: fifty are still extant from Leo III. to Leo IX., with the addition of the reigning emperor none remain of Gregory VII. or Urban II.; but in those of Paschal II. he seems to have renounced this badge of dependence.]

Of her two sovereigns, the emperor had precariously reigned by the right of conquest; but the authority of the pope was founded on the soft, though more solid, basis of opinion and habit. The removal of a foreign influence restored and endeared the shepherd to his flock. Instead of the arbitrary or venal nomination of a German court, the vicar of Christ was freely chosen by the college of cardinals, most of whom were either natives or inhabitants of the city. The applause of the magistrates and people confirmed his election, and the ecclesiastical power that was obeyed in Sweden and Britain had been ultimately derived from the suffrage of the Romans. The same suffrage gave a prince, as well as a pontiff, to the capital. It was universally believed, that Constantine had invested the popes with the temporal dominion of Rome; and the boldest civilians, the most profane skeptics, were satisfied with disputing the right of the emperor and the validity of his gift. The truth of the fact, the authenticity of his donation, was deeply rooted in the ignorance and tradition of four centuries; and the fabulous origin was lost in the real and permanent effects. The name of Dominus or Lord was inscribed on the coin of the bishops: their title was acknowledged by acclamations and oaths of allegiance, and with the free, or reluctant, consent of the German Cæsars, they had long exercised a supreme or subordinate jurisdiction over the city and patrimony of St. Peter. The reign of the popes, which gratified the prejudices, was not incompatible with the liberties, of Rome; and a more critical inquiry would have revealed a still nobler source of their power; the gratitude of a nation, whom they had rescued from the heresy and oppression of the Greek tyrant. In an age of superstition, it should seem that the union of the royal and sacerdotal characters would mutually fortify each other; and that the keys of Paradise would be the surest pledge of earthly obedience. The sanctity of the office might indeed be degraded by the personal vices of the man. But the scandals of the tenth century were obliterated by the austere and more dangerous virtues of Gregory the Seventh and his successors; and in the ambitious contests which they maintained for the rights of the church, their sufferings or their success must equally tend to increase the popular veneration. They sometimes wandered in poverty and exile, the victims of persecution; and the apostolic zeal with which they offered themselves to martyrdom must engage the favor and sympathy of every Catholic breast. And sometimes, thundering from the Vatican, they created, judged, and deposed the kings of the world; nor could the proudest Roman be disgraced by submitting to a priest, whose feet were kissed, and whose stirrup was held, by the successors of Charlemagne. [6] Even the temporal interest of the city should have protected in peace and honor the residence of the popes; from whence a vain and lazy people derived the greatest part of their subsistence and riches. The fixed revenue of the popes was probably impaired; many of the old patrimonial estates, both in Italy and the provinces, had been invaded by sacrilegious hands; nor could the loss be compensated by the claim, rather than the possession, of the more ample gifts of Pepin and his descendants. But the Vatican and Capitol were nourished by the incessant and increasing swarms of pilgrims and suppliants: the pale of Christianity was enlarged, and the pope and cardinals were overwhelmed by the judgment of ecclesiastical and secular causes. A new jurisprudence had established in the Latin church the right and practice of appeals; [7] and from the North and West the bishops and abbots were invited or summoned to solicit, to complain, to accuse, or to justify, before the threshold of the apostles. A rare prodigy is once recorded, that two horses, belonging to the archbishops of Mentz and Cologne, repassed the Alps, yet laden with gold and silver: [8] but it was soon understood, that the success, both of the pilgrims and clients, depended much less on the justice of their cause than on the value of their offering. The wealth and piety of these strangers were ostentatiously displayed; and their expenses, sacred or profane, circulated in various channels for the emolument of the Romans.

[Footnote 6: See Ducange, Gloss. mediæ et infimæ Latinitat. tom. vi. p. 364, 365, Staffa. This homage was paid by kings to archbishops, and by vassals to their lords, (Schmidt, tom. iii. p. 262;) and it was the nicest policy of Rome to confound the marks of filial and of feudal subjection.]

[Footnote 7: The appeals from all the churches to the Roman pontiff are deplored by the zeal of St. Bernard (de Consideratione, l. iii. tom. ii. p. 431—442, edit. Mabillon, Venet. 1750) and the judgment of Fleury, (Discours sur l'Hist. Ecclésiastique, iv. et vii.) But the saint, who believed in the false decretals condemns only the abuse of these appeals; the more enlightened historian investigates the origin, and rejects the principles, of this new jurisprudence.]

[Footnote 8: Germanici.... summarii non levatis sarcinis onusti nihilominus repatriant inviti. Nova res! quando hactenus aurum Roma refudit? Et nunc Romanorum consilio id usurpatum non credimus, (Bernard, de Consideratione, l. iii. c. 3, p. 437.) The first words of the passage are obscure, and probably corrupt.]

Such powerful motives should have firmly attached the voluntary and pious obedience of the Roman people to their spiritual and temporal father. But the operation of prejudice and interest is often disturbed by the sallies of ungovernable passion. The Indian who fells the tree, that he may gather the fruit, [9] and the Arab who plunders the caravans of commerce, are actuated by the same impulse of savage nature, which overlooks the future in the present, and relinquishes for momentary rapine the long and secure possession of the most important blessings. And it was thus, that the shrine of St. Peter was profaned by the thoughtless Romans; who pillaged the offerings, and wounded the pilgrims, without computing the number and value of similar visits, which they prevented by their inhospitable sacrilege. Even the influence of superstition is fluctuating and precarious; and the slave, whose reason is subdued, will often be delivered by his avarice or pride. A credulous devotion for the fables and oracles of the priesthood most powerfully acts on the mind of a Barbarian; yet such a mind is the least capable of preferring imagination to sense, of sacrificing to a distant motive, to an invisible, perhaps an ideal, object, the appetites and interests of the present world. In the vigor of health and youth, his practice will perpetually contradict his belief; till the pressure of age, or sickness, or calamity, awakens his terrors, and compels him to satisfy the double debt of piety and remorse. I have already observed, that the modern times of religious indifference are the most favorable to the peace and security of the clergy. Under the reign of superstition, they had much to hope from the ignorance, and much to fear from the violence, of mankind. The wealth, whose constant increase must have rendered them the sole proprietors of the earth, was alternately bestowed by the repentant father and plundered by the rapacious son: their persons were adored or violated; and the same idol, by the hands of the same votaries, was placed on the altar, or trampled in the dust. In the feudal system of Europe, arms were the title of distinction and the measure of allegiance; and amidst their tumult, the still voice of law and reason was seldom heard or obeyed. The turbulent Romans disdained the yoke, and insulted the impotence, of their bishop: [10] nor would his education or character allow him to exercise, with decency or effect, the power of the sword. The motives of his election and the frailties of his life were exposed to their familiar observation; and proximity must diminish the reverence which his name and his decrees impressed on a barbarous world. This difference has not escaped the notice of our philosophic historian: "Though the name and authority of the court of Rome were so terrible in the remote countries of Europe, which were sunk in profound ignorance, and were entirely unacquainted with its character and conduct, the pope was so little revered at home, that his inveterate enemies surrounded the gates of Rome itself, and even controlled his government in that city; and the ambassadors, who, from a distant extremity of Europe, carried to him the humble, or rather abject, submissions of the greatest potentate of the age, found the utmost difficulty to make their way to him, and to throw themselves at his feet." [11]

[Footnote 9: Quand les sauvages de la Louisiane veulent avoir du fruit, ils coupent l'arbre au pied et cueillent le fruit. Voila le gouvernement despotique, (Esprit des Loix, l. v. c. 13;) and passion and ignorance are always despotic.]

[Footnote 10: In a free conversation with his countryman Adrian IV., John of Salisbury accuses the avarice of the pope and clergy: Provinciarum diripiunt spolia, ac si thesauros Crsi studeant reparare. Sed recte cum eis agit Altissimus, quoniam et ipsi aliis et sæpe vilissimis hominibus dati sunt in direptionem, (de Nugis Curialium, l. vi. c. 24, p. 387.) In the next page, he blames the rashness and infidelity of the Romans, whom their bishops vainly strove to conciliate by gifts, instead of virtues. It is pity that this miscellaneous writer has not given us less morality and erudition, and more pictures of himself and the times.]

[Footnote 11: Hume's History of England, vol. i. p. 419. The same writer has given us, from Fitz-Stephen, a singular act of cruelty perpetrated on the clergy by Geoffrey, the father of Henry II. "When he was master of Normandy, the chapter of Seez presumed, without his consent, to proceed to the election of a bishop: upon which he ordered all of them, with the bishop elect, to be castrated, and made all their testicles be brought him in a platter." Of the pain and danger they might justly complain; yet since they had vowed chastity he deprived them of a superfluous treasure.]

Since the primitive times, the wealth of the popes was exposed to envy, their powers to opposition, and their persons to violence. But the long hostility of the mitre and the crown increased the numbers, and inflamed the passions, of their enemies. The deadly factions of the Guelphs and Ghibelines, so fatal to Italy, could never be embraced with truth or constancy by the Romans, the subjects and adversaries both of the bishop and emperor; but their support was solicited by both parties, and they alternately displayed in their banners the keys of St. Peter and the German eagle. Gregory the Seventh, who may be adored or detested as the founder of the papal monarchy, was driven from Rome, and died in exile at Salerno. Six-and-thirty of his successors, [12] till their retreat to Avignon, maintained an unequal contest with the Romans: their age and dignity were often violated; and the churches, in the solemn rites of religion, were polluted with sedition and murder. A repetition [13] of such capricious brutality, without connection or design, would be tedious and disgusting; and I shall content myself with some events of the twelfth century, which represent the state of the popes and the city. On Holy Thursday, while Paschal officiated before the altar, he was interrupted by the clamors of the multitude, who imperiously demanded the confirmation of a favorite magistrate. His silence exasperated their fury; his pious refusal to mingle the affairs of earth and heaven was encountered with menaces, and oaths, that he should be the cause and the witness of the public ruin. During the festival of Easter, while the bishop and the clergy, barefooted and in procession, visited the tombs of the martyrs, they were twice assaulted, at the bridge of St. Angelo, and before the Capitol, with volleys of stones and darts. The houses of his adherents were levelled with the ground: Paschal escaped with difficulty and danger; he levied an army in the patrimony of St. Peter; and his last days were embittered by suffering and inflicting the calamities of civil war. The scenes that followed the election of his successor Gelasius the Second were still more scandalous to the church and city. Cencio Frangipani, [14] a potent and factious baron, burst into the assembly furious and in arms: the cardinals were stripped, beaten, and trampled under foot; and he seized, without pity or respect, the vicar of Christ by the throat. Gelasius was dragged by the hair along the ground, buffeted with blows, wounded with spurs, and bound with an iron chain in the house of his brutal tyrant. An insurrection of the people delivered their bishop: the rival families opposed the violence of the Frangipani; and Cencio, who sued for pardon, repented of the failure, rather than of the guilt, of his enterprise. Not many days had elapsed, when the pope was again assaulted at the altar. While his friends and enemies were engaged in a bloody contest, he escaped in his sacerdotal garments. In this unworthy flight, which excited the compassion of the Roman matrons, his attendants were scattered or unhorsed; and, in the fields behind the church of St. Peter, his successor was found alone and half dead with fear and fatigue. Shaking the dust from his feet, the apostle withdrew from a city in which his dignity was insulted and his person was endangered; and the vanity of sacerdotal ambition is revealed in the involuntary confession, that one emperor was more tolerable than twenty. [15] These examples might suffice; but I cannot forget the sufferings of two pontiffs of the same age, the second and third of the name of Lucius. The former, as he ascended in battle array to assault the Capitol, was struck on the temple by a stone, and expired in a few days. The latter was severely wounded in the person of his servants. In a civil commotion, several of his priests had been made prisoners; and the inhuman Romans, reserving one as a guide for his brethren, put out their eyes, crowned them with ludicrous mitres, mounted them on asses with their faces towards the tail, and extorted an oath, that, in this wretched condition, they should offer themselves as a lesson to the head of the church. Hope or fear, lassitude or remorse, the characters of the men, and the circumstances of the times, might sometimes obtain an interval of peace and obedience; and the pope was restored with joyful acclamations to the Lateran or Vatican, from whence he had been driven with threats and violence. But the root of mischief was deep and perennial; and a momentary calm was preceded and followed by such tempests as had almost sunk the bark of St. Peter. Rome continually presented the aspect of war and discord: the churches and palaces were fortified and assaulted by the factions and families; and, after giving peace to Europe, Calistus the Second alone had resolution and power to prohibit the use of private arms in the metropolis. Among the nations who revered the apostolic throne, the tumults of Rome provoked a general indignation; and in a letter to his disciple Eugenius the Third, St. Bernard, with the sharpness of his wit and zeal, has stigmatized the vices of the rebellious people. [16] "Who is ignorant," says the monk of Clairvaux, "of the vanity and arrogance of the Romans? a nation nursed in sedition, untractable, and scorning to obey, unless they are too feeble to resist. When they promise to serve, they aspire to reign; if they swear allegiance, they watch the opportunity of revolt; yet they vent their discontent in loud clamors, if your doors, or your counsels, are shut against them. Dexterous in mischief, they have never learned the science of doing good. Odious to earth and heaven, impious to God, seditious among themselves, jealous of their neighbors, inhuman to strangers, they love no one, by no one are they beloved; and while they wish to inspire fear, they live in base and continual apprehension. They will not submit; they know not how to govern faithless to their superiors, intolerable to their equals, ungrateful to their benefactors, and alike impudent in their demands and their refusals. Lofty in promise, poor in execution; adulation and calumny, perfidy and treason, are the familiar arts of their policy." Surely this dark portrait is not colored by the pencil of Christian charity; [17]

yet the features, however harsh or ugly, express a lively resemblance of the Roman of the twelfth century. [18]

[Footnote 12: From Leo IX. and Gregory VII. an authentic and contemporary series of the lives of the popes by the cardinal of Arragon, Pandulphus Pisanus, Bernard Guido, &c., is inserted in the Italian Historians of Muratori, (tom. iii. P. i. p. 277—685,) and has been always before my eyes.]

[Footnote 13: The dates of years in the contents may throughout his this chapter be understood as tacit references to the Annals of Muratori, my ordinary and excellent guide. He uses, and indeed quotes, with the freedom of a master, his great collection of the Italian Historians, in xxviii. volumes; and as that treasure is in my library, I have thought it an amusement, if not a duty, to consult the originals.]

[Footnote 14: I cannot refrain from transcribing the high-colored words of Pandulphus Pisanus, (p. 384.) Hoc audiens inimicus pacis atque turbator jam fatus Centius Frajapane, more draconis immanissimi sibilans, et ab imis pectoribus trahens longa suspiria, accinctus retro gladio sine more cucurrit, valvas ac fores confregit. Ecclesiam furibundus introiit, inde custode remoto papam per gulam accepit, distraxit pugnis calcibusque percussit, et tanquam brutum animal intra limen ecclesiæ acriter calcaribus cruentavit; et latro tantum dominum per capillos et brachia, Jesû bono interim dormiente, detraxit, ad domum usque deduxit, inibi catenavit et inclusit.]

[Footnote 15: Ego coram Deo et Ecclesiâ dico, si unquam possibile esset, mallem unum imperatorem quam tot dominos, (Vit. Gelas. II. p. 398.)]

[Footnote 16: Quid tam notum seculis quam protervia et cervicositas Romanorum? Gens insueta paci, tumultui assueta, gens immitis et intractabilis usque adhuc, subdi nescia, nisi cum non valet resistere, (de Considerat. l. iv. c. 2, p. 441.) The saint takes breath, and then begins again: Hi, invisi terræ et clo, utrique injecere manus, &c., (p. 443.)]

[Footnote 17: As a Roman citizen, Petrarch takes leave to observe, that Bernard, though a saint, was a man; that he might be provoked by resentment, and possibly repent of his hasty passion, &c. (Mémoires sur la Vie de Pétrarque, tom. i. p. 330.)]

[Footnote 18: Baronius, in his index to the xiith volume of his Annals, has found a fair and easy excuse. He makes two heads, of Romani Catholici and Schismatici: to the former he applies all the good, to the latter all the evil, that is told of the city.]

The Jews had rejected the Christ when he appeared among them in a plebeian character; and the Romans might plead their ignorance of his vicar when he assumed the pomp and pride of a temporal sovereign. In the busy age of the crusades, some sparks of curiosity and reason were rekindled in the Western world: the heresy of Bulgaria, the Paulician sect, was successfully transplanted into the soil of Italy and France; the Gnostic visions were mingled with the simplicity of the gospel; and the enemies of the clergy reconciled their passions with their conscience, the desire of freedom with the profession of piety. [19] The trumpet of Roman liberty was first sounded by Arnold of Brescia, [20] whose promotion in the church was confined to the lowest rank, and who wore the monastic habit rather as a garb of poverty than as a uniform of obedience. His adversaries could not deny the wit and eloquence which they severely felt; they confess with reluctance the specious purity of his morals; and his errors were recommended to the public by a mixture of important and beneficial truths. In his theological studies, he had been the disciple of the famous and unfortunate Abelard, [21] who was likewise involved in the suspicion of heresy: but the lover of Eloisa was of a soft and flexible nature; and his ecclesiastic judges were edified and disarmed by the humility of his repentance. From this master, Arnold most probably imbibed some metaphysical definitions of the Trinity, repugnant to the taste of the times: his ideas of baptism and the eucharist are loosely censured; but a political heresy was the source of his fame and misfortunes. He presumed to quote the declaration of Christ, that his kingdom is not of this world: he boldly maintained, that the sword and the sceptre were intrusted to the civil magistrate; that temporal honors and possessions were lawfully vested in secular persons; that the abbots, the bishops, and the pope himself, must renounce either their state or their salvation; and that after the loss of their revenues, the voluntary tithes and oblations of the faithful would suffice, not indeed for luxury and avarice, but for a frugal life in the exercise of spiritual labors. During a short time, the preacher was revered as a patriot; and the discontent, or revolt, of Brescia against her bishop, was the first fruits of his dangerous lessons. But the favor of the people is less permanent than the resentment of the priest; and after the heresy of Arnold had been condemned by Innocent the Second, [22] in the general council of the Lateran, the magistrates themselves were urged by prejudice and fear to execute the sentence of the church. Italy could no longer afford a refuge; and the disciple of Abelard escaped beyond the Alps, till he found a safe and hospitable shelter in Zurich, now the first of the Swiss cantons. From a Roman station, [23] a royal villa, a chapter of noble virgins, Zurich had gradually increased to a free and flourishing city; where the appeals of the Milanese were sometimes tried by the Imperial commissaries. [24] In an age less ripe for reformation, the precursor of Zuinglius was heard with applause: a brave and simple people imbibed, and long retained, the color of his opinions; and his art, or merit, seduced the bishop of Constance, and even the pope's legate, who forgot, for his sake, the interest of their master and their order. Their tardy zeal was quickened by the fierce exhortations of St. Bernard; [25] and the enemy of the church was driven by persecution to the desperate measures of erecting his standard in Rome itself, in the face of the successor of St. Peter.

[Footnote 19: *The heresies of the xiith century may be found in Mosheim, (Institut. Hist. Ecclés. p. 419—427,) who entertains a favorable opinion of Arnold of Brescia. In the vth volume I have described the sect of the Paulicians, and followed their migration from Armenia to Thrace and Bulgaria, Italy and France.*]

[Footnote 20: *The original pictures of Arnold of Brescia are drawn by Otho, bishop of Frisingen, (Chron. l. vii. c. 31, de Gestis Frederici I. l. i. c. 27, l. ii. c. 21,) and in the iiid book of the Ligurinus, a poem of Gunthur, who flourished A.D. 1200, in the monastery of Paris near Basil, (Fabric. Bibliot. Latin. Med. et Infimæ Ætatis, tom. iii. p. 174, 175.) The long passage that relates to Arnold is produced by Guilliman, (de Rebus Helveticis, l. iii. c. 5, p. 108.)* Note: Compare Franke, Arnold von Brescia und seine Zeit. Zurich, 1828—M.]

[Footnote 21: *The wicked wit of Bayle was amused in composing, with much levity and learning, the articles of Abelard, Foulkes, Heloise, in his Dictionnaire Critique. The dispute of Abelard and St. Bernard, of scholastic and positive divinity, is well understood by Mosheim, (Institut. Hist. Ecclés. p. 412—415.)*]

[Footnote 22: —*Damnatus ab illo Præsule, qui numeros vetitum contingere nostros Nomen ad innocuâ ducit laudabile vitâ.*

We may applaud the dexterity and correctness of Ligurinus, who turns the unpoetical name of Innocent II. into a compliment.]

[Footnote 23: A Roman inscription of Statio Turicensis has been found at Zurich, (D'Anville, Notice de l'ancienne Gaul, p. 642—644;) but it is without sufficient warrant, that the city and canton have usurped, and even monopolized, the names of Tigurum and Pagus Tigurinus.]

[Footnote 24: Guilliman (de Rebus Helveticis, l. iii. c. 5, p. 106) recapitulates the donation (A.D. 833) of the emperor Lewis the Pious to his daughter the abbess Hildegardis. Curtim nostram Turegum in ducatû Alamanniæ in pago Durgaugensi, with villages, woods, meadows, waters, slaves, churches, &c.; a noble gift. Charles the Bald gave the jus monetæ, the city was walled under Otho I., and the line of the bishop of Frisingen, Nobile Turegum multarum copia rerum, is repeated with pleasure by the antiquaries of Zurich.]

[Footnote 25: Bernard, Epistol. cxcv. tom. i. p. 187—190. Amidst his invectives he drops a precious acknowledgment, qui, utinam quam sanæ esset doctrinæ quam districtæ est vitæ. He owns that Arnold would be a valuable acquisition for the church.]

PART II

Yet the courage of Arnold was not devoid of discretion: he was protected, and had perhaps been invited, by the nobles and people; and in the service of freedom, his eloquence thundered over the seven hills. Blending in the same discourse the texts of Livy and St. Paul, uniting the motives of gospel, and of classic, enthusiasm, he admonished the Romans, how strangely their patience and the vices of the clergy had degenerated from the primitive times of the church and the city. He exhorted them to assert the inalienable rights of men and Christians; to restore the laws and magistrates of the republic; to respect the name of the emperor; but to confine their shepherd to the spiritual government of his flock. [26] Nor could his spiritual government escape the censure and control of the reformer; and the inferior clergy were taught by his lessons to resist the cardinals, who had usurped a despotic command over the twenty-eight regions or parishes of Rome. [27] The revolution was not accomplished without rapine and violence, the diffusion of blood and the demolition of houses: the victorious faction was enriched with the spoils of the clergy and the adverse nobles. Arnold of Brescia enjoyed, or deplored, the effects of his mission: his reign continued above ten years, while two popes, Innocent the Second and Anastasius the Fourth, either trembled in the Vatican, or wandered as exiles in the adjacent cities. They were succeeded by a more vigorous and fortunate pontiff. Adrian the Fourth, [28] the only Englishman who has ascended the throne of St. Peter; and whose merit emerged from the mean condition of a monk, and almost a beggar, in the monastery of St. Albans. On the first provocation, of a cardinal killed or wounded in the streets, he cast an interdict on the guilty people; and from Christmas to Easter, Rome was deprived of the real or imaginary comforts of religious worship. The Romans had despised their temporal prince: they submitted with grief and terror to the censures of their spiritual father: their guilt was expiated by penance, and the banishment of the seditious preacher was the price of their absolution. But the revenge of Adrian was yet unsatisfied, and the approaching coronation of Frederic Barbarossa was fatal to the bold reformer, who had offended, though not in an equal degree, the heads of the church and state. In their interview at Viterbo, the pope represented to the emperor the furious, ungovernable spirit of the Romans; the insults, the injuries, the fears, to which his person and his clergy were continually exposed; and the pernicious tendency of the heresy of Arnold, which must subvert the principles of civil, as well as ecclesiastical, subordination. Frederic was convinced by these arguments, or tempted by the desire of the Imperial crown: in the balance of ambition, the innocence or life of an individual is of small account; and their common enemy was sacrificed to a moment of political concord.

After his retreat from Rome, Arnold had been protected by the viscounts of Campania, from whom he was extorted by the power of Cæsar: the præfect of the city pronounced his sentence: the martyr of freedom was burned alive in the presence of a careless and ungrateful people; and his ashes were cast into the Tyber, lest the heretics should collect and worship the relics of their master. [29] The clergy triumphed in his death: with his ashes, his sect was dispersed; his memory still lived in the minds of the Romans. From his school they had probably derived a new article of faith, that the metropolis of the Catholic church is exempt from the penalties of excommunication and interdict. Their bishops might argue, that the supreme jurisdiction, which they exercised over kings and nations, more especially embraced the city and diocese of the prince of the apostles. But they preached to the winds, and the same principle that weakened the effect, must temper the abuse, of the thunders of the Vatican.

[Footnote 26: He advised the Romans, Consiliis armisque sua moderamina summa Arbitrio tractare suo: nil juris in hâc re Pontifici summo, modicum concedere regi Suadebat populo. Sic læsâ stultus utrâque Majestate, reum geminæ se fecerat aulæ. Nor is the poetry of Gunther different from the prose of Otho.]

[Footnote 27: See Baronius (A.D. 1148, No. 38, 39) from the Vatican MSS. He loudly condemns Arnold (A.D. 1141, No. 3) as the father of the political heretics, whose influence then hurt him in France.]

[Footnote 28: The English reader may consult the Biographia Britannica, Adrian IV.; but our own writers have added nothing to the fame or merits of their countrymen.]

[Footnote 29: Besides the historian and poet already quoted, the last adventures of Arnold are related by the biographer of Adrian IV. (Muratori. Script. Rerum Ital. tom. iii. P. i. p. 441, 442.)]

The love of ancient freedom has encouraged a belief that as early as the tenth century, in their first struggles against the Saxon Othos, the commonwealth was vindicated and restored by the senate and people of Rome; that two consuls were annually elected among the nobles, and that ten or twelve plebeian magistrates revived the name and office of the tribunes of the commons. [30] But this venerable structure disappears before the light of criticism. In the darkness of the middle ages, the appellations of senators, of consuls, of the sons of consuls, may sometimes be discovered. [31] They were bestowed by the emperors, or assumed by the most powerful citizens, to denote their rank, their honors, [32] and perhaps the claim of a pure and patrician descent: but they float on the surface, without a series or a substance, the titles of men, not the orders of government; [33] and it is only from the year of Christ one thousand one hundred and forty-four that the establishment of the senate is dated, as a glorious æra, in the acts of the city. A new constitution was hastily framed by private ambition or popular enthusiasm; nor could Rome, in the twelfth century, produce an antiquary to explain, or a legislator to restore, the harmony and proportions of the ancient model. The assembly of a free, of an armed, people, will ever speak in loud and weighty acclamations. But the regular distribution of the thirty-five tribes, the nice balance of the wealth and numbers of the centuries, the debates of the adverse orators, and the slow operations of votes and ballots, could not easily be adapted by a blind multitude, ignorant of the arts, and insensible of the benefits, of legal government. It was proposed by Arnold to revive and discriminate the equestrian order; but what could be the motive or measure of such distinction? [34] The pecuniary qualification of the knights must have been reduced to the poverty of the times: those times no longer required their civil functions of judges and farmers of the revenue; and their primitive duty, their military service on horseback, was more nobly supplied by feudal tenures and the spirit of chivalry. The jurisprudence of the republic was useless and unknown: the nations and families of Italy who lived under the Roman and Barbaric laws were insensibly mingled in a common mass; and some faint tradition, some imperfect fragments, preserved the memory of the Code and

Pandects of Justinian. With their liberty the Romans might doubtless have restored the appellation and office of consuls; had they not disdained a title so promiscuously adopted in the Italian cities, that it has finally settled on the humble station of the agents of commerce in a foreign land. But the rights of the tribunes, the formidable word that arrested the public counsels, suppose or must produce a legitimate democracy. The old patricians were the subjects, the modern barons the tyrants, of the state; nor would the enemies of peace and order, who insulted the vicar of Christ, have long respected the unarmed sanctity of a plebeian magistrate. [35]

[Footnote 30: Ducange (Gloss. Latinitatis Mediæ et Infimæ Ætatis, Decarchones, tom. ii. p. 726) gives me a quotation from Blondus, (Decad. ii. l. ii.:) Duo consules ex nobilitate quotannis fiebant, qui ad vetustum consulum exemplar summærerum præessent. And in Sigonius (de Regno Italiæ, l. v. Opp. tom. ii. p. 400) I read of the consuls and tribunes of the xth century. Both Blondus, and even Sigonius, too freely copied the classic method of supplying from reason or fancy the deficiency of records.]

[Footnote 31: In the panegyric of Berengarius (Muratori, Script. Rer. Ital. tom. ii. P. i. p. 408) a Roman is mentioned as consulis natus in the beginning of the xth century. Muratori (Dissert. v.) discovers, in the years 952 and 956, Gratianus in Dei nomine consul et dux, Georgius consul et dux; and in 1015, Romanus, brother of Gregory VIII., proudly, but vaguely, styles himself consul et dux et omnium Roma norum senator.]

[Footnote 32: As late as the xth century, the Greek emperors conferred on the dukes of Venice, Naples, Amalphi, &c., the title of upatoV or consuls, (see Chron. Sagornini, passim;) and the successors of Charlemagne would not abdicate any of their prerogative. But in general the names of consul and senator, which may be found among the French and Germans, signify no more than count and lord, (Signeur, Ducange Glossar.) The monkish writers are often ambitious of fine classic words.]

[Footnote 33: The most constitutional form is a diploma of Otho III., (A. D 998,) consulibus senatûs populique Romani; but the act is probably spurious. At the coronation of Henry I., A.D. 1014, the historian Dithmar (apud Muratori, Dissert. xxiii.) describes him, a senatoribus duodecim vallatum, quorum sex rasi barbâ, alii prolixâ, mystice incedebant cum baculis. The senate is mentioned in the panegyric of Berengarius, (p. 406.)]

[Footnote 34: In ancient Rome the equestrian order was not ranked with the senate and people as a third branch of the republic till the consulship of Cicero, who assumes the merit of the establishment, (Plin. Hist. Natur. xxxiii. 3. Beaufort, République Romaine, tom. i. p. 144—155.)]

[Footnote 35: The republican plan of Arnold of Brescia is thus stated by Gunther:— Quin etiam titulos urbis renovare vetustos; Nomine plebeio secernere nomen equestre, Jura tribunorum, sanctum reparare senatum, Et senio fessas mutasque reponere leges. Lapsa ruinosis, et adhuc pendentia muris Reddere primævo Capitolia prisca nitori. But of these reformations, some were no more than ideas, others no more than words.]

In the revolution of the twelfth century, which gave a new existence and æra to Rome, we may observe the real and important events that marked or confirmed her political independence. I. The Capitoline hill, one of her seven eminences, [36] is about four hundred yards in length, and two hundred in breadth. A flight of a hundred steps led to the summit of the Tarpeian rock; and far steeper was the ascent before the declivities had been smoothed and the precipices filled by the ruins of fallen edifices. From the earliest ages, the Capitol had been used as a temple in peace, a fortress in war: after the loss of the city, it maintained a siege against the victorious Gauls, and the sanctuary of the empire was occupied, assaulted, and burnt, in the civil wars of Vitellius and Vespasian. [37] The temples of Jupiter and his kindred deities had crumbled into dust; their place was supplied by monasteries and houses; and the solid walls, the long and shelving porticos, were decayed or ruined by the lapse of time. It was the first act of the Romans, an act of freedom, to restore the strength, though not the beauty, of the Capitol; to fortify the seat of their arms and counsels; and as often as they ascended the hill, the coldest minds must have glowed with the remembrance of their ancestors. II. The first Cæsars had been invested with the exclusive coinage of the gold and silver; to the senate they abandoned the baser metal of bronze or copper: [38] the emblems and legends were inscribed on a more ample field by the genius of flattery; and the prince was relieved from the care of celebrating his own virtues. The successors of Diocletian despised even the flattery of the senate: their royal officers at Rome, and in the provinces, assumed the sole direction of the mint; and the same prerogative was inherited by the Gothic kings of Italy, and the long series of the Greek, the French, and the German dynasties. After an abdication of eight hundred years, the Roman senate asserted this honorable and lucrative privilege; which was tacitly renounced by the popes, from Paschal the Second to the establishment of their residence beyond the Alps. Some of these republican coins of the twelfth and thirteenth centuries are shown in the cabinets of the curious. On one of these, a gold medal, Christ is depictured holding in his left hand a book with this inscription: "The vow of the Roman senate and people: Rome the capital of the world;" on the reverse, St. Peter delivering a banner to a kneeling senator in his cap and gown, with the name and arms of his family impressed on a shield. [39] III. With the empire, the præfect of the city had declined to a municipal officer; yet he still exercised in the last appeal the civil and criminal jurisdiction; and a drawn sword, which he received from the successors of Otho, was the mode of his investiture and the emblem of his functions. [40] The dignity was confined to the noble families of Rome: the choice of the people was ratified by the pope; but a triple oath of fidelity must have often embarrassed the præfect in the conflict of adverse duties. [41] A servant, in whom they possessed but a third share, was dismissed by the independent Romans: in his place they elected a patrician; but this title, which Charlemagne had not disdained, was too lofty for a citizen or a subject; and, after the first fervor of rebellion, they consented without reluctance to the restoration of the præfect. About fifty years after this event, Innocent the Third, the most ambitious, or at least the most fortunate, of the Pontiffs, delivered the Romans and himself from this badge of foreign dominion: he invested the præfect with a banner instead of a sword, and absolved him from all dependence of oaths or service to the German emperors. [42] In his place an ecclesiastic, a present or future cardinal, was named by the pope to the civil government of Rome; but his jurisdiction has been reduced to a narrow compass; and in the days of freedom, the right or exercise was derived from the senate and people. IV. After the revival of the senate, [43] the conscript fathers (if I may use the expression) were invested with the legislative and executive power; but their views seldom reached beyond the present day; and that day was most frequently disturbed by violence and tumult. In its utmost plenitude, the order or assembly consisted of fifty-six senators, [44] the most eminent of whom were distinguished by the title of counsellors: they were nominated, perhaps annually, by the people; and a previous choice of their electors, ten persons in each region, or parish, might afford a basis for a free and permanent constitution. The popes, who in this tempest submitted rather to bend than to break, confirmed by treaty the establishment and privileges of the senate, and expected from time, peace, and religion, the restoration of their government. The motives of public and private interest might sometimes draw from the Romans an occasional and temporary sacrifice of their claims; and they renewed their oath of allegiance to the successor of St. Peter and Constantine, the lawful head of the church and the republic. [45]

[Footnote 36: *After many disputes among the antiquaries of Rome, it seems determined, that the summit of the Capitoline hill next the river is strictly the Mons Tarpeius, the Arx; and that on the other summit,* the church and convent of Araceli, the barefoot friars of St. Francis occupy the temple of Jupiter, (Nardini, Roma Antica, l. v. c. 11—16. Note: The authority of Nardini is now vigorously impugned, and the question of the Arx and the Temple of Jupiter revived, with new arguments by Niebuhr and his accomplished follower, M. Bunsen. Roms Beschreibung, vol. iii. p. 12, et seqq—M.]

[Footnote 37: Tacit. Hist. iii. 69, 70.]

[Footnote 38: This partition of the noble and baser metals between the emperor and senate must, however, be adopted, not as a positive fact, but as the probable opinion of the best antiquaries, (see the Science des Medailles of the Père Joubert, tom. ii. p. 208—211, in the improved and scarce edition of the Baron de la Bastie. Note: Dr. Cardwell (Lecture on Ancient Coins, p. 70, et seq.) assigns convincing reasons in support of this opinion—M.]

[Footnote 39: In his xxviith dissertation on the Antiquities of Italy, (tom. ii. p. 559—569,) Muratori exhibits a series of the senatorian coins, which bore the obscure names of Affortiati, Infortiati, Provisini, Paparini. During this period, all the popes, without excepting Boniface VIII, abstained from the right of coining, which was resumed by his successor Benedict XI., and regularly exercised in the court of Avignon.]

[Footnote 40: A German historian, Gerard of Reicherspeg (in Baluz. Miscell. tom. v. p. 64, apud Schmidt, Hist. des Allemands, tom. iii. p. 265) thus describes the constitution of Rome in the xith century: Grandiora urbis et orbis negotia spectant ad Romanum pontificem itemque ad Romanum Imperatorem, sive illius vicarium urbis præfectum, qui de suâ dignitate respicit utrumque, videlicet dominum papam cui facit hominum, et dominum imperatorem a quo accipit suæ potestatis insigne, scilicet gladium exertum.]

[Footnote 41: The words of a contemporary writer (Pandulph. Pisan. in Vit. Paschal. II. p. 357, 358) describe the election and oath of the præfect in 1118, inconsultis patribus.... loca præfectoria.... Laudes præfectoriæ.... comitiorum applausum.... juraturum populo in ambonem sublevant.... confirmari eum in urbe præfectum petunt.]

[Footnote 42: Urbis præfectum ad ligiam fidelitatem recepit, et per mantum quod illi donavit de præfecturâ eum publice investivit, qui usque ad id tempus juramento fidelitatis imperatori fuit obligatus et ab eo præfecturæ tenuit honorem, (Gesta Innocent. III. in Muratori, tom. iii. P. i. p. 487.)]

[Footnote 43: See Otho Frising. Chron. vii. 31, de Gest. Frederic. I., l. i. c. 27.]

[Footnote 44: Cur countryman, Roger Hoveden, speaks of the single senators, of the Capuzzi family, &c., quorum temporibus melius regebatur Roma quam nunc (A.D. 1194) est temporibus lvi. senatorum, (Ducange, Gloss. tom. vi. p. 191, Senatores.)]

[Footnote 45: Muratori (dissert. xlii. tom. iii. p. 785—788) has published an original treaty: Concordia inter D. nostrum papam Clementem III. et senatores populi Romani super regalibus et aliis dignitatibus urbis, &c., anno 44º senatûs. The senate speaks, and speaks with authority: Reddimus ad præsens.... habebimus.... dabitis presbetria.... jurabimus pacem et fidelitatem, &c. A chartula de Tenementis Tusculani, dated in the 47th year of the same æra, and confirmed decreto amplissimi ordinis senatûs, acclamatione P. R. publice Capitolio consistentis. It is there we find the difference of senatores consiliarii and simple senators, (Muratori, dissert. xlii. tom. iii. p. 787—789.)]

The union and vigor of a public council was dissolved in a lawless city; and the Romans soon adopted a more strong and simple mode of administration. They condensed the name and authority of the senate in a single magistrate, or two colleagues; and as they were changed at the end of a year, or of six months, the greatness of the trust was compensated by the shortness of the term. But in this transient reign, the senators of Rome indulged their avarice and ambition: their justice was perverted by the interest of their family and faction; and as they punished only their enemies, they were obeyed only by their adherents. Anarchy, no longer tempered by the pastoral care of their bishop, admonished the Romans that they were incapable of governing themselves; and they sought abroad those blessings which they were hopeless of finding at home. In the same age, and from the same motives, most of the Italian republics were prompted to embrace a measure, which, however strange it may seem, was adapted to their situation, and productive of the most salutary effects. [46] They chose, in some foreign but friendly city, an impartial magistrate of noble birth and unblemished character, a soldier and a statesman, recommended by the voice of fame and his country, to whom they delegated for a time the supreme administration of peace and war. The compact between the governor and the governed was sealed with oaths and subscriptions; and the duration of his power, the measure of his stipend, the nature of their mutual obligations, were defined with scrupulous precision. They swore to obey him as their lawful superior: he pledged his faith to unite the indifference of a stranger with the zeal of a patriot. At his choice, four or six knights and civilians, his assessors in arms and justice, attended the Podesta, [47] who maintained at his own expense a decent retinue of servants and horses: his wife, his son, his brother, who might bias the affections of the judge, were left behind: during the exercise of his office he was not permitted to purchase land, to contract an alliance, or even to accept an invitation in the house of a citizen; nor could he honorably depart till he had satisfied the complaints that might be urged against his government.

[Footnote 46: Muratori (dissert. xlv. tom. iv. p. 64—92) has fully explained this mode of government; and the Occulus Pastoralis, which he has given at the end, is a treatise or sermon on the duties of these foreign magistrates.]

[Footnote 47: In the Latin writers, at least of the silver age, the title of Potestas was transferred from the office to the magistrate:—
Hujus qui trahitur prætextam sumere mavis;
An Fidenarum Gabiorumque esse Potestas.
Juvenal. Satir. x. 99.11]

PART III

It was thus, about the middle of the thirteenth century, that the Romans called from Bologna the senator Brancaleone, [48] whose fame and merit have been rescued from oblivion by the pen of an English historian. A just anxiety for his reputation, a clear foresight of the difficulties of the task, had engaged him to refuse the honor of their choice: the statutes of Rome were suspended, and his office prolonged to the term of three years. By the guilty and licentious he was accused as cruel; by the clergy he was suspected as partial; but the friends of peace and order applauded the firm and upright magistrate by whom those blessings were restored. No criminals were so powerful as to brave, so obscure as to elude, the justice of the senator. By his sentence two nobles of the Annibaldi family were executed on a gibbet; and he inexorably demolished, in the city and neighborhood, one hundred and forty towers, the strong shelters of rapine and mischief. The bishop, as a simple bishop, was compelled to reside in his diocese; and the standard of Brancaleone was displayed in the field with terror and effect. His services were repaid by the ingratitude of a people unworthy of the happiness which they enjoyed. By the public robbers, whom he had provoked for their sake, the Romans were excited to depose and imprison their benefactor; nor would his life have been spared, if Bologna had not possessed a pledge for his safety. Before his departure, the prudent senator had required the exchange of thirty hostages of the noblest families of Rome: on the news of his danger, and at the prayer of his wife, they were more strictly guarded; and Bologna, in the cause of honor, sustained the thunders of a papal interdict. This generous resistance allowed the Romans to compare the present with the past; and Brancaleone was conducted from the prison to the Capitol amidst the acclamations of a repentant people. The remainder of his government was firm and fortunate; and as soon as envy was appeased by death, his head, enclosed in a precious vase, was deposited on a lofty column of marble. [49]

[Footnote 48: See the life and death of Brancaleone, in the Historia Major of Matthew Paris, p. 741, 757, 792, 797, 799, 810, 823, 833, 836, 840. The multitude of pilgrims and suitors connected Rome and St. Albans, and the resentment of the English clergy prompted them to rejoice when ever the popes were humbled and oppressed.]

[Footnote 49: Matthew Paris thus ends his account: Caput vero ipsius Brancaleonis in vase pretioso super marmoream columnam collocatum, in signum sui valoris et probitatis, quasi reliquias, superstitiose nimis et pompose sustulerunt. Fuerat enim superborum potentum et malefactorum urbis malleus et extirpator, et populi protector et defensor veritatis et justitiæ imitator et amator, (p. 840.) A biographer of Innocent IV. (Muratori, Script. tom. iii. P. i. p. 591, 592) draws a less favorable portrait of this Ghibeline senator.]

The impotence of reason and virtue recommended in Italy a more effectual choice: instead of a private citizen, to whom they yielded a voluntary and precarious obedience, the Romans elected for their senator some prince of independent power, who could defend them from their enemies and themselves. Charles of Anjou and Provence, the most ambitious and warlike monarch of the age, accepted at the same time the kingdom of Naples from the pope, and the office of senator from the Roman people. [50] As he passed through the city, in his road to victory, he received their oath of allegiance, lodged in the Lateran palace, and smoothed in a short visit the harsh features of his despotic character. Yet even Charles was exposed to the inconstancy of the people, who saluted with the same acclamations the passage of his rival, the unfortunate Conradin; and a powerful avenger, who reigned in the Capitol, alarmed the fears and jealousy of the popes. The absolute term of his life was superseded by a renewal every third year; and the enmity of Nicholas the Third obliged the Sicilian king to abdicate the government of Rome. In his bull, a perpetual law, the imperious pontiff asserts the truth, validity, and use of the donation of Constantine, not less essential to the peace of the city than to the independence of the church; establishes the annual election of the senator; and formally disqualifies all emperors, kings, princes, and persons of an eminent and conspicuous rank. [51] This prohibitory clause was repealed in his own behalf by Martin the Fourth, who humbly solicited the suffrage of the Romans. In the presence, and by the authority, of the people, two electors conferred, not on the pope, but on the noble and faithful Martin, the dignity of senator, and the supreme administration of the republic, [52] to hold during his natural life, and to exercise at pleasure by himself or his deputies. About fifty years afterwards, the same title was granted to the emperor Lewis of Bavaria; and the liberty of Rome was acknowledged by her two sovereigns, who accepted a municipal office in the government of their own metropolis.

[Footnote 50: The election of Charles of Anjou to the office of perpetual senator of Rome is mentioned by the historians in the viiith volume of the Collection of Muratori, by Nicholas de Jamsilla, (p. 592,) the monk of Padua, (p. 724,) Sabas Malaspina, (l. ii. c. 9, p. 308,) and Ricordano Malespini, (c. 177, p. 999.)]

[Footnote 51: The high-sounding bull of Nicholas III., which founds his temporal sovereignty on the donation of Constantine, is still extant; and as it has been inserted by Boniface VIII. in the Sexte of the Decretals, it must be received by the Catholics, or at least by the Papists, as a sacred and perpetual law.]

[Footnote 52: I am indebted to Fleury (Hist. Ecclés. tom. xviii. p. 306) for an extract of this Roman act, which he has taken from the Ecclesiastical Annals of Odericus Raynaldus, A.D. 1281, No. 14, 15.]

In the first moments of rebellion, when Arnold of Brescia had inflamed their minds against the church, the Romans artfully labored to conciliate the favor of the empire, and to recommend their merit and services in the cause of Cæsar. The style of their ambassadors to Conrad the Third and Frederic the First is a mixture of flattery and pride, the tradition and the ignorance of their own history. [53] After some complaint of his silence and neglect, they exhort the former of these princes to pass the Alps, and assume from their hands the Imperial crown. "We beseech your majesty not to disdain the humility of your sons and vassals, not to listen to the accusations of our common enemies; who calumniate the senate as hostile to your throne, who sow the seeds of discord, that they may reap the harvest of destruction. The pope and the Sicilian are united in an impious league to oppose our liberty and your coronation. With the blessing of God, our zeal and courage has hitherto defeated their attempts. Of their powerful and factious adherents, more especially the Frangipani, we have taken by assault the houses and turrets: some of these are occupied by our troops, and some are levelled with the ground. The Milvian bridge, which they had broken, is restored and fortified for your safe passage; and your army may enter the city without being annoyed from the castle of St. Angelo. All that we have done, and all that we design, is for your honor and service, in the loyal hope, that you will speedily appear in person, to vindicate those rights which have been invaded by the clergy, to revive the dignity of the empire, and to surpass the fame and glory of your predecessors. May you fix your residence in Rome, the capital of the world; give laws to Italy, and the Teutonic kingdom; and imitate the example of Constantine and Justinian, [54] who, by the vigor of the senate and people, obtained the sceptre of the earth." [55] But these splendid and fallacious wishes were not cherished by Conrad the Franconian, whose eyes were fixed on the Holy Land, and who died without visiting Rome soon after his return from the Holy Land.

[Footnote 53: These letters and speeches are preserved by Otho bishop of Frisingen, (Fabric. Bibliot. Lat. Med. et Infim. tom. v. p. 186, 187,) perhaps the noblest of historians: he was son of Leopold marquis of Austria; his mother, Agnes, was daughter of the emperor Henry IV., and he was half-brother and uncle to Conrad III. and Frederic I. He has left, in seven books, a Chronicle of the Times; in two, the Gesta Frederici I., the last of which is inserted in the vith volume of Muratori's historians.]

[Footnote 54: We desire (said the ignorant Romans) to restore the empire in um statum, quo fuit tempore Constantini et Justiniani, qui totum orbem vigore senatûs et populi Romani suis tenuere manibus.]

[Footnote 55: Otho Frising. de Gestis Frederici I. l. i. c. 28, p. 662—664.]

His nephew and successor, Frederic Barbarossa, was more ambitious of the Imperial crown; nor had any of the successors of Otho acquired such absolute sway over the kingdom of Italy. Surrounded by his ecclesiastical and secular princes, he gave audience in his camp at Sutri to the ambassadors of Rome, who thus addressed him in a free and florid oration: "Incline your ear to the queen of cities; approach with a peaceful and friendly mind the precincts of Rome, which has cast away the yoke of the clergy, and is impatient to crown her legitimate emperor. Under your auspicious influence, may the primitive times be restored. Assert the prerogatives of the eternal city, and reduce under her monarchy the insolence of the world. You are not ignorant, that, in former ages, by the wisdom of the senate, by the valor and discipline of the equestrian order, she extended her victorious arms to the East and West, beyond the Alps, and over the islands of the ocean. By our sins, in the absence of our princes, the noble institution of the senate has sunk in oblivion; and with our prudence, our strength has likewise decreased. We have revived the senate, and the equestrian order: the counsels of the one, the arms of the other, will be devoted to your person and the service of the empire. Do you not hear the language of the Roman matron? You were a guest, I have adopted you as a citizen; a Transalpine stranger, I have elected you for my sovereign; [56] and given you myself, and all that is mine. Your first and most sacred duty is to swear and subscribe, that you will shed your blood for the republic; that you will maintain in peace and justice the laws of the city and the charters of your predecessors; and that you will reward with five thousand pounds of silver the faithful senators who shall proclaim your titles in the Capitol. With the name, assume the character, of Augustus." The flowers of Latin rhetoric were not yet exhausted; but Frederic, impatient of their vanity, interrupted the orators in the high tone of royalty and conquest. "Famous indeed have been the fortitude and wisdom of the ancient Romans; but your speech is not seasoned with wisdom, and I could wish that fortitude were conspicuous in your actions. Like all sublunary things, Rome has felt the vicissitudes of time and fortune. Your noblest families were translated to the East, to the royal city of Constantine; and the remains of your strength and freedom have long since been exhausted by the Greeks and Franks. Are you desirous of beholding the ancient glory of Rome, the gravity of the senate, the spirit of the knights, the discipline of the camp, the valor of the legions? you will find them in the German republic. It is not empire, naked and alone, the ornaments and virtues of empire have likewise migrated beyond the Alps to a more deserving people: [57] they will be employed in your defence, but they claim your obedience. You pretend that myself or my predecessors have been invited by the Romans: you mistake the word; they were not invited, they were implored. From its foreign and domestic tyrants, the city was rescued by Charlemagne and Otho, whose ashes repose in our country; and their dominion was the price of your deliverance. Under that dominion your ancestors lived and died. I claim by the right of inheritance and possession, and who shall dare to extort you from my hands? Is the hand of the Franks [58] and Germans enfeebled by age? Am I vanquished? Am I a captive? Am I not encompassed with the banners of a potent and invincible army? You impose conditions on your master; you require oaths: if the conditions are just, an oath is superfluous; if unjust, it is criminal. Can you doubt my equity? It is extended to the meanest of my subjects. Will not my sword be unsheathed in the defence of the Capitol? By that sword the northern kingdom of Denmark has been restored to the Roman empire. You prescribe the measure and the objects of my bounty, which flows in a copious but a voluntary stream. All will be given to patient merit; all will be denied to rude importunity." [59] Neither the emperor nor the senate could maintain these lofty pretensions of dominion and liberty. United with the pope, and suspicious of the Romans, Frederic continued his march to the Vatican; his coronation was disturbed by a sally from the Capitol; and if the numbers and valor of the Germans prevailed in the bloody conflict, he could not safely encamp in the presence of a city of which he styled himself the sovereign. About twelve years afterwards, he besieged Rome, to seat an antipope in the chair of St. Peter; and twelve Pisan galleys were introduced into the Tyber: but the senate and people were saved by the arts of negotiation and the progress of disease; nor did Frederic or his successors reiterate the hostile attempt. Their laborious reigns were exercised by the popes, the crusades, and the independence of Lombardy and Germany: they courted the alliance of the Romans; and Frederic the Second offered in the Capitol the great standard, the Caroccio of Milan. [60] After the extinction of the house of Swabia, they were banished beyond the Alps: and their last coronations betrayed the impotence and poverty of the Teutonic Cæsars. [61]

[Footnote 56: Hospes eras, civem feci. Advena fuisti ex Transalpinis partibus principem constitui.]

[Footnote 57: Non cessit nobis nudum imperium, virtute sua amictum venit, ornamenta sua secum traxit. Penes nos sunt consules tui, &c. Cicero or Livy would not have rejected these images, the eloquence of a Barbarian born and educated in the Hercynian forest.]

[Footnote 58: Otho of Frisingen, who surely understood the language of the court and diet of Germany, speaks of the Franks in the xiith century as the reigning nation, (Proceres Franci, equites Franci, manus Francorum:) he adds, however, the epithet of Teutonici.]

[Footnote 59: Otho Frising. de Gestis Frederici I., l. ii. c. 22, p. 720—733. These original and authentic acts I have translated and abridged with freedom, yet with fidelity.]

[Footnote 60: From the Chronicles of Ricobaldo and Francis Pipin, Muratori (dissert. xxvi. tom. ii. p. 492) has translated this curious fact with the doggerel verses that accompanied the gift:— Ave decus orbis, ave! victus tibi destinor, ave! Currus ab Augusto Frederico Cæsare justo. Væ Mediolanum! jam sentis spernere vanum Imperii vires, proprias tibi tollere vires. Ergo triumphorum urbs potes memor esse priorum Quos tibi mittebant reges qui bella gerebant. Ne si dee tacere (I now use the Italian Dissertations, tom. i. p. 444) che nell' anno 1727, una copia desso Caroccio in marmo dianzi ignoto si scopri, nel campidoglio, presso alle carcere di quel luogo, dove Sisto V. l'avea falto rinchiudere. Stava esso posto sopra quatro colonne di marmo fino colla sequente inscrizione, &c.; to the same purpose as the old inscription.]

[Footnote 61: The decline of the Imperial arms and authority in Italy is related with impartial learning in the Annals of Muratori, (tom. x. xi. xii.;) and the reader may compare his narrative with the Histoires des Allemands (tom. iii. iv.) by Schmidt, who has deserved the esteem of his countrymen.]

Under the reign of Adrian, when the empire extended from the Euphrates to the ocean, from Mount Atlas to the Grampian hills, a fanciful historian [62] amused the Romans with the picture of their ancient wars. "There was a time," says Florus, "when Tibur and Præneste, our summer retreats, were the objects of hostile vows in the Capitol, when we dreaded the shades of the Arician groves, when we could triumph without a blush over the nameless villages of the Sabines and Latins, and even Corioli could afford a title not unworthy of a victorious general." The pride of his contemporaries was gratified by the contrast of the past and the present: they would have been humbled by the prospect of futurity; by the prediction, that after a thousand years, Rome, despoiled of empire, and contracted to her primæval limits, would renew the same hostilities, on the same ground which was then decorated with her villas and gardens. The adjacent territory on either side of the Tyber was always claimed, and sometimes possessed, as the patrimony of St. Peter; but the barons assumed a lawless independence, and the cities too faithfully copied the revolt and discord of the metropolis. In the twelfth and thirteenth centuries the Romans incessantly labored to reduce or destroy the contumacious vassals of the church and senate; and if their headstrong and selfish ambition was moderated by the pope, he often encouraged their zeal by the alliance of his spiritual arms. Their warfare was that of the first consuls and dictators, who were taken from the plough. The assembled in arms at the foot of the Capitol; sallied from the gates, plundered or burnt the harvests of their neighbors, engaged in tumultuary conflict, and returned home after an expedition of fifteen or twenty days. Their sieges were tedious and unskilful: in the use of victory, they indulged the meaner passions of jealousy and revenge; and instead of adopting the valor, they trampled on the misfortunes, of their adversaries. The captives, in their shirts, with a rope round their necks, solicited their pardon: the fortifications, and even the buildings, of the rival cities, were demolished, and the inhabitants were scattered in the adjacent villages. It was thus that the seats of the cardinal bishops, Porto, Ostia, Albanum, Tusculum, Præneste, and Tibur or Tivoli, were successively overthrown by the ferocious hostility of the Romans. [63] Of these, [64] Porto and Ostia, the two keys of the Tyber, are still vacant and desolate: the marshy and unwholesome banks are peopled with herds of buffaloes, and the river is lost to every purpose of navigation and trade. The hills, which afford a shady retirement from the autumnal heats, have again smiled with the blessings of peace; Frescati has arisen near the ruins of Tusculum; Tibur or Tivoli has resumed the honors of a city, [65] and the meaner towns of Albano and Palestrina are decorated with the villas of the cardinals and princes of Rome. In the work of destruction, the ambition of the Romans was often checked and repulsed by the neighboring cities and their allies: in the first siege of Tibur, they were driven from their camp; and the battles of Tusculum [66] and Viterbo [67] might be compared in their relative state to the memorable fields of Thrasymene and Cannæ. In the first of these petty wars, thirty thousand Romans were overthrown by a thousand German horse, whom Frederic Barbarossa had detached to the relief of Tusculum: and if we number the slain at three, the prisoners at two, thousand, we shall embrace the most authentic and moderate account. Sixty-eight years afterwards they marched against Viterbo in the ecclesiastical state with the whole force of the city; by a rare coalition the Teutonic eagle was blended, in the adverse banners, with the keys of St. Peter; and the pope's auxiliaries were commanded by a count of Thoulouse and a bishop of Winchester. The Romans were discomfited with shame and slaughter: but the English prelate must have indulged the vanity of a pilgrim, if he multiplied their numbers to one hundred, and their loss in the field to thirty, thousand men. Had the policy of the senate and the discipline of the legions been restored with the Capitol, the divided condition of Italy would have offered the fairest opportunity of a second conquest. But in arms, the modern Romans were not above, and in arts, they were far below, the common level of the neighboring republics. Nor was their warlike spirit of any long continuance; after some irregular sallies, they subsided in the national apathy, in the neglect of military institutions, and in the disgraceful and dangerous use of foreign mercenaries.

[Footnote 62: Tibur nunc suburbanum, et æstivæ Præneste deliciæ, nuncupatis in Capitolio votis petebantur. The whole passage of Florus (l. i. c. 11) may be read with pleasure, and has deserved the praise of a man of genius, (uvres de Montesquieu, tom. iii. p. 634, 635, quarto edition.)]

[Footnote 63: Ne a feritate Romanorum, sicut fuerant Hostienses, Portuenses, Tusculanenses, Albanenses, Labicenses, et nuper Tiburtini destruerentur, (Matthew Paris, p. 757.) These events are marked in the Annals and Index (the xviiith volume) of Muratori.]

[Footnote 64: For the state or ruin of these suburban cities, the banks of the Tyber, &c., see the lively picture of the P. Labat, (Voyage en Espagne et en Italiæ,) who had long resided in the neighborhood of Rome, and the more accurate description of which P. Eschinard (Roma, 1750, in octavo) has added to the topographical map of Cingolani.]

[Footnote 65: Labat (tom. iii. p. 233) mentions a recent decree of the Roman government, which has severely mortified the pride and poverty of Tivoli: in civitate Tiburtinâ non vivitur civiliter.]

[Footnote 66: I depart from my usual method, of quoting only by the date the Annals of Muratori, in consideration of the critical balance in which he has weighed nine contemporary writers who mention the battle of Tusculum, (tom. x. p. 42—44.)]

[Footnote 67: Matthew Paris, p. 345. This bishop of Winchester was Peter de Rupibus, who occupied the see thirty-two years, (A.D. 1206—1238.) and is described, by the English historian, as a soldier and a statesman. (p. 178, 399.)]

Ambition is a weed of quick and early vegetation in the vineyard of Christ. Under the first Christian princes, the chair of St. Peter was disputed by the votes, the venality, the violence, of a popular election: the sanctuaries of Rome were polluted with blood; and, from the third to the twelfth century, the church was distracted by the mischief of frequent schisms. As long as the final appeal was determined by the civil magistrate, these mischiefs were transient and local: the merits were tried by equity or favor; nor could the unsuccessful competitor long disturb the triumph of his rival. But after the emperors had been divested of their prerogatives, after a maxim had been established that the vicar of Christ is amenable to no earthly tribunal, each vacancy of the holy see might involve Christendom in controversy and war. The claims of the cardinals and inferior clergy, of the nobles and people, were vague and litigious: the freedom of choice was overruled by the tumults of a city that no longer owned or obeyed a superior. On the decease of a pope, two factions proceeded in different churches to a double election: the number and weight of votes, the priority of time, the merit of the candidates, might balance each other: the most respectable of the clergy were divided; and the distant princes, who bowed before the spiritual throne, could not distinguish the spurious, from the legitimate, idol. The emperors were often the authors of the schism, from the political motive of opposing a friendly to a hostile pontiff; and each of the competitors was reduced to suffer the insults of his enemies, who were not awed by conscience, and to purchase the support of his adherents, who were instigated by avarice or ambition a peaceful and perpetual succession was ascertained by Alexander the Third, [68] who finally abolished the tumultuary votes of the clergy and people, and defined the right of election in the sole college of cardinals. [69] The three orders of bishops, priests, and deacons, were assimilated to each other by this important privilege; the parochial clergy of Rome obtained the first rank in the hierarchy: they were indifferently chosen among the nations of Christendom; and the possession of the richest benefices, of the most important bishoprics, was not incompatible with their title and office. The senators of the Catholic church, the coadjutors and legates of the supreme pontiff, were robed in purple, the symbol of martyrdom or royalty; they claimed a proud equality with kings; and their dignity was enhanced by the smallness of their number, which, till the reign of Leo the Tenth, seldom exceeded twenty or twenty-five persons. By this wise regulation, all doubt and scandal were removed, and the root of schism was so effectually destroyed, that in a period of six hundred years a double choice has only once divided the unity of the sacred college. But as the concurrence of two thirds of the votes had been made necessary, the election was often delayed by the private interest and passions of the cardinals; and while they prolonged their independent reign, the Christian world was left destitute of a head. A vacancy of almost three years had preceded the elevation of George the Tenth, who resolved to prevent the future abuse; and his bull, after some opposition, has been consecrated in the code of the canon law. [70] Nine days are allowed for the obsequies of the deceased pope, and the arrival of the absent cardinals; on the tenth, they are imprisoned, each with one domestic, in a common apartment or conclave, without any separation of walls or curtains: a small window is reserved for the introduction of necessaries; but the door is locked on both sides and guarded by the magistrates of the city, to seclude them from all correspondence with the world. If the election be not consummated in three days, the luxury of their table is contracted to a single dish at dinner and supper; and after the eighth day, they are reduced to a scanty allowance of bread, water, and wine. During the vacancy of the holy see, the cardinals are prohibited from touching the revenues, or assuming, unless in some rare emergency, the government of the church: all agreements and promises among the electors are formally annulled; and their integrity is fortified by their solemn oath and the prayers of the Catholics. Some articles of inconvenient or superfluous rigor have been gradually relaxed, but the principle of confinement is vigorous and entire: they are still urged, by the personal motives of health and freedom, to accelerate the moment of their deliverance; and the improvement of ballot or secret votes has wrapped the struggles of the conclave [71] in the silky veil of charity and politeness. [72] By these institutions the Romans were excluded from the election of their prince and bishop; and in the fever of wild and precarious liberty, they seemed insensible of the loss of this inestimable privilege. The emperor Lewis of Bavaria revived the example of the great Otho. After some negotiation with the magistrates, the Roman people were assembled [73] in the square before St. Peter's: the pope of Avignon, John the Twenty-second, was deposed: the choice of his successor was ratified by their consent and applause. They freely voted for a new law, that their bishop should never be absent more than three months in the year, and two days' journey from the city; and that if he neglected to return on the third summons, the public servant should be degraded and dismissed. [74] But Lewis forgot his own debility and the prejudices of the times: beyond the precincts of a German camp, his useless phantom was rejected; the Romans despised their own workmanship; the antipope implored the mercy of his lawful sovereign; [75] and the exclusive right of the cardinals was more firmly established by this unseasonable attack.

[Footnote 68: See Mosheim, Institut. Histor. Ecclesiast. p. 401, 403. Alexander himself had nearly been the victim of a contested election; and the doubtful merits of Innocent had only preponderated by the weight of genius and learning which St. Bernard cast into the scale, (see his life and writings.)]

[Footnote 69: The origin, titles, importance, dress, precedency, &c., of the Roman cardinals, are very ably discussed by Thomassin, (Discipline de l'Eglise, tom. i. p. 1262—1287;) but their purple is now much faded. The sacred college was raised to the definite number of seventy-two, to represent, under his vicar, the disciples of Christ.]

[Footnote 70: See the bull of Gregory X. approbante sacro concilio, in the Sexts of the Canon Law, (l. i. tit. 6, c. 3,) a supplement to the Decretals, which Boniface VIII. promulgated at Rome in 1298, and addressed in all the universities of Europe.]

[Footnote 71: The genius of Cardinal de Retz had a right to paint a conclave, (of 1665,) in which he was a spectator and an actor, (Mémoires, tom. iv. p. 15—57;) but I am at a loss to appreciate the knowledge or authority of an anonymous Italian, whose history (Conclavi de' Pontifici Romani, in 4to. 1667) has been continued since the reign of Alexander VII. The accidental form of the work furnishes a lesson, though not an antidote, to ambition. From a labyrinth of intrigues, we emerge to the adoration of the successful candidate; but the next page opens with his funeral.]

[Footnote 72: The expressions of Cardinal de Retz are positive and picturesque: On y vecut toujours ensemble avec le même respect, et la même civilité que l'on observe dans le cabinet des rois, avec la même politesse qu'on avoit dans la cour de Henri III., avec la même familiarité que l'on voit dans les colleges; avec la même modestie, qui se remarque dans les noviciats; et avec la même charité, du moins en apparence, qui pourroit être entre des frères parfaitement unis.]

[Footnote 73: Richiesti per bando (says John Villani) sanatori di Roma, e 52 del popolo, et capitani de' 25, e consoli, (consoli?) et 13 buone huomini, uno per rione. Our knowledge is too imperfect to pronounce how much of this constitution was temporary, and how much ordinary and permanent. Yet it is faintly illustrated by the ancient statutes of Rome.]

*[Footnote 74: Villani (l. x. c. 68—71, in Muratori, Script. tom. xiii. p. 641—645) relates this law, and the whole transaction, with much less abhorrence than the prudent Muratori. Any one conversant with the darker ages must have observed how much the sense (I mean the nonsense) of superstition is fluctuating and inconsistent.]*

*[Footnote 75: In the first volume of the Popes of Avignon, see the second original Life of John XXII. p. 142—145, the confession of the antipope p. 145—152, and the laborious notes of Baluze, p. 714, 715.]*

Had the election been always held in the Vatican, the rights of the senate and people would not have been violated with impunity. But the Romans forgot, and were forgotten. in the absence of the successors of Gregory the Seventh, who did not keep as a divine precept their ordinary residence in the city and diocese. The care of that diocese was less important than the government of the universal church; nor could the popes delight in a city in which their authority was always opposed, and their person was often endangered. From the persecution of the emperors, and the wars of Italy, they escaped beyond the Alps into the hospitable bosom of France; from the tumults of Rome they prudently withdrew to live and die in the more tranquil stations of Anagni, Perugia, Viterbo, and the adjacent cities. When the flock was offended or impoverished by the absence of the shepherd, they were recalled by a stern admonition, that St. Peter had fixed his chair, not in an obscure village, but in the capital of the world; by a ferocious menace, that the Romans would march in arms to destroy the place and people that should dare to afford them a retreat. They returned with timorous obedience; and were saluted with the account of a heavy debt, of all the losses which their desertion had occasioned, the hire of lodgings, the sale of provisions, and the various expenses of servants and strangers who attended the court. [76] After a short interval of peace, and perhaps of authority, they were again banished by new tumults, and again summoned by the imperious or respectful invitation of the senate. In these occasional retreats, the exiles and fugitives of the Vatican were seldom long, or far, distant from the metropolis; but in the beginning of the fourteenth century, the apostolic throne was transported, as it might seem forever, from the Tyber to the Rhône; and the cause of the transmigration may be deduced from the furious contest between Boniface the Eighth and the king of France. [77] The spiritual arms of excommunication and interdict were repulsed by the union of the three estates, and the privileges of the Gallican church; but the pope was not prepared against the carnal weapons which Philip the Fair had courage to employ. As the pope resided at Anagni, without the suspicion of danger, his palace and person were assaulted by three hundred horse, who had been secretly levied by William of Nogaret, a French minister, and Sciarra Colonna, of a noble but hostile family of Rome. The cardinals fled; the inhabitants of Anagni were seduced from their allegiance and gratitude; but the dauntless Boniface, unarmed and alone, seated himself in his chair, and awaited, like the conscript fathers of old, the swords of the Gauls. Nogaret, a foreign adversary, was content to execute the orders of his master: by the domestic enmity of Colonna, he was insulted with words and blows; and during a confinement of three days his life was threatened by the hardships which they inflicted on the obstinacy which they provoked. Their strange delay gave time and courage to the adherents of the church, who rescued him from sacrilegious violence; but his imperious soul was wounded in the vital part; and Boniface expired at Rome in a frenzy of rage and revenge. His memory is stained with the glaring vices of avarice and pride; nor has the courage of a martyr promoted this ecclesiastical champion to the honors of a saint; a magnanimous sinner, (say the chronicles of the times,) who entered like a fox, reigned like a lion, and died like a dog. He was succeeded by Benedict the Eleventh, the mildest of mankind. Yet he excommunicated the impious emissaries of Philip, and devoted the city and people of Anagni by a tremendous curse, whose effects are still visible to the eyes of superstition. [78]

[Footnote 76: Romani autem non valentes nec volentes ultra suam celare cupiditatem gravissimam, contra papam movere cperunt questionem, exigentes ab eo urgentissime omnia quæ subierant per ejus absentiam damna et jacturas, videlicet in hispitiis locandis, in mercimoniis, in usuris, in redditibus, in provisionibus, et in aliis modis innumerabilibus. Quòd cum audisset papa, præcordialiter ingemuit, et se comperiens muscipulatum, &c., Matt. Paris, p. 757. For the ordinary history of the popes, their life and death, their residence and absence, it is enough to refer to the ecclesiastical annalists, Spondanus and Fleury.]

[Footnote 77: Besides the general historians of the church of Italy and of France, we possess a valuable treatise composed by a learned friend of Thuanus, which his last and best editors have published in the appendix (Histoire particulière du grand Différend entre Boniface VIII et Philippe le Bel, par Pierre du Puis, tom. vii. P. xi. p. 61—82.)]

[Footnote 78: It is difficult to know whether Labat (tom. iv. p. 53—57) be in jest or in earnest, when he supposes that Anagni still feels the weight of this curse, and that the cornfields, or vineyards, or olive-trees, are annually blasted by Nature, the obsequious handmaid of the popes.]

PART IV

After his decease, the tedious and equal suspense of the conclave was fixed by the dexterity of the French faction. A specious offer was made and accepted, that, in the term of forty days, they would elect one of the three candidates who should be named by their opponents. The archbishop of Bourdeaux, a furious enemy of his king and country, was the first on the list; but his ambition was known; and his conscience obeyed the calls of fortune and the commands of a benefactor, who had been informed by a swift messenger that the choice of a pope was now in his hands. The terms were regulated in a private interview; and with such speed and secrecy was the business transacted, that the unanimous conclave applauded the elevation of Clement the Fifth. [79] The cardinals of both parties were soon astonished by a summons to attend him beyond the Alps; from whence, as they soon discovered, they must never hope to return. He was engaged, by promise and affection, to prefer the residence of France; and, after dragging his court through Poitou and Gascony, and devouring, by his expense, the cities and convents on the road, he finally reposed at Avignon, [80] which flourished above seventy years [81] the seat of the Roman pontiff and the metropolis of Christendom. By land, by sea, by the Rhône, the position of Avignon was on all sides accessible; the southern provinces of France do not yield to Italy itself; new palaces arose for the accommodation of the pope and cardinals; and the arts of luxury were soon attracted by the treasures of the church. They were already possessed of the adjacent territory, the Venaissin county, [82] a populous and fertile spot; and the sovereignty of Avignon was afterwards purchased from the youth and distress of Jane, the first queen of Naples and countess of Provence, for the inadequate price of fourscore thousand florins. [83] Under the shadow of a French monarchy, amidst an obedient people, the popes enjoyed an honorable and tranquil state, to which they long had been strangers: but Italy deplored their absence; and Rome, in solitude and poverty, might repent of the ungovernable freedom which had driven from the Vatican the successor of St. Peter. Her repentance was tardy and fruitless: after the death of the old members, the sacred college was filled with French cardinals, [84] who beheld Rome and Italy with abhorrence and contempt, and perpetuated a series of national, and even provincial, popes, attached by the most indissoluble ties to their native country.

[Footnote 79: See, in the Chronicle of Giovanni Villani, (l. viii. c. 63, 64, 80, in Muratori, tom. xiii.,) the imprisonment of Boniface VIII., and the election of Clement V., the last of which, like most anecdotes, is embarrassed with some difficulties.]

[Footnote 80: The original lives of the eight popes of Avignon, Clement V., John XXII., Benedict XI., Clement VI., Innocent VI., Urban V., Gregory XI., and Clement VII., are published by Stephen Baluze, (Vitæ Paparum Avenionensium; Paris, 1693, 2 vols. in 4to.,) with copious and elaborate notes, and a second volume of acts and documents. With the true zeal of an editor and a patriot, he devoutly justifies or excuses the characters of his countrymen.]

[Footnote 81: The exile of Avignon is compared by the Italians with Babylon, and the Babylonish captivity. Such furious metaphors, more suitable to the ardor of Petrarch than to the judgment of Muratori, are gravely refuted in Baluze's preface. The abbé de Sade is distracted between the love of Petrarch and of his country. Yet he modestly pleads, that many of the local inconveniences of Avignon are now removed; and many of the vices against which the poet declaims, had been imported with the Roman court by the strangers of Italy, (tom. i. p. 23—28.)]

[Footnote 82: The comtat Venaissin was ceded to the popes in 1273 by Philip III. king of France, after he had inherited the dominions of the count of Thoulouse. Forty years before, the heresy of Count Raymond had given them a pretence of seizure, and they derived some obscure claim from the xith century to some lands citra Rhodanum, (Valesii Notitia Galliarum, p. 495, 610. Longuerue, Description de la France, tom. i. p. 376—381.)]

[Footnote 83: If a possession of four centuries were not itself a title, such objections might annul the bargain; but the purchase money must be refunded, for indeed it was paid. Civitatem Avenionem emit.... per ejusmodi venditionem pecuniâ redundates, &c., (iida Vita Clement. VI. in Baluz. tom. i. p. 272. Muratori, Script. tom. iii. P. ii. p. 565.) The only temptation for Jane and her second husband was ready money, and without it they could not have returned to the throne of Naples.]

[Footnote 84: Clement V immediately promoted ten cardinals, nine French and one English, (Vita ivta, p. 63, et Baluz. p. 625, &c.) In 1331, the pope refused two candidates recommended by the king of France, quod xx. Cardinales, de quibus xvii. de regno Franciæ originem traxisse noscuntur in memorato collegio existant, (Thomassin, Discipline de l'Eglise, tom. i. p. 1281.)]

The progress of industry had produced and enriched the Italian republics: the æra of their liberty is the most flourishing period of population and agriculture, of manufactures and commerce; and their mechanic labors were gradually refined into the arts of elegance and genius. But the position of Rome was less favorable, the territory less fruitful: the character of the inhabitants was debased by indolence and elated by pride; and they fondly conceived that the tribute of subjects must forever nourish the metropolis of the church and empire. This prejudice was encouraged in some degree by the resort of pilgrims to the shrines of the apostles; and the last legacy of the popes, the institution of the holy year, [85] was not less beneficial to the people than to the clergy. Since the loss of Palestine, the gift of plenary indulgences, which had been applied to the crusades, remained without an object; and the most valuable treasure of the church was sequestered above eight years from public circulation. A new channel was opened by the diligence of Boniface the Eighth, who reconciled the vices of ambition and avarice; and the pope had sufficient learning to recollect and revive the secular games which were celebrated in Rome at the conclusion of every century. To sound without danger the depth of popular credulity, a sermon was seasonably pronounced, a report was artfully scattered, some aged witnesses were produced; and on the first of January of the year thirteen hundred, the church of St. Peter was crowded with the faithful, who demanded the customary indulgence of the holy time. The pontiff, who watched and irritated their devout impatience, was soon persuaded by ancient testimony of the justice of their claim; and he proclaimed a plenary absolution to all Catholics who, in the course of that year, and at every similar period, should respectfully visit the apostolic churches of St. Peter and St. Paul. The welcome sound was propagated through Christendom; and at first from the nearest provinces of Italy, and at length from the remote kingdoms of Hungary and Britain, the highways were thronged with a swarm of pilgrims who sought to expiate their sins in a journey, however costly or laborious, which was exempt from the perils of military service. All exceptions of rank or sex, of age or infirmity, were forgotten in the common transport; and in the streets and churches many persons were trampled to death by the eagerness of devotion. The calculation of their numbers could not be easy nor accurate; and they have probably been magnified by a dexterous clergy, well apprised of the contagion of example: yet we are assured by a judicious historian, who assisted at the ceremony, that Rome was never replenished with less than two hundred thousand strangers; and another spectator has fixed at two millions the total concourse of the year. A trifling oblation from each individual would accumulate a royal treasure; and two priests stood night and day, with rakes in their hands, to collect, without counting, the heaps of gold and silver that were poured on the altar of St. Paul. [86] It was fortunately a season of peace and plenty; and if forage was scarce, if inns and lodgings were extravagantly dear, an inexhaustible supply of bread and wine, of meat and fish, was provided by the policy of Boniface and the venal hospitality of the Romans. From a city without trade or industry, all casual riches will speedily evaporate: but the avarice and envy of the next generation solicited Clement the Sixth [87] to anticipate the distant period of the century. The gracious pontiff complied with their wishes; afforded Rome this poor consolation for his loss; and justified the change by the name and practice of the Mosaic Jubilee. [88] His summons was obeyed; and the number, zeal, and liberality of the pilgrims did not yield to the primitive festival. But they encountered the triple scourge of war, pestilence, and famine: many wives and virgins were violated in the castles of Italy; and many strangers were pillaged or murdered by the savage Romans, no longer moderated by the presence of their bishops. [89] To the impatience of the popes we may ascribe the successive reduction to fifty, thirty-three, and twenty-five years; although the second of these terms is commensurate with the life of Christ. The profusion of indulgences, the revolt of the Protestants, and the decline of superstition, have much diminished the value of the jubilee; yet even the nineteenth and last festival was a year of pleasure and profit to the Romans; and a philosophic smile will not disturb the triumph of the priest or the happiness of the people. [90]

[Footnote 85: *Our primitive account is from Cardinal James Caietan, (Maxima Bibliot. Patrum, tom. xxv.;) and I am at a loss to determine whether the nephew of Boniface VIII. be a fool or a knave: the uncle is a much clearer character.*]

[Footnote 86: *See John Villani (l. viii. c. 36) in the xiith, and the Chronicon Astense, in the xith volume (p. 191, 192) of Muratori's Collection Papa innumerabilem pecuniam ab eisdem accepit, nam duo clerici, cum rastris, &c.*]

[Footnote 87: *The two bulls of Boniface VIII. and Clement VI. are inserted on the Corpus Juris Canonici, Extravagant. (Commun. l. v. tit. ix c 1, 2.)*]

[Footnote 88: *The sabbatic years and jubilees of the Mosaic law, (Car. Sigon. de Republica Hebræorum, Opp. tom. iv. l. iii. c. 14, 14, p. 151, 152,) the suspension of all care and labor, the periodical release of lands, debts, servitude, &c., may seem a noble idea, but the execution would be impracticable in a profane republic; and I should be glad to learn that this ruinous festival was observed by the Jewish people.]*

*[Footnote 89: See the Chronicle of Matteo Villani, (l. i. c. 56,) in the xivth vol. of Muratori, and the Mémoires sur la Vie de Pétrarque, tom. iii. p. 75—89.]*

*[Footnote 90: The subject is exhausted by M. Chais, a French minister at the Hague, in his Lettres Historiques et Dogmatiques, sur les Jubilés et es Indulgences; la Haye, 1751, 3 vols. in 12mo.; an elaborate and pleasing work, had not the author preferred the character of a polemic to that of a philosopher.]*

In the beginning of the eleventh century, Italy was exposed to the feudal tyranny, alike oppressive to the sovereign and the people. The rights of human nature were vindicated by her numerous republics, who soon extended their liberty and dominion from the city to the adjacent country. The sword of the nobles was broken; their slaves were enfranchised; their castles were demolished; they assumed the habits of society and obedience; their ambition was confined to municipal honors, and in the proudest aristocracy of Venice on Genoa, each patrician was subject to the laws. [91] But the feeble and disorderly government of Rome was unequal to the task of curbing her rebellious sons, who scorned the authority of the magistrate within and without the walls. It was no longer a civil contention between the nobles and plebeians for the government of the state: the barons asserted in arms their personal independence; their palaces and castles were fortified against a siege; and their private quarrels were maintained by the numbers of their vassals and retainers. In origin and affection, they were aliens to their country: [92] and a genuine Roman, could such have been produced, might have renounced these haughty strangers, who disdained the appellation of citizens, and proudly styled themselves the princes, of Rome. [93] After a dark series of revolutions, all records of pedigree were lost; the distinction of surnames was abolished; the blood of the nations was mingled in a thousand channels; and the Goths and Lombards, the Greeks and Franks, the Germans and Normans, had obtained the fairest possessions by royal bounty, or the prerogative of valor. These examples might be readily presumed; but the elevation of a Hebrew race to the rank of senators and consuls is an event without a parallel in the long captivity of these miserable exiles. [94] In the time of Leo the Ninth, a wealthy and learned Jew was converted to Christianity, and honored at his baptism with the name of his godfather, the reigning Pope. The zeal and courage of Peter the son of Leo were signalized in the cause of Gregory the Seventh, who intrusted his faithful adherent with the government of Adrian's mole, the tower of Crescentius, or, as it is now called, the castle of St. Angelo. Both the father and the son were the parents of a numerous progeny: their riches, the fruits of usury, were shared with the noblest families of the city; and so extensive was their alliance, that the grandson of the proselyte was exalted by the weight of his kindred to the throne of St. Peter. A majority of the clergy and people supported his cause: he reigned several years in the Vatican; and it is only the eloquence of St. Bernard, and the final triumph of Innocence the Second, that has branded Anacletus with the epithet of antipope. After his defeat and death, the posterity of Leo is no longer conspicuous; and none will be found of the modern nobles ambitious of descending from a Jewish stock. It is not my design to enumerate the Roman families which have failed at different periods, or those which are continued in different degrees of splendor to the present time. [95] The old consular line of the Frangipani discover their name in the generous act of breaking or dividing bread in a time of famine; and such benevolence is more truly glorious than to have enclosed, with their allies the Corsi, a spacious quarter of the city in the chains of their fortifications; the Savelli, as it should seem a Sabine race, have maintained their original dignity; the obsolete surname of the Capizucchi is inscribed on the coins of the first senators; the Conti preserve the honor, without the estate, of the counts of Signia; and the Annibaldi must have been very ignorant, or very modest, if they had not descended from the Carthaginian hero. [96]

[Footnote 91: Muratori (Dissert. xlvii.) alleges the Annals of Florence, Padua, Genoa, &c., the analogy of the rest, the evidence of Otho of Frisingen, (de Gest. Fred. l. l. ii. c. 13,) and the submission of the marquis of Este.]

[Footnote 92: As early as the year 824, the emperor Lothaire I. found it expedient to interrogate the Roman people, to learn from each individual by what national law he chose to be governed. (Muratori, Dissertat xxii.)]

[Footnote 93: Petrarch attacks these foreigners, the tyrants of Rome, in a declamation or epistle, full of bold truths and absurd pedantry, in which he applies the maxims, and even prejudices, of the old republic to the state of the xivth century, (Mémoires, tom. iii. p. 157—169.)]

[Footnote 94: The origin and adventures of the Jewish family are noticed by Pagi, (Critica, tom. iv. p. 435, A.D. 1124, No. 3, 4,) who draws his information from the Chronographus Maurigniacensis, and Arnulphus Sagiensis de Schismate, (in Muratori, Script. Ital. tom. iii. P. i. p. 423—432.) The fact must in some degree be true; yet I could wish that it had been coolly related, before it was turned into a reproach against the antipope.]

[Footnote 95: Muratori has given two dissertations (xli. and xlii.) to the names, surnames, and families of Italy. Some nobles, who glory in their domestic fables, may be offended with his firm and temperate criticism; yet surely some ounces of pure gold are of more value than many pounds of base metal.]

[Footnote 96: The cardinal of St. George, in his poetical, or rather metrical history of the election and coronation of Boniface VIII., (Muratori Script. Ital. tom. iii. P. i. p. 641, &c.,) describes the state and families of Rome at the coronation of Boniface VIII., (A.D. 1295.) Interea titulis redimiti sanguine et armis Illustresque viri Romanâ a stirpe trahentes Nomen in emeritos tantæ virtutis honores Insulerant sese medios festumque colebant Aurata fulgente togâ, sociante catervâ. Ex ipsis devota domus præstantis ab Ursâ Ecclesiæ, vultumque gerens demissius altum Festa Columna jocis, necnon Sabellia mitis; Stephanides senior, Comites, Annibalica proles, Præfectusque urbis magnum sine viribus nomen. (l. ii. c. 5, 100, p. 647, 648.) The ancient statutes of Rome (l. iii. c. 59, p. 174, 175) distinguish eleven families of barons, who are obliged to swear in concilio communi, before the senator, that they would not harbor or protect any malefactors, outlaws, &c—a feeble security!]

But among, perhaps above, the peers and princes of the city, I distinguish the rival houses of Colonna and Ursini, whose private story is an essential part of the annals of modern Rome. I. The name and arms of Colonna [97] have been the theme of much doubtful etymology; nor have the orators and antiquarians overlooked either Trajan's pillar, or the columns of Hercules, or the pillar of Christ's flagellation, or the luminous column that guided the Israelites in the desert. Their first historical appearance in the year eleven hundred and four attests the power and antiquity, while it explains the simple meaning, of the name. By the usurpation of Cavæ, the Colonna provoked the arms of Paschal the Second; but they lawfully held in the Campagna of Rome the hereditary fiefs of Zagarola and Colonna; and the latter of these towns was probably adorned with some lofty pillar, the relic of a villa or temple. [98] They likewise possessed one moiety of the neighboring city of Tusculum, a strong presumption of their descent from the counts of Tusculum, who in the tenth century were the tyrants of the apostolic see. According to their own and the public opinion, the primitive and remote source was derived from the banks of the Rhine; [99] and the sovereigns of Germany were not ashamed of a real or fabulous affinity with a noble race, which in the revolutions of seven hundred years has been often illustrated by merit and always by fortune. [100] About the end of the thirteenth century, the most powerful branch was composed of an uncle and six bothers, all conspicuous in arms, or in the honors of the church. Of these, Peter was elected senator of Rome, introduced to the Capitol in a triumphal car, and hailed in some vain acclamations with the title of Cæsar; while John and Stephen were declared marquis of Ancona and count of Romagna, by Nicholas the Fourth, a patron so partial to their family, that he has been delineated in satirical portraits, imprisoned as it were in a hollow pillar. [101] After his decease their haughty behavior provoked the displeasure of the most implacable of mankind. The two cardinals, the uncle and the nephew, denied the election of Boniface the Eighth; and the Colonna were oppressed for a moment by his temporal and spiritual arms. [102] He proclaimed a crusade against his personal enemies; their estates were confiscated; their fortresses on either side of the Tyber were besieged by the troops of St. Peter and those of the rival nobles; and after the ruin of Palestrina or Præneste, their principal seat, the ground was marked with a ploughshare, the emblem of perpetual desolation. Degraded, banished, proscribed, the six brothers, in disguise and danger, wandered over Europe without renouncing the hope of deliverance and revenge. In this double hope, the French court was their surest asylum; they prompted and directed the enterprise of Philip; and I should praise their magnanimity, had they respected the misfortune and courage of the captive tyrant. His civil acts were annulled by the Roman people, who restored the honors and possessions of the Colonna; and some estimate may be formed of their wealth by their losses, of their losses by the damages of one hundred thousand gold florins which were granted them against the accomplices and heirs of the deceased pope. All the spiritual censures and disqualifications were abolished [103] by his prudent successors; and the fortune of the house was more firmly established by this transient hurricane. The boldness of Sciarra Colonna was signalized in the captivity of Boniface, and long afterwards in the coronation of Lewis of Bavaria; and by the gratitude of the emperor, the pillar in their arms was encircled with a royal crown. But the first of the family in fame and merit was the elder Stephen, whom Petrarch loved and esteemed as a hero superior to his own times, and not unworthy of ancient Rome. Persecution and exile displayed to the nations his abilities in peace and war; in his distress he was an object, not of pity, but of reverence; the aspect of danger provoked him to avow his name and country; and when he was asked, "Where is now your fortress?" he laid his hand on his heart, and answered, "Here." He supported with the same virtue the return of prosperity; and, till the ruin of his declining age, the ancestors, the character, and the children of Stephen Colonna, exalted his dignity in the Roman republic, and at the court of Avignon.

II. The Ursini migrated from Spoleto; [104] the sons of Ursus, as they are styled in the twelfth century, from some eminent person, who is only known as the father of their race. But they were soon distinguished among the nobles of Rome, by the number and bravery of their kinsmen, the strength of their towers, the honors of the senate and sacred college, and the elevation of two popes, Celestin the Third and Nicholas the Third, of their name and lineage. [105] Their riches may be accused as an early abuse of nepotism: the estates of St. Peter were alienated in their favor by the liberal Celestin; [106] and Nicholas was ambitious for their sake to solicit the alliance of monarchs; to found new kingdoms in Lombardy and Tuscany; and to invest them with the perpetual office of senators of Rome. All that has been observed of the greatness of the Colonna will likewise redeemed to the glory of the Ursini, their constant and equal antagonists in the long hereditary feud, which distracted above two hundred and fifty years the ecclesiastical state. The jealously of preeminence and power was the true ground of their quarrel; but as a specious badge of distinction, the Colonna embraced the name of Ghibelines and the party of the empire; the Ursini espoused the title of Guelphs and the cause of the church. The eagle and the keys were displayed in their adverse banners; and the two factions of Italy most furiously raged when the origin and nature of the dispute were long since forgotten. [107] After the retreat of the popes to Avignon they disputed in arms the vacant republic; and the mischiefs of discord were perpetuated by the wretched compromise of electing each year two rival senators. By their private hostilities the city and country were desolated, and the fluctuating balance inclined with their alternate success. But none of either family had fallen by the sword, till the most renowned champion of the Ursini was surprised and slain by the younger Stephen Colonna. [108] His triumph is stained with the reproach of violating the truce; their defeat was basely avenged by the assassination, before the church door, of an innocent boy and his two servants. Yet the victorious Colonna, with an annual colleague, was declared senator of Rome during the term of five years. And the muse of Petrarch inspired a wish, a hope, a prediction, that the generous youth, the son of his venerable hero, would restore Rome and Italy to their pristine glory; that his justice would extirpate the wolves and lions, the serpents and bears, who labored to subvert the eternal basis of the marble column. [109]

[Footnote 97: It is pity that the Colonna themselves have not favored the world with a complete and critical history of their illustrious house. I adhere to Muratori, (Dissert. xlii. tom. iii. p. 647, 648.)]

[Footnote 98: Pandulph. Pisan. in Vit. Paschal. II. in Muratori, Script. Ital. tom. iii. P. i. p. 335. The family has still great possessions in the Campagna of Rome; but they have alienated to the Rospigliosi this original fief of Colonna, (Eschinard, p. 258, 259.)]

[Footnote 99: Te longinqua dedit tellus et pascua Rheni, says Petrarch; and, in 1417, a duke of Guelders and Juliers acknowledges (Lenfant, Hist. du Concile de Constance, tom. ii. p. 539) his descent from the ancestors of Martin V., (Otho Colonna:) but the royal author of the Memoirs of Brandenburg observes, that the sceptre in his arms has been confounded with the column. To maintain the Roman origin of the Colonna, it was ingeniously supposed (Diario di Monaldeschi, in the Script. Ital. tom. xii. p. 533) that a cousin of the emperor Nero escaped from the city, and founded Mentz in Germany.]

[Footnote 100: I cannot overlook the Roman triumph of ovation on Marce Antonio Colonna, who had commanded the pope's galleys at the naval victory of Lepanto, (Thuan. Hist. l. 7, tom. iii. p. 55, 56. Muret. Oratio x. Opp. tom. i. p. 180—190.)]

[Footnote 101: Muratori, Annali d'Italia, tom. x. p. 216, 220.]

[Footnote 102: Petrarch's attachment to the Colonna has authorized the abbé de Sade to expatiate on the state of the family in the fourteenth century, the persecution of Boniface VIII., the character of Stephen and his sons, their quarrels with the Ursini, &c., (Mémoires sur Pétrarque, tom. i. p. 98—110, 146—148, 174—176, 222—230, 275—280.) His criticism often rectifies the hearsay stories of Villani, and the errors of the less diligent moderns. I understand the branch of Stephen to be now extinct.]

[Footnote 103: Alexander III. had declared the Colonna who adhered to the emperor Frederic I. incapable of holding any ecclesiastical benefice, (Villani, l. v. c. 1;) and the last stains of annual excommunication were purified by Sixtus V., (Vita di Sisto V. tom. iii. p. 416.) Treason, sacrilege, and proscription are often the best titles of ancient nobility.]

[Footnote 104: —Vallis te proxima misit, Appenninigenæ qua prata virentia sylvæ Spoletana metunt armenta gregesque protervi. Monaldeschi (tom. xii. Script. Ital. p. 533) gives the Ursini a French origin, which may be remotely true.]

[Footnote 105: In the metrical life of Celestine V. by the cardinal of St. George (Muratori, tom. iii. P. i. p. 613, &c.,) we find a luminous, and not inelegant, passage, (l. i. c. 3, p. 203 &c.:)—genuit quem nobilis

Ursæ (Ursi?) Progenies, Romana domus, veterataque magnis Fascibus in clero, pompasque experta senatûs, Bellorumque manû grandi stipata parentum Cardineos apices necnon fastigia dudum Papatûs iterata tenens. Muratori (Dissert. xlii. tom. iii.) observes, that the first Ursini pontificate of Celestine III. was unknown: he is inclined to read Ursi progenies.]

[Footnote 106: Filii Ursi, quondam Clestini papæ nepotes, de bonis ecclesiæ Romanæ ditati, (Vit. Innocent. III. in Muratori, Script. tom. iii. P. i.) The partial prodigality of Nicholas III. is more conspicuous in Villani and Muratori. Yet the Ursini would disdain the nephews of a modern pope.]

[Footnote 107: In his fifty-first Dissertation on the Italian Antiquities, Muratori explains the factions of the Guelphs and Ghibelines.]

[Footnote 108: Petrarch (tom. i. p. 222—230) has celebrated this victory according to the Colonna; but two contemporaries, a Florentine (Giovanni Villani, l. x. c. 220) and a Roman, (Ludovico Monaldeschi, p. 532—534,) are less favorable to their arms.]

[Footnote 109: The abbé de Sade (tom. i. Notes, p. 61—66) has applied the vith Canzone of Petrarch, Spirto Gentil, &c., to Stephen Colonna the younger: Orsi, lupi, leoni, aquile e serpi Al una gran marmorea colexna Fanno noja sovente e à se danno. 11]


CHAPTER LXX

FINAL SETTLEMENT OIF THE ECCLESIASTICAL STATE

PART I

CHARACTER AND CORONATION OF PETRARCH—RESTORATION OF THE FREEDOM AND GOVERNMENT OF ROME BY THE TRIBUNE RIENZI—HIS VIRTUES AND VICES, HIS EXPULSION AND DEATH—RETURN OF THE POPES FROM AVIGNON—GREAT SCHISM OF THE WEST—REUNION OF THE LATIN CHURCH—LAST STRUGGLES OF ROMAN LIBERTY—STATUES OF ROME—FINAL SETTLEMENT OF THE ECCLESIASTICAL STATE

In the apprehension of modern times, Petrarch [1] is the Italian songster of Laura and love. In the harmony of his Tuscan rhymes, Italy applauds, or rather adores, the father of her lyric poetry; and his verse, or at least his name, is repeated by the enthusiasm, or affectation, of amorous sensibility. Whatever may be the private taste of a stranger, his slight and superficial knowledge should humbly acquiesce in the judgment of a learned nation; yet I may hope or presume, that the Italians do not compare the tedious uniformity of sonnets and elegies with the sublime compositions of their epic muse, the original wildness of Dante, the regular beauties of Tasso, and the boundless variety of the incomparable Ariosto. The merits of the lover I am still less qualified to appreciate: nor am I deeply interested in a metaphysical passion for a nymph so shadowy, that her existence has been questioned; [2] for a matron so prolific, [3] that she was delivered of eleven legitimate children, [4] while her amorous swain sighed and sung at the fountain of Vaucluse. [5] But in the eyes of Petrarch, and those of his graver contemporaries, his love was a sin, and Italian verse a frivolous amusement. His Latin works of philosophy, poetry, and eloquence, established his serious reputation, which was soon diffused from Avignon over France and Italy: his friends and disciples were multiplied in every city; and if the ponderous volume of his writings [6] be now abandoned to a long repose, our gratitude must applaud the man, who by precept and example revived the spirit and study of the Augustan age. From his earliest youth, Petrarch aspired to the poetic crown. The academical honors of the three faculties had introduced a royal degree of master or doctor in the art of poetry; [7] and the title of poet-laureate, which custom, rather than vanity, perpetuates in the English court, [8] was first invented by the Cæsars of Germany. In the musical games of antiquity, a prize was bestowed on the victor: [9] the belief that Virgil and Horace had been crowned in the Capitol inflamed the emulation of a Latin bard; [10] and the laurel [11] was endeared to the lover by a verbal resemblance with the name of his mistress. The value of either object was enhanced by the difficulties of the pursuit; and if the virtue or prudence of Laura was inexorable, [12] he enjoyed, and might boast of enjoying, the nymph of poetry. His vanity was not of the most delicate kind, since he applauds the success of his own labors; his name was popular; his friends were active; the open or secret opposition of envy and prejudice was surmounted by the dexterity of patient merit. In the thirty-sixth year of his age, he was solicited to accept the object of his wishes; and on the same day, in the solitude of Vaucluse, he received a similar and solemn invitation from the senate of Rome and the university of Paris. The learning of a theological school, and the ignorance of a lawless city, were alike unqualified to bestow the ideal though immortal wreath which genius may obtain from the free applause of the public and of posterity: but the candidate dismissed this troublesome reflection; and after some moments of complacency and suspense, preferred the summons of the metropolis of the world.

[Footnote 1: The Mémoires sur la Vie de François Pétrarque, (Amsterdam, 1764, 1767, 3 vols. in 4to.,) form a copious, original, and entertaining work, a labor of love, composed from the accurate study of Petrarch and his contemporaries; but the hero is too often lost in the general history of the age, and the author too often languishes in the affectation of politeness and gallantry. In the preface to his first volume, he enumerates and weighs twenty Italian biographers, who have professedly treated of the same subject.]

[Footnote 2: The allegorical interpretation prevailed in the xvth century; but the wise commentators were not agreed whether they should understand by Laura, religion, or virtue, or the blessed virgin, or—. See the prefaces to the first and second volume.]

[Footnote 3: Laure de Noves, born about the year 1307, was married in January 1325, to Hugues de Sade, a noble citizen of Avignon, whose jealousy was not the effect of love, since he married a second wife within seven months of her death, which happened the 6th of April, 1348, precisely one-and-twenty years after Petrarch had seen and loved her.]

[Footnote 4: Corpus crebris partubus exhaustum: from one of these is issued, in the tenth degree, the abbé de Sade, the fond and grateful biographer of Petrarch; and this domestic motive most probably suggested the idea of his work, and urged him to inquire into every circumstance that could affect the history and character of his grandmother, (see particularly tom. i. p. 122—133, notes, p. 7—58, tom. ii. p. 455—495 not. p. 76—82.)]

[Footnote 5: Vaucluse, so familiar to our English travellers, is described from the writings of Petrarch, and the local knowledge of his biographer, (Mémoires, tom. i. p. 340—359.) It was, in truth, the retreat of a hermit; and the moderns are much mistaken, if they place Laura and a happy lover in the grotto.]

[Footnote 6: Of 1250 pages, in a close print, at Basil in the xvith century, but without the date of the year. The abbé de Sade calls aloud for a new edition of Petrarch's Latin works; but I much doubt whether it would redound to the profit of the bookseller, or the amusement of the public.]

[Footnote 7: Consult Selden's Titles of Honor, in his works, (vol. iii. p. 457—466.) A hundred years before Petrarch, St. Francis received the visit of a poet, qui ab imperatore fuerat coronatus et exinde rex versuum dictus.]

[Footnote 8: From Augustus to Louis, the muse has too often been false and venal: but I much doubt whether any age or court can produce a similar establishment of a stipendiary poet, who in every reign, and at all events, is bound to furnish twice a year a measure of praise and verse, such as may be sung in the chapel, and, I believe, in the presence, of the sovereign. I speak the more freely, as the best time for abolishing this ridiculous custom is while the prince is a man of virtue and the poet a man of genius.]

[Footnote 9: Isocrates (in Panegyrico, tom. i. p. 116, 117, edit. Battie, Cantab. 1729) claims for his native Athens the glory of first instituting and recommending the alwnaV—kai ta aqla megista—mh monon tacouV kai rwmhV, alla kai logwn kai gnwmhV. The example of the Panathenæa was imitated at Delphi; but the Olympic games were ignorant of a musical crown, till it was extorted by the vain tyranny of Nero, (Sueton. in Nerone, c. 23; Philostrat. apud Casaubon ad locum; Dion Cassius, or Xiphilin, l. lxiii. p. 1032, 1041. Potter's Greek Antiquities, vol. i. p. 445, 450.)]

[Footnote 10: The Capitoline games (certamen quinquenale, musicum, equestre, gymnicum) were instituted by Domitian (Sueton. c. 4) in the year of Christ 86, (Censorin. de Die Natali, c. 18, p. 100, edit. Havercamp.) and were not abolished in the ivth century, (Ausonius de Professoribus Burdegal. V.) If the crown were given to superior merit, the exclusion of Statius (Capitolia nostræ inficiata lyræ, Sylv. l. iii. v. 31) may do honor to the games of the Capitol; but the Latin poets who lived before Domitian were crowned only in the public opinion.]

[Footnote 11: Petrarch and the senators of Rome were ignorant that the laurel was not the Capitoline, but the Delphic crown, (Plin. Hist. Natur p. 39. Hist. Critique de la République des Lettres, tom. i. p. 150—220.) The victors in the Capitol were crowned with a garland of oak eaves, (Martial, l. iv. epigram 54.)]

[Footnote 12: The pious grandson of Laura has labored, and not without success, to vindicate her immaculate chastity against the censures of the grave and the sneers of the profane, (tom. ii. notes, p. 76—82.)]

The ceremony of his coronation [13] was performed in the Capitol, by his friend and patron the supreme magistrate of the republic. Twelve patrician youths were arrayed in scarlet; six representatives of the most illustrious families, in green robes, with garlands of flowers, accompanied the procession; in the midst of the princes and nobles, the senator, count of Anguillara, a kinsman of the Colonna, assumed his throne; and at the voice of a herald Petrarch arose. After discoursing on a text of Virgil, and thrice repeating his vows for the prosperity of Rome, he knelt before the throne, and received from the senator a laurel crown, with a more precious declaration, "This is the reward of merit." The people shouted, "Long life to the Capitol and the poet!" A sonnet in praise of Rome was accepted as the effusion of genius and gratitude; and after the whole procession had visited the Vatican, the profane wreath was suspended before the shrine of St. Peter. In the act or diploma [14] which was presented to Petrarch, the title and prerogatives of poet-laureate are revived in the Capitol, after the lapse of thirteen hundred years; and he receives the perpetual privilege of wearing, at his choice, a crown of laurel, ivy, or myrtle, of assuming the poetic habit, and of teaching, disputing, interpreting, and composing, in all places whatsoever, and on all subjects of literature. The grant was ratified by the authority of the senate and people; and the character of citizen was the recompense of his affection for the Roman name. They did him honor, but they did him justice. In the familiar society of Cicero and Livy, he had imbibed the ideas of an ancient patriot; and his ardent fancy kindled every idea to a sentiment, and every sentiment to a passion. The aspect of the seven hills and their majestic ruins confirmed these lively impressions; and he loved a country by whose liberal spirit he had been crowned and adopted. The poverty and debasement of Rome excited the indignation and pity of her grateful son; he dissembled the faults of his fellow-citizens; applauded with partial fondness the last of their heroes and matrons; and in the remembrance of the past, in the hopes of the future, was pleased to forget the miseries of the present time. Rome was still the lawful mistress of the world: the pope and the emperor, the bishop and general, had abdicated their station by an inglorious retreat to the Rhône and the Danube; but if she could resume her virtue, the republic might again vindicate her liberty and dominion. Amidst the indulgence of enthusiasm and eloquence, [15] Petrarch, Italy, and Europe, were astonished by a revolution which realized for a moment his most splendid visions. The rise and fall of the tribune Rienzi will occupy the following pages: [16] the subject is interesting, the materials are rich, and the glance of a patriot bard [17] will sometimes vivify the copious, but simple, narrative of the Florentine, [18] and more especially of the Roman, historian. [19]

[Footnote 13: The whole process of Petrarch's coronation is accurately described by the abbé de Sade, (tom. i. p. 425—435, tom. ii. p. 1—6, notes, p. 1—13,) from his own writings, and the Roman diary of Ludovico, Monaldeschi, without mixing in this authentic narrative the more recent fables of Sannuccio Delbene.]

[Footnote 14: The original act is printed among the Pieces Justificatives in the Mémoires sur Pétrarque, tom. iii. p. 50—53.]

[Footnote 15: To find the proofs of his enthusiasm for Rome, I need only request that the reader would open, by chance, either Petrarch, or his French biographer. The latter has described the poet's first visit to Rome, (tom. i. p. 323—335.) But in the place of much idle rhetoric and morality, Petrarch might have amused the present and future age with an original account of the city and his coronation.]

[Footnote 16: It has been treated by the pen of a Jesuit, the P. de Cerceau whose posthumous work (Conjuration de Nicolas Gabrini, dit de Rienzi, Tyran de Rome, en 1347) was published at Paris, 1748, in 12mo. I am indebted to him for some facts and documents in John Hocsemius, canon of Liege, a contemporary historian, (Fabricius Bibliot. Lat. Med. Ævi, tom. iii. p. 273, tom. iv. p. 85.)]

[Footnote 17: The abbé de Sade, who so freely expatiates on the history of the xivth century, might treat, as his proper subject, a revolution in which the heart of Petrarch was so deeply engaged, (Mémoires, tom. ii. p. 50, 51, 320—417, notes, p. 70—76, tom. iii. p. 221—243, 366—375.) Not an idea or a fact in the writings of Petrarch has probably escaped him.]

[Footnote 18: Giovanni Villani, l. xii. c. 89, 104, in Muratori, Rerum Italicarum Scriptores, tom. xiii. p. 969, 970, 981—983.]

[Footnote 19: In his third volume of Italian antiquities, (p. 249—548,) Muratori has inserted the Fragmenta Historiæ Romanæ ab Anno 1327 usque ad Annum 1354, in the original dialect of Rome or Naples in the xivth century, and a Latin version for the benefit of strangers. It contains the most particular and authentic life of Cola (Nicholas) di Rienzi; which had been printed at Bracciano, 1627, in 4to., under the name of Tomaso Fortifiocca, who is only mentioned in this work as having been punished by the tribune for forgery. Human nature is scarcely capable of such sublime or stupid impartiality: but whosoever in the author of these Fragments, he wrote on the spot and at the time, and paints, without design or art, the manners of Rome and the character of the tribune. Note: Since the publication of my first edition of Gibbon, some new and very remarkable documents have been brought to light in a life of Nicolas Rienzi,—Cola di Rienzo und seine Zeit,—by Dr. Felix Papencordt. The most important of these documents are letters from Rienzi to Charles the Fourth, emperor and king of Bohemia, and to the archbishop of Praque; they enter into the whole history of his adventurous career during its first period, and throw a strong light upon his extraordinary character. These documents were first discovered and made use of, to a certain extent, by Pelzel, the historian of Bohemia. The originals have disappeared, but a copy made by Pelzel for his own use is now in the library of Count Thun at Teschen. There seems no doubt of their authenticity. Dr. Papencordt has printed the whole in his Urkunden, with the exception of one long theological paper—M. 1845.]

In a quarter of the city which was inhabited only by mechanics and Jews, the marriage of an innkeeper and a washer woman produced the future deliverer of Rome. [20] [201] From such parents Nicholas Rienzi Gabrini could inherit neither dignity nor fortune; and the gift of a liberal education, which they painfully bestowed, was the cause of his glory and untimely end. The study of history and eloquence, the writings of Cicero, Seneca, Livy, Cæsar, and Valerius Maximus, elevated above his equals and contemporaries the genius of the young plebeian: he perused with indefatigable diligence the manuscripts and marbles of antiquity; loved to dispense his knowledge in familiar language; and was often provoked to exclaim, "Where are now these Romans? their virtue, their justice, their power? why was I not born in those happy times?" [21] When the republic addressed to the throne of Avignon an embassy of the three orders, the spirit and eloquence of Rienzi recommended him to a place among the thirteen deputies of the commons. The orator had the honor of haranguing Pope Clement the Sixth, and the satisfaction of conversing with Petrarch, a congenial mind: but his aspiring hopes were chilled by disgrace and poverty and the patriot was reduced to a single garment and the charity of the hospital. [211] From this misery he was relieved by the sense of merit or the smile of favor; and the employment of apostolic notary afforded him a daily stipend of five gold florins, a more honorable and extensive connection, and the right of contrasting, both in words and actions, his own integrity with the vices of the state. The eloquence of Rienzi was prompt and persuasive: the multitude is always prone to envy and censure: he was stimulated by the loss of a brother and the impunity of the assassins; nor was it possible to excuse or exaggerate the public calamities. The blessings of peace and justice, for which civil society has been instituted, were banished from Rome: the jealous citizens, who might have endured every personal or pecuniary injury, were most deeply wounded in the dishonor of their wives and daughters: [22] they were equally oppressed by the arrogance of the nobles and the corruption of the magistrates; [22/1] and the abuse of arms or of laws was the only circumstance that distinguished the lions from the dogs and serpents of the Capitol. These allegorical emblems were variously repeated in the pictures which Rienzi exhibited in the streets and churches; and while the spectators gazed with curious wonder, the bold and ready orator unfolded the meaning, applied the satire, inflamed their passions, and announced a distant hope of comfort and deliverance. The privileges of Rome, her eternal sovereignty over her princes and provinces, was the theme of his public and private discourse; and a monument of servitude became in his hands a title and incentive of liberty. The decree of the senate, which granted the most ample prerogatives to the emperor Vespasian, had been inscribed on a copper plate still extant in the choir of the church of St. John Lateran. [23] A numerous assembly of nobles and plebeians was invited to this political lecture, and a convenient theatre was erected for their reception. The notary appeared in a magnificent and mysterious habit, explained the inscription by a version and commentary, [24] and descanted with eloquence and zeal on the ancient glories of the senate and people, from whom all legal authority was derived. The supine ignorance of the nobles was incapable of discerning the serious tendency of such representations: they might sometimes chastise with words and blows the plebeian reformer; but he was often suffered in the Colonna palace to amuse the company with his threats and predictions; and the modern Brutus [25] was concealed under the mask of folly and the character of a buffoon. While they indulged their contempt, the restoration of the good estate, his favorite expression, was entertained among the people as a desirable, a possible, and at length as an approaching, event; and while all had the disposition to applaud, some had the courage to assist, their promised deliverer.

[Footnote 20: The first and splendid period of Rienzi, his tribunitian government, is contained in the xviiith chapter of the Fragments, (p. 399—479,) which, in the new division, forms the iid book of the history in xxxviii. smaller chapters or sections.]

[Footnote 201: But see in Dr. Papencordt's work, and in Rienzi's own words, his claim to be a bastard son of the emperor Henry the Seventh, whose intrigue with his mother Rienzi relates with a sort of proud shamelessness. Compare account by the editor of Dr. Papencordt's work in Quarterly Review vol. lxix—M. 1845.]

[Footnote 21: The reader may be pleased with a specimen of the original idiom: Fò da soa juventutine nutricato di latte de eloquentia, bono gramatico, megliore rettuorico, autorista bravo. Deh como et quanto era veloce leitore! moito usava Tito Livio, Seneca, et Tullio, et Balerio Massimo, moito li dilettava le magnificentie di Julio Cesare raccontare. Tutta la die se speculava negl' intagli di marmo lequali iaccio intorno Roma. Non era altri che esso, che sapesse lejere li antichi pataffii. Tutte scritture antiche vulgarizzava; quesse fiure di marmo justamente interpretava. On come spesso diceva, "Dove suono quelli buoni Romani? dove ene loro somma justitia? poleramme trovare in tempo che quessi fiuriano!"]

[Footnote 21/1: Sir J. Hobhouse published (in his Illustrations of Childe Harold) Rienzi's joyful letter to the people of Rome on the apparently favorable termination of this mission—M. 1845.]

[Footnote 22: Petrarch compares the jealousy of the Romans with the easy temper of the husbands of Avignon, (Mémoires, tom. i. p. 330.)]

[Footnote 221: All this Rienzi, writing at a later period to the archbishop of Prague, attributed to the criminal abandonment of his flock by the supreme pontiff. See Urkunde apud Papencordt, p. xliv. Quarterly Review, p. 255—M. 1845.]

[Footnote 23: The fragments of the Lex regia may be found in the Inscriptions of Gruter, tom. i. p. 242, and at the end of the Tacitus of Ernesti, with some learned notes of the editor, tom. ii.]

[Footnote 24: I cannot overlook a stupendous and laughable blunder of Rienzi. The Lex regia empowers Vespasian to enlarge the Pomrium, a word familiar to every antiquary. It was not so to the tribune; he confounds it with pomarium, an orchard, translates lo Jardino de Roma cioene Italia, and is copied by the less excusable ignorance of the Latin translator (p. 406) and the French historian, (p. 33.) Even the learning of Muratori has slumbered over the passage.]

[Footnote 25: Priori (Bruto) tamen similior, juvenis uterque, longe ingenio quam cujus simulationem induerat, ut sub hoc obtentû liberator ille P R. aperiretur tempore suo.... Ille regibus, hic tyrannis *contemptus, (Opp. p. 536.) Note: Fatcor attamen quod-nunc fatuum. nunc hystrionem, nunc gravem nunc simplicem, nunc astutum, nunc fervidum, nunc timidum simulatorem, et dissimulatorem ad hunc caritativum finem, quem dixi, constitusepius memet ipsum. Writing to an archbishop, (of Prague,) Rienzi alleges scriptural examples. Saltator coram archa David et insanus apparuit coram Rege; blanda, astuta, et tecta Judith astitit Holoferni; et astute Jacob meruit benedici, Urkunde xlix—M. 1845.]*

A prophecy, or rather a summons, affixed on the church door of St. George, was the first public evidence of his designs; a nocturnal assembly of a hundred citizens on Mount Aventine, the first step to their execution. After an oath of secrecy and aid, he represented to the conspirators the importance and facility of their enterprise; that the nobles, without union or resources, were strong only in the fear nobles, of their imaginary strength; that all power, as well as right, was in the hands of the people; that the revenues of the apostolical chamber might relieve the public distress; and that the pope himself would approve their victory over the common enemies of government and freedom. After securing a faithful band to protect his first declaration, he proclaimed through the city, by sound of trumpet, that on the evening of the following day, all persons should assemble without arms before the church of St. Angelo, to provide for the reestablishment of the good estate. The whole night was employed in the celebration of thirty masses of the Holy Ghost; and in the morning, Rienzi, bareheaded, but in complete armor, issued from the church, encompassed by the hundred conspirators. The pope's vicar, the simple bishop of Orvieto, who had been persuaded to sustain a part in this singular ceremony, marched on his right hand; and three great standards were borne aloft as the emblems of their design. In the first, the banner of liberty, Rome was seated on two lions, with a palm in one hand and a globe in the other; St. Paul, with a drawn sword, was delineated in the banner of justice; and in the third, St. Peter held the keys of concord and peace. Rienzi was encouraged by the presence and applause of an innumerable crowd, who understood little, and hoped much; and the procession slowly rolled forwards from the castle of St. Angelo to the Capitol. His triumph was disturbed by some secret emotions which he labored to suppress: he ascended without opposition, and with seeming confidence, the citadel of the republic; harangued the people from the balcony; and received the most flattering confirmation of his acts and laws. The nobles, as if destitute of arms and counsels, beheld in silent consternation this strange revolution; and the moment had been prudently chosen, when the most formidable, Stephen Colonna, was absent from the city. On the first rumor, he returned to his palace, affected to despise this plebeian tumult, and declared to the messenger of Rienzi, that at his leisure he would cast the madman from the windows of the Capitol. The great bell instantly rang an alarm, and so rapid was the tide, so urgent was the danger, that Colonna escaped with precipitation to the suburb of St. Laurence: from thence, after a moment's refreshment, he continued the same speedy career till he reached in safety his castle of Palestrina; lamenting his own imprudence, which had not trampled the spark of this mighty conflagration. A general and peremptory order was issued from the Capitol to all the nobles, that they should peaceably retire to their estates: they obeyed; and their departure secured the tranquillity of the free and obedient citizens of Rome.

But such voluntary obedience evaporates with the first transports of zeal; and Rienzi felt the importance of justifying his usurpation by a regular form and a legal title. At his own choice, the Roman people would have displayed their attachment and authority, by lavishing on his head the names of senator or consul, of king or emperor: he preferred the ancient and modest appellation of tribune; [251] the protection of the commons was the essence of that sacred office; and they were ignorant, that it had never been invested with any share in the legislative or executive powers of the republic. In this character, and with the consent of the Roman, the tribune enacted the most salutary laws for the restoration and maintenance of the good estate. By the first he fulfils the wish of honesty and inexperience, that no civil suit should be protracted beyond the term of fifteen days. The danger of frequent perjury might justify the pronouncing against a false accuser the same penalty which his evidence would have inflicted: the disorders of the times might compel the legislator to punish every homicide with death, and every injury with equal retaliation. But the execution of justice was hopeless till he had previously abolished the tyranny of the nobles. It was formally provided, that none, except the supreme magistrate, should possess or command the gates, bridges, or towers of the state; that no private garrisons should be introduced into the towns or castles of the Roman territory; that none should bear arms, or presume to fortify their houses in the city or country; that the barons should be responsible for the safety of the highways, and the free passage of provisions; and that the protection of malefactors and robbers should be expiated by a fine of a thousand marks of silver. But these regulations would have been impotent and nugatory, had not the licentious nobles been awed by the sword of the civil power. A sudden alarm from the bell of the Capitol could still summon to the standard above twenty thousand volunteers: the support of the tribune and the laws required a more regular and permanent force. In each harbor of the coast a vessel was stationed for the assurance of commerce; a standing militia of three hundred and sixty horse and thirteen hundred foot was levied, clothed, and paid in the thirteen quarters of the city: and the spirit of a commonwealth may be traced in the grateful allowance of one hundred florins, or pounds, to the heirs of every soldier who lost his life in the service of his country. For the maintenance of the public defence, for the establishment of granaries, for the relief of widows, orphans, and indigent convents, Rienzi applied, without fear of sacrilege, the revenues of the apostolic chamber: the three branches of hearth-money, the salt-duty, and the customs, were each of the annual produce of one hundred thousand florins; [26] and scandalous were the abuses, if in four or five months the amount of the salt-duty could be trebled by his judicious economy. After thus restoring the forces and finances of the republic, the tribune recalled the nobles from their solitary independence; required their personal appearance in the Capitol; and imposed an oath of allegiance to the new government, and of submission to the laws of the good estate. Apprehensive for their safety, but still more apprehensive of the danger of a refusal, the princes and barons returned to their houses at Rome in the garb of simple and peaceful citizens: the Colonna and Ursini, the Savelli and Frangipani, were confounded before the tribunal of a plebeian, of the vile buffoon whom they had so often derided, and their disgrace was aggravated by the indignation which they vainly struggled to disguise. The same oath was successively pronounced by the several orders of society, the clergy and gentlemen, the judges and notaries, the merchants and artisans, and the gradual descent was marked by the increase of sincerity and zeal. They swore to live and die with the republic and the church, whose interest was artfully united by the nominal association of the bishop of Orvieto, the pope's vicar, to the office of tribune. It was the boast of Rienzi, that he had delivered the throne and patrimony of St. Peter from a rebellious aristocracy; and Clement the Sixth, who rejoiced in its fall, affected to believe the professions, to applaud the merits, and to confirm the title, of his trusty servant. The speech, perhaps the mind, of the tribune, was inspired with a lively regard for the purity of the faith: he insinuated his claim to a supernatural mission from the Holy Ghost; enforced by a heavy forfeiture the annual duty of confession and communion; and strictly guarded the spiritual as well as temporal welfare of his faithful people. [27]

[Footnote 25/1: *Et ego, Deo semper auctore, ipsa die pristinâ (leg. primâ) Tribunatus, quæ quidem dignitas a tempore deflorati Imperii, et per annos Vo et ultra sub tyrannicà occupatione vacavit, ipsos omnes potentes indifferenter Deum at justitiam odientes, a meâ, ymo a Dei facie fugiendo vehementi Spiritu dissipavi, et nullo effuso cruore trementes expuli, sine ictu remanente Romane terre facie renovatâ.* Libellus Tribuni ad Cæsarem, p. xxxiv—M. 1845.]

[Footnote 26: In one MS. I read (l. ii. c. 4, p. 409) *perfumante quatro solli,* in another, *quatro florini,* an important variety, since the florin was worth ten Roman solidi, (Muratori, dissert. xxviii.) The former reading would give us a population of 25,000, the latter of 250,000 families; and I much fear, that the former is more consistent with the decay of Rome and her territory.]

[Footnote 27: Hocsemius, p. 498, apud du Cerçeau, Hist. de Rienzi, p. 194. The fifteen tribunitian laws may be found in the Roman historian (whom for brevity I shall name) Fortifiocca, l. ii. c. 4.]

## PART II

Never perhaps has the energy and effect of a single mind been more remarkably felt than in the sudden, though transient, reformation of Rome by the tribune Rienzi. A den of robbers was converted to the discipline of a camp or convent: patient to hear, swift to redress, inexorable to punish, his tribunal was always accessible to the poor and stranger; nor could birth, or dignity, or the immunities of the church, protect the offender or his accomplices. The privileged houses, the private sanctuaries in Rome, on which no officer of justice would presume to trespass, were abolished; and he applied the timber and iron of their barricades in the fortifications of the Capitol. The venerable father of the Colonna was exposed in his own palace to the double shame of being desirous, and of being unable, to protect a criminal. A mule, with a jar of oil, had been stolen near Capranica; and the lord of the Ursini family was condemned to restore the damage, and to discharge a fine of four hundred florins for his negligence in guarding the highways. Nor were the persons of the barons more inviolate than their lands or houses; and, either from accident or design, the same impartial rigor was exercised against the heads of the adverse factions. Peter Agapet Colonna, who had himself been senator of Rome, was arrested in the street for injury or debt; and justice was appeased by the tardy execution of Martin Ursini, who, among his various acts of violence and rapine, had pillaged a shipwrecked vessel at the mouth of the Tyber. [28] His name, the purple of two cardinals, his uncles, a recent marriage, and a mortal disease were disregarded by the inflexible tribune, who had chosen his victim. The public officers dragged him from his palace and nuptial bed: his trial was short and satisfactory: the bell of the Capitol convened the people: stripped of his mantle, on his knees, with his hands bound behind his back, he heard the sentence of death; and after a brief confession, Ursini was led away to the gallows. After such an example, none who were conscious of guilt could hope for impunity, and the flight of the wicked, the licentious, and the idle, soon purified the city and territory of Rome. In this time (says the historian,) the woods began to rejoice that they were no longer infested with robbers; the oxen began to plough; the pilgrims visited the sanctuaries; the roads and inns were replenished with travellers; trade, plenty, and good faith, were restored in the markets; and a purse of gold might be exposed without danger in the midst of the highway. As soon as the life and property of the subject are secure, the labors and rewards of industry spontaneously revive: Rome was still the metropolis of the Christian world; and the fame and fortunes of the tribune were diffused in every country by the strangers who had enjoyed the blessings of his government.

[Footnote 28: Fortifiocca, l. ii. c. 11. From the account of this shipwreck, we learn some circumstances of the trade and navigation of the age. 1. The ship was built and freighted at Naples for the ports of Marseilles and Avignon. 2. The sailors were of Naples and the Isle of naria less skilful than those of Sicily and Genoa. 3. The navigation from Marseilles was a coasting voyage to the mouth of the Tyber, where they took shelter in a storm; but, instead of finding the current, unfortunately ran on a shoal: the vessel was stranded, the mariners escaped. 4. The cargo, which was pillaged, consisted of the revenue of Provence for the royal treasury, many bags of pepper and cinnamon, and bales of French cloth, to the value of 20,000 florins; a rich prize.]

The deliverance of his country inspired Rienzi with a vast, and perhaps visionary, idea of uniting Italy in a great federative republic, of which Rome should be the ancient and lawful head, and the free cities and princes the members and associates. His pen was not less eloquent than his tongue; and his numerous epistles were delivered to swift and trusty messengers. On foot, with a white wand in their hand, they traversed the forests and mountains; enjoyed, in the most hostile states, the sacred security of ambassadors; and reported, in the style of flattery or truth, that the highways along their passage were lined with kneeling multitudes, who implored Heaven for the success of their undertaking. Could passion have listened to reason; could private interest have yielded to the public welfare; the supreme tribunal and confederate union of the Italian republic might have healed their intestine discord, and closed the Alps against the Barbarians of the North. But the propitious season had elapsed; and if Venice, Florence, Sienna, Perugia, and many inferior cities offered their lives and fortunes to the good estate, the tyrants of Lombardy and Tuscany must despise, or hate, the plebeian author of a free constitution. From them, however, and from every part of Italy, the tribune received the most friendly and respectful answers: they were followed by the ambassadors of the princes and republics; and in this foreign conflux, on all the occasions of pleasure or business, the low born notary could assume the familiar or majestic courtesy of a sovereign. [29] The most glorious circumstance of his reign was an appeal to his justice from Lewis, king of Hungary, who complained, that his brother and her husband had been perfidiously strangled by Jane, queen of Naples: [30] her guilt or innocence was pleaded in a solemn trial at Rome; but after hearing the advocates, [31] the tribune adjourned this weighty and invidious cause, which was soon determined by the sword of the Hungarian. Beyond the Alps, more especially at Avignon, the revolution was the theme of curiosity, wonder, and applause. [31/1] Petrarch had been the private friend, perhaps the secret counsellor, of Rienzi: his writings breathe the most ardent spirit of patriotism and joy; and all respect for the pope, all gratitude for the Colonna, was lost in the superior duties of a Roman citizen. The poet-laureate of the Capitol maintains the act, applauds the hero, and mingles with some apprehension and advice, the most lofty hopes of the permanent and rising greatness of the republic. [32]

[Footnote 29: It was thus that Oliver Cromwell's old acquaintance, who remembered his vulgar and ungracious entrance into the House of Commons, were astonished at the ease and majesty of the protector on his throne, (See Harris's Life of Cromwell, p. 27—34, from Clarendon Warwick, Whitelocke, Waller, &c.) The consciousness of merit and power will sometimes elevate the manners to the station.]

[Footnote 30: See the causes, circumstances, and effects of the death of Andrew in Giannone, (tom. iii. l. xxiii. p. 220—229,) and the Life of Petrarch (Mémoires, tom. ii. p. 143—148, 245—250, 375—379, notes, p. 21—37.) The abbé de Sade wishes to extenuate her guilt.]

[Footnote 31: The advocate who pleaded against Jane could add nothing to the logical force and brevity of his master's epistle. Johanna! inordinata vita præcedens, retentio potestatis in regno, neglecta vindicta, vir alter susceptus, et excusatio subsequens, necis viri tui te probant fuisse participem et consortem. Jane of Naples, and Mary of Scotland, have a singular conformity.]

[Footnote 31/1]: In his letter to the archbishop of Prague, Rienzi thus describes the effect of his elevation on Italy and on the world: "Did I not restore real peace among the cities which were distracted by factions? did I not cause all the citizens, exiled by party violence, with their wretched wives and children, to be readmitted? had I not begun to extinguish the factious names (scismatica nomina) of Guelf and Ghibelline, for which countless thousands had perished body and soul, under the eyes of their pastors, by the reduction of the city of Rome and all Italy into one amicable, peaceful, holy, and united confederacy? the consecrated standards and banners having been by me collected and blended together, and, in witness to our holy association and perfect union, offered up in the presence of the ambassadors of all the cities of Italy, on the day of the assumption of our Blessed Lady." p. xlvii. —In the Libellus ad Cæsarem: "I received the homage and submission of all the sovereigns of Apulia, the barons and counts, and almost all the people of Italy. I was honored by solemn embassies and letters by the emperor of Constantinople and the king of England. The queen of Naples submitted herself and her kingdom to the protection of the tribune. The king of Hungary, by two solemn embassies, brought his cause against his queen and his nobles before my tribunal; and I venture to say further, that the fame of the tribune alarmed the soldan of Babylon. When the Christian pilgrims to the sepulchre of our Lord related to the Christian and Jewish inhabitants of Jerusalem all the yet unheard-of and wonderful circumstances of the reformation in Rome, both Jews and Christians celebrated the event with unusual festivities. When the soldan inquired the cause of these rejoicings, and received this intelligence about Rome, he ordered all the havens and cities on the coast to be fortified, and put in a state of defence," p. xxxv—M. 1845.]

[Footnote 32: See the Epistola Hortatoria de Capessenda Republica, from Petrarch to Nicholas Rienzi, (Opp. p. 535—540,) and the vth eclogue or pastoral, a perpetual and obscure allegory.]

While Petrarch indulged these prophetic visions, the Roman hero was fast declining from the meridian of fame and power; and the people, who had gazed with astonishment on the ascending meteor, began to mark the irregularity of its course, and the vicissitudes of light and obscurity. More eloquent than judicious, more enterprising than resolute, the faculties of Rienzi were not balanced by cool and commanding reason: he magnified in a tenfold proportion the objects of hope and fear; and prudence, which could not have erected, did not presume to fortify, his throne. In the blaze of prosperity, his virtues were insensibly tinctured with the adjacent vices; justice with cruelty, cruelty, liberality with profusion, and the desire of fame with puerile and ostentatious vanity. [32/1] He might have learned, that the ancient tribunes, so strong and sacred in the public opinion, were not distinguished in style, habit, or appearance, from an ordinary plebeian; [33] and that as often as they visited the city on foot, a single viator, or beadle, attended the exercise of their office. The Gracchi would have frowned or smiled, could they have read the sonorous titles and epithets of their successor, "Nicholas, severe and merciful; deliverer of Rome; defender of Italy; [34] friend of mankind, and of liberty, peace, and justice; tribune august:" his theatrical pageants had prepared the revolution; but Rienzi abused, in luxury and pride, the political maxim of speaking to the eyes, as well as the understanding, of the multitude. From nature he had received the gift of a handsome person, [35] till it was swelled and disfigured by intemperance: and his propensity to laughter was corrected in the magistrate by the affectation of gravity and sternness. He was clothed, at least on public occasions, in a party-colored robe of velvet or satin, lined with fur, and embroidered with gold: the rod of justice, which he carried in his hand, was a sceptre of polished steel, crowned with a globe and cross of gold, and enclosing a small fragment of the true and holy wood. In his civil and religious processions through the city, he rode on a white steed, the symbol of royalty: the great banner of the republic, a sun with a circle of stars, a dove with an olive branch, was displayed over his head; a shower of gold and silver was scattered among the populace, fifty guards with halberds encompassed his person; a troop of horse preceded his march; and their tymbals and trumpets were of massy silver.

[Footnote 32/1: An illustrious female writer has drawn, with a single stroke, the character of Rienzi, Crescentius, and Arnold of Brescia, the fond restorers of Roman liberty: 'Qui ont pris les souvenirs pour les espérances.' Corinne, tom. i. p. 159. "Could Tacitus have excelled this?" Hallam, vol i p. 418—M.]

[Footnote 33: In his Roman Questions, Plutarch (Opuscul. tom. i. p. 505, 506, edit. Græc. Hen. Steph.) states, on the most constitutional principles, the simple greatness of the tribunes, who were not properly magistrates, but a check on magistracy. It was their duty and interest omoiousqai schmati, kai stolh kai diaithtoiV epitugcanousi tvn politvn.... katapateisqai dei (a saying of C. Curio) kai mh semnon einai th oyei mhde dusprosodon... osw de mallon ektapeinoutai tv swmati, tosoutw mallon auxetai th dunamei, &c. Rienzi, and Petrarch himself, were incapable perhaps of reading a Greek philosopher; but they might have imbibed the same modest doctrines from their favorite Latins, Livy and Valerius Maximus.]

[Footnote 34: I could not express in English the forcible, though barbarous, title of Zelator Italiæ, which Rienzi assumed.]

[Footnote 35: Era bell' homo, (l. ii. c. l. p. 399.) It is remarkable, that the riso sarcastico of the Bracciano edition is wanting in the Roman MS., from which Muratori has given the text. In his second reign, when he is painted almost as a monster, Rienzi travea una ventresca tonna trionfale, a modo de uno Abbate Asiano, or Asinino, (l. iii. c. 18, p. 523.)]

The ambition of the honors of chivalry [36] betrayed the meanness of his birth, and degraded the importance of his office; and the equestrian tribune was not less odious to the nobles, whom he adopted, than to the plebeians, whom he deserted. All that yet remained of treasure, or luxury, or art, was exhausted on that solemn day. Rienzi led the procession from the Capitol to the Lateran; the tediousness of the way was relieved with decorations and games; the ecclesiastical, civil, and military orders marched under their various banners; the Roman ladies attended his wife; and the ambassadors of Italy might loudly applaud or secretly deride the novelty of the pomp. In the evening, which they had reached the church and palace of Constantine, he thanked and dismissed the numerous assembly, with an invitation to the festival of the ensuing day. From the hands of a venerable knight he received the order of the Holy Ghost; the purification of the bath was a previous ceremony; but in no step of his life did Rienzi excite such scandal and censure as by the profane use of the porphyry vase, in which Constantine (a foolish legend) had been healed of his leprosy by Pope Sylvester. [37] With equal presumption the tribune watched or reposed within the consecrated precincts of the baptistery; and the failure of his state-bed was interpreted as an omen of his approaching downfall. At the hour of worship, he showed himself to the returning crowds in a majestic attitude, with a robe of purple, his sword, and gilt spurs; but the holy rites were soon interrupted by his levity and insolence. Rising from his throne, and advancing towards the congregation, he proclaimed in a loud voice: "We summon to our tribunal Pope Clement: and command him to reside in his diocese of Rome: we also summon the sacred college of cardinals. [38] We again summon the two pretenders, Charles of Bohemia and Lewis of Bavaria, who style themselves emperors: we likewise summon all the electors of Germany, to inform us on what pretence they have usurped the inalienable right of the Roman people, the ancient and lawful sovereigns of the empire." [39] Unsheathing his maiden sword, he thrice brandished it to the three parts of the world, and thrice repeated the extravagant declaration, "And this too is mine!" The pope's vicar, the bishop of Orvieto, attempted to check this career of folly; but his feeble protest was silenced by martial music; and instead of withdrawing from the assembly, he consented to dine with his brother tribune, at a table which had hitherto been reserved for the supreme pontiff. A banquet, such as the Cæsars had given, was prepared for the Romans. The apartments, porticos, and courts of the Lateran were spread with innumerable tables for either sex, and every condition; a stream of wine flowed from the nostrils of Constantine's brazen horse; no complaint, except of the scarcity of water, could be heard; and the licentiousness of the multitude was curbed by discipline and fear. A subsequent day was appointed for the coronation of Rienzi; [40] seven crowns of different leaves or metals were successively placed on his head by the most eminent of the Roman clergy; they represented the seven gifts of the

Holy Ghost; and he still professed to imitate the example of the ancient tribunes. [40/1] These extraordinary spectacles might deceive or flatter the people; and their own vanity was gratified in the vanity of their leader. But in his private life he soon deviated from the strict rule of frugality and abstinence; and the plebeians, who were awed by the splendor of the nobles, were provoked by the luxury of their equal. His wife, his son, his uncle, (a barber in name and profession,) exposed the contrast of vulgar manners and princely expense; and without acquiring the majesty, Rienzi degenerated into the vices, of a king.

[Footnote 36: Strange as it may seem, this festival was not without a precedent. In the year 1327, two barons, a Colonna and an Ursini, the usual balance, were created knights by the Roman people: their bath was of rose-water, their beds were decked with royal magnificence, and they were served at St. Maria of Araceli in the Capitol, by the twenty-eight buoni huomini. They afterwards received from Robert, king of Naples, the sword of chivalry, (Hist. Rom. l. i. c. 2, p. 259.)]

[Footnote 37: All parties believed in the leprosy and bath of Constantine (Petrarch. Epist. Famil. vi. 2,) and Rienzi justified his own conduct by observing to the court of Avignon, that a vase which had been used by a Pagan could not be profaned by a pious Christian. Yet this crime is specified in the bull of excommunication, (Hocsemius, apud du Cerçeau, p. 189, 190.)]

[Footnote 38: This verbal summons of Pope Clement VI., which rests on the authority of the Roman historian and a Vatican MS., is disputed by the biographer of Petrarch, (tom. ii. not. p. 70—76), with arguments rather of decency than of weight. The court of Avignon might not choose to agitate this delicate question.]

[Footnote 39: The summons of the two rival emperors, a monument of freedom and folly, is extant in Hocsemius, (Cerçeau, p. 163—166.)]

[Footnote 40: It is singular, that the Roman historian should have overlooked this sevenfold coronation, which is sufficiently proved by internal evidence, and the testimony of Hocsemius, and even of Rienzi, (Cercean p. 167—170, 229.)]

[Footnote 40/1: It was on this occasion that he made the profane comparison between himself and our Lord; and the striking circumstance took place which he relates in his letter to the archbishop of Prague. In the midst of all the wild and joyous exultation of the people, one of his most zealous supporters, a monk, who was in high repute for his sanctity, stood apart in a corner of the church and wept bitterly! A domestic chaplain of Rienzi's inquired the cause of his grief. "Now," replied the man of God, "is thy master cast down from heaven—never saw I man so proud. By the aid of the Holy Ghost he has driven the tyrants from the city without drawing a sword; the cities and the sovereigns of Italy have submitted to his power. Why is he so arrogant and ungrateful towards the Most High? Why does he seek earthly and transitory rewards for his labors, and in his wanton speech liken himself to the Creator? Tell thy master that he can only atone for this offence by tears of penitence." In the evening the chaplain communicated this solemn rebuke to the tribune: it appalled him for the time, but was soon forgotten in the tumult and hurry of business—M. 1845.]

A simple citizen describes with pity, or perhaps with pleasure, the humiliation of the barons of Rome. "Bareheaded, their hands crossed on their breast, they stood with downcast looks in the presence of the tribune; and they trembled, good God, how they trembled!" [41] As long as the yoke of Rienzi was that of justice and their country, their conscience forced them to esteem the man, whom pride and interest provoked them to hate: his extravagant conduct soon fortified their hatred by contempt; and they conceived the hope of subverting a power which was no longer so deeply rooted in the public confidence. The old animosity of the Colonna and Ursini was suspended for a moment by their common disgrace: they associated their wishes, and perhaps their designs; an assassin was seized and tortured; he accused the nobles; and as soon as Rienzi deserved the fate, he adopted the suspicions and maxims, of a tyrant. On the same day, under various pretences, he invited to the Capitol his principal enemies, among whom were five members of the Ursini and three of the Colonna name. But instead of a council or a banquet, they found themselves prisoners under the sword of despotism or justice; and the consciousness of innocence or guilt might inspire them with equal apprehensions of danger. At the sound of the great bell the people assembled; they were arraigned for a conspiracy against the tribune's life; and though some might sympathize in their distress, not a hand, nor a voice, was raised to rescue the first of the nobility from their impending doom. Their apparent boldness was prompted by despair; they passed in separate chambers a sleepless and painful night; and the venerable hero, Stephen Colonna, striking against the door of his prison, repeatedly urged his guards to deliver him by a speedy death from such ignominious servitude. In the morning they understood their sentence from the visit of a confessor and the tolling of the bell. The great hall of the Capitol had been decorated for the bloody scene with red and white hangings: the countenance of the tribune was dark and severe; the swords of the executioners were unsheathed; and the barons were interrupted in their dying speeches by the sound of trumpets. But in this decisive moment, Rienzi was not less anxious or apprehensive than his captives: he dreaded the splendor of their names, their surviving kinsmen, the inconstancy of the people the reproaches of the world, and, after rashly offering a mortal injury, he vainly presumed that, if he could forgive, he might himself be forgiven. His elaborate oration was that of a Christian and a suppliant; and, as the humble minister of the commons, he entreated his masters to pardon these noble criminals, for whose repentance and future service he pledged his faith and authority. "If you are spared," said the tribune, "by the mercy of the Romans, will you not promise to support the good estate with your lives and fortunes?" Astonished by this marvellous clemency, the barons bowed their heads; and while they devoutly repeated the oath of allegiance, might whisper a secret, and more sincere, assurance of revenge. A priest, in the name of the people, pronounced their absolution: they received the communion with the tribune, assisted at the banquet, followed the procession; and, after every spiritual and temporal sign of reconciliation, were dismissed in safety to their respective homes, with the new honors and titles of generals, consuls, and patricians. [42]

[Footnote 41: Puoi se faceva stare denante a se, mentre sedeva, li baroni tutti in piedi ritti co le vraccia piecate, e co li capucci tratti. Deh como stavano paurosi! (Hist. Rom. l. ii. c. 20, p. 439.) He saw them, and we see them.]

[Footnote 42: The original letter, in which Rienzi justifies his treatment of the Colonna, (Hocsemius, apud du Cerçeau, p. 222—229,) displays, in genuine colors, the mixture of the knave and the madman.]

During some weeks they were checked by the memory of their danger, rather than of their deliverance, till the most powerful of the Ursini, escaping with the Colonna from the city, erected at Marino the standard of rebellion. The fortifications of the castle were instantly restored; the vassals attended their lord; the outlaws armed against the magistrate; the flocks and herds, the harvests and vineyards, from Marino to the gates of Rome, were swept away or destroyed; and the people arraigned Rienzi as the author of the calamities which his government had taught them to forget. In the camp, Rienzi appeared to less advantage than in the rostrum; and he neglected the progress of the rebel barons till their numbers were strong, and their castles impregnable. From the pages of Livy he had not imbibed the art, or even the courage, of a general: an army of twenty thousand Romans returned without honor or effect from the attack of Marino; and his vengeance was amused by painting his enemies, their heads downwards, and drowning two dogs (at least they should have been bears) as the representatives of the Ursini. The belief of his incapacity encouraged their operations: they were invited by their secret adherents; and the barons attempted, with four thousand foot, and sixteen hundred horse, to enter Rome by force or surprise. The city was prepared for their reception; the alarm-bell rung all night; the gates were strictly guarded, or insolently open; and after some hesitation they sounded a retreat. The two first divisions had passed along the walls, but the prospect of a free entrance tempted the headstrong valor of the nobles in the rear; and after a successful skirmish, they were overthrown and massacred without quarter by the crowds of the Roman people. Stephen Colonna the younger, the noble spirit to whom Petrarch ascribed the restoration of Italy, was preceded or accompanied in death by his son John, a gallant youth, by his brother Peter, who might regret the ease and honors of the church, by a nephew of legitimate birth, and by two bastards of the Colonna race; and the number of seven, the seven crowns, as Rienzi styled them, of the Holy Ghost, was completed by the agony of the deplorable parent, and the veteran chief, who had survived the hope and fortune of his house. The vision and prophecies of St. Martin and Pope Boniface had been used by the tribune to animate his troops: [43] he displayed, at least in the pursuit, the spirit of a hero; but he forgot the maxims of the ancient Romans, who abhorred the triumphs of civil war. The conqueror ascended the Capitol; deposited his crown and sceptre on the altar; and boasted, with some truth, that he had cut off an ear, which neither pope nor emperor had been able to amputate. [44] His base and implacable revenge denied the honors of burial; and the bodies of the Colonna, which he threatened to expose with those of the vilest malefactors, were secretly interred by the holy virgins of their name and family. [45] The people sympathized in their grief, repented of their own fury, and detested the indecent joy of Rienzi, who visited the spot where these illustrious victims had fallen. It was on that fatal spot that he conferred on his son the honor of knighthood: and the ceremony was accomplished by a slight blow from each of the horsemen of the guard, and by a ridiculous and inhuman ablution from a pool of water, which was yet polluted with patrician blood. [46]

[Footnote 43: Rienzi, in the above-mentioned letter, ascribes to St. Martin the tribune, Boniface VIII. the enemy of Colonna, himself, and the Roman people, the glory of the day, which Villani likewise (l. 12, c. 104) describes as a regular battle. The disorderly skirmish, the flight of the Romans, and the cowardice of Rienzi, are painted in the simple and minute narrative of Fortifiocca, or the anonymous citizen, (l. i. c. 34—37.)]

[Footnote 44: In describing the fall of the Colonna, I speak only of the family of Stephen the elder, who is often confounded by the P. du Cerçeau with his son. That family was extinguished, but the house has been perpetuated in the collateral branches, of which I have not a very accurate knowledge. Circumspice (says Petrarch) familiæ tuæ statum, Columniensium domos: solito pauciores habeat columnas. Quid ad rem modo fundamentum stabile, solidumque permaneat.]

[Footnote 45: The convent of St. Silvester was founded, endowed, and protected by the Colonna cardinals, for the daughters of the family who embraced a monastic life, and who, in the year 1318, were twelve in number. The others were allowed to marry with their kinsmen in the fourth degree, and the dispensation was justified by the small number and close alliances of the noble families of Rome, (Mémoires sur Pétrarque, tom. i. p. 110, tom. ii. p. 401.)]

[Footnote 46: Petrarch wrote a stiff and pedantic letter of consolation, (Fam. l. vii. epist. 13, p. 682, 683.) The friend was lost in the patriot. Nulla toto orbe principum familia carior; carior tamen respublica, carior Roma, carior Italia. —Je rends graces aux Dieux de n'être pas Romain.]

A short delay would have saved the Colonna, the delay of a single month, which elapsed between the triumph and the exile of Rienzi. In the pride of victory, he forfeited what yet remained of his civil virtues, without acquiring the fame of military prowess. A free and vigorous opposition was formed in the city; and when the tribune proposed in the public council [47] to impose a new tax, and to regulate the government of Perugia, thirty-nine members voted against his measures; repelled the injurious charge of treachery and corruption; and urged him to prove, by their forcible exclusion, that if the populace adhered to his cause, it was already disclaimed by the most respectable citizens. The pope and the sacred college had never been dazzled by his specious professions; they were justly offended by the insolence of his conduct; a cardinal legate was sent to Italy, and after some fruitless treaty, and two personal interviews, he fulminated a bull of excommunication, in which the tribune is degraded from his office, and branded with the guilt of rebellion, sacrilege, and heresy. [48] The surviving barons of Rome were now humbled to a sense of allegiance; their interest and revenge engaged them in the service of the church; but as the fate of the Colonna was before their eyes, they abandoned to a private adventurer the peril and glory of the revolution. John Pepin, count of Minorbino, [49] in the kingdom of Naples, had been condemned for his crimes, or his riches, to perpetual imprisonment; and Petrarch, by soliciting his release, indirectly contributed to the ruin of his friend. At the head of one hundred and fifty soldiers, the count of Minorbino introduced himself into Rome; barricaded the quarter of the Colonna: and found the enterprise as easy as it had seemed impossible. From the first alarm, the bell of the Capitol incessantly tolled; but, instead of repairing to the well-known sound, the people were silent and inactive; and the pusillanimous Rienzi, deploring their ingratitude with sighs and tears, abdicated the government and palace of the republic.

[Footnote 47: This council and opposition is obscurely mentioned by Pollistore, a contemporary writer, who has preserved some curious and original facts, (Rer. Italicarum, tom. xxv. c. 31, p. 798—804.)]

[Footnote 48: The briefs and bulls of Clement VI. against Rienzi are translated by the P. du Cerçeau, (p. 196, 232,) from the Ecclesiastical Annals of Odericus Raynaldus, (A.D. 1347, No. 15, 17, 21, &c.,) who found them in the archives of the Vatican.]

[Footnote 49: Matteo Villani describes the origin, character, and death of this count of Minorbino, a man da natura inconstante e senza fede, whose grandfather, a crafty notary, was enriched and ennobled by the spoils of the Saracens of Nocera, (l. vii. c. 102, 103.) See his imprisonment, and the efforts of Petrarch, (tom. ii. p. 149—151.)]

PART III

Without drawing his sword, count Pepin restored the aristocracy and the church; three senators were chosen, and the legate, assuming the first rank, accepted his two colleagues from the rival families of Colonna and Ursini. The acts of the tribune were abolished, his head was proscribed; yet such was the terror of his name, that the barons hesitated three days before they would trust themselves in the city, and Rienzi was left above a month in the castle of St. Angelo, from whence he peaceably withdrew, after laboring, without effect, to revive the affection and courage of the Romans. The vision of freedom and empire had vanished: their fallen spirit would have acquiesced in servitude, had it been smoothed by tranquillity and order; and it was scarcely observed, that the new senators derived their authority from the Apostolic See; that four cardinals were appointed to reform, with dictatorial power, the state of the republic. Rome was again agitated by the bloody feuds of the barons, who detested each other, and despised the commons: their hostile fortresses, both in town and country, again rose, and were again demolished: and the peaceful citizens, a flock of sheep, were devoured, says the Florentine historian, by these rapacious wolves. But when their pride and avarice had exhausted the patience of the Romans, a confraternity of the Virgin Mary protected or avenged the republic: the bell of the Capitol was again tolled, the nobles in arms trembled in the presence of an unarmed multitude; and of the two senators, Colonna escaped from the window of the palace, and Ursini was stoned at the foot of the altar. The dangerous office of tribune was successively occupied by two plebeians, Cerroni and Baroncelli. The mildness of Cerroni was unequal to the times; and after a faint struggle, he retired with a fair reputation and a decent fortune to the comforts of rural life. Devoid of eloquence or genius, Baroncelli was distinguished by a resolute spirit: he spoke the language of a patriot, and trod in the footsteps of tyrants; his suspicion was a sentence of death, and his own death was the reward of his cruelties. Amidst the public misfortunes, the faults of Rienzi were forgotten; and the Romans sighed for the peace and prosperity of their good estate. [50]

*[Footnote 50: The troubles of Rome, from the departure to the return of Rienzi, are related by Matteo Villani (l. ii. c. 47, l. iii. c. 33, 57, 78) and Thomas Fortifiocca, (l. iii. c. 1—4.) I have slightly passed over these secondary characters, who imitated the original tribune.]*

After an exile of seven years, the first deliverer was again restored to his country. In the disguise of a monk or a pilgrim, he escaped from the castle of St. Angelo, implored the friendship of the king of Hungary at Naples, tempted the ambition of every bold adventurer, mingled at Rome with the pilgrims of the jubilee, lay concealed among the hermits of the Apennine, and wandered through the cities of Italy, Germany, and Bohemia. His person was invisible, his name was yet formidable; and the anxiety of the court of Avignon supposes, and even magnifies, his personal merit. The emperor Charles the Fourth gave audience to a stranger, who frankly revealed himself as the tribune of the republic; and astonished an assembly of ambassadors and princes, by the eloquence of a patriot and the visions of a prophet, the downfall of tyranny and the kingdom of the Holy Ghost. [51] Whatever had been his hopes, Rienzi found himself a captive; but he supported a character of independence and dignity, and obeyed, as his own choice, the irresistible summons of the supreme pontiff. The zeal of Petrarch, which had been cooled by the unworthy conduct, was rekindled by the sufferings and the presence, of his friend; and he boldly complains of the times, in which the savior of Rome was delivered by her emperor into the hands of her bishop. Rienzi was transported slowly, but in safe custody, from Prague to Avignon: his entrance into the city was that of a malefactor; in his prison he was chained by the leg; and four cardinals were named to inquire into the crimes of heresy and rebellion. But his trial and condemnation would have involved some questions, which it was more prudent to leave under the veil of mystery: the temporal supremacy of the popes; the duty of residence; the civil and ecclesiastical privileges of the clergy and people of Rome. The reigning pontiff well deserved the appellation of Clement: the strange vicissitudes and magnanimous spirit of the captive excited his pity and esteem; and Petrarch believes that he respected in the hero the name and sacred character of a poet. [52] Rienzi was indulged with an easy confinement and the use of books; and in the assiduous study of Livy and the Bible, he sought the cause and the consolation of his misfortunes.

*[Footnote 51: These visions, of which the friends and enemies of Rienzi seem alike ignorant, are surely magnified by the zeal of Pollistore, a Dominican inquisitor, (Rer. Ital. tom. xxv. c. 36, p. 819.) Had the tribune taught, that Christ was succeeded by the Holy Ghost, that the tyranny of the pope would be abolished, he might have been convicted of heresy and treason, without offending the Roman people. Note: So far from having magnified these visions, Pollistore is more than confirmed by the documents*

published by Papencordt. The adoption of all the wild doctrines of the Fratricelli, the Spirituals, in which, for the time at least, Rienzi appears to have been in earnest; his magnificent offers to the emperor, and the whole history of his life, from his first escape from Rome to his imprisonment at Avignon, are among the most curious chapters of his eventful life—M. 1845.]

[Footnote 52: The astonishment, the envy almost, of Petrarch is a proof, if not of the truth of this incredible fact, at least of his own veracity. The abbé de Sade (Mémoires, tom. iii. p. 242) quotes the vith epistle of the xiiith book of Petrarch, but it is of the royal MS., which he consulted, and not of the ordinary Basil edition, (p. 920.)]

The succeeding pontificate of Innocent the Sixth opened a new prospect of his deliverance and restoration; and the court of Avignon was persuaded, that the successful rebel could alone appease and reform the anarchy of the metropolis. After a solemn profession of fidelity, the Roman tribune was sent into Italy, with the title of senator; but the death of Baroncelli appeared to supersede the use of his mission; and the legate, Cardinal Albornoz, [53] a consummate statesman, allowed him with reluctance, and without aid, to undertake the perilous experiment. His first reception was equal to his wishes: the day of his entrance was a public festival; and his eloquence and authority revived the laws of the good estate. But this momentary sunshine was soon clouded by his own vices and those of the people: in the Capitol, he might often regret the prison of Avignon; and after a second administration of four months, Rienzi was massacred in a tumult which had been fomented by the Roman barons. In the society of the Germans and Bohemians, he is said to have contracted the habits of intemperance and cruelty: adversity had chilled his enthusiasm, without fortifying his reason or virtue; and that youthful hope, that lively assurance, which is the pledge of success, was now succeeded by the cold impotence of distrust and despair. The tribune had reigned with absolute dominion, by the choice, and in the hearts, of the Romans: the senator was the servile minister of a foreign court; and while he was suspected by the people, he was abandoned by the prince. The legate Albornoz, who seemed desirous of his ruin, inflexibly refused all supplies of men and money; a faithful subject could no longer presume to touch the revenues of the apostolical chamber; and the first idea of a tax was the signal of clamor and sedition. Even his justice was tainted with the guilt or reproach of selfish cruelty: the most virtuous citizen of Rome was sacrificed to his jealousy; and in the execution of a public robber, from whose purse he had been assisted, the magistrate too much forgot, or too much remembered, the obligations of the debtor. [54] A civil war exhausted his treasures, and the patience of the city: the Colonna maintained their hostile station at Palestrina; and his mercenaries soon despised a leader whose ignorance and fear were envious of all subordinate merit. In the death, as in the life, of Rienzi, the hero and the coward were strangely mingled. When the Capitol was invested by a furious multitude, when he was basely deserted by his civil and military servants, the intrepid senator, waving the banner of liberty, presented himself on the balcony, addressed his eloquence to the various passions of the Romans, and labored to persuade them, that in the same cause himself and the republic must either stand or fall. His oration was interrupted by a volley of imprecations and stones; and after an arrow had transpierced his hand, he sunk into abject despair, and fled weeping to the inner chambers, from whence he was let down by a sheet before the windows of the prison. Destitute of aid or hope, he was besieged till the evening: the doors of the Capitol were destroyed with axes and fire; and while the senator attempted to escape in a plebeian habit, he was discovered and dragged to the platform of the palace, the fatal scene of his judgments and executions. A whole hour, without voice or motion, he stood amidst the multitude half naked and half dead: their rage was hushed into curiosity and wonder: the last feelings of reverence and compassion yet struggled in his favor; and they might have prevailed, if a bold assassin had not plunged a dagger in his breast. He fell senseless with the first stroke: the impotent revenge of his enemies inflicted a thousand wounds: and the senator's body was abandoned to the dogs, to the Jews, and to the flames. Posterity will compare the virtues and failings of this extraordinary man; but in a long period of anarchy and servitude, the name of Rienzi has often been celebrated as the deliverer of his country, and the last of the Roman patriots. [55]

[Footnote 53: Ægidius, or Giles Albornoz, a noble Spaniard, archbishop of Toledo, and cardinal legate in Italy, (A.D. 1353—1367,) restored, by his arms and counsels, the temporal dominion of the popes. His life has been separately written by Sepulveda; but Dryden could not reasonably suppose, that his name, or that of Wolsey, had reached the ears of the Mufti in Don Sebastian.]

[Footnote 54: From Matteo Villani and Fortifiocca, the P. du Cerçeau (p. 344—394) has extracted the life and death of the chevalier Montreal, the life of a robber and the death of a hero. At the head of a free company, the first that desolated Italy, he became rich and formidable be had money in all the banks,— 60,000 ducats in Padua alone.]

[Footnote 55: The exile, second government, and death of Rienzi, are minutely related by the anonymous Roman, who appears neither his friend nor his enemy, (l. iii. c. 12—25.) Petrarch, who loved the tribune, was indifferent to the fate of the senator.]

The first and most generous wish of Petrarch was the restoration of a free republic; but after the exile and death of his plebeian hero, he turned his eyes from the tribune, to the king, of the Romans. The Capitol was yet stained with the blood of Rienzi, when Charles the Fourth descended from the Alps to obtain the Italian and Imperial crowns. In his passage through Milan he received the visit, and repaid the flattery, of the poet-laureate; accepted a medal of Augustus; and promised, without a smile, to imitate the founder of the Roman monarchy. A false application of the name and maxims of antiquity was the source of the hopes and disappointments of Petrarch; yet he could not overlook the difference of times and characters; the immeasurable distance between the first Cæsars and a Bohemian prince, who by the favor of the clergy had been elected the titular head of the German aristocracy. Instead of restoring to Rome her glory and her provinces, he had bound himself by a secret treaty with the pope, to evacuate the city on the day of his coronation; and his shameful retreat was pursued by the reproaches of the patriot bard. [56]

[Footnote 56: The hopes and the disappointment of Petrarch are agreeably described in his own words by the French biographer, (Mémoires, tom. iii. p. 375—413;) but the deep, though secret, wound was the coronation of Zanubi, the poet-laureate, by Charles IV.]

After the loss of liberty and empire, his third and more humble wish was to reconcile the shepherd with his flock; to recall the Roman bishop to his ancient and peculiar diocese. In the fervor of youth, with the authority of age, Petrarch addressed his exhortations to five successive popes, and his eloquence was always inspired by the enthusiasm of sentiment and the freedom of language. [57] The son of a citizen of Florence invariably preferred the country of his birth to that of his education; and Italy, in his eyes, was the queen and garden of the world. Amidst her domestic factions, she was doubtless superior to France both in art and science, in wealth and politeness; but the difference could scarcely support the epithet of barbarous, which he promiscuously bestows on the countries beyond the Alps. Avignon, the mystic Babylon, the sink of vice and corruption, was the object of his hatred and contempt; but he forgets that her scandalous vices were not the growth of the soil, and that in every residence they would adhere to the power and luxury of the papal court. He confesses that the successor of St. Peter is the bishop of the universal church; yet it was not on the banks of the Rhône, but of the Tyber, that the apostle had fixed his everlasting throne; and while every city in the Christian world was blessed with a bishop, the metropolis alone was desolate and forlorn. Since the removal of the Holy See, the sacred buildings of the Lateran and the Vatican, their altars and their saints, were left in a state of poverty and decay; and Rome was often painted under the image of a disconsolate matron, as if the wandering husband could be reclaimed by the homely portrait of the age and infirmities of his weeping spouse. [58] But the cloud which hung over the seven hills would be dispelled by the presence of their lawful sovereign: eternal fame, the prosperity of Rome, and the peace of Italy, would be the recompense of the pope who should dare to embrace this generous resolution. Of the five whom Petrarch exhorted, the three first, John the Twenty-second, Benedict the Twelfth, and Clement the Sixth, were importuned or amused by the boldness of the orator; but the memorable change which had been attempted by Urban the Fifth was finally accomplished by Gregory the Eleventh. The execution of their design was opposed by weighty and almost insuperable obstacles. A king of France, who has deserved the epithet of wise, was unwilling to release them from a local dependence: the cardinals, for the most part his subjects, were attached to the language, manners, and climate of Avignon; to their stately palaces; above all, to the wines of Burgundy. In their eyes, Italy was foreign or hostile; and they reluctantly embarked at Marseilles, as if they had been sold or banished into the land of the Saracens. Urban the Fifth resided three years in the Vatican with safety and honor: his sanctity was protected by a guard of two thousand horse; and the king of Cyprus, the queen of Naples, and the emperors of the East and West, devoutly saluted their common father in the chair of St. Peter. But the joy of Petrarch and the Italians was soon turned into grief and indignation. Some reasons of public or private moment, his own impatience or the prayers of the cardinals, recalled Urban to France; and the approaching election was saved from the tyrannic patriotism of the Romans. The powers of heaven were interested in their cause: Bridget of Sweden, a saint and pilgrim, disapproved the return, and foretold the death, of Urban the Fifth: the migration of Gregory the Eleventh was encouraged by St. Catharine of Sienna, the spouse of Christ and ambassadress of the Florentines; and the popes themselves, the great masters of human credulity, appear to have listened to these visionary females. [59] Yet those celestial admonitions were supported by some arguments of temporal policy. The residents of Avignon had been invaded by hostile violence: at the head of thirty thousand robbers, a hero had extorted ransom and absolution from the vicar of Christ and the sacred college; and the maxim of the French warriors, to spare the people and plunder the church, was a new heresy of the most dangerous import. [60] While the pope was driven from Avignon, he was strenuously invited to Rome. The senate and people acknowledged him as their lawful sovereign, and laid at his feet the keys of the gates, the bridges, and the fortresses; of the quarter at least beyond the Tyber. [61] But this loyal offer was accompanied by a declaration, that they could no longer suffer the scandal and calamity of his absence; and that his obstinacy would finally provoke them to revive and assert the primitive right of election. The abbot of Mount Cassin had been consulted, whether he would accept the triple crown [62] from the clergy and people: "I am a citizen of Rome," [63] replied that venerable ecclesiastic, "and my first law is, the voice of my country." [64]

[Footnote 57: See, in his accurate and amusing biographer, the application of Petrarch and Rome to Benedict XII. in the year 1334, (Mémoires, tom. i. p. 261—265,) to Clement VI. in 1342, (tom. ii. p. 45—47,) and to Urban V. in 1366, (tom. iii. p. 677—691:) his praise (p. 711—715) and excuse (p. 771) of the last of these pontiffs. His angry controversy on the respective merits of France and Italy may be found, Opp. p. 1068—1085.]

[Footnote 58: Squalida sed quoniam facies, neglectaque cultû Cæsaries; multisque malis lassata senectus Eripuit solitam effigiem: vetus accipe nomen; Roma vocor. (Carm. l. 2, p. 77.) He spins this allegory beyond all measure or patience. The Epistles to Urban V in prose are more simple and persuasive, (Senilium, l. vii. p. 811—827 l. ix. epist. i. p. 844—854.)]

[Footnote 59: I have not leisure to expatiate on the legends of St. Bridget or St. Catharine, the last of which might furnish some amusing stories. Their effect on the mind of Gregory XI. is attested by the last solemn words of the dying pope, who admonished the assistants, ut caverent ab hominibus, sive viris, sive mulieribus, sub specie religionis loquentibus visiones sui capitis, quia per tales ipse seductus, &c., (Baluz. Not ad Vit. Pap. Avenionensium, tom. i. p. 1224.)]

[Footnote 60: This predatory expedition is related by Froissard, (Chronique, tom. i. p. 230,) and in the life of Du Guesclin, (Collection Générale des Mémoires Historiques, tom. iv. c. 16, p. 107—113.) As early as the year 1361, the court of Avignon had been molested by similar freebooters, who afterwards passed the Alps, (Mémoires sur Pétrarque, tom. iii. p. 563—569.)]

[Footnote 61: Fleury alleges, from the annals of Odericus Raynaldus, the original treaty which was signed the 21st of December, 1376, between Gregory XI. and the Romans, (Hist. Ecclés. tom. xx. p. 275.)]

[Footnote 62: The first crown or regnum (Ducange, Gloss. Latin. tom. v. p. 702) on the episcopal mitre of the popes, is ascribed to the gift of Constantine, or Clovis. The second was added by Boniface VIII., as the emblem not only of a spiritual, but of a temporal, kingdom. The three states of the church are represented by the triple crown which was introduced by John XXII. or Benedict XII., (Mémoires sur Pétrarque, tom. i. p. 258, 259.)]

[Footnote 63: Baluze (Not. ad Pap. Avenion. tom. i. p. 1194, 1195) produces the original evidence which attests the threats of the Roman ambassadors, and the resignation of the abbot of Mount Cassin, qui, ultro se offerens, respondit se civem Romanum esse, et illud velle quod ipsi vellent.]

[Footnote 64: The return of the popes from Avignon to Rome, and their reception by the people, are related in the original lives of Urban V. and Gregory XI., in Baluze (Vit. Paparum Avenionensium, tom. i. p. 363—486) and Muratori, (Script. Rer. Italicarum, tom. iii. P. i. p. 613—712.) In the disputes of the schism, every circumstance was severely, though partially, scrutinized; more especially in the great inquest, which decided the obedience of Castile, and to which Baluze, in his notes, so often and so largely appeals from a MS. volume in the Harley library, (p. 1281, &c.)]

If superstition will interpret an untimely death, [65] if the merit of counsels be judged from the event, the heavens may seem to frown on a measure of such apparent season and propriety. Gregory the Eleventh did not survive above fourteen months his return to the Vatican; and his decease was followed by the great schism of the West, which distracted the Latin church above forty years. The sacred college was then composed of twenty-two cardinals: six of these had remained at Avignon; eleven Frenchmen, one Spaniard, and four Italians, entered the conclave in the usual form. Their choice was not yet limited to the purple; and their unanimous votes acquiesced in the archbishop of Bari, a subject of Naples, conspicuous for his zeal and learning, who ascended the throne of St. Peter under the name of Urban the Sixth. The epistle of the sacred college affirms his free, and regular, election; which had been inspired, as usual, by the Holy Ghost; he was adored, invested, and crowned, with the customary rites; his temporal authority was obeyed at Rome and Avignon, and his ecclesiastical supremacy was acknowledged in the Latin world. During several weeks, the cardinals attended their new master with the fairest professions of attachment and loyalty; till the summer heats permitted a decent escape from the city. But as soon as they were united at Anagni and Fundi, in a place of security, they cast aside the mask, accused their own falsehood and hypocrisy, excommunicated the apostate and antichrist of Rome, and proceeded to a new election of Robert of Geneva, Clement the Seventh, whom they announced to the nations as the true and rightful vicar of Christ. Their first choice, an involuntary and illegal act, was annulled by fear of death and the menaces of the Romans; and their complaint is justified by the strong evidence of probability and fact. The twelve French cardinals, above two thirds of the votes, were masters of the election; and whatever might be their provincial jealousies, it cannot fairly be presumed that they would have sacrificed their right and interest to a foreign candidate, who would never restore them to their native country. In the various, and often inconsistent, narratives, [66] the shades of popular violence are more darkly or faintly colored: but the licentiousness of the seditious Romans was inflamed by a sense of their privileges, and the danger of a second emigration. The conclave was intimidated by the shouts, and encompassed by the arms, of thirty thousand rebels; the bells of the Capitol and St. Peter's rang an alarm: "Death, or an Italian pope!" was the universal cry; the same threat was repeated by the twelve bannerets or chiefs of the quarters, in the form of charitable advice; some preparations were made for burning the obstinate cardinals; and had they chosen a Transalpine subject, it is probable that they would never have departed alive from the Vatican. The same constraint imposed the necessity of dissembling in the eyes of Rome and of the world; the pride and cruelty of Urban presented a more inevitable danger; and they soon discovered the features of the tyrant, who could walk in his garden and recite his breviary, while he heard from an adjacent chamber six cardinals groaning on the rack. His inflexible zeal, which loudly censured their luxury and vice, would have attached them to the stations and duties of their parishes at Rome; and had he not fatally delayed a new promotion, the French cardinals would have been reduced to a helpless minority in the sacred college. For these reasons, and the hope of repassing the Alps, they rashly violated the peace and unity of the church; and the merits of their double choice are yet agitated in the Catholic schools. [67] The vanity, rather than the interest, of the nation determined the court and clergy of France. [68] The states of Savoy, Sicily, Cyprus, Arragon, Castille, Navarre, and Scotland were inclined by their example and authority to the obedience of Clement the Seventh, and after his decease, of Benedict the Thirteenth. Rome and the principal states of Italy, Germany, Portugal, England, [69] the Low Countries, and the kingdoms of the North, adhered to the prior election of Urban the Sixth, who was succeeded by Boniface the Ninth, Innocent the Seventh, and Gregory the Twelfth.

*[Footnote 65: Can the death of a good man be esteemed a punishment by those who believe in the immortality of the soul? They betray the instability of their faith. Yet as a mere philosopher, I cannot agree with the Greeks, on oi Jeoi jilousin apoqnhskei neoV, (Brunck, Poetæ Gnomici, p. 231.) See in Herodotus (l. i. c. 31) the moral and pleasing tale of the Argive youths.]*

*[Footnote 66: In the first book of the Histoire du Concile de Pise, M. Lenfant has abridged and compared the original narratives of the adherents of Urban and Clement, of the Italians and Germans, the French and Spaniards. The latter appear to be the most active and loquacious, and every fact and word in the original lives of Gregory XI. and Clement VII. are supported in the notes of their editor Baluze.]*

*[Footnote 67: The ordinal numbers of the popes seems to decide the question against Clement VII. and Benedict XIII., who are boldly stigmatized as antipopes by the Italians, while the French are content with authorities and reasons to plead the cause of doubt and toleration, (Baluz. in Præfat.) It is singular, or rather it is not singular, that saints, visions and miracles should be common to both parties.]*

*[Footnote 68: Baluze strenuously labors (Not. p. 1271—1280) to justify the pure and pious motives of Charles V. king of France: he refused to hear the arguments of Urban; but were not the Urbanists equally deaf to the reasons of Clement, &c.?]*

*[Footnote 69: An epistle, or declamation, in the name of Edward III., (Baluz. Vit. Pap. Avenion. tom. i. p. 553,) displays the zeal of the English nation against the Clementines. Nor was their zeal confined to*

words: *the bishop of Norwich led a crusade of 60,000 bigots beyond sea,* (Hume's History, vol. iii. p. 57, 58.)]

From the banks of the Tyber and the Rhône, the hostile pontiffs encountered each other with the pen and the sword: the civil and ecclesiastical order of society was disturbed; and the Romans had their full share of the mischiefs of which they may be arraigned as the primary authors. [70] They had vainly flattered themselves with the hope of restoring the seat of the ecclesiastical monarchy, and of relieving their poverty with the tributes and offerings of the nations; but the separation of France and Spain diverted the stream of lucrative devotion; nor could the loss be compensated by the two jubilees which were crowded into the space of ten years. By the avocations of the schism, by foreign arms, and popular tumults, Urban the Sixth and his three successors were often compelled to interrupt their residence in the Vatican. The Colonna and Ursini still exercised their deadly feuds: the bannerets of Rome asserted and abused the privileges of a republic: the vicars of Christ, who had levied a military force, chastised their rebellion with the gibbet, the sword, and the dagger; and, in a friendly conference, eleven deputies of the people were perfidiously murdered and cast into the street. Since the invasion of Robert the Norman, the Romans had pursued their domestic quarrels without the dangerous interposition of a stranger. But in the disorders of the schism, an aspiring neighbor, Ladislaus king of Naples, alternately supported and betrayed the pope and the people; by the former he was declared gonfalonier, or general, of the church, while the latter submitted to his choice the nomination of their magistrates. Besieging Rome by land and water, he thrice entered the gates as a Barbarian conqueror; profaned the altars, violated the virgins, pillaged the merchants, performed his devotions at St. Peter's, and left a garrison in the castle of St. Angelo. His arms were sometimes unfortunate, and to a delay of three days he was indebted for his life and crown: but Ladislaus triumphed in his turn; and it was only his premature death that could save the metropolis and the ecclesiastical state from the ambitious conqueror, who had assumed the title, or at least the powers, of king of Rome. [71]

[Footnote 70: *Besides the general historians, the Diaries of Delphinus Gentilia Peter Antonius, and Stephen Infessura, in the great collection of Muratori, represented the state and misfortunes of Rome.*]

[Footnote 71: *It is supposed by Giannone (tom. iii. p. 292) that he styled himself Rex Romæ, a title unknown to the world since the expulsion of Tarquin. But a nearer inspection has justified the reading of Rex Ramæ, of Rama, an obscure kingdom annexed to the crown of Hungary.*]

I have not undertaken the ecclesiastical history of the schism; but Rome, the object of these last chapters, is deeply interested in the disputed succession of her sovereigns. The first counsels for the peace and union of Christendom arose from the university of Paris, from the faculty of the Sorbonne, whose doctors were esteemed, at least in the Gallican church, as the most consummate masters of theological science. [72] Prudently waiving all invidious inquiry into the origin and merits of the dispute, they proposed, as a healing measure, that the two pretenders of Rome and Avignon should abdicate at the same time, after qualifying the cardinals of the adverse factions to join in a legitimate election; and that the nations should subtract [73] their obedience, if either of the competitor preferred his own interest to that of the public. At each vacancy, these physicians of the church deprecated the mischiefs of a hasty choice; but the policy of the conclave and the ambition of its members were deaf to reason and entreaties; and whatsoever promises were made, the pope could never be bound by the oaths of the cardinal. During fifteen years, the pacific designs of the university were eluded by the arts of the rival pontiffs, the scruples or passions of their adherents, and the vicissitudes of French factions, that ruled the insanity of Charles the Sixth. At length a vigorous resolution was embraced; and a solemn embassy, of the titular patriarch of Alexandria, two archbishops, five bishops, five abbots, three knights, and twenty doctors, was sent to the courts of Avignon and Rome, to require, in the name of the church and king, the abdication of the two pretenders, of Peter de Luna, who styled himself Benedict the Thirteenth, and of Angelo Corrario, who assumed the name of Gregory the Twelfth. For the ancient honor of Rome, and the success of their commission, the ambassadors solicited a conference with the magistrates of the city, whom they gratified by a positive declaration, that the most Christian king did not entertain a wish of transporting the holy see from the Vatican, which he considered as the genuine and proper seat of the successor of St. Peter. In the name of the senate and people, an eloquent Roman asserted their desire to cooperate in the union of the church, deplored the temporal and spiritual calamities of the long schism, and requested the protection of France against the arms of the king of Naples. The answers of Benedict and Gregory were alike edifying and alike deceitful; and, in evading the demand of their abdication, the two rivals were animated by a common spirit. They agreed on the necessity of a previous interview; but the time, the place, and the manner, could never be ascertained by mutual consent. "If the one advances," says a servant of Gregory, "the other retreats; the one appears an animal fearful of the land, the other a creature apprehensive of the water. And thus, for a short remnant of life and power, will these aged priests endanger the peace and salvation of the Christian world." [74]

[Footnote 72: The leading and decisive part which France assumed in the schism is stated by Peter du Puis in a separate history, extracted from authentic records, and inserted in the seventh volume of the last and best edition of his friend Thuanus, (P. xi. p. 110—184.)]

[Footnote 73: Of this measure, John Gerson, a stout doctor, was the author of the champion. The proceedings of the university of Paris and the Gallican church were often prompted by his advice, and are copiously displayed in his theological writings, of which Le Clerc (Bibliothèque Choisie, tom. x. p. 1—78) has given a valuable extract. John Gerson acted an important part in the councils of Pisa and Constance.]

[Footnote 74: Leonardus Brunus Aretinus, one of the revivers of classic learning in Italy, who, after serving many years as secretary in the Roman court, retired to the honorable office of chancellor of the republic of Florence, (Fabric. Bibliot. Medii Ævi, tom. i. p. 290.) Lenfant has given the version of this curious epistle, (Concile de Pise, tom. i. p. 192—195.)]

The Christian world was at length provoked by their obstinacy and fraud: they were deserted by their cardinals, who embraced each other as friends and colleagues; and their revolt was supported by a numerous assembly of prelates and ambassadors. With equal justice, the council of Pisa deposed the popes of Rome and Avignon; the conclave was unanimous in the choice of Alexander the Fifth, and his vacant seat was soon filled by a similar election of John the Twenty-third, the most profligate of mankind. But instead of extinguishing the schism, the rashness of the French and Italians had given a third pretender to the chair of St. Peter. Such new claims of the synod and conclave were disputed; three kings, of Germany, Hungary, and Naples, adhered to the cause of Gregory the Twelfth; and Benedict the Thirteenth, himself a Spaniard, was acknowledged by the devotion and patriotism of that powerful nation. The rash proceedings of Pisa were corrected by the council of Constance; the emperor Sigismond acted a conspicuous part as the advocate or protector of the Catholic church; and the number and weight of civil and ecclesiastical members might seem to constitute the states-general of Europe. Of the three popes, John the Twenty-third was the first victim: he fled and was brought back a prisoner: the most scandalous charges were suppressed; the vicar of Christ was only accused of piracy, murder, rape, sodomy, and incest; and after subscribing his own condemnation, he expiated in prison the imprudence of trusting his person to a free city beyond the Alps. Gregory the Twelfth, whose obedience was reduced to the narrow precincts of Rimini, descended with more honor from the throne; and his ambassador convened the session, in which he renounced the title and authority of lawful pope. To vanquish the obstinacy of Benedict the Thirteenth or his adherents, the emperor in person undertook a journey from Constance to Perpignan. The kings of Castile, Arragon, Navarre, and Scotland, obtained an equal and honorable treaty; with the concurrence of the Spaniards, Benedict was deposed by the council; but the harmless old man was left in a solitary castle to excommunicate twice each day the rebel kingdoms which had deserted his cause. After thus eradicating the remains of the schism, the synod of Constance proceeded with slow and cautious steps to elect the sovereign of Rome and the head of the church. On this momentous occasion, the college of twenty-three cardinals was fortified with thirty deputies; six of whom were chosen in each of the five great nations of Christendom,—the Italian, the German, the French, the Spanish, and the English: [75] the interference of strangers was softened by their generous preference of an Italian and a Roman; and the hereditary, as well as personal, merit of Otho Colonna recommended him to the conclave. Rome accepted with joy and obedience the noblest of her sons; the ecclesiastical state was defended by his powerful family; and the elevation of Martin the Fifth is the æra of the restoration and establishment of the popes in the Vatican. [76]

[Footnote 75: I cannot overlook this great national cause, which was vigorously maintained by the English ambassadors against those of France. The latter contended, that Christendom was essentially distributed into the four great nations and votes, of Italy, Germany, France, and Spain, and that the lesser kingdoms (such as England, Denmark, Portugal, &c.) were comprehended under one or other of these great divisions. The English asserted, that the British islands, of which they were the head, should be considered as a fifth and coördinate nation, with an equal vote; and every argument of truth or fable was introduced to exalt the dignity of their country. Including England, Scotland, Wales, the four kingdoms of Ireland, and the Orkneys, the British Islands are decorated with eight royal crowns, and discriminated by four or five languages, English, Welsh, Cornish, Scotch, Irish, &c. The greater island from north to south measures 800 miles, or 40 days' journey; and England alone contains 32 counties and 52,000 parish churches, (a bold account!) besides cathedrals, colleges, priories, and hospitals. They celebrate the mission of St. Joseph of Arimathea, the birth of Constantine, and the legatine powers of the two primates, without forgetting the testimony of Bartholomey de Glanville, (A.D. 1360,) who reckons only four Christian kingdoms, 1. of Rome, 2. of Constantinople, 3. of Ireland, which had been transferred to the English monarchs, and 4, of Spain. Our countrymen prevailed in the council, but the victories of Henry V. added much weight to their arguments. The adverse pleadings were found at Constance by Sir Robert Wingfield, ambassador of Henry VIII. to the emperor Maximilian I., and by him printed in 1517 at Louvain. From a Leipsic MS. they are more correctly published in the collection of Von der Hardt, tom. v.; but I have only seen Lenfant's abstract of these acts, (Concile de Constance, tom. ii. p. 447, 453, &c.)]

[Footnote 76: The histories of the three successive councils, Pisa, Constance, and Basil, have been written with a tolerable degree of candor, industry, and elegance, by a Protestant minister, M. Lenfant, who retired from France to Berlin. They form six volumes in quarto; and as Basil is the worst, so Constance is the best, part of the Collection.]

PART IV

The royal prerogative of coining money, which had been exercised near three hundred years by the senate, was first resumed by Martin the Fifth, [77] and his image and superscription introduce the series of the papal medals. Of his two immediate successors, Eugenius the Fourth was the last pope expelled by the tumults of the Roman people, [78] and Nicholas the Fifth, the last who was importuned by the presence of a Roman emperor. [79] I. The conflict of Eugenius with the fathers of Basil, and the weight or apprehension of a new excise, emboldened and provoked the Romans to usurp the temporal government of the city. They rose in arms, elected seven governors of the republic, and a constable of the Capitol; imprisoned the pope's nephew; besieged his person in the palace; and shot volleys of arrows into his bark as he escaped down the Tyber in the habit of a monk. But he still possessed in the castle of St. Angelo a faithful garrison and a train of artillery: their batteries incessantly thundered on the city, and a bullet more dexterously pointed broke down the barricade of the bridge, and scattered with a single shot the heroes of the republic. Their constancy was exhausted by a rebellion of five months. Under the tyranny of the Ghibeline nobles, the wisest patriots regretted the dominion of the church; and their repentance was unanimous and effectual. The troops of St. Peter again occupied the Capitol; the magistrates departed to their homes; the most guilty were executed or exiled; and the legate, at the head of two thousand foot and four thousand horse, was saluted as the father of the city. The synods of Ferrara and Florence, the fear or resentment of Eugenius, prolonged his absence: he was received by a submissive people; but the pontiff understood from the acclamations of his triumphal entry, that to secure their loyalty and his own repose, he must grant without delay the abolition of the odious excise. II. Rome was restored, adorned, and enlightened, by the peaceful reign of Nicholas the Fifth. In the midst of these laudable occupations, the pope was alarmed by the approach of Frederic the Third of Austria; though his fears could not be justified by the character or the power of the Imperial candidate. After drawing his military force to the metropolis, and imposing the best security of oaths [80] and treaties, Nicholas received with a smiling countenance the faithful advocate and vassal of the church. So tame were the times, so feeble was the Austrian, that the pomp of his coronation was accomplished with order and harmony: but the superfluous honor was so disgraceful to an independent nation, that his successors have excused themselves from the toilsome pilgrimage to the Vatican; and rest their Imperial title on the choice of the electors of Germany.

[Footnote 77: See the xxviith Dissertation of the Antiquities of Muratori, and the 1st Instruction of the Science des Medailles of the Père Joubert and the Baron de la Bastie. The Metallic History of Martin V. and his successors has been composed by two monks, Moulinet, a Frenchman, and Bonanni, an Italian: but I understand, that the first part of the series is restored from more recent coins.]

[Footnote 78: Besides the Lives of Eugenius IV., (Rerum Italic. tom. iii. P. i. p. 869, and tom. xxv. p. 256,) the Diaries of Paul Petroni and Stephen Infessura are the best original evidence for the revolt of the Romans against Eugenius IV. The former, who lived at the time and on the spot, speaks the language of a citizen, equally afraid of priestly and popular tyranny.]

[Footnote 79: The coronation of Frederic III. is described by Lenfant, (Concile de Basle, tom. ii. p. 276—288,) from Æneas Sylvius, a spectator and actor in that splendid scene.]

[Footnote 80: The oath of fidelity imposed on the emperor by the pope is recorded and sanctified in the Clementines, (l. ii. tit. ix.;) and Æneas Sylvius, who objects to this new demand, could not foresee, that in a few years he should ascend the throne, and imbibe the maxims, of Boniface VIII.]

A citizen has remarked, with pride and pleasure, that the king of the Romans, after passing with a slight salute the cardinals and prelates who met him at the gate, distinguished the dress and person of the senator of Rome; and in this last farewell, the pageants of the empire and the republic were clasped in a friendly embrace. [81] According to the laws of Rome, [82] her first magistrate was required to be a doctor of laws, an alien, of a place at least forty miles from the city; with whose inhabitants he must not be connected in the third canonical degree of blood or alliance. The election was annual: a severe scrutiny was instituted into the conduct of the departing senator; nor could he be recalled to the same office till after the expiration of two years. A liberal salary of three thousand florins was assigned for his expense and reward; and his public appearance represented the majesty of the republic. His robes were of gold brocade or crimson velvet, or in the summer season of a lighter silk: he bore in his hand an ivory sceptre; the sound of trumpets announced his approach; and his solemn steps were preceded at least by four lictors or attendants, whose red wands were enveloped with bands or streamers of the golden color or livery of the city. His oath in the Capitol proclaims his right and duty to observe and assert the laws, to control the proud, to protect the poor, and to exercise justice and mercy within the extent of his jurisdiction. In these useful functions he was assisted by three learned strangers; the two collaterals, and the judge of criminal appeals: their frequent trials of robberies, rapes, and murders, are attested by the laws; and the weakness of these laws connives at the licentiousness of private feuds and armed associations for mutual defence. But the senator was confined to the administration of justice: the Capitol, the treasury, and the government of the city and its territory, were intrusted to the three conservators, who were changed four times in each year: the militia of the thirteen regions assembled under the banners of their respective chiefs, or caporioni; and the first of these was distinguished by the name and dignity of the prior. The popular legislature consisted of the secret and the common councils of the Romans. The former was composed of the magistrates and their immediate predecessors, with some fiscal and legal officers, and three classes of thirteen, twenty-six, and forty, counsellors: amounting in the whole to about one hundred and twenty persons. In the common council all male citizens had a right to vote; and the value of their privilege was enhanced by the care with which any foreigners were prevented from usurping the title and character of Romans. The tumult of a democracy was checked by wise and jealous precautions: except the magistrates, none could propose a question; none were permitted to speak, except from an open pulpit or tribunal; all disorderly acclamations were suppressed; the sense of the majority was decided by a secret ballot; and their decrees were promulgated in the venerable name of the Roman senate and people. It would not be easy to assign a period in which this theory of government has been reduced to accurate and constant practice, since the establishment of order has been gradually connected with the decay of liberty. But in the year one thousand five hundred and eighty the ancient statutes were collected, methodized in three books, and adapted to present use, under the pontificate, and with the approbation, of Gregory the Thirteenth: [83] this civil and criminal code is the modern law of the city; and, if the popular assemblies have been abolished, a foreign senator, with the three conservators, still resides in the palace of the Capitol. [84] The policy of the Cæsars has been repeated by the popes; and the bishop of Rome affected to maintain the form of a republic, while he reigned with the absolute powers of a temporal, as well as a spiritual, monarch.

[Footnote 81: *Lo senatore di Roma, vestito di brocarto con quella beretta, e con quelle maniche, et ornamenti di pelle, co' quali va alle feste di Testaccio e Nagone,* might escape the eye of Æneas Sylvius, but he is viewed with admiration and complacency by the Roman citizen, (Diario di Stephano Infessura, p. 1133.)]

[Footnote 82: See, in the statutes of Rome, the senator and three judges, (l. i. c. 3—14,) the conservators, (l. i. c. 15, 16, 17, l. iii. c. 4,) the caporioni (l. i. c. 18, l. iii. c. 8,) the secret council, (l. iii. c. 2,) the common council, (l. iii. c. 3.) The title of feuds, defiances, acts of violence, &c., is spread through many a chapter (c. 14—40) of the second book.]

[Footnote 83: Statuta alm Urbis Rom Auctoritate S. D. N. Gregorii XIII Pont. Max. a Senatu Populoque Rom. reformata et edita. Rom, 1580, in folio. The obsolete, repugnant statutes of antiquity were *confounded in five books, and Lucas Pætus, a lawyer and antiquarian, was appointed to act as the modern Tribonian. Yet I regret the old code, with the rugged crust of freedom and barbarism.]*

*[Footnote 84: In my time (1765) and in M. Grosley's, (Observations sur l'Italie tom. ii. p. 361,) the senator of Rome was M. Bielke, a noble Swede and a proselyte to the Catholic faith. The pope's right to appoint the senator and the conservator is implied, rather than affirmed, in the statutes.]*

It is an obvious truth, that the times must be suited to extraordinary characters, and that the genius of Cromwell or Retz might now expire in obscurity. The political enthusiasm of Rienzi had exalted him to a throne; the same enthusiasm, in the next century, conducted his imitator to the gallows. The birth of Stephen Porcaro was noble, his reputation spotless: his tongue was armed with eloquence, his mind was enlightened with learning; and he aspired, beyond the aim of vulgar ambition, to free his country and immortalize his name. The dominion of priests is most odious to a liberal spirit: every scruple was removed by the recent knowledge of the fable and forgery of Constantine's donation; Petrarch was now the oracle of the Italians; and as often as Porcaro revolved the ode which describes the patriot and hero of Rome, he applied to himself the visions of the prophetic bard. His first trial of the popular feelings was at the funeral of Eugenius the Fourth: in an elaborate speech he called the Romans to liberty and arms; and they listened with apparent pleasure, till Porcaro was interrupted and answered by a grave advocate, who pleaded for the church and state. By every law the seditious orator was guilty of treason; but the benevolence of the new pontiff, who viewed his character with pity and esteem, attempted by an honorable office to convert the patriot into a friend. The inflexible Roman returned from Anagni with an increase of reputation and zeal; and, on the first opportunity, the games of the place Navona, he tried to inflame the casual dispute of some boys and mechanics into a general rising of the people. Yet the humane Nicholas was still averse to accept the forfeit of his life; and the traitor was removed from the scene of temptation to Bologna, with a liberal allowance for his support, and the easy obligation of presenting himself each day before the governor of the city. But Porcaro had learned from the younger Brutus, that with tyrants no faith or gratitude should be observed: the exile declaimed against the arbitrary sentence; a party and a conspiracy were gradually formed: his nephew, a daring youth, assembled a band of volunteers; and on the appointed evening a feast was prepared at his house for the friends of the republic. Their leader, who had escaped from Bologna, appeared among them in a robe of purple and gold: his voice, his countenance, his gestures, bespoke the man who had devoted his life or death to the glorious cause. In a studied oration, he expiated on the motives and the means of their enterprise; the name and liberties of Rome; the sloth and pride of their ecclesiastical tyrants; the active or passive consent of their fellow-citizens; three hundred soldiers, and four hundred exiles, long exercised in arms or in wrongs; the license of revenge to edge their swords, and a million of ducats to reward their victory. It would be easy, (he said,) on the next day, the festival of the Epiphany, to seize the pope and his cardinals, before the doors, or at the altar, of St. Peter's; to lead them in chains under the walls of St. Angelo; to extort by the threat of their instant death a surrender of the castle; to ascend the vacant Capitol; to ring the alarm bell; and to restore in a popular assembly the ancient republic of Rome. While he triumphed, he was already betrayed. The senator, with a strong guard, invested the house: the nephew of Porcaro cut his way through the crowd; but the unfortunate Stephen was drawn from a chest, lamenting that his enemies had anticipated by three hours the execution of his design. After such manifest and repeated guilt, even the mercy of Nicholas was silent. Porcaro, and nine of his accomplices, were hanged without the benefit of the sacraments; and, amidst the fears and invectives of the papal court, the Romans pitied, and almost applauded, these martyrs of their country. [85] But their applause was mute, their pity ineffectual, their liberty forever extinct; and, if they have since risen in a vacancy of the throne or a scarcity of bread, such accidental tumults may be found in the bosom of the most abject servitude.

[Footnote 85: Besides the curious, though concise, narrative of Machiavel, (Istoria Florentina, l. vi. Opere, tom. i. p. 210, 211, edit. Londra, 1747, in 4to.) the Porcarian conspiracy is related in the Diary of Stephen Infessura, (Rer. Ital. tom. iii. P. ii. p. 1134, 1135,) and in a separate tract by Leo Baptista Alberti, (Rer. Ital. tom. xxv. p. 609—614.) It is amusing to compare the style and sentiments of the courtier and citizen. Facinus profecto quo.... neque periculo horribilius, neque audaciâ detestabilius, neque crudelitate tetrius, a quoquam perditissimo uspiam excogitatum sit.... Perdette la vita quell' huomo da bene, e amatore dello bene e libertà di Roma.]

But the independence of the nobles, which was fomented by discord, survived the freedom of the commons, which must be founded in union. A privilege of rapine and oppression was long maintained by the barons of Rome; their houses were a fortress and a sanctuary: and the ferocious train of banditti and criminals whom they protected from the law repaid the hospitality with the service of their swords and daggers. The private interest of the pontiffs, or their nephews, sometimes involved them in these domestic feuds. Under the reign of Sixtus the Fourth, Rome was distracted by the battles and sieges of the rival houses: after the conflagration of his palace, the prothonotary Colonna was tortured and beheaded; and Savelli, his captive friend, was murdered on the spot, for refusing to join in the acclamations of the victorious Ursini. [86] But the popes no longer trembled in the Vatican: they had strength to command, if they had resolution to claim, the obedience of their subjects; and the strangers, who observed these partial disorders, admired the easy taxes and wise administration of the ecclesiastical state. [87]

[Footnote 86: The disorders of Rome, which were much inflamed by the partiality of Sixtus IV. are exposed in the Diaries of two spectators, Stephen Infessura, and an anonymous citizen. See the troubles of the year 1484, and the death of the prothonotary Colonna, in tom. iii. P. ii. p. 1083, 1158.]

[Footnote 87: Est toute la terre de l'église troublée pour cette partialité (des Colonnes et des Ursins) come nous dirions Luce et Grammont, ou en Hollande Houc et Caballan; et quand ce ne seroit ce différend la terre de l'église seroit la plus heureuse habitation pour les sujets qui soit dans toute le monde (car ils ne payent ni tailles ni guères autres choses,) et seroient toujours bien conduits, (car toujours les papes sont sages et bien conselliés;) mais très souvent en advient de grands et cruels meurtres et pilleries.]

The spiritual thunders of the Vatican depend on the force of opinion; and if that opinion be supplanted by reason or passion, the sound may idly waste itself in the air; and the helpless priest is exposed to the brutal violence of a noble or a plebeian adversary. But after their return from Avignon, the keys of St. Peter were guarded by the sword of St. Paul. Rome was commanded by an impregnable citadel: the use of cannon is a powerful engine against popular seditions: a regular force of cavalry and infantry was enlisted under the banners of the pope: his ample revenues supplied the resources of war: and, from the extent of his domain, he could bring down on a rebellious city an army of hostile neighbors and loyal subjects. [88] Since the union of the duchies of Ferrara and Urbino, the ecclesiastical state extends from the Mediterranean to the Adriatic, and from the confines of Naples to the banks of the Po; and as early as the sixteenth century, the greater part of that spacious and fruitful country acknowledged the lawful claims and temporal sovereignty of the Roman pontiffs. Their claims were readily deduced from the genuine, or fabulous, donations of the darker ages: the successive steps of their final settlement would engage us too far in the transactions of Italy, and even of Europe; the crimes of Alexander the Sixth, the martial operations of Julius the Second, and the liberal policy of Leo the Tenth, a theme which has been adorned by the pens of the noblest historians of the times. [89] In the first period of their conquests, till the expedition of Charles the Eighth, the popes might successfully wrestle with the adjacent princes and states, whose military force was equal, or inferior, to their own. But as soon as the monarchs of France, Germany and Spain, contended with gigantic arms for the dominion of Italy, they supplied with art the deficiency of strength; and concealed, in a labyrinth of wars and treaties, their aspiring views, and the immortal hope of chasing the Barbarians beyond the Alps. The nice balance of the Vatican was often subverted by the soldiers of the North and West, who were united under the standard of Charles the Fifth: the feeble and fluctuating policy of Clement the Seventh exposed his person and dominions to the conqueror; and Rome was abandoned seven months to a lawless army, more cruel and rapacious than the Goths and Vandals. [90] After this severe lesson, the popes contracted their ambition, which was almost satisfied, resumed the character of a common parent, and abstained from all offensive hostilities, except in a hasty quarrel, when the vicar of Christ and the Turkish sultan were armed at the same time against the kingdom of Naples. [91] The French and Germans at length withdrew from the field of battle: Milan, Naples, Sicily, Sardinia, and the sea-coast of Tuscany, were firmly possessed by the Spaniards; and it became their interest to maintain the peace and dependence of Italy, which continued almost without disturbance from the middle of the sixteenth to the opening of the eighteenth century. The Vatican was swayed and protected by the religious policy of the Catholic king: his prejudice and interest disposed him in every dispute to support the prince against the people; and instead of the encouragement, the aid, and the asylum, which they obtained from the adjacent states, the friends of liberty, or the enemies of law, were enclosed on all sides within the iron circle of despotism. The long habits of obedience and education subdued the turbulent spirit of the nobles and commons of Rome. The barons forgot the arms and factions of their ancestors, and insensibly became the servants of luxury and government. Instead of maintaining a crowd of tenants and followers, the produce of their estates was consumed in the private expenses which multiply the pleasures, and diminish the power, of the lord. [92] The Colonna and Ursini vied with each other in the decoration of their palaces and chapels; and their antique splendor was rivalled or surpassed by the sudden opulence of the papal families. In Rome the voice of freedom and discord is no longer heard; and, instead of the foaming torrent, a smooth and stagnant lake reflects the image of idleness and servitude.

[Footnote 88: By the conomy of Sixtus V. the revenue of the ecclesiastical state was raised to two millions and a half of Roman crowns, (Vita, tom. ii. p. 291—296;) and so regular was the military establishment, that in one month Clement VIII. could invade the duchy of Ferrara with three thousand horse and twenty thousand foot, (tom. iii. p. 64) Since that time (A.D. 1597) the papal arms are happily rusted: but the revenue must have gained some nominal increase. Note: On the financial measures of Sixtus V. see Ranke, Dio Römischen Päpste, i. p. 459—M.]

[Footnote 89: More especially by Guicciardini and Machiavel; in the general history of the former, in the Florentine history, the Prince, and the political discourses of the latter. These, with their worthy successors, Fra Paolo and Davila, were justly esteemed the first historians of modern languages, till, in the present age, Scotland arose, to dispute the prize with Italy herself.]

[Footnote 90: In the history of the Gothic siege, I have compared the Barbarians with the subjects of Charles V., (vol. iii. p. 289, 290;) an anticipation, which, like that of the Tartar conquests, I indulged with the less scruple, as I could scarcely hope to reach the conclusion of my work.]

[Footnote 91: The ambitious and feeble hostilities of the Caraffa pope, Paul IV. may be seen in Thuanus (l. xvi—xviii.) and Giannone, (tom. iv p. 149—163.) Those Catholic bigots, Philip II. and the duke of Alva, presumed to separate the Roman prince from the vicar of Christ, yet the holy character, which would have sanctified his victory was decently applied to protect his defeat. Note: But compare Ranke, Die Römischen Päpste, i. p. 289—M.]

[Footnote 92: This gradual change of manners and expense is admirably explained by Dr. Adam Smith, (Wealth of Nations, vol. i. p. 495—504,) who proves, perhaps too severely, that the most salutary effects have flowed from the meanest and most selfish causes.]

A Christian, a philosopher, [93] and a patriot, will be equally scandalized by the temporal kingdom of the clergy; and the local majesty of Rome, the remembrance of her consuls and triumphs, may seem to imbitter the sense, and aggravate the shame, of her slavery. If we calmly weigh the merits and defects of the ecclesiastical government, it may be praised in its present state, as a mild, decent, and tranquil system, exempt from the dangers of a minority, the sallies of youth, the expenses of luxury, and the calamities of war. But these advantages are overbalanced by a frequent, perhaps a septennial, election of a sovereign, who is seldom a native of the country; the reign of a young statesman of threescore, in the decline of his life and abilities, without hope to accomplish, and without children to inherit, the labors of his transitory reign. The successful candidate is drawn from the church, and even the convent; from the mode of education and life the most adverse to reason, humanity, and freedom. In the trammels of servile faith, he has learned to believe because it is absurd, to revere all that is contemptible, and to despise whatever might deserve the esteem of a rational being; to punish error as a crime, to reward mortification and celibacy as the first of virtues; to place the saints of the calendar [94] above the heroes of Rome and the sages of Athens; and to consider the missal, or the crucifix, as more useful instruments than the plough or the loom. In the office of nuncio, or the rank of cardinal, he may acquire some knowledge of the world, but the primitive stain will adhere to his mind and manners: from study and experience he may suspect the mystery of his profession; but the sacerdotal artist will imbibe some portion of the bigotry which he inculcates. The genius of Sixtus the Fifth [95] burst from the gloom of a Franciscan cloister. In a reign of five years, he exterminated the outlaws and banditti, abolished the profane sanctuaries of Rome, [96] formed a naval and military force, restored and emulated the monuments of antiquity, and after a liberal use and large increase of the revenue, left five millions of crowns in the castle of St. Angelo. But his justice was sullied with cruelty, his activity was prompted by the ambition of conquest: after his decease the abuses revived; the treasure was dissipated; he entailed on posterity thirty-five new taxes and the venality of offices; and, after his death, his statue was demolished by an ungrateful, or an injured, people. [97] The wild and original character of Sixtus the Fifth stands alone in the series of the pontiffs; the maxims and effects of their temporal government may be collected from the positive and comparative view of the arts and philosophy, the agriculture and trade, the wealth and population, of the ecclesiastical state. For myself, it is my wish to depart in charity with all mankind, nor am I willing, in these last moments, to offend even the pope and clergy of Rome. [98]

[Footnote 93: Mr. Hume (Hist. of England, vol. i. p. 389) too hastily conclude that if the civil and ecclesiastical powers be united in the same person, it is of little moment whether he be styled prince or prelate since the temporal character will always predominate.]

[Footnote 94: A Protestant may disdain the unworthy preference of St. Francis or St. Dominic, but he will not rashly condemn the zeal or judgment of Sixtus V., who placed the statues of the apostles St. Peter and St. Paul on the vacant columns of Trajan and Antonine.]

[Footnote 95: A wandering Italian, Gregorio Leti, has given the Vita di Sisto-Quinto, (Amstel. 1721, 3 vols. in 12mo.,) a copious and amusing work, but which does not command our absolute confidence. Yet the character of the man, and the principal facts, are supported by the annals of Spondanus and Muratori, (A.D. 1585—1590,) and the contemporary history of the great Thuanus, (l. lxxxii. c. 1, 2, l. lxxxiv. c. 10, l. c. c. 8.) Note: The industry of M. Ranke has discovered the document, a kind of scandalous chronicle of the time, from which Leti wrought up his amusing romances. See also M. Ranke's observations on the Life of Sixtus. by Tempesti, b. iii. p. 317, 324— M.]

[Footnote 96: These privileged places, the quartieri or franchises, were adopted from the Roman nobles by the foreign ministers. Julius II. had once abolished the abominandum et detestandum franchitiarum hujusmodi nomen: and after Sixtus V. they again revived. I cannot discern either the justice or magnanimity of Louis XIV., who, in 1687, sent his ambassador, the marquis de Lavardin, to Rome, with an armed force of a thousand officers, guards, and domestics, to maintain this iniquitous claim, and insult Pope Innocent XI. in the heart of his capital, (Vita di Sisto V. tom. iii. p. 260—278. Muratori, Annali d'Italia, tom. xv. p. 494—496, and Voltaire, Siecle de Louis XIV. tom. i. c. 14, p. 58, 59.)]

[Footnote 97: This outrage produced a decree, which was inscribed on marble, and placed in the Capitol. It is expressed in a style of manly simplicity and freedom: Si quis, sive privatus, sive magistratum gerens de collocandâ vivo pontifici statuâ mentionem facere ausit, legitimo S. P. Q. R. decreto in perpetuum infamis et publicorum munerum expers esto. MDXC. mense Augusto, (Vita di Sisto V. tom. iii. p. 469.) I believe that this decree is still observed, and I know that every monarch who deserves a statue should himself impose the prohibition.]

[Footnote 98: The histories of the church, Italy, and Christendom, have contributed to the chapter which I now conclude. In the original Lives of the Popes, we often discover the city and republic of Rome: and the events of the xivth and xvth centuries are preserved in the rude and domestic chronicles which I have carefully inspected, and shall recapitulate in the order of time.

1. Monaldeschi (Ludovici Boncomitis) Fragmenta Annalium Roman. A.D. 1328, in the Scriptores Rerum Italicarum of Muratori, tom. xii. p. 525. N. B. The credit of this fragment is somewhat hurt by a singular interpolation, in which the author relates his own death at the age of 115 years.

2. Fragmenta Historiæ Romanæ (vulgo Thomas Fortifioccæ) in Romana Dialecto vulgari, (A.D. 1327—1354, in Muratori, Antiquitat. Medii Ævi Italiæ, tom. iii. p. 247—548;) the authentic groundwork of the history of Rienzi.

3. Delphini (Gentilis) Diarium Romanum, (A.D. 1370—1410,) in the Rerum Italicarum, tom. iii. P. ii. p. 846.

4. Antonii (Petri) Diarium Rom., (A.D. 1404—1417,) tom. xxiv. p. 699.

5. Petroni (Pauli) Miscellanea Historica Romana, (A.D. 1433—1446,) tom. xxiv. p. 1101.

6. Volaterrani (Jacob.) Diarium Rom., (A.D. 1472—1484,) tom. xxiii p. 81.

7. Anonymi Diarium Urbis Romæ, (A.D. 1481—1492,) tom. iii. P. ii. p. 1069.

8. Infessuræ (Stephani) Diarium Romanum, (A.D. 1294, or 1378—1494,) tom. iii. P. ii. p. 1109.

9. Historia Arcana Alexandri VI. sive Excerpta ex Diario Joh. Burcardi, (A.D. 1492—1503,) edita a Godefr. Gulielm. Leibnizio, Hanover, 697, in 14to. The large and valuable Journal of Burcard might be completed from the MSS. in different libraries of Italy and France, (M. de Foncemagne, in the Mémoires de l'Acad. des Inscrip. tom. xvii. p. 597—606.)

Except the last, all these fragments and diaries are inserted in the Collections of Muratori, my guide and master in the history of Italy. His country, and the public, are indebted to him for the following works on that subject: 1. Rerum Italicarum Scriptores, (A.D. 500—1500,) quorum potissima pars nunc primum in lucem prodit, &c., xxviii. vols. in folio, Milan, 1723—1738, 1751. A volume of chronological and alphabetical tables is still wanting as a key to this great work, which is yet in a disorderly and defective state. 2. Antiquitates Italiæ Medii Ævi, vi. vols. in folio, Milan, 1738—1743, in lxxv. curious dissertations, on the manners, government, religion, &c., of the Italians of the darker ages, with a large supplement of charters, chronicles, &c. 3. Dissertazioni sopra le Antiquita Italiane, iii. vols. in 4to., Milano, 1751, a free version by the author, which may be quoted with the same confidence as the Latin text of the Antiquities. Annali d' Italia, xviii. vols. in octavo, Milan, 1753—1756, a dry, though accurate and useful, abridgment of the history of Italy, from the birth of Christ to the middle of the xviiith century. 5. Dell' Antichita Estense ed Italiane, ii. vols. in folio, Modena, 1717, 1740. In the history of this illustrious race, the parent of our Brunswick kings, the critic is not seduced by the loyalty or gratitude of the subject. In all his works, Muratori approves himself a diligent and laborious writer, who aspires above the prejudices of a Catholic priest. He was born in the year 1672, and died in the year 1750, after passing near 60 years in the libraries of Milan and Modena, (Vita del Proposto Ludovico Antonio Muratori, by his nephew and successor Gian. Francesco Soli Muratori Venezia, 1756 m 4to.)]

CHAPTER LXXI

PROSPECT OF THE RUINS OF ROME IN THE FIFTEENTH CENTURY

PART I

PROSPECT OF THE RUINS OF ROME IN THE FIFTEENTH CENTURY—FOUR CAUSES OF DECAY AND DESTRUCTION—EXAMPLE OF THE COLISEUM—RENOVATION OF THE CITY—CONCLUSION OF THE WHOLE WORK

In the last days of Pope Eugenius the Fourth, [101] two of his servants, the learned Poggius [1] and a friend, ascended the Capitoline hill; reposed themselves among the ruins of columns and temples; and viewed from that commanding spot the wide and various prospect of desolation. [2] The place and the object gave ample scope for moralizing on the vicissitudes of fortune, which spares neither man nor the proudest of his works, which buries empires and cities in a common grave; and it was agreed, that in proportion to her former greatness, the fall of Rome was the more awful and deplorable. "Her primeval state, such as she might appear in a remote age, when Evander entertained the stranger of Troy, [3] has been delineated by the fancy of Virgil. This Tarpeian rock was then a savage and solitary thicket: in the time of the poet, it was crowned with the golden roofs of a temple; the temple is overthrown, the gold has been pillaged, the wheel of fortune has accomplished her revolution, and the sacred ground is again disfigured with thorns and brambles. The hill of the Capitol, on which we sit, was formerly the head of the Roman empire, the citadel of the earth, the terror of kings; illustrated by the footsteps of so many triumphs, enriched with the spoils and tributes of so many nations. This spectacle of the world, how is it fallen! how changed! how defaced! The path of victory is obliterated by vines, and the benches of the senators are concealed by a dunghill. Cast your eyes on the Palatine hill, and seek among the shapeless and enormous fragments the marble theatre, the obelisks, the colossal statues, the porticos of Nero's palace: survey the other hills of the city, the vacant space is interrupted only by ruins and gardens. The forum of the Roman people, where they assembled to enact their laws and elect their magistrates, is now enclosed for the cultivation of pot-herbs, or thrown open for the reception of swine and buffaloes. The public and private edifices, that were founded for eternity, lie prostrate, naked, and broken, like the limbs of a mighty giant; and the ruin is the more visible, from the stupendous relics that have survived the injuries of time and fortune." [4]

[Footnote 101: It should be Pope Martin the Fifth. See Gibbon's own note, ch. lxv, note 51 and Hobhouse, Illustrations of Childe Harold, p. 155—M.]

[Footnote 1: I have already (notes 50, 51, on chap. lxv.) mentioned the age, character, and writings of Poggius; and particularly noticed the date of this elegant moral lecture on the varieties of fortune.]

[Footnote 2: Consedimus in ipsis Tarpeiæ arcis ruinis, pone ingens portæ cujusdam, ut puto, templi, marmoreum limen, plurimasque passim confractas columnas, unde magnâ ex parte prospectus urbis patet, (p. 5.)]

[Footnote 3: Æneid viii. 97—369. This ancient picture, so artfully introduced, and so exquisitely finished, must have been highly interesting to an inhabitant of Rome; and our early studies allow us to sympathize in the feelings of a Roman.]

[Footnote 4: Capitolium adeo.... immutatum ut vineæ in senatorum subsellia successerint, stercorum ac purgamentorum receptaculum factum. Respice ad Palatinum montem..... vasta rudera.... cæteros colles perlustra omnia vacua ædificiis, ruinis vineisque oppleta conspicies, (Poggius, de Varietat. Fortunæ p. 21.)]

These relics are minutely described by Poggius, one of the first who raised his eyes from the monuments of legendary, to those of classic, superstition. [5] 1.Besides a bridge, an arch, a sepulchre, and the pyramid of Cestius, he could discern, of the age of the republic, a double row of vaults, in the salt-office of the Capitol, which were inscribed with the name and munificence of Catulus. 2. Eleven temples were visible in some degree, from the perfect form of the Pantheon, to the three arches and a marble column of the temple of Peace, which Vespasian erected after the civil wars and the Jewish triumph. 3. Of the number, which he rashly defines, of seven therm, or public baths, none were sufficiently entire to represent the use and distribution of the several parts: but those of Diocletian and Antoninus Caracalla still retained the titles of the founders, and astonished the curious spectator, who, in observing their solidity and extent, the variety of marbles, the size and multitude of the columns, compared the labor and expense with the use and importance. Of the baths of Constantine, of Alexander, of Domitian, or rather of Titus, some vestige might yet be found. 4. The triumphal arches of Titus, Severus, and Constantine, were entire, both the structure and the inscriptions; a falling fragment was honored with the name of Trajan; and two arches, then extant, in the Flaminian way, have been ascribed to the baser memory of Faustina and Gallienus. [501] 5. After the wonder of the Coliseum, Poggius might have overlooked small amphitheatre of brick, most probably for the use of the prætorian camp: the theatres of Marcellus and Pompey were occupied in a great measure by public and private buildings; and in the Circus, Agonalis and Maximus, little more than the situation and the form could be investigated. 6. The columns of Trajan and Antonine were still erect; but the Egyptian obelisks were broken or buried. A people of gods and heroes, the workmanship of art, was reduced to one equestrian figure of gilt brass, and to five marble statues, of which the most conspicuous were the two horses of Phidias and Praxiteles. 7. The two mausoleums or sepulchres of Augustus and Hadrian could not totally be lost: but the former was only visible as a mound of earth; and the latter, the castle of St. Angelo, had acquired the name and appearance of a modern fortress. With the addition of some separate and nameless columns, such were the remains of the ancient city; for the marks of a more recent structure might be detected in the walls, which formed a circumference of ten miles, included three hundred and seventy-nine turrets, and opened into the country by thirteen gates.

[Footnote 5: See Poggius, p. 8—22.]

[Footnote 501: One was in the Via Nomentana; est alter præterea Gallieno principi dicatus, ut superscriptio indicat, Viâ Nomentana. Hobhouse, p. 154. Poggio likewise mentions the building which Gibbon ambiguously says be "might have overlooked."—M.]

This melancholy picture was drawn above nine hundred years after the fall of the Western empire, and even of the Gothic kingdom of Italy. A long period of distress and anarchy, in which empire, and arts, and riches had migrated from the banks of the Tyber, was incapable of restoring or adorning the city; and, as all that is human must retrograde if it do not advance, every successive age must have hastened the ruin of the works of antiquity. To measure the progress of decay, and to ascertain, at each æra, the state of each edifice, would be an endless and a useless labor; and I shall content myself with two observations, which will introduce a short inquiry into the general causes and effects. 1. Two hundred years before the eloquent complaint of Poggius, an anonymous writer composed a description of Rome. [6] His ignorance may repeat the same objects under strange and fabulous names. Yet this barbarous topographer had eyes and ears; he could observe the visible remains; he could listen to the tradition of the people; and he distinctly enumerates seven theatres, eleven baths, twelve arches, and eighteen palaces, of which many had disappeared before the time of Poggius. It is apparent, that many stately monuments of antiquity survived till a late period, [7] and that the principles of destruction acted with vigorous and increasing energy in the thirteenth and fourteenth centuries. 2. The same reflection must be applied to the three last ages; and we should vainly seek the Septizonium of Severus; [8] which is celebrated by Petrarch and the antiquarians of the sixteenth century. While the Roman edifices were still entire, the first blows, however weighty and impetuous, were resisted by the solidity of the mass and the harmony of the parts; but the slightest touch would precipitate the fragments of arches and columns, that already nodded to their fall.

[Footnote 6: Liber de Mirabilibus Romæ ex Registro Nicolai Cardinalis de Arragoniâ in Bibliothecâ St. Isidori Armario IV., No. 69. This treatise, with some short but pertinent notes, has been published by Montfaucon, (Diarium Italicum, p. 283—301,) who thus delivers his own critical opinion: Scriptor xiiimi. circiter sæculi, ut ibidem notatur; antiquariæ rei imperitus et, ut ab illo ævo, nugis et anilibus fabellis refertus: sed, quia monumenta, quæ iis temporibus Romæ supererant pro modulo recenset, non parum inde lucis mutuabitur qui Romanis antiquitatibus indagandis operam navabit, (p. 283.)]

[Footnote 7: The Père Mabillon (Analecta, tom. iv. p. 502) has published an anonymous pilgrim of the ixth century, who, in his visit round the churches and holy places at Rome, touches on several buildings, especially porticos, which had disappeared before the xiiith century.]

[Footnote 8: On the Septizonium, see the Mémoires sur Pétrarque, (tom. i. p. 325,) Donatus, (p. 338,) and Nardini, (p. 117, 414.)]

After a diligent inquiry, I can discern four principal causes of the ruin of Rome, which continued to operate in a period of more than a thousand years. I. The injuries of time and nature. II. The hostile attacks of the Barbarians and Christians. III. The use and abuse of the materials. And, IV. The domestic quarrels of the Romans.

I. The art of man is able to construct monuments far more permanent than the narrow span of his own existence; yet these monuments, like himself, are perishable and frail; and in the boundless annals of time, his life and his labors must equally be measured as a fleeting moment. Of a simple and solid edifice, it is not easy, however, to circumscribe the duration. As the wonders of ancient days, the pyramids [9] attracted the curiosity of the ancients: a hundred generations, the leaves of autumn, have dropped [10] into the grave; and after the fall of the Pharaohs and Ptolemies, the Cæsars and caliphs, the same pyramids stand erect and unshaken above the floods of the Nile. A complex figure of various and minute parts to more accessible to injury and decay; and the silent lapse of time is often accelerated by hurricanes and earthquakes, by fires and inundations. The air and earth have doubtless been shaken; and the lofty turrets of Rome have tottered from their foundations; but the seven hills do not appear to be placed on the great cavities of the globe; nor has the city, in any age, been exposed to the convulsions of nature, which, in the climate of Antioch, Lisbon, or Lima, have crumbled in a few moments the works of ages into dust. Fire is the most powerful agent of life and death: the rapid mischief may be kindled and propagated by the industry or negligence of mankind; and every period of the Roman annals is marked by the repetition of similar calamities. A memorable conflagration, the guilt or misfortune of Nero's reign, continued, though with unequal fury, either six or nine days. [11] Innumerable buildings, crowded in close and crooked streets, supplied perpetual fuel for the flames; and when they ceased, four only of the fourteen regions were left entire; three were totally destroyed, and seven were deformed by the relics of smoking and lacerated edifices. [12] In the full meridian of empire, the metropolis arose with fresh beauty from her ashes; yet the memory of the old deplored their irreparable losses, the arts of Greece, the trophies of victory, the monuments of primitive or fabulous antiquity. In the days of distress and anarchy, every wound is mortal, every fall irretrievable; nor can the damage be restored either by the public care of government, or the activity of private interest. Yet two causes may be alleged, which render the calamity of fire more destructive to a flourishing than a decayed city. 1. The more combustible materials of brick, timber, and metals, are first melted or consumed; but the flames may play without injury or effect on the naked walls, and massy arches, that have been despoiled of their ornaments. 2. It is among the common and plebeian habitations, that a mischievous spark is most easily blown to a conflagration; but as soon as they are devoured, the greater edifices, which have resisted or escaped, are left as so many islands in a state of solitude and safety. From her situation, Rome is exposed to the danger of frequent inundations. Without excepting the Tyber, the rivers that descend from either side of the Apennine have a short and irregular course; a shallow stream in the summer heats; an impetuous torrent, when it is swelled in the spring or winter, by the fall of rain, and the melting of the snows. When the current is repelled from the sea by adverse winds, when the ordinary bed is inadequate to the weight of waters, they rise above the banks, and overspread, without limits or control, the plains and cities of the adjacent country. Soon after the triumph of the first Punic war, the Tyber was increased by unusual rains; and the inundation, surpassing all former measure of time and place, destroyed all the buildings that were situated below the hills of Rome. According to the variety of ground, the same mischief was produced by different means; and the edifices were either swept away by the sudden impulse, or dissolved and undermined by the long continuance, of the flood. [13] Under the reign of Augustus, the same calamity was renewed: the lawless river overturned the palaces and temples on its banks; [14] and, after the labors of the emperor in cleansing and widening the bed that was encumbered with ruins, [15] the vigilance of his successors was exercised by similar dangers and designs. The project of diverting into new channels the Tyber itself, or some of the dependent streams, was long opposed by superstition and local interests; [16] nor did the use compensate the toil and cost of the tardy and imperfect execution. The servitude of rivers is the noblest and most important victory which man has obtained over the licentiousness of nature; [17] and if such were the ravages of the Tyber under a firm and active government, what could oppose, or who can enumerate, the injuries of the city, after the fall of the Western empire? A remedy was at length produced by the evil itself: the accumulation of rubbish and the earth, that has been washed down from the hills, is supposed to have elevated the plain of Rome, fourteen or fifteen feet, perhaps, above the ancient level; [18] and the modern city is less accessible to the attacks of the river. [19]

[Footnote 9: The age of the pyramids is remote and unknown, since Diodorus Siculus (tom. i l. i. c. 44, p. 72) is unable to decide whether they were constructed 1000, or 3400, years before the clxxxth Olympiad. Sir John Marsham's contracted scale of the Egyptian dynasties would fix them about 2000 years before Christ, (Canon. Chronicus, p. 47.)]

[Footnote 10: See the speech of Glaucus in the Iliad, (Z. 146.) This natural but melancholy image is peculiar to Homer.]

[Footnote 11: The learning and criticism of M. des Vignoles (Histoire Critique de la République des Lettres, tom. viii. p. 47—118, ix. p. 172—187) dates the fire of Rome from A.D. 64, July 19, and the subsequent persecution of the Christians from November 15 of the same year.]

[Footnote 12: Quippe in regiones quatuordecim Roma dividitur, quarum quatuor integræ manebant, tres solo tenus dejectæ: septem reliquis pauca testorum vestigia supererant, lacera et semiusta. Among the old relics that were irreparably lost, Tacitus enumerates the temple of the moon of Servius Tullius; the fane and altar consecrated by Evander præsenti Herculi; the temple of Jupiter Stator, a vow of Romulus; the palace of Numa; the temple of Vesta cum Penatibus populi Romani. He then deplores the opes tot victoriis quæsitæ et Græcarum artium decora.... multa quæ seniores meminerant, quæ reparari nequibant, (Annal. xv. 40, 41.)]

[Footnote 13: A. U. C. 507, repentina subversio ipsius Romæ prævenit triumphum Romanorum.... diversæ ignium aquarumque clades pene absumsere urbem Nam Tiberis insolitis auctus imbribus et ultra opinionem, vel diuturnitate vel magnitudine redundans, omnia Romæ ædificia in plano posita delevit. Diversæ qualitates locorum ad unam convenere perniciem: quoniam et quæ segnior inundatio tenuit madefacta dissolvit, et quæ cursus torrentis invenit impulsa dejecit, (Orosius, Hist. l. iv. c. 11, p. 244, edit. Havercamp.) Yet we may observe, that it is the plan and study of the Christian apologist to magnify the calamities of the Pagan world.]

[Footnote 14:
Vidimus flavum Tiberim, retortis Littore Etrusco violenter undis, Ire dejectum monumenta Regis Templaque Vestæ. (Horat. Carm. I. 2.)

If the palace of Numa and temple of Vesta were thrown down in Horace's time, what was consumed of those buildings by Nero's fire could hardly deserve the epithets of vetustissima or incorrupta.]

[Footnote 15: Ad coercendas inundationes alveum Tiberis laxavit, ac repurgavit, completum olim ruderibus, et ædificiorum prolapsionibus coarctatum, (Suetonius in Augusto, c. 30.)]

[Footnote 16: Tacitus (Annal. i. 79) reports the petitions of the different towns of Italy to the senate against the measure; and we may applaud the progress of reason. On a similar occasion, local interests would undoubtedly be consulted: but an English House of Commons would reject with contempt the arguments of superstition, "that nature had assigned to the rivers their proper course," &c.]

[Footnote 17: See the Epoques de la Nature of the eloquent and philosophic Buffon. His picture of Guyana, in South America, is that of a new and savage land, in which the waters are abandoned to themselves without being regulated by human industry, (p. 212, 561, quarto edition.)]

[Footnote 18: In his travels in Italy, Mr. Addison (his works, vol. ii. p. 98, Baskerville's edition) has observed this curious and unquestionable fact.]

[Footnote 19: Yet in modern times, the Tyber has sometimes damaged the city, and in the years 1530, 1557, 1598, the annals of Muratori record three mischievous and memorable inundations, (tom. xiv. p. 268, 429, tom. xv. p. 99, &c.) Note: The level of the Tyber was at one time supposed to be considerably raised: recent investigations seem to be conclusive against this supposition. See a brief, but satisfactory statement of the question in Bunsen and Platner, Roms Beschreibung. vol. i. p. 29—M.]

II. The crowd of writers of every nation, who impute the destruction of the Roman monuments to the Goths and the Christians, have neglected to inquire how far they were animated by a hostile principle, and how far they possessed the means and the leisure to satiate their enmity. In the preceding volumes of this History, I have described the triumph of barbarism and religion; and I can only resume, in a few words, their real or imaginary connection with the ruin of ancient Rome. Our fancy may create, or adopt, a pleasing romance, that the Goths and Vandals sallied from Scandinavia, ardent to avenge the flight of Odin; [20] to break the chains, and to chastise the oppressors, of mankind; that they wished to burn the records of classic literature, and to found their national architecture on the broken members of the Tuscan and Corinthian orders. But in simple truth, the northern conquerors were neither sufficiently savage, nor sufficiently refined, to entertain such aspiring ideas of destruction and revenge. The shepherds of Scythia and Germany had been educated in the armies of the empire, whose discipline they acquired, and whose weakness they invaded: with the familiar use of the Latin tongue, they had learned to reverence the name and titles of Rome; and, though incapable of emulating, they were more inclined to admire, than to abolish, the arts and studies of a brighter period. In the transient possession of a rich and unresisting capital, the soldiers of Alaric and Genseric were stimulated by the passions of a victorious army; amidst the wanton indulgence of lust or cruelty, portable wealth was the object of their search; nor could they derive either pride or pleasure from the unprofitable reflection, that they had battered to the ground the works of the consuls and Cæsars. Their moments were indeed precious; the Goths evacuated Rome on the sixth, [21] the Vandals on the fifteenth, day: [22] and, though it be far more difficult to build than to destroy, their hasty assault would have made a slight impression on the solid piles of antiquity. We may remember, that both Alaric and Genseric affected to spare the buildings of the city; that they subsisted in strength and beauty under the auspicious government of Theodoric; [23] and that the momentary resentment of Totila [24] was disarmed by his own temper and the advice of his friends and enemies. From these innocent Barbarians, the reproach may be transferred to the Catholics of Rome. The statues, altars, and houses, of the dæmons, were an abomination in their eyes; and in the absolute command of the city, they might labor with zeal and perseverance to erase the idolatry of their ancestors. The demolition of the temples in the East [25] affords to them an example of conduct, and to us an argument of belief; and it is probable that a portion of guilt or merit may be imputed with justice to the Roman proselytes. Yet their abhorrence was confined to the monuments of heathen superstition; and the civil structures that were dedicated to the business or pleasure of society might be preserved without injury or scandal. The change of religion was accomplished, not by a popular tumult, but by the decrees of the emperors, of the senate, and of time. Of the Christian hierarchy, the bishops of Rome were commonly the most prudent and least fanatic; nor can any positive charge be opposed to the meritorious act of saving or converting the majestic structure of the Pantheon. [26] [26/1]

[Footnote 20: I take this opportunity of declaring, that in the course of twelve years, I have forgotten, or renounced, the flight of Odin from Azoph to Sweden, which I never very seriously believed, (vol. i. p. 283.) The Goths are apparently Germans: but all beyond Cæsar and Tacitus is darkness or fable, in the antiquities of Germany.]

[Footnote 21: History of the Decline, &c., vol. iii. p. 291.]

[Footnote 22: History of the Decline, &c., vol. iii. p. 464.]

[Footnote 23: History of the Decline, &c., vol. iv. p. 23—25.]

[Footnote 24: History of the Decline, &c., vol. iv. p. 258.]

[Footnote 25: History of the Decline, &c., vol. iii. c. xxviii. p. 139—148.]

[Footnote 26: Eodem tempore petiit a Phocate principe templum, quod appellatur Pantheon, in quo fecit ecclesiam Sanctæ Mariæ semper Virginis, et omnium martyrum; in quâ ecclesiæ princeps multa bona obtulit, (Anastasius vel potius Liber Pontificalis in Bonifacio IV., in Muratori, Script. Rerum Italicarum, tom. iii. P. i. p. 135.) According to the anonymous writer in Montfaucon, the Pantheon had been vowed by Agrippa to Cybele and Neptune, and was dedicated by Boniface IV., on the calends of November, to the Virgin, quæ est mater omnium sanctorum, (p. 297, 298.)]

[Footnote 26/1: The popes, under the dominion of the emperor and of the exarchs, according to Feas's just observation, did not possess the power of disposing of the buildings and monuments of the city according to their own will. Bunsen and Platner, vol. i. p. 241—M.]

III. The value of any object that supplies the wants or pleasures of mankind is compounded of its substance and its form, of the materials and the manufacture. Its price must depend on the number of persons by whom it may be acquired and used; on the extent of the market; and consequently on the ease or difficulty of remote exportation, according to the nature of the commodity, its local situation, and the temporary circumstances of the world. The Barbarian conquerors of Rome usurped in a moment the toil and treasure of successive ages; but, except the luxuries of immediate consumption, they must view without desire all that could not be removed from the city in the Gothic wagons or the fleet of the Vandals. [27] Gold and silver were the first objects of their avarice; as in every country, and in the smallest compass, they represent the most ample command of the industry and possessions of mankind. A vase or a statue of those precious metals might tempt the vanity of some Barbarian chief; but the grosser multitude, regardless of the form, was tenacious only of the substance; and the melted ingots might be readily divided and stamped into the current coin of the empire. The less active or less fortunate robbers were reduced to the baser plunder of brass, lead, iron, and copper: whatever had escaped the Goths and Vandals was pillaged by the Greek tyrants; and the emperor Constans, in his rapacious visit, stripped the bronze tiles from the roof of the Pantheon. [28] The edifices of Rome might be considered as a vast and various mine; the first labor of extracting the materials was already performed; the metals were purified and cast; the marbles were hewn and polished; and after foreign and domestic rapine had been satiated, the remains of the city, could a purchaser have been found, were still venal. The monuments of antiquity had been left naked of their precious ornaments; but the Romans would demolish with their own hands the arches and walls, if the hope of profit could surpass the cost of the labor and exportation. If Charlemagne had fixed in Italy the seat of the Western empire, his genius would have aspired to restore, rather than to violate, the works of the Cæsars; but policy confined the French monarch to the forests of Germany; his taste could be gratified only by destruction; and the new palace of Aix la Chapelle was decorated with the marbles of Ravenna [29] and Rome. [30] Five hundred years after Charlemagne, a king of Sicily, Robert, the wisest and most liberal sovereign of the age, was supplied with the same materials by the easy navigation of the Tyber and the sea; and Petrarch sighs an indignant complaint, that the ancient capital of the world should adorn from her own bowels the slothful luxury of Naples. [31] But these examples of plunder or purchase were rare in the darker ages; and the Romans, alone and unenvied, might have applied to their private or public use the remaining structures of antiquity, if in their present form and situation they had not been useless in a great measure to the city and its inhabitants. The walls still described the old circumference, but the city had descended from the seven hills into the Campus Martius; and some of the noblest monuments which had braved the injuries of time were left in a desert, far remote from the habitations of mankind. The palaces of the senators were no longer adapted to the manners or fortunes of their indigent successors: the use of baths [32] and porticos was forgotten: in the sixth century, the games of the theatre, amphitheatre, and circus, had been interrupted: some temples were devoted to the prevailing worship; but the Christian churches preferred the holy figure of the cross; and fashion, or reason, had distributed after a peculiar model the cells and offices of the cloister. Under the ecclesiastical reign, the number of these pious foundations was enormously multiplied; and the city was crowded with forty monasteries of men, twenty of women, and sixty chapters and colleges of canons and priests, [33] who aggravated, instead of relieving, the depopulation of the tenth century. But if the forms of ancient architecture were disregarded by a people insensible of their use and beauty, the plentiful materials were applied to every call of necessity or superstition; till the fairest columns of the Ionic and Corinthian orders, the richest marbles of Paros and Numidia, were degraded, perhaps to the support of a convent or a stable. The daily havoc which is perpetrated by the Turks in the cities of Greece and Asia may afford a melancholy example; and in the gradual destruction of the monuments of Rome, Sixtus the Fifth may alone be excused for employing the stones of the Septizonium in the glorious edifice of St. Peter's. [34] A fragment, a ruin, howsoever mangled or profaned, may be viewed with pleasure and regret; but the greater part of the marble was deprived of substance, as well as of place and proportion; it was burnt to lime for the purpose of cement. [34/1] Since the arrival of Poggius, the temple of Concord, [35] and many capital structures, had vanished from his eyes; and an epigram of the same age expresses a just and pious fear, that the continuance of this practice would finally annihilate all the monuments of antiquity. [36] The smallness of their numbers was the sole check on the demands and depredations of the Romans. The imagination of Petrarch might create the presence of a mighty people; [37] and I hesitate to believe, that, even in the fourteenth century, they could be reduced to a contemptible list of thirty-three thousand inhabitants. From that period to the reign of Leo the Tenth, if they multiplied to the amount of eighty-five thousand, [38] the increase of citizens was in some degree pernicious to the ancient city.

[Footnote 27: Flaminius Vacca (apud Montfaucon, p. 155, 156. His memoir is likewise printed, p. 21, at the end of the Roman Antica of Nardini) and several Romans, doctrinâ graves, were persuaded that the Goths buried their treasures at Rome, and bequeathed the secret marks filiis nepotibusque. He relates some anecdotes to prove, that in his own time, these places were visited and rifled by the Transalpine pilgrims, the heirs of the Gothic conquerors.]

[Footnote 28: Omnia quæ erant in ære ad ornatum civitatis deposuit, sed e ecclesiam B. Mariæ ad martyres quæ de tegulis æreis cooperta discooperuit, (Anast. in Vitalian. p. 141.) The base and sacrilegious Greek had not even the poor pretence of plundering a heathen temple, the Pantheon was already a Catholic church.]

[Footnote 29: For the spoils of Ravenna (musiva atque marmora) see the original grant of Pope Adrian I. to Charlemagne, (Codex Carolin. epist. lxvii. in Muratori, Script. Ital. tom. iii. P. ii. p. 223.)]

[Footnote 30: I shall quote the authentic testimony of the Saxon poet, (A.D. 887—899,) de Rebus gestis Caroli magni, l. v. 437—440, in the Historians of France, (tom. v. p. 180:)

Ad quæ marmoreas præstabat Roma columnas, Quasdam præcipuas pulchra Ravenna dedit. De tam longinquâ poterit regione vetustas Illius ornatum, Francia, ferre tibi.

And I shall add from the Chronicle of Sigebert, (Historians of France, tom. v. p. 378,) extruxit etiam Aquisgrani basilicam plurimæ pulchritudinis, ad cujus structuram a Roma et Ravenna columnas et marmora devehi fecit.]

[Footnote 31: I cannot refuse to transcribe a long passage of Petrarch (Opp. p. 536, 537) in Epistolâ hortatoriâ ad Nicolaum Laurentium; it is so strong and full to the point: Nec pudor aut pietas continuit quominus impii spoliata Dei templa, occupatas arces, opes publicas, regiones urbis, atque honores magistratûum inter se divisos; (habeant?) quam unâ in re, turbulenti ac seditiosi homines et totius reliquæ vitæ consiliis et rationibus discordes, inhumani fderis stupendà societate convenirent, in pontes et mnia atque immeritos lapides desævirent. Denique post vi vel senio collapsa palatia, quæ quondam ingentes tenuerunt viri, post diruptos arcus triumphales, (unde majores horum forsitan corruerunt,) de ipsius vetustatis ac propriæ impietatis fragminibus vilem quæstum turpi mercimonio captare non puduit. Itaque nunc, heu dolor! heu scelus indignum! de vestris marmoreis columnis, de liminibus templorum, (ad quæ nuper ex orbe toto concursus devotissimus fiebat,) de imaginibus sepulchrorum sub quibus patrum vestrorum venerabilis civis (cinis?) erat, ut reliquas sileam, desidiosa Neapolis adornatur. Sic paullatim ruinæ ipsæ deficiunt. Yet King Robert was the friend of Petrarch.]

[Footnote 32: Yet Charlemagne washed and swam at Aix la Chapelle with a hundred of his courtiers, (Eginhart, c. 22, p. 108, 109,) and Muratori describes, as late as the year 814, the public baths which were built at Spoleto in Italy, (Annali, tom. vi. p. 416.)]

[Footnote 33: See the Annals of Italy, A.D. 988. For this and the preceding fact, Muratori himself is indebted to the Benedictine history of Père Mabillon.]

[Footnote 34: Vita di Sisto Quinto, da Gregorio Leti, tom. iii. p. 50.]

[Footnote 34/1: From the quotations in Bunsen's Dissertation, it may be suspected that this slow but continual process of destruction was the most fatal. Ancient Rome eas considered a quarry from which the church, the castle of the baron, or even the hovel of the peasant, might be repaired—M.]

[Footnote 35: Porticus ædis Concordiæ, quam cum primum ad urbem accessi vidi fere integram opere marmoreo admodum specioso: Romani postmodum ad calcem ædem totam et porticûs partem disjectis columnis sunt demoliti, (p. 12.) The temple of Concord was therefore not destroyed by a sedition in the xiiith century, as I have read in a MS. treatise del' Governo civile di Rome, lent me formerly at Rome, and ascribed (I believe falsely) to the celebrated Gravina. Poggius likewise affirms that the sepulchre of Cæcilia Metella was burnt for lime, (p. 19, 20.)]

[Footnote 36: Composed by Æneas Sylvius, afterwards Pope Pius II., and published by Mabillon, from a MS. of the queen of Sweden, (Musæum Italicum, tom. i. p. 97.)

Oblectat me, Roma, tuas spectare ruinas: Ex cujus lapsû gloria prisca patet. Sed tuus hic populus muris defossa vetustis Calcis in obsequium marmora dura coquit. Impia tercentum si sic gens egerit annos Nullum hinc indicium nobilitatis erit.]

[Footnote 37: Vagabamur pariter in illâ urbe tam magnâ; quæ, cum propter spatium vacua videretur, populum habet immensum, (Opp p. 605 Epist. Familiares, ii. 14.)]

[Footnote 38: These states of the population of Rome at different periods are derived from an ingenious treatise of the physician Lancisi, de Romani Cli Qualitatibus, (p. 122.)]

IV. I have reserved for the last, the most potent and forcible cause of destruction, the domestic hostilities of the Romans themselves. Under the dominion of the Greek and French emperors, the peace of the city was disturbed by accidental, though frequent, seditions: it is from the decline of the latter, from the beginning of the tenth century, that we may date the licentiousness of private war, which violated with impunity the laws of the Code and the Gospel, without respecting the majesty of the absent sovereign, or the presence and person of the vicar of Christ. In a dark period of five hundred years, Rome was perpetually afflicted by the sanguinary quarrels of the nobles and the people, the Guelphs and Ghibelines, the Colonna and Ursini; and if much has escaped the knowledge, and much is unworthy of the notice, of history, I have exposed in the two preceding chapters the causes and effects of the public disorders. At such a time, when every quarrel was decided by the sword, and none could trust their lives or properties to the impotence of law, the powerful citizens were armed for safety, or offence, against the domestic enemies whom they feared or hated. Except Venice alone, the same dangers and designs were common to all the free republics of Italy; and the nobles usurped the prerogative of fortifying their houses, and erecting strong towers, [39] that were capable of resisting a sudden attack. The cities were filled with these hostile edifices; and the example of Lucca, which contained three hundred towers; her law, which confined their height to the measure of fourscore feet, may be extended with suitable latitude to the more opulent and populous states. The first step of the senator Brancaleone in the establishment of peace and justice, was to demolish (as we have already seen) one hundred and forty of the towers of Rome; and, in the last days of anarchy and discord, as late as the reign of Martin the Fifth, forty-four still stood in one of the thirteen or fourteen regions of the city. To this mischievous purpose the remains of antiquity were most readily adapted: the temples and arches afforded a broad and solid basis for the new structures of brick and stone; and we can name the modern turrets that were raised on the triumphal monuments of Julius Cæsar, Titus, and the Antonines. [40] With some slight alterations, a theatre, an amphitheatre, a mausoleum, was transformed into a strong and spacious citadel. I need not repeat, that the mole of Adrian has assumed the title and form of the castle of St. Angelo; [41] the Septizonium of Severus was capable of standing against a royal army; [42] the sepulchre of Metella has sunk under its outworks; [43] [43/1] the theatres of Pompey and Marcellus were occupied by the Savelli and Ursini families; [44] and the rough fortress has been gradually softened to the splendor and elegance of an Italian palace. Even the churches were encompassed with arms and bulwarks, and the military engines on the roof of St. Peter's were the terror of the Vatican and the scandal of the Christian world. Whatever is fortified will be attacked; and whatever is attacked may be destroyed. Could the Romans have wrested from the popes the castle of St. Angelo, they had resolved by a public decree to annihilate that monument of servitude. Every building of defence was exposed to a siege; and in every siege the arts and engines of destruction were laboriously employed. After the death of Nicholas the Fourth, Rome, without a sovereign or a senate, was abandoned six months to the fury of civil war. "The houses," says a cardinal and poet of the times, [45] "were crushed by the weight and velocity of enormous stones; [46] the walls were perforated by the strokes of the battering-ram; the towers were involved in fire and smoke; and the assailants were stimulated by rapine and revenge." The work was consummated by the tyranny of the laws; and the factions of Italy alternately exercised a blind and thoughtless vengeance on their adversaries, whose houses and castles they razed to the ground. [47] In comparing the days of foreign, with the ages of domestic, hostility, we must pronounce, that the latter have been far more ruinous to the city; and our opinion is confirmed by the evidence of Petrarch. "Behold," says the laureate, "the relics of Rome, the image of her pristine greatness! neither time nor the Barbarian can boast the merit of this stupendous destruction: it was perpetrated by her own citizens, by the most illustrious of her sons; and your ancestors (he writes to a noble Annabaldi) have done with the battering-ram what the Punic hero could not accomplish with the sword." [48] The influence of the two last principles of decay must in some degree be multiplied by each other; since the houses and towers, which were subverted by civil war, required by a new and perpetual supply from the monuments of antiquity. [481]

[Footnote 39: All the facts that relate to the towers at Rome, and in other free cities of Italy, may be found in the laborious and entertaining compilation of Muratori, Antiquitates Italiæ Medii Ævi, dissertat. xxvi., (tom. ii. p. 493—496, of the Latin, tom.. p. 446, of the Italian work.)]

[Footnote 40: As for instance, templum Jani nunc dicitur, turris Centii Frangipanis; et sane Jano impositæ turris lateritiæ conspicua hodieque vestigia supersunt, (Montfaucon Diarium Italicum, p. 186.) The anonymous writer (p. 285) enumerates, arcus Titi, turris Cartularia; arcus Julii Cæsaris et Senatorum, turres de Bratis; arcus Antonini, turris de Cosectis, &c.]

[Footnote 41: Hadriani molem.... magna ex parte Romanorum injuria.... disturbavit; quod certe funditus evertissent, si eorum manibus pervia, absumptis grandibus saxis, reliqua moles exstisset, (Poggius de Varietate Fortunæ, p. 12.)]

[Footnote 42: Against the emperor Henry IV., (Muratori, Annali d' Italia, tom. ix. p. 147.)]

[Footnote 43: I must copy an important passage of Montfaucon: Turris ingens rotunda.... Cæciliæ Metellæ.... sepulchrum erat, cujus muri tam solidi, ut spatium perquam minimum intus vacuum supersit; et Torre di Bove dicitur, a boum capitibus muro inscriptis. Huic sequiori ævo, tempore intestinorum bellorum, ceu urbecula adjuncta fuit, cujus mnia et turres etiamnum visuntur; ita ut sepulchrum Metellæ quasi arx oppiduli fuerit. Ferventibus in urbe partibus, cum Ursini atque Columnenses mutuis cladibus perniciem inferrent civitati, in utriusve partis ditionem cederet magni momenti erat, (p. 142.)]

[Footnote 43/1: This is inaccurately expressed. The sepulchre is still standing See Hobhouse, p. 204—M.]

[Footnote 44: See the testimonies of Donatus, Nardini, and Montfaucon. In the Savelli palace, the remains of the theatre of Marcellus are still great and conspicuous.]

[Footnote 45: James, cardinal of St. George, ad velum aureum, in his metrical life of Pope Celestin V., (Muratori, Script. Ital. tom. i. P. iii. p. 621, l. i. c. l. ver. 132, &c.)

Hoc dixisse sat est, Romam caruisee Senatû Mensibus exactis heu sex; belloque vocatum (vocatos) In scelus, in socios fraternaque vulnera patres; Tormentis jecisse viros immania saxa; Perfodisse domus trabibus, fecisse ruinas Ignibus; incensas turres, obscuraque fumo Lumina vicino, quo sit spoliata supellex.]

[Footnote 46: Muratori (Dissertazione sopra le Antiquità Italiane, tom. i. p. 427—431) finds that stone bullets of two or three hundred pounds' weight were not uncommon; and they are sometimes computed at xii. or xviii cantari of Genoa, each cantaro weighing 150 pounds.]

[Footnote 47: The vith law of the Visconti prohibits this common and mischievous practice; and strictly enjoins, that the houses of banished citizens should be preserved pro communi utilitate, (Gualvancus de la Flamma in Muratori, Script. Rerum Italicarum, tom. xii. p. 1041.)]

[Footnote 48: Petrarch thus addresses his friend, who, with shame and tears had shown him the mnia, laceræ specimen miserable Romæ, and declared his own intention of restoring them, (Carmina Latina, l. ii. epist. Paulo Annibalensi, xii. p. 97, 98.)

Nec te parva manet servatis fama ruinis Quanta quod integræ fuit olim gloria Romæ Reliquiæ testantur adhuc; quas longior ætas Frangere non valuit; non vis aut ira cruenti Hostis, ab egregiis franguntur civibus, heu! heu'—Quod ille nequivit (Hannibal.) Perficit hic aries.]

[Footnote 481: Bunsen has shown that the hostile attacks of the emperor Henry the Fourth, but more particularly that of Robert Guiscard, who burned down whole districts, inflicted the worst damage on the ancient city Vol. i. p. 247—M.]

PART II

These general observations may be separately applied to the amphitheatre of Titus, which has obtained the name of the Coliseum, [49] either from its magnitude, or from Nero's colossal statue; an edifice, had it been left to time and nature, which might perhaps have claimed an eternal duration. The curious antiquaries, who have computed the numbers and seats, are disposed to believe, that above the upper row of stone steps the amphitheatre was encircled and elevated with several stages of wooden galleries, which were repeatedly consumed by fire, and restored by the emperors. Whatever was precious, or portable, or profane, the statues of gods and heroes, and the costly ornaments of sculpture which were cast in brass, or overspread with leaves of silver and gold, became the first prey of conquest or fanaticism, of the avarice of the Barbarians or the Christians. In the massy stones of the Coliseum, many holes are discerned; and the two most probable conjectures represent the various accidents of its decay. These stones were connected by solid links of brass or iron, nor had the eye of rapine overlooked the value of the baser metals; [50] the vacant space was converted into a fair or market; the artisans of the Coliseum are mentioned in an ancient survey; and the chasms were perforated or enlarged to receive the poles that supported the shops or tents of the mechanic trades. [51] Reduced to its naked majesty, the Flavian amphitheatre was contemplated with awe and admiration by the pilgrims of the North; and their rude enthusiasm broke forth in a sublime proverbial expression, which is recorded in the eighth century, in the fragments of the venerable Bede: "As long as the Coliseum stands, Rome shall stand; when the Coliseum falls, Rome will fall; when Rome falls, the world will fall." [52] In the modern system of war, a situation commanded by three hills would not be chosen for a fortress; but the strength of the walls and arches could resist the engines of assault; a numerous garrison might be lodged in the enclosure; and while one faction occupied the Vatican and the Capitol, the other was intrenched in the Lateran and the Coliseum. [53]

[Footnote 49: *The fourth part of the Verona Illustrata of the marquis Maffei professedly treats of amphitheatres, particularly those of Rome and Verona, of their dimensions, wooden galleries, &c. It is from magnitude that he derives the name of Colosseum, or Coliseum; since the same appellation was applied to the amphitheatre of Capua, without the aid of a colossal statue; since that of Nero was erected in the court (in atrio) of his palace, and not in the Coliseum, (P. iv. p. 15—19, l. i. c. 4.)]*

[Footnote 50: *Joseph Maria Suarés, a learned bishop, and the author of a history of Præneste, has composed a separate dissertation on the seven or eight probable causes of these holes, which has been since reprinted in the Roman Thesaurus of Sallengre. Montfaucon (Diarium, p. 233) pronounces the rapine of the Barbarians to be the unam germanamque causam foraminum. Note: The improbability of this theory is shown by Bunsen, vol. i. p. 239—M.]*

[Footnote 51: *Donatus, Roma Vetus et Nova, p. 285. Note: Gibbon has followed Donatus, who supposes that a silk manufactory was established in the xiith century in the Coliseum. The Bandonarii, or Bandererii, were the officers who carried the standards of their school before the pope. Hobhouse, p. 269—M.]*

[Footnote 52: *Quamdiu stabit Colyseus, stabit et Roma; quando cadet Coly seus, cadet Roma; quando cadet Roma, cadet et mundus, (Beda in Excerptis seu Collectaneis apud Ducange Glossar. Med. et Infimæ Latinitatis, tom. ii. p. 407, edit. Basil.) This saying must be ascribed to the Anglo-Saxon pilgrims who visited Rome before the year 735 the æra of Bede's death; for I do not believe that our venerable monk ever passed the sea.]*

[Footnote 53: *I cannot recover, in Muratori's original Lives of the Popes, (Script Rerum Italicarum, tom. iii. P. i.,) the passage that attests this hostile partition, which must be applied to the end of the xiith or the beginning of the xiith century. Note: "The division is mentioned in Vit. Innocent. Pap. II. ex Cardinale Aragonio, (Script. Rer. Ital. vol. iii. P. i. p. 435,) and Gibbon might have found frequent other records of it at other dates." Hobhouse's Illustrations of Childe Harold. p. 130—M.]*

The abolition at Rome of the ancient games must be understood with some latitude; and the carnival sports, of the Testacean mount and the Circus Agonalis, [54] were regulated by the law [55] or custom of the city. The senator presided with dignity and pomp to adjudge and distribute the prizes, the gold ring, or the pallium, [56] as it was styled, of cloth or silk. A tribute on the Jews supplied the annual expense; [57] and the races, on foot, on horseback, or in chariots, were ennobled by a tilt and tournament of seventy-two of the Roman youth. In the year one thousand three hundred and thirty-two, a bull-feast, after the fashion of the Moors and Spaniards, was celebrated in the Coliseum itself; and the living manners are painted in a diary of the times. [58] A convenient order of benches was restored; and a general proclamation, as far as Rimini and Ravenna, invited the nobles to exercise their skill and courage in this perilous adventure. The Roman ladies were marshalled in three squadrons, and seated in three balconies, which, on this day, the third of September, were lined with scarlet cloth. The fair Jacova di Rovere led the matrons from beyond the Tyber, a pure and native race, who still represent the features and character of antiquity. The remainder of the city was divided as usual between the Colonna and Ursini: the two factions were proud of the number and beauty of their female bands: the charms of Savella Ursini are mentioned with praise; and the Colonna regretted the absence of the youngest of their house, who had sprained her ankle in the garden of Nero's tower. The lots of the champions were drawn by an old and respectable citizen; and they descended into the arena, or pit, to encounter the wild bulls, on foot as it should seem, with a single spear. Amidst the crowd, our annalist has selected the names, colors, and devices, of twenty of the most conspicuous knights. Several of the names are the most illustrious of Rome and the ecclesiastical state: Malatesta, Polenta, della Valle, Cafarello, Savelli, Capoccio, Conti, Annibaldi, Altieri, Corsi: the colors were adapted to their taste and situation; the devices are expressive of hope or despair, and breathe the spirit of gallantry and arms. "I am alone, like the youngest of the Horatii," the confidence of an intrepid stranger: "I live disconsolate," a weeping widower: "I burn under the ashes," a discreet lover: "I adore Lavinia, or Lucretia," the ambiguous declaration of a modern passion: "My faith is as pure," the motto of a white livery: "Who is stronger than myself?" of a lion's hide: "If am drowned in blood, what a pleasant death!" the wish of ferocious courage. The pride or prudence of the Ursini restrained them from the field, which was occupied by three of their hereditary rivals, whose inscriptions denoted the lofty greatness of the Colonna name: "Though sad, I am strong:" "Strong as I am great:" "If I fall," addressing himself to the spectators, "you fall with me;"—intimating (says the contemporary writer) that while the other families were the subjects of the Vatican, they alone were the supporters of the Capitol. The combats of the amphitheatre were dangerous and bloody. Every champion successively encountered a wild bull; and the victory may be ascribed to the quadrupeds, since no more than eleven were left on the field, with the loss of nine wounded and eighteen killed on the side of their adversaries. Some of the noblest families might mourn, but the pomp of the funerals, in the churches of St. John Lateran and St. Maria Maggiore, afforded a second holiday to the people. Doubtless it was not in such conflicts that the blood of the Romans should have been shed; yet, in blaming their rashness, we are compelled to applaud their gallantry; and the noble volunteers, who display their magnificence, and risk their lives, under the balconies of the fair, excite a more generous sympathy than the thousands of captives and malefactors who were reluctantly dragged to the scene of slaughter. [59]

[Footnote 54: Although the structure of the circus Agonalis be destroyed, it still retains its form and name, (Agona, Nagona, Navona;) and the interior space affords a sufficient level for the purpose of racing. But the Monte Testaceo, that strange pile of broken pottery, seems only adapted for the annual practice of hurling from top to bottom some wagon-loads of live hogs for the diversion of the populace, (Statuta Urbis Romæ, p. 186.)]

[Footnote 55: See the Statuta Urbis Romæ, l. iii. c. 87, 88, 89, p. 185, 186. I have already given an idea of this municipal code. The races of Nagona and Monte Testaceo are likewise mentioned in the Diary of Peter Antonius from 1404 to 1417, (Muratori, Script. Rerum Italicarum, tom. xxiv. p. 1124.)]

[Footnote 56: The Pallium, which Menage so foolishly derives from Palmarius, is an easy extension of the idea and the words, from the robe or cloak, to the materials, and from thence to their application as a prize, (Muratori, dissert. xxxiii.)]

[Footnote 57: For these expenses, the Jews of Rome paid each year 1130 florins, of which the odd thirty represented the pieces of silver for which Judas had betrayed his Master to their ancestors. There was a foot-race of Jewish as well as of Christian youths, (Statuta Urbis, ibidem.)]

[Footnote 58: This extraordinary bull-feast in the Coliseum is described, from tradition rather than memory, by Ludovico Buonconte Monaldesco, on the most ancient fragments of Roman annals,

(Muratori, Script Rerum Italicarum, tom. xii. p. 535, 536;) and however fanciful they may seem, they are deeply marked with the colors of truth and nature.]

[Footnote 59: Muratori has given a separate dissertation (the xxixth) to the games of the Italians in the Middle Ages.]

This use of the amphitheatre was a rare, perhaps a singular, festival: the demand for the materials was a daily and continual want which the citizens could gratify without restraint or remorse. In the fourteenth century, a scandalous act of concord secured to both factions the privilege of extracting stones from the free and common quarry of the Coliseum; [60] and Poggius laments, that the greater part of these stones had been burnt to lime by the folly of the Romans. [61] To check this abuse, and to prevent the nocturnal crimes that might be perpetrated in the vast and gloomy recess, Eugenius the Fourth surrounded it with a wall; and, by a charter long extant, granted both the ground and edifice to the monks of an adjacent convent. [62] After his death, the wall was overthrown in a tumult of the people; and had they themselves respected the noblest monument of their fathers, they might have justified the resolve that it should never be degraded to private property. The inside was damaged: but in the middle of the sixteenth century, an æra of taste and learning, the exterior circumference of one thousand six hundred and twelve feet was still entire and inviolate; a triple elevation of fourscore arches, which rose to the height of one hundred and eight feet. Of the present ruin, the nephews of Paul the Third are the guilty agents; and every traveller who views the Farnese palace may curse the sacrilege and luxury of these upstart princes. [63] A similar reproach is applied to the Barberini; and the repetition of injury might be dreaded from every reign, till the Coliseum was placed under the safeguard of religion by the most liberal of the pontiffs, Benedict the Fourteenth, who consecrated a spot which persecution and fable had stained with the blood of so many Christian martyrs. [64]

[Footnote 60: In a concise but instructive memoir, the abbé Barthelemy (Mémoires de l'Académie des Inscriptions, tom. xxviii. p. 585) has mentioned this agreement of the factions of the xivth century de Tiburtino faciendo in the Coliseum, from an original act in the archives of Rome.]

[Footnote 61: Coliseum.... ob stultitiam Romanorum majori ex parte ad calcem deletum, says the indignant Poggius, (p. 17:) but his expression too strong for the present age, must be very tenderly applied to the xvth century.]

[Footnote 62: Of the Olivetan monks. Montfaucon (p. 142) affirms this fact from the memorials of Flaminius Vacca, (No. 72.) They still hoped on some future occasion, to revive and vindicate their grant.]

[Footnote 63: After measuring the priscus amphitheatri gyrus, Montfaucon (p. 142) only adds that it was entire under Paul III.; tacendo clamat. Muratori (Annali d'Italia, tom. xiv. p. 371) more freely reports the guilt of the Farnese pope, and the indignation of the Roman people. Against the nephews of Urban VIII. I have no other evidence than the vulgar saying, "Quod non fecerunt Barbari, fecere Barberini," which was perhaps suggested by the resemblance of the words.]

[Footnote 64: As an antiquarian and a priest, Montfaucon thus deprecates the ruin of the Coliseum: Quòd si non suopte merito atque pulchritudine dignum fuisset quod improbas arceret manus, indigna res utique in locum tot martyrum cruore sacrum tantopere sævitum esse.]

When Petrarch first gratified his eyes with a view of those monuments, whose scattered fragments so far surpass the most eloquent descriptions, he was astonished at the supine indifference [65] of the

Romans themselves; [66] he was humbled rather than elated by the discovery, that, except his friend Rienzi, and one of the Colonna, a stranger of the Rhône was more conversant with these antiquities than the nobles and natives of the metropolis. [67] The ignorance and credulity of the Romans are elaborately displayed in the old survey of the city which was composed about the beginning of the thirteenth century; and, without dwelling on the manifold errors of name and place, the legend of the Capitol [68] may provoke a smile of contempt and indignation. "The Capitol," says the anonymous writer, "is so named as being the head of the world; where the consuls and senators formerly resided for the government of the city and the globe. The strong and lofty walls were covered with glass and gold, and crowned with a roof of the richest and most curious carving. Below the citadel stood a palace, of gold for the greatest part, decorated with precious stones, and whose value might be esteemed at one third of the world itself. The statues of all the provinces were arranged in order, each with a small bell suspended from its neck; and such was the contrivance of art magic, [69] that if the province rebelled against Rome, the statue turned round to that quarter of the heavens, the bell rang, the prophet of the Capitol repeated the prodigy, and the senate was admonished of the impending danger." A second example, of less importance, though of equal absurdity, may be drawn from the two marble horses, led by two naked youths, who have since been transported from the baths of Constantine to the Quirinal hill. The groundless application of the names of Phidias and Praxiteles may perhaps be excused; but these Grecian sculptors should not have been removed above four hundred years from the age of Pericles to that of Tiberius; they should not have been transferred into two philosophers or magicians, whose nakedness was the symbol of truth or knowledge, who revealed to the emperor his most secret actions; and, after refusing all pecuniary recompense, solicited the honor of leaving this eternal monument of themselves. [70] Thus awake to the power of magic, the Romans were insensible to the beauties of art: no more than five statues were visible to the eyes of Poggius; and of the multitudes which chance or design had buried under the ruins, the resurrection was fortunately delayed till a safer and more enlightened age. [71] The Nile which now adorns the Vatican, had been explored by some laborers in digging a vineyard near the temple, or convent, of the Minerva; but the impatient proprietor, who was tormented by some visits of curiosity, restored the unprofitable marble to its former grave. [72] The discovery of a statue of Pompey, ten feet in length, was the occasion of a lawsuit. It had been found under a partition wall: the equitable judge had pronounced, that the head should be separated from the body to satisfy the claims of the contiguous owners; and the sentence would have been executed, if the intercession of a cardinal, and the liberality of a pope, had not rescued the Roman hero from the hands of his barbarous countrymen. [73]

[Footnote 65: Yet the statutes of Rome (l. iii. c. 81, p. 182) impose a fine of 500 aurei on whosoever shall demolish any ancient edifice, ne ruinis civitas deformetur, et ut antiqua ædificia decorem urbis perpetuo representent.]

[Footnote 66: In his first visit to Rome (A.D. 1337. See Mémoires sur Pétrarque, tom. i. p. 322, &c.) Petrarch is struck mute miraculo rerum tantarum, et stuporis mole obrutus.... Præsentia vero, mirum dictû nihil imminuit: vere major fuit Roma majoresque sunt reliquiæ quam rebar. Jam non orbem ab hâc urbe domitum, sed tam sero domitum, miror, (Opp. p. 605, Familiares, ii. 14, Joanni Columnæ.)]

[Footnote 67: He excepts and praises the rare knowledge of John Colonna. Qui enim hodie magis ignari rerum Romanarum, quam Romani cives! Invitus dico, nusquam minus Roma cognoscitur quam Romæ.]

[Footnote 68: After the description of the Capitol, he adds, statuæ erant quot sunt mundi provinciæ; et habebat quælibet tintinnabulum ad collum. Et erant ita per magicam artem dispositæ, ut quando aliqua regio Romano Imperio rebellis erat, statim imago illius provinciæ vertebat se contra illam; unde *tintinnabulum resonabat quod pendebat ad collum; tuncque vates Capitolii qui erant custodes senatui, &c.* He mentions an example of the Saxons and Suevi, who, after they had been subdued by Agrippa, again rebelled: *tintinnabulum sonuit; sacerdos qui erat in speculo in hebdomada senatoribus nuntiavit: Agrippa marched back and reduced the*—Persians, (Anonym. in Montfaucon, p. 297, 298.)]

[Footnote 69: The same writer affirms, that *Virgil captus a Romanis invisibiliter exiit, ivitque Neapolim.* A Roman magician, in the xith century, is introduced by William of Malmsbury, (de Gestis Regum Anglorum, l. ii. p. 86;) and in the time of Flaminius Vacca (No. 81, 103) it was the vulgar belief that the strangers (the Goths) invoked the dæmons for the discovery of hidden treasures.]

[Footnote 70: Anonym. p. 289. Montfaucon (p. 191) justly observes, that if Alexander be represented, these statues cannot be the work of Phidias (Olympiad lxxxiii.) or Praxiteles, (Olympiad civ.,) who lived before that conqueror (Plin. Hist. Natur. xxxiv. 19.)]

[Footnote 71: William of Malmsbury (l. ii. p. 86, 87) relates a marvellous discovery (A.D. 1046) of Pallas the son of Evander, who had been slain by Turnus; the perpetual light in his sepulchre, a Latin epitaph, the corpse, yet entire, of a young giant, the enormous wound in his breast, (pectus perforat ingens,) &c. If this fable rests on the slightest foundation, we may pity the bodies, as well as the statues, that were exposed to the air in a barbarous age.]

[Footnote 72: *Prope porticum Minervæ, statua est recubantis, cujus caput integrâ effigie tantæ magnitudinis, ut signa omnia excedat. Quidam ad plantandas arbores scrobes faciens detexit. Ad hoc visendum cum plures in dies magis concurrerent, strepitum adeuentium fastidiumque pertæsus, horti patronus congestâ humo texit,* (Poggius de Varietate Fortunæ, p. 12.)]

[Footnote 73: See the Memorials of Flaminius Vacca, No. 57, p. 11, 12, at the end of the Roma Antica of Nardini, (1704, in 4to.)]

But the clouds of barbarism were gradually dispelled; and the peaceful authority of Martin the Fifth and his successors restored the ornaments of the city as well as the order of the ecclesiastical state. The improvements of Rome, since the fifteenth century, have not been the spontaneous produce of freedom and industry. The first and most natural root of a great city is the labor and populousness of the adjacent country, which supplies the materials of subsistence, of manufactures, and of foreign trade. But the greater part of the Campagna of Rome is reduced to a dreary and desolate wilderness: the overgrown estates of the princes and the clergy are cultivated by the lazy hands of indigent and hopeless vassals; and the scanty harvests are confined or exported for the benefit of a monopoly. A second and more artificial cause of the growth of a metropolis is the residence of a monarch, the expense of a luxurious court, and the tributes of dependent provinces. Those provinces and tributes had been lost in the fall of the empire; and if some streams of the silver of Peru and the gold of Brazil have been attracted by the Vatican, the revenues of the cardinals, the fees of office, the oblations of pilgrims and clients, and the remnant of ecclesiastical taxes, afford a poor and precarious supply, which maintains, however, the idleness of the court and city. The population of Rome, far below the measure of the great capitals of Europe, does not exceed one hundred and seventy thousand inhabitants; [74] and within the spacious enclosure of the walls, the largest portion of the seven hills is overspread with vineyards and ruins. The beauty and splendor of the modern city may be ascribed to the abuses of the government, to the influence of superstition. Each reign (the exceptions are rare) has been marked by the rapid elevation of a new family, enriched by the childish pontiff at the expense of the church and country. The palaces of these fortunate nephews are the most costly monuments of elegance and servitude: the perfect arts of architecture, sculpture, and painting, have been prostituted in their service; and their galleries and gardens are decorated with the most precious works of antiquity, which taste or vanity has prompted them to collect. The ecclesiastical revenues were more decently employed by the popes themselves in the pomp of the Catholic worship; but it is superfluous to enumerate their pious foundations of altars, chapels, and churches, since these lesser stars are eclipsed by the sun of the Vatican, by the dome of St. Peter, the most glorious structure that ever has been applied to the use of religion. The fame of Julius the Second, Leo the Tenth, and Sixtus the Fifth, is accompanied by the superior merit of Bramante and Fontana, of Raphael and Michael Angelo; and the same munificence which had been displayed in palaces and temples was directed with equal zeal to revive and emulate the labors of antiquity. Prostrate obelisks were raised from the ground, and erected in the most conspicuous places; of the eleven aqueducts of the Cæsars and consuls, three were restored; the artificial rivers were conducted over a long series of old, or of new arches, to discharge into marble basins a flood of salubrious and refreshing waters: and the spectator, impatient to ascend the steps of St. Peter's, is detained by a column of Egyptian granite, which rises between two lofty and perpetual fountains, to the height of one hundred and twenty feet. The map, the description, the monuments of ancient Rome, have been elucidated by the diligence of the antiquarian and the student: [75] and the footsteps of heroes, the relics, not of superstition, but of empire, are devoutly visited by a new race of pilgrims from the remote, and once savage countries of the North.

[Footnote 74: In the year 1709, the inhabitants of Rome (without including eight or ten thousand Jews,) amounted to 138,568 souls, (Labat Voyages en Espagne et en Italie, tom. iii. p. 217, 218.) In 1740, they had increased to 146,080; and in 1765, I left them, without the Jews 161,899. I am ignorant whether they have since continued in a progressive state.]

[Footnote 75: The Père Montfaucon distributes his own observations into twenty days; he should have styled them weeks, or months, of his visits to the different parts of the city, (Diarium Italicum, c. 8—20, p. 104—301.) That learned Benedictine reviews the topographers of ancient Rome; the first efforts of Blondus, Fulvius, Martianus, and Faunus, the superior labors of Pyrrhus Ligorius, had his learning been equal to his labors; the writings of Onuphrius Panvinius, qui omnes obscuravit, and the recent but imperfect books of Donatus and Nardini. Yet Montfaucon still sighs for a more complete plan and description of the old city, which must be attained by the three following methods: 1. The measurement of the space and intervals of the ruins. 2. The study of inscriptions, and the places where they were found. 3. The investigation of all the acts, charters, diaries of the middle ages, which name any spot or building of Rome. The laborious work, such as Montfaucon desired, must be promoted by princely or public munificence: but the great modern plan of Nolli (A.D. 1748) would furnish a solid and accurate basis for the ancient topography of Rome.]

Of these pilgrims, and of every reader, the attention will be excited by a History of the Decline and Fall of the Roman Empire; the greatest, perhaps, and most awful scene in the history of mankind. The various causes and progressive effects are connected with many of the events most interesting in human annals: the artful policy of the Cæsars, who long maintained the name and image of a free republic; the disorders of military despotism; the rise, establishment, and sects of Christianity; the foundation of Constantinople; the division of the monarchy; the invasion and settlements of the Barbarians of Germany and Scythia; the institutions of the civil law; the character and religion of Mahomet; the temporal sovereignty of the popes; the restoration and decay of the Western empire of Charlemagne; the crusades of the Latins in the East: the conquests of the Saracens and Turks; the ruin of the Greek empire; the state and revolutions of Rome in the middle age. The historian may applaud the importance and variety of his subject; but while he is conscious of his own imperfections, he must often accuse the deficiency of his materials. It was among the ruins of the Capitol that I first conceived the idea of a work which has amused and exercised near twenty years of my life, and which, however inadequate to my own wishes, I finally delivere to the curiosity and candor of the public.

**Lausanne, June 27$^{th}$, 1787**


EDWARD GIBBON – A SHORT BIOGRAPHY

Edward Gibbon was born on 8$^{th}$ May, 1737, the son of Edward and Judith Gibbon at Lime Grove, in the town of Putney, Surrey. He had six siblings, all of whom died in infancy. His grandfather, also named Edward, had lost everything as a result of the South Sea Bubble collapse in 1720, but eventually regained much of his wealth, so that Gibbon's father was able to inherit a substantial estate.

As a youth, Gibbon's health was under constant threat. He described himself as "a puny child, neglected by my Mother, starved by my nurse". At age nine, he was sent to Dr. Woddeson's school at Kingston-upon-Thames, shortly after which his mother died. He was then moved to the Westminster School boarding house, owned by his adored "Aunt Kitty", Catherine Porten.

By 1751, Gibbon's reading was already extensive and certainly pointed toward his future pursuits having covered such works as Laurence Echard's Roman History (1713), William Howell's An Institution of General History (1680–85), and several of the 65 volumes of the acclaimed Universal History from the Earliest Account of Time (1747–1768).

Following a stay at Bath, at age 15, in 1752 to improve his health, Gibbon was sent by his father to Magdalen College, Oxford, where he was enrolled as a gentleman-commoner (a rank of student above commoners i.e. normal students who paid the normal rate for tuition and boarding but below noblemen. They paid double the tuition fee and enjoyed more privileges). He was ill-suited, however, to the college atmosphere and later rued his 14 months there as the "most idle and unprofitable" of his life. Because of his autobiography, it used to be thought that his penchant for "theological controversy" (his aunt's influence) fully bloomed when he came under the spell of the deist or rationalist theologian Conyers Middleton, the author of Free Inquiry into the Miraculous Powers (1749). In that tract, Middleton denied the validity of such powers; Gibbon promptly objected, or so the argument used to run. The product of that disagreement, with some assistance from the work of Catholic Bishop Jacques-Bénigne Bossuet, and that of the Elizabethan Jesuit Robert Parsons, yielded the most memorable event of his time at Oxford: his conversion to Roman Catholicism on 8th June 1753. He was further 'corrupted' by the 'free thinking' deism of the playwright/poet couple David and Lucy Mallet; and finally Gibbon's father, already deeply in despair, had had enough.

However, this story has fallen somewhat into disrepute only being introduced to the final draft of Gibbon's "Memoirs" in 1792–93. There are also other accounts as to why Gibbons may have given a new 'backstory' to his conversion.

Within weeks of his conversion, the Gibbons was removed from Oxford and sent to live under the care and tutelage of Daniel Pavillard, Reformed pastor of Lausanne in Switzerland.

Here he made great friendships with Jacques Georges Deyverdun (the French-language translator of Goethe's The Sorrows of Young Werther), and John Baker Holroyd (later Lord Sheffield).

Just a year and a half later, after his father threatened to disinherit him, on Christmas Day, 1754, he reconverted to Protestantism. "The various articles of the Romish creed," he wrote, "disappeared like a dream".

He remained in Lausanne for five intellectually productive years, a period that greatly enriched Gibbon's already immense aptitude for scholarship and erudition: he read Latin literature; travelled throughout Switzerland studying its cantons' constitutions; and studied the works of Hugo Grotius, Samuel von Pufendorf, John Locke, Pierre Bayle, and Blaise Pascal.

He also met the one love in his life: the daughter of the pastor of Crassy; Suzanne Curchod. As the two developed an ever-closer relationship; Gibbon raised the question of marriage, but ultimately wedlock was out of the question, blocked both by his father's staunch disapproval and Curchod's refusal to leave Switzerland.

Gibbon returned to England in August 1758 to face his father. There was to be no refusal of his wishes. Gibbon put it rather poetically: "I sighed as a lover, I obeyed as a son." He proceeded to cut off all contact with Suzanne, even as she vowed to wait for him.

Upon his return to England, Gibbon published his first book, Essai sur l'Étude de la Littérature in 1761, which produced an initial taste of celebrity and distinguished him, in Paris at least, as a man of letters.

Interestingly to add to his interests and talents he had, from 1759 to 1770, served on active duty and then in reserve with the South Hampshire militia, his deactivation in December 1762 coinciding with the militia's dispersal after the Seven Years' War.

In 1763, he began as many men of privilege of class then did to round out and embellish their education on the Grand Tour, which included a visit to Rome. In his autobiography Gibbon vividly records his rapture when he finally neared "the great object of my pilgrimage": ...at the distance of twenty-five years I can neither forget nor express the strong emotions which agitated my mind as I first approached and entered the eternal City. After a sleepless night, I trod, with a lofty step the ruins of the Forum; each memorable spot where Romulus stood, or Tully spoke, or Caesar fell, was at once present to my eye; and several days of intoxication were lost or enjoyed before I could descend to a cool and minute investigation.

And it was here that Gibbon first conceived the idea of composing a history of the city, later extended to the entire empire, a moment known to history as the Capitoline vision: "It was at Rome, on the 15th of October 1764, as I sat musing amidst the ruins of the Capitol, while the barefooted fryars were singing Vespers in the temple of Jupiter, that the idea of writing the decline and fall of the City first started to my mind".

In June 1765, Gibbon returned to his father's house. He would remain there for the following five years until his father's death. He always considered this span of time as the worst of his life. He busied himself with various writing projects which failed to reach fruition. His first historical narrative, the History of Switzerland, was neither published nor finished. Gibbon had become too self-critical and abandoned the work a mere 60 pages in.

His second work, Memoires Litteraires de la Grande Bretagne, in two volumes, described both the literary and the social conditions of England at the time. When published it failed to gain any traction.

With the death of his father and the settling of the estate Gibbon had enough of a legacy to be free of any financial problems. He moved to Bentinck Street in London and began to live the life that suited him. He joined a number of clubs, including Dr. Johnson's Literary Club. He succeeded Oliver Goldsmith at the Royal Academy as 'professor in ancient history' (honorary but nonetheless prestigious). And he was writing. The work for which he would gain worldwide fame was under way.

But still other interests would divert his attention.

In late 1774, he was initiated a freemason of the Premier Grand Lodge of England. That same year he was returned to Parliament for the seat of Liskeard in Cornwall through the intervention of his relative and patron, Edward Eliot. Gibbon became a typical backbencher, mute and indifferent to his responsibilities, apart from routinely voting for the Whig Administration.

After several rewrites usually brought on by self-doubt and seven years of work the first volume of The History of the Decline and Fall of the Roman Empire, was published on 17th February 1776.

It was an immediate success. Within a year it had gone through three editions and the royalties were very handsome indeed.

Further volumes followed quickly and with the same measure of success; Volumes II and III were published on 1st March 1781, and volume IV was released in June 1784. Volumes V and VI were completed during a second Lausanne sojourn (September 1783 to August 1787) where Gibbon reunited with his friend Deyverdun. By early 1787, he was "straining for the goal" and with great relief the project was finished in June. Gibbon later wrote: "It was on the day, or rather the night, of 27th June 1787, between the hours of eleven and twelve, that I wrote the last lines of the last page in a summer-house in my garden...I will not dissemble the first emotions of joy on the recovery of my freedom, and perhaps the establishment of my fame. But my pride was soon humbled, and a sober melancholy was spread over my mind by the idea that I had taken my everlasting leave of an old and agreeable companion, and that, whatsoever might be the future date of my history, the life of the historian must be short and precarious".

Volumes V, and VI finally reached the press in May 1788, their publication having been delayed since March, so it could coincide with a dinner party on the 8th celebrating Gibbon's 51st birthday.

Praise came from all directions. Leading it were such contemporary luminaries as Adam Smith, Lord Camden, and Horace Walpole. Smith remarked that Gibbon's triumph had positioned him "at the very head of Europe's literary tribe."

In November of that year, he was elected a Fellow of the Royal Society, the main proposer being his good friend Lord Sheffield.

But the high-water mark had been reached and for Gibbon the following years were of sorrow and increasing health problems.

In 1789 he returned to Lausanne only to learn of and be "deeply affected" by the death of Deyverdun, who had willed Gibbon his home, La Grotte. He resided there with little commotion, took in the local society, received a visit from Sheffield in 1791, and "shared the common abhorrence" of the French Revolution.

In a letter to Lord Sheffield on 5th February 1791, Gibbon praised Burke's Reflections on the Revolution in France: "Burke's book is a most admirable medicine against the French disease, which has made too much progress even in this happy country. I admire his eloquence, I approve his politics, I adore his chivalry, and I can even forgive his superstition...The French spread so many lyes about the sentiments of the English nation, that I wish the most considerable men of all parties and descriptions would join in some public act declaring themselves satisfied with, and resolved to support, our present constitution."

In 1793, word came of Lady Sheffield's death; Gibbon immediately left Lausanne and set sail to comfort a grieving but composed Sheffield. But for Gibbon too, time was failing. His health began to fail critically in December, and at the turn of the new year, he was in rapid decline.

Gibbon is believed to have suffered from an extreme case of scrotal swelling, probably a hydrocele testis, a condition in which the scrotum swell with fluid in a compartment overlying either testicle. In an age when close-fitting clothes were fashionable, his condition led to a chronic and disfiguring inflammation that left Gibbon a lonely figure. As his condition worsened, he underwent numerous procedures to alleviate the condition, but with no enduring success. In early January, the last of a series of three operations caused an unremitting peritonitis to set in and spread, from which he died.

Edward Gibbon, the "English giant of the Enlightenment" finally succumbed at 12:45 pm, 16 January 1794 at age 56. He was buried in the Sheffield Mausoleum attached to the north transept of the Church of St Mary and St Andrew, Fletching, East Sussex.

### EDWARD GIBBON – A CONCISE BIBLIOGRAPHY

Essai sur l'Étude de la Littérature (1761)
Critical Observations on the Sixth Book of Vergil's 'The Aeneid' (1770)
The History of the Decline and Fall of the Roman Empire (Vol. I, 1776; Vols. II, III, 1781; Vols. IV, V, VI, 1788–1789)
A Vindication of some passages in the fifteenth and sixteenth chapters of the History of the Decline and Fall of the Roman Empire (1779)
Mémoire Justificatif pour servir de Réponse à l'Exposé, etc. de la Cour de France (1779)
Mémoires Littéraires de la Grande-Bretagne. co-author: Georges Deyverdun (2 vols: vol. 1, 1767; vol. 2, 1768)
Miscellaneous Works of Edward Gibbon, Esq., ed. John Lord Sheffield (2 vols., 1796; 5 vols., 1814; 3 vols., 1815) Includes Memoirs of the Life and Writings of Edward Gibbon, Esq.
Autobiographies of Edward Gibbon, ed. John Murray (1896). Edward Gibbon's complete memoirs (six drafts) from the original manuscripts.
The Private Letters of Edward Gibbon, 2 vols., ed. Rowland E. Prothero (1896)
The works of Edward Gibbon (Volume 3, 1906)
Gibbon's Journal to 28 January 1763, ed. D.M. Low (1929)
Le Journal de Gibbon à Lausanne, ed. Georges A. Bonnard (1945)

Miscellanea Gibboniana, eds. G.R. de Beer, L. Junod, G.A. Bonnard (1952)
The Letters of Edward Gibbon, 3 vols., ed. J.E. Norton (1956). vol. 1: 1750–1773; vol. 2: 1774–1784; vol. 3: 1784–1794. cited as 'Norton, Letters'
Gibbon's Journey from Geneva to Rome, ed. G.A. Bonnard (1961) Journal
Edward Gibbon: Memoirs of My Life, ed. G.A. Bonnard (1969; 1966). portions of Edward Gibbon's memoirs arranged chronologically, omitting repetition.
The English Essays of Edward Gibbon, ed. Patricia Craddock (1972)

www.ingramcontent.com/pod-product-compliance
Lightning Source LLC
Chambersburg PA
CBHW050123170426
43197CB00011B/1698